Sport in America Series

SPORT
in
AMERICA

From Colonial Leisure to Celebrity Figures and Globalization

VOLUME II

David K. Wiggins, PhD

George Mason University

Editor

HUMAN KINETICS

Library of Congress Cataloging-in-Publication Data

Sport in America: from colonial leisure to celebrity figures and globalization / David
K. Wiggins, editor. -- 2nd ed.
    p. cm.
  Includes bibliographical references and index.
  ISBN-13: 978-0-7360-7886-3 (hard cover)
  ISBN-10: 0-7360-7886-X (hard cover)
  1. Sports--United States--History. 2. Sports--Social aspects--United States--History. I.
Wiggins, David Kenneth, 1951-
  GV583.S6823 2010
  796'.0973--dc20

                                    94-16363
                                      CIP

ISBN-10: 0-7360-7886-X (print)   ISBN-10: 0-7360-8561-0 (Adobe PDF)
ISBN-13: 978-0-7360-7886-3 (print)   ISBN-13: 978-0-7360-8561-8 (Adobe PDF)

Acquisitions Editor: Myles Schrag; **Developmental Editor:** Amanda S. Ewing; **Assistant Editors:**
Casey A. Gentis and Steven Calderwood; **Copyeditor:** Joanna Hatzopoulos Portman; **Indexer:** Dan
Connolly; **Permission Manager:** Dalene Reeder; **Graphic Designer:** Bob Reuther; **Graphic Artist:**
Denise Lowry; **Cover Designer:** Bob Reuther; **Photo Asset Manager:** Laura Fitch; **Photo Produc-
tion Manager:** Jason Allen; **Printer:** Thomson-Shore, Inc.

Printed in the United States of America   10 9 8 7 6 5 4 3 2 1

The paper in this book is certified under a sustainable forestry program.

The cover photo shows a 1921 game between Georgia Tech and Penn State. The photograph is courtesy
of the Library of Congress, LC-USZ62-99631.

Human Kinetics
Web site: www.HumanKinetics.com

United States: Human Kinetics, P.O. Box 5076, Champaign, IL 61825-5076
800-747-4457
e-mail: humank@hkusa.com

Canada: Human Kinetics, 475 Devonshire Road Unit 100, Windsor, ON N8Y 2L5
800-465-7301 (in Canada only)
e-mail: info@hkcanada.com

Europe: Human Kinetics, 107 Bradford Road, Stanningley, Leeds LS28 6AT, United Kingdom
+44 (0) 113 255 5665
e-mail: hk@hkeurope.com

Australia: Human Kinetics, 57A Price Avenue, Lower Mitcham, South Australia 5062
08 8372 0999
e-mail: info@hkaustralia.com

New Zealand: Human Kinetics, Division of Sports Distributors NZ Ltd.
P.O. Box 300 226 Albany, North Shore City, Auckland
0064 9 448 1207
e-mail: info@humankinetics.co.nz

E4671

To the memory of my mother,
Lurline Wiggins (1927-2008),
who helped instill in me
a love of sport and the good life.

CONTENTS

PREFACE

Some 15 years have passed since the publication of *Sport in America: From Wicked Amusement to National Obsession*. During that time significant progress has been made in sport history; an increasing number of articles, book chapters, and monographs are being published on a variety of compelling topics. These aforementioned works, written by well-known academicians from disciplines such as history, kinesiology, and American studies, have been disseminated in prestigious peer-reviewed academic journals, more popular commercial presses, and notable university presses that have, in some cases, established special series devoted to various aspects of sport.

Volume II of *Sport in America: From Colonial Leisure to Celebrity Figures and Globalization* includes, with some notable exceptions, many works that have been published since the 1995 edition. Although it is impossible to include works that cover every topic and use every methodological approach, I have chosen essays that are well written and thoroughly researched and cover a wide range of timely and thought-provoking topics. The essays include diverse topics such as horse racing among the Virginia gentry, Muhammad Ali's involvement in the Nation of Islam, and the interconnection between sport and the World War I military experience and the role of Jews in the reintegration of Major League Baseball.

Intended Audience

Volume II can be used as a stand-alone text in undergraduate and graduate sport history courses. However, it is primarily designed to supplement the survey texts assigned for those courses. For example, it can serve as an accompaniment to such standard survey texts as Benjamin Rader's *American Sports: From the Age of Folk Games to the Age of Spectators* (2008); Elliott J. Gorn and Warren Goldstein's *A Brief History of American Sports* (2004); and Gerald R. Gems, Linda J. Borish, and Gertrude Pfister's *Sports in American History: From Colonization to Globalization* (2008). Such use of this work will allow students an opportunity to examine topics in more depth and realize a greater understanding of sport and how it is intertwined with other societal institutions. It both reflects and illuminates deep-seated stereotypic notions about such sensitive and controversial issues as race, gender, and masculinity. This book can have a wider audience than just those students enrolled in sport history courses. The larger public will have an interest in and benefit from the essays because they are easily accessible, are devoid of the jargon that sometimes characterizes academic work, and include information that is relevant to contemporary sport specifically and today's world in general.

Notes on Volume II

This book includes 18 reprinted essays, all of which contain their original footnotes and are divided into six parts. (The photographs that accompany each article are not original to the article but are added to illustrate the chapter.) To provide the proper historical context and to give readers a better idea of the changes that have taken place in sport over time, the articles are arranged chronologically from the early American period to the present day. At the same time, the articles in each of the six parts of the book provide readers with an understanding of the role and pattern of sport at particular moments in American history and how sport is interconnected with other societal institutions and cultural changes. After a brief introduction, each section includes a list of suggested readings to give readers an understanding of the quality and wide-ranging nature of the secondary literature dealing with the history of American sport.

ACKNOWLEDGMENTS

I would like to thank a few people who assisted me in the completion of this project. A special thanks to Myles Schrag, who expressed enthusiasm for this book from the very beginning and graciously answered all my questions and patiently guided me through every step of the process. I would also like to thank Jill Singleton for the many hours she spent correcting scanned documents and for typing and formatting articles for publication. This book could not have been completed without her help and assistance. I would also like to express my appreciation to three of my colleagues, Alison Wrynn, Mark Dyreson, and Dan Nathan, who provided cogent comments and suggestions regarding recent publications and selections of essays. Lastly, I would like to thank the various publishers who granted me reprint permission for all the essays that are included in this second volume.

PART I

THE PATTERN OF SPORT IN EARLY AMERICA, 1607-1776

Sport in early America was marked by significant geographical differences. Religion, climate, topography, patterns of work, and a host of other factors would have a profound effect on where sport would flourish. Some parts of the country received sport well and others were less receptive, ambivalent, or even opposed to sport. Perhaps no part of the country was more ambivalent about sport than New England. As Bruce C. Daniels notes in chapter 1, "Sober Mirth and Pleasant Poisons: Puritan Ambivalence Toward Leisure and Recreation in Colonial New England," the Puritans provided "ambiguous messages to their own society and to future generations" in regard to leisure, recreation, and sport. Although they could support these activities in principle, particularly if they refreshed the body and soul, the Puritans often cautioned or railed against them for a combination of religious, economic, sociological, and political reasons. For example, they were adamantly opposed to the theater, believing it was unproductive and led to homosexuality. They believed the Sabbath should be devoted to religious observance and not festive celebrations, recreation, or sport. They condemned all forms of gambling and blood sports as well as football because they believed these activities fostered idleness and resulted in injuries and bitter rivalries. The Puritans condemned such games as handball and tennis because of their association with the Roman Catholic Church and the idle nobility. However, they supported activities and competitions that they considered productive or virtuous. For example, hunting and fishing produced food, and the competitions of running, wrestling, and marksmanship were part of military training and led to the "civic virtue of promoting health and defense as well as providing recreation for the men on militia training days."

This skepticism and condemnation of many types of recreation and sport were nowhere to be found in the colonial South. Because of the heterogeneous nature of its population, religious background, racial composition, rural environment, and agricultural economy, the South generally took its leisure very seriously and was enthusiastic about participation in an assortment of recreation and sports. One group that was particularly enthusiastic about these activities was the gentry of late seventeenth- and early eighteenth-century Virginia, especially if it included making bets with large sums of money and tobacco on horse racing. In chapter 2 Timothy Breen provides a provocative explanation about why gambling, especially on horse racing, was so important to the gentlemen of Virginia during this time period in his essay "Horses and Gentlemen: The Cultural Significance of Gambling Among the Gentry of Virginia." Taking a cue from Clifford Geertz's famous analysis of the Balinese cockfight, Breen argues that when the great planters of Virginia staked large amounts of money and tobacco on a favorite horse, it was not simply a pastime but a reflection of the "core elements of late seventeenth and early eighteenth century gentry values." These core elements consisted of competitiveness, individualism, and materialism.

Suggested Readings

Blanchard, Kendall. *The Mississippi Choctaws at Play*. Urbana, IL: University of Illinois Press, 1981.

Brailsford, Dennis. *Sport and Society: Elizabeth to Anne*. London: Routledge & Kegan Paul, 1969.

Bridenbaugh, Carl. "Baths and Watering Places of Colonial America," *William and Mary Quarterly*, 3(1946): 153-181.

Brobeck, Stephen. "Revolutionary Change in Colonial Philadelphia: The Brief Life of the Proprietary Gentry." *William and Mary Quarterly*, 33(1976): 410-434.

Carson, Jane. *Colonial Virginians at Play*. Charlottesville, VA: University of Virginia Press, 1965.

Cheska, Alyce. "Native Americans Games as Strategies of Societal Maintenance." In *Forms of Play of Native North Americans*, edited by Edward Norbeck and Claire R. Farrer. St. Paul, MN: West Publishing, 1979, 227-247.

Culin, Stewart. *Games of the North American Indians*. Washington, DC: U.S. Government Printing Office, 1907.

Daniels, Bruce. *Puritans at Play: Leisure and Recreation in Colonial New England*. New York: Palgrave Macmillan, 1996.

Isaac, Rhys. *The Transformation of Virginia, 1740-1790.* Chapel Hill: University of North Carolina Press, 1982.

Jable, J. Thomas. "The English Puritans: Suppressors of Sport and Amusement?" *Canadian Journal of History of Sport and Physical Education,* 7(1976): 33-40.

Jable, J. Thomas. "Pennsylvania's Blue Laws: A Quaker Experiment in Suppression of Sport and Amusements, 1682-1740." *Journal of Sport History,* 1(1974). 107-121.

Kennard, June A. "Maryland Colonials at Play: Their Sports and Games." *Research Quarterly,* 41(1970): 389-395.

Ledbetter, Bonnie S. "Sports and Games of the American Revolution." *Journal of Sport History,* 6(1979): 29-40.

Oxendine, Joseph. *American Indian Sports Heritage.* Champaign, IL: Human Kinetics, 1988.

Salter, Michael A. "Play in Ritual: An Ethnohistorical Overview of Native North America." *Stadion,* 3(1977): 230-243.

Struna, Nancy L. "The Formalizing of Sport and the Formation of an Elite: The Chesapeake Gentry, 1650-1720." *Journal of Sport History,* 13(1986): 212-234.

Struna, Nancy L. "Gender and Sporting Practice in Early America." *Journal of Sport History,* 18(1991): 10-31.

Struna, Nancy L. *People of Prowess: Sport, Leisure and Labor in Early Anglo-America,* Urbana, IL: University of Illinois Press, 1996.

Struna, Nancy L. "Puritans and Sport: The Irrevitable Tide of Change." *Journal of Sport History,* 4(1977): 1-21.

Struna, Nancy L. "Sport and Society in Early America." *The International Journal of the History of Sport,* 5(1988): 292-311.

Wagner, Peter. "Literary Evidence of Sport in Colonial New England." *Stadion,* 2(1976):233-249.

Wagner, Peter. "Puritan Attitudes Toward Physical Recreation in Seventeenth Century New England." *Journal of Sport History,* 6(1979): 29-40.

Wagner, Peter. *Puritan Attitudes Toward Recreation in Seventeenth-Century New England.* Frankfurt: Peter Lang, 1982.

CHAPTER 1

SOBER MIRTH AND PLEASANT POISONS

Puritan Ambivalence Toward Leisure and Recreation in Colonial New England

■ *Bruce C. Daniels* ■

A culture at play tells much about itself. Patterns of leisure and recreation do not develop by accident; invariably they are manifestations of a society's core values. Unfortunately, assaying the meaning of specific patterns of leisure and recreation is seldom easy. Scholars often assert—virtually as a matter of faith—that pleasurable pastimes provide significant clues to a culture's inner workings, but then find the meaning of the clues puzzling and elusive.[1]

In particular, people have sought to understand the culture of the United States by analyzing how its citizens relax.[2] Americans at play, however, send ambivalent signals both to themselves and to the international community. On the one hand, they pursue pleasure relentlessly—even wantonly. Licentious, narcissistic, hedonistic—all of these adjectives could be used to describe behavior that revolves around sexuality, individual gratification, and conspicuous consumption of everything. A large portion of music and film exaggerate reality and promote a picture of American decadence. Yet, on the other hand, many people, particularly foreigners, feel that Americans do not know how to play *properly*. According to this view, the seeming American hedonism in truth camouflages an inability to relax. Co-existing with the American attitudes of freedom of expression and behavior are deeper feelings that bespeak a repressive, censorious morality. Thus, bath-tub gin can be explained as a product of abstemious temperance; sex on the movie screen reflects sophomoric insecurities; the frenetic chase for fun parallels the rat-race pace of work. Americans

Reprinted with permission of Mid America American Studies Association.

work too hard at play, a sure sign that they are not very good at it. They take their leisure and recreation like they take their role in the world— too seriously.[3]

When either foreign or American commentators search the past for clues to the American identity, a number of explanatory factors surface with regularity; among these, for example, are the frontier, abundance, immigration, and the short span of American history. Predictably, considerations of morality and pleasure begin with a short discussion about or diatribe against Puritanism. Something about Puritanism has fascinated— perhaps fixated is a more appropriate term—the historical imagination. The general storyline of the popular analysis goes as follows. Political freedom, individualism, a fluid class structure, prosperity, geographical mobility—all of these factors and others fuel an American drive towards hedonism. But, lurking just beneath this surface gaiety, a cluster of attitudes derived from the Puritan origins prevent Americans from truly enjoying themselves. Despite their apparent carefree pursuit of pleasure, Americans have always been and still are chained to guilt, sanctimony, harsh judgments and hypocrisy by their Puritan past. As the French paper *Le Monde* wrote recently in a front page editorial on the Clarence Thomas/Anita Hill scandal, "since the arrival of the pilgrim fathers, America has never truly settled its account with sin. The old Puritan heritage periodically surges forth from the collective memory."[4] Much of the popular culture, however, still associates Puritanism with dour prudery. And, modern literary figures as distinguished as Arthur Miller and Robert Lowell reinforce this perception.[5]

Contemporary historians have developed a view of Puritanism in opposition to this popularly-held view. Puritans enjoyed sex, beer, and time free from work. They may have been harsh in judging sinners, but they were clear and fair-minded when they applied standards, not bigoted and hypocritical. Most professional historians attribute any ascetic, prudish qualities in American life to double-standards created by Victorian Americans in the late nineteenth century. Puritans have been relieved of blame by scholars who have reassigned the historical burden to the more recent past.

Why are literary and popular cultures at such odds with recent historical interpretations? Have historians overstated Puritanism's capacity to pursue pleasure through leisure and recreation? These questions have been raised by several recent analyses of Puritan attitudes towards sex which suggest that professional historians may have "over corrected" in their efforts to rehabilitate the Puritans. In an attempt to place Puritan attitude in a more sophisticated context, historians may have replaced one stereotype with another: both the gloomy, religious fanatic and the relaxed, moderate Puritan may be equally ahistorical images.[6]

I believe that both of these historical figures—the gloomy fanatic and the relaxed moderate—fail to personify the complexity of Puritan attitudes towards leisure and recreation. And, by this I do not mean that Puritans said one thing but did another. That was to be expected. Scholars know, as did Puritans, that a gap existed between ideals and practice in all societies; such a gap merely reflects the human condition. Recent social historians have done much to measure the distance between practice and preaching in New England by assessing criminality and deviance. It was within the preaching itself, however, that the real complexity existed. The Puritan ideal of leisure and recreation contained an ambivalence of profound importance. Puritans had a problem articulating their ideal of appropriate leisure and recreation. This problem resulted in ambiguous messages to their own society and to future generations.

Puritan Ambivalence

For a people remarkably consistent in their commitment to build a society based on Scriptural blueprint, New England's Puritans pursued their grand goal with a high degree of ambivalence over strategies, values, and secondary purposes. A series of conflicting, contradictory impulses underlay much of this ambivalence: Puritans believed in conformity to doctrine but also in liberty of conscience; they worked for material prosperity but wanted to avoid worldly temptations; they prized social communalism but asserted economic individualism. Each of these pairs (among others) provided alternatives that competed for loyalty both within society as a whole and within the hearts and mind of individuals. The leadership usually pretended no conflict existed and tried to fit these divisions into a coherent whole. They argued, for example, that people should use their liberty of conscience to arrive at the same doctrine as the ministerial elite. Yet, the contradictions did not go away in the seventeenth century; they resurfaced continually in both ideology and in practice. In reality, they resurfaced because Puritans neither had the desire nor the ability to make these hard choices. Hence, they did not line up on either side of the alternatives for a showdown, but tried instead to make all the contradictions fit together comfortably. They could not.

Puritan attitudes towards recreation and leisure reflected the ambivalence produced by those conflicting impulses. On the one hand, Puritans were virtually unanimous in stressing that all people needed relaxation to refresh their body and soul. As John Cotton, the most influential minister of the founding generation wrote, "life is not life, if it be overwhelmed with discouragements...wine it [is] to be drunken with a cheerful heart...thy wife beloved and she be joyfully lived withal, all the days of thy vanity." Cotton was quick to add, however, that enjoyment of drink and love did not extend to "gluttony and drunkenness... swaggering and debauch ruffians."[7] In these cautions we see the manifestations of the Puritan's general ambivalence towards relaxation. Support of recreation and leisure in rhetoric was almost always accompanied by cautions against ungodly, unlawful, unreasonable or unproductive activities. As if the very assertion threatened to open the floodgates to Hell, almost every endorsement of pleasure and fun was hedged about with restrictions of its actual exercise. William Bradford, John Winthrop, Thomas Shepard, Thomas Hooker, among most other early leaders, took great care in their writings to identify the limits of lawful recreation and to cite the many examples of fellow New Englanders who had exceeded these limits. A generation later in 1684, Increase Mather echoed these sentiments when he wrote, "Lawful recreation…moderately and reasonably used are good and in some cases a duty." Yet, people "often spend more time therein than God allowth of. And, too many indulge themselves in sinful sports and pastimes…The Scriptures commend unto Christians, gravity and sobriety in their carriage at all times; and condemn all levity." Mather concluded with a blanket requirement that virtually negated everything he had said earlier in praise of recreation.[8]

This tradition of give and take in moral rhetoric continued into the eighteenth century. In 1707 the tradition received its most comprehensive statement in Benjamin Coleman's 170-page tract, *The Government and Improvement of Mirth, According to the Laws of Christianity, in Three Sermons.*[9] Coleman's *tour de force* is the only book-length study devoted exclusively to the subject of recreation and leisure published in colonial New England's history. Written at a time when the Puritan impulse seemed to be waning, *The Government and Improvement of Mirth* became the ideal text of its time.[10] Its influence derived not just from its bulk but also from the care, judiciousness, and moderation Coleman brought to his analysis, giving it a legal-like quality of calm rationality.

As did John Cotton and Increase Mather before him, Coleman extolled the virtues of recreation in the abstract. "I am far from inveighing against sober mirth," he wrote, "on the contrary, I justify, applaud, and recommend it. Let it be pure and grave, serious and devout, all which it may be and yet free and cheerful." The concept of "sober mirth" which Coleman returned to continually, embodied in two words the ambivalence at the heart of Puritan attitudes towards recreation and leisure. Almost no page passed without a reminder that "mirth may and generally does degenerate into sin: tis ordinarily the froth and noxious blast of a corrupt heart." Mirth is "graceful and charming so far as it is innocent," Coleman admitted. But then he felt compelled to add, "tis pity that sin should mix with it to make it nauseous and destructive and make it end in shame and sorrow." Yet, continuing in this vein of give and take, Coleman reminded ascetics that Christ, himself, did not scorn mirth on proper occasions nor censor it in others; thus, "we read of his tears but never of his laughing." A reflexive caution against giddiness or sensuality, however, invariably followed an endorsement of joviality. In the final analysis, Coleman did not want readers to forget that above all, Jesus was "a man of sorrow."[11]

In its overall thrust, Coleman's thoughts rehashed what must have been a familiar message to New Englanders: have fun but not too much. Unlike other Puritan moralists who freely gave advice on the pleasures/dangers of recreation, however, Coleman was systematic and precise in his attempt to separate the joyful from the sinful. He was a list maker and his lists of rules provide a detailed guide—almost a manual—of the rights and wrongs of sober mirth. Coleman's rhetorical commitments to recreation and leisure were qualified only by a few basic restrictions: they must be "innocent"; "do no injury to God or our neighbor"; and "must not transgress sobriety, holiness, or charity." If his analysis had ended with the above caveats, Coleman's work would stand as a monument to the happy, moderate Puritan. But, after rhetorically establishing his support for the principal of pursuing pleasure in Sermon One, Coleman examines the reality of the pursuit in Sermon Two. Lurking within the innocent pastimes of "sober mirth," "virtuous mirth," and "profitable mirth" are always their natural enemies, "carnal and vicious mirths." Although these two types of mirth stood at opposing poles of good and evil values, Coleman argued that they were not far apart in the realities of daily life. And herein lay the danger that was at the heart of Puritan ambivalence towards recreation and leisure. Once a

> Licentious manner of expressing our mirth takes over, all possibilities of innocence, neighborly love, or sobriety vanish. The pretence of restraint may be outwardly maintained but disdain is sneered from the eye and contempt is in the smile; tho indeed envy and spite are under the paint; the look is pleasing enough and gay but tis only disguise, a forced laugh while a man's galled and mad at the heart…a wretch cannot be overjoyed to see a friend but he must curse him and every cup of drink he damns himself….the wanton man's mirth is ridiculous. He lays aside the man and the gravity of reason and acts the part of a frolic colt. He roars and frisks and leaps.[12]

Coleman's list of licentious mirths— the attributes of the "frolic cold"—was inclusive and more detailed than the list of acceptable sober mirths. Among the commonplace practices that he found unacceptable were: playing the part of the "merry drunkard"; "mirth ill-timed" on fast days, days of sorrow or the Sabbath; "idle or impertinent mirth—as sport to a fool"; "making ourselves merry with sin"; "to make religion and goodness the object of our mirth"; "to make merry at the judgment of God"; mirth that "stops devotion, cramps industry and is big with idleness…[is] evil and unlawful." None of these "lewd practices" could be lawfully tolerated according to Coleman, because to allow them to exist, even if they were held in contempt, would expose the community to the dangers of contamination by one bad example. "Sensual lust love company," he argued. "Men can't game and drink and be lewd and laugh alone. They provoke and spurt on one another." Throughout the substantive heart of Sermon Two, one searches in vain for any specific non-religion recreations that Coleman found proper and lawful. Undoubtedly there were some, but Coleman left these unspecified. In the final third of his book, Sermon Three, however, Coleman described what he believed to be the greatest recreation of all: rejoicing in God. The worship of God was the source of true relaxation for a regenerate Christian.[13] Thus, for Coleman, the apparently paradoxical phrase, "sober mirth," was more than a convenient literary device: it was a statement of an ideal—an ideal from which he was not prepared to condone much deviation in practice.

This idea of sober mirth animated the writings of most respectable moralists. A statement jointly written by 22 ministers in 1726, nearly two decades after Coleman's tract appeared, shows the enduring quality of Puritan ambivalence. In *A Serious Address to Those Who Unnecessarily Frequent the Tavern…*, one of the last great Puritan manifestos on morality, a group of Boston-area ministers prefaced their diatribe against tavern and liquor abuse with a perfunctory endorsement of the need for leisure and relations: "We would not be misunderstood, as if we meant to insinuate that a due pursuit of religion is inconsistent with all manner of diversion. There are diversions, undoubtedly innocent, yet profitable and of use, to fit us for service." Then, however, they list some of the appropriate attributes of acceptable innocent diversion. "Harmless recreation," they argued, should "be governed by reason and virtue," "convenient, sparing, prudent," "give place to business," "observe proper rules," "subserve religion," and "minister to the Glory of God." Not surprisingly, these ministers believed that few people satisfied these requirements for "sanctifying recreation" and for "resisting the temptations that mingle with their diversions." Most, instead, "drink down poison in their pleasant cups and perceive it not."[14]

Puritan Attitudes Towards Specific Activities

Only a few types of activities were categorically condemned as "poisons" by Puritans. Theatre was one of these. Puritans opposed the staging of plays with a vehemence that comes close to defying modern comprehension. Considered false recreations because they exhausted rather than relaxed the audience and actors, plays wasted labor, led to wantonness and homosexuality, and invariably were represented by Puritans as a foreign—particularly French and Italian—disease of a similar enervating nature as syphilis. To a seventeenth century New Englander a play was as horrible as a Catholic Mass; both represented a special snare of Satan—public gatherings that promoted the anti-Christ. [15]

Probably only the concept of Sabbatarianism had as strong an ideological charge as the Puritan's hatred for the theatre. Most of the English colonies practiced some form of Sabbatarianism, but Puritans were its leading colonial proponents and quite probably the most strict Sabbath observers in all of Christendom. A "Day of Joy," was their term for the Sabbath which ran from sunset on Saturday to sunset on Sunday; but joy's manifestations were holy rather than festive. Normally lawful recreations or productive practices were forbidden on the Sabbath. Sexual intercourse, unnecessary travelling, and any type of banter or conversational frivolities were proscribed. Opportunities to hunt had to be forsworn even if food was scarce. Crimes usually regarded as minor such as using profanity or stealing apples from a tree were punished with great severity if committed on a Sunday. Brandings and mutilations for crimes committed on the Sabbath were not unusual and a few ministers and civil leaders believed the death penalty appropriate for Sabbath breaking. New Haven Colony provided fodder for generations of jests by punishing a husband and wife who kissed on Sunday. And, Michael Wigglesworth, the popular Puritan poet and quintessential neurotic, added to his historical fame by agonizing in his diary over whether closing a stable door that was blowing in the wind constituted an act of work which would profane the Sabbath. New Haven and Wigglesworth, of course, were extremes within New England, being akin to the spirit that moved one English wag to charge a Puritan with the "hanging of his cat on Monday for killing a mouse on Sunday." But, all of the region, with the exception of Rhode Island, embraced Sabbatarianism with a ferocious sobriety.[16]

Nothing quite matched their hatred of theatre and Sabbath-breaking, but Puritan moralists also condemned all forms of gambling. "An enchanting witchery," as one Englishman called it, "gotten betwixt idleness and avarice." Gambling seemed to strike at the heart of the values of family, work, and honesty.[17] More than that, however, Puritans found gambling theologically offensive because it appealed to God to intervene in trivial matters. Implicating "Providence in frivolity" violated the Third Commandment against taking the Lord's name in vain since gamblers implicitly asked him to intervene on their behalf. Given the compelling social and religious reasons for despising gambling, it might seem surprising that Puritans devoted much less energy and emotion to combating it than they did to fighting the scourge of theatre. However, little needed to be said about gambling; its ills were manifestly evident. Theatre had a more innocent appearance and hence a greater propensity to lure the unwarned into the life of debauchery that lay beneath the surface. The fact that all of the early Puritan law codes made gambling illegal did not deter some from its practice. The courts routinely fined card-players, dice-throwers, and others who seemed smitten with the "itching disease." Gambling held no special horrors for Puritans; it was wrong but inevitably some people out of weakness or greed would do it. And, in the same matter-of-fact way, those people must be punished.[18]

Puritan ideology also condemned music, art, and dancing as illegitimate recreational or leisure activities but made one or two important exceptions about each. Secular singing and the playing of instruments, moralists thought, had little to offer spiritual growth and ran the danger of leading to ribaldry. Hence, only music that could be regarded as an "effective, divinely given tool" to help worship God, as Calvin said, had a claim to legitimacy. And only those songs that God had revealed in Scriptures, the Psalms, should be used in worship. These should be sung without the direction of a choir director and without the accompaniment of instruments since both of these aids were created by the Catholic Church to promote music as a form of sensual rather than spiritual arousal. The net result of all these strictures was that, in early New England, music played no morally acceptable role outside of church, and within church only a limited one. Tunes were forgotten, no training took place, and creativity was indulged only to the extent that each singer in the congregation anarchically dealt with each Psalm on his or her own terms.[19]

Similarly, the world of art afforded little in the way of legitimate relaxation to Puritans. They opposed almost all iconography as part of the Catholic apostasy and inasmuch as most European art reflected religious symbolism, Puritans opposed it as part of their warfare with Rome. Stained glass, ornate churches and alters, steeples, pictures of saints and of Christ, stood at the opposite end of the continuum to the end containing the small, unpainted, undecorated Puritan meetinghouse. This rejection of "craven images" joined with the Puritan contempt of beauty for beauty's sake—which they regarded as a form of idleness—to produce a hostility to most forms of artistic expression.

Gravestone decorations and portraiture were the two important exceptions that Puritan ideology allowed. Moralists encouraged both activities because they had an instructive quality that served society. Decorating gravestones with religious images or messages did not constitute idolatry since one did not worship gravestones, but instead learned a sobering lesson of temporality from them. Portraiture performed the useful function of preserving the images of worthy men and women to inculcate respect among the rest of the present and future population. Puritans considered portraitist more as craftsmen than as artists and they received the wages of middle-of-the-road artisans. As did other craftsmen, portrait painters did something useful for society; they moved "men towards virtue" by marking the historical accomplishment of great people. If painters were regarded in any way as outside the regular bounds of crafts, it was more as historians than as artists. A few Puritan leaders owned landscape paintings which were painted in New England and were, indeed, closer to examples of art for pleasure than of art for purposes of moral instruction. Also, artists painted a few pictures of funeral processions of great men; these had the same function as portraits. Both landscape and funery paintings were rare and seldom seen by most New Englanders.[20]

"Dancing or leaping," Increase Mather wrote in his famous and much-quoted morality tract of 1684, "is a natural expression of joy; so that there is no more sin in it, than in laughter." This endorsement may make the Puritans sound more liberal on the matter than many modern religious groups; however, closer examination of Mather's definition of "dancing and leaping" reveals otherwise. The dancing of "men with men", or of "women with women" was a reasonable form of recreation as long as done, "without offense, in due season, and with moderations." Problems occurred, however, with what Matter termed "gynecandrical dancing" or what was more commonly called "mixed" or "promiscuous dancing." Mixed dancing between men and women could not be tolerated in respectable society, according to Mather. Men and women dancing together or even in each other's sight invariably would succumb to the "unchaste touches and gesticulation…[that] have a palpable tendency to that which is evil." Mather argued that dancers did not always realize the seductive quality of dancing—its perceived innocence made mixed dancing all the more dangerous.[21] A few of the seventeenth-century divines, including John Cotton, thought mixed dancing acceptable under a few select circumstances, but agreed that it was not a practice to be encouraged. Even when men and women leaped about merely in the *presence* of the other gender, dancing posed danger. In particular, Puritans condemned organized dancing at weddings or on holidays such as the infamous dancing around the Maypole. Dancing at taverns was forbidden by law in each of the Puritan colonies because of the "many arouses and disorders' it provoked.[22] When all these restrictions were added together, they created a large moral barrier to most forms of dancing as an acceptable recreation.

Similarly, sports and games played a surprisingly small role in recreational thought and practice. Puritans had no theological quarrel with them if they did not involve gambling; but, many of the English sports and games with which they were familiar, such as billiards, shuffleboard, horseracing, bowling, and cards, usually did. At the very least, sports and games were felt to provide a ready opportunity for gambling. By 1650 all of the above mentioned activities were outlawed in New England because of their collateral propensities. Puritans also had serious social questions about other aspects of sporting activities commonly practiced in England. For example, sports had been played on Sundays and posed a constant threat to Sabbatarianism. Few New Englanders could forget that the greatest symbol of the royal repression of their movement was the *Book of Sports* issued in 1618 by James I and reissued in 1633 by Charles I.[23] Moreover, sports in England frequently involved injury-producing violence as an inherent part of the activity and engendered rowdy behavior among both participants and spectators. Puritans opposed the "blood sports" of cockfighting, cudgel-fighting and bearbaiting and had serious reservations about team sports such as football because they encouraged idleness, produced injuries, and created bitter rivalries. Football also was traditionally played on holidays, especially Epiphany Day, which made the sport even more compromising to Puritan sensibilities.[24] Some organized sports that drew on the medieval traditions of the jousting tournament with costumes, rituals, and cheering spectators smacked more of theatre than of sport to Puritans. Still other games such as tennis and handball had been the preserve of the English elite and the Puritans disdained them because of their association with the Established Church and the idle nobility.[25] In the final analysis, despite the fact that Puritan rhetoric did not generally condemn the concept of sport and games, it did specifically condemn all those most commonly played in England. A few sporting activities escaped Puritan proscription and were practiced in New England: hunting and fishing, because they were productive and did not normally tend toward immoderation; and competitions of marksmanship, running, and wrestling held intramurally within the membership of militia companies. These latter sports, of course, had the civic virtue of promoting health and defense as well as providing recreation for the men on militia training days.[26]

One should not infer from the Puritan opposition to most forms of sport and dancing, however, that they did not prize sociability. Puritans were communalists whose social ideals were founded in groups: the family, the congregation,

One activity that was acceptable to the Puritans was hunting.

Photo courtesy of Library of Congress. LC-USZ62-8357.

the town, the colony, and the way of life that knit them together in New England. They visited each other a great deal and much of their recreation and leisure derived from the informal give and take of everyday conversation in the homes, the fields, the streets, the meeting house, and the tavern. Covenant theology forced upon the Puritans a required sociability that sat easily upon these pioneers and pilgrims who had been removed by distance and dissent from many of England's familiar pleasures. The Puritan landscape was dotted with central places that brought them together as a people who believed in sharing life's joys and hardships as well as in helping one another in the business of moral regeneration.[27]

A quiet sort of *congregational recreation* provided the truest relaxation experienced by the most respectable Puritans. Church and town meetings were the two most obvious examples of group activities, but family prayers and meals produced daily meetings of a more intimate nature. Puritan sermons may have warned of the dangers of gluttony, but feasting was a popular and thoroughly legitimate pastime to the people who held the first Thanksgiving in American history. Puritans did not celebrate most traditional holidays such as Christmas, Easter, May Day or personal annual holidays such as birthdays and anniversaries, but they did celebrate special occasions of note—military victories, ample harvests, good news from abroad, ordinations, weddings, births and so forth. Almost all of these celebrations centered around food and conversation. This pattern of behavior explains the importance of the tavern in Puritan social life. It provided a warm place to gather together and enjoy good fellowship. Beer, ale, and cider played the same role as bread and cakes did at the dinner table. Drunkenness was a crime just as glutton was a sin; but both alcohol and food promoted conviviality—a virtue as well as a necessity to people living in cramped houses and austere ideological quarters.[28]

At the other end of the spectrum from congregational recreation lay another strand of Puritan thought that prized the solitary activities of reading and writing. Puritans were a reflective people and extolled the virtues of contemplative leisure. Just as sociability lay at the heart of Puritan group recreation, literature provided the ideal vehicle for individual leisure. Scriptures, of course, were read for quiet pleasure and profit, but so were a whole host of other acceptable materials. History was a favorite subject, natural science another. One of the most literate groups in the early modern world, Puritans not only read, they also wrote a great deal. Spiritual diaries, autobiographies, daily journals, accounts of the weather, letters to friends in New and old England, poetry, commentaries on the New World landscape; all of these things commended themselves to Puritans who prized education highly for its theological as well as its economic and social benefits.[29] Puritan society espoused an intellectuality that made reading and writing its ideal form of quiet leisure. Despite its attractiveness, however, some practical problems made literary pursuits less perfect in practice than in theory. Although literacy rates were high by seventeenth-century standards, only about sixty percent of New England could read with ease. Books and other printed matter were expensive and in short supply. Finally, reading/writing did not have a sufficiently robust appeal to all.[30]

Literature, however, added an ideological advantage of posing only a few dangers to the Puritan mind. Although one could, of course, read or write sacrilegious materials, in general, worries about the type of literature being consumed or produced did not weigh heavily upon Puritan moralists. Puritans perceived fewer potential problems in literature than in almost all other ways of having fun. Most forms of recreation or leisure were laden with lures, hidden ever so slightly, ready to trap the unwarned "like silly birds [who] hasten to the snare, not knowing that it is for life." The natural propensities of people (especially men) inclined them to pursue sinful pleasures. Increase Mather's famous warning against the snares prepared by passion put the proposition point-blank in his title, *Solemn Advice to Young Men Not to Walk In The Way of Their Heart* (1695).[31] Puritans wrote much about the need for recreation and leisure to have a positive side—it must refresh, it must be uplifting—but, they wrote much more about the negative side always lurking just beneath the surface of even the most innocent appearing of activities. Warning to the unwary—the duty of all figures of authority from ministers to town leaders to fathers of families to neighbors—freighted so many social activities with ambivalence that even the most pure of heart was likely to have a cautious soul. And, of course, this was the whole idea of Puritanism: to make all people aware of the need for constant vigilance against a descent into sin that could –and usually did—begin with the slightest immoderate step.

Certain specific circumstances or situations added to the danger inherent in all activities. Travel away from family and friends could easily loosen the bonds of restraint imposed by the familiar community. England and Europe provided particularly bad examples of conduct to ensnare the young. Youth, in general, and especially adolescents, were at much greater risk than were adults who had developed greater powers of resistance.[32]

According to Puritan theology, women all had traces of the Eve temptress in them and, thus, had a larger burden placed upon them by original sin. Since women could more easily lure men into sinful situations than vice-versa, women had to guard themselves more closely against boisterous, excessive behavior. The Puritan fear of latent Eves built a double-standard into their ideas of social conduct for the sexes. Puritans also believed women to be more vain. A woman's pride in appearance became the particular "snare of her soul," wrote Cotton Mather in a sermon entitled, *Ornaments for the Daughters of Zion or the Character and Happiness of a Virtuous Woman.*[33]

The winter season with its shorter days, longer nights and less essential farm work also held special dangers. Idleness and darkness, two winter products, made abuses of recreation both more likely and more possible. "The frothy diversions of bad company;" "spending the night in the telling of tales;" "dancing, drunkenness, and chambering and wantonness;" "games of pure lot;" "books of debauchery, tales and songs;" were just a few of the frightful seasonal possibilities that Cotton Mather warned of in his sermon *Winter Meditations* (1693).[34] Winter days were regarded as especially appropriate times for fasts either by the entire community or by individual families. In general, summer was much less a season of temptation than was winter, but it did have its special problems of providing sylvan opportunities for improper behavior.

Erosion and Change

Determining how long these patterns of Puritan thought persisted is difficult. Attempts to define the chronological era of Puritanism have challenged the minds of the best historians, but, as of yet, no consensus on either dates or criteria has emerged. Nor is one likely to arrive very soon. Nevertheless, some aspects of the evolution of the Puritan mind may be described with a reasonable degree of certitude.

Puritan thought did not end at any grand moment or event, but instead eroded over the entire colonial period. The erosion started when New England began its two primary settlements in 1620 and 1629 and was still going on in 1790 when the regional identity became submerged in a national polity. The first governors of Plymouth and Massachusetts Bay, William Bradford and John Winthrop, lived in societies where practice sustained unusually high standards of moral conduct, yet both complained of licentiousness and expressed fears that their colonies were backsliding into English degeneracy. On the other hand, in the 1790s, when moral conduct had significantly deteriorated by Puritan standards, the opponents of theatre in Boston expressed their contempt with the same words used by their great grandfathers of the early seventeenth century.[35] Thus, despite being continually worn down, despite a perceived fragility from its very beginning, Puritan thought had an extraordinary tenacity and a very real influence long after any pretence of Puritan political and religious hegemony had ended. Along this continuum, however, it is possible to identify a few periods in which a shift in emphasis occurred and also to identify a few of the agents of change. A tension between the forces of self-denial and self-gratification—between austerity and pleasure—characterized all of the years on the continuum. In the first generation, the forces of self-denial had the upper hand. In a collection of fifty-six letters sent from Massachusetts to England in the decade of the 1630s (all those known to be extant), the subject of recreation and leisure rarely surfaced. Descriptions of land, climate, natives, daily work, news of self, family and colony crowd the pages but little mention was made of having fun. Small talk abounded in the letters but the only frequent reference to any form of relaxation came in discussions of food and joy of worship.[36] Without any conscious historical intent, the ordinary Puritans painted a somber picture of an austere Puritan milieu of ideology and practice.

This golden era of Puritanism ended about 1660. As students of the ministerial literature point out, a new type of sermon began to appear in the 1640s. The "jeremiad," a lament that extolled the virtues of the past and bewailed the vices of the present, castigated congregations for their declension—for their inability to maintain the purity and glorious intent of the founding generation. By 1660, almost all of that founding generation lay in the grave. The second generation seemed less sure of itself and more convinced that the moral leadership of the ministers was losing sway over average people. On the distant horizon, the secular trends in Restoration England promoted what appeared to Puritans to be licentious, hedonistic behavior. Cards, dice, foppish clothes, idleness, theatre, circuses, and ribald literature returned to England with renewed vigor along with the return of the Stuarts to the throne. Closer to home, the growth and dispersion of population in New England, the passing of the spirit of martyr-dom among those who fled the oppression of James I and Charles I, and the pursuit of "God land and God trade" by the sons and daughters of pilgrims all combined to create a world of alternative counterpoints to the stern morality of the early years. The plaintive cry of the jeremiads indicate that the second generation knew something was wrong but did not know how to fix it. Along with the increased shrillness of the warnings went an increase in prosecutions for crimes associated with the pursuit of pleasure: illegal sex, drunkenness, Sabbath-breaking, the wearing of vain clothes and so forth.[37] Michael Wigglesworth's poem published in 1662, *God's Controversy with New England,* is the most famous indictment of a New England "overgrown with many noisome weeds."[38]

From the 1660s to approximately the end of the 1720s, the second and third generation Puritan moralists struggled against what they regarded as the forces of laxity. Published sermons of the great ministers, always a barometer of their fears and insecurities but not a reliable guide to either popular thought or societal practices, repeatedly warned of the growth of sin and tried to maintain the proscriptions and prescriptions of the founding era. Several manifestos are of particular note. A Massachusetts church synod in 1679 issued a statement entitled, *The Necessity of Reformation,* which was a sort of official jeremiad bearing the moral authority not of one minister or congregation but of the churches of the entire colony. Among the recreational practices the authors found horrify-ing were: "walking abroad and travelling on the Sabbath;" "having unsuitable discourses;" "sinful drinking;" "days of training and other public solemnities… abused;" "mixed dancing, light behavior and expressions;" "unlawful gaming;" and "an abundance of idleness."[39]

The father/son team of Increase and Cotton Mather, the two most respected and prolific moralists of the second and third generation, wrote sermon after sermon trying to stem the tide of licentiousness that they perceived. Yet, chang-ing circumstances forced even the Mathers to make concessions to more relaxed standards. In 1684, Increase railed against mixed dancing; in 1700, Cotton condemned organized balls but implicitly accepted some types of dancing between the sexes as long as they did not abuse the practice. By 1719, Cotton, as the first author listed of a collectively-written jeremiad, was forced to argue against the creation of dancing schools, dancing at the ordination ceremonies of ministers, "immodest irregularities at weddings," parishioners who move from the "House of God unto the Tavern after worship," and "other revels." As they tried to resist laxity by excoriating what they regarded as the most horrible of practices, however, the Mathers and other members of the ministerial elite grudgingly softened the ideology to condone in one decade what would have been unacceptable in the previous one.[40]

This form of damage control received its last great statement in the 1726 collective jeremiad mentioned earlier in which twenty-two ministers combined their talents to blast the misuse of taverns. It contained an appended letter on the topic written by Increase Mather who had died three years earlier in 1723 and was organized by Cotton Mather who died two years later in 1728. The death of the Mathers and the ending of this type of jeremiad symbolizes the passing of the Puritan era. Hereafter, important traces of the austere moralism survived but did so as individual fragments of an earlier unified ethos. Cautions against many practices continued into the mid-eighteenth century in New England, but, in general, the ideology of recreation and leisure entered into a new, more permissive phase in the 1730s. The moral arbiters, tired of waging a Sisyphean battle, began to make ideological concessions to reality and practice. In the second quarter of the eighteenth century, New England was still relatively decorous and certainly appeared "puritanical" compared to urbane New York or cavalier Virginia. But a variety of recent analyses by social historians show that New England became increasingly less isolated and distinctive and more integrated into an Atlantic-Anglo world of culture and behavior.[41]

Conclusion

Many forces without and within New England created the shift in emphasis. Events near the end of the seventeenth century weakened Puritanism both politically and emotionally. Massachusetts' charter was revoked in 1684 and when a new one was issued in 1691 it contained aspects of royal government including a governor appointed by the crown. New Hampshire had an even stronger royal presence and Connecticut and Rhode Island had to function with the knowledge that they also would lose their charters if they behaved too independently. The debacle of the Salem witch trials made the established church look foolish and antiquated in the eyes of many. And, in general, religious, social, and economic trends militated against the maintenance of Puritan hegemony. By 1730, the Congregational church no longer had a monopoly on religion but had to compete with Anglicans, Baptists, and, in a few places, Quakers. The population had grown to approximately 120,000 persons in Massachusetts, 60,000 in Connecticut, 18,000 in Rhode Island, and 10,000 in New Hampshire, the vast majority of whom lived on isolated farmsteads whose locations ranged from the coastline to the White Mountains in the North and the Berkshires in the West. Over 250 incorporated towns existed with their own local governments. And, sophisticated urban centers began to emerge: Boston and Newport were preeminent among these, but Portsmouth, Newburyport, Salem, Springfield, Providence, New London, Norwich, New Haven, Middletown, and Hartford developed into secondary cities as their trade burgeoned and their social structures grew much more varied by class and occupation. In short, the relative homogeneity of New England's churches, governments and economy, gave way to a society of much greater heterogeneity as the sprinkling of Puritan villages evolved into a large, bustling region. Not surprisingly, the morality of the Puritan village also gave way to more heterogeneous views and practices of recreation and leisure. Of course, some areas of New England, most notably the small settlements of Rhode Island, had from the beginning departed a great deal from Puritan morality. Conversely, some Puritan villages based on one church, one community, and one shared restrictive vision of morality remained throughout the eighteenth century. And, some vestiges of Puritan morality remained in all communities, including the cities. Thus, a residue of the earliest ambivalence survived, but, overall, a new set of more permissive standards for recreation and leisure had become ensconced in New England by the fourth decade of the century. This more secular, relaxed view of morality carried the region into the Revolutionary era. In the years after 1730, New England still felt some of the tension between self-denial and self-gratification but the best mirth was no longer defined as sober, virtuous, or profitable. In an encompassing range of activities—courtship, tavern-life, social gatherings, holiday celebrations, music, the arts, games and so forth—New Englanders pursued mirth actively for the sheer sake of pleasure.

Notes

The author would like to thank the Social Sciences and Humanities Research Council of Canada for its support in the form of a research grant.

1. For some general statements about the role of leisure and recreation in society, see J.S. Hans, *The Play of the World* (Amherst, Massachusetts, 1981); N.H. Cheek, Jr. and W.R. Burch, *The Social Organization of Leisure in Human Society* (New York, 1976); and D.J. Tinsley, "A Theory of the Attributes, Benefits, and Causes of Leisure Experience," *Leisure Studies*, 8 (1986), 1-6.

2. See the most well known general history of American leisure and recreation, Foster Rhea Dulles, *A History of Recreation: America Learns to Play* (New York, 2nd ed., 1965) especially the two chapters added in the 2nd edition, "The Changing Scene," 366-385 and "The New Leisure," 386-397. For the unusual emphasis placed on analyses of American play see Walter Podilchak, "Establishing the Fun in Leisure," *Leisure Studies*, 13 (1991), 124.

3. Some of the well known commentators who have described America's "desperate drive for leisure," are discussed in Daniel Bell, *The End of Ideology: On the Exhaustion of Political Ideas in the Fifties* (New York, 1962), 257-269. Americans "work easily; play hard," Bell argued. This is also implicitly argued in another scholarly analysis aimed at the mass market: John Kenneth Galbraith, *The Affluent Society* (Boston, 1958), 259-269, and passim.

4. For the quotation from *Le Monde* and for a wonderful statement of the association of Puritanism with an enduring prudery see the recent editorial by Strobe Talbot in *Time Magazine*, "America Abroad: How Tout Le Monde Missed the Story." Talbot's piece features a graphic which shows eight Puritans questioning Prof. Anita Hill on her morality and quotes extensively from the international press about the pernicious effect of Puritanism on modern-day American morality. See Talbot, "America Abroad," *Time*, Oct. 28 (1991), 15.

5. See among others the major revisionist histories of Puritanism by Perry Miller, *The New England Mind in the Seventeenth Century* (Cambridge, Massachusetts, 1939); Samuel Eliot Morison, *Builders of the Bay Colony* (Boston, 1930); and Edmund Morgan, *The Puritan Family: Religion and Domestic Relations in Seventeenth-Century New England* (New York, 1966). Many recent general interpretations of Puritanism disagree with important aspects of the Miller/Morison view but still agree with the

conclusion that Puritans were not ascetic prudes. See, for example, the following diverse analyses: Sacvan Bercovitch, *The American Jeremiad* (Madison, Wisconsin, 1978); Francis Bremer, *The Puritan Experiment* (New York, 1976). See also the following recent discussions of Miller's work: Francis Butts, "Norman Fiering and the Revision of Perry Miller," *Canadian Review of American Studies*, 17 (1986), 1-25; and Bruce Tucker, "Early American Intellectual History After Perry Miller," *Canadian Review of American Studies*, 13 (1982), 145-157. Miller, *The Crucible* (New York, 1953); and Robert Lowell, *Endecott and the Red Cross* (New York, 1968).

6. See Roger Thompson, *Sex in Middlesex: Popular Mores in the Massachusetts County, 1649-1699* (Amherst, Massachusetts, 1986), 92-94; and Kathleen Verdun, "'Our Cursed Natures': Sexuality and the Puritan Conscience," *New England Quarterly* (hereafter cited as N.E.O.) 56 (1983), 222-224, 229-230.

7. *The New England Mind*, 61.

8. Increase Mather, *An Arrow Against Profane and Promiscuous Dancing, Drawn Out of the Quiver of the Scriptures* (Boston, 1684), 6.

9. Coleman, *The Government of Mirth* (Boston, 1707).

10. See Richard Bushman, *From Puritan to Yankee: Character and the Social Order in Connecticut, 1690-1765* (Boston, 1967), for a general discussion of the changes associated with this transition.

11. Coleman, *The Government of Mirth*, 1, 12, 18, 19.

12. *Ibid.*, 19-20, 46-47.

13. *Ibid.*, 46-47, 87, 89-120.

14. Cotton Mather, et al., *A Serious Address to Those Who Unnecessarily Frequent the Tavern, and Often Spend the Evening in Public Houses. By several ministers to Which is added, a private letter on the subject, by the Late Reverend Dr. Increase Mather* (Boston, 1726), 10.

15. For some general statements of the Puritan opposition to theatre see, James Barriskill, "The Newburyport Theatre in the Eighteenth Century," *Essex Institute Historical Collections*, 91 (1955), 211-245; B.W. Brown, "The Colonial Theatre in New England," *Newport Historical Society Bulletin* 76 (1930), 2-25; Brooks MacNamara, *The American Playhouse in the Eighteenth Century* (Cambridge, Massachusetts, 1969); Edmund S. Morgan, "Puritan Hostility to the Theatre," *Proceedings of the American Philosophical Society*, 110 (1966), 340-347.

16. Winton U. Solberg, *Redeem the Time: The Puritan Sabbath in America* (Cambridge, Massachusetts and London, 1977), 2-8, 9, 31-32, 76-77, 88, 107-113, 131-174 and passim. Solberg's extraordinary book is one of the few pieces of historical work to merit the term definitive.

17. Charles Cotton, *The Complete Gamester or Instructions How to Play at Billiards, Trucks, Bowls, and Chess, Together With All Manner of Useful and Most Gentile Games Either on Cards or Dice* (London, 1674: repub. London, 1930), XXVI.

18. John Findlay, *People of Chance: Gambling in American Society from Jamestown to Las Vegas* (New York: Oxford Univ. Press, 1986), 21; Nancy Struna, "Puritans and Sport: The Irretrievable Tide of Change," *Journal of Sport History*, 4 (1977), 12-13.

19. Joyce Irwin, "The Theology of Regular Singing," *N.E.Q.* L1 (1978), 177-178. See also, Lowell P. Beveridge, "Music in New England from John Cotton to Cotton Mather, 1640-1726," *Historical Magazine of the Protestant Episcopal Church*, 48 (1979), 145-165; and Cyclone Covey, "Puritanism and Music in Early America," *William and Mary Quarterly* (hereafter cited as W.M.Q.), VIII (1951), 377-388.

20. For general discussions of Puritan attitudes towards art, see Miller, *The New England Mind*, 157-167; Jonathan Fairbanks, "Portrait Painting in Seventeenth-Century Boston," in Fairbanks, et. al., *New England Begins: The Seventeenth Century*, 3 vols. (Boston, 1982), 413-415; Lynn Haims, "The Face of God: Puritan Iconography in Early American Poetry, Sermons, and Tombstone Carving," *Early American Literature*, 14, (1979), 15-47; Lillian B. Miller, "The Puritan Portrait: Its Function in Old and New England," in David D. Hall and David Grayson Allen (eds.), *Seventeenth-Century New England* (Boston, 1984), 157-165; and Dickran and Ann Tashjean, *Memorials for Children of Change: The Art of Early New England Stonecarving* (Middletown, Connecticut, 1974), 3-7.

21. Mather, *An Arrow Against Profane and Promiscuous Dancing*, 21-22.

22. Struna, "Puritans and Sport," 10-11. John Cotton was also more liberal on the role of music than were his contemporaries, although as with his view of dancing, Cotton made only the slightest of concessions. See Everett Emerson, *John Cotton* (New York, 1965), 27.

23. See Solberg, *The Puritan Sabbath*, 47-48, 70-77, for discussions of the dangers of sports and gambling in general and on the Sabbath especially.

24. R.M. Wiles, "Crowd-Pleasing Spectacles in 18ᵗʰ Century England," *Journal of Popular Culture*, 1 (1967), 93-95; Thomas Henricks, "Sport and Social Hierarchy in Medieval England," *Journal of Sport History*, 9 (1982), 21-23; Struna, "Puritans and Sport," 6-7.

25. Henricks, "Sport and Social Hierarchy," 25-30.

26. Struna, "Puritans and Sport," 6-7.

27. The urban quality of the puritan ideal is well known. Perry Miller in chapter V, "Puritan State and Puritan Society," in his *Errand Into The Wilderness* (Cambridge, Massachusetts, 1956), 141-152 provides the best intellectual analysis of their communal nature. Ola Winslow, *Meetinghouse Hill, 1630-1783* (New York, 1952), demonstrates the social, economic, and political importance of meeting places throughout the work.

28. For a wide-ranging examination of the social role played by meals and food see the essays in Peter Benes (ed.), *Foodways in the Northeast* (Boston, 1984). See also Kym S. Rice, "Early American Taverns: For the Entertainment of Friends and Strangers," *Early American Life*, 14 (1983), 46-55.

29. The importance of reading and writing to Puritans is well known to New England historians. For a few general views see David Grayson Allen, "The Social and Cultural Landscape of Seventeenth-Century New England," in Fairbanks, *New England Begins, I*, 1-9; George Littlefield, *Early Boston Booksellers, 1642-1711* (Boston, 1900); and especially the collection of essays in William Joyce (ed.), *Printing and Society in Early America* (Worcester, Massachusetts, 1983).

30. Kenneth Lockridge, *Literacy in Colonial New England: An Enquiry into the Social Context of Literacy in the Early Modern West* (New York, 1974), remains the best book on the subject. Lockridge's estimates of literacy rates have been adjusted upward slightly by some other scholars. See Ross Bealos, "Studying Literacy at the Community Level: A Research Note," *Journal of Interdisciplinary History*, 9 (1987), 93-102.

31. Mather, *Solemn Advice To Young Men Not To Walk In the Way of Their Hearts* (Boston: B. Green, 1695), 47.

32. For a particularly sharp warning aimed entirely at describing the dangers of travel see, Ebenezer Pemberton, *Advice to a Son: A Sermon Preached at the Request of a Gentleman in New England, Upon His Sons Going to Europe* (Boston, 1705). Warnings in the sermon literature were often targeted at adolescents. See Thompson, *Sex in Middlesex*, (1986), 71-96.

33. Mary Maples Dunn, "Saints and Sisters: Congregational and Quaker Women in the Early Colonial Period," *American Quarterly* (hereafter cited as A.Q.), XXX (1978), 584-601; Laurel Thatcher Ulrich, "Virtuous Women Found: New England Ministerial Literature, 1668-1755" A.Q. , XXVIII (1976), 20-40; Margaret Masson, "The Typology of the Female as a Model for the Regenerate: Puritan Preaching, 1690-1730," *Signs*, 2 (1986), 304-315; Cotton Mather, *Ornaments for the Daughters of Zion or the Character and Happiness of a Virtuous Woman* (Cambridge, Massachusetts, 1692), 1-11.

34. Cotton Mather, *Winter Meditations. Directions How to Employ the Leisure of the Winter for the Glory of God* (Boston, 1693), 3-15.

35. Theatre was one of the most hotly debated morality issues in post Revolutionary New England. See Morgan, "Puritan Hostility to the Theatre," 340-347; Brown, "The Colonial Theatre," 2-10; and John Gardiner, *The Speech of John Gardiner, Esq. Delivered in the House of Representatives on Thursday the 26ᵗʰ of January 1792 on the Subject…of Theatrical Exhibitions* (Boston, 1792), passim.

36. These letters are collected in Everett Emerson, *Letters from New England: The Massachusetts Bay Colony, 1629-1638* (Amherst, Massachusetts, 1976) passim.

37. Probably more than anyone else, Perry Miller has made historians aware of the function and nature of the jeremiad. See Miller, *The New England Mind*, 471-475. For some recent analysis of the jeremiads see, Sacvan Bereovitch, *The American Jeremiad* (Madison, Wisconsin, 1978), 3-30; Harry S. Stout, *The New England Soul: Preaching and Religious Culture in Colonial New England* (New York, 1986) passim, and Peter Wagner, "American Puritan Literature," *Canadian Journal of History and Sport and Physical Education*, 8 (1977), 62-75.

38. Wigglesworth, *God's controversy with New England,* (Boston, 1662); reprinted in *The American Puritans: Their Prose and Poetry,* ed. Perry Miller (New York: Doubleday and Co., 1956), 298.

39. See Wagner, American Puritan Literature, 64-65 for a discussion of this collective warning.

40. Cotton Mather, *A Cloud of Witness Against Balls and Dances* (Boston, 1700), 3-10; "Cotton Mather, et. al., *A Testimony Against Evil Customs Given by Several Ministers* (Boston, 1719), passim.

41. Cotton Mather, et. al., *A Serious Address to those Who Unnecessarily Frequent the Taverns.*

CHAPTER 2

HORSES AND GENTLEMEN

The Cultural Significance of Gambling Among the Gentry of Virginia

▪ *T. H. Breen* ▪

In the fall of 1686 Durand of Dauphiné, a French Huguenot, visited the capital of colonial Virginia. Durand regularly recorded in a journal what he saw and heard, providing one of the few firsthand accounts of late seventeenth-century Virginia society that has survived to the present day. When he arrived in Jamestown the House of Burgesses was in session. "I saw there fine-looking men," he noted, "sitting in judgment booted and with belted sword." But to Durand's surprise, several of these Virginia gentlemen "started gambling" soon after dinner, and it was not until midnight that one of the players noticed the Frenchman patiently waiting for the contest to end. The Virginian—obviously a veteran of long nights at the gaming table—advised Durand to go to bed. "For, said he, 'it is quite possible that we shall be here all night,' and in truth I found them still playing the next morning."[1]

The event Durand witnessed was not unusual. In late seventeenth- and early eighteenth-century Virginia, gentlemen spent a good deal of time gambling. During this period, in fact, competitive gaming involving high stakes became a distinguishing characteristic of gentry culture. Whenever the great planters congregated, someone inevitably produced a deck of cards, a pair of dice, or a backgammon board; and quarter-horse racing was a regular event throughout the colony. Indeed, these men hazarded money and tobacco on almost any proposition in which there was an element of chance. Robert Beverley, a member of one of Virginia's most prominent families, made a wager "with the gentlemen of the country" that if he could produce seven hundred gallons of

Reprinted, by permission, from T. Breen, "Horses and gentlemen: The cultural significance of gambling among the gentry of Virginia," *William and Mary Quarterly* By permission of Omohundro Institute of Early American History and Culture.

wine on his own plantation, they would pay him the handsome sum of one thousand guineas. Another leading planter offered six-to-one odds that Alexander Spotswood could not procure a commission as the colony's governor. And in 1671 one disgruntled gentleman asked a court of law to award him his winnings from a bet concerning "a Servant maid." The case of this suspect-sounding wager—unfortunately not described in greater detail—dragged on until the colony's highest court ordered the loser to pay the victor a thousand pounds of tobacco.[2]

The great planters' passion for gambling, especially on quarter-horse racing, coincided with a period of far-reaching social change in Virginia. Before the mid-1680s constant political unrest, servant risings both real and threatened, plant-cutting riots, and even a full-scale civil war had plagued the colony. But by the end of the century Virginia had achieved internal peace. Several elements contributed to the growth of social tranquility. First, by 1700 the ruling gentry were united as they had never been before. The great planters of the seventeenth century had been for the most part aggressive English immigrants. They fought among themselves for political and social dominance, and during Bacon's Rebellion in 1676 various factions within the gentry attempted to settle their differences on the battlefield. By the end of the century, however, a sizable percentage of the Virginia gentry, perhaps a majority, had been born in the colony. The members of this native-born elite—one historian calls them a "creole elite"—cooperated more frequently to unite in resistance against a series of interfering royal governors such as Thomas Lord Culpeper, Francis Nicholson, and Alexander Spotswood. After Bacon's Rebellion the leading planters—the kind of men whom Durand watched gamble the night away—successfully consolidated their control over Virginia's civil, military, and ecclesiastical institutions. They monopolized the most important offices; they patented the best lands.[3]

A second and even more far-reaching element in the creation of this remarkable solidarity among the gentry was the shifting racial composition of the plantation labor force. Before the 1680s the planters had relied on large numbers of white indentured servants to cultivate Virginia's sole export crop, tobacco. These impoverished, often desperate servants disputed their masters' authority and on several occasions resisted colonial rulers with force of arms. In part because of their dissatisfaction with the indenture system, and in part because changes in the international slave trade made it easier and cheaper for Virginians to purchase black laborers, the major planters increasingly turned to Africans. The blacks' cultural disorientation made them less difficult to control than the white servants. Large-scale collective violence such as Bacon's Rebellion and the 1682 plant-cutting riots consequently declined markedly. By the beginning of the eighteenth century Virginia had been transformed into a relatively peaceful, biracial society in which a few planters exercised almost unchallenged hegemony over both their slaves and their poorer white neighbors.[4]

The growth of gambling among the great planters during a period of significant social change raises important questions not only about gentry values but also about the social structure of late seventeenth-century Virginia. Why did gambling, involving high stakes, become so popular among the gentlemen at precisely this time? Did it reflect gentry values or have symbolic connotations for the people living in this society? Did this activity serve a social function, contributing in some manner to the maintenance of group cohesion? Why did quarter-horse racing, in particular, become a gentry sport? And finally, did public displays such as this somehow reinforce the great planters' social and political dominance?

In part, of course, gentlemen laid wagers on women and horses simply because they enjoyed the excitement of competition. Gambling was a recreation, like a good meal among friends or a leisurely hunt in the woods—a pleasant pastime when hard-working planters got together. Another equally acceptable explanation for the gentry's fondness for gambling might be the transplanting of English social mores. Certainly, the upper classes in the mother country loved betting for high stakes, and it is possible that the all-night cardgames and the frequent horse races were staged attempts by a provincial gentry to transform itself into a genuine landed aristocracy. While both views possess merit, neither is entirely satisfactory. The great planters of Virginia presumably could have favored less risky forms of competition. Moreover, even though several planters deliberately emulated English social styles, the widespread popularity of gambling among the gentry indicates that this type of behavior may have had deeper, more complex cultural roots than either of these explanations would suggest.[5]

In many societies competitive gaming is a device by which the participants transform abstract cultural values into observable social behavior. In his now-classic analysis of the Balinese cockfight Clifford Geertz describes contests for extremely high stakes as intense social dramas. These battles not only involve the honor of important villagers and their kin groups but also reflect in symbolic form the entire Balinese social structure. Far from being a simple pastime, betting on cocks turns out to be an expression of the way the Balinese perceive social reality. The rules of the fight, the patterns of wagering, the reactions of winners and losers—all these elements help us to understand more profoundly the totality of Balinese culture.[6]

The Virginia case is analogous to the Balinese. When the great planter staked his money and tobacco on a favorite horse or spurred a sprinter to victory, he displayed some of the central elements of gentry culture—its competitiveness, individualism, and materialism. In fact, competitive gaming was for many gentlemen a means of translating a particular set of values into action, a mechanism for expressing a loose but deeply felt bundle of ideas and assumptions about the nature of society. The quarter-horse races of Virginia were intense contests involving personal honor, elaborate rules, heavy betting, and wide community interest; and just as the cockfight opens up hidden dimensions of Balinese culture, gentry gambling offers an opportunity to improve our understanding of the complex interplay between cultural values and social behavior in Virginia.

Gambling reflected core elements of late seventeenth- and early eighteenth-century gentry values. From diaries, letters, and travel accounts we discover that despite their occasional cooperation in political affairs, Virginia gentlemen placed extreme emphasis upon personal independence. This concern may in part have been the product of the colony's peculiar settlement patterns. The great planters required immense tracts of fresh land for their tobacco. Often thousands of acres in size, their plantations were scattered over a broad area from the Potomac River to the James. The dispersed planters lived in their "Great Houses" with their families and slaves, and though they saw friends from time to time, they led for the most part isolated, routine lives. An English visitor in 1686 noted with obvious disapproval that "Their Plantations run over vast Tracts of Ground…whereby the Country is thinly inhabited; the Living solitary and unsociable." Some planters were uncomfortably aware of the problems created by physical isolation. William Fitzhugh, for example, admitted to a correspondent in the mother country, "Society that is good and ingenious is very scarce, and seldom to be come at except in books."[7]

Yet despite such apparent cultural privation, Fitzhugh and his contemporaries refused to alter their life styles in any way that might compromise their freedom of action. They assumed it their right to give commands, and in the ordering of daily plantation affairs they rarely tolerated outside interference. Some of these planters even saw themselves as lawgivers out of the Old Testament. In 1726 William Byrd II explained that "like one of the Patriarchs, I have my Flocks and my Herds, my Bond-men and Bond-women, and every sort of Trade amongst my own Servants, so that I live in a kind of independence on every one but Providence." Perhaps Byrd exaggerated for literary effect, but forty years earlier Durand had observed, "There are no lords [in Virginia], but each is sovereign on his own plantation." Whatever the origins of this independent spirit, it bred excessive individualism in a wide range of social activities. While these powerful gentlemen sometimes worked together to achieve specific political and economic ends, they bristled at the least hint of constraint. Andrew Burnaby later noted that "the public or political character of the Virginians corresponds with their private one: they are haughty and jealous of their liberties, impatient of restraint, and can scarcely bear the thought of being controlled by any superior power."[8]

The gentry expressed this uncompromising individualism in aggressive competitiveness, engaging in a constant struggle against real and imagined rivals to obtain more lands, additional patronage, and high tobacco prices. Indeed, competition was a major factor shaping the character of face-to-face relationships among the colony's gentlemen, and when the stakes were high the planters were not particular about the methods they employed to gain victory. In large part, the goal of the competition within the gentry group was to improve social position by increasing wealth.[9]

Some gentlemen believed that personal honor was at stake as well. Robert "King" Carter, by all accounts the most successful planter of his generation, expressed his anxiety about losing out to another Virginian in a competitive market situation. "In discourse with Colonel Byrd, Mr. Armistead, and a great many others," he explained, "I understand you [an English merchant] had sold their tobacco in round parcels and at good rates. I cannot allow myself to come behind any of these gentlemen in the planter's trade." Carter's pain arose not so much from the lower price he had received as from the public knowledge that he had been bested by respected peers. He believed he had lost face. This kind of intense competition was sparked, especially among the less affluent members of the gentry, by a dread of slipping into the ranks of what one eighteenth-century Virginia historian called the "common Planters." Gov. Francis Nicholson, an acerbic English placeman, declared that the "ordinary sort of planters" knew full well "from whence these mighty dons derive their originals." The governor touched a nerve; the efforts of "these mighty dons" to outdo one another were almost certainly motivated by a desire to disguise their "originals," to demonstrate anew through competitive encounters that they could legitimately claim gentility.[10]

Another facet of Virginia gentry culture was materialism. This certainly does not mean that the great planters lacked spiritual concerns. Religion played a vital role in the lives of men like Robert Carter and William Byrd II. Nevertheless, piety was largely a private matter. In public these men determined social standing not by a man's religiosity or philosophic knowledge but by his visible estate—his lands, slaves, buildings, even by the quality of his garments. When John Bartram, one of America's first botanists, set off in 1737 to visit two of Virginia's most influential planters, a London friend advised him to purchase a new set of clothes, "for though I should not esteem thee less, to come to me in what dress thou will,—yet these Virginians are a very gentle, well-dressed people—and look, perhaps, more at a man's outside than his inside." This perception of gentry values was accurate. Fitzhugh's desire to maintain outward appearances drove him to collect a stock of monogrammed silver plate and to import at great expense a well-crafted, though not very practical, English carriage. One even finds hints that the difficulty of preserving the image of material success weighed heavily upon some planters. When he described local Indian customs in 1705, Robert Beverley noted that native Americans lived an easy, happy existence "without toiling and perplexing their mind for Riches, which other people often trouble themselves to provide for uncertain and ungrateful Heirs."[11]

The gentry were acutely sensitive to the element of chance in human affairs, and this sensitivity influenced their attitudes toward other men and society. Virginians knew from bitter experience that despite the best-laid plans, nothing in their lives was certain. Slaves suddenly sickened and died. English patrons forgot to help their American friends. Tobacco prices fell without warning. Cargo ships sank. Storms and droughts ruined the crop. The list was endless. Fitzhugh warned an English correspondent to think twice before allowing a son to become a Virginia planter, for even "if the best husbandry and the greatest forecast and skill were used, yet ill luck at sea, a fall of a Market, or twenty other accidents may ruin and overthrow the best Industry." Other planters, even those who had risen to the top of colonial society, longed for greater security. "I could wish," declared William Byrd I in 1685, "we had some more certain commodity [than tobacco] to rely on but see no hopes of it." However desirable such certainty may have appeared, the planters always put their labor and money into tobacco, hoping for a run of luck. One simply learned to live with chance. In 1710 William Byrd II confided in his secret diary, "I dreamed last night that I won a tun full of money and might win more if I had ventured."[12]

Gaming relationships reflected these strands of gentry culture. In fact, gambling in Virginia was a ritual activity. It was a form of repetitive, patterned behavior that not only corresponded closely to the gentry's values and assumptions but also symbolized the realities of everyday planter life. This congruence between actions and belief, between form and experience, helps to account for the popularity of betting contests. The wager, whether over cards or horses, brought together in a single, focused act the great planters' competitiveness, independence, and materialism, as well as the element of chance. It represented a social agreement in which each individual was free to determine how he would play, and the gentleman who accepted a challenge risked losing his material possessions as well as his personal honor.[13]

The favorite household or tavern contests during this period included cards, backgammon, billiards, nine-pins, and dice. The great planters preferred card games that demanded skill as well as luck. Put, piquet, and whist provided

William Byrd III was one of the Virginia gentry's most avid participants in horse racing.

Virginia Historical Society.

the necessary challenge, and Virginia gentlemen—Durand's hosts, for example—regularly played these games for small sums of money and tobacco. These activities brought men together, stimulated conversation, and furnished a harmless outlet for aggressive drives. They did not, however, become for the gentry a form of intense, symbolic play such as the cockfight in Bali. William Byrd II once cheated his wife in a game of piquet, something he would never have dared to do among his peers at Williamsburg. By and large, he showed little emotional involvement in these types of household gambling. The exception here proves the rule. After an unusually large loss at the gaming tables of Williamsburg, Byrd drew a pointed finger in the margin of his secret diary and swore a "solemn resolution never at once to lose more than 50 shillings and to spend less time in gaming, and I beg the God Almighty to give me grace to keep so good a resolution...." Byrd's reformation was short-lived, for within a few days he dispassionately noted losing another four pounds at piquet.[14]

Horse racing generated far greater interest among the gentry than did the household games. Indeed, for the great planters and the many others who came to watch, these contests were preeminently a social drama. To appreciate the importance of racing in seventeenth-century Virginia, we must understand the cultural significance of horses. By the turn of the century possession of one of these animals had become a social necessity. Without a horse, a planter felt despised, an object of ridicule. Owning even a slow-footed saddle horse made the common planter more of a man in his own eyes as well as in those of his neighbors; he was reluctant to venture forth on foot for fear of making an adverse impression. As the Rev. Hugh Jones explained in 1724, "almost every ordinary person keeps a horse; and I have known some spend the morning in ranging several miles in the woods to find and catch their horses only to ride two or three miles to church, to the court-house, or to a horse-race, where they generally appoint to meet upon business." Such behavior seems a waste of time and energy only to one who does not comprehend the symbolic importance which the Virginians attached to their horses. A horse was an extension of its owner; indeed, a man was only as good as his horse. Because of the horse's cultural significance, the gentry attempted to set its horsemanship apart from that of the common planters. Gentlemen took better care of their animals, and, according to John Clayton, who visited Virginia in 1688, they developed a distinctive riding style. "They ride pretty sharply," Clayton reported; "a planters' pace is a proverb, which is a good sharp hand-gallop." A fast-rising cloud of dust far down a Virginia road probably alerted the common planter that he was about to encounter a social superior.[15]

The contest that generated the greatest interest among the gentry was the quarter-horse race, an all-out sprint by two horses over a quarter-mile dirt track. The great planters dominated these events. In the records of the county courts—our most important source of information about specific races—we find the names of some of the colony's most prominent planter families—Randolph, Eppes, Jefferson, Swan, Kenner, Hardiman, Parker, Cocke, Batte, Harwick (Hardidge), Youle (Yowell), and Washington. Members of the House of Burgesses, including its powerful speaker, William Randolph, were frequently mentioned in the contests that came before the courts. On at least one occasion the Rev James Blair, Virginia's most eminent clergyman and a founder of the College of William and Mary, gave testimony in a suit arising from a race run between Capt. William Soane and Robert Napier. The tenacity with which the gentry pursued these cases, almost continuations of the race itself, suggests that victory was no less sweet when it was gained in court.[16]

Many elements contributed to the exclusion of lower social groups from these contests. Because of the sheer size of wagers, poor freemen and common planters could not have participated regularly. Certainly, the members of the Accomack County Court were embarrassed to discover that one Thomas Davis, "a very poor man," had lost 500 pounds of tobacco or a cow and calf in a horse race with an adolescent named Mr. John Andrews. Recognizing that Davis bore "a great charge of wife and children," the justices withheld final judgment until the governor had an opportunity to rule on the legality of the wager. The Accomack court noted somewhat gratuitously that if the governor declared the action unlawful, it would fine Davis five days' work on a public bridge. In such cases county justices ordinarily made no comment upon a plaintiff's or defendant's financial condition, assuming, no doubt, that most people involved in racing were capable of meeting their gaming obligation.[17]

The gentry actively enforced its exclusive control over quarter-horse racing. When James Bullocke, a York County tailor, challenged Mr. Mathew Slader to a race in 1674, the county court informed Bullocke that it was "contrary to law for a labourer to make a race being a sport for gentlemen" and fined the presumptuous tailor two hundred pounds of tobacco and cask. Additional evidence of exclusiveness is found in early eighteenth-century Hanover County. In one of the earliest issues of the colony's first newspaper, the Virginia Gazette, an advertisement appeared announcing that "some merry-disposed gentlemen" in Hanover planned to celebrate St. Andrew's Day with a race for quarter-milers. The Hanover gentlemen explained in a later, fuller description that "all Persons resorting there are desired to behave themselves with decency and sobriety, the subscribers being resolved to discountenance all immorality with the utmost rigor." The purpose of these contests was to furnish the county's "considerable number of gentlemen, merchants, and credible planters" an opportunity for "cultivating friendship." Less affluent persons apparently were welcome to watch the proceedings provided they acted like gentlemen.[18]

In most match races the planter rode his own horse, and the exclusiveness of these contests meant that racing created intensely competitive confrontations. There were two ways to set up a challenge. The first was a regularly scheduled affair usually held on Saturday afternoon. By 1700 there were at least a dozen tracks, important enough to be known by name, scattered through the counties of the Northern Neck and the James River valley. The records are filled with references to contests held at such places as Smith's Field, Coan Race Course, Devil's Field, Yeocomico, and Varina. No doubt, many races also occurred on nameless country roads or convenient pastures. On the appointed day the planter simply appeared at the race track and waited for a likely challenge. We know from a dispute heard before the Westmoreland County Court in 1693 that John Gardner baldly "challenged all the horses then upon the ground to run with any of them for a thousand pounds of tobo and twenty shillings in money." A second type of contest was a more spontaneous challenge. When gentlemen congregated over a jug of hard cider or peach brandy, the talk frequently turned to horses. The owners presumably bragged about the superior speed of their animals, and if one planter called another's bluff, the men cried out "done, and done," marched to the nearest field, and there discovered whose horse was in fact the swifter.[19]

Regardless of the outcome, quarter-horse races in Virginia were exciting spectacles. The crowds of onlookers seem often to have been fairly large, as common planters, even servants, flocked to the tracks to watch the gentry challenge one another for what must have seemed immense amounts of money and tobacco. One witness before a Westmoreland County Court reported in 1674 that Mr. Stone and Mr. Youle had run a challenge for 10 pounds sterling "in sight of many people." Attendance at race days was sizable enough to support a brisk trade in cider and brandy. In 1714 the Richmond County Court fined several men for peddling "by retaile in the race ground." Judging from the popularity of horses throughout planter society, it seems probable that the people who attended these events dreamed of one day riding a local champion such as Prince or Smoaker.[20]

The magnitude of gentry betting indicates that racing must have deeply involved the planters' self-esteem. Wagering took place on two levels. The contestants themselves made a wager on the outcome, a main bet usually described in a written statement. In addition, side wagers were sometimes negotiated between spectators or between a contestant and spectator. Of the two, the main bet was far the more significant. From accounts of disputed races reaching the county courts we know that gentlemen frequently risked very large sums. The most extravagant contest of the period was a race run between John Baker and John Haynie in Northumberland County in 1693, in which the two men wagered 4000 pounds of tobacco and 40 shillings sterling on the speed of their sprinters, Prince and Smoaker. Some races involved only twenty or thirty shillings, but a substantial number were run for several pounds sterling and hundreds of pounds of tobacco. While few, if any, of the seventeenth-century gentlemen were what we would call gambling addicts, their betting habits seem irrational even by the more prudential standards of their own day; in conducting normal business transactions, for example, they would never have placed so much money in such jeopardy.[21]

To appreciate the large size of these bets we must interpret them within the context of Virginia's economy. Between 1660 and 1720 a planter could anticipate receiving about ten shillings per hundredweight of tobacco. Since the average grower seldom harvested more than 1500 pounds of tobacco a year per man, he probably never enjoyed an annual income from tobacco in excess of eight pounds sterling. For most Virginians the conversion of tobacco into sterling occurred only in the neat columns of account books. They themselves seldom had coins in their pockets. Specie was extremely scarce, and planters ordinarily paid their taxes and conducted business transactions with tobacco notes—written promises to deliver to the bearer a designated amount of tobacco. The great preponderance of seventeenth-century planters were quite poor, and even the great planters estimated their income in hundreds, not thousands, of pounds sterling. Fitzhugh, one of the wealthier men of his generation, described his financial situation in detail. "Thus I have given you some particulars," he wrote in 1686, "which I thus deduce, the yearly crops of corn and tobo together with the surplusage of meat more than will serve the family's use, will amount annually to 60000 lb. tobo which at 10 shillings per ct, is 300 pounds annum." These facts reveal that the Baker-Haynie bet—to take a notable example—amounted to approximately 22 pounds sterling, more than 7 percent of Fitzhugh's annual cash return. It is therefore not surprising that the common planters seldom took part in quarter-horse racing; this wager alone amounted to approximately three times the income they could expect to receive in a good year. Even a modest wager of a pound or two sterling represented a substantial risk.[22]

Gentlemen sealed these gaming relationships with a formal agreement, either a written statement laying out the terms of the contest or a declaration before a disinterested third party of the nature of the wager. In either case the participants carefully stipulated what rules would be in effect. Sometimes the written agreements were quite elaborate. In 1698, for example, Richard Ward and John Steward, Jr., "covenanted and agreed" to race at a quarter-mile track in Henrico County known as Ware. Ward's mount was to enjoy a ten-yard handicap, and if it crossed the finish line within five lengths of Steward's horse, Ward would win five pounds sterling; if Steward's obviously superior animal won by a greater distance, Ward promised to pay six pounds sterling. In another contest William Eppes and Stephen Cocke asked William Randolph to witness an agreement for a ten-shilling race: "each horse was to keep his path, they not being to crosse unlesse Stephen Cocke could get the other riders path at the start at two or three jumps."[23]

Virginia's county courts treated race covenants as binding legal contracts. If a gentleman failed to fulfill the agreement, the other party had legitimate grounds to sue; and the county justices' first consideration during a trial was whether the planters had properly recorded their agreement. The Henrico court summarily dismissed one gambling suit because "Noe money was stacked down nor Contract in writing made[,] one of which in such cases is by the law required." Because any race might generate legal proceedings, it was necessary to have a number of people present at the track not only to assist in the running of the contest but also to act as witnesses if anything went wrong. The two riders normally appointed an official starter, several judges, and someone to hold the stakes.[24]

Almost all of the agreements included a promise to ride a fair race. Thus two men in 1698 insisted upon "fair Rideing"; another pair pledged "they would run fair horseman's play." By such agreements the planters waived their customary right to jostle, whip, or knee an opponent, or to attempt to unseat him. During the last decades of the seventeenth century the gentry apparently attempted to substitute riding skill and strategy for physical violence. The demand for "fair Rideing" also suggests that the earliest races in Virginia were wild, no-holds-barred affairs that afforded contestants ample opportunity to vent their aggressions.[25]

The intense desire to win sometimes undermined a gentleman's written promise to run a fair race. When the stakes were large, emotions ran high. One man complained in a York County court that an opponent had interfered with his horse in the middle of the race, "by means whereof the s[ai]d Plaintiff lost the said race." Joseph Humphrey told a Northumberland County court that he would surely have come in first in a challenge for 1500 pounds of tobacco had not Capt. Rodham Kenner (a future member of the House of Burgesses) "held the defendt horses bridle in running his race." Other riders testified that they had been "josselled" while the race was in progress. An unusual case of interference grew out of a 1694 race which Rodham Kenner rode against John Hartly for one pound sterling and 575 pounds of tobacco. In a Westmoreland County Court Hartly explained that after a fair start and without using "whipp or spurr" he found himself "a great distance" in front of Kenner. But as Hartly neared the finish line, Kenner's brother, Richard, suddenly jumped onto the track and "did hollow and shout and wave his hat over his head in the plts [plaintiff's] horse's face." The animal panicked, ran outside the posts marking the finish line, and lost the race. After a lengthy trial a Westmoreland jury decided that Richard Kenner "did no foule play in his hollowing and waveing his hatt." What exactly occurred during this race remains a mystery, but since no one denied that Richard acted very strangely, it seems likely that the Kenner brothers were persuasive as well as powerful.[26]

Planters who lost large wagers because an opponent jostled or "hollowed" them off the track were understandably angry. Yet instead of challenging the other party to a duel or allowing gaming relationships to degenerate into blood feuds, the disappointed horsemen invariably took their complaints to the courts. Such behavior indicates not only that the gentlemen trusted the colony's formal legal system—after all, members of their group controlled it—but also that they were willing to place institutional limitations on their own competitiveness. Gentlemen who felt they had been cheated or abused at the track immediately collected witnesses and brought suit before the nearest county court. The legal machinery available to the aggrieved gambler was complex; and no matter how unhappy he may have been with the final verdict, he could rarely claim that the system had denied due process.[27]

The plaintiff brought charges before a group of justices of the peace sitting as a county court; if these men found sufficient grounds for a suit, the parties—in the language of seventeenth-century Virginia—could "put themselves upon the country." In other words, they could ask that a jury of twelve substantial freeholders hear the evidence and decide whether the race had in fact been fairly run. If the sums involved were high enough, either party could appeal a local decision to the colony's general court, a body consisting of the governor and his council. Several men who hotly insisted that they had been wronged followed this path. For example, Joseph Humphrey, loser in a race for 1500 pounds of tobacco, stamped out of a Northumberland County Court, demanding a stop to "farther proceedings in the Common Law till a hearing in Chancery." Since most of the General Court records for the seventeenth century were destroyed during the Civil War, it is impossible to follow these cases beyond the county level. It is apparent from the existing documents, however, that all the men involved in these race controversies took their responsibilities seriously, and there is no indication that the gentry regarded the resolution of a gambling dispute as less important than proving a will or punishing a criminal. It seems unlikely that the colony's courts would have adopted such an indulgent attitude toward racing had these contests not in some way served a significant social function for the gentry.[28]

Competitive activities such as quarter-horse racing served social as well as symbolic functions. As we have seen, gambling reflected core elements of the culture of late seventeenth-century Virginia. Indeed, if it had not done so, horse racing would not have become so popular among the colony's gentlemen. These contests also helped the gentry to maintain group cohesion during a period of rapid social change. After 1680 the great planters do not appear to have become significantly less competitive, less individualistic, or less materialistic than their predecessors had been. But while the values persisted, the forms in which they were expressed changed. During the last decades of the century unprecedented external pressures, both political and economic, coupled with a major shift in the composition of the colony's labor force, caused the Virginia gentry to communicate these values in ways that would not lead to deadly physical violence or spark an eruption of blood feuding. The members of the native-born elite, anxious to preserve their autonomy over local affairs, sought to avoid the kinds of divisions within their ranks that had contributed to the outbreak of Bacon's Rebellion. They found it increasingly necessary to cooperate against meddling royal governors. Moreover, such earlier unrest among the colony's plantation workers as Bacon's Rebellion and the plant-cutting riots had impressed upon the great planters the need to present a common face to their dependent laborers, especially to the growing number of black slaves who seemed more and more menacing as the years passed.[29]

Gaming relationships were one of several ways by which the planters, no doubt unconsciously, preserved class cohesion. By wagering on cards and horses they openly expressed their extreme competitiveness, winning temporary emblematic victories over their rivals without thereby threatening the social tranquility of Virginia. These non-lethal competitive devices, similar in form to what social anthropologists have termed "joking relationships," were a kind of functional alliance developed by the participants themselves to reduce dangerous, but often inevitable, social tensions.[30]

Without rigid social stratification racing would have lost much of its significance for the gentry. Participation in these contests publicly identified a person as a member of an elite group. Great planters raced against their social peers. They certainly had no interest in competing with social inferiors, for in this kind of relationship victory carried no positive meaning: The winner gained neither honor nor respect. By the same token, a defeat by someone like James Bullocke, the tailor from York, was painful, and to avoid such incidents gentlemen rarely allowed poorer whites to enter their gaming relationships—particularly the heavy betting on quarter horses. The common planters certainly gambled among themselves. Even the slaves may have laid wagers. But when the gentry competed for high stakes, they kept their inferiors at a distance, as spectators but never players.

The exclusiveness of horse racing strengthened the gentry's cultural dominance. By promoting these public displays the great planters legitimized the cultural values which racing symbolized—materialism, individualism, and competitiveness. These colorful, exclusive contests helped persuade subordinate white groups that gentry culture was desirable, something worth emulating; and it is not surprising that people who conceded the superiority of this culture readily accepted the gentry's right to rule. The wild sprint down a dirt track served the interests of Virginia's gentlemen better than they imagined.

Notes

1. [Durand of Dauphiné], A Huguenot Exile in Virginia or Voyages of a Frenchman exiled for his Religion with a Description of Virginia and Maryland, ed. Gilbert Chinard (New York, 1934 [orig. publ. The Hague, 1687]),148.

2. Rev. James Fontaine, Memoirs of a Huguenot Family...,ed. Ann Maury (Baltimore, 1967 [orig. publ. 1853]), 265-266; John Mercer, cited in Jane Carson; Colonial Virginians at Play (Williamsburg, 1965), 49, n. 1; H. R. McIlwaine, ed., Minutes of the Council and General Court of Colonial Virginia, 1622-1632, 1670-1676 . . . (Richmond, 1924), 252, 281, 285.

3. Throughout this essay I use the terms gentry, gentlemen, and great planters as synonyms. In each Virginia county a few gentry families dominated civil, ecclesiastical, and military affairs. While the members of these families were substantially wealthier than the great majority of white planters, they were not a class in a narrow economic sense. Their cultural style as well as their financial position set them apart. The great planters and their families probably accounted for less than 2% of the colony's white population. Louis B. Wright, The First Gentlemen of Virginia; Intellectual Qualities of the Early Colonial Ruling Class (San Marino, Calif., 1940), 57, estimates their number at "fewer than a hundred families." While entrance into the gentry was not closed to newcomers, upward mobility into that group became increasingly difficult after the 1690s. See Philip A. Bruce, Social Life of Virginia in the Seventeenth Century (New York, 1907), 39-100; Aubrey C. Land, "Economic Base and Social Structure: The Northern Chesapeake in the Eighteenth Century," Journal of Economic History, XXV (1965), 639-654; Bernard Bailyn, "Politics and Social Structure in Virginia," in James Morton Smith, ed., Seventeenth-Century America: Essays in Colonial History (Chapel Hill, NC., 1959), 90-115; and Jack P. Greene, "Foundations of Political Power in the Virginia House of Burgesses, 1720-1776," William and Mary Quarterly, 3d Ser., XVI (1959), 485-506. These disturbances are described in T. H. Breen, "A Changing Labor Force and Race Relations in Virginia 1660-1710," Journal of Social History, VII (1973), 3-25. The fullest account of Bacon's Rebellion remains Wilcomb E. Washburn, The Governor and the Rebel: A History of Bacon's Rebellion in Virginia (Chapel Hill, NC., 1957). Several historians have remarked on the unusual political stability of 18th-century Virginia. See, for example, Jack P. Greene, "Changing Interpretations of Early American Politics," in Ray Allen Billington, ed., The Reinterpretation of Early American History: Essays in Honor of John Edwin Pomfret (San Marino, Calif., 1966), l67-168, and Gordon S. Wood, "Rhetoric and Reality in the American Revolution," WMQ, 3d Ser., XXIII (1966), 27-30. The phrase "creole elite" comes from Carole Shammas, "English-Born and Creole Elites in Turn- of-the-Century Virginia," in Thad W. Tate and David L. Ammerman, eds., Essays on the Seventeenth-Century Chesapeake (Chapel Hill, NC., forthcoming). See also David W. Jordan, "Political Stability and the Emergence of a Native Elite in Maryland, 1660-1715," ibid. The process of forming a native-born elite is also discussed in Bailyn, "Politics and Social Structure," in Smith, ed., Seventeenth-Century America, 90-115; John C. Rainbolt, "The Alteration in the Relationship between Leadership and Constituents in Virginia, 1660 to 1720." WMQ, 3rd Ser., XXVII (1970), 411-434; and Martin H. Quitt, "Virginia House of Burgesses 1660-1706: The Social, Educational, and Economic Bases of Political Power" (Ph.D. Diss., Washington University, 1970).

4. Breen, "Changing Labor Force," Jour. Soc. Hist., VII (1973) 2-25; Edmund S. Morgan, American Slavery—American Freedom: The Ordeal of Colonial Virginia (New York, 1975), 295-362; Rainbolt, "Leadership and Constituents," WMQ, 3d Ser., XXVII (1970), 428-429. On the social attitudes of the small planters see David Alan Williams, "Political Alignments in Colonial Virginia, 1698-1750" (Ph.D. Diss., Northwestern University, 1959), chap. I.

5. A sudden growth of gambling for high stakes in pre-Civil War England is discussed in Lawrence Stone, The Crisis of the Aristocracy, 1558-1641 (Oxford, 1965.) For the later period see Robert W. Malcolmson, Popular Recreations in English Society, 1700-1850 (Cambridge, 1973); G. E. Mingay, English Landed Society in the Eighteenth Century (London, 1963), 151-153, 249-250; and E. D. Cuming, "Sports and Games," in A. S. Turberville, ed., Johnson's England: An Account of the Life

and Manners of his Age, I (London, 1933), 362-383. It is important to stress here that the Virginia gentry did not simply copy English customs. As I argue in this essay, a specific, patterned form of behavior, such as gambling, does not become popular in a society or among the members of a subgroup of that society unless the activity reflects or expresses values indigenous to that culture. In 17th-century Massachusetts Bay, for example, heavy betting did not develop. A small amount of gambling seems to have occurred among the poor, especially among servants, but I can find no incidence of gambling among the colony's social, political, or religious leaders. See Nathaniel B. Shurtleff, ed. Records of the Governor and Company of the Massachusetts Bay… (Boston, 1853-1854), II, 180, III, 201, IV, p1. 1, 366; Records of the Suffolk County Court, 1671 1680 (Colonial Society of Massachusetts, Publications [Boston], 1933), XXIX, 131, 259, 263, XXX, 1162; and Joseph H. Smith, ed., Colonial Justice in Western Massachusetts, 1693-1702: The Pynchon Court Record (Cambridge, Mass., 1961), 109.

6. Two of Clifford Geertz's essays here helped shape my ideas about Virginia society: "Thick Description: Toward an Interpretive Theory of Culture" and "Deep Play: Notes on the Balinese Cockfight" in Geertz, The Interpretation of Cultures (New York, 1973), 3-30, 412-453. Also see Erving Goffman's "Fun in Games" in Goffmann, Encounters: Two Studies in the Sociology of Interaction (Indianapolis, 1961), 17-81; Raymond Firth, "A Dart Match in Tikopia: A Study in the Sociology of Primitive Sport," Oceania, 1(1930), 64-96; and H. A. Powell, "Cricket in Kiriwina," Listener, XLVIII (1952), 384-385.

7. Philip A. Bruce, Economic History of Virginia in the Seventeenth Century…, II (New York, 1935 [Orig. publ. 1895]), 1511. "A Letter from Mr. John Clayton Rector of Crofton at Wakefield in Yorkshire, to the Royal Society, May 12, 1688," in Peter Force, ed., Tracts and Other Papers Relating Principally to the Origin, Settlement and Progress of the Colonies in North America, III (Washington. D.C.. 1844), no. 12, 21. Richard Beale Davis, ed., William Fitzhugh and His Chesapeake World 1676-1701: The Fitzhugh Letters and Other Documents (Chapel Hill, N.C., 1963).

8. On the independence of the Virginia gentry see Gerald W. Mullin, Flight and Rebellion: Slave Resistance in Eighteenth-Century Virginia (New York, 1972), chap. I. William Byrd II to Charles, Earl of Orrery, July 5, 1726, in "Virginia Council Journals, 1726-1753," Virginia Magazine of History and Biography, XXXJJ (1924), 27. [Durand], A Huguenot Exile, ed. Chinard, 1210. I discuss this theme in greater detail in a paper entitled "Looking Out For Number One: Cultural Values and Social Behavior in Early Seventeenth-Century Virginia" (paper delivered at the Thirty-Second Conference in Early American History, Nov. 1974). Rev. Andrew Burnaby, Travels through the Middle Settlements in North America, in the Years 1759 and 1760; With Observations Upon the State of the Colonies, in John Pinkerton, ed., A General Collection of the Best and Most interesting Voyages and Travels in All Ports of the World…, XIII (London, 1812), 715.

9. According to John Rainbolt, the gentry's "striving for land, wealth, and position was intense and, at times, ruthless" ("Leadership and Constituents," WMQ, 3d Ser., XXVII [1970], 414). See Carole Shammas, "English-Born and Creole Elites," in Tate and Ammerman, eds., Seventeenth-Century Chesapeake; Morgan, American Slavery—American Freedom, 288-289; and Rhys Isaac, "Evangelical Revolt: The Nature of the Baptists' Challenge to the Traditional Order in Virginia, 1765 to 1775," WMQ, 3d Ser., XXXI (1974), 345-353.

10. Louis B. Wright, ed., Letters of Robert Carter, 1720-1727: The Commercial Interests of a Virginia Gentleman (San Marino, Calif., 1940), 93-94. Hugh Jones, The Present State of Virginia Giving a Particular and short Account of the Indian, English, and Negroe Inhabitants of that Colony… (New York, 1865 [Orig. publ 1724]), 48. Quoted in Thomas Jefferson Werten-baker, The Old South: The Founding of American Civilization (New York, 1942),19.

11. Peter Collinson to John Bartram, Feb. 17, 1737, WMQ, 3d Ser., VI (1926), 304. Davis, ed., Fitzhugh Letters, 229, 241-242, 244, 246, 249-250, 257-259. For another example of the concern about outward appearances see the will of Robert Cole (1674), in WMQ, 3d Ser., XXXI (1974), 139. Robert Beverley, The History and Present State of Virginia, ed., Louis B. Wright (Chapel Hill, N.C , 1947), 226.

12. William Fitzhugh to Oliver Luke, Aug. 15, 1690, in Davis, ed., Fitzhugh Letters, 280. The favorite household or tavern contests during this period included William Byrd to Perry and Lane, July 8, 1686, in "Letters of William Byrd I," VMHB, XXV (1917), 132. Louis B. Wright and Marion Tinling, eds., The Secret Diary of William Byrd of Westover, 1709-1712 (Richmond, Va., 1941), 223-224.

13. Gaming was so popular among the gentry, so much an expression of their culture, that it became a common metaphor in their discussion of colonial politics. For example, an unsigned essay

entitled "The History of Bacon's and Ingram's Rebellion, 1676" described the relationship between Nathaniel Bacon and Gov. William Berkeley as a card game. Charles M. Andrews, ed., Narratives of the Insurrections, 1675-1690 (New York, 1915), 57. In another account of Bacon's Rebellion, written in 1705, Thomas Mathew noted that several members of the House of Burgesses were "not docile enough to Gallop the future Races, that Court seed dispo'd to lead'em." Ibid., 32. In May 1697 William Fitzhugh explained to Capt. Roger Jones: "your self will see what a hard game we have to play the contrary party that is our opposers, having the best cards and the trumps to boot especially the Honor. Yet would my Lord Fairfax there [in England], take his turn in Shuffling and Dealing the cards and his Lordship with the rest see that we were not cheated in our game, I question not but we should gain the Sett, tho' the game is so far plaid" (Davis, ed., Fitzhugh Letters, 352). Rhys Isaac provides a provocative analysis of the relationship between games and gentry culture on the eve of the Revolution in "Evangelical Revolt," WMQ, 3d Ser., XXXI (1974), 348-353. See also Mark Anthony deWolfe Howe, ed., "Journal of Josiah Quincy, Junior, 1773," Massachusetts Historical Society, Proceedings, XLIX (1915-1916), 467, and William Stith, The Sinfulness and pernicious Nature of Gaming. A Sermon Preached before the General Assembly of Virginia: At Williamsburg, March 1st 1752 (Williamsburg, 1752), 5-26.

14. The best discussion of these household games is Carson, Virginians at Play, 49-89. See also Charles Cotton, The Compleat Gamester or Instructions How to Play at Billiards, Trucks, Bowls, and Chess .. (1674), in Cyril H. Hartmann, ed., Games and Gamesters of the Restoration: The Compleat Gamester by Charles Cotton, 1674, and Lives of the Gamesters, by Theophilus Lucas, 1714 (London, 1930). After 1750, however, the gentry's attitude toward household or tavern games seems to have changed. The betting became so heavy that several eminent planters lost fortunes at the gaming tables. A visitor at Williamsburg in 1765 wrote of these men that "they are all professed gamesters, Especially Colonel Burd [William Byrd III], who is never happy but when he has the box and Dice in hand. [T]his Gentleman from a man of the greatest poverty of any in America has reduced himself to the Degree by gaming, that few or nobody will Credit him for Ever so small a sum of money. [H]e was obliged to sel 400 fine Negroes a few Days before my arrival." "Journal of a French Traveller in the Colonies, 1765, I," American Historical Review, CCVI (1920-1921), 742. Byrd was not alone. Robert Wormeley Carter and Robert Burwell were excessive gamblers, and as the aging Landon Carter (Robert "King" Carter's son) observed the wagering of the gentry on the eve of the Revolution, he sadly mused, "they play away and play it all away," Jack P. Greene, ed., The Diary of Colonel Landon Carter of Sabine Hall, 1752-1778, II (Charlottesville, Va., 1965), 830. On this generation's addiction to gambling see Emory G. Evans, "The Rise and Decline of the Virginia Aristocracy in the Eighteenth Century: The Nelsons," in Darrett B. Rutman, ed., The Old Dominion: Essay for Thomas Perkins Abernethy (Charlottesville, Va., 1964), 68-70. Wright and Tinling, eds., Secret Diary, 75, 442, 449.

15. Only one mention of cockfighting before 1730 has come to my attention, and that one refers to contests among the "common planters." Jones, Present State of Virginia, 48. See Carson, Virginians at Play, 151-152. Jones, Present State of Virginia, 48. This observation was repeated in other accounts of Virginia society throughout the 18th century. William Byrd II wrote "my Dear Countymen have so great a Passion for riding, that they will often walk two miles to catch a Horse, in Order to ride One." William K. Boyd, ed., William Byrd's Histories of the Dividing Line Betwixt Virginia and North Carolina (Raleigh, N.C. 1928), 258. See also Carson, Virginians at Play, 102-105. "A Letter from Clayton," in Force, ed., Tracts and Other Papers, no. 12, 35.

16. On the development of racing in Virginia, especially the transition from the quarter-mile straight track to the oval course, see W. G. Stanard, "Racing in Colonial Virginia," VMHB, II (1894-1895), 293-305, and Fairfax Harrison, "The Equine F.F.V.'s: A study of the Evidence for the English Horses Imported into Virginia before the Revolution," Ibid., XXXV (1927), 329-370. I suspect that quarter-horse racing was a sport indigenous to Virginia. Besides Randolph, there were John Stone, William Hardidge, Thomas Yowell, John Hardiman, Daniel Sullivant, Thomas Chamberlain, Rodham Kenner, Richard Kenner, William Soan, and Alexander Swan. Aug. 1690, Henrico County, Order Book, 1978-1693, 340. All references to manuscript county records are to the photostat copies at the Virginia State Library, Richmond.

17. Jan. 16, 1666, Accomack Co., Orders, 1666-1670, 9.

18. Sept. 10, 1674, York Co., Deeds, Orders, Wills, 1672-1694, 85. Virginia Gazette, Nov. 19-26, 1736, Sept. 30 – Oct. 7, 1737.

19. Bruce, *Social Life*, 195-209; Carson, *Virginians at Play*, 108-110. Apr. 7, 1693, Westmoreland Co., Order Book, 1690-1698, 92; "Racing in Virginia in 1700-05," *VMHB*, X (1902-1903), 320. Aug. 1683, Henrico Co. Records [Deeds and Wills], 1677-1692, 254.

20. Oct. 16, 1674, Westmoreland Co., Deeds, Patents, Etc., 1655-1677, 211; Bruce, *Social Life*, 197-198; Carson, *Virginians at Play*, 109. Beverley Fleet, Ed., *Richmond County Records, 1704-1724*, Virginia Colonial Abstracts, XVII (Richmond, VA, 1943), 95-96.

21. Carson, *Virginians at Play*, 105. See Aug. 29, 1694, Westmoreland Co., Order Book, 1690-1698, 146. Aug. 22, 1695, Northumberland Co., Order Book, 1678-1698. Pt. 2, 707-708.

22. Morgan, *American Slavery—American Freedom*, 142, 198, 204. Bruce, *Economic History*, II, 495-512. Aubrey Land's analysis of the probate records in a tobacco-producing area in nearby Maryland between 1690 and 1699 reveals that 74.6% of the estates there were worth less than 100 pounds sterling. According to Land, the difference between the social structures of Maryland and Virginia at the time were not "very great." Land, "Economic Base and Social Structure," *Jour. Econ. Hist.*, XXV (1965), 641-644. William Fitzhugh to Dr. Ralph Smith, Apr. 22, 1686, in Davis, ed., *Fitzhugh Letters*, 176.

23. The full covenant is reproduced in Stanard, "Racing in Colonial Virginia," *VMHB*, II (1894-1895), 296-298.

24. Virginia law prohibited fraudulent gaming, certain kinds of side bets, and gambling by persons who had "no visible estate, profession or calling, to maintain themselves." William Waller Hening, ed., *The Statutes at Large; Being a Collection of all the Laws of Virginia…*, IV (Richmond, 1820), 214-218; George Webb, *Office and Authority of a Justice of Peace…* (Williamsburg, VA 1736), 165-167. Wagers made between two gainfully employed colonists were legal agreements and enforceable as contracts. The courts of Virginia, both common law and chancery, apparently followed what they believed to be standard English legal procedure. Whether they were correct is difficult to ascertain. Sir William Holdsworth explains that acts passed by Parliament during the reigns of Charles II and Anne allowed individuals to sue for gaming debts, but he provides no evidence that English courts regularly settled disputed contests such as horse races. Holdsworth, *A History of English Law* (London, 1966), VI, 404, XI, 539-542. Not until the 1750s did Virginians begin to discuss gambling as a social vice. See Stith, *The Sinfulness…of Gaming*; R. A. Brock, ed., *The Official Records of Robert Dinwiddie*, I (Richmond, VA 1883); Samuel Davies, *Virginia's Danger and Remedy. Two Discourses Occasioned by the Severe Drought…* (Williamsburg, 1756). Oct. 1690, Henrico Co., Order Book, 1678-1693, 351. See also Aug. 28, 1674, Northampton Co., Order Book No. 9, 1664-1674, 269, and Nov. 4, 1674, *Ibid.*, No. 10, 1674-1679.

25. Stanard, "Racing in Colonial Virginia," *VMHB*, II (1894-1895), 267; Henrico Co. Records [Deeds and Wills], 1677-1692, 466. Carson, *Virginians at Play*, 109-110.

26. "Some Extracts from the Records of York Co., Virginia," WMQ, 1st Ser., IX (1900-1901), 178-179 Jan. 1694, Northumberland Co., Order Book, 1678-1698, Pt. 2, 643. Aug. 29, 1694, Westmoreland Co., Order Book, 1690-1698, 146-146a. Also see Oct. 1689, Henrico Co., Order Book, 1678-1693, 313, and Stanard, "Racing in Virginia," VMHB, II(1894-1895), 296.

27. A gentleman could have challenged an opponent to a duel. Seventeenth and early 18th-century Virginians recognized a code of honor of which dueling was a part, but they did everything possible to avoid such potentially lethal combats. I have found only four cases before 1730 in which dueling was even discussed. County courts fined two of the challengers before they could do any harm. ("A Virginian Challenge in the Seventeenth Century," VMHB, II [1894-1895, 96-97; Lower Norfolk County Antiquarian, IV [1904], 106.) And two comic-opera challenges that only generated blustery rhetoric are described in William Stevens Perry, ed., Historical Collections Relating to the American Colonial Church, I (Hartford, Conn., 1870), 25-28, and Bond, ed., Byrd's Histories of the Dividing Line, 173-175. On the court system see Philip A. Bruce, Institutional History of Virginia in the Seventeenth Century…, I(Gloucester, 1910), 484-632, 647-689.

28. Aug. 29, 1694, Westmoreland Co., Order Book, 1690-1698, 146a. Jan. 1694, Northumberland Co., Order Book, 1678-1698, Pit. 2, 643. Sometimes the courts had an extremely difficult time deciding exactly what had occurred at a race. A man testified in 1675 that he had served as the official judge for a contest, and that while he knew which horse had finished first, he was "not able to say much less to Sweare that the Horse did Cary his Rider upon his back over the path." Sept. 16, 1675, Surry County, Deeds, Wills and Orders, 1671-1684, 133. For another complex case see Mar. 5, 1685, Rappahannock Co. Order [no. 1], 1683-1686, 103, 120, 153.

29. For evidence of the persistence of these values among the gentry in the Revolutionary period see Isaac, "Evangelical Revolt," WMQ, 3d Ser., XXXI (1974), 348-353.

30. The planters' aggressive hospitality may have served a similar function. Hospitality in Virginia should be analyzed to discover its relationship to gentry culture. Robert Beverley makes some suggestive comments about this custom in his History and Present State of Virginia, 312-313. An interesting comparison to the Virginia practice is provided in Michael W. Young, Fighting with Food: Leadership, Values and Social Control in a Massim Society (Cambridge, 1971). A. R. Radcliffe-Brown, Structure and Function in Primitive Society: Essays and Addresses (New York, 1964), Chaps. 4, 5.

PART II

TRANSFORMATION OF SPORT IN A RAPIDLY CHANGING SOCIETY, 1776-1870

Between 1776 and 1870 America experienced an assortment of rapid changes. An influx of immigrants, war between the North and the South, religious revivalism, growing industrialization and urbanization, the common school movement, the women's rights crusade, the health reform movement, and a host of other transformative events all combined to make changes in this country's attitudes toward exercise, fitness, and sport at various levels of competition. The latter stages of this period in particular saw sport assume more modern trappings, including the birth of sporting periodicals, prearranged athletic contests, formalization of rules and record keeping, and founding of sport organizations.

These changes in sport were probably most noticeable in New York City. The city emerged as a great center for sport, which is made clear in chapter 3, in Melvin Adelman's essay "Pedestrianism, Billiards, Boxing, and Animal Sports." Using an impressive list of primary source materials, including newspaper accounts, journal entries, and committee reports, Adelman analyzes the growth of four dissimilar yet culturally important sports in the city founded by the Dutch West India Company. Adelman's central point is that pedestrianism, billiards, boxing, and animal sports all had modern elements but were not transformed into modern sports by 1870. Of the four sports, commercial pedestrianism, most significantly the Caledonian Games, became the most modern in regard to organizational structure.

During this period, croquet became popular among both men and women. Although the precise origins of the game are not known, croquet apparently found its way from Ireland to England in the 1850s and sometime later arrived in America. The common characterization of the game is that it was ideally suited for women who followed a strict code of behavior and participated in the sport with good manners while emphasizing proper etiquette and the social graces over winning and unbridled competition. Jon Sterngass turns that characterization on its head in chapter 4, "Cheating, Gender Roles, and the Nineteenth-Century Croquet Craze." Acknowledging that "female grace and good manners" were the ideal standards codified in croquet manuals, Sterngass argues that in reality women were temporarily able to "jettison their passive role and dominate if not humiliate men. They played the game very seriously, strove for victory, and commonly used deception and stretched the rules when competing."

Generating far more public appeal than croquet was the sport of baseball. A highly competitive game that demands an extraordinary amount of athletic skill and teamwork, baseball was transformed in the 1860s from a local club sport in the New York City area to a network of clubs located throughout the Midwest and Northeast. Warren Goldstein nicely analyzes this nationalization of the sport in chapter 5, "The National Game." With much insight, Goldstein makes clear that the Cincinnati Red Stockings were very important in baseball's expansion. Under the guidance of legendary baseball man Harry Wright, and with outstanding players from different parts of the country, the Red Stockings dominated the sport long enough to garner enormous attention from a sporting press who "was creating a baseball public whose interest was acquiring national scope."

Suggested Readings

Adelman, Melvin L. *A Sporting Time: New York City and the Rise of Modern Athletics.* Urbana, IL: University of Illinois Press, 1986.

Adelman, Melvin L. "The First Modern Sport in America: Harness Racing in New York City, 1825-1870." *Journal of Sport History*, 8(1981): 5-32.

Barney, Robert Knight. "Knights of Cause and Exercise: German Forty-Eighters and Turnvereine in the United States During the Ante-Bellum Period." *Canadian Journal of History of Sport*, 13(1982): 62-79.

Berryman, Jack W. "Sport, Health, and the Rural-Urban Conflict: Baltimore and John Stuart Skinner's American Farmer, 1919-1820." *Conspectus of History*, 1(1982). 43-61.

Berryman, Jack W. "The Tenuous Attempts of Americans to 'Catch up with John Bull': Specialty Magazines and Sporting Journalism, 1800-1835." *Canadian Journal of History of Sport and Physical Education*, 10(1979): 33-61.

Block, David. *Baseball Before We Knew It: A Search for the Roots of the Game.* Lincoln, NE: University of Nebraska Press, 2005.

Chisholm, Ann. "The Disciplinary Dimensions of Nineteenth-Century Gymnastics for U.S. Women." *The International Journal of History of Sport,* 24(2007): 432-479.

Durick, William G. "The Gentlemen's Race: An Examination of the 1868 Harvard-Oxford Boat Race." *Journal of Sport History,* 15(1988): 41-63.

Fielding, Lawrence W. "War and Trifles: Sport in the Shadows of Civil War Army Life." *Journal of Sport History,* 4(1977): 151-168.

Folsom, Ed. "The Manly and Healthy Game: Walt Whitman and the Development of American Baseball." *Arete: The Journal of Sport Literature.* 2(1984):43-62.

Gorn, Elliott J. "Good-Bye Boys, I Die a True American: Homicide, Nativism and Working-Class Culture in Antebellum New York City." *Journal of American History,* 74(1987): 388-410.

Gorn, Elliott J. " 'Gouge and Bite, Pull Hair and Scratch': The Social Significance of Fighting in the Southern Backcountry." *American Historical Review,* 90(1985): 18-43.

Gorn, Elliott J. *The Manly Art: Bareknuckle Prize Fighting in America.* Ithaca, NY: Cornell University Press, 1986.

Green, Harvey. *Fit for America: Health, Fitness, Sport and American Society.* Baltimore, MD: The Johns Hopkins University Press, 1988.

Jable, J. Thomas. "Social Class and the Sport of Cricket in Philadelphia, 1850-1880." *Journal of Sport History,* 18(1991): 205-223.

Kirsch, George B. *Baseball in Blue and Gray: The National Pastime During the Civil War.* Princeton: Princeton University Press, 2003.

Kirsch, George B. *The Creation of American Team Sports: Baseball and Cricket, 1838-1872.* Urbana, IL: University of Illinois Press, 1989.

Lewis, Guy. "The Muscular Christianity Movement," *Journal of Health, Physical Education and Recreation,* 5(1966): 27-42.

Lewis, R.M. "American Croquet in the 1860s: Playing the Game and Winning." *Journal of Sport History,* 18(1991): 365-386.

Lockley, Timothy. " 'The Manly Game': Cricket and Masculinity in Savannah Georgia in 1859." *The International Journal of the History of Sport,* 20(2003): 77-98.

Lucas, John A. "A Prelude to the Rise of Sport: Ante-bellum America, 1850-1860." *Quest,* 11(1968): 50-57.

Park, Roberta J. " 'Embodied Selves': The Rise and Development of Concern for Physical Education, Active Games and Recreation for American Women, 1776-1865." *Journal of Sport History,* 5(1978): 5-41.

Park, Roberta J. "Harmony and Cooperation: Attitudes Toward Physical Education and Recreation in Utopian Social Thought and American Communitarian Experiments, 1825-1865." *Research Quarterly,* 45(1974): 276-292.

Park, Roberta J. "The Attitudes of Leading New England Transcendentalists Toward Healthful Exercise, Active Recreations, and Proper Care of the Body, 1830-1860." *Journal of Sport History,* 4(1977): 355-369.

Rader, Benjamin G. "The Quest for Subcommunities and the Rise of American Sports." *American Quarterly,* 29(1977): 355-369.

Redmond, Gerald. *The Caledonian Games in Nineteenth Century America.* Rutherford, NJ: Fairleigh Dickinson University Press, 1982.

Rosenzweig, Roy and Blackmar, Elizabeth. *The Park and the People: A History of Central Park*. Ithaca, NY: Cornell University Press, 1992.

Smith, Kevin R. *Black Genesis: The History of the Black Prize Fighter, 1760-1870*. New York: I Universe, Inc., 2003.

Struna, Nancy L. "The North-South Races: American Thoroughbred Racing in Transition, 1823-1850." *Journal of Sport History*, 8(1981): 28-57.

Todd, Jan. *Physical Culture and the Body Beautiful: Purposive Exercise in the Lives of American Women, 1800-1875*. Macon, GA: Mercer University Press, 1998.

Verbrugge, Martha A. *Able-Bodied Womanhood: Personal Health and Social Change in Nineteenth-Century Boston*. New York: Oxford University Press, 1988.

Vertinsky, Patricia. "Sexual Equality and the Legacy of Catherine Beecher." *Journal of Sport History*, 6(1979): 39-49.

Whorton, James. *Crusaders for Fitness: The History of American Health Reformers*. Princeton, NJ: Princeton Unversity Press, 1982.

Wiggins, David K. "The Play of Slave Children in the Plantation Communities of the Old South, 1820-1860." *Journal of Sport History*, 7(1980): 21-39.

Yates, Norris W. *William T. Porter and the Spirit of the Times*. Baton Rouge: Louisiana State University Press, 1957.

CHAPTER 3

PEDESTRIANISM, BILLIARDS, BOXING, AND ANIMAL SPORTS

■ *Melvin L. Adelman* ■

Running and walking races, billiards, boxing, and animal sports were all part of life in New York during the colonial period, and city residents increasingly followed these sports between 1820 and 1870, particularly after 1840. The four sports had much in common, including the fact that they were all primarily spectator sports dominated by a small group of professionals who came overwhelmingly from the working classes and were mostly foreign-born. The growth of each of these sports, with the exception of pedestrianism, was intimately bound up with shifts in the concept of manhood and concomitant changes in male social institutions. Their premodern structures gradually took on certain modern elements, but unlike baseball or harness racing none of them were transformed into truly modern sports despite professional and commercial influences. Their limited modernization raises some questions concerning the assumed relationship between the commercial, professional, and modern aspects of sport.

Pedestrianism

Professional running and walking contests, which I refer to here as pedestrianism, following nineteenth-century terminology, became one of the leading spectator sports in New York City and other parts of America between 1835 and 1860. Interest continued in the post-Civil War period, although to a lesser extent. As was the case with rowing, the tone and direction of track and field changed in the last part of the nineteenth century, marked by the formation of the New York Athletic Club in 1868.

Between 1820 and 1835 the New York press noted several local pedestrian races. These were generally arranged privately and always for side bets; on a few occasions they were held in conjunction with horse races, with the track proprietors putting up the purses.[1] The major stimulant to the rise of pedestrianism as a leading spectator sport was a ten-mile race held at the Union Course in April 1835. The contest originated with a sizable wager between John C. Stevens and Samuel L. Gouveneur that Stevens could find a man capable of running ten miles in one hour. He was allowed to start any number of runners, of any nationality or color. To attract competitors Stevens initially offered $1,000 to be divided equally among all those who covered the distance in the required time. By the time of the race, however, it was decided that the first person to cross the finish line in an hour or less would receive the entire $1,000. An extra $100 was offered to the first-, second-, and third-place finishers provided each completed the distance in the allocated time. If only one runner accomplished the feat, he would collect all $300 in bonus money.[2]

The novelty of the experience, the prize money offered, and the sporting reputations of the sponsors produced considerable interest in the contest. Men like Phillip Hone were swept up by the excitement. In his diary he wrote that "without intending it by any means, when I arose this morning I found myself with Robert [his son]…on the race course, jostled by every description of people. The crowd on the ground was as great, I think, as at the famous *Eclipse* race, and immense sums were being bet."[3] Nine men, ranging in age from eighteen to thirty-three, started the race. The majority of them were artisans from New York City and vicinity, one was an unskilled laborer, two were foreign-born (Prussia and Ireland), and a couple were farmers from upstate New York and Connecticut. Only three men finished the race, and only Henry Stannard, a 165-pound Connecticut farmer, completed the distance in the required time, finishing in 59:48 minutes. Although Stevens had opened up the race to men of all nationalities and colors, he hoped that an American would win. Thus, Stannard's victory proved doubly rewarding, since the success of this native-born-and-bred farmer was for many confirmation of the superiority of the "true American way," rural living.[4]

The number of pedestrian contests markedly increased in the decade following the "Great Footrace" of 1835, by the mid-1840s emerging behind harness racing as the number two spectator sport in New York. The growing popularity of pedestrianism was linked to the decline of thoroughbred racing, which became unprofitable in the late 1830s. Proprietors of racetracks, seeking financial alternatives, began sponsoring running contests. The Beacon Course in Hoboken, New Jersey, was the classic example of this shift. Having failed miserably as a thoroughbred track, the course became the scene of many pedestrian races until its demise in 1845.[5]

The willingness of entrepreneurs to sponsor such races does not automatically explain the growing interest in these athletic activities. Americans had long been intrigued by feats of skill and strength, and the more formal contests of the 1830s built on this existing interest by giving the sport greater publicity and providing greater opportunity for betting on the outcome. The popularity of pedestrianism in England and two modernizing elements—records and nationalism—further encouraged the sport's growth. While these variables acted independently they were interrelated in the sense that John Bull often served as the standard by which Americans measured their own sports achievements.[6] Precisely when men began timing running races is unknown, yet this procedure was an integral part of English running and walking contests by the start of the nineteenth century and probably earlier. A letter to a New York newspaper in 1821 indicates the stimulant of time in the growth of pedestrianism and its relationship to nationalistic feelings. The author noted that he had witnessed an Englishman run 10 ¼ miles in 58:23 minutes. He believed that American runners were equal, if not superior, to any on earth and hoped to see an American lop 23 seconds off this time. The requirement that Stevens's runners in the 1835 race go a shorter distance in more time indicates the absence of permanent records at this stage of the sport's development in America. After 1835, however, the public was made aware of the fastest times via the growing number of sports journals.[7]

Nationalism undoubtedly played a part in the growth of pedestrianism. Evident in the 1835 contest, it was instrumental in a series of important long-distance races held at the Beacon Course in 1844. The $1,000 in prize money attracted a large field of American runners to the first contest, again won by Stannard. Before the race the *Herald* noted that "nothing is talked of now, in the sport circle, but this race," and the *Spirit* predicted that "all the world and his wife will be assembled." The huge crowd, estimated at 30,000 spectators, was enough to convince the promoter to sponsor another contest. He again offered $1,000 in prize money and this time placed notices of the upcoming race in newspapers here and abroad to lure an international field. The race attracted thirty-seven entrants (only seventeen started), including three Englishmen, three Irishmen, and an American Indian, John Steeprock, of the Seneca tribe. Stannard was the runner to beat, which is exactly what John Gildersleeve, a New York chair builder, did. He overtook John Barlow and John Greenlaugh, both Englishmen, on the tenth and final mile in a race one newspaper asserted was one of the greatest that ever took place in America or England.[8]

Newspaperman Nathaniel P. Willis, exploring the implications of the race and why it was the talk of the town even among New York's elite, noted that unlike horse racing, which at least had some *"submerged utility,"* there was "no utility in speed of foot, no dignity in it, and no improvement of the race." Although the novelty of the contest partially contributed to the enthusiasm, the tremendous interest *"arose from the accidental contact of several of the circumstances of the race with strong under-current of natural interest."* Elaborating on this theme he claimed, "It was a trial of the Indian against the white man, on the point in which the red man most boasts his superiority. It was the trial of the peculiar American *physique* against the long held supremacy of the English muscular endurance." The excitement derived from the fact that the white man beat the red man and the American defeated the Englishman.[9]

Two more races were held in 1844, with Englishmen prevailing on each occasion. Of the first of these contests the *Spirit* doubted "if so many spectators have ever been assembled on an American race course as was present on this occasion." In an extraordinary performance Barlow covered the ten miles in what was considered a world record time of 54:21 minutes. The other contest took place in mid-December, with inclement weather holding down both the number of competitors and the size of the crowd. The hardy spectators witnessed a classic confrontation as Greenlaugh and Gildersleeve battled neck and neck until the last few yards, when the Englishman pulled ahead to win the twelve-mile race.[10]

The tremendous excitement created by the Beacon Course contests spurred the rise of pedestrianism throughout the nation. During the next decade all kinds of pedestrian events were held, most of them between competitors but a few solely against time. On several occasions both elements were employed with extra money to be won if a runner completed a certain distance in a specific time. Endurance races remained the most popular, although sprints and hurdle races did take place. At times these contests took on a carnival atmosphere. For example, on one occasion a man was matched against a horse in a hurdle race. Besides running races, walking contests also occurred in New York City, although they were not as popular. The latter were solely endurance races, and distances of twenty miles or more were common.[11]

With the national growth of the sport, professional pedestrians began touring the country in search of financial rewards. Major races usually were run for $1,000, but the prize money was frequently divided, although unequally, among a certain number of finishers. Most contests were for less than $200, and sprints and dashes could earn the winner as little as $30. Besides races for prize money put up by promoters, professional runners also issued challenges in the leading sports journals. Match races generally went for $100-$500. As was the case in rowing, backers usually put up the money for these races and reaped most of the profits. It is difficult to say how much money professional runners earned. While the incomes of leading pedestrians probably exceeded the national norm, there is no evidence to support the conclusion of one scholar that these "were affluent men by contemporary standards, with annual incomes many times above the average."[12]

The limited biographical information on New York's professional runners suggests that they came from the manual classes, but how many were artisans or semiskilled and unskilled laborers cannot be determined. Very few of them, such as John Gildersleeve, toured the country; most confined their racing to the metropolitan area. For the latter group running served as a means of supplementing their regular incomes. Most of the professional runners in New York were from the lower-middle class, although members of respectable society also engaged in walking and running contests, even if they did not enter purse races.[13]

While the Beacon Course races of 1844 may have spurred the growth of pedestrianism they represented at the same time, paradoxically, the climax of professional pedestrianism in antebellum New York. The number of running and walking contests increased, but none attracted the interest or crowds of the 1844 races. These contradictory trends persisted until the mid-1850s when the popularity of the sport declined severely in New York.[14] Among other contributing factors, in early 1845 the Beacon Course proprietor, who was the major promoter of the sport, was forced to close the track. Other groups continued to sponsor races, but the prize money they offered was far less than what the Hoboken proprietor had put up. With the loss of this entrepreneur there was a sharp rise in match races and a corresponding decrease in purse races between 1845 and 1855. The shift reflected the economic weakness of pedestrianism since the promotion of the sport and the profits that derived from it now depended on those directly involved (runners and backers) rather than commercial interests (spectators).[15] Simultaneously, and quite possibly because of it, there was a decrease in the number of good runners, and the absence of native-born American runners with national reputations further reduced interest in long-distance running. The sport also suffered from charges of fixed races, its association with gambling, and certain carnival-like and dangerous contests.[16] Finally, the continued growth of harness racing, the revival of thoroughbred racing, and the surge of baseball also added to the decline of professional pedestrianism in New York just prior to the Civil War.

The rise of the Scottish Caledonian games in the mid-1850s corresponded with the decline of professional pedestrianism. The sponsors compensated the winners; hence, the games were considered professional affairs. The nature of the sport at that time and the organizational structure of the games radically differed from earlier pedestrianism. The Caledonian games, as Gerald Redmond accurately notes, had "an important influence in the early development of track and field in the United States." They marked the beginning of organized track and field in this country, nurtured interest in the sport, and influenced its development on both the collegiate and club level.[17]

The first reference to the traditional Scottish games being held in America dates back to 1836 when the Highland Society of New York met to "renew the Sport of their Native Land." Although other Scottish societies held games from time to time during the next decade and a half, the Highland games in America became identified mainly with the Caledonian clubs. In 1853 the first such club was organized in Boston, and three years later another was established in New York. During the next twenty-five years the number of Caledonian clubs increased until they and their games became a national institution. As early as 1867 Caledonian clubs in the United States and Canada held the first international games in New York, and three years later they established the North American Caledonian Association in an attempt to standardize the rules governing the games. The birth of what was the first international sporting organization indicated "the tremendous popularity of the Caledonian games in both countries and the financial benefits of consistent public patronage."[18]

The New York Caledonian Club was the wealthiest and probably the most influential Scottish society in America. Although the annual games were not its only concern, they became an ever-increasing source of publicity and a major source of revenue. Initially the admission fee was a quarter, but by the post-Civil War years the price had risen to fifty cents. Spectators came mainly from the city's Scottish community, although contingents from Scottish societies outside the metropolitan area were also represented. The large crowds that were attracted to these events would not have materialized except for the presence of a significant number of Americans and other non-Scottish foreigners.[19]

The Caledonian clubs represented a new form of sponsorship for commercialized spectator sports. Heretofore, such sports were universally promoted by entrepreneurs seeking personal profit, with the occasional exception of horse racing. The sponsorship of commercialized track and field meetings by these quasi-athletic clubs marked an important break with this policy, however. During the Civil War decade other athletic organizations, most notably baseball clubs, began to charge admission to their contests, and by the 1870s almost all athletic clubs with commercial potential had ventured into the business side of sport.[20]

The program of the New York Caledonian Club varied significantly from the pedestrianism with which Americans had become familiar. The major contribution of the Scots to American track and field was the emphasis they placed on the field events, such as putting the heavy stone and the long jump. Following the traditions of their native land Caledonian clubs offered prize money as an incentive to compete. While the amount was small at first, it increased markedly in the post-Civil War years as commercialism took hold of the games. Even in the later years, however, the winnings per event rarely exceeded $100 and certainly never approached the amounts earlier runners had won in major long-distance races. An athlete still could earn a tidy sum in a single day by winning several events, which often occurred because of their similarity. With the rising number of games, several participants were able to join the circuit, although from their inception the games in New York always attracted competitors from outside the metropolitan area. In 1869 the chieftain of the New York club recommended that it bring over Donald Dinnie, the champion athlete of Scotland, in the hopes that he would lure an even larger crowd. Dinnie first competed in New York in 1871, and during the remainder of the decade other Scottish athletes crossed the Atlantic as well.[21]

Naturally, the majority of the competitors at the New York games were Scottish, although participants of other nationalities and races were permitted, to varying degrees, to compete in the annual affair. Biographical information on the competitors is nonexistent, but it can be assumed that their social backgrounds differed from earlier runners in that the Scots were more likely to be drawn from the middle class. Although the Caledonian games in the post-Civil War years took on an increasingly professional dimension as they grew nationally and added to the prize money, the majority of the competitors used their winnings merely to supplement their regular incomes. Only a small number of star athletes made a considerable sum from a tour of the Caledonian games, and this probably did not occur until the 1870s.[22]

From its inception the New York Caledonian Club was praised by the sports and daily presses. Journalists felt that Americans should emulate these Scots since their activities promoted health and fostered patriotism. In 1858 *Porter's Spirit* clearly articulated this sentiment, maintaining that these manly pastimes "give not only health and vigor to the frame, but place a large share on contentment in the mind, and make men fond of the soil on which they are enjoyed." Such athletic activities "are wiser than statesmanship, and more wholesome to the heart than preachers' prayers." The press also took note of the club's meticulous organization, the perfect decorum that existed despite the huge crowds, and its concern for, and encouragement of, the physical training of youth.[23]

After the Civil War long-distance races among professionals reemerged as a spectator sport in New York City and other parts of the country, although these contests were mainly walking races. Edward P. Weston's walk in 1867 from Portland, Maine, to Chicago in twenty-six days, for which he won $10,000, was the major impetus to "pedestrian mania." A year later the *Clipper* noted an increase in the number of walking contests. However, the *Times* wondered why the public sustained Weston or "what particular gratification they derived from the spectacle of a usually unattractive looking person in tights, doing in excess what each of them is in the habit of doing in moderation everyday of his life." It also rejected the argument that professional walking contests were "an incentive to physical culture," claiming that they were "an incentive to idle young men to get a shiftless living in a desultory way, and to be generally as useless as possible." Others disapproved of these contests because of the suspicion of a fix.[24]

The seeds for the destruction of professional pedestrianism had been sown prior to 1870 with the beginnings of amateur track and field on both the club and collegiate levels. Informal footraces had long taken place at American colleges, and the first formal intercollegiate track and field program was established at Columbia College in New York City. In 1868 George Rives, a Columbia graduate who was visiting England, was so impressed with the track meets held there that he penned an enthusiastic letter to friends back home advocating the formation of an athletic association. The result was the creation in 1869 of the Columbia College Athletic Association and the holding of the first intercollegiate track meet there in June of that year.[25]

The creation of the New York Athletic Club in 1868 was far more significant to the future of track and field. The brainchild of John C. Babcock, Henry Buermeyer, and William C. Curtis, the new club was influenced by English sports developments as well as the local Caledonian games. Modeled after the London Athletic Club, the New York Club actively sponsored several sports, rather than focusing on only one sport as earlier athletic clubs had done. From the outset, however, its major emphasis was track and field, although its influence on amateur athletics ranged far and wide.[26] *Wilkes' Spirit* asserted in the club's first year that although still in its infancy it showed "remarkable promise of becoming the leading institution of its kind in this country, and will, doubtlessly, in the course of time, fill the same position in this country occupied by the London Athletic Club in England." Another sports journal maintained that the recently organized club was already "making its influence felt in the community." While such praiseworthy statements proved accurate in the long run, the club was less successful than predicted in its first three years. The track and field meets it sponsored drew little public attention and small crowds. For example, the games of the New York Caledonian Club attracted crowds of 10,000 or more, compared to less than 2,000 spectators at New York Athletic Club meets. The increase in the athletic club's membership was the only bright spot, with over a hundred names on the roster by 1870.[27]

The social composition of the New York Athletic Club varied significantly from the clubs of Caledonian competitors and professional pedestrians. Athletic club members were mainly from respectable society, and some of them were descendants of leading New York families, such as the Roosevelts and DePeysters. It is highly unlikely, however, that the New York Athletic Club included the men of wealth who joined other elite sports organizations, such as the New York Yacht Club, the American Jockey Club, or the New York Racquet Club; rather, the majority of them, like their rowing counterparts, were from New York's upper-middle class.[28]

As opposed to professional rowing, which declined because of its inherent inability to emerge as a commercial endeavor, track and field had the potential to become commercialized; yet amateurism triumphed in that sport during the last decades of the nineteenth century. A major reason for this development was the absence of sufficient popular appeal to encourage entrepreneurs to promote professional pedestrians on a regular basis. The economic weakness of the sport was already evident during the antebellum period, at a time when runners and walkers faced fewer challenges from other spectator sports, and the ongoing reliance on match races indicates that the earlier problems persisted even in the post-Civil War period. While a spectacular performance, such as achieved by Stannard and Weston, produced a burst of interest, the absence of adequate commercialization made it difficult to nurture professional pedestrianism on a continuing basis and contributed to the cyclical character of the sport in the years prior to 1870.[29]

Amateur track and field made rapid advances against the backdrop of the economic weakness of commercialized-professional pedestrianism, prompted in part by the rising number of amateur clubs. By the end of the 1870s nearly a hundred athletic clubs existed in the New York metropolitan area, many of which sponsored their own track and field meets. These amateur contests never drew the vast crowds that were attracted to the Caledonian games, but they were under no economic pressure to do so since their expenses were far less. While amateur clubs were concerned with the business side of sport, their real motivation for sponsoring meets was prestige and power rather than profit—their goal was to break even, or at least not lose too much money. More numerous, better organized, and better financed than professional groups, these amateur clubs had another distinct advantage: by eliminating professionals from their meets, collectively they appealed solely to the athlete's reason for existence— his desire to compete and demonstrate his skills. With limited opportunity to compete elsewhere, trackmen easily came under the control of amateur clubs.[30]

Billiards

Until the post-World War II years billiards in America consisted of two generally mutually exclusive styles: the first, associated with the upper class, was played mainly in their homes and in private clubs; the other, associated with the hoi polloi, was played in neighborhood poolhalls. The former predominated until the 1820s and quite possibly until 1840; but by the mid-nineteenth century the latter tradition set the tone and direction of the sport. Between 1850 and 1870 this shift coincided with the emergence of pool as a commercialized spectator sport dominated by a small group of professional players.[31]

Since the 1730s wealthy New Yorkers had engaged in billiards in the comfort of their homes. Public poolrooms, as adjuncts to taverns and roadside inns, also date back to the colonial period; however, poolhalls per se did not come into existence until the beginning of the nineteenth century. Charles Haswell recalled in 1896 that two such establishments existed in the city in 1816, but both appear to have been connected with other types of businesses. A small number of public billiard tables were set up in New York coffeehouses and hotels: in 1808 there were eight such tables, which one observer insisted was more than in any other American city; by 1824 between twelve and twenty-four tables were available to the public in New York.[32]

Between 1820 and 1850 billiards remained an informal recreation, although the emergence of leading, possibly professional, players during the 1820s indicated the beginning of more formal contests. During this period the press totally ignored the activities of these skilled performers, and the advertisements of billiard table manufacturers were the only references to the sport in either daily newspapers or sports journals.[33] The limited evidence available suggests that playing pool became more common in New York in the 1830s, but the information on the development of the sport in the subsequent decade appears conflicting. The *Clipper* later claimed that the popularity of billiards waned during the mid-1840s because "blacklegs and professional sharpers, those vampyres of the sporting world, had begun to frequent the public billiard rooms, and men of respectability and integrity were driven from it." Clearly, the sport came under increasing criticism as a result of its association with gambling. Nevertheless, there are reasons to assume that the number of public billiard halls did not decrease—in fact, it quite possibly increased— during these years.[34]

The presence of a gambling element and the moral indignation against the sport in the 1840s drove respectable New Yorkers out of the public poolhalls, although they did not curtail their gentlemanly participation in the sport. It was no coincidence that this trend away from public play corresponded with the rise of a new institution, the elite social club, where billiard tables were usually available to members. Further insulated from the masses, upper-class involvement subsequently had no influence on the development of the sport, with one notable exception: gentlemanly participation, even in private, provided an important ideological sanction, a point to be discussed later in greater detail.[35]

The atmosphere of public poolrooms also changed during the 1840s. Ned Polsky points out that from the beginning these places "were always associated with gambling and various forms of low life." While there is some merit to his thesis, it is nonetheless true that prior to the 1840s poolrooms did not carry their later social stigma. In general, the places gentlemen frequented to play pool were attached to respectable business establishments, such as hotels. What emerged during the 1840s was a different type of billiard parlor, where pool tables were the owner's major source of revenue. These places became overwhelmingly lower-middle-class institutions and served as the focal point for the development of the sport.[36]

Billiards made significant advances as both a competitive and recreational sport during the 1850s. Michael Phelan was the major figure behind the rising interest in billiards and from 1850 until his death in 1871 was the sport's dominant personality and promoter.[37] In 1850 Phelan was responsible for two significant developments. Through the *Spirit* he issued a challenge to the English billiard champion, John Roberts, to a home-and-home series for $500 per match. The challenge, which remained open for a year, went unanswered. Phelan was probably not disturbed by the course of events, for in proposing the contests he asserted that his desire was merely to prove that he was not only the best pool player in America but worldwide. He had agreed to forego financial gain, promising to give his winnings, above his expenses, to the treasury of the New York Fire Department,[38] a curiously noble action in view of the fact that he later engaged in money contests and kept the proceeds. Ever the promoter, his challenge to Roberts was a shrewd one, for he quite possibly recognized from the outset that the matches would not take place and he would be proclaimed America's foremost player without ever picking up a cue. As the owner of a billiard parlor he succeeded in arousing public interest in the sport—his challenge was the first reference to billiards (outside of advertisements) in the New York press. He also managed to call attention to himself and the fact that he was in the midst of writing a book on billiards.

The publication of Phelan's *Billiards Without Masters* marked the second major development in the sport in 1850. The first work of its kind in America, the book examined the history of the sport, explained the rules of the various billiard games, provided instruction and diagrams on how to play them, and supplied the usual homilies on the moral and social benefits of the sport. In reviewing the book the *Spirit* claimed that "it was unquestionably the best and most complete work of its kind ever published." Relatively expensive at three dollars, the book nonetheless went through ten editions during the next quarter-century, illustrating its enduring popularity and the interest of the "better class" in the sport.[39] Phelan left New York for the gold fields of California around 1851 or 1852, returning to the city in 1854 or 1855. He soon began manufacturing billiard tables, entering into a partnership with Hugh Collender. In 1856 he published the *Billiard Cue*, the first billiard periodical. A four-page monthly, the publication went out of print in 1874. There do not appear to be any copies still in existence.[40]

In 1855 Phelan and his partner proposed a grand billiard tournament if eight or ten leading players could be assembled, another case of an unanswered challenge that did more to promote business than determine skill. In 1858 Phelan defeated Ralph Benjamin of Philadelphia for $1,000 in the first recorded billiard match in America. And his contest with John Seeriter of Detroit the following year evoked considerable interest in, and discussion about, the sport, probably for the first time. Even the *Times,* which heretofore had virtually ignored billiards, noted the tremendous public excitement and devoted several columns to the match, which Phelan won. Originally scheduled for $5,000, the purse was later raised to $15,000 per man, and admission was charged for the first time. All 500 seats in Detroit's Fireman Hall were filled, and it was reported that more tickets could have been sold if there had been additional space.[41]

With Phelan's title as America's billiard champion firmly established, reports of an upcoming confrontation with Roberts began to circulate in the sports journals. These proved to be nothing but rumors.[42] The arrival of Monsieur Berger, reputed to be the French champion, the following year caused a sensation in New York sports circles. *Wilkes' Spirit* noted that the "desire to witness his extraordinary performances, had brought a large number of billiards celebrities to this neighborhood." Phelan took advantage of the unique situation by promoting a week-long round-robin tournament among the leading players. In early 1861 the *Clipper* wrote that billiards "had been the subject of much attention during the past few months" and the arrival of Berger, coupled with Phelan's tournament, gave "an impetus to the game, and popularized it to an extent hitherto unknown."[43]

The increasing number of professional contests revealed one side of the sport's growth; the rise in the number of billiard manufacturers and public poolrooms revealed another. By 1858 at least four firms were producing billiard tables in New York and the rivalry was often bitter. In a letter to the *Clipper* one manufacturer took exception to Phelan's recent involvement in the business, conceding that he himself was not a "crack player" but instead had devoted his entire life to his trade and no other. While hard data are not available, most observers believed that, for better or worse, the number of poolrooms increased annually in New York City. In 1861 the *Clipper* stated that "where billiard tables, billiard rooms and billiard players were a few years since numbered by the tens, they may now be counted by hundreds."[44]

Several factors contributed to the rise of billiards in the mid-nineteenth century. In addition to the forces that stimulated the growth of sport in general, pool emerged as a popular pastime at the same time that bowling was declining in popularity. In 1869 Dudley Kavanaugh, a professional pool player and billiard manufacturer, claimed that during the previous decade the appeal of tenpins had "yielded to the superior attraction of billiards." His economic interest may have clouded his perspective, although two other observers also suggested that the greater skill required in billiards contributed to the respective fates of the two sports. These statements are credible but they run counter to our general knowledge of the relationship between skill level and participation in a recreational activity.[45] While there is no confirming evidence, billiards quite possibly was a less expensive sport than bowling. In addition, the upper-class tradition in billiards, which was absent in bowling, may have made the former more appealing to the masses.

Ned Polsky has already demonstrated that the popularity of pool and poolhalls was intimately tied to a "bachelor subculture," which was linked to various institutions ranging from fraternal organizations and middle and upper-middle-class men's clubs to boardinghouses and hobo life. These urban residents regularly visited prostitutes and sustained all-male gathering places such as gambling parlors and saloons. They cultivated a variety of sports while playing an important, although less critical, role in the development of others. Of the numerous refuges from women, Polsky insists, the poolroom "was not just one of these places: it was *the* one, the keystone."[46] His thesis is convincing, but it requires certain minor modifications as an explanation for the initial surge of billiards, since this development occurred prior to the rise of the bachelor subculture. What Polsky does not recognize is that the creation of a bachelor subculture in the last quarter of the nineteenth century was itself part of a broader change in male—female relations.[47]

The profound impact of the changing nineteenth-century economy on masculine values and masculine institutions played a paramount role in the growth of billiards. Several scholars have shown recently that industrialization altered masculine values and "heightened the importance of defining the criteria of manhood and of fulfilling those criteria." While the masculine response to this change depended on social class, there emerged among working-class youth in particular a vigorous subculture designed to prove masculinity through fighting, wenching, and sometimes drinking. In addition, the shifting modes of production created a division of leisure that was based increasingly on sex.[48] The all-male recreational pattern, although present among all classes, emerged initially and was most firmly entrenched within the life-style of the working class.

Cultural influences alone do not explain why pool and the poolhall became such an important part of the lower-middle-class masculine subculture. The inexpensive and individualistic nature of billiards provided an advantage over some sports, but it was not the only one to possess these characteristics. The historical association of billiards with the tavern and with lowlifes played a part, but even more important was the atmosphere of the poolhall; secluded, open day and night, in use all year long, and in virtually all neighborhoods. The poolhall was unmatched by any other sports facility, with the exception of the gymnasium and the bowling alley. However, the gym could be eliminated as a serious competitor because of the unpopularity of the activities that took place there, because it catered to the middle class and to ethnic groups, and because its members were required to pay an annual subscription fee. The bowling alley, even when the sport was popular, never seemed to better the poolhall as a place to hang out.

Since colonial days moralists had attacked billiards because they associated the sport with gambling and idleness. However, as long as the game remained essentially the prerogative of the wealthy it was an acceptable diversion. Criticism of billiards did not intensify until its public form became popular among the masses. The president of the New York Society for the Suppression of Gambling claimed that fewer games are of "a more deceptive character than billiards." Its perception "as an elegant and innocent amusement, in which even persons of the most respectable character can indulge in without damage to their reputations made the sport particularly dangerous." This pretense of fashion made "verdant youth" susceptible to the "nefarious swindles of the professed gamblers."[49]

While gambling remained the essential reason for objections to billiards a more subtle factor entered into the debate. At a time when new social forces were creating all-male institutions, the view of women as refining and civilizing agents of society was also taking hold. Thus, it is not surprising that throughout the nineteenth century sports promoters actively encouraged the presence of women at their athletic events as a means of tempering the crowd and providing middle-class respectability.[50] Furthermore, moral and social reformers believed that since they and people like them, obviously meaning the middle class, had provided their children and society with the proper principles of morality and discipline, their all-masculine institutions would not create deviant behavior or threaten home and family. The lower class was a different story, however. They did not possess the proper characteristics of control, so moralists viewed their masculine hangouts, whether taverns or billiard parlors, as evil, not just because of the activity that occurred there but because such places were perceived as breeding grounds for other and more serious social ills.

Supporters of billiards responded to such criticism by drawing on the sport's upper-class tradition and ignoring the issue of the public poolhall as a den of iniquity. Billiard promoters frequently pointed to the famous men who played the game in a never-ending search for respectability. The *Herald* noted that even clergymen, such as Henry Ward Beecher, participated in the sport and attended billiard matches. Proponents also sought to downplay the association of the sport with gambling. When two professional players donated the gate receipts from their match to charity, *Wilkes' Spirit* happily noted that "billiards does not in America, as in other countries, lead to the practice of gambling among its votaries, but on the contrary, when any great match among its professors take place, the cause of charity is served." Others conceded that gambling on billiard games took place, but they justified the practice on the grounds that wagering was not an inherent part of billiards and therefore did not detract from its value. Dudley Kavanaugh pointed out the divergent view of baseball's versus billiards' association with gambling and wondered why betting tarnished one and not the other.[51]

Besides refuting the negative, devotees of billiards emphasized the positive contributions of the sport. The *Clipper* maintained that no other game was "so well adapted to the needs of dwellers in the cities as that of billiards." *Wilkes' Spirit* voiced a similar theme, noting that "billiards is a mathematical game, and affords scope and exercise for those faculties which discipline and strengthen the mind. A steady hand, a clear head, quick perception and a pleasurable exercise of the calculation powers are the requisite of an accomplished billiard-player." While promoters and sports journals were the major proponents of the positive value of billiards, some daily newspapers also encouraged the sport. The *Herald* insisted that billiards was "well worth introducing into the household" and that it was particularly well suited for women since it forced them to walk, use their arms, and expand their chest. It was "much better for ladies and gentlemen to sit together in a game of 'pool' after dinner, than for gentlemen to sit discussing politics in the dining room, while the ladies are left to amuse themselves in the drawingroom." Finally, all billiard supporters insisted that a major benefit of the sport was that it could be played during all seasons, as well as at night. The *Clipper* called billiards the best winter amusement.[52]

Billiards made significant advances as both a recreational and competitive sport during the 1860s. Unlike many other sports it did not suffer during the Civil War years, thanks to the individualistic nature of participation, the inexpensiveness, and the fact that it could be played at any time or in any season. Hard data on the rise of billiards are not available, but reports from contemporary observers are clear with regard to this development. In 1861 the *Clipper* claimed that billiards "has attained a degree of popularity in this country that is truly marvelous." Four years later the *Times* wrote that the game "was never in a more prosperous condition than at the present time, and it is really becoming a most popular amusement." By the end of the decade the *Herald* insisted that the "popularity which the game of billiards has already attained in this city is largely on the increase. Unquestionably it stands number one as a scientific and recreative amusement."[53]

The low cost of playing pool was a major factor in its widespread popularity and contributed to the easy access almost all social classes had to the game. Prior to the Civil War New Yorkers were charged an average of twenty-five cents per game; after the war proprietors began charging sixty cents per hour to prevent customers from playing "short" (i.e., intentionally delaying the end of the game). The hourly rate was hardly universal, however, and as late as the end of the 1860s some poolhall owners still charged as little as ten cents per game.[54]

The comfortable living that proprietors of billiard parlors reportedly earned also suggests the popularity of this recreational activity. First-class establishments were especially rewarding, and *Wilkes' Spirit* claimed that half a dozen poolrooms in New York City cleared $11,000-$15,000 annually. In 1862 Michael Phelan asserted that the capital investment in billiards was $2 million; four years later it was reported that 12,000 people nationwide supposedly earned their livelihood from pool. Recognizing that these figures were probably inflated, they nonetheless point to the prosperity of billiards.[55]

The growth of billiards as a professional–commercial spectator sport corresponded with an increase in recreational participation. In 1862 *Wilkes' Spirit* maintained that the tremendous excitement generated by the activities of professional players settled "any lingering doubts about the great popularity of the game of billiards among our people." Michael Phelan's retirement from active competition in 1863 sparked further interest in the sport and even more contests. The *Clipper* claimed that the tournament held to establish a new champion, won by Dudley Kavanaugh, "was the most important that has ever taken place in connection with this scientific game."[56]

Problems associated with professional billiards soon surfaced, with Phelan at the center of the controversy. Although his playing days had ended he remained the sport's leading figure both in New York and nationally. By 1865 several sports journals and players accused him of heading a clique which sought to dominate professional pool. In March of that year Kavanaugh, still the American champion, sharply criticized Phelan for monopolizing the sport. Three months later he was forced to forfeit his champion cue, although it is not perfectly clear what the grounds for forfeiture were. In September Phelan was the prime mover behind the formation of the American Billiard Players Association, open to professional players, poolroom proprietors, and skilled amateurs. The association's stated objectives were the "supervision of the interest of billiards, the encouragement and advancement of players, and the general welfare of the billiard profession at large," which was Phelan's way of solidifying his position in the face of mounting criticism. One sports journal charged that the group had been formed with the interests of certain manufacturers, not the players, in mind. Anti-Phelan forces established their own group, the National American Billiards Association, a year later, electing Kavanaugh their president and promising to revise the rules of the game and regulate competition in an open and free manner.[57]

Although championship contests on a state and national level took place with increased frequency in the years immediately following the Civil War, the controversy between the Phelan- and Kavanaugh-led groups quieted down until 1870. Then *Wilkes' Spirit* led a savage attack against Phelan, charging that he sought to dominate the sport, control all the professional players, dictate the winners of all matches, and claim the right to manufacture and sell all the billiard tables used in America. The journal further asserted that Phelan had collected a ring of leading players "between whom he fostered matches, and by whose assistance he constructed tournaments in his name, putting up, for the most part, paltry ornaments as prizes." Phelan also supposedly cheated players out of their winnings: on one occasion a tournament winner was to earn roughly $1,250 but eventually received only $364 after expenses were deducted. Finally, *Wilkes' Spirit* maintained that Phelan encouraged a luxurious life-style among professionals in order to keep his minions in bondage.[58] The exposé naturally won the support of the anti-Phelan faction, but since the issue was otherwise ignored the accuracy of the charges is open to speculation. While *Wilkes' Spirit* probably overstated certain points there appears to be little doubt that at times Phelan used his influence and well-established reputation to serve his own financial interests.

Despite the Phelan controversy billiards was comparatively free of the criticism that accompanied the professionalization of other sports. For example, the press usually reported that crowds at the leading matches were respectable and orderly. Although participation was widely based, spectators were mostly white-collar workers since an admission fee of at least $1.00, sometimes more, was charged. When ruffians attended one contest *Wilkes' Spirit* recommended that the price be raised to $2.50 and possibly $5.00 to ensure that such groups would be excluded. Charges of fixed contests also were rarely heard. Almost on principle the *Times* disapproved of professional billiards, but it admitted that, like baseball, billiards was in its proper sphere an enjoyable recreation; however, "converted into a trade it fosters idleness and ultimately depravity." The more democratic newspapers offered no criticism of the players or, like the *Clipper,* noted that they were generally honorable men.[59]

While billiards grew nationally during the 1860s New York remained the sport's capital. Many of the major matches and tournaments were held there despite the charge that the city lacked good playing facilities, and thirteen of the twenty-seven leading professional players resided at one time or another in New York (although Maurice Daly is the only known player to have been born there). Of the migrants to the city half came prior to 1860, arriving with their families while still quite young; others moved there in the 1860s to open, or more likely be employed in, billiard parlors. The late arrivals generally stayed only briefly in New York before moving on to other cities where they engaged in the same line of work.[60]

Wilkes' Spirit insisted that the large majority of the leading billiard players were of "Hibernian extraction." Phelan and Kavanaugh, the two dominant figures, were Irish by birth, but only two other players (of the twenty-three whose birthplaces could be ascertained) were from Ireland; of the remaining nineteen, eight were American-born, six were either French or French-Canadian, four were born in Germany, and one in England. Kavanaugh's nephew, Maurice Daly, was born in America but of Irish descent. The ethnic backgrounds of other players are unknown, although their names are as much English or German as Irish.[61] In spite of differences in players' nationalities, their class backgrounds were probably very similar. Of five players for whom biographical data are available, four had fathers or close relatives in the billiard business. It would not be surprising if this pattern held true for most skilled players. Both Kavanaugh, in 1869, and Polsky, in 1969, noted that the overwhelming majority of professional players of their respective eras were playing pool regularly by at least their early teens. Polsky further points out that many of the more recent great players, including Willie Hoppe and Willie Mosconi, were the sons of poolroom owners. If this was true for the earlier period, then it may be suggested that the majority of billiard players during the 1860s came from lower-middle- to middle-class backgrounds.[62]

The income of a professional player during the 1860s was comparable to that from most middle-class occupations. Many older players whose active careers ended in the 1860s already were involved in a billiard-related business, either as poolhall owners or billiard manufacturers, prior to the first decade of professional billiards. For this group, their business, not the money won in competition, was their major source of income, providing them, by all accounts, a comfortable, although not opulent, life-style. Younger players derived their income from two sources: as a supervisor or "house pro" for a certain billiard parlor—although how widespread this practice was is unknown—and via contest money. In 1866 Melvin Foster received $2,000 for supervising Kavanaugh Hall, an amount that was, according to one sports journal, about twice the going rate for this type of job. The amount earned in a contest depended on who won, and professional players in most cases had backers who put up the money in match contests and reaped most of the profits. Discrepancies between the amounts reportedly won in tournaments and the amounts actually received make it difficult to calculate the annual earnings of these professionals, but $1,500-$2,500 per year would probably be a reasonable figure.[63]

Despite this commercial–professional growth and the creation of two national billiard organizations, as late as 1870 the rules of the sport remained "an unknown quantity, varying at the caprice of irresponsible and interested parties." The various games that could be played on a billiard table further complicated the codification of rules. (Interestingly and uncharacteristically, *Wilkes' Spirit* believed that the French version was superior to the American since it required more skill.[64]) Clearly, the sport was still in a transitional stage between premodern and modern by 1870, as evidenced by the lack of standardized rules but the presence of national organizations, national champions, and coverage in national sports journals. These latter modern elements did not yet exist at a sophisticated enough level, however. The national organizations were weak in the sense that the development of the sport was more a result of Michael Phelan's personal power and influence than an effective central administration. When one considers that by 1870 professional–commercial billiards was only a decade old, that it had been marred by personal and financial squabbles, and that the sport faced middle-class disapproval, it is somewhat amazing that it had progressed so far as both a competitive and recreational sport. The foundation for the tremendous growth of billiards during the last three decades of the nineteenth century was clearly in place.[65]

Boxing

Boxing matches which occurred during the colonial period were generally of the rough-and-tumble sort and were not governed by anything approaching stringent rules. During the Jacob Hyer–Tom Beasley fight in 1816, recognized as the first American boxing match, "some attempt at uniform observance of rules were kept in view"; hence the significance of the contest in the history of American boxing.[66] Over the next fifty-five years the sport grew significantly in New York City and throughout America, mainly in two waves: slow but steady gains until the early 1840s, and rapid advances after 1850 as the number of contests and combatants markedly increased. Various social, economic, and communications changes that stimulated the development of other sports were also at work here, as was the fact that boxing was an urban product and New York was the sport's capital. In addition, massive immigration and the beginning of the modern political system influenced the rise of pugilism. By 1870 prize-fighters emerged as leading sports figures despite public criticism and various legal attempts to prohibit the sport altogether.

During the 1820s boxing was linked to the emergence of the gymnasium movement. One of several skills taught in the gym, boxing was proclaimed the "manly art of self defense," a frequently echoed justification for teaching young men to fight. At least one proprietor claimed that "sparring with gloves is an athletic amusement, and not withstanding the hue and cry that has often been raised against it," there is "no reason why the Gymnasium should be discouraged because some of its members may choose to include this among their exercise."[67] Gentlemanly sparring declined during the 1830s, however, as the popularity of the gym waned and boxing came under increasing criticism. A small number of respectable New Yorkers continued to spar, but as with billiards this had almost nothing to do with the essential development of the sport except that it provided supporters with an important justification for boxing and a key to the never-ending search for respectability.

Several prizefights, each marked by an increasing regard for rules, characterized boxing in the 1820s. The press ignored local bouts, however, and when they discussed the sport at all it was always in negative terms. In 1824 one writer noted in the *Spectator* that he had accidentally witnessed a boxing match and judged it a brutal affair, rife with foul play. He advocated that measures be taken to stop prizefighting. A letter to the *Post* two years later expressed a similar opposition to boxing: "Such practices are brutal and detestable in themselves and disgraceful to the country in which they are suffered to take place. What is called by its advocates the science of defense, is only the commission, always of horrible violence, and sometimes murder."[68]

During the 1830s prizefighting in New York increased despite constant criticism. Although the number of contests never exceeded more than three annually, by 1835 the *Mirror* was warning that "the detestable practice of prize fighting" threatened to take root in America. The *Herald* expressed the opinion that prizefighting was "not without merit" and "in some degree tends to benefit the community at large." While possessing certain demoralizing tendencies the sport also elicited "a feeling of courage—of proud manly self-dependence" and was "far preferable to the insidious knife…, or the cowardly and brutal practice of biting, kicking or gouging, now so prevalent."[69] The number of boxing contests and exhibitions rose further still in the early 1840s. Tom Hyer, Jacob's son, defeated Country McCleester in 1841 to become the first recognized heavyweight champion of America, and by the summer of 1842 the "rage for prize fighting" had reached new heights —"scarcely a week passed that there was not a grand set-to at some public house about town, at which hundreds were in attendance, giving their countenance and support." Then tragedy struck in September when Thomas McCoy became America's first boxing fatality in a fight in nearby Westchester County.[70]

The light heavyweight battle between McCoy and Christopher Lilly evolved from a personal quarrel, as so many fights of this period did. Each man represented a different New York boxing faction, and the fight took on nationalistic overtones as well (McCoy was Irish and Lilly was British). The contest lasted 120 rounds, slightly more than two hours and forty minutes. McCoy, who was obviously no match for Lilly, was urged to leave the ring as early as the 60th round, but he reportedly had committed himself to win or die. By the 86th round both of McCoy's eyes were swollen shut. In the 120th round he died after receiving eighty-one heavy blows.[71]

To the opponents of boxing McCoy's death was not an unfortunate accident but the logical extension of the sport's brutality and a reflection of the kind of people involved and the overall environment in which fighting occurred. The *Tribune,* a leading critic, noted that McCoy and Lilly met in a grogshop "where pugilism is the stable of excitement and…the promoters of the sport are gamblers, brothelkeepers and saloonkeepers." It found comfort only in the fact that boxing's promoters and participants were almost entirely foreigners and that the American environment itself was not congenial to the growth of the sport.[72] Now, in the aftermath of the Lilly–McCoy fight, the rest of the press and many New Yorkers joined the *Tribune* in condemning boxing. Over the next several years a few second-rate matches took place, but pugilism virtually disappeared from the New York sports scene until Tom Hyer and James "Yankee" Sullivan met for the heavyweight championship in 1849. The first of four heavyweight championship fights between 1849 and 1860, these battles indicated the revived interest in boxing as well as the changing character and setting of the sport.[73]

The Hyer–Sullivan battle had been brewing since Sullivan's arrival in New York City a decade earlier. In fact, several newspapers insisted that the increasing pugilistic activity of the early 1840s was directly linked to his presence in New York. Arrested as a result of his part in the Lilly–McCoy fight, Sullivan promised never to fight again, but in 1847 he returned to the ring to defeat Robert Caunt at Harper's Ferry for $1,000. While Hyer had not fought since 1841 he remained in the minds of many the best fighter in America. In early 1848 the two met in a saloon, drank too much, and got into a scuffle, all of which led to a proposed match for $5,000 per man.[74] The upcoming fight became the talk of the town for nearly six months, with heavy betting on both sides. Large throngs, including many respectable gentlemen, paid fifty cents each to witness the prefight sparring exhibitions of each of the combatants. The actual contest, held in February 1849 near Baltimore, was "a hurricane fight." Hyer won in only sixteen rounds (seventeen minutes and eighteen seconds) when Sullivan failed to answer the bell. *American Fistiana* noted that "never had the American ring shown so much fighting in so little time."[75]

The personal nature of the feud, the large amount of money staked and wagered, and the reputations of the fighters all contributed to the tremendous interest in the Hyer–Sullivan bout. Foreshadowing great battles of the future, the excitement this prizefight generated was in part due to a perception of the combatants as symbols of certain social groups. The *Herald* noted that Sullivan "had been the chief and champion of a class of society comprised of persons similar in every respect to himself—not refined." By contrast, Hyer was "the pet of fashionable society in this city...and in appearance and symmetry of person, almost equals the statue of Apollo." While certain class differences existed between Hyer's and Sullivan's fans, partisanship was not divided mainly along economic lines. Instead, the fighters' nationalities were the symbolic key: Sullivan, the representative of Irish immigrants, and Hyer, the native New Yorker and "Great American Hope," made the contest not just a prizefight but an extension of the growing tension between these two groups.[76]

In the late l850s *Porter's Spirit* asserted that the Hyer–Sullivan match marked "the actual rise of pugilism in America, into anything like importance." Before this battle fights were few and far between; now they were innumerable, and by the eve of the Civil War one newspaper noted that four sparring matches took place in New York each week. The gradual shift of the boxing arena from taverns to theaters, to accommodate more fans, further indicated the rising spectator appeal of the sport during the l850s. Since the admission fee to these exhibitions ranged from fifty cents to a dollar, boxing's spectators did not come from the economically deprived class but mainly from the bachelor subculture discussed earlier. Although many of these Runyonesque characters were of lower-class origin, they had money in their pockets, even if it often burned a hole there.[77]

Of all the boxing matches that took place, heavyweight championship fights generated the most excitement and attracted the largest number of spectators, even though they were held far away from population centers to avoid police interference. The title bout between Sullivan and John Morrissey in 1853 "made as much town talk as if it were some great achievement of science or wonderful exhibition of strategic skill on the battlefield." The fight between the two Irishmen had an interesting twist to it which added to the general appeal: since Morrissey had become Hyer's rival, Sullivan was seen as the bearer of American pride in a "comical juxtaposition of...the usual lines of popular partisanship." The stakes were $1,000 per man and the match attracted an estimated 2,000-6,000 spectators to the New York–Massachusetts border. Morrissey won the fight in the thirty-seventh round when Sullivan was disqualified on a foul.[78] When Morrissey fought John Camel Heenan in 1858 for $2,500 per man, the contest was "looked upon with the keenness of interest" in every city throughout the nation. *Porter's Spirit* pointed out that "not only are the usual sporting circles much excited about the issue, but the interest is rapidly pervading classes of society which are in the habit of viewing ordinary contests with indifference, if not distaste." More money supposedly was wagered than on any previous boxing match, and the *Times* claimed that every major sports figure attended the battle. In eleven rounds, lasting just twenty-one minutes, Morrissey easily whipped the challenger, whereupon he retired and the "Benica Boy," as Heenan was called, assumed the championship.[79]

The surge of boxing at the end of the antebellum period reached a roaring, dramatic climax in 1860 with the first international heavyweight championship fight. Heenan's confrontation with Tom Sayers, England's titleholder, for $1,000 and the championship belt, drew more public comment than any other single sports event between 1820 and 1870. *Wilkes' Spirit* and Frank Leslie's

Illustrated News sent reporters to England to cover the fight, while the *Times* and *Herald* received regular reports from their English correspondents. The *Times* noted that "all classes of people seem to share this anxiety to hear the results—not all in the same degree or the same extent, but with the masses of the people it is just now the great topic of speculation of interest—eclipsing the Charleston Convention and throwing completely into shade all political themes, and everything else which can afford to wait." While this development was "not very creditable to our tastes or culture," the paper felt that it was due in part "to the fact that we are a very excitable people—always craving a sensation of some sort—and partly to the equally palpable and still important fact that Muscle is King."[80]

The nationalistic overtones surrounding the contest were the major stimulant for this great concern over the outcome. "The ordinary objections to vulgar pugilism are waived in the real importance of this first-class struggle," *Wilkes' Spirit* wrote, "and there is scarcely a mind that is amenable to the influence of national pride, which does not once lay aside its prejudice against fighting, in the hope to see the

The great American pugilist, John C. Heenan. On April 17, 1860, Heenan battled Tom Sayers in a championship bout that lasted 42 rounds spread out over 2 hours and 20 minutes.

Photo courtesy of Library of Congress. LC-USZ62-840.

American champion win." The reason for this attitude, it continued, stemmed from the longstanding British assumption that physical vigor had deteriorated on this continent. An American victory would therefore testify to the nation's physical superiority. The *Herald* poked fun at such sentiment: "In the language of the bruisers' and dog beaters' organization, this fight will settle the question of national superiority between England and the United States. If Heenan whips Sayers then the commercial importance of the United States is greater than that of England, then the British government is humbug, and our Congress are the only palledum of popular liberty." While this rebuttal illustrates the ludicrous association of sports supremacy with a certain superior national character, the theme has been a pervasive one for modern sport and lends itself readily to boxing because of its highly combative nature. Not until the Joe Louis–Max Schmeling fight in the 1930s was any boxing match, or quite possibly any international sports contest in which an American was involved, so highly charged with nationalistic sentiments.[81]

The fight pitted Heenan's youth and his height and weight advantage against Sayers's experience and savvy. The American broke Sayers's arm early in the fight while the Englishman cut one of Heenan's eyes, yet both fighters continued gamely until the thirty-seventh round when the ropes were mysteriously cut and the police rushed in to break up the fight. Who was winning at the time depended on which side of the Atlantic you lived on. English journalists believed that Sayers would have eventually won; American reporters were even more adamant that Heenan was on the verge of victory. The *Times* correspondent reported that an Englishman had told him before the fight that there was "too much money bet at odds in favor of Sayers for Heenan to be permitted to gain the contest." Other New York newspapers were unanimous in their belief that a conspiracy had deprived Heenan of the victory even as they overlooked the financial consequences of the fight. *Wilkes' Spirit* dramatically placed full responsibility for the debacle squarely on the doorstep of the British government, since it was "thoroughly alive to the great political injury it might work to English prestige, should the people of the Continent, over whose race she has always domineered in physical comparison, should behold some stranger from beyond the seas bear off the emblem of her superiority in prowess." The *Times*, while not as passionate, echoed a similar theme: "England has lost so much prestige in great matters during the last few years, that the trivial circumstances of an English boxer found physically inferior to an American had evidently assumed in English eyes an importance ludicrously disproportionate to its real significance…They have been worsened by sea and land in so many diverse ways and sundry manners that they cling with desperation to the ropes of the Prize Ring."[82]

The fight was declared a draw and each fighter was awarded a championship belt. Then Sayers retired and Heenan emerged as the heavyweight champion, an inadequate solution for most Americans. With nationalism running high only a firm English acceptance of Heenan's victory would suffice. Amid increasing anti-English sentiments on other fronts, Americans seemed to feel that the fight reflected the true English character, that the English applied their oft-stated belief in fair play only to themselves. The *Eagle* picked up the theme and paralleled the conspiracy against Heenan to the "foul play" of British foreign policy. Although the controversy gradually subsided the issue was often revived on the pages of *Wilkes' Spirit*, which for the next decade repeatedly pointed to the outcome of this fight as an indication of the "true" English character.[83]

Ever since the days of Tom Hyer pugilists had been popular sports figures, and the reception New Yorkers gave Heenan on his return to the city did not prove otherwise. An estimated crowd of 50,000 turned out to honor Heenan, much to the dismay of the *Herald*, which complained that the reception was a "glorification of brutality and vice and its exaltation over the noblest sentiments of the human heart." The presence of the sports fraternity was understood, but participation by city officials and other politicians was unwarranted, according to the paper—which nonetheless devoted four columns on the front page to the occasion.[84]

Just as changing urban forces stimulated the rise of boxing in the two decades prior to the Civil War, so did immigration and politics. At first the press generally insisted that neither boxers nor their sport were indigenous to America. In 1837 the *Herald* claimed that it was erroneous to suggest that the sport was confined solely to foreigners, but twenty years later *Porter's Spirit* still asserted that the majority of professional boxers in America were of European descent. An examination of the nationalities of thirty-two New York boxers between 1840 and 1860 confirms the latter thesis: twenty-four of these men were Irish (56.3 percent) or English (18.8 percent) by birth; five of the eight Americans were sons of immigrants, and another was black. The Irish clearly dominated New York boxing, with 71.9 percent of the boxers having at least one Irish parent.[85]

The nationalities of New York boxers and the data on their occupations between 1840 and 1860, while limited, indicate that they came from the lower and lower-middle classes.[86] The general absence of American-born fighters, as *Porter's Spirit* recognized, stemmed from their ability to find "more profitable ways of using their physical advantages, than standing up to be knocked about a twenty-four foot ring for a few scores of dollars." While money lured lower-class youth to boxing, ethnic, personal, and political animosities also played a part in bringing fighters into the ring. Moreover, most boxers did not as yet perceive the sport as a career. Even the leading fighters rarely entered the ring more than five times in a lifetime, excluding sparring exhibitions, but when they did fight they could earn in one contest, if they won, as much as a skilled craftsman made in a year or more.[87] Although boxing has traditionally provided lower-class youth with a means of escaping the ghetto, it has long been noted that at best the sport serves as a temporary source of mobility, even among those who fight for large purses. Despite limited data this appears to have been the case in the two decades preceding the Civil War. The *Clipper* clearly felt that most boxers wound up poor, although exceptions did exist.[88]

Historians have paid almost no attention to the relationship between the emergence of mass politics and the growth of boxing,[89] a connection that was not lost on early observers of the sport. In 1842 the *Tribune* insisted that our citizens should "ascertain what terms of mutual consideration and service exists between the most lawless and dangerous combination of our city on the one hand, and our highest Executive authority." At times the press went so far as to claim that the prizefighters in this country would be "its governing class in due course of time, if they are not so already." The *Clipper* denied this, noting that fighters "have been used and abused by politicians as the occasion demanded." While both statements are exaggerations, they reflect what was the accepted relationship between boxing and politics, a connection that played a subtle, but definite, part in the opposition of the press to the sport during these years.[90]

The link between pugilists and politicians grew out of the New York gangs that were spawned in the second quarter of the nineteenth century amid the dismal tenements of a growing immigrant community, although they also existed in other sections of the city. Many of the same social forces that produced these urban gangs also changed the very nature of New York politics. By the early 1820s Tammany Hall was the vanguard of increased democratization in the political process and the development of the modern party system. In the next decade Tammany Hall politicians began to actively seek the immigrant vote, just as they began to see "the practical value of the [gang member], and to realize the advisability of providing them meeting and hiding places, that their favors might be curried and their peculiar talents employed on election day to assure government of, by, and for Tammany." Capt. Isaiah Rynders, the Tammany boss of the Sixth Ward and a leading sports figure, was the first to organize the gang chieftains. His powerful Empire Club, established in 1843, was the center of political activity in his ward as well as "the clearing house of all [gang] activities which had to do with politics." By 1855 an estimated 30,000 men owed their allegiance to the gang leaders. And while these political "repeaters" and performers of other political services were tied mainly to Tammany Hall, other factions of the Democratic party, the Know-Nothing (or Nativist) party, and even to some extent the Whig and Republican parties, all had their "shoulder hitters."[91]

Almost all of the leading boxers and probably quite a few other sporting figures were aligned with one or another of these quasi-political gangs. For example, John Morrissey and Country McCleester were members of Rynders's Empire Club; the Bowery Boys' Tom Hyer and Bill Harrington, a leader in New York sports, were connected with the Nativist party. Many prizefights actually originated in and took their symbolic importance from these political and ethnic differences. Even more importantly the new political system gave aid and comfort to the environment that nurtured the pugilist, making politicians and elected officials indirect patrons of the sport. These men either owned or had a strong influence on the owners of the boxers' hangouts, and they provided young fighters with jobs when they were not in the ring. Some of Rynders's men, such as Morrissey (during his early years in New York), were emigrant runners; others worked in saloons, either as taverners or bouncers; and some were given patronage jobs, such as Dan Kerrigan, who was a policeman on New York's docks.[92]

By and large these fighters were heroes in wards where violence was a way of life and a man was measured by his physical prowess. In 1863 Morrissey enhanced his position in the Irish community when he brought together Irish fighters for an exhibition, with the proceeds going for the relief of the poor in his native country.[93] The funeral procession of the Bowery Boys' "Butcher" Billy Poole, which was one of the largest ever in New York, indicated that such hero worship was not confined solely to the immigrant community. Shot by a member of Rynders's gang, Poole stated on his deathbed, "Good-bye boys, I die a true

American." The political overtones of the murder of this native street fighter and close friend of Tom Hyer was largely responsible for his cannonization. While the press was disgruntled by Poole's emergence as a political martyr, there is little doubt that he, along with Hyer and Harrington, were quite influential within the butcher community and among other segments of the city's lusty street life.[94] It is no wonder that politicians courted such men.

The changing nature of the urban press and the emergence of sports journals also aided the rise of boxing. In 1867 the *Chronicle* declared that there was "no incentive to the growth of prize fighting, like that presented by the notoriety given pugilists in the long, detailed reports of their brutal meeting which appear in the metropolitan dailies." This claim exaggerated the impact of the press on boxing, since it responded to the growth of the sport as much as caused it. Nevertheless, from 1840 to 1870 boxing received more newspaper coverage than any other sport, with the exception of baseball.[95] Granted, a good deal of newspaper space was devoted to denouncing the sport because of its brutality, including calls for stricter laws to prevent fights from taking place. Boxing was proclaimed anti-religion, anti-civilization, and anti-American; its intended purpose, as far as the press was concerned, was to encourage gambling. Objection to the sport also derived from the press's dim view of the class and ethnic backgrounds of the participants, sponsors, and spectators, and from the belief that boxers held a "privileged position" within the community and wielded undue political influence. Yet despite their disapproval of boxing many newspapers, most notably the *Herald*, provided detailed accounts of the leading matches. When a letter to the *Times* asked why a respectable paper carried so much news on the Heenan–Sayers fight, the editors replied—perhaps speaking for the media—that boxing was news and therefore must be reported; that details of such events would convince the public of the essential brutality of boxing; and that the public interest in the results of fights would cause them to go to other newspapers for the information if the *Times* did not cover the sport.[96]

The lion's share of boxing news was found in the sports journals, however, such as the *Clipper,* which catered to the more "democratic element."[97] From the very beginning Frank Queen, the *Clipper's* editor, was the leading supporter of boxers and boxing. On several occasions he argued that the character of these men had been grossly misrepresented, and he railed against the hypocrisy of the press, which gave details of the fights but decried boxing in editorials and other articles in the "bitterest manner." The *Clipper* frequently pointed to the positive contribution of pugilism, maintaining that knowledge of the sport led to manliness, confidence, and courage, and furthermore discouraged the use of knives and guns during street fights. In addition, boxers led Spartan lives—"the privation, the hardship, and the self-denial, which a man must practice before he can arrive at his physical climax"—in preparation for a fight.[98]

Such arguments did not induce any vocal supporters among the press, but there was a slow, subtle shift in the media's attitude toward the sport. While newspapers continued to carry denunciations of pugilism, they also began to include articles that spoke of the positive values of boxing. In 1848 the *Herald* declared that a boxing contest could teach a moral lesson, that the self-denial, temperance, daily exercise, and beautiful regimentation fighters undergo for months prior to a match "present the elements of a system of life which is equal to any system of morality or human conduct that can be picked out of the historical romances of the last thirty centuries." By the post-Civil War years the same paper described boxing as a "judicious, healthful and manly exercise," and insisted that knowledge of the sport infuses a feeling of confidence and gives strength to the weak and courage to the timid. It distinguished between two kinds of prizefighters, the bruiser and the scientific fighter: while the "punch-it-out" style was more common, the latter style involved "intellectual operations" and raised "the combat from its brutal character."[99]

Even the conservative *Times* found some positive value in boxing, pointing out that the sport encouraged physical development and helped banish the knife. By 1870 the *Times* was ready to admit that there were two sides to the boxing question, a change of heart influenced by a doctor who noted that prizefighting was beneficial because of the severe training it required, that it did for man what racing did for horses. While the paper conceded that "prize fighting has its merits," it nonetheless insisted that "its demerits greatly outweigh them." It acknowledged a certain admiration for "the physical advantage of training for the ring" but felt that "the moral disadvantages which are its inseparable concomitants are immensely greater." In exploring the negative consequences of boxing it is noteworthy that the *Times* focused as much, if not more, on the lifestyle of boxers as on the brutality of the sport.[100]

The contention that boxing had positive values originated in the concept of the sport as the "manly art of self defense," but it was not until the middle of the nineteenth century that respectable newspapers cautiously acknowledged the benefits of the sport. This gradual shift in attitude derived from several factors, including the growing concern for the physical well-being of urban residents. The evolving concept of manhood during the nineteenth century—from moral to physical—was the major impetus behind the changing perception of boxing.[101] While proponents of other sports claimed that their activities also contributed to physical well-being and manliness, this was the prime argument for boxing advocates. The rigorous discipline and training required of a fighter, and the courage and confidence that emerged from the ability to defend oneself, appealed to even those who denounced pugilism. Opponents could not point to any other sport that inculcated these characteristics to the same degree as boxing.

During the 1860s, as prizefighting continued to grow in terms of the number of contests and combatants, interest in the sport leveled off. Major contests still attracted considerable attention but none created the excitement of the Hyer–Sullivan or the Heenan–Sayers bouts. Boxing in New York declined during the first year of the Civil War, but this may have been a natural letdown following the excitement of the 1860 international contest. By 1862 pugilistic activity was on the rise, and the following year the *Clipper* noted that the two previous seasons would "long be remembered for the number and character of sparring exhibitions in this city." In 1863 New Yorker Joe Coburn defeated St. Louisan Mike McCool for the heavyweight championship, a fight that sparked considerable interest because of its intersectional overtones.[102]

When John Heenan came out of retirement in late 1863 to fight English champion Tom King, the international character of the contest, the high stakes, and the heavy wagering produced considerable discussion but did not create nearly the same degree of interest that the earlier international contest had, probably because of the war and a distrust of the English sporting character. Heenan's unwillingness to join the North in its battle also resulted in sharp criticism of this American-born heavyweight fighter and made it difficult for his former supporters to accept him as the champion of the American cause.[103] The out-of-shape Heenan was no match for his English challenger, leading some people to suggest that Heenan, or more likely his trainers and backers, had dumped the fight; others blamed British injustice for the outcome, as they had done earlier. The public outcry was limited, however, in both duration and scope, with most of the post-fight analysis confined to sports journals.[104]

Boxing underwent a three-year period of general inactivity, the *Clipper* claiming that "the palmy days of the prize ring have gone forever." In 1867 there was a resurgence in interest and the number of contests, causing that same journal to state that it did not "remember a time when the prize ring was in such favor as it is at present, or when there was such animation among the young lambs." The *Herald* echoed these sentiments, noting that "papers team with accounts of fights…and benefits are held even in our theatres." *Wilkes' Spirit* maintained that the excitement created by the scheduled rematch in 1868 between Colburn and McCool was comparable to that which had surrounded the Hyer–Sullivan fight. At the last minute, however, the fight was cancelled when threats were made that the police would intervene.[105] When a contest was proposed in 1870 between two recent English immigrants, heavyweights Jem Mace and Tom Allen, the *Herald* hoped that it would not take place in New York, an attitude that did not prevent them, along with the *New York Sun* and *Wilkes' Spirit*, from sending reporters to New Orleans to cover the fight. The tremendous nationwide interest in a contest between two foreign fighters testified to the appeal of boxing, particularly major heavyweight bouts.[106]

Animal Sports

Various animal sports, also called blood sports, had existed in New York since the earliest colonial days, although in the generation following the Revolution efforts were made to curtail such activity. Some citizens characterized these cruel diversions as "disgraceful and beastly," believing that they "debase the mind of the spectator, deaden the feelings and extinguish every spark of benevolence." By 1820 bear and bull baiting had virtually disappeared from

New York's sporting scene, their demise a result of the physical growth of the city and the dangers such large animals presented to the expanding urban population.[107] Influenced primarily by those who encouraged billiards and boxing, cockfighting and other animal sports continued and experienced significant growth between 1850 and 1870. In the immediate post-Civil War years, however, changing attitudes and various social forces, symbolized by the formation in 1866 of the American Society for the Prevention of Cruelty to Animals, began to undermine these bloody sports, although their full impact would not be felt for another two decades.

In 1823 an English visitor pointed out that in New York "it is perfectly common for two or three cockfights to regularly take place every week." Although the sport no doubt was commonplace, nearly a quarter-century passed before it was referred to in the New York press. In 1847 the *Spirit* noted a battle between New York and Philadelphia cocks, and two years later it mentioned a cockfight between Troy and New York birds, strongly suggesting that intercity cockfights were also a common practice.[108] During the 1850s the media took note of other animal sports as well, a reflection of not only the changing nature of the urban press and the increasing number of sports journals but the growth of these sports. Promoters of animal sports began advertising in various sports journals, and in 1857 the *Clipper* even devoted an entire section to rat baiting and dogfighting. Although New York State had banned all blood sports the previous year, law enforcement was lax and "hardly a night passed in the city without a tournament held in amateur or professional pits."[109]

Animal sports continued to be popular during the Civil War decade, as the *Clipper* noted in 1861: "notwithstanding the arrests that have been made from time to time, the Fancy still continue their canine 'sport' as if regardless of all laws." Cockfighting was said to be "very exciting and is becoming more popular than formerly."[110] Kit Burns's Sportsman Hall was the best known of New York's numerous animal pits. A barroom hangout for some of the city's leading ruffians and criminals, its location behind the bar and through a narrow passage made it easy to defend against the police and other intruders. The amphitheater seated 250 comfortably, although usually 400 spectators were packed around the center pit to witness rat baiting and dogfighting. Another attraction was Jack the Rat, who would bite off the head of a mouse for a dime and decapitate a rat for a quarter.[111]

Most of the spectators at Kit Burns's hall and other such places were from the lower and lower-middle classes, although individuals from other social strata did not hesitate to pay as much as three dollars to see a cockfight. Among the spectators at one of these events the *Herald* noted "several members of our past and present municipal board, a bevy of junior members of the bar, certain ward politicians [and] a considerable assortment of fast and fancy men." In 1861 some 250 people paid three dollars each to witness a cockfight between birds owned by John Morrissey, the boxer, and Mr. Genet, the president of the board of alderman. Reporting the event under the derogatory title "Amusements of the Ruling Class," the *Times* maintained that $50,000 had changed hands on the outcome. Frederick Van Wyck claimed in his memoirs that attendance at animal contests and other bawdy sporting events was a rite de passage for the sons of the old aristocracy. At Tommy Norris's livery stable he witnessed rat baiting, a cockfight, a prizefight between two billy goats, and a boxing match between two topless women: "Certainly, for a lad of 17, such as I, a night with Tommy Norris and his attraction was quite a night."[112]

In the five years following the Civil War animal sports remained a popular pastime in the New York City area, although the law prohibiting these bloody contests became stricter and was more readily enforced. *Wilkes' Spirit* claimed that cockfighting was "all the rage and embraces all sorts of people from the millionaires of the highest respectability down to the lowest roughs." The *Herald* agreed, noting that "never before was there such universal interest in the sport" both in New York and nationally. Other animal sports also had their devotees, which prompted one writer to declare, "Those who are not interested in such contests can form but little idea of the excitement which such produce among one class of the sporting fraternity, nor will they probably appreciate the delight with which they are enjoyed and the amount of money which is staked upon the results."[113]

Objections to these cruel, bloody sports date to colonial days. During the antebellum period an infiltration of changing English attitudes toward animal sports, a general national reform movement, and the effects of urbanization and a shifting economy reinforced these older objections. The various social and intellectual pressures coalesced in 1866 with the formation of the American Society for the Prevention of Cruelty to Animals (ASPCA) in New York. Henry Bergh, the son of a wealthy New York shipbuilder, was for more than twenty years the major force behind the ASPCA, which was modeled after England's Royal Society for the Prevention of Cruelty to Animals, founded forty-two years earlier. Few public figures "labored with a greater zest for battle, or a more flamboyant sense of the dramatic."[114]

The policies of the ASPCA with regard to animal sports of all kinds took on class overtones. Although the organization condemned many upper-class activities such as pigeon shooting and fox hunting, Bergh was forced against his best judgment to prosecute "the 5th Avenue 'Sport' with greater caution than those of Water Street," since many gentlemen sportsmen were also friends and supporters of the ASPCA. His battles with the upper class took on the nature of a sparring match, according to his biographer, with Bergh frequently retreating and only occasionally "driving home a body blow to the slow-changing public opinion."[115] This pressure to focus on the lower classes' involvement in animal sports was indicative of the general nature of criticism of blood sports. While many people had long been disgusted by the cruelty involved, others were equally, if not more, concerned with gambling and misspent time among the working class and the unemployed. The *Times*, the most outspoken critic of blood sports, noted that these contests existed solely for gambling purposes and that the amusement was "reprobrated by decent people."[116] As in many other things, participation by the upper class was often overlooked when fingers were being pointed.

Bergh and the ASPCA, bolstered by changing attitudes and a more enforceable anticruelty law, began an intensive campaign to shut down the various animal pits in New York, particularly Kit Burns's place. By 1870 only a modicum of success had been achieved, for despite numerous raids the organization was unable to count on many prosecutions. The failure of Bergh and his cohorts "reflected less upon the zeal of these stout-hearted crusaders than upon the political affiliations of the sporting tribe." The *Herald* believed that "as far as preventing this sort of sport is concerned Mr. Bergh and his numerous corp of deputies may well throw up the sponge...; for beyond causing a little inconvenience and conveyance to those who frequent and participate in the enjoyment, they will never accomplish anything." Although unable to win many convictions, Bergh's efforts proved to be more than minor inconveniences. One raid set Burns back $800, while other New York sportsmen, always fearful that Bergh was waiting in the wings, began to frequent pits in Brooklyn, Williamsburgh, and Hoboken for their evening entertainment.[117]

By 1870 Bergh's harassments placed animal sports on the defensive. Although certain segments of New York's sporting society continued to frequent various pits, the power of public sentiment, the clergy, and the ASPCA became too great in the 1880s. By the last decade of the nineteenth century animal sports disappeared from the city's sporting scene for all intents and purposes. Having existed in New York for more than 250 years, these cruel, bloody sports were no longer compatible with urban society.[118]

Professional Athletes and the Modernization of Sport

The premodern character of pedestrianism, billiards, boxing, and animal sports broke down with their emergence as spectator sports both in New York and nationally. By 1870 all four sports contained certain modern elements, but none of them were transformed into a modern sport despite the presence of a professional element. Although the professional athlete emerged as one of the dominant symbols of modern sport, the limited impact that professionalization had on the modernization of sport is not surprising since there were paid athletes even during the premodern period. For those sports in which professional athletes comparatively flourished in earlier times, elements similar to modern sports can be discovered and to a certain degree were linked to the presence of these paid athletes. For example, as far back as ancient Greece professional athletes were involved in specialization, training routines, and coaching. While professional athletes sought to rationalize their sport skills, their presence did not affect the rationalization of the sporting institution.[119]

The inability of professionalization to act as an agent of rationalization derives from the fact that professional athletes merely affect the sports contest, not the institution of sport. In essence, the professional athlete is a specialized sports product (i.e., a better or more skilled player). The changing nature of ownership or sponsorship of the "means of production" (or contest) provides the impetus for the rationalization of the sport. What distinguished the sponsorship of pre-modern professional sport from modern professional sport was the shift from match or private sponsorship to commercial sponsorship.[120] It was precisely because of the limited commercial growth of these sports that modern elements, most notably the organizational structure, emerged so slowly.

The reasons for the limited commercialization of these professional sports varied. Legal sanctions inhibited the commercialization of boxing. While pugilism was a spectator sport, there was no admission fee charged to boxing contests held in open fields usually far away from police intervention. Gate receipts were collected at local sparring matches, but these fights were exhibitions, not contests. Pedestrianism was a commercial–spectator sport, but interest in it was insufficient to nurture entrepreneurship to any significant degree. Where commercial pedestrianism was profitable, notably the Caledonian games, the maturation of modern structures, especially on the organizational level, made significant advances. Similarly, it is no coincidence that billiards was the only other sport among these four to have a national organization, even if it was ineffective in regulating the sport. While the creation of the American Billiard Players Association was rooted in part in the recreational growth of the sport and the economic interest of billiard manufacturers, the commercialization of billiard contests also played a role in this development.

Notes

1. *New York Post*, 8 July, 3 Sept. 1824, 3 June 1834; *New York American*, 2, 23 July 1824. Also see John Cumming, *Runners and Walkers: A Nineteenth Century Sports Chronicle* (Chicago: Regnery Gateway, 1981), 5-8; John R. Betts, *America's Sporting Heritage, 1850-1950* (Reading, Mass.: Addison-Wesley, 1974), 36; George Moss, "The Long Distance Runners of Ante-Bellum America," *Journal of Popular Culture* 8 (1974): 370; Jennie Holliman, *American Sport, 1785-1835* (Durham, NC.: Seeman, 1931), 152-54. For running races prior to 1820, see ibid., 152; Foster R. Dulles, *A History of Recreation: America Learns to Play* (New York: Appleton-Century-Crofts, 1965), 26, 34.

2. *Post*, 14 Jan., 17 Apr. 1835; *Spirit of the Times* 5 (18 Apr. 1835). Also see Allan Nevins, ed., *The Diary of Philip Hone, 1828-1851* (New York: Arno, 1970), 156; Archibald D. Turnbull, *John Stevens: An American Record* (New York: Century, 1928), 510-11. Samuel L. Gouveneur was from one of New York's wealthiest families and an active member of the city's horse-racing community during the 1820s and 1830s. The exact amount of the Gouveneur–Stevens wager is unknown.

3. Nevins, *Diary*, 156-57. The *Post* reported that the crowd at this contest was not as large as the one at the Eclipse–Henry race; this race attracted 16,000-20,000 spectators. See *Post*, 25 Apr. 1835.

4. *Post*, 17, 25 Apr. 1835; *American Turf Register and Sporting Magazine* 6 (May 1835): 478; *Spirit* 14 (1 June 1844): 162; *New York Spectator*, 27 Apr.1835. For the background of the runners, see *Post*, 2S Apr. 1835. Francis Smith, a black runner, wanted to compete but was declared ineligible because he had not filled out the entry form before the deadline. See Moss, "Long Distance," 371, 378; *American Turf Register* 6 (June 1835): 518-20.

5. For pedestrianism in New York between 1835 and 1844, see *Spirit* 8 (16 June 1838): 140, (8 Sept. 1838): 236, 10 (6 Aug. 1840): 265, 11(11 Dec. 1841): 468.

6. For the lure of gambling, see Henry Chafetz, *Play the Devil: A History of Gambling in the United States, 1492-1955* (New York: Potter, 1960), 223-24; Moss, "Long Distance," 370. For pedestrianism in England, see Melvyn Waterman, *History of British Athletics* (London: Hale, 1968), 15-18; Harold Harris, *Sport in Britain: Its Origins and Development* (London: Paul, 1975), 136-38.

7. *American, 15* June 1821. Richard Mandell claims that the first use of the term "record" in connection with a sporting event appeared in an 1868 track and field manual. See "The Invention of the Sports Record," *Stadion* 2 (1976): 259. Prior to this date, however, Americans were familiar with both the term and the concept of a sports record. See *Spirit* 24(23 Nov. 1844): 462. Nevertheless, there was at this time no agency for keeping records, authenticating performances, or making sure of standardized conditions. While all records were unofficial and a published list of sports records did not as yet exist, the swiftest times could be found by consulting back issues of sports journals.

8. *Spirit* 14 (1 June 1844): 162, (8 June 1844): 169; *New York Herald*, 1, 4 June, 13, 17-18 Oct. 1844; *American Turf Register* 15 (July 1844): 436-38, (Nov. 1844): 684-90.

9. *Spirit* 14 (2 Nov. 1844): 426.

10. Ibid., (23 Nov. 1844): 462-63, (21 Dec. 1844): 510; *American Turf Register* 15 (Dec. 1844): 730-35, 738-43; *Herald*, 18, 20 Nov. 1844.

11. *Spirit* 14 (22 June 1844): 202, 19 (1 Dec. 1849): 486, 15 (9 Aug. 1845): 278; *Herald*, 14 July 1841. For walking contests, see *Spirit* 7 (16 Sept. 1837): 244, 10 (4 Apr. 1840): 49, 11 (6 Mar. 1841): 6; *American Turf Register* 12 (Mar. 1841): 162. For the growth of pedestrianism nationally, see Moss, "Long Distance," 375-82; Cumming, *Runners*, 30-34, 40-41, 48-62; Betts, *Sporting Heritage*, 36; Dulles, *Recreation*, 143-44; Dale A, Somers, *The Rise of Sport in New Orleans, 1850-1900* (Baton Rouge: Louisiana State University Press, 1972), 61-62.

12. Moss, "Long Distance," 373. For examples of the size of New York purses, see *Spirit* 8 (8 June 1838): 128, 11(11 Dec. 1841): 468, 14 (12 Oct. 1844): 387, 15 (5 July 1845): 213, 18 (18 Nov. 1848): 462, 24 (18 Mar. 1854): 54; *Herald*, 12 Apr. 1856.

13. For the involvement of respectable New Yorkers in the sport, see *Spirit* 14 (8 June 1844): 169, 11 (6 Mar. 1841): 6; *American Turf Register* 12 (Mar. 1841): 162.

14. For racing in New York between 1845 and *1855*, see *Spirit* 15 (5 July 1845): 213, 18 (18 Nov. 1845): 462, 20 (10 Aug. 1850): 294, 24 (18 Mar. 1854): 54; *Herald*, 3 Jan., 25 Mar., 9, 26 June, 8 July 1845, *5* Sept. 1854; *New York Times*, 4 Aug., 5 Sept. 1854; *New York Clipper* 2 (12 Aug. 1854).

15. The economic implications of commercial versus participant money is discussed in chapter 3. The Beacon Course was closed "because most of the inhabitants of its surrounding area did not like races or the characters that patronize them." See Harry B. Weiss and Grace M. Weiss, *Early Pastimes in New Jersey* (Trenton, N.J.: Pastime, 1960), 124. While these elements quite possibly contributed to the demise of the Beacon Course, the death of Cyrus Browning, the proprietor, was probably more significant. Whatever the exact reason, the closing of the Beacon Course raises questions of the profitability of the racecourse—if it had been a financial success, other investors would have stepped in to challenge the closing; and if it was not a profitable venture, then the crowd sizes must have been grossly exaggerated. In any event it is easier to understand why there was a shift from promoter to match money.

16. *Times*, 1 June 1857; *Herald*, 25 Mar., 1, 10 July, 4 Oct. 1845; *Clipper* 1 (18 Mar. 1854), (25 Mar. 1854).

17. Gerald Redmond, *The Caledonian Games in Nineteenth-Century America* (Cranbury, N.J.: Associated University Press, 1971), 20. Also see Rowland Berthoff, *British Immigrants in Industrial America, 1790-1950* (New York: Russell and Russell, *1953)*, 151; Robert Korsgaard, "A History of the Amateur Athletic Union of the United States" (Ed.D. diss., Teacher's College, Columbia University, *1952)*, 28-29.

18. Redmond, *Caledonian*, 37-45, 59-60; Berthoff, *British, 151*, 168; *Times*, 2 July 1867; Korsgaard, "Amateur," 22-23.

19. Redmond, *Caledonian*, 40-41; Berthoff, *British*, 151. Crowds at the Caledonian games in New York during the 1860s were almost always estimated at 10,000 or more. For examples, see *Wilkes' Spirit of the Times* 23 (10 Sept. 1870): 54; *Times*, 10 Sept. 1864.

20. Sport historians have easily linked the commercialization of sport with professionalization. Unfortunately, they have paid scant attention to the role that amateur athletic clubs played in this development.

21. *Clipper* 7 (24 Sept. 1859): 183; *Wilkes' Spirit* 23 (10 Sept. 1870): 54; Redmond, *Caledonian*, 20-21, 42, 62-66, 116-17. Field events were known in America before the Caledonian games but rarely engaged in at track and field meets. Similarly, running races in the Scottish games were more on the order of dashes, in contrast to the passion of Americans for endurance races.

22. Redmond, *Caledonian*, 53-54, 59-60, 62-67; Melvin L. Adelman, "The Development of Modern Athletics: Sport in New York City, 1820-1870" (Ph.D. diss., University of Illinois, 1980), 593.

23. *Porter's Spirit of the Times* 5 (4 Sept. 1858): 9; *Clipper* 4 (29 Nov. 1856): 252, 13 (16 Sept. 1865): 176; *Wilkes' Spirit* 11 (17 Sept. 1864): 36, 1 (24 Sept. 1859): 45, 23 (10 Sept. 1870): 54; *Times*, 12 Oct. 1867, 24 Sept. 1858, 10 Sept. 1864; *Herald*, 8 Oct. 1858, 16 Sept. 1859.

24. *Clipper* 16 (30 May 1868): 58, 15 (14 Dec. 1867): 282, 17 (10 Apr. 1869): 5; *Times*, 24 Sept. 1870, 28 July 1868, 1 Dec. 1867; *Herald*, 24 Nov. 1869; *Wilkes' Spirit* 15 (1 Sept. 1866): 8, 18 (9 May 1868): 195, (30 May 1868): 252. Also see, Cummings, *Runners*, 77-100.

25. Redmond, *Caledonian*, 76. Korsgaard notes that informal track meets took place at Columbia College as early as 1864. See "Amateur," 32-33.

26. John A. Krout, *Annals of American Sport* (New Haven, Conn.: Yale University Press, 1929), 186; Redmond, *Caledonian*, 51-52; Frederick W. Janssen, *A History of American Athletics and Aquatics, 1829-1886* (New York: Outing, 1888), 31.

27. *Wilkes' Spirit* 19 (10 Oct. 1868): 121; *Turf, Field and Farm* 7 (13 Nov. 1868): 736; *Clipper* 17 (19 Mar. 1870): 397.

28. The New York Athletic Club emerged as a sports club of the New York elite in the 1880s. See Benjamin G. Rader, *American Sports: From the Age of Folk Games to the Age of Spectators* (Englewood Cliffs, N.J.: Prentice-Hall, 1983), 55-57.

29. Redmond also pointed out that financial considerations were an important reason for the decline of the Caledonian games during the 1880s. See *Caledonian*, 99-110.

30. For the rise of athletic clubs in New York during the 1870s, see Korsgaard, "Amateur," 32-33, 50. As was the case with rowing, amateur control over track and field did not occur overnight. See ibid., 43-69; Redmond, *Caledonian*, 67.

31. Ford discussion of the two billiard styles, see Ned Polsky, *Hustlers, Beats and Others* (Garden City, N.Y.: Anchor, 1969), 7-18. While professional pool players dominated the sport after 1850, billiards is the only sport discussed in this chapter to also have a significant recreational dimension. In this chapter the terms "billiards" and "pool" are used interchangeably to describe various types of billiard and pool games.

32. Ibid., 6-16, 24; Louise C. Belden, "Billiards in America Before 1830," *Antiques* 87 (Jan. 1965): 99-101; Charles Haswell, *Reminiscence of New York by an Octogenarian, 1816-1860* (New York: Harper, 1896), 59; *Clipper* 9 (23 Nov. 1861): 250, 16 (9 May 1868): 37, (16 May 1868): 44.

33. For a discussion of skilled pool players in the 1820s, see *Clipper* 9 (23 Nov. 1861): 250, 16 (16 May 1868): 44. For billiard advertisements, see *Herald*, 21 Dec. 1837, 5 June 1846; *Spirit* 7 (2 Sept. 1836): 231.

34. *Clipper* 16 (16 May 1868): 44, (23 May 1868): 5; J. H. Green, *An Exposure of the Arts and Miseries of Gambling; Designed Especially as a Warning to the Youthful and Inexperienced Against the Evils of that Odious and Destructive Vice*, 5th ed. (Philadelphia: Zieber, 1847), 206-7.

35. For the growth of club life in New York, see Edward Pessen, *Riches, Class and Power Before the Civil War* (Lexington, Mass.: Heath, 1973), 225-29.

36. Polsky, *Hustlers*, 6, 17-21. New York merchant N. T. Hubbard fondly recalled that he played billiards at the New York Hotel. See *Autobiography of N. T. Hubbard with Personal Reminiscences of New York City from 1795-1875* (New York: Trow, 1875), 69-70.

37. Phelan was born in Ireland around 1814, and his family emigrated to America when he was seven or eight years old. At one time an apprentice jeweler, Phelan became the proprietor of the Arcade Billiard Saloon in New York in 1846, if not earlier. See *Herald*, 5 June 1846, 8 Oct. 1871; *Times*, 7 Oct. 1871; Betts, *Sporting Heritage*, 41-42.

38. *Spirit* 20 (23 Feb. 1850): 6, (1 Mar. 1851): 18.

39. Michael Phelan, *Billiards Without Masters* (New York: Winant, 1850); *Spirit* 20 (17 Aug. 1850): 312.

40. Polsky, *Hustlers*, 24; Betts, *Sporting Heritage*, 75.

41. *Spirit* 25 (8 Dec. 1855): 516, 27 (30 May 1857): 187, 29 (16 Apr. 1859): 109; *Times,* 19 Mar., 11 Apr. 1859; *Porter's Spirit* 3 (9 Jan. 1858): 293, 6 (26 Mar. 1859): 53, (23 Apr. 1859): 115-17; Michael Phelan, *The American Billiard Record. A Compendium of Important Matches since 1854* (New York: Phelan and Collender, 1870), 11.

42. *Spirit* 29 (27 Aug. 1859): 342; *Wilkes' Spirit* 1 (15 Oct. 1859): 89.

43. *Wilkes' Spirit* 3 (10 Nov. 1860): 153, (6 Oct. 1860): 73, (13 Oct. 1860): 88, (27 Oct. 1860): 121, 5 (21 Sept. 1861): 37; *Clipper* 8 (12 Jan. 1860): 314. Also see *Times,* 1 Oct. 1860; Phelan, *American Billiard,* 12. Americans were led to believe that Berger was the champion billiard player of France, and the ease with which he defeated professional pool players in America gave credence to the claim. However, a letter written to the editor of *Wilkes' Spirit* from Paris claimed that Berger was not the best French player. See *Wilkes' Spirit* 5 (28 Sept. 1861): 57.

44. *Clipper* 6 (29 Jan. 1859): 327, (12 Feb. 1859): 343, 9 (23 Nov. 1861): 252, 7 (21 Jan. 1860): 314; *Herald,* 4 Feb. 1858; *Spirit* 29 (12 Mar. 1859): 60; Phelan, *American Billiard,* 12.

45. Dudley Kavanaugh, *The Billiard World: Containing the Rules of the Games of Billiard as Played in the United States and Europe* (New York: Kavanaugh and Decker, 1869), 27; *Wilkes' Spirit* 7 (10 Jan. 1863): 292, 11 (26 Nov. 1864): 202. For similar developments in New Orleans, see Somers, *Rise,* 65. It is interesting to note that one of the explanations offered for bowling being more popular today than billiards is that it is easier to learn. For the relationship between mastery of a physical skill and involvement in a recreational activity, see p. 111.

46. Polsky coined the term "bachelor subculture" to describe a group "that has become increasingly rare and unimportant to America—the hetero-sexual but all male subculture." The bachelor subculture originated from the increasing proportion of single males in the population during the latter part of the nineteenth century. See Polsky, *Hustlers,* 20-25. For the bachelor subculture and its relation to sport, see Somers, *Rise,* 52-53; Rader, *American Sports,* 97-98.

47. Polsky points out that American historians "seem never to have assayed, indeed to be oblivious of, the swiftly growing role of a confirmed bachelor subculture in the social history of nineteenth-century America." Unfortunately, he does not explore this theme in any depth. He simply shows that a casual relationship existed between marriage statistics and the emergence of the bachelor subculture and states that changing economic conditions and immigration affected America's sexual patterns. See *Hustlers,* 21-24. For a discussion of the changing sexual patterns, see Jayme A. Sokolow, *Eros and Modernization: Sylvester Graham, Health Reform, and the Origins of Victorian Sexuality in America* (Cranbury, N.J.: Associated University Press, 1983), 11-39, 77-99; Stephen W. Nissenbaum, *Sex, Diet, and Debility in Jacksonian America: Sylvester Graham and Health Reform* (Westport, Conn.: Greenwood, 1980), 3-38; Charles N. Rosenberg, "Sexuality, Class and Role in 19th Century America," *American Quarterly* 25 (1973): 131-53; Barbara Welter, "The Culture of True Womanhood, 1820-1860," ibid. 18 (1966): 151-74; Nancy Cott, "Passionlessness: An Interpretation of Victorian Sexual Ideology, 1790-1850," *Signs* 4 (1978-79): 219-36; Ronald G. Walters, *Primers for Prudency: Sexual Advice to Victorian America* (Englewood Cliffs, N.J.: Prentice-Hall, 1974). Dale Somers applies the concept of the bachelor subculture to explain sporting developments in antebellum New Orleans. He avoids the problem found in Polsky's argument by merely pointing to the discrepancy in the number of men and women in that city's population. See *Rise,* 52-53. In New York, however, the male–female ratio was roughly even. See United States Bureau of the Census, *Eighth Census of the United States (1860): Population of the United States in 1860* (Washington, D.C., 1864), 322, 328, 337.

48. Peter Stearns, *Be a Man! Males in Modern Society* (New York: Meier and Holmes, 1979), 39-112 (quote from p. 38); Joe L. Dubbert, *A Man's Place: Masculinity in Transition* (Englewood Cliffs, N.J.: Prentice-Hall, 1979), 29-30, 111-12; E. Anthony Rotundo, "Body and Soul: Changing Ideals of American Middle-Class Manhood, 1770-1920," *Journal of Social History* 16 (1983): 23-38.

49. Green, *Art and Miseries,* 206-7; J. H. Green, *Green's Report No. I on Gambling and Gambling Houses in New York* (New York, 1851), 79-81; *New York Tribune,* 25 Dec. 1850; Polsky, *Hustlers, 6;* Marshall B. Davidson, *Life in America,* 2 vols. (Boston: Houghton-Mifflin, *1951),* 2:31.

50. Welter, "Cult," 151-74; Barbara Welter, "The Feminization of American Religion, 1800-1860," in Lois Banner and Mary Hartman, eds., *Clio's Consciousness Raised* (New York: Harper and Row, 1974), 137-57; Nancy Cott, *Bonds of Womanhood: "Woman's Sphere" in New England, 1780-1835* (New Haven, Conn.: Yale University Press, 1977), 149-54. In 1866 *Wilkes' Spirit* claimed, "We have always advocated the presence of ladies at these matches,…as the most reliable means of conferring tone upon the necessarily heterogeneous masculine assemblage." See *Wilkes' Spirit* 14 (19 May 1866).

51. Michael Phelan, *The Game of Billiards*, 3d ed. (New York: Appleton, 1858), 13-28; *Herald*, 5 Apr. 1862; *Wilkes' Spirit* 10(16 Apr. 1864): 99; Kavanaugh, *Billiard World*, 68.

52. *Clipper* 11(19 Dec. 1863): 29, 5 (19 Dec. 1857): 276; *Wilkes' Spirit* 15 (24 Nov. 1866): 204; *Herald*, 11 June 1864; *Times*, 13 Feb. 1870.

53. *Clipper* 9 (23 Nov. 1861): 252; *Times*, 17 Jan. 1865; *Herald*, 21 Feb. 1869, 11 June 1864. Also see *Wilkes' Spirit* 5 (21 Sept. 1861): 37, 6 (28 June 1862): 260, 11(21 Jan. 1865): 324.

54. *Clipper* 7 (21 Jan. 1860): 314, 12 (1 Oct. 1864): 194; *Turf, Field and Farm* 5 (31 Aug. 1867): 138; Kavanaugh, *Billiard World*, 67.

55. *Wilkes' Spirit* 6 (22 Mar. 1862): 37, 15 (5 Jan. 1867): 292; *Clipper* 14 (3 Nov. 1866): 235.

56. *Wilkes' Spirit* 6 (12 Apt. 1862): 89, (15 Mar. 1862): 20-21, 8 (2 May 1863): 141; *Clipper* 11(27 June 1863): 84; *Times*, 19 Mar., 10 June 1863, 21 June 1861; *Herald*, 5 Apr. 1862; Phelan, *American Billiard*, 18.

57. *Wilkes' Spirit* 12 (4 Mar. 1865): 4, (17 June 1865): 249, 15 (15 Sept. 1866): 41, 48, (29 Sept. 1866): 77, (3 Nov. 1866): 156; *Clipper* 12 (11 Feb. 1865): 347, (25 Feb. 1865): 362, 14 (3 Nov. 1866): 235; *Times*, 2 Sept. 1865; Phelan, *American Billiard*, 34.

58. *Wilkes' Spirit* 23 (1 Oct. 1870): 101, 105, (8 Oct. 1870): 117, 120, (22 Oct. 1870): 155-56, (7 Jan. 1871): 325, 22 (23 July 1870): 356-57.

59. Ibid. 10 (25 June 1864): 260; *Herald*, 5 Apr. 1862, 11 June 1864; *Times*, 20 Jan. 1871; *Clipper* 11(24 Oct. 1863): 218.

60. For a discussion of professional billiard players coming to New York, see *Wilkes' Spirit* 6 (12 Apr. 1862): 84. The names of leading players were taken mainly from newspaper accounts of major billiard contests. Also see ibid. 13 (23 Dec. 1865); Phelan, *American Billiard*, 11; Kavanaugh, *Billiard World*, 23-64.

61. *Wilkes' Spirit* 8 (2 May 1863): 141. Polsky also shares the view that "most of the early non-WASP billiard professionals are of Irish origin," although he realizes that German-Americans were involved in the sport to a far greater extent than earlier billiard historians recognized. See *Hustlers*, 25. Polsky makes no mention, however, of the contribution of the French or French-Canadians to the development of the sport in America, possibly because their influence was not far-reaching and was confined to the initial decade of professional billiards, and because these skilled performers, unlike other immigrant players, rarely stayed in the United States for any extended period of time.

62. Polsky, *Hustlers*, 19; Kavanaugh, *Billiard World*, 69.

63. *Wilkes' Spirit* 15 (29 Sept. 1866): 77, 6 (12 Apr. 1862): 84-85; Kavanaugh, *Billiard World*, 54. For further discussion of the financing and earnings of professional poolplayers, see Melvin L. Adelman, "Neglected Sports in American History: The Rise of Billiards in New York City, 1850-1 870," *Canadian Journal of History of Sport* 12 (Dec. 1981): 23, n. 67.

64. *Wilkes' Spirit* 20 (22 May 1869): 201, 23 (20 Aug. 1870): 4, 13 (14 Oct. 1865): 104. Also see *Times*, 13 Feb. 1870. For the rules and various types of billiard games, see Phelan, *Billiard*, 172-97.

65. Betts, *Sporting Heritage*, 205; Polsky, *Hustlers*, 19, 25-26.

66. For boxing in America prior to 1820, see Elliott Jacob Corn, "The Manly Art: Bare-Knuckle Prize Fighting and the Rise of American Sport" (Ph.D. diss., Yale University, 1983), 1-61, 118-26; Holliman, *American Sport*, 138-43; *American Fistiana, Containing All the Fights in the United States from 1816 to 1860* (New York: DeWitt, 1860), 5-6; Nat Fleischer, *The Heavyweight Championship: An Informal History of Heavy-Weight Boxing from 1719 to the Present Day* (New York: Putnam, 1961), 41. Newspapers during the antebellum period agreed that the Hyer–Beasley fight was the first American prizefight. See *Herald*, 24 Sept. 1842, 9 Feb. 1849; *Times*, 13 Dec. 1855; *Porter's Spirit* 5 (23 Oct. 1858): 118.

67. *American*, 19, 1 Mar, 1822. Also see Gorn, "Manly Art," 141-54.

68. *Spectator*, 19 Oct. 1824; *Post*, 14 Dec. 1826, 28 June 1823. For boxing contests during the 1820s, see *American Fistiana*, 6-7; *Herald*, 9 Feb. 1849; Gorn, "Manly Art," 126-32; Holliman, *American Sport*, 143.

69. For the *New York Mirror's* criticism of boxing, see Davidson, *Life*, 2:33; *Herald*, 22 Aug. 1837. Also see *Spirit* 6 (15 Oct. 1836): 275. For boxing contests in New York in the 1830s, see *Herald*, 21 Aug. 1837, 24 Sept. 1842, 9 Feb. 1849; *Porter's Spirit* 5 (23 Oct. 1858): 118; *Post*, 30 Aug. 1830; Holliman, *American Sport*, 147; Gorn, "Manly Art," 135-41.

70. *Herald*, 24 Sept. 1842; *Spirit* 12 (3 Sept. 1842): 322; *Times*, 13 Dec. 1855; *Clipper* 9 (4 Jan. 1862): 304; Fleischer, *Heavyweight*, 41,

71. *Herald*, 13-16 Sept. 1842; *Tribune*, 19 Sept. 1842; *Spirit* 12 (17 Sept. 1842): 342; *Clipper* 1 (25 Feb. 1854); Thomas M. McDade, "Death in the Afternoon," *Westchester Historian* 46 (Winter 1970): 2-4. Some writers claimed that McCoy's mother told him not to return home a loser, but others insisted that his mother opposed his fighting. See *Herald*, 15 Sept. 1842; *Spirit* 12 (17 Sept. 1842): 342; *Tribune*, 17 Sept. 1842. Under the boxing rules of the day a round lasted until one of the fighters was knocked down; the next round started thirty seconds later.

72. *Tribune*, 19-20 Sept. 1842; *Herald*, 16-17 Sept. 1842.

73. For the negative view of pugilism, see Nevins, *Diary*, 619-20, 636-37, 640; George T. Strong, *The Diary of George Templeton Strong*, ed. Alan Nevins and Milton H. Thomas, 4 vols. (New York: Macmillan, 1952), 1:185-86. For the damper the Lilly–McCoy fight put on pugilism and second-rate fights in New York, see *Porter's Spirit* 5 (23 Oct. 1858): 118; *Herald*, 26 June 1843; *Tribune*, 27 June 1843, 1 Sept., 19 Oct. 1847.

74. Sullivan was neither a Yankee nor a Sullivan—he was born James Ambrose in Ireland in 1813. For biographical material on Sullivan, his impact on the rise of pugilism, and his boxing career, see Gorn, "Manly Art," 172-80; Fleischer, *Heavyweight*, 51-59; *Times*, 30 June 1856, 13 Dec. 1855; *American Fistiana*, 16-17; *Herald*, 9 July, 14 May 1847, 9 Feb. 1849, 22 Oct. 1858; *Spirit* 16 (19 Sept. 1846): 354; *Clipper* 4 (5 July 1856): 82-83; *Porter's Spirit* 5 (23 Oct. 1858): 118; *Times*, 13 Dec. 1855.

75. *American Fistiana*, 19; *Herald*, 11 Jan., 9 Feb. 1849; *Spirit* 18 (23 Sept. 1848): 366, (25 Nov. 1848): 474, (17 Feb. 1849): 615, 618-19; *Times*, 13 Dec. 1855; *Clipper* 9 (8 Feb. 1862): 341.

76. *Herald*, 7, 9, 11 Feb. 1849; *Porter's Spirit* (23 Oct. 1858): 118; *American Fistiana*, 19.

77. For the impact of the Hyer–Sullivan fight, see *Porter's Spirit* 5 (23 Oct. 1858): 118; *Clipper* 9 (8 Feb. 1862): 341. For the growth of boxing during the 1850s, see ibid. 1 (25 Feb. 1854), (15 Apr. 1854), 4 (9 Aug. 1856): 122, 7 (11 June 1859): 58; *Herald*, 23 Feb. 1858; *Tribune*, 7 Feb. 1855. Also see *Clipper* 1 (4 Feb. 1854), 5 (12 Dec. 1857): 267, 6 (13 Nov. 1858): 234; *Wilkes' Spirit* 1 (10 Dec. 1859): 221.

78. *Herald*, 13-14 Oct. 1853; *Times*, 11, 14 Oct. 1853; *American Fistiana*, 20-21; *Tribune*, 20 Oct. 1853; *Spirit* 23 (22 Oct. 1853): 421; *Clipper* 1 (15 Oct. 1854), (22 Oct. 1854). The heavyweight championship fights between Floyd Patterson and Muhammad Ali, and Ali and Sonny Liston, had some of the same symbolic characteristics as the Sullivan–Morrissey contest a century earlier. See Adelman, "Modern Athletics," 600.

79. *Porter's Spirit* 4 (31 July 1858): 345, 349, (7 Aug. 1858): 357; *Times*, 18 Sept., 18, 22-23 Oct. 1858; *Herald*, 22 July, 26 Sept., 15, 21 Oct. 1858; *American Fistiana*, 59; *Clipper* 6 (30 Oct. 1858): 222-23, (13 Nov. 1858): 234. The backgrounds of Heenan and Morrissey were remarkably similar: both grew up in Troy, New York; both had Irish parents; and both went to California during the 1850s, eventually returning to New York. For biographical material on Heenan, see *John C. Heenan of Troy, N. Y., Champion Pugilist of America* (New York: Fox, 1882), 6-9; *Herald*, 22 Oct. 1858. Heenan was the American representative in this fight because he was born in America and because nativists disliked Morrissey.

80. *Times*, 25, 28, 30 Apr., 9 Mar. 1860; *Herald*, 11 Mar., 24 Apr., 13, 28 May, 9 Nov. 1859, 13, 18 Feb., 30 Apr. 1860; *Wilkes' Spirit* 2 (14 Apr. 1860): 84-85; *Clipper* 7 (12 Nov. 1859): 234, (7 Jan. 1860): 398; *Harper's Magazine* 20 (May 1860): 844. For a popular history of the Heenan–Sayers fight, see Alan Lloyd, *The Great Prize Fight* (New York: Coward, McCann and Geoghegan, 1977).

81. *Herald*, 8 Dec. 1859, 25 Apr. 1860; *Clipper* 7 (24 Mar. 1860): 386; *Wilkes' Spirit* 1 (21 Jan. 1860): 313. Also see Anthony O. Edmonds, "The Second Louis-Schmeling Fight," *Journal of Popular Culture* 7 (1973): 42-50.

82. For an American view of the fight, see *Times*, 30 Apr., 3, 17 May, 16 July 1860; *Herald*, 29 Apr. 1860; *Wilkes' Spirit* 2 (5 May 1860): 129-35, 137-41, (12 May 1860): 143-49, 153, (2 June 1860): 201, (21 July 1860): 330, *S* (28 Dec. 1861): 264. For a discussion of the fight, see ibid. 2 (29 Apr. 1860): 114-20; *Clipper* 8 (5 May 1860): 18-20, (12 May 1860): 26-27; Lloyd, *Great*, 137-59; Fleischer, *Heavyweight*, 64-66.

83. *Brooklyn Eagle*, 12 May 1860; *Herald*, 30 Apr., 2, 8 May 1860; *Clipper* 8 (2 June 1860.): 50, 52, (9 June 1860): 71, (23 June 1860): 106. For an anti-English view and a discussion of the English sporting character, see *Wilkes' Spirit* 22 (21 May 1870): 216-17.

84. *Herald*, 30 June, 15 May, 16 June 1860; *Clipper* 8 (19 May 1860): 34, (25 Aug. 1860): 145-47; *Times*, 8 May 1860.

85. *Tribune,* 20 Sept. 1842; *Herald,* 24 Aug. 1837; *Porter's Spirit* 5 (23 Oct. 1858): 118. Of the six English-born fighters in New York, it is noteworthy that four were from minority groups—two were Irish or part Irish, and two were Jewish. While there were several black fighters in New York between 1840 and 1860, Samuel Freedman was the only one on whom any information exists. Black fighters competed at times against whites in exhibitions. For black boxing in New York, see *Clipper* 9 (3 Aug. 1861): 122, 16 (27 Feb. 1869): 371; *Times,* 18 Oct. 1859.

86. The evidence on occupation indicates that boxers were employed in unskilled and semiskilled jobs, which is not surprising given the high proportion of Irish fighters. Native-born fighters were more likely to come from the artisan class, particularly the butcher community. Although many of the fighters were of lower-class origins, a few owned their own taverns and others were probably managers or bouncers. Some fighters were given patronage jobs. Even among the fighters who held white-collar jobs, the evidence strongly suggests that they had lower- or lower-middle-class origins.

87. *Porter's Spirit* 5 (23 Oct. 1858): 118. The average fighter in New York earned money by participating in numerous sparring exhibitions. How much of the gate receipts he was given is unknown, but in all probability it was not more than $25 and quite possibly as little as $10 for an evening's work.

88. *Clipper* 8 (6 Oct. 1860): 195. For this view of boxers, see S. Kirson Weinberg and Henry Arond, "The Occupational Culture of the Boxer," *American Journal of Sociology* 58 (1951): 460-69; Nathan Hare, "A Study of the Black Fighter," *Black Scholar* 3 (Nov. 1971): 2-8; John Ford, *Prizefighting: The Age of Regency Boximania* (New York: Great Albion, 1972), 57-59.

89. The connection between pugilism and politics was briefly touched on by Fleischer, *Heavyweight,* 50-51; Alvin F. Harlow, *Old Bowery Days: The Chronicle of a Famous Street* (New York: Appleton, 1931), 296, 299-301; Herbert Asbury, *The Gangs of New York: An Informal History of the Underworld* (New York: Capricorn, 1970), 95; Edward K. Spann, *The New Metropolis, New York City, 1840-1857* (New York: Columbia University Press, 1981), 345-48.

90. *Tribune,* 20 Sept. 1842, 1 Mar. 1855; *Times,* 28 July 1858, 28 Apr. 1860, 18 May 1871; *Herald,* 22, 30 Oct. 1858, 6 July, 12 Aug. 1860; *Eagle,* 27 Sept. 1858; *Clipper* 4 (14 Feb. 1857): 338, (15 Nov. 1856): 234. The amount of space given to the political ramifications of pugilism appeared to be equal to the amount given for other reasons for disapproval of the sport.

91. For the formation of New York gangs, see Asbury, *Gangs,* 1-86. For the development of Tammany Hall and the shifting nature of politics, see Jerome Mushkat, *Tammany: The Evolution of a Political Machine, 1789-1865* (Syracuse, N.Y.: Syracuse University Press, 1971), 76, 101, 202; Alexander B. Callow, Jr., *The Tweed Ring* (New York: Oxford University Press, 1965), 6-7; Spann, *The New Metropolis,* 45-66, 341-63. For the connection between gangs and politics, see Ashury, *Gangs,* 37-44, 105-6; Callow, *Tweed,* 57-59. For the declining political importance of fighters in the post-Civil War period, see Adelman, "Modern Athletics," 573-75.

92. Harlow, *Bowery,* 296-301; Fleischer, *Heavyweight,* 50-51; Callow, *Tweed,* 56-57; Asbury, *Gangs,* 95.

93. *Clipper* 11(25 Apr. 1863): 10; *Wilkes' Spirit* 8 (25 Apr. 1863): 122.

94. *Herald,* 23 Jan., 26-27 Feb., 9, 11, 19-20 Mar., 1855, 28 July 1854; *Tribune,* 26 July 1854, 27 Feb., 9-10 Mar. 1855; *Times,* 28 July 1854, 26-27 Feb., 12 Mar., 13, 15, 17 Dec. 1855; Asbury, *Gangs,* 99-100; Spann, *New Metropolis,* 254-55. One journal noted that Bill Harrington won the respect of the better class. See *Porter's Spirit* 6 (2 Apr. 1859): 68. A member of old-line Knickerbocker society declared that Harrington was "a protector of the weak and timid, a terror to sneak thieves and ruffians." See Abram C. Dayton, *The Last Days of Knickerbocker Life in New York* (New York: Putnam, 1897), 338-39. Also see Harlow, *Bowery,* 151; *American Fistiana,* 80.

95. *Chronicle* 1 (22 Aug. 1867): *Turf, Field and Farm* 5 (31 Aug. 1867): 137.

96. *Times,* 20 Apr. 1860.

97. The increasing coverage boxing received in the daily press reflected the changing nature of the urban press. See James L. Crouthamel, "The Newspaper Revolution in New York, 1830-1860," *New York History* 45 (1964): 91-113; Crouthamel, "James Gordon Bennett, the *New York Herald* and the Development of Newspaper Sensationalism," ibid. 54 (1973): 294-316; Dan Schiller, *Objectivity and the News: The Public and the Rise of Commercial Journalism* (Philadelphia: University of Pennsylvania Press, 1981).

98. *American Fistiana,* 24; *Clipper* 6 (27 Nov. 1858): 250, (2 Oct. 1856): 186, (22 Jan. 1859): 314, 1 (28 Jan. 1854), 4 (23 Aug. 1856): 138, (27 Dec. 1856): 284, 5 (26 Dec. 1857): 252, 7 (25 Feb. 1860): 356, 8 (2 Feb. 1861): 330, (9 Mar. 1861); 372, 16 (6 June 1868): 68.

99. *Herald,* 26 Sept. 1848, 9 Feb., 2 June 1866, ii May 1870, 22 Aug. 1837.

100. *Times,* 18 Sept. 1858, 9 Sept. 1870, 13 Dec. 1855, 26 Mar. 1862.

101. Rotundo, "Body and Soul," 123-38.

102. *Clipper* 11 (20 June 1863): 79; *Herald,* 20 July 1860; *Wilkes' Spirit* 8 (25 Apr. 1863): 122. For the Coburn–McCool fight, see *Herald,* 29 Apr., 6 May 1863; *Clipper* 11 (16 May 1863): 335; *Times,* 26 Mar. 1863; Fleischer, *Heavyweight,* 71.

103. *Herald,* 24 Nov. 1863; *Times,* 22 Dec. 1863; *Eagle,* 23 Aug. 1861.

104. *Clipper* 11(21 Jan. 1864); 314, (13 Feb. 1864); 346, (27 Feb. 1864): 362, (19 Mar. 1864): 386, 12 (23 Apr. 1864): 10; *Wilkes' Spirit* 9 (2 Jan. 1864); 273-74, 280, 284-85, (9 Jan. 1864): 296-97; *Times,* 26 Dec. 1863.

105. *Clipper* 13 (16 Dec. 1865): 282, 15 (18 May 1867): 421; *Herald,* 23 Aug. 1867, 25 Aug. 1868. For the Coburn–McCool fight, see *Clipper* 16 (18 Apr. 1868): 11, (6 June 1868): 667; *Wilkes' Spirit* 18 (25 Apr. 1868); 153.

106. *Herald,* 8 Jan., ii May 1870; *Times,* 11 May 1870; *Wilkes' Spirit* 22 (14 May 1870); 201; Fleischer, *Heavyweight,* 72-73; Somers, *Rise,* 162-63.

107. For animal sports prior to 1820, see Jack Berryman, "The Ending of American Blood Sports," paper presented at the 86th meeting of the American Historical Association, 1971, 4-7; Krout, *Annals,* 15, 23; Holliman, *American Sport,* 128, 130, 134; Ester Singleton, *Social New York under the Georges, 1714-1776* (New York; Appleton, 1902), 266-67.

108. Isaac Holmes, *An Account of the United States* (London, 1823), quoted in Berryman, "Ending," 6; *Spirit* 17 (20 Mar. 1847); 4, 19 (10 Nov. 1849); 450; Gerald Carson, *Men, Beasts and Gods: A History of Cruelty and Kindness to Animals* (New York; Scribner, 1972), 65.

109. *Spirit* 22 (25 Dec. 1852); 540, 19 (12 Jan. 1850); 558, 20 (25 Jan. 1851); 582, 29 (8 Oct. 1859); 414; Zula Steele, *Angel in Top Hat* (New York; Harper, 1942), 141; *Tribune,* 24 Jan. 1855; *Herald,* 8 Feb., 28 May 1858; *Porter's Spirit* 6 (5 Mar. 18S9); 12; *Wilkes' Spirit* 1 (17 Dec. 1859); 229, (24 Dec. 1859); 253; *Times,* 24 May 1855; *Clipper* 4 (31 Jan. 1857); 327, 6 (26 Feb. 1859); 355.

110. *Clipper* 8 (16 Mar. 1861); 378, 10 (8 Nov. 1862); 234, 12 (25 Feb. 1865); 362; *Herald,* 21 Feb. 1862; *Times,* 22 Jan., 23 Aug. 1861; *Wilkes' Spirit* 4 (22 June 1861); 245.

111. Asbury, *Gangs,* 49-51; Steele, *Angel,* 142-43; Martin and Herbert J. Kaufman, "Henry Bergh, Kit Burns, and the Sportsmen of New York," *New York Folklore Quarterly* 28 (1972); 15-20. For biographical material on Burns, see *Herald,* 24 Dec. 1870; *Clipper* 18 (31 Dec. 1870); 306; *Wilkes' Spirit* 23 (24 Dec. 1870); 293.

112. *Herald,* 8 Feb. 1858; *Times,* 22 Jan. 1861; Frederick Van Wyck, *Recollections of an Old New Yorker* (New York; Liveright, 1932), 113-14; *Tribune,* 24 Jan. 1855; *Wilkes' Spirit* 3 (2 Feb. 1861); 340.

113. *Herald,* 19, 27 Jan., 13 Mar., 1 Nov. 1870, 14 Dec. 1869, 12 Mar., 18 May 1868; *Wilkes' Spirit* 22 (19 Mar. 1870); 68, 21 (12 Feb. 1870); 406-7; Berryman, "Ending," 5, 8-9.

114. Carson, *Men,* 96-97. For biographical material on Bergh, see ibid., 97-100; Steele, *Angel,* 3; Charles B. Morris, ed., *Makers of New York* (Philadelphia; Hammersly, 1895), 66. For changing attitudes toward animal sports in England, see Robert W. Malcolmson, *Popular Recreations in English Society, 1700-1850* (Cambridge; Cambridge University Press, 1973), 123-38; Brian Harrison, "Religion and Recreation in Nineteenth Century England," *Past and Present* 38 (1968); 118-23; Carson, *Men,* 43-54.

115. Steele, *Angel,* 7, 218.

116. *Times,* 22 Mar, 1866, 7 Mar. 1867.

117. Kaufman and Kaufman, "Henry Bergh," 26——; *Herald,* 1 Nov. 1870; Steele, *Angel,* 144-48. Also see Berryman, "Ending," 8-9, 11.

118. Berryman, "Ending," 8, 11, 13; Somers, *Rise,* 205-6.

119. For the relationship between professional athletes and the emergence of certain modern sporting characteristics prior to the nineteenth century, see Allen Guttmann, *From Ritual to Record: The Nature of Modern Sports* (New York: Columbia University Press, 1978), 36-38; Dennis Brailsford, *Sport and Society: Elizabeth to Anne* (London: Routledge and Kegan Paul, 1969), 210-17. Sport scholars have asserted that the rationalization of sport "had been greatly facilitated by commercialization and professionalization." See Alan G. Ingham, "Occupational Subculture in the Work World of Sport," in Donald W. Ball and John W. Loy, eds., *Sport and Social Order: Contributions to the Sociology of Sport* (Reading, Mass.: Addison-Wesley, 1975), 353. In examining the influence of commercialization and professionalization on sporting developments, scholars have too easily tended to perceive

them as two sides of the same coin. While there has been a growing interrelationship between these two elements during this century, historically they have been divergent traditions.

120. In both the private (or match) and commercial system the promoter's objective is to make a profit; however, the means to this end vary. In the former system the backer achieves his profit only through victory; in the latter system the winner is unimportant. For the entrepreneur the size of the crowd and gate receipts are the key to his profits. The differences between the two systems produces different relationships to the contest. While the backer is concerned with "outcome," the entrepreneur is concerned with "spectacle." It is this shifting relationship to the promotion of sporting contests that marks the initial step in the emerging rationalization of the sporting institution.

CHAPTER 4

CHEATING, GENDER ROLES, AND THE NINETEENTH-CENTURY CROQUET CRAZE

■ Jon Sterngass ■

Croquet is usually stereotyped as a genteel game, less a sport than a social function, and more suited to genial conversation and unfettered flirtation than strident competition. Nineteenth- century American periodicals and croquet manuals emphasized the sport's placidity, as opposed to male working-class sports such as football, baseball, and rowing, which often seemed infected with the time-discipline or rationality of the workaday world. The Newport (Rhode Island) Croquet Club's 1865 handbook proclaimed that the game owed its popularity to "the delights of out-of-doors exercise and social enjoyment, fresh air and friendship—two things which are of all others most effective for promoting happiness." Croquet was portrayed as a morally improving and rational recreation; the *New York Galaxy* declared that "amiability and unselfishness are the first requisites of a good player." Because croquet was not a particularly athletic game, it was considered ideal for children, older people, and mixed gender groupings. Thus, one recent historian of the sport decisively concluded, "In the 1860s, in a family and female sport like croquet, the etiquette of playing the game with grace and good manners took precedence over winning, sociable play triumphed over unprincipled competition."[1]

Yet was this, in fact, how the game was played on the croquet lawns of the nineteenth century? While authors of croquet manuals and magazines propounded trite encomiums to honesty, rationality, and fellowship, a perusal of visual and literary evidence reveals that a great deal of competitive spirit existed in the typical croquet match, that the use of deception to win was common, and that women were particularly guilty transgressors. Modern reliance on croquet manuals and a handful of periodical articles recalls the limitations of other

Article appears by permission of the *Journal of Sport History*.

nineteenth-century hortatory literature such as etiquette and advice manuals; that is, the ethos was only a code, not an accurate depiction of reality. Female grace and good manners may have been the ideal for the rule- and taste-makers, but on the croquet ground, a peculiar sort of gender reversal enabled women to temporarily jettison their passive role and dominate, if not humiliate, men. Women played the game seriously, enjoyed matching skills with men, and often emerged victorious. The fact that this image runs contrary to "Victorian" gender stereotypes suggests that a more nuanced approach is needed, rather than to declare some sports to be "male" and other sports "female" with all the formulaic and oversimplified preconceptions these adjectives imply.[2]

The origins of croquet are obscure, but some version apparently migrated from Ireland to England in the 1850s, where it proved a favorite amusement at fashionable lawn parties. An ivory turner named John Jaques, whose firm had been in the games business since 1795, may have introduced the sport at the Great Exhibition of 1851. It spread rapidly enough that in 1864, Jaques declared that croquet had "won a popularity which has almost revolutionized our out-door social life." By 1867, he had published sixty-five thousand copies of his rule book, with a female croquet-player adorning the cover of most editions. The game reached its English apogee in 1871, when spectators crowded five deep to witness Walter Jones Whitmore's unforgettable croquet tournament/extravaganza, complete with ten thousand troops parading around the courts, a full dress ball, and brilliant aristocratic company.[3]

Americans imported croquet from Victorian England some time during the Civil War. In 1864, the *American Boy's Book of Sports and Games* reported croquet "has been only recently introduced into this country." By April 1865, *Godey's Lady's Book* felt obligated to publish some rules of croquet because the game was "now becoming very fashionable." The following April, Milton Bradley patented his version of croquet socket bridges and indexical balls and then obtained court injunctions against competitors who infringed his rights. *The Nation* concluded in 1866 that "of all the epidemics that have swept over our land, the swiftest and most infectious is croquet." Manufacturers even produced sets with candle-sockets attached to the wickets to facilitate night games.[4]

The game made inroads far beyond the young and single set. Supporters suggested that the sport enjoyed wide American success because it matched the spirit of the aggressive, achievement-minded nation, "and nowhere else is the family circle so certain to appreciate its purity and give it full patronage." Ulysses Grant was supposedly playing croquet when informed of the gold crisis instigated by Jim Fisk and Jay Gould; Rutherford Hayes later allocated six dollars from the government treasury to buy "good quality" croquet balls, a profligacy vigorously condemned by Democrats in Congress. Croquet players overran Martha's Vineyard campgrounds, and the game was also popular with the Shakers. At the utopian Oneida Community, John Noyes theorized that croquet served as "a field for the development and manifestation of character and individual power and destiny, and competition, instead of being a mere exhibition of antagonism, becomes a harmonic cooperation with God."[5]

The majority of croquet players were female; "they are its disciples," declared the *Galaxy,* "and from them it claims great homage." Official explanations for the affinity of women for croquet emphasized the facts that the game required delicate skill rather than strength, flattered bodily appearance, and was played in places suitable for courtship. The *New Orleans Picayune* commented, "There are few prettier sights than a number of young ladies and gentlemen upon some level greensward pursuing a painted croquet ball, and entering fully into the spirit of the game." Women players dominated the plethora of croquet images produced from 1860 to 1900, whether lithographs or sheet music, stereograph views or plaster figurines; Winslow Homer's five oil paintings *(1865-69)* featuring croquet depicted seventeen players of which fourteen are female. Women's magazines such as *Godey's, Demorest's,* and *Peterson's* highlighted croquet rules and fashions, while croquet manuals returned the favor by conspicuously advertising women's and children's magazines, home amusements, and piano music. By 1869, *Appleton's* could report, "there is no doubt that croquet has, during the last few years, done more than anything else to promote with young ladies a liking for open-air games..." One newspaper asserted, "never in the history of outdoor sports in this country has any game achieved so suddenly a popularity with both sexes, but especially with the Ladies, as Croquet has." In Charlotte Yonge's novel *The Trial* (1864), some young women "seemed at a loss what life had to offer" when they found no croquet mallets in the garden. One of these women declared, "I used to garden once, but we have no flower-beds now, they spoilt the lawn for croquet."[6]

The croquet craze also had its opponents. Although an early guidebook claimed croquet was "too refined, too intellectual, ever to become a gambler's game," Julia Ward Howe's daughter complained that wagering on the outcome was exceedingly common. Others supported the abolition of croquet on the grounds that its enticements were addictive. The sport was momentarily banned in Boston, and the authorities at both the Oneida Community and Martha's Vineyard took the drastic step of restricting the game or forbidding it altogether.[7]

It was the infatuation of women with croquet, however, that caused the most cultural dissonance in a nation only a generation removed from Lydia Child's caution that activities such as skating and sliding should not take place in mixed company. Although croquet seemed to be a simple and innocent family game— Mark Twain called it "ineffably insipid"—the novel idea that men and women could play together, whether at archery, roller skating, mixed bathing, or croquet, raised the specter of extreme sexual danger for women unregulated by "traditional" social norms. In Charlotte Yonge's *The Clever Woman of the Family* (1865), croquet was enthusiastically received by the younger set and especially the girls, but several of the adults fretted over its wickedness "as an engine for flirtation." At a croquet party in 1869, female competitors altered their dresses "that they might form no impediment to the progress of the game," and the *New Orleans Picayune* confirmed that women actually cut short their dresses while playing "to allow perfect freedom of action." Another magazine condemned the mendacious game in purple prose, claiming croquet was a "source of slumbering depravity, a veritable Frankenstein monster of recreation" and suggesting that "it would be well if the enthusiasm of the clergy and laity were enlisted for suppressing the immoral practice of croquet."[8]

For a putatively sociable and noncompetitive pastime, even croquet's popularizers agreed that the game engendered a great deal of controversy. That all did not go smoothly at matches was implied by Milton Bradley's first "suggestion to beginners" in capital and bold letters: "KEEP YOUR TEMPER, and remember when your turn comes." Walter Whitmore Jones listed eight principles of play, of which the fifth was "whatever you do, never lose your temper." A turn-of-the-century etiquette book included only two sentences on croquet, of which one reminded social aspirants, "Never dispute, or show any temper over the outcome of any game." Almost every Gilded Age resort hotel had a croquet lawn, according to William Dix's reminiscences, where "people wrangled and bickered and—let it be whispered—sometimes cheated over that effete game." *The Nation* lamented that croquet transformed respectable adults into "dogs, barking and biting," and a sketch in the *Philadelphia Evening Bulletin* called it the "destroyer of life-long friendships and a ruiner of happy homes." The latter accusation was confirmed in a separation hearing reported in the *International Herald Tribune.* The wife testified that when playing croquet, her husband became so annoyed when she raised a question as to whether his ball had gone through a hoop that he did not speak to her for days. Commented the judge, "I do not think there is any game which is so liable to put one out of humour as croquet."[9]

The croquet-ground-as-battlefield was a common motif in croquet descriptions. Mayne Reid, author of one of the most widely read croquet guides and a former captain in the British military, specifically denoted the opposing sides as "enemies" whose duty was to "marshall" the opposing sides and "strike for first play," and this militaristic metaphor received widespread acceptance. Matches could end in complete chaos, as parodied on the "curious croquet-ground" in Wonderland where Alice met the Queen of Hearts. Lewis Carroll was a connoisseur of the game, and he had published his own complex croquet variant anonymously in 1863. The runaway popularity of *Alice in Wonderland* [1865] implied not only that every reader could be expected to know something of the rules of croquet, but also that they would recognize Alice's reproach that, "The players all played at once, without waiting for turns, quarreling all the while." Was it a croquet ground in Wonderland or a summer resort where Alice described players who don't "play at all fairly…and they quarrel so dreadfully one can't hear oneself speak—and they don't seem to have any rules in particular: at least, if there are, nobody attends to them…"[10]

The issue of cheating was greatly complicated by the widespread diversity of methods of playing the game. At one time, more than ten different croquet manuals offered competing sets of rules, to the dismay of many men in that order-obsessed age. Milton Bradley's manual insisted, "in order to have peace and harmony on any Croquet ground, some authority must be adopted…"; and when *Scribner's* published its own clarifications in 1876, the writer felt compelled to declare, "It's a mistaken idea that complication of rules makes it 'more interesting'." In Anthony Trollope's *The Small House at Allington* [1862], competition between the heroine Lily Dale and Mr. Crosbie inevitably led to a squabble over the proper rules. But even when rules were mutually agreed upon, arguments frequently ensued over whether balls had been pushed rather than struck, or whether they had been moved at all. A frustrated writer for the *Galaxy* especially decried those who played out of turn, claiming that croquet attracted "individuals who are by nature mysteriously gifted with stupidity in a larger and more provoking degree" than nonplayers.[11]

This anarchic period opened the door for a variant known as 'tight croquet' to become all the rage. In this version of croquet, players were permitted in certain situations to place their ball next to their opponent's, plant their foot firmly on their own ball, and use the mallet to smash it with all their might. The shock transmitted by this action to the opponent's ball would send it spinning away into the lake or the rhododendrons. Although not permitted in the modern game, the dramatic tight croquet stroke became the instantly recognizable iconic image of croquet between 1860 and 1900, enshrined in numerous illustrations and descriptions. In many of these pictures, visually dominant and athletic women outnumbered subservient or passive men, completely reversing the doctrine of separate spheres that assigned noncompetitive roles to women. For example, Thomas Hill's *Palo Alto Spring* [1878] depicted the Stanford family and their friends at croquet. In the painting, young Leland Jr., the family's powerful heir apparent, was relegated to a garden chair while his female companions actively engaged in the game.[12]

A game of croquet illustrated in *Harper's Weekly*, September 8, 1866.
Photo courtesy of Library of Congress. LC-USZ62-7927.

When performed by female players, the tight croquet stroke could be interpreted as an act of symbolic castration. Men were 'forced' to look on helplessly as their female opponent lined up the two balls, lifted her skirt, placed her dainty foot on her own ball, and with a resounding thwack, hammered the other ball to parts unknown. Winslow Homer's first treatment of croquet seized upon the game's most salient moment, and he returned to it numerous times in his croquet series. The inherent titillation of this action was personified in an illustration in *Harper's Weekly* in which the revelation of a minuscule portion of a woman's ankle and leg tantalized and transfixed her fellow male players. John Leech's much reproduced cartoon for *Punch* the next year, entitled "A Nice Game for Two," reprised the same theme. Beneath a similar picture, subsequently reproduced ad infinitum, the caption read: "—Fixing her eyes on his, and placing her pretty little foot on the ball, she said, 'Now, then, I am going to croquet you!' and croquet'd he was completely." Even worse, the man often had to set the balls in place for the croquet shot as an act of courtesy. In theory, a bending woman clad in stiff hoops and petticoats violated the game's emphasis on graceful attitudes, but the act also underscored male obeisance.[13]

The gesture of raising one's skirt to reveal one's leg carried vast psychosexual meaning in the nineteenth century, for within the strict moral codes of the period, the socially acceptable feet often displaced the genitals as a focus of eroticism. In George Du Maurier's *Trilby*, the heroine's animal innocence, beauty, and sexuality were all symbolized by the exquisite shape of her naked feet, which were the focus of whatever sexuality the novel's three Englishmen express. The book was an international best-seller, selling nearly 300,000 copies its first year of publication. Du Maurier's biographer noted of the resulting *Trilby-mania*, "The scene in the novel that was most thoroughly exploited for commercial purposes was the one in which Little Billee sketched Trilby's perfect foot on the wall of his apartment." The feet of croquet players received the same sort of attention; in the poem "The Croquet Queen," Mayne Reid described the heroine's attractions:

> Her figure was faultless—nor tall, nor petite—
> Her skirt barely touched the top lace of her boot;
> I've seen in my time some remarkable feet,
> But never one equalling that little foot.
> Its tournure was perfect, from ankle to toe—
> Praxitiles ne'er had such a model for art—
> No arrow so sharp ever shot Cupid's bow;
> When poised on the ball it seemed pressing your heart!
> It crushed more than one, as I sadly remember—

Sigmund Freud directly linked this type of fetishism—when the normal sexual object is replaced by another that bears some relation to it but is entirely unsuited to serve the normal sexual aim—to castration anxiety. The combination of these two suppressed symbolic images meant that croquet could be a very unsettling game for male players.[14]

The definitive moment of the croquet stroke often took on great significance in the literature. In Daisy Ventnor's story "Pet Leighton's Game of Croquet," the willful heroine flirtatiously declared that she would give Major St. John an answer to his marriage proposal only if he could defeat her in croquet. The Major conceded he was "a very poor player" but he played so well that "Miss Pet saw it behooved her to be careful. Privately, she would not have missed winning the game for worlds..." At the game's end, only Pet and the Major's ball remained, of course, and Pet must croquet the Major or "she would inevitably lose the game." Her teammate (another suitor) egged her on to do the deed: "send him to the other end of the field, Miss Pet, and the game is your own." At the climax of the story,

> Pet placed her foot on the ball, and lifted her mallet to strike, when she glanced up at the Major, the first time she had looked him fairly in the eyes that afternoon. She blushed violently, and to cover her confusion, struck in haste. His ball went flying off, but alas! poor Pet! As she turned, her foot slipped from her own ball to the ground; an agonizing pain shot through her whole frame, and she quietly fainted away.

Pet's failure to complete the ritually castrating stroke with sufficient panache or gleeful malice clearly symbolized the end of her independent and flirtatious ways. In the brief denouement, she was ultimately described as "a meek and submissive victim," a "dear little penitent" who had surrendered to the Major.[15]

The linkage between flirtation and croquet underlined the fact that both were 'sports' which reversed 'traditional' gender roles by allowing women to play against and defeat men. Many nineteenth-century men had interpreted physical differences to imply the superiority of men and inferiority of women in leisure activity, but on both the hotel lawn and the championship course, women players proved themselves equal to or better than their male counterparts. Croquet even encouraged competition between the sexes, since the game could "be played with equal facility by ladies and gentlemen, skill and ingenuity being of much more importance to success than mere physical strength." The sport challenged the superiority of males and undermined the concept of separate spheres propounded as late as 1906 by noted psychologist and educator G. Stanley Hall: "The presence of the fair sex gives tonicity to youth's muscles... [a teenage girl] performs her best service in the true role of sympathetic spectator rather than as fellow player." In the late nineteenth century, Americans envisioned themselves playing, as popular poet John Saxe entitled one of his poems, "the game of life." The sporting metaphor, which often replaced the concept of life as a battle or journey, raised 'the game' to quasi-religious importance. In this highly charged rhetorical atmosphere, many men believed women brought confusion to sport. Competition, toughness, and winning at all costs were presumed to be not only culturally valued aspects of masculinity, but inherently masculine traits. Yet in *Lothair* [1870], Benjamin Disraeli described a situation probably typical on both sides of the Atlantic:

> Lord Montairy was passionately devoted to croquet. He flattered himself that he was the most accomplished male performer existing. He would have thought absolutely the most accomplished, were it not for the unrivalled feats of Lady Montairy. She was the queen of croquet.[16]

Exasperated male commentators complained incessantly about the propensity of women to cheat at croquet. In *Sylvie and Bruno Concluded* [1893], Lewis Carroll declared, "Look at the way Croquet is demoralising Society. Ladies are beginning to cheat at it, terribly: and, if they're found out, they only laugh and call it fun." Women were held to have various tricks up their sleeve, and magazines frequently alluded to the effectiveness of feminine wiles in winning the game. The 'push shot' was a particularly feared trick employed by women, and double-tapping acquired the slang appellation of "spooning," linking croquet to the verb's sexual implications of amorous fondling. English champion Lily Gower, who regularly played with and defeated the top men in the game, was officially accused of spooning in 1901. The ensuing controversy centered not on whether she was guilty of the widely practiced offense, but whether it was ungentlemanly of her opponent to protest. The *New York Times* explained away the shortage of male croquet players by reporting that women constantly cheated, and therefore men would not play with them. The "last words" of an 1865 croquet manual reminded players:

> Another important piece of advice is, don't cheat. We are aware that young ladies are proverbially fond of cheating at this game; but as they only do it because 'it is such fun,' and also because they think that men like it...The practice spoils the game so much, that, if it is allowed, the rules may as well be done way with at once.[17]

The distinctive clothing of women was also suspect in their ability to play croquet. An early historian of the game complained in 1872 of "the disgraceful practice of certain ladies to stand over a ball and conceal it with their clothes, while they scuffle it along with their feet to where they wish it to lie." An American periodical called this subterfuge "a very common practice and a very effective one." Some croquet manuals charitably assumed this to be an inadvertent tactic: "The ladies will very much oblige all their associates in croquet by avoiding long dresses, which are continually dragging the balls about over the ground to the annoyance of the players and the disturbance of the game." The charge was so widely disseminated that another writer despairingly pleaded:

> Ladies, be honorable, and reform this trick altogether, for in most cases you do not need these little helps: you are generally better players than men; you play more frequently than they do; besides your nerves are steadier, and croquet is more the business of life with you than with them...Surely these are advantages enough; why, then, take any unfair ones.[18]

Within a decade of the sport's arrival in America, cheating in croquet had become a literary commonplace. For example, in 1868, *Harper's Bazaar* offered tongue-in-cheek hints on croquet gamesmanship, "drawn up in accordance with several successful players of our acquaintance." In considerable detail, the author mocked the conventional advice manuals by advocating the use of "tricks and delicate stratagems," "clever sleights of hand," disputation of the rules, hinting "to a lady partner to trail her dress" over the croquet balls, and even outright lying and cheating. The satirist suggested:

if you have the ill luck to be found out, not to apologize or say that it was done unintentionally, or for a joke, or to plead ignorance of the rules. Put a bold front upon it, and, if your opponent says positively that you did so or so, answer him that you did not; tell him that he is strangely mistaken; pledge your honor to what you say; tell him any thing you will but go on. People generally give way rather than have a disturbance.

The article concluded, "while others are merely amusing themselves, be you wide awake to your own interests...the single object of the croquet player being to win the game." Although intended in jest, this comic caricature reinforces anecdotal evidence from other sources, and implies considerable grounding in reality.[19]

Similarly, in an article titled "The Immorality of Croquet," another writer fulminated against widespread cheating in the sport. The jeremiad described the actions of the participants in a mixed doubles match:

One pushes his ball to a more convenient spot when nobody is looking that way; another declares that hers touched somebody else's in passing well knowing that she is the only person in a position to have seen daylight between them; the third is busy knocking in the second hoop, so that her ball may pass through more easily; number four is lying low, awaiting a convenient opportunity to deceive the rest. Stage the first, everybody has degenerated into a cheat.

The author described a game in which "such words as liar, cheat, brute, scoundrel or viper have passed into currency. Rules are improvised as the game proceeds, and the basest subterfuges resorted to in order to gain a point." Even allowing for hyperbole and/or satire, cheating by women in croquet seems to have been taken for granted.[20]

As early as 1860, the British novel *Sylvan Holt's Daughter* caught the essence of a typical mixed-gender croquet match. In a chapter-long description, the female author described players who "talked, one against the other from first to last, contradicting, wrangling, and arguing vociferously." The imperious older daughter, victorious in the first match, ran from one to another of the onlookers, shouting out with exuberant glee, "We have won! We have won!...I told you we should: we will play you again, and beat you again too." Although the two main participants engaged in some flirtation, when he mis-hit a ball, she "ventured on a rebuke, telling him that her ball was first, and that, if he did his best, perhaps they should win the game." Her male partner responded, "Would you like to win?...well, then I won't risk our chance again." When they did win, their female opponent "flung down her mallet and said she would play no more that day, everybody was so stupid!"[21]

The croquet party depicted in Louisa May Alcott's *Little Women* represents a slightly different example of competition in croquet. The opposing four-person teams obviously were playing to win; "The English played well, but the Americans played better and contested every inch of ground...Jo and Fred had several skirmishes and once narrowly escaped high words." Inevitably, the issue of cheating arises. Fred gave his ball "a sly nudge with his toe, which put it just an inch on the right side." When Jo accused him of cheating, he brazenly denied it just as suggested by *Harper's Bazaar*, declaring, "Upon my word, I didn't move it; it rolled a bit, perhaps, but that is allowed; so stand off, please, and let me have a go at the stake." Despite Fred's manipulations, Jo's team emerged victorious through her superior play, and far from chastising Jo, Laurie tossed up his hat in exultation, while Meg praised her actions. Although in this case the perpetrator was male, in *Little Women*, another female novelist clearly represents a competitive situation in which a young woman wants to win, and succeeds.[22]

The question of how 'seriously' women took croquet, or whether or not they actually beguiled their opponents, evades an easy answer. Despite the longstanding belief that women were "first in transgression" dating back to Eve's accusation against the serpent, the tradition that women possessed a special affinity for lying was not a nineteenth-century commonplace. Scientists occasionally promulgated the belief that females were less mentally and morally developed than males, and that a savage and childlike nature in women was a hallmark of civilization.[23] On the other hand, the more widely accepted 'cult of true womanhood' propounded women's moral superiority as a counterbalance to the ruthless and competitive economic world of men. At least in theory, women's nurturing spirit and intuitive morality sanctified the domestic sphere and made them, if anything, less likely to lie than men. Women were incessantly called upon to be passive and submissive (morally positive traits for them) in the face of life's vicissitudes. Although issues of hypocrisy and sincerity transfixed nineteenth-century America, there was no particular emphasis on an innate female propensity to lie, nor were there widespread accusations against women's truthfulness in other endeavors except flirtation—significantly, another venue in which women held a modicum of power.[24]

In reality, antebellum American women occupied the slipstream between the poles of ethereal and earthy, angel of light and painted lady. If they all did not seethe with indignation over the prescribed ideals of ladyhood, neither did they totally acquiesce or become 'nervous' invalids. The doctrine of separate spheres enabled women to hold the reins of influence inside the family, the church, and the social world, and dominate child-rearing, religious morality, and fashion. From there, it was just a short step to membership in the reform movements that took women out of the home into the public world, where they sought to correct problems invariably created by men. In the meantime, the denial of direct political representation and equal economic opportunity forced women to exercise what degree of power they could in cultural choices such as reading, shopping, making social calls, or creating crafts. The tension created by nineteenth-century changes in gender roles, masked or repressed in more restrictive institutions, was revealed in cultural forms—everyday acts, rhetorical devices, and unconscious patterns of behavior.[25]

The numerous accusations or descriptions of female deception at croquet by both male and female writers, and the lack of reciprocally passionate denials and pleas of innocence, seems to imply that women did in fact cheat. Yet this flies in the face of common knowledge about gender-related variations in 'truth-telling.' Women, as the social and emotional specialists in American culture, are supposedly more expressive, approachable, and people-oriented than men. Where men's fabrications are often self-centered, women apparently use lies to focus on the feelings of others or put a positive gloss on events. When women were accused of cheating at croquet in the nineteenth century, however, the denunciation implied not that women were falsely derogating their abilities in order to prop up fragile male egos, but that they hoodwinked opponents in order to win. Maud Howe Elliot conceded, "There was cheating in croquet. It is hardly human to resist the temptation of pushing the ball into a position where one stroke will carry it through a wicket, when the other player is busy at the far end." Her rationalization for using 'immoral' means to gain victory at any cost fits none of the stereotypes of demure, insecure women lowering their self-esteem to become better adjusted to occupying a subordinate status.[26]

Nor does the accusation that women cheated "because they think that men like it" appear reasonable. Men emphatically did not like it; they complained about women cheating all the time. I know of no case where a man implied that a woman was cute, more desirable, or would make a better marriage prospect because she was a devious croquet player. On the contrary, this rare justification appears to be an explicitly narcissistic male view of female actions; when men could not understand a woman's motivations, men automatically assumed it must be done on some level to please them. Since the authors of most if not all croquet guides were male, their admonitions to "amiability and unselfishness" are better interpreted as another example of men directing objectified women how to act, rather than an actual depiction of the way the game was played. And cheating could exasperate women as well as men. Katherine Rice, who enjoyed playing croquet while attending Albany [NY] Female Seminary, complained in her diary in 1873 that in an unspecified game, "Mattie cheated! cheated! cheated! cheated! cheated!!!!!! But no one seems to think that very unusual in her." [exclamations in text][27]

A better approach to this croquet conundrum centers on the ethical ambiguity of American attitudes toward deception in the nineteenth century. The confidence man represented the threat of social disorder and moral vacuity, yet comic and satiric literature presented a society in which shrewd, roguish operators delighted in swindles and living by their wits. On the frontier, backwoodsmen like hunter Davy Crockett or Mississippi boatman Mike Fink bragged of their deceptions while telling self-aggrandizing tall tales. In the east, the Yankee peddler was a peripatetic trickster figure, supposedly achieving his goals through constant theatricality. Southern humorist Johnson Hooper created the popular Simon Suggs, whose "whole ethical system lies snugly in his favorite aphorism—'IT IS GOOD TO BE SHIFTY IN A NEW COUNTRY'." In 1849, the *Spirit of the Times* reported, not without admiration, of one Mississippi turfman who had "acquired some celebrity for making and unmaking rules as they would happen best to suit him at the times." After 1865, Horatio Alger personified this tradition by encouraging readers to cultivate the art of the confidence man in order to seize the main chance. The trickster became a covert cultural hero, and although the role was usually filled by males, women too could play the 'confidence' game. Thus, Americans did not universally condemn deception at all times in all places.[28]

In particular, dishonesty in sports was/is not always viewed as a morally reprehensible act, even if it undermines the moral argument for character development. Games theoretically have binding rules; historian Johann Huizinga implied, "as soon as the rules are transgressed the whole play-world collapses." But these rules are paper commandments only. Cheating may stem from a variety of motivations and serve many purposes, but morally charged actions are situationally specific, and different domains of social life exhibit different expectations of truthfulness. No matter the size of the rulebook, all ambiguity cannot possibly be eliminated from a sport, and players learn or are even taught to 'bend' the rules; games teach children (and adults) to distinguish between the fairness of some forms of deception and the unfairness of others. Cheating may callously further the cheater's self-interest, but at a safe distance, many cultures enjoy the wit and audacity of successful liars and glorify the cheater (or trickster) who outwits others through outright fraud. As Samuel Butler noted several centuries earlier: "Doubtless, The pleasure is as great Of being cheated as to cheat."[29]

The concept of liminality helps explain the curious anomaly of theoretically pedestal-bound paragons of public virtue cheating to win at croquet. According to anthropologists Victor and Edith Turner, individuals longing for a deeper and less restrictive range of experience and meaning participate in 'liminoid rituals' whose symbols are in some way antithetical to the existing rules, hierarchies, and duties that typically govern social life. Certain intervals and actions acquire special meaning and become demarcated from the mundane and specific sites become associated with unusual experiences. This passage through a limen (Latin for 'threshold') situates the participant in a period of transition and potentiality. In the twilight-zone world of liminality, the ritualist sheds normal responses and behaves speculatively without anxiety.[30]

In the early days of the American croquet craze, the croquet field served as such a liminal site, providing a venue where women could tentatively challenge, in a semi-ritual setting, the so-called 'cult of domesticity.' Nowhere is this better expressed than in Alice Brown's story "Dooryards" [1899], set "in the days when croquet first inundated the land." A shy and lonely housewife, married to a farmer "who never learned to smile…duller than the ox," fell in love with croquet after defeating the minister at a Fourth of July picnic. Without the money to buy a croquet set, Della created her own grassless court between the barn and the pump, with wickets cut from willows, potatoes or apples for balls, and a clothes-prop for a mallet. She imperiously warned her husband when he returned from the fields, "Don't you drive over them wickets!," at which point, "Eben looked at her and then at his path to the barn, and he turned his horse aside." Thereafter, she daily played her solitary game with faithful joy after her chores were completed, a deliberate "leaping [of] the bounds of domestic custom."[31]

A comparable liminality existed in nineteenth-century fiction, where female novelists could express covert and aberrant sentiments such as hostility toward men, religious faith, traditional authority marriage, and the class-order, which were unacceptable in conventional society. But the croquet lawn possessed tangible form, and the sport presented a rare field of endeavor in which women could not only compete on absolutely equal terms with men but tweak their noses as well. In croquet, sublimated aggression between the sexes took the form of knocking the other player's balls around the field and transgressing the rules in order to win. "What is the reason women tell such outrageous fibs?" asks Major St. John in "Pet Leighton's Game of Croquet." "They don't," replied Pet promptly. "Or," she added, "they wouldn't if you men didn't provoke them into it." Perhaps Jean Jacques Rousseau was correct when he speculated that it was "the law of obedience which produces the necessity of lying, because since obedience is irksome, it is secretly dispensed with as much as possible." For both genders, the croquet lawn was a liminal site where previous orderings of thought and behavior (such as morally superior, athletically inferior, or noncompetitive women) could be criticized or revised, and unprecedented modes of ordering relations between people became possible and/or desirable. "All thoughts of business or other cares must be thrown off," claimed *The Round Table*, "before putting foot upon this magical [croquet] lawn."[32]

The setting also lent itself to rule-breaking, for although croquet could be played in suburban backyards, it was the summer resort game nonpareil. At Saratoga and Newport, women emerged from an idealized role as dependents and noncompetitors to explicitly organize and perpetuate the amusements. At cities of play, women resided in public domiciles with minimal domestic duties and assumed a freedom of movement and activity often suppressed in private parlors and proscribed in etiquette books. The resort experience broke down established canons of female propriety, and women took advantage of the partial escape from mundane rules and expectations to play at croquet, archery, badminton, and bowl, swim, roller skate, and even gamble. Joanna Anthon, for example, meticulously recorded in her diary from 1867 to 1883 her activities (including croquet) at a variety of summer watering places, including few other details except the deaths of acquaintances. For Anthon, the watering place not only offered an idealized vision of the possibilities of life, it was life itself. And like the grand summer hotel, the croquet ground served as a legitimate meeting ground for flirtatious encounters, an opportunity, according to British Consul George Towle, for "whispered asides, blithe merry-making at blunders, [and] eager espousals of the partner's cause." Summer resorts were often female bastions and centers of flirtation, and it would not be surprising if women were sexually forward and/or extremely competitive under these atypical circumstances, so far and so different from everyday life.[33]

Of course, the croquet lawn was not a complete anomaly as a site of social change and contradictions in gender roles. The sport first appeared in the United States, perhaps not coincidentally, during the Civil War, an upheaval which brought gender issues into bold relief. In the 1850s, feminist sympathy with the abolitionist movement led to a sexualized debate over secession and slavery and Northerners and Southerners frequently berated each other for violating natural and immutable patterns of male and female behavior. The Civil War itself, by making different demands on men and women, initiated new attitudes toward gender roles, and especially opened up the question as to what it meant 'to be a man.' Women played vital roles in the economic and social mobilization for both sides and gained a certain independence and sense of assertiveness amidst the wartime crisis. Soldiers depended on them to manage their households, outfit them in the field, or nurse them when wounded. Historian Ann Douglas commented on

> the strongly aggressive, not to say belligerent gestures, conspicuous in the careers of not a few of the most famous nurses during the war [which] seem to unmask the element of competitive attack in their volunteer crusade. They said they wanted to take care of men: but did not they also want to take them over? Onlookers may have wondered.[34]

Economic and social changes in the second half of the nineteenth century continued to batter the "separate spheres" ideology and create other liminal spaces for women. Rapid industrialization radically transformed men's relationship to their work, making an endangered species out of the independent artisan, the autonomous farmer, and the small shopkeeper. The proliferation of women's colleges, a delayed age of marriage, and upward social mobility gave rise to the articulation of new claims and demands by women for expanded opportunities. This in turn prompted a reevaluation of gender roles by both sexes and an obsession with 'manliness' at the turn of the century. Nineteenth-century leisure entrepreneurs actively sought to cultivate the vast potential female audience and targeted American women who craved "to be actively amused, if not blissfully excited." Vaudeville managers (and later movie exhibitors) provided social spaces where women could impinge on 'traditionally' male public space and blurred the gender categories so carefully constructed earlier in the century. The 'New Woman'—vigorous, economically autonomous, and desirous of personal pleasure and self-expression—could be seen as early as the 1880s wearing bloomer outfits and playing tennis aggressively at the Newport Casino, where once croquet courts had flourished.[35]

This educated and self-assured 'New Woman' could play with men, but to defeat them was another matter. It is significant that when lawn tennis began to supplant croquet in the late 1870s, accusations against women were not simply transplanted to the new sport. In an 1893 article entitled "Will Croquet Come Again?," *Harper's Weekly* declared that "as a direct cause of…'foul play,' croquet overshadows lawn tennis as a mountain overshadows a valley." Croquet was a sport where your opponent will openly charge fraud, and "criminations and recriminations will fly about." In defense of their claim, *Harper's* related the story of a disputed croquet match between two Iowa farmers. One participant accused the other of cheating, a fight ensued, and the wronged party struck his accuser on the head with a mallet. The victim staggered home, where he collapsed and died. Things like this did not seem to occur in tennis matches.[36]

The fact that men and women did not compete equally at the more 'athletic' tennis meant the same sense of cultural dissonance and individual anxiety was not present among players. George Powell said as much in a 1901 article in *Temple Bar* in which he railed against superior female croquet players. On the croquet ground, Powell complained, there was nothing that men could do that women could not do better. No wonder he supported the new vogue for tennis, where women could "scarcely play with the athletic violence of the first-class male, and [women] remain what we should like them to be." Walter Wingfield, an astute tennis promoter, appealed to just this instinct in men in 1874: "Croquet, which of late years has monopolized the attention of the public, lacks the healthy and **manly** excitement of Lawn Tennis [emphasis added]." Disquietude with equality in mixed-gender competition helps explain the collapse of the croquet craze. If women played croquet better than men, women may have even accepted the accusation of cheating as a way to cover the embarrassment of that superiority that defied so many American preconceptions.[37]

For whatever reason, croquet did not sustain its initial popular momentum. By the time an American National Croquet Association was finally formed in 1882 to standardize the rules, the enthusiasm had already peaked, and croquet lawns in America and Europe were being madly converted into tennis courts as depicted in Leo Tolstoy's *Anna Karenina* [1877]. The sport's decline opened the door for the game of 'roque,' a bastard offspring of croquet that was marketed specifically to men by appealing to their superior physical prowess and familiarity with billiard-like strategy. Despite an Olympic appearance in 1904, roque hardly lived up to its appellation as the "game of the century," although like croquet, it continues to be played beyond the fringes of mass appeal.[38]

As a contest of skill, however, croquet retained a feminine aura as well as a reputation for the prevalence of dishonesty and fraud. The eponymous hero of H.G. Wells' *The Croquet Player* noted that many people found him "a trifle effeminate and ridiculous because I make croquet my game…soft hands and an ineffective will." In Vladimir Nabokov's *Pnin*, the Russian professor held "his mallet very low and daintily swinging it between his parted spindly legs." When Pnin "croqueted, or rather rocketed, an adversary's ball," an argument broke out; "Susan said it was completely against the rules, but Madame Shpolyanski insisted it was perfectly acceptable." A Spalding Manual from 1916 still issued a two- page warning against cheating, reminding beginners, "Let every movement be one of fairness and honor. Let your adherence to the rules be observed in all cases of even the greatest interest." Modern guides continue to contain similar admonitions; Gill's *Croquet* (1988) advises, "The one thing you really do have to be is honest."[39]

The nineteenth century was undeniably composed of heavily gendered space, a realm of sporting men and double standards, parlors and taverns. But this paradigm is not the entire story, and all evidence is not consistent with this stereotype. Authors of croquet manuals and magazine articles may have believed that limits needed to be set to marketplace values in their sport, but on the actual croquet lawn, coquetry did not always eclipse competition, nor did etiquette necessarily take precedence over winning. The evidence does not substantiate the typical judgment of croquet as a sport that had "little competitive edge, and was primarily recreative, offering relief and release from stress in the quiet and sheltered confines of the private suburban yard." On the contrary, the croquet lawn was a site where middle-class gender roles and upper-class gentility were ambiguous and contested.[40]

Of course, a microcosmic activity such as croquet could not alone dismantle the idea of separate spheres so prevalent in the nineteenth century. For all the emphasis on rupture and breach, the concept of liminality is essentially functionalist, concluding in the re-incorporation of the participants. Women may have cheated at croquet, but ultimately the game ended, and everyone returned to the strictures and boredom of everyday life. But for a moment, with the grass closely cut and the turf smoothly rolled, with mallet in hand and dress cut short, with steady eye and practiced stroke, women occupied the same moral plane as men, for better and for worse.

Notes

1. R. Lewis, "American Croquet in the 1860s: Playing the Game and Winning," *Journal of Sport History* 18 (Winter 1991): 386, 373 81. For the croquet stereotype, see *Croquet as Played by The Newport Croquet Club by One of the Members* (New York, 1865); L. Clarke Davis, "Croquet," *New York Galaxy* 4 (August 1867): 413-15; Henry Hall, ed., *The Tribune Book of Open-Air Sports* (New York, 1887) in Kathryn Grover, ed., *Hard at Play: Leisure in America, 1840-1940* (Amherst: Univ. of Massachusetts Press, 1992), 230; "Summer in the Country," *Appleton's Journal of Literature, Science, and Art* 2 (10 July 1869): 465; "Never Too Old To Play at Croquet—Nor Yet Too Young," *Harper's Weekly*, 9 August 1873.

2. Frances Cogan, *All-America Girl: The Ideal of Real Womanhood in Mid-Nineteenth Century America* (Athens: Univ. of Georgia Press, 1989), 3-7.

3. A.E. Gill, *Croquet: The Complete Guide* (London: Heinnemann Kingswood, 1988), 1-23; Davis, 415; Mayne Reid, *Croquet: A Treatise, With Notes and Commentaries* (New York, 1869), 11-14, 46; John Jaques, *Croquet. The Laws and Regulations of the Game...* (London, 1864), 5 [the copy in the New York State Library [NYSL], Albany, is inscribed "For my Daughters...Christmas 1864"]; D. Prichard, *The History of Croquet* (London: Cassell, 1981), 1-54, 171-83; John Lowcrson, *Sport and the English Middle Classes, 1870-1 914* (Manchester: Manchester Univ. Press, 1993), 101-03.

4. *American Boy's Book of Sports and Games* (New York, 1864) in Grover, 231; H. Vernon, "Croquet and Troco," *Peterson's* 46 (June 1864): 451; *Godey's Lady's Book* 70 (April 1865): 377; 'American Croquet," *The Nation* 3 (9 August 1866): 113-15; "Amusements: Croquet," *Round Table*, 2 July 1864; Nancy Rhoades, *Croquet: An Annotated Bibliography from the Rendell Rhoades Croquet Collection* (London: Scarecrow Press, 1992), 140.

5. A. Rover, *Croquet: Its Principles and Rules* 13th ed. (Springfield, Mass.: Milton Bradley, 1874), 9-11; Reid, 14; *New York Daily Graphic*, 24 June 1882; Rhoades, 70; Two Englishmen [Rivington, pseud.] *Reminiscences of America in 1869* (London, 1870), 63- 66; Constance Noyes Robertson, ed., *Oneida Community: An Autobiography, 1851-1876* (Syracuse: Syracuse Univ. Press, 1970), 189, 201, 208; *Shaker Girls Playing Croquet, Mt. Lebanon*, JVY Shaker Museum and Library, Old Chatham, NY; Donald Richardson, *Croquet: The Art and Elegance of Playing the Game* (New York: Harmony Books, 1988), 20-31; Dona Brown, *Inventing New England: Regional Tourism in the Nineteenth Century* (Washington, DC: Smithsonian Press, 1995), 100, 78-79.

6. "Summer" *Appleton's* 2 (10 July 1869): 465; *How To Play Croquet* (Boston, 1865), 6-7; *Harper's Weekly*, 22 July 1871; Davis, 414 (never); A. Rover 9-10; *Picayune* in Dale Somers, *The Rise of Sports in New Orleans, 1850-1900* (Baton Rouge: L.S.U. Press, 1971), 209-10; newspaper in Melvin Adelman, *A*

Sporting Time: New York City and the Rise of Modern Athletics, 1820-1870 (Urbana: Univ. of Illinois Press, 1990), 255; Harvey Green, *The Light of Home: An Intimate View of the Lives of Women in Victorian America* (New York: Pantheon, 1983), 152; "What Shall We Do Next," *Harper's Bazaar* (31 July 1869): 488; Charlotte Yonge, *The Trial* (London, 1864) in Rhoades, 64.

7. Reid, 5 (refined), 30, 42-43; Maud Howe Elliott, *This Was My Newport* (Cambridge: Mythology, 1944), 205; Robertson, 207.

8. Cogan, 29-61; "The Immorality of Croquet," *Living Age* 1 (25 October 1898): 199-200; Mark Twain, *Innocents Abroad*, Chapter 61; Lydia Child, *The Mothers Book* (Boston, 1831), 59; "Editor's Easy Chair," *Harper's Monthly* 34 (March 1867): 528-29; *Picayune* in Somers, 209-10; Charlotte Yonge, *The Clever Woman of the Family* (London, 1865), 1:220-22; Gill, 69 (impediment).

9. William Dix, "American Summer Resorts in the Seventies," *Independent* 70 (June 1911): 1214; *How To Play Croquet*, 34; A. Rover, 43; *International Herald Tribune*, 29 October 1909; croquet cartoon in *Harper's Young People* 9 (31 July 1888): 684 entitled "An Unfinished Game, and a Quarrel For Which Both are Sorry;" Maude Cooke, *Social Etiquette or Manners and Customs of Polite Society* (Boston, 1896), 312; William Stevenson, *The Joys of Sport* (Philadelphia, 1900) in Rhoades, 60 (destroyer). See James Chariton and William Thompson, *Croquet: Its History, Strategy, Rules, and Records* (Lexington, MA: Stephen Greene, 1988), 98, for a Connecticut couple married thirty-three years who received a legal separation in 1974, the man explaining, "his wife was not aggressive enough in croquet mixed-doubles."

10. Reid, 25; Curry, 25; Yonge, *Clever*, 1:229, 231; *Round Table*, 2 July 1864; Lewis Carroll, *Alice's Adventures in Wonderland*, Chapter 8; see Carroll's castle croquet reprinted in Horace Scudder, *The Game of Croquet: Its Appointment and Laws* (New York: Abercrombie and Fitch, 1968 [1865]), 46-52.

11. Anthony Trollope, *The Small House at Allington* (New York, 1864), Chapter 2; for diverse rules, see Rhoades, 113-36; "Croquet: Its Implements and Laws," *Godey's Lady's Book* 74 (February 1867): 141-43; "The Game of Croquet," *Peterson's* 51 (June 1867): 462-63; 52 (July 1867): 78-80; 52 (August 1867): 156-57; Uncle Charley, "The Rules of Croquet," *Scribner's* 12 (August 1876): 597 98; "American Croquet," *The Nation* 3 (9 August 1866): 113-15; A Rover, iii, 11; Davis, 416-20.

12. Thomas Hill, *Palo Alto Spring*, 1878, Stanford Univ. Museum of Art; "The Game of Croquet. No. 2," 52 (July 1867): 78; Curry, 7-18; Gill, 29-31; Tight croquet lives on in the backyard variety of the American game; Jack Osborn, *Croquet: The Sport* (Palm Beach Gardens: Farsight, 1989), 11, 34, 37; Scudder, 17; Chariton and Thompson, 64.

13. Winslow Homer, *Croquet Scene*, 1865, Art Institute of Chicago; *Croquet Player*, 1865, National Academy of Design [NY]; *A Game of Croquet*, 1866, Yale Univ. Art Gallery [New Haven]; "Summer," *Appleton's* 2 (10 July 1869): 465; *Harper's Weekly*, 8 September 1866; 9 August 1873; *Punch*, 6 July 1867; Reid, 8; "Croquet," *Harper's Bazaar* 1 (24 October 1868): 827-28; for other illustrations, see *How To*, 28; Rover, 20, frontpiece; *Every Saturday*, 13 July 1870; R. Valentine, ed., *The Home Book of Pleasure and instruction* (New York, 1868?) in Grover, 231.

14. Reid, 8; George Du Maurier, *Trilby* (New York, 1894), 15-50; Richard Kelly, *George Du Maunier* (Boston: Twayne, 1983), 112, 121; Sigmund Freud, "Fetishism," in *Sexuality and the Psychology of Love*, Ed. P. Rieff (New York: Collier, 1963), 214-19; Sigmund Freud, *Three Essays on Sexuality*, Trans. J. Strachey. (New York: Basic Books, 1962), 19-23; R. Kress, "Femininity, Castration, and the Phallus," *Literature and Psychology* 42 (1996): 1-14.

15. Daisy Ventnor, "Pet Leighton's Game of Croquet," *Peterson's* 49 (March 1866): 181-84.

16. Stanley Hall, *Youth: It's Education, Regimen, and Hygiene* (New York: Appleton, 1906), 103; John Saxe, *Poetical Works of John Saxe* (Boston, 1889), 40-41; Benjamin Disraeli, *Lothair* (London, 1927 [1870]), 11; *Round Table* 2 (2 July 1864): 42; Michel Oriard, *Sporting with the Gods: The Rhetoric of Play and Game in American Culture* (Cambridge: Cambridge Univ. Press, 1991), 161-91; Cynthia Russett, *Sexual Science: The Victorian Construction of Womanhood* (Cambridge: Harvard Univ. Press, 1989), 146-49; Kathleen McCrone, *Playing the Game: Sport and the Physical Emancipation of English Women, 1870-1914* (Lexington: Univ. Press of Kentucky 1988), 155; Gail Bederman, *Manliness and Civilization: A Cultural History of Gender and Race in the United States, 1880-1917* (Chicago: Univ. of Chicago Press, 1995), 77-120.

17. "The Game of Croquet. No. 3," *Peterson's* 52 (August 1867): 156-57; Lewis Carroll, *Complete Works* (New York: Modern Library 1936), 597; *New York Times*, 30 July 1876; *Croquet as Played by the Newport Croquet Club*, 52; *Nation* 3 (1866): 115; Prichard, 67-70, 90-91; *Punch*, 17 August 1861; 14 October 1865.

18. R. Prior *Notes on Croquet...*, 1872, in Gill, 10-11; Davis, 420 (innocent); "Hints Upon Croquet. By a Committee of Croakers," *Harper's Bazaar* 1 (12 September 1868): 727 (common); Scudder, 42; A. Rover, 45; for croquet fashions, see *Godey's Lady's Book* 72 (April 1866): 297-98.

19. "Hints," 727.

20. Immorality, 199-200.

21. Holme Lee, *Sylvan Holt's Daughter* (New York, 1860), 58-68.

22. Louisa May Alcott, *Little Women,* Chapter 12.

23. Lorna Duffin, "Prisoners of Progress: Women and Evolution," in S. Delamont and L. Duffin, eds., *The Nineteenth-Century Woman: Her Cultural and Physical World* (New York: Barnes and Noble, 1978), 65-81; Russett, 42-63, 80-81, 100-03. Chaucer's Wife of Bath observed (*Canterbury Tales:* Wife of Bath's Prologue, Lines 233-34): For half so boldely can there no man Swere and lien as a woman can.

24. Nancy Cott, *The Bonds of Womanhood: "Woman's Sphere" in New England, 1780-1835* (New Haven: Yale Univ. Press, 1977), 64-74; Karen Haltunen, *Confidence Men and Painted Women: A Study of Middle Class Culture in America, 1830-1970* (New Haven: Yale Univ. Press, 1982), 33-55; Kathleen De Grave, *Swindler, Spy, Rebel: The Confidence Woman in Nineteenth Century America* (Columbia: Univ. of Missouri Press, 1995), 21-22; E. Anthony Rotundo, "Learning About Manhood: Gender Ideals and the Middle-Class Family in Nineteenth-Century America," in J. Mangan and J. Walvin, eds., *Manliness and Morality: Middle-Class Masculinity in Britain and America, 1800-1940* (New York: St. Martins, 1987), 35-51.

25. Peter Filene, *Him/Her/Self: Sex Roles in Modern America* (Baltimore: Johns Hopkins Univ. Press, 1986 [1972]), 6-18; Karen Hansen, "Helped Put in a Quilt': Men's Work and Male Intimacy in Nineteenth Century New England," in J. Lorber and S. Farrell, eds., *The Social Construction of Gender* (London: Sage, 1991), 83-103; Caroll Smith-Rosenberg, *Disorderly Conduct: Visions of Gender in Victorian America* (New York: Alfred Knopf, 1985), 53-76, 109-13, 129-31.

26. Elliott, 205. On women and lying, see Bella De Paulo, Jennifer Epstein, and Melissa Wyer, "Sex Differences in Lying: How Women and Men Deal with the Dilemma of Deceit," in Michael Lewis and Carolyn Saarni, eds., *Lying and Deception in Everyday Life* (New York: Guilford, 1993), 19-21, 126-47; Gillian Mitchell, "Women and Lying" in Azizah Al-Hibri and Margaret Simons, *Hypatia Reborn: Essays in Feminist Philosophy* (Bloomington: Indiana Univ. Press, 1990), 175-91; Joan Hartung, "Deceiving Down: Conjectures on the Management of Subordinate Status," in Joan Lockard and Delroy Paulus, *Self-Deception: An Adaptive Mechanism?* (Englewood Cliffs: Prentice Hall, 1988), 173-77; Daniel Goleman, *Vita/Lies, Simple Truths: The Psychology of Self-Deception* (New York: Simon and Schuster, 1985), 218-23.

27. Katherine Rice diary, 29 June, 14 August 1873, NYSL.

28. Gary Lindberg, *The Confidence Man in American Literature* (New York: Oxford Univ. Press, 1982), 3-11; Johnson Hooper, *Adventures of Captain Simon Suggs* (Chapel Hill: Univ. of North Carolina Press, 1969 [1845]), 8; De Grave, 55-107; *Spirit of the Times* (14 April 1849) in John Dizikes, *Sportsmen and Gamesmen* (Boston: Houghton-Mifflin, 1981), 39-41.

29. Samuel Butler, *Hudibras,* II: Canto III; J. Barnes, *A Pack of Lies: Towards a Sociology of Lying* (Cambridge: Cambridge Univ. Press, 1994), 4, 10-19, 109-10; Marie Vasek, "Lying as a Skill: The Development of Deception in Children," in Robert Mitchell and Nicholas Thompson, eds., *Deception: Perspectives on Human and Nonhuman Deceit* (Albany: SUNY Press, 1986), 285-91. Johan Huizinga, *Homo Ludens: A Study of the Play Element in Culture* (Boston: Beacon, 1950), 11, 52, noted that society prefers the cheater, who at least pretends to play by the rules, to the spoil sport, who robs play of its illusion by withdrawing from the game. Shakespeare observed (Sonnet 138): When my love swears that she is made of truth, I do believe her though I know she lies.

30. On liminality, see Arnold van Gennep, *The Rites of Passage* Trans. M. Vizedom and G. Caffee (Chicago: Univ. of Chicago Press, 1960 [1908]), 1-25, 189-94; Victor and Edith Turner, *Image and Pilgrimage in Christian Culture* (New York: Columbia Univ. Press, 1978), 1-34, 231-54; Victor Turner, "Liminal to Liminoid, in Play, Flo and Ritual: An Essay in Comparative Symbology," *Rice University Studies* 60 (Summer 1974): 53-92; Donald Weber, "From Limen to Border: A Meditation on the Legacy of Victor Turner for American Cultural Studies," *American Quarterly* 47 (September 1995): 525-36.

31. Alice Brown, *Tiverton Tales* (Boston: Houghton Mifflin, 1927 [1899]), 3-8.

32. Ventnor, 182; *Round Table,* 2 July 1864; Jean Jacques Rousseau, *Emile, or on Education* Trans. A. Bloom (New York: Basic Books, 1979 [1762]), 101.

33. George Towle, *American Society* (London, 1870), II: 40; Joanna Anthon diary [1867-83], NYPL, (especially 9 August 1871 when in the middle of a croquet party, someone fell down the hotel steps). See also Jemima Morrell, *Miss Jemima's Swiss Journal: The First Conducted Tour of Switzerland* (London: Putnam, 1963 [1863]), 67-68: "Our lives needed no other romance than was afforded by the perfect freedom we enjoyed. It was an entire change; the usual routine of life was gone. All memories of times and seasons faded away and we lived only in the enjoyment of the present. We all felt that the recollection of these pleasant days would form a precious possession for the rest of our life."

34. Ann Douglas Wood, "The War Within a War: Women Nurses in the Union Army," *Civil War History* 18 (September 1972): 197-212; C. Clinton and N. Silber eds., *Divided Houses: Gender and the Civil War* (New York: Oxford Univ. Press, 1992), essays by Jeanie Attie, Leeann Whites, Reid Mitchell, David Blight, and Nina Silber.

35. Robert Grant, "The Art of Living: The Summer Problem," *Scribner's* 18 (July 1895): 56 (amused); Lois Banner, *American Beauty* (New York: Alfred Knopf 1983), 142-46, 187. By 1911, Frederick Martin claimed that both men and women at Newport virtually fetishized physical exercise; *Passing of the Idle Rich* (New York, 1911), 230-31. See also Kathy Peiss, "Leisure and the 'Woman Question'," in Richard Butsch, ed., *For Fan and Profit: The Transformation of Leisure into Consumption* (Philadelphia: Temple Univ. Press, 1990), 105-117; Green, 144-64; Bederman, 10-20; Michael Kimmel, "Men's Responses to Feminism at the Turn of the Century," *Gender and Society* 1 (September 1987): 262; Filene, 18-38; Smith-Rosenberg, 245-96; Cogan, 257-62.

36. *Harper's Weekly,* 26 August 1893.

37. Wingfseld in Gill, 47; Powell in Rhoades, 164; McCrone, 156-66.

38. Leo Tolstoy, *Anna Karenina,* Part 6, Chapter 22; also Part 3, Chapter 17; Lynn Abbott, "Outdoor Recreation at Night," *Suburban Life 5* (August 1907): 72-74; E. Farrington, "How To Play Croquet, An Improved Form of Croquet Which is Winning Sure Favor," *Outing* 62 (April1913): 100-04; W. Wahly, "Roque—Modern Croquet," *Outing* 38 (September 1901): 662-66; Prichard, 52-71; Osborne, 19-23; Charlton and Thompson, 111.

39. Vladimir Nabokov *Pnin* (New York: Avon, 1969), 129-30; HG. Wells, *The Croquet Player* (New York: Viking, 1937), 10-13; Gill, xviii; *Lawn Sports: Comprising Roque, Croquet, Golf-Croquet...* (New York: American Sports, 1916, 3-42; Curry, 24-25; J. W. Solomon, *Croquet* (London: B. Batsford, 1966), 9.

40. Lewis, 386 (little).

CHAPTER 5

THE NATIONAL GAME

■ *Warren Goldstein* ■

Home and Away

The 1860s proved to be a momentous decade in the history of baseball. At the beginning of this short period the game was centered in the New York metropolitan area and embedded in the rich social life of fraternal clubs. Ten years later the game had escaped the confines of both New York and club fraternalism. Baseball's transformation from a local club sport into an association of "clubs" scattered over the Northeast and Midwest was encouraged by the very structure of the game's play and organization. More than any other American game, baseball was built on a geographical and psychological sense of localism—if we take localism to be simultaneously an attachment to one place and fear, antipathy, or competitiveness toward other places. There had always been a "home" club or nine and a "visiting" club or nine in baseball, and the action of the game alternated between the home and visiting sides. From the earliest days of the organized game, nearly every club had its own, home ground.[1]

Challengers were visitors from another neighborhood or town, strangers sometimes literally as well as figuratively. They were also frequently identified by the locales of their clubs. The Brooklyn Atlantics, for example, were named for Atlantic Avenue—one of the major thoroughfares of the city—and were known familiarly as the "Bedford boys," for the section of Brooklyn in which they played. Other Brooklyn clubs also bore the names of streets (Putnams, Clintons) or neighborhoods (Williamsburgh, Green Point). Far more than among New York-area cricket clubs, rivalry in baseball quickly assumed a territorial form and language. For a full decade after the Fashion Course all-star matches in 1858 (and in the minds of some fans, for most of the following century), baseball's strongest rivalry remained that between New York and Brooklyn clubs.[2]

The game itself internalized the play of locale and loyalty. Many contemporary commentators, remarking on the differences between baseball and cricket, argued that baseball was a much faster game than its English counterpart—not only because it took a few hours instead of an entire day or two days to play one match, but because the game itself was livelier. Melvin Adelman has pointed to baseball's more rapid alternation of offense and defense as the key to this perception. But in a baseball game, offense and defense were not abstractions: they were the home club and the visitors, or our boys and the out-of-towners, or us and them. In each inning sides alternated in possession of territory (although territory itself was not the object of the struggle). The actual competition was over one side's passage through a field patrolled by the opposition. Players at bat began their would-be circuit in the safety of "home base" and ventured (if they were successful) out to the three points of "safety" in the entire field—the three bases—in the hope of completing the circuit and coming back "home" to score in safety.[3]

The game was a constant play of safety and danger, intensified by the need to get "home" both in order to be "safe" and in order to win. Such safety and danger depended on an imaginative rendering of the field which took "home" at least as seriously as the "real" club took its geographical home. The travel of the visitors was analogized into the necessary travel of all players through the territory of their adversaries, while the proud possession of the home club—their "ground"—was by turns not theirs at all, a region where they could be put "out" for the slightest error of skill or judgment. What local rivalry existed between neighborhoods, towns, or cities, then, received particular intensification and dramatization on the ballfield.

That dramatic focusing of local rivalries helps explain the excitement generated by the game, as well as the tendency of spectators to express dissatisfaction

A 1866 Currier and Ives print of "The American National Game of Base Ball" at the Elysian Fields in Hoboken, New Jersey.
Photo courtesy of Library of Congress. LC-USZ62-640.

with umpires, the opposing club, or even their own club. It also provides a way of seeing the contradictions inherent in the attachment to a local club. For the desire for a winning nine could and did conflict strongly with the feelings of localism. The tension between these two sets of feelings, held in uneasy balance during the late 1850s and early 1860s, began to shift in favor of winning, as neighborhoods, followed by towns and cities, began to "import" players and claim them as their own.[4]

Numerous paradoxes attended this development, not the least of which was that the intensity of neighborhood (increasingly, urban) baseball rivalries in the late nineteenth century grew in inverse proportion to the local nativity of the home team. The more intense the rivalry, the more likely a club's ability to raise the sums necessary to attract a professional nine to "represent" the club. And by the late 1860s, the distance between "constituent" and "representative" was widening in baseball almost as rapidly as it was in politics. (That baseball remained closer to the people—at least in their imaginations—than politics is suggested by the eagerness with which politicians sought at the time, and have continued to seek, to associate themselves with baseball clubs.) As American cities began a period of unparalleled and accelerated growth, the local imagination was subjected to serious strains, which produced contradictory altitudes toward baseball "representatives."

The Birth of the Cincinnati Red Stockings

It is at this point, then, and in this context that we should approach the Cincinnati Red Stockings, known to fans and historians alike as the first "all-professional" club, or the first "all-salaried" professional club, or the first "admittedly" all-professional club.[5] However we choose to acknowledge their firstness, there can be no doubt that the Red Stockings marked a turning point in the history of the game.

Their legendary status is best explained by the fact that so many strands of baseball history came together in the relatively short history of the club. The most important of these threads may very well have been the career of Harry Wright. One of the truly dominant figures of the baseball world between the late 1860s and early 1880s, Wright carried a good portion of American sport history in his own life. Born in England in 1835, the son of the noted cricketer Sam Wright, Harry was brought to the United States as a baby. Like his father, Harry was engaged as a professional bowler by the St. George Cricket Club in 1856. (Although cricket professionals often played in matches, they resembled teaching pros in modern tennis and golf clubs.) The grounds of the St. George Cricket Club were at the Elysian Fields at this time, and there Harry began to play a different game with another occupant of the Fields, the Knickerbocker Base Ball Club. Joining the Knickerbockers in 1858, he quickly became one of their more valued players.[6]

In 1866 Wright moved to Cincinnati as the professional of the Union Cricket Club, hired at a salary of $1,200 a year. Later that year he was involved in organizing the Cincinnati Base Ball Club, which played its matches on the field owned by his employer. The new baseball club borrowed more than grounds. At least four members of the Union Cricket Club also played on the baseball club's first nine, including pitcher Harry Wright. Many more members of the cricket club doubtless belonged to the newer club.[7]

The relationship between cricket and baseball in Cincinnati recapitulated that between the two sports in New York, but more rapidly. At the end of the 1867 season Harry Wright switched games and went to work—at the same salary—for the Cincinnati Base Ball Club. This change, while it could not have seemed especially consequential at the time either for the clubs, for Harry Wright, or for the history of baseball and cricket, in fact constituted one of the most significant events in the history of all three. Wright, the English-born professional cricketer (who later referred to cricket as "my first love"), astutely shifted his paid allegiance from a sport that was gradually losing its popularity to the fast-growing, increasingly profitable game of baseball. The decision to play as a professional did not have to be made in the face of strong feelings in favor of amateur play—he and his father had been earning their livings from manly sports for years. Wright's skill and reputation meshed perfectly with the growing ambitions of the Cincinnati club.

In 1867 the club defeated all but one of its opponents. The exception, the Washington Nationals, walloped the Cincinnatis 53 to 10, partly as a result of the assistance of Harry Wright's younger brother George. That defeat by an eastern club seems to have determined the Cincinnati directors to begin employing professionals. So, interestingly, did the club's indebtedness. According to a later report, the club owed some $600 to $700 at the beginning of 1868, exclusive of what they still owed on the lease for the Union Grounds. For the 1868 season, accordingly, the club decided to fence in the grounds, charge admission, and employ some professional players. Thus, in order to get the club out of debt, the directors incurred larger liabilities in the form of players' salaries and improvements to the grounds.[8]

Urban rivalry and local attachments were important factors in this decision as well. The Buckeye Club, also of Cincinnati, was the Red Stockings' major local competitor; both clubs fielded semiprofessional nines in 1868. Henry Chadwick suggested in 1870 that this city rivalry had been the major force behind the professionalization of Cincinnati baseball. To challenge the Red Stockings, the Buckeyes engaged two professional players. The Red Stockings then procured two more (in addition to Harry Wright), whereupon the Buckeyes added four professionals, inducing the Cincinnatis to add two more, in addition to Charley Gould, who left the Buckeyes for the Red Stockings. When the Red Stockings won the first match, the Buckeyes promptly imported three players from Washington, D.C., for the next contest, though to no avail.

Having established their local superiority, the Cincinnatis broadened their sights. They traveled east to take on the best-known and most successful clubs in the fraternity, but without notable success. Victories over the Philadelphia

Olympics and Washington Nationals and a split with the champion Morrisania Unions whetted the club's appetite for a better nine. Club members may have been pushing for a more successful club, too. In late 1868, the *Clipper* reported, the Union Cricket Club gave up the ghost and "resigned to the Cincinnati Base Ball Club all their rights, title and interests to and in the Union grounds and the improvements, provided the base ball club would guarantee to them the use of the grounds at certain times for practice, and assume all the indebtedness."[9]

According to the former president of the Cincinnati club, the grounds had been held under joint lease by the two clubs for eight years at $2,000 a year. Each club furnished half the outlay, "both being represented in the management by delegates to a Board of Directors." They also spent $10,000 in 1867 for buildings and other improvements. These figures, he asserted at the time, were "sufficiently heavy to warrant the statement that the clubs have exhibited considerable courage in pledging themselves to an undertaking of such magnitude." Evidently the cricketers had more courage than prudence. When they ceded their interest in the ground to their baseball partners, over $7,500 was still owed on the field alone. The baseball club formed a stock association with $15,000 capital and authorized the sale of $7,500 worth of stock in order to help meet the club's total indebtedness of "$8,500 or $9,000." Buyers were found for only about $3,000 worth, however, and the club began the 1869 season owing about $6,000. Or rather, it would have owed that much if it had not decided to undertake an even greater obligation and risk.[10]

Given the size of the club's debt, some of the members very likely argued against getting deeper into the baseball business. Others no doubt claimed that only investment in a first-class nine could make enough money to bring the club out of the red. Still others were probably unconcerned about the money the club owed. After all, the club counted 380 members in 1867, among whom were many men of considerable means. The elements were certainly there for a dispute between traditionalists and modernizers, although the only evidence that one took place lies in the resignation of an unpaid member of the 1868 nine who was unhappy with the mix of professionals and amateurs on the same team. The club directors may have shared the sentiment, but if so, they went in the opposite direction. "Still bent on obtaining a leading position as the most successful nine in the country," according to Chadwick, the club "went to work in a business-like manner, and got together the first *regularly trained* professional nine which had ever been placed in the field."[11]

Baseball histories sometimes give the impression that the Cincinnati club emerged full-blown and previously unknown to the baseball fraternity. This was hardly the case. Ohio baseball had grown strong enough to provide a National Association president in 1867, and city baseball clubs, particularly the Cincinnatis and the Buckeyes, received a good deal of press attention. Aaron B. Champion, president of the Cincinnati club, was also head of the Ohio State Base-Ball Association in 1868; he had, according to one account, "the reputation of having done as much toward advancing base-ball in the West as any other individual." The rivalry between the Buckeyes and Red Stockings was a matter of journalistic interest, and both clubs' professional additions in 1868 were covered in detail.[12]

But there is a more striking point in the interest taken in Cincinnati baseball. The dominance of New York teams was broken by the Red Stockings, who were only one of several teams, including the Philadelphia Athletics that could have done the same thing. On the other hand, to say that "Cincinnati" dominated baseball implied the successful appropriation of baseball relationships by the ideology of urban boosterism. Fewer and fewer of the first-nine players of either the Buckeyes or the Cincinnatis were genuine residents of the city. As each club hired more players in turn, the two clubs became increasingly "represented" in the field by eastern (largely New York) players. So the eastern eyes watching the Cincinnati game were also focused on New York players who had relocated in the Midwest. Interest in baseball as a national game, then, depended in part on the nationalization of formerly regional ballplayers.

For all of locals fans' interest in the home club, the sporting press was creating a baseball public whose interest was acquiring national scope. This expansion was assisted by the mobility of ballplayers, the same ballplayers fans castigated as traitorous for revolving away from their home clubs. Spectators read about Cincinnati baseball not only to see how the game was progressing out West. The size of the coverage—and the amount of readers' interest—had more to do with the exploits of players already well known to eastern audiences "The Cincinnatis have strengthened their nine with two first-class New York players," observed *Wilkes' Spirit of the Times* in early 1868, "Harry Wright, who pitched for them last year, and John Hatfield, late of the New York Mutuals." In another story on Cincinnati the next week the eastern origins of the professional Red Stockings and Buckeyes figured prominently. The new players came from the Mutuals, the Nationals, the Eurekas of Newark, the Irvingtons of New Jersey, and the West Philadelphia Club. When the Buckeyes met the Cincinnatis for the city championship, the spectators' excitement was attributed by one reporter to the fact "that these two clubs strengthened themselves for the contest by the introduction into their organizations of no less than seven first-class players from the Eastern States."[13]

Baseball fans, commentators, and promoters were caught, then, in a series of contradictions that admitted of resolution only in unsatisfactory ways. They chose by and large to ignore the fact (or repress the knowledge) that these were contradictions, and preferred to rail at one side or the other, nominally in service to the opposing ideal, in fact depending on a vision of the game free of difficulty and conflict. Desire to see the game as national conflicted with their strong attachment to the game as an expression of local environments and loyalties. Paradoxically, that very loyalty was strengthened by the widening scope of competition, but the geographic expansion of the competitive sphere seriously undermined the extent to which players themselves expressed those loyalties other than as, in effect, actors playing roles.

Uniform Identities

Baseball's nationalization in the late 1860s thus strained the localism that had sustained the game in its early years. Institutionalized revolving supported by widespread professionalism confused spectators, who were suspicious of players who could move so easily from club to club, city to city. If players could exchange one club's uniform for that of its rival from one season to the next, wondered fans, who were they?

The baseball uniform itself offers some clues. Even in the early 1860s reporters noticed particularly attractive or striking uniforms. Clubs whose members were lax about suiting up for games or practices came in for criticism. Club feeling and pride were at stake in the members' public appearance as club representatives. At such times, uniforms helped legitimate the game that these men were playing, by referring visually to the ritual dress of other manly fraternal organizations, such as fire companies and volunteer military companies. Uniforms helped enforce members' sense of comradeship—that they were all fellows in the same club—as well as a sense of apartness. Partial or mixed uniforms, then, broke the spell cast by such regalia. Reporters were sensitive to these issues, having a stake themselves in the creation and maintenance of distinctiveness on the ballfield. Like the fences around enclosed grounds, the ropes that kept back spectators, and the foul lines on the field, uniforms were boundaries between what was baseball and what was not, between who belonged on the playing field and who did not. Men inside the uniform belonged to a club. Men outside of it were onlookers.

"There is more importance attached to the selection of a regular uniform for a base ball club than the fraternity generally think there is," argued the indefatigable Chadwick, for whom the importance of everything in the baseball world was greater than "the fraternity generally think." Chadwick had two principal concerns: that "one of the last things a club should…do, is to change the colors or form of its uniform"; and that therefore when "a club is first organized," particular care should be taken to adopt a tasteful and appropriate uniform. That his first comment on the importance of uniforms emphasized the dangers of changing them suggests that Chadwick had revolving and the problem of local attachments very much on his mind. It was hard enough to keep track of players who moved from club to club. One of the anchors that made such movement bearable was a certain club continuity, the relative stability of clubs' names, in some cases their officers, and usually their uniforms. Even a spectator whose knowledge of team lineups was not fully up to date could tell which clubs were playing just by recognizing the uniforms. Club nicknames were often derived from club uniforms: aside from the Cincinnati Red Stockings and Chicago White Stockings, the Mutuals were commonly referred to as the Green Stockings, and the Olympics of Washington, D.C., as the Blue Stockings. Changes in uniforms—those of individual clubs as well as of the entire fraternity—have often produced commotion in the baseball world, much more than seems appropriate to a simple change of shirt or pants style. Fans' allegiance to particular insignia or styles was (and remains) a sign of the intensity with which the emotional pull of a desired stability has been felt throughout the history of the game.[14]

In the heyday of the baseball club, then, with its rituals, suppers, soirees, and winter balls, uniforms served as expressions of club sentiment, of fraternal feeling and pride. Deviations from the ideal were criticized for reflecting poorly on the club. *Wilkes' Spirit of the Times* complained in 1864 that "for a season or two past...our ball clubs have grown negligent in regard to their appearance...A reform is needed in this matter." The reporter went on to discuss the issue at length, making some important connections:

> One of the attractive features of a ball-ground on a match-day is the appropriate uniforms of the players; in fact, to see a nine come on the ground and play a regular match in their club suit, others in a portion of it only, and others again merely in their shirt sleeves, has the appearance of poverty in the club, not creditable to any respectable organization. There is nothing to prevent a base-ball player's uniform from being as well known as that of a United States soldier. It is only requisite that each club should have a distinct style of cap, the pants and shirt can be the same for all, blue and white being the desirable colors...But whether these colors are chosen... is of secondary importance, so that each club own a distinctive uniform and, what is more, wears it at all times on the ball-field...Get new uniforms, gentlemen, if you can afford it, and wear them whenever you play ball, if you want to look like ball-players.[15]

The keys here were a combination of consistency (in pants and shirts) and distinctiveness, so that players were identified first as members of the ballplaying fraternity ("if you want to look like ball-players") and second as members of a particular club. Although taste was an issue, it was not nearly so important as the fact of having uniforms.

Specifically, uniforms were one of the means by which a "respectable organization" established its distance from the "appearance of poverty." Ever concerned to solidify baseball's position in the world of respectability, the reporter clearly identified the world he feared (poverty) even as he acknowledged its proximity in his final admonition: "Get new uniforms, gentlemen, if you can afford it."

The reportorial advice about uniforms, then, drew on a powerful set of fears and antagonisms by suggesting that sloppy, incomplete, or nonexistent uniforms gave the "appearance of poverty." Uniforms served the seekers after respectability quite well as they sought to distinguish themselves from the poor and the roughs—men, boys, and would-be gentlemen who could not afford uniforms.[16]

But if uniforms began as measures and badges of club (and overall fraternal) identification, by the late 1860s and 1870s they had acquired a new function. Now, it was hoped, they would provide ballplayers and clubs with an outward sign of the identity that appeared to be lacking in so many areas. Even though the horses had escaped, Chadwick was still trying to close the barn door. By concentrating on uniforms, commentators were adopting a device from the theater. Uniforms came off just as easily as they went on. But if distinctive dress could not change the players, it could give the anxious spectator something to grasp.

It would not be the last time in baseball history that this illusion was fostered by baseball's promoters and seized upon by a confused public.

Chadwick's second point about uniforms, "that particular care should be taken to adopt a tasteful and appropriate uniform," was likewise revealing. He mentioned four possible styles, the last of which was "the mixed, circus-style of dress, generally worn by junior clubs and country village organizations, in which bright red is a conspicuous color." Clearly he hoped to distinguish the more "manly," or more mature and advanced, organizations from the relatively unsophisticated junior and country clubs.

Here we can see the beginnings of an otherwise curious phenomenon in baseball history: the cultural prejudice against the country. Baseball myth, after all, is firmly rural. Yet players from the country, or from small towns, have been considered hicks, yokels, or hay-seeds since the 1860s. Recall that, according to Chadwick in 1867, it was mainly the insufficiently self-controlled "country" spectators who still hooted at umpires. The "villagers" of Louisville, Kentucky, had been the most partisan and least "well-bred" of all the audiences encountered by the Washington Nationals on their tour that year. This development is partially explained by the fact that New York was the center of the baseball world during these years. The rest of the explanation lies in the way professional baseball grew: nearly always in larger towns and cities with populations large enough to support an entertainment business based on gate receipts, but drawing players from the entire surrounding region, or even (occasionally) from across the country. So the very fact that a disproportionate number of professional ballplayers had come from rural areas to play on teams based in cities produced prejudice against the country boy.

In the metropolis itself, the "conspicuous color" of the fire company uniforms was a very bright red. It was fire company runners, like the baseball club followers, who were the most visible representatives of the city's "untrained" residents. This chain of associations was less extended for nineteenth-century urban residents than it may seem over a hundred years later. Uniforms were more remarkable then than now; volunteer fire companies had been prominent sources of "disorder" in the 1840s and 1850s; and their uniforms were a distinctive red. Associating juvenile, lower-class partisanship with bumpkins and the "untrained," all dressed in flaming red, was easy and natural for Chadwick and his readers. George Wilkes's reporter had recommended the adoption of blue and white. The taste and propriety of baseball uniforms, then, were meant to anchor the increasingly drifting identity of ballplayers, and to strengthen the permeable barrier between the respectable game and the bawdier aspects of urban recreational culture.[17]

Management, Triumph, and Defeat: The Red Stockings of 1869 and 1870

By an interesting coincidence, the first issue of *Beadle's Dime Base-Ball Player* to carry Chadwick's advice about uniforms appeared in 1869, the year of the team known for its uniform, for its first-rate eastern ballplayers, and for its extraordinary season-long string of victories. Let us look closely at the Red Stockings of that year and try to see what converged in this team full of firsts.

Perhaps most important of all, the Red Stockings were, in Chadwick's words, the first "regularly trained" all-professional club. For if the language and ideology of management had come to organized baseball in 1867, its first triumph was Harry Wright's management of the Cincinnati club. Wright offered a model of baseball management that was matched by few (if any) others. What we understand today as a team manager was the team "captain" in the 1860s and 1870s— the player responsible for making tactical decisions about the game on the field. The "manager" of the club in these years was its business manager, the club official—often the corresponding secretary—in charge of making arrangements with other clubs for games, handling travel plans, reserving hotel rooms for the players, and the like. It is important to remember that all through this period clubs did not have prearranged playing schedules the way nearly all clubs (even Little League teams) do today. As a result, the conscientious manager spent an enormous amount of time writing letters and sending telegrams to his counterparts in other clubs just to arrange matches. It fell on Wright to arrange club tours that were filled not only with games but with contests that would pay enough to make the trip worthwhile. He performed this task for the Cincinnati club better than it had ever been done before by anyone, for any club. The Red Stockings' 1869 tour was the most extensive ever undertaken, and the club ended up turning a profit.[18]

Though largely unheralded, Wright's business management was an outstanding contribution to Cincinnati's success and ought to be listed in the catalogue of firsts. His efforts to subject an extremely irregular and unpredictable set of encounters (baseball games) to the systematic supervision of business management carved out new territory in the material history of the game.

Some people besides members of the Cincinnati club must have been aware of Wright's tireless work in these matters. Baseball men knew how difficult it was to arrange such a lengthy tour as the one announced in the papers in early 1869. They were also the recipients of his letters. But most of the praise that came his way—and there was a substantial amount during and after that season—centered on his management of the nine itself, on his captaincy of his men on and off the field. That is what Chadwick meant when he said that the Red Stockings were the first "regularly trained" professional nine. Harry Wright was more involved in the lives of his players than any previous captain had ever been. He directed and supervised their practices, decided who played where and when, maintained morale, and kept an eye on their eating, drinking, and sleeping habits. He was, in effect, the first modern baseball manager.[19]

This point has been understood only partially by students of the game. Emphasis has fallen primarily on Wright simply as baseball's "first professional manager," or on his "zeal as a field manager and trainer." But the key to Wright's importance as baseball's first real manager was the way he altered relations among the nine, firmly establishing his authority over the players in every aspect of the game. Wright negotiated contracts with them, and he ordered them about on the ballfield and off. His control over the players' lives off the field was never as complete as he would have liked, but he did establish the *principle* of that authority.[20]

Backed by the directors of the club and his years of experience in the game, Wright's authority partook simultaneously of a variety of hierarchical relationships. First, although not strictly an employer, he acted as the employer's representative. Whether or not a player actually worked—that is, played—was up to Wright. Second, he was the club provider: by arranging games, Wright put bread on the table for everyone. So in dealing with a particular player or group of players, he spoke for the welfare of the club as a whole.

Finally, Wright was thirty-four in 1869, almost twelve years older than the average Red Stocking. All but one of the other players were between twenty and twenty-three years old, and the oldest, Asa Brainard, was twenty-seven. When Wright referred to the nine as "the boys," he may have been including himself as well, but the term had more force as an acknowledgment of age difference that implicitly asserted a form of paternal authority. Wright's managerial style was firmly rooted in the complex of emotions generated by the tensions between men and boys, or imagined tensions between manliness and boyishness. His paternalism may have been strengthened further by the presence of his much younger brother George. Only twenty-two years old in 1869, George Wright was already widely known as one of the finest shortstops, batters, and all-round players in the game. That Harry traced his lineage back to the professional cricketer Sam Wright and forward to his brother George (and later his even younger brother Sam, Jr.) gave his voice the added force of the sporting past.[21]

If the Red Stockings represented a departure in some areas, they were firmly within baseball tradition in others. The first nine consisted for the most part of well-known players who came from the ranks of skilled artisans and clerks, including two "in insurance," one bookkeeper, two hatters, a marble cutter, a pianomaker, a jeweler, and an engraver. (The last two were Harry and George Wright, who, although they made their livings from baseball, also had trades.) Their salaries were discussed in the press, and deserve some attention. "Captain Harry" received $1,200. George Wright was the team's highest paid player, at $1,400. Asa Brainard, the pitcher, and Fred Waterman, the third baseman, were paid $1,100 and $1,000, respectively. The five remaining starters got $800 apiece, while the substitute was paid either $600 or $800.[22]

Such figures are not very informative, however, unless they are put in the context of the work world of the late 1860s and early 1870s. Because the fluctuations of the economy could radically affect the number of days worked and wage rates, the income of skilled workers varied widely—from around $525 a year at the lower end of the scale to as much as $750 at the upper end. Since the lowest-paid of the regular players on the Cincinnatis earned $800—and that on a contract that ran for only eight months (March 15 to November 15)—it is clear that professional ballplayers were doing quite well. Yet with the exception of George Wright, who earned nearly twice as much as most of his teammates, the

Red Stockings did not make so much more than their fellow artisans as to be considered wealthy. The five or six at $800 made in eight months what it took the best-paid and most regularly employed skilled craftsman a year to earn. Nevertheless, the potential clearly existed to make considerably more than even a very well-paid artisan. The four best-paid Red Stockings, for example, earned from 15 to about 70 percent more than the top craftsman's wage.[23]

These salaries, though noted in the press in June, excited less comment than the remarkable play of the Red Stockings. The momentous eastern tour began on May 31, and the club's first big victory came a week later, when the Cincinnatis beat the surprised Troy Haymakers. They then made their way into the metropolis, the lion's den for any western or country ball club. Taking on the "champion" New York Mutuals, Cincinnati squeaked out a 4-to-2 win, an extremely close game by the standards of the time and "the best-played game ever witnessed," according to the *Spirit of the Times.* Doubtless buoyed by this stunning victory, the Cincinnatis proceeded to administer a "crushing defeat" to the Atlantics (32 to 10) the next day, and an even more lopsided whipping to the Eckfords the day after. At this point the club vaulted into new prominence, exciting the admiration and envy of the baseball world. The "marvelous" Red Stockings, enthused one reporter, "are the only true exponents of the game to-day. Full of courage, free from intemperance, they have conducted themselves in every city they visited in a manner to challenge admiration, and their exhibitions of skill in the art of handling both ball and bat call for unexampled praise. Their present tour has done more to elevate the game than any trip of the kind ever before known." Although New York was the equal of Cincinnati "in manly, courageous, and gentlemanly players," the story continued, "our own clubs will profit by the example set them by the Red Stockings in the matter of playing and organizing a nine."[24]

This theme appeared repeatedly in game stories and editorials. Even though the club was "composed almost entirely of Eastern *materiel,*" according to one account, it was only "by the most assiduous training, and under the management of the first, best, and only trainer of a club nine—Harry Wright—[that] the men were brought to a degree of perfection—physically and otherwise—never before witnessed." Audiences in Buffalo were impressed by another aspect of this training: except for their captain, none of the Red Stockings uttered a word on the field. The "lesson" taught New York was "that steady, temperate habits and constant training are all conditions precedent to a first-class organization."[25]

The *Spirit of the Times* directly addressed the question of Cincinnati's right to the championship in an editorial following the club's New York victories. "CINCINNATI THE CHAMPION CITY," ran the headline, an honor that could not "fairly be abated by the fact that many of the players went to the West from New York." Even though the players might have come from the New York area, their "capital play is mainly to be attributed to their organization, and, as that originated and was perfected in Cincinnati, that city is fully entitled to credit therefor."[26]

This assertion ratified the nationalizing of players and the game. On the one hand, players "from" New York populated the other clubs, so that the spread of New York players across the Northeast and Midwest reenacted the spread of the "New York game" across the same areas on the road to become the "national game." Yet writers were apparently willing to give up their claims to departed players, ascribing loyalties and granting claiming rights to the player's new "home" club or city. In return, of course, any player who revolved into New York baseball circles could be considered a New Yorker by virtue of playing on a New York nine. Such a reformulation of player citizenship, although never quite completed, helped local fans accommodate themselves emotionally to the growing irrelevance of players' cities of origin.

One could turn this observation around and argue that the stress on an urban "home" occasioned by the nationalization of the players and clubs more accurately resembled propaganda designed to disguise real developments in the game, and thus contributed to the beginning of the mythmaking that has characterized so much baseball reporting and commentary ever since. Of course, even the notion of an urban home rested on social quicksand. Forty percent of New York's population in 1850 was foreign-born. And the well-documented furious pace of geographical mobility among city residents in the mid-nineteenth century meant that anyone's hold on a particular "hometown" had to be tenuous. These analyses need not be mutually exclusive. What to some was an emotional accommodation to a changing reality was for others (or even to the same people) a more or less deliberate refusal to look at the changes head on.

In any event, such accommodation or refusal has continued to structure fans' attitudes toward the problem of locality in baseball. Each fan, it seems, must, in the course of his or her private loss of baseball innocence, see a favorite player depart, a hometown boy traded, a quintessential Yankee or Dodger or Cardinal suddenly move to another team, don another uniform, and appear to forget his previous home. That movement is painful for a fan to watch, and it causes pain each time it happens, at least partly because, as we have seen, the game internalizes that very problem—home and away, at bat or in the field, our boys and the visitors. Only by remaining immune to the emotional pull of the game could its followers not be affected by apparent violations of this impulse to claim a home territory and home players. In other words, for fans little was to be gained by seeing the fraternity of professional ballplayers as they were: potentially, universally interchangeable. Rather than face the complete industrialization of the game, a development for which there was little emotional support, it was far easier to participate in a fictive process of hometown identification.

Cincinnati's dominance of the baseball world turned out to be short-lived. Although the season of 1870 began with much promise, the club's undefeated streak finally came to an end in New York, as the Atlantics narrowly beat the champions in an eleven-inning contest. That game broke the Cincinnati spell over the rest of the baseball world. Suddenly the Red Stockings became just another first-class club that could be beaten now and then. Five more defeats followed during the season, still an excellent record, but hometown enthusiasm was beginning to fall off.[27]

Pleading the "claims of their private business," the president and secretary of the club resigned in August. Although they (and Harry Wright) had pulled the Cincinnatis out of debt, their final financial report predicted no profit, and when the year was over the balance sheet showed that the club had just broken even. More serious changes followed the close of the season. Amid reports that the club would be "thoroughly reorganized" for the next season to eliminate the "growlers and shirkers of the present nine," as well as those who would "not contract to abstain from the use of intoxicating beverages at all times unless prescribed by a physician in good standing," the club leadership went a step further and resolved to abandon the professional arena altogether.[28]

The circular with which the club directors announced their decision touched on so many aspects of the club that it is worth a close look. Apparently intending at first to continue the course of the past two seasons, the board had been in "communication with many of the leading professional ball players throughout the country, as well as with the various members of our former nine." Unfortunately, they concluded, paying the "enormous salaries" now demanded by professional players would "plunge our club deeply in debt." The past two years had shown that a nine with a payroll in excess of $6,000 to $8,000 "cannot, even with the strictest economy, be self-sustaining." With current salary demands, the "maximum sum... would be very nearly doubled." To avoid bankruptcy the club would have to impose a "heavy levy" on its members to make up the difference.[29]

Not that the club had refused to call on its members in the past. In fact, the members had "year after year contributed liberally for the liquidation of the expenses incurred in the employment of players." This year, however, the directors did "not feel justified in calling on them again." Money—that is, meeting the salaries of a professional nine—was an issue, but not the only one. The recipients of the salaries had failed to live up to expected standards. "Payment of large salaries causes jealousy," argued the directors, not making it clear whether they meant jealousy among players or between players and other club members, "and leads to extravagance and dissipation on the part of the players." Such behavior, "injurious to them," was also "destructive of the subordination and good feeling necessary to the success of a nine."

Whether these charges accurately described the 1869 and 1870 Red Stockings is another matter. Jealousy, extravagance, and dissipation notwithstanding, the club lost no games in 1869 and only six the following year. While some of the players were apparently given to occasional nighttime sprees, there is very little evidence to suggest widespread dissipation. Wright, while not tyrannical, did not look kindly upon flagrantly unrespectable behavior.[30]

The circular can be read more usefully as a statement (if a belated one) about the transformation of baseball from a fraternal club sport into an entertainment business. Even its language was mixed, dominated by turns by a concern for business accounting and by the spirit of club fraternalism. This confusion was particularly evident in the claim that high salaries had destroyed "that subordination and good feeling necessary to the success of a nine." Three or four years earlier the word "subordination" would not have been used. "Harmony and good feeling" might have been, or perhaps "discipline"—understood as self-discipline—and "good feeling," but not "subordination." The directors were talking about their employees' failure to behave as subordinates, and in so far as they were serious about the good feeling, they were talking about the club members, and about the bygone days of genuinely fraternal clubs.[31]

It was to that prior state of grace that the directors made their concluding appeal, expressed in the new language of amateurism: "We believe that there will be a development of the amateur talent of our club, such as has not been displayed since we employed paid professionals, and that we will still enjoy the pleasure of witnessing many exciting contests on our grounds."

Inasmuch as the club had employed professionals almost since its founding, the reference to its early amateur days must be taken with a grain of salt. The club, evidently frustrated by its failure to make money even with an outstanding championship club, was blaming its problems on the uppity players—jealous, extravagant, dissipated, and insubordinate—and retreating from the heartless world of professional baseball into the sheltered glen of amateurism. Although the directors appealed to the club's experience of "good feeling," the circular indicated their major focus: dollars, cents, and the management of their player–employees.

Their appeal to amateurism, and to its supposed affinity with the simpler fraternal days of the game, could be made only disingenuously. They had tried something very different, and when it failed to satisfy the club in either emotional or material terms, they recoiled from professionalism like lovers scorned, wrapping themselves in the cloak of amateurism. Even so, the circular concluded with gestures in another direction. The club and its grounds, the directors pointed out proudly, were "entirely free from debt." Despite their best efforts to reclaim baseball "tradition," the club directors had been so greatly influenced by their experience as pioneers that they could speak only in the language of baseball's modernity. Lest anyone think that withdrawal from the professional arena would diminish the quality of Cincinnati baseball, they expressed confidence in the "many exciting contests" sure to follow.

Notes

1. So, of course, did cricket clubs, but cricketers commonly belonged to more than one club at a time. The attempt to restrict cricketers to one club was a relatively late development in cricket's American history, attributable mostly to the effort to Americanize the game. It failed. From nearly the beginning of the NABBP, however, the association insisted that membership could be held in only one club. For an excellent discussion of cricket in America, see Melvin L. Adelman, *A Sporting Time: New York City and the Rise of Modern Athletics, 1820-1870* (Urbana: University of Illinois Press, 1986), chap. 5.

2. The baseball world was not alone in identifying its favorites by their home territory. Politicians, for example, frequently had nicknames drawn from their hometowns or states. Others in the world of amusement carried such badges, both to allow hometown identification and to indicate a certain exoticism. Prizefighters in particular often carried the names of their hometowns: the Benicia Boy, the Manassa Mauler. Cricket clubs outside of New York frequently took the names of their towns or counties. Within the metropolitan area, however, clubs seem not to have sought local

identifications, preferring instead a national label of origin. Nor did the most prominent eastern cricket clubs adopt neighborhood names, apparently preferring names of cities or ungrounded names: New York, St. George, Satellite, American. Moreover, the important conflicts in American cricket took place over national and international issues. First, the sport drew much criticism as being too "English"—not because it originated in England but because most of the best players were English immigrants. This dispute led to the founding of the American Cricket Club, an explicit attempt to encourage native American cricketers. Second, the major event of each cricket season was a series of "international matches" with a representative eleven from Canada, or, as in 1859, the visit of the All-England Eleven.

Less rooted in metropolitan neighborhoods or particular workplaces, the clubs relied on a broader, more geographically dispersed public of a somewhat higher class. One reason, then, that baseball was able to supplant cricket in the late 1850s and early 1860s was that the proliferation of local clubs in New York and Brooklyn tapped just those sources of support—in a purposeful and direct manner—that cricket clubs overlooked. See George B. Kirsch, "The Rise of Modern Sports: New Jersey Cricketers, Baseball Players, and Clubs, 1845-1860," *New Jersey History* 101 (Spring-Summer 1983): 53-84; and his "American Cricket: Players and Clubs before the Civil War," *Journal of Sport History* 11 (Spring 1984): 28-49.

3. In a cricket "innings," every player but one on each side must bat until he is put out. A team comes to the bat only after the entire other side has been put out. A game thus consists of just two full innings, and matches commonly take more than a day to complete. Baseball, by contrast, consists of nine innings, but only three players on each side need be put out in each inning, and the defense has more advantages than in cricket. In 1860 baseball games usually took from two and a half to three and a half hours.

4. The wide use of the term "import" indicates the extent of baseball's convergence with the world of commerce.

5. On the Cincinnati Red Stockings, see Harold Seymour, *Baseball*, vol. I (New York: Oxford University Press, 1960), pp. 56-59; David Quentin Voigt, *American Baseball*, vol. I (Norman: University of Oklahoma Press, 1966), pp. 23-24; Irving Leitner, *Baseball: Diamond in the Rough* (New York: Abelard-Schuman, 1972), pp. 83-97; Preston D. Orem, *Baseball (1845-1881)* (Altadena, Calif: By the author, 1961), pp. 87-97, 100, 102-103. See also Harold Seymour, "Baseball's First Professional Manager," *Ohio Historical Quarterly* 64 (October 1955): 406-423; David Quentin Voigt, "America's First Red Scare: The Cincinnati Reds of 1869," *Ohio History* 78 (Winter 1969), 12-24, 68-69; Adelman, *A Sporting Time*, pp. 170-172. Nearly every popular history of the game includes several paragraphs on the team, and numerous articles talk about their contribution. Few of these accounts can be trusted.

6. Knickerbocker Base Ball Club of New York Club Book, 2 vols., 1854-1859, 1859-1868, cited in Seymour, "Baseball's First Professional Manager," pp. 406-407: John Kieran, "Henry Wright," *Dictionary of American Biography* (New York, 1936), 20:554.

7. For the nine of the Cincinnati Base Ball Club in the late 1860s, see Henry Chadwick, ed., *Beadle's Dime Base-Ball Player* (New York, 1870), pp. 61-62. For the Union Cricket Club players, see *Wilkes' Spirit of the Times*, August 4, 1866, p. 365. Actually, the Cincinnati Base Ball Club began to play on the grounds of the Live Oak Base Ball Club. It was not until the following year that the baseball club began to play on the cricket club's grounds. The arrangement was not simply fraternal: the ballplayers paid their cricket comrades $2,000 for the use of their field.

8. Joseph S. Stern, Jr., "The Team That Couldn't Be Beat," *Bulletin of the Cincinnati Historical Society* 27 (1969): 30; Seymour, "Baseball's First Professional Manager," p 412; clipping from *New York Clipper*, August 1870, in John Hadley Doyle Scrapbooks, vol. 2, National Baseball Library, Cooperstown, N.Y.

9. *New York Clipper*, August 1870, in Doyle Scrapbooks, vol. 2.

10. *Ball Players' Chronicle*, August 18, 1867, p 6; July 18, 1867, p. July 25, 1867, p. 1.

11. Stern, "Team That Couldn't Be Beat," pp. 28, 30; *Ball Players' Chronicle*, October 31, 1867, p. 4; Henry Chadwick, ed., *Beadle's* (1870), p. 62 (emphasis in original). Recall also that, as indicated in the Judiciary Committee hearing cited in chap. 5, it was implied that every club had its wealthy backers—"a class of members in every club who do the paying part of the business, and but little else."

12. *Wilkes' Spirit of the Times*, April 4, 1868, p. 99; April 11, 1868, pp. 115-116.

13. Ibid., April 11, 1868, p. 116; May 30, 1868, p. 252.

14. Chadwick, ed., *Beadle's* (1869), p. 99. Uniforms of the 1860s and 1870s carried no numbers and no players' names. Both of these innovations—the former later in the nineteenth century, the latter not until the mid-twentieth—were accompanied by controversy. Some teams still do not put players' names on their uniforms.

15. *Wilkes' Spirit of the Times*, May 28, 1864, p. 196.

16. That gentlemen might not have been able to afford new uniforms raises an important issue. It is difficult to overstate the extent to which the misinterpretation of this term has skewed the popular and scholarly history of baseball. Most historians of the game have simply assumed that "gentleman" meant a member of the upper class, and have therefore argued that baseball was originally controlled by a genteel upper crust, and was gradually appropriated by the masses. Thus Harold Seymour describes the Knickerbockers as having "a distinctively exclusive flavor—somewhat similar to what country clubs represented in the 1920s and 1930s, before they became popular with the middle class in general." In this view, "the Knickerbockers wanted to restrict baseball to their own social class," but were eventually "thrust aside" by the Eckford Club, among others (Seymour, *Baseball*, 1:15, 23-24). Following Seymour's lead and making the argument much more strongly, David Quentin Voigt claims that the "aristocratic" Knickerbockers "took a condescending view of other clubs…and it soon became apparent that they were out to establish themselves as the social arbiters of baseball." This effort failed, according to Voigt, as the other clubs in the New York area, unconvinced of the Knickerbockers' "superior pedigrees," "bluntly rejected [them] as baseball's fashion dictators" (Voigt, American *Baseball*, 1:8). Melvin Adelman has demonstrated that these accounts are without historical foundation. After looking at the social composition of the early baseball clubs, including the Knickerbockers, Adelman concludes, first, that "gentlemen" referred primarily to the prosperous middle class rather than to an upper class, and second, that it had less of an economic meaning than a social one—that is, it was an indicator less of class than of culture (Adelman, *A Sporting Time*, pp. 122-125). Although this conclusion represents a real advance in baseball scholarship, it does not go quite far enough. There were well-off merchants and professional men in early baseball clubs who styled themselves "gentlemen," but there were also large numbers of clerks and skilled workers whose interest in being called gentlemen was attributable mainly to their desire for respectability. This longing for respectability, and not players' status as members of the prosperous middle class, presents the real key to the puzzle of "gentlemen." Gentility, understood as an upper-class Victorian delicacy and priggishness, played only a minor part in the culture of baseball during these years. The cult of respectability among artisans, clerks, and petty proprietors gave them just as much dread of "the poor" and the "roughs" as was expressed by those much farther up the class ladder.

17. In fact, given the common associations of the color, a surprisingly large proportion of the sporting and theatrical clothes offered by Peck & Snyder was partly or wholly made of bright-red material. It is tempting to speculate further about the psychological significance of this color in baseball, especially since to Chadwick it suggested children and the insufficiently repressed "yokels" and "roughs." Bright red had for many years been used to indicate sexual passion or sexual commerce. Red dresses (or petticoats) could identify prostitutes, who worked in red-light districts. Hester Prynne's badge of adultery partook of the same symbolism, as did the "lady of the scarlet petticoat" in Hawthorne's "My Kinsman, Major Molineux." Garish as well as naughty, red carried both meanings in the nineteenth century. Might the prominence of red in baseball uniforms and team names (the Red Stockings, the Red Sox, the Redlegs, the Cardinals, or Redbirds) have been a way of maintaining a relationship to a younger, naughtier culture, if only by a kind of visual suggestiveness? The political implications of the color, in any event, are a matter of record. The Cincinnati Reds of 1944 changed their name to the Redlegs precisely to deflect public feelings about political "reds."

18. Or rather, the tour turned a profit of about $1,700. At the beginning of the 1869 season the club had incurred liabilities (including the current players' salaries) of over $15,000. By the end of the year all but about $1,000 of this debt had been paid off. See clipping from New *York Clipper*, August 1870, in Doyle Scrapbooks, vol. 2.

19. *Spirit of the Times*, June , 1869, p. 246.

20. Voigt, *American Baseball*, 1:27.

21. The only other team captain of long enough tenure to have "Captain" placed before his name in newspaper stories was Robert Ferguson of the Mutuals and Atlantics. Ferguson, however, was fully ten years younger than "Captain Harry," and though he commanded respect on the ballfield and off, he simply did not exercise the same authority as the Cincinnati (later Boston) captain.

22. Seymour, *Baseball,* 1:56-57; Voigt, "America's First Red Scare," p. 18.

23. Wage figures for these years vary a good deal, but some general ranges can be established. Though lower than they were in 1866-1867, wages were still relatively high in the late 1860s and early 1870s. We can calculate an upper limit on yearly income for five groups studied—blacksmiths, carpenters, engineers, machinists, and painters—by taking the highest daily wage earned in any of these occupations in the twenty-year period from 1860 to 1880 and multiplying it by the largest possible number of working days—312, at six days a week. The figure thus arrived at is just under $86. For a number of reasons this figure is much higher than what skilled craftsmen could expect to earn during these years. Few if any worked the maximum number of days, and most worked at well below this wage level. These calculations are based on Series D, 728-734, "Daily Wages of Five Skilled Occupations and of Laborers, in Manufacturing Establishments: 1860 to 1880," in *Historical Statistics of the United States, Colonial Times to 1870,* 2 vols. (Washington, D.C.: Bureau of the Census, 1975), 1:165; and two tables in Stephen Thernstrom, *Poverty and Progress: Social Mobility in a Nineteenth-Century City* (New York: Atheneum, 1970), pp. 93-94.

24. *Spirit of the Times,* June 12, 1869, p. 261; June 26, 1869, p. 291.

25. Joseph M. Overfield, "Baseball in Buffalo—1865 to 1870: Heyday of the Niagaras," *Niagara Frontier* 47 (1965): 10; *Spirit of the Times,* June 19, 1869, p. 281.

26. *Spirit of the Times,* June 26, 1869, p. 296.

27. Ibid., June 11, 1870, p. 263; June 18, 1870, p. 277.

28. *New York Clipper,* August 1870 and August 27, 1870, in Doyle Scrapbooks, vol. 2; Seymour, "Baseball's First Professional Manager," p. 415. Actually the club netted a total of $1.39 for the season.

29. The circular, dated November 21, 1870, was reprinted in the *New York Clipper,* December 3, 1870; the clipping is in Doyle Scrapbooks, vol. 2.

30. Voigt, *American Baseball,* 1:31-32.

31. There is some evidence that the club's stated inability to pay players' salaries was actually a negotiating ploy designed to force players to accept lower salaries: Seymour, *Baseball,* 1:59.

PART III

SPORT IN THE ERA OF INDUSTRIALIZATION AND REFORM, 1870-1915

During the latter part of the nineteenth century and early years of the twentieth century, sport in America evolved from a more informal and unorganized activity to a highly structured and organized phenomenon. The massive flow of immigration, increased urbanization and industrialization, new technologies, decline of religious opposition to recreation and leisure activities, expanding middle and working classes, and influence of the British on this country's nouveau riche all contributed to the establishment of governing bodies in intercollegiate athletics, increased organization and controls of amateur sport, and growing bureaucracy in professional sport. This period alone saw the founding of the American Association for the Advancement of Physical Education, organization of the League of American Wheelmen, formation of the National Croquet Association, founding of the Amateur Athletic Union, staging of the first national women's singles tennis championship, invention of basketball and volleyball, beginning of the Davis Cup tennis competition, formation of the Playground Association of America, and founding of the National Collegiate Athletic Association.

Contributing to the transformation of sport during this period was an emerging class of extraordinarily rich Americans. Realizing great wealth embedded in industrial capitalism, the very rich were responsible for the emergence of sports that required a great deal of money for equipment and facilities and their upkeep. As Donald Mrozek makes clear in chapter 6, "Sporting Life as Consumption, Fashion, and Display—The Pastimes of the Rich," the ultrarich established prestige and social exclusiveness through their participation in such sports as polo, yachting, fox hunting, tennis, and golf. These sports, performed in a deliberately stylized way and with special regard to proper etiquette and social customs, "took place in distinctive environments shaped for their pursuit."

Among the "distinctive environments" that sprang up in increasing numbers in late nineteenth- and early twentieth-century America were country clubs. One of the more famous of these country clubs was Pinehurst. Founded by James Tufts in 1895, Pinehurst was taken over by James' son Leonard in 1906 and soon blossomed into one of the great country clubs in America. As Larry R. Youngs notes in chaper 7, "Creating America's Winter Golfing Mecca at Pinehurst, North Carolina: National Marketing and Local Control," from the moment he took control of Pinehurst, Leonard Tufts "invested heavily in developing Pinehurst into a haven for a certain segment of America's sporting enthusiasts—those with the necessary time, disposable wealth, and proper wealth." Although various activities, such as skeet shooting, tennis, and horseback riding, were available to its patrons, the Donald Ross–designed golf courses and the club's annual golf tournaments were always the drawing cards. To ensure that those features remained so, Tufts, his brother-in-law, and Ross officially organized the Pinehurst Golf Club. Tufts also sold numerous properties in an effort to encourage golf enthusiasts to winter in Pinehurst for its entire season and, along with other officers in the Pinehurst Golf Club, began what they called the "Pinehurst System." This system, which adopted a set of rules to regulate tournament entries and handicaps, was particularly important because it restricted "Pinehurst's tournaments to only those people" Tufts and his colleagues "considered authentic golfers."

While golf had emerged as the main attraction at Pinehurst and other country clubs across America, the epicenter of college football during this period was among the Big Three colleges: Harvard, Yale, and Princeton. Among the Big Three, Yale was the undisputed king of college football, largely as a result of the influence of one man, Walter Camp. Michael Oriard provides details about Camp in chapter 8, "The Father of American Football." Born to a schoolteacher in New Haven, Connecticut, Camp was a star running back at Yale for a little over six years. After a brief stint in Yale's medical school, Camp first took a position with the Manhattan Watch Company and then later assumed a four-decade-long career with the New Haven Clock Company while continuing to serve "as Yale's unofficial, unpaid, unquestioned chief mentor and arbiter" of football. Apart from serving as the "unofficial" leader of Yale football, Camp was instrumental in changing the very nature of the sport through his implementation of several important rule changes: creation of a line of scrimmage, point scoring system, and proposal of 11 players on a side. According to Oriard, these rule changes, along with the plethora of articles Camp wrote on the sport for some of this country's major periodicals, make clear the direct connection Camp drew between football and "modern business civilization," particularly the "scientific management" system promoted by Frederick Winslow Taylor.

Suggested Readings

Balf, Todd. *Major: A Black Athlete, a White Era, and the Fight to Be the World's Fastest Human Being.* New York: Crown Publishers, 2008.

Berryman, Jack W. "Early Black Leadership in Collegiate Football: Massachusetts as a Pioneer." *Historical Journal of Massachusetts*, 9(1981): 17-28.

Borish, Linda. "The Cradle of American Champions, Woman Champions, Swim Champions: Charlotte Epstein, Gender and Jewish Identity, and the Physical Emancipation of Women in Aquatic Sports." *The International Journal of the History of Sport*, 21(2004): 197-235.

Captain Gwendolyn. "Enter Ladies and Gentlemen of Color: Gender, Sport and the Ideal of African American Manhood and Womanhood During the Late Nineteenth and Early Twentieth Century." *Journal of Sport History*, 18(1991): 81-102.

Cavallo, Dominick. *Muscles and Morals: Organized Playgrounds and Urban Reform, 1880-1920.* Philadelphia: University of Pennsylvania Press, 1981.

Chapman, David L. *Sandow the Magnificent: Eugen Sandow and the Beginnings of Bodybuilding.* Urbana, IL: University of Illinois Press, 2006.

Dyreson, Mark. "Nature by Design: Modern American Ideas About Sport Energy, Evolution and Republics, 1865-1920." *Journal of Sport History*, 26(1999): 447-469.

Dyreson, Mark. *Making the American Team: Sport, Culture and the Olympic Experience.* Urbana, IL: University of Illinois Press, 1998.

Eisen, George. "Sport, Recreation and Gender: Jewish Immigrant Women in Turn-of-the-Century America." *Journal of Sport History*, 18(1991): 103-120.

Eisenberg, Michael T. *John L. Sullivan and His America.* Urbana, IL: University of Illinois Press: 1988.

Fielding, Lawrence W. and Pitts, Brenda G. "The Battle Over Athletic Priorities in Louisville YMCA, 1892-1916." *Canadian Journal of History of Sport*, 20(1989): 64-78.

Gelber, Steven M. "Their Hands Are All Out Playing: Business and Amateur Baseball, 1845-1917." *Journal of Sport History*, 11(1984): 5-27.

Grover, Kathryn. (Ed). *Fitness in American Culture: Images of Health, Sport, and the Body, 1830-1940.* Rochester, NY: The Margaret Woodbury Strong Museum, 1989.

Grover, Kathryn. (Ed.) *Hard at Play: Leisure in America, 1840-1940.* Rochester, NY: The Margaret Woodbury Strong Museum, 1992.

Hardy Stephen H. "Adopted by All the Leading Clubs: Sporting Goods and the Shaping of Leisure." In Richard Butsch (ed.) *For Fun and Profit.* Philadelphia, PA: Temple University Press, 1990, pp. 71-101.

Hardy, Stephen H. *How Boston Played: Sport, Recreation and Community, 1865-1915.* Knoxville, TN: University of Tennessee Press, 2003.

Hardy, Stephen H. "Memory, Performance, and History: The Making of American Ice Hockey at St. Paul's School, 1860-1915." *The International Journal of the History of Sport*, 14(1997): 97-115.

Hardy, Stephen H. and Ingham, Alan G. "Games, Structures and Agencies: Historians on the American Play Movement." *Journal of Social History*, 17(1983): 285-301.

Harmond, Richard. "Progress and Flight: An Interpretation of the American Cycle Craze of the 1890s." *Journal of Social History*, 5(1971): 235-257.

Jenkins, Sally. *The Real All Americans: The Team that Changed the Game, a People, a Nation.* New York: Doubleday, 2007.

Kirsch, George B. "Municipal Golf Courses in the United States: 1895 to 1930." *Journal of Sport History*, 32(2005): 23-44.

LeCompte, Mary Lou. "Cowgirls at the Crossroads: Women in Professional Rodeo, 1885-1992." *Canadian Journal of History of Sport*, 20(1989): 27-48.

Levine, Peter, *A.G. Spalding and the Rise of Baseball: The Promise of American Sport.* New York: Oxford University Press, 1985.

Lomax, Michael E. *Black Baseball Entrepreneurs, 1860-1901: Operating by Any Means Necessary.* Syracuse, NY: Syracuse University Press, 2003.

Lucas, John. "The Hegemonic Rule of the American Amateur Athletic Union, 1888-1914: James Edward Sullivan as Prime Mover." *The International Journal of the History of Sport.* 11(1994): 355-371.

MacAloon, John J. *This Great Symbol: Pierre de Coubertin and the Origins of the Modern Olympic Games.* Chicago: University of Chicago Press, 1981.

Markels, Robin Bell. "Bloomer Basketball and Its Suspender Suppressions: Women's Intercollegiate Competition at Ohio State University, 1904-1907." *Journal of Sport History*, 27(2000): 30-49.

Moore, Glenn. "The Great Baseball Tour of 1888-89." *The International Journal of the History of Sport.* 11(1994): 431-456.

Moss, Richard J. *Golf and the American Country Club.* Urbana, IL: University of Illinois Press, 2001.

Oriard, Michael. *Reading Football: Sport, Popular Journalism, and American Culture.* Chapel Hill: University of North Carolina Press, 1993.

Park, Roberta J. "From Football to Rugby—and Back, 1906-1919: The University of California-Stanford University Response to the Football Crisis of 1905." *Journal of Sport History*, 11(1984): 5-40.

Paul, Joan. "The Health Reformers: George Barker Windship and Boston's Strength Seekers." *Journal of Sport History*, 10(1983): 41-57.

Peavy, Linda and Smith, Ursula. " 'Leav[ing] the White[s]…Far Behind Them': The Girls from Fort Shaw (Montana) Indian School, Basketball Champions of the 1904 World's Fair." *The International Journal of the History of Sport*, 24(2007): 819-840.

Peiss, Kathy. *Cheap Amusements: Working Women and Leisure in Turn-of-the-Century New York.* Philadelphia: Temple University Press, 1986.

Pesavento, Wilma J. "Sport and Recreation in the Pullman Experiment, 1880-1900." *Journal of Sport History*, 9(1982): 38-62.

Pruter, Robert. "Chicago High School Football Struggles, the Fight for Faculty Control, and the War against Secret Societies, 1898-1908." *Journal of Sport History*, 30(2003): 47-72.

Putney, Clifford. *Muscular Christianity: Manhood and Sports in Protestant America, 1880-1920.* Cambridge, MA: Harvard University Press, 2001.

Riess, Steven A. *Touching Base: Professional Baseball and American Culture in the Progressive Era.* Westport, CT: Greenwood Press, 1980.

Ritchie, Andrew. "Amateur World Champion, 1893: The International Cycling Career of American Arthur Augustus Zimmerman, 1888-1896." *The International Journal of the History of Sport,* 22(2005): 563-581.

Ritchie, Andrew. *Major Taylor: The Extraordinary Career of a Champion Bicycle Racer.* San Francisco: Bicycle Books, 1988.

Roberts, Randy. *Papa Jack: Jack Johnson and the Era of White Hopes.* New York: The Free Press, 1983.

Shattuck, Debra S. "Bats, Balls, and Books: Baseball and Higher Education for Women at Three Eastern Women's Colleges, 1866-1900." *Journal of Sport History,* 19(1992): 91-109.

Smith, Ronald A. "Preludes to the NCAA: Early Failures of Faculty Intercollegiate Athletic Control." *Research Quarterly for Exercise and Sport,* 54(1983): 372-382.

Smith, Ronald A. *Sports and Freedom: The Rise of Big-Time College Athletics.* New York: Oxford University Press, 1988.

Somers, Dale A. *The Rise of Sports in New Orleans, 1850-1900.* Baton Rouge: Louisiana State University Press, 1972.

Story, Ronald. "The Country of the Young: The Meaning of Baseball in Early American Culture," in Alvin Hall, (ed.) *Cooperstown Symposium on Baseball.* Westport, CT: Meckler, 1991, pp. 324-342.

Ward, Geoffrey C. *Unforgivable Blackness: The Rise and Fall of Jack Johnson.* New York: Alfred A. Knopf, 2004.

Zeiler, Thomas W. *Ambassadors in Pinstripes: The Spalding World Baseball Tour and the Birth of the American Empire.* New York: Roman & Littlefield, 2006.

CHAPTER 6

SPORTING LIFE AS CONSUMPTION, FASHION, AND DISPLAY—THE PASTIMES OF THE RICH

■ *Donald J. Mrozek* ■

It has been argued that the newly emerging class of extravagantly rich Americans whose wealth was rooted in industrial capitalism came to challenge the role of social leadership and political power of the traditional American gentility. Later historians have questioned the degree of antipathy between old and new wealth.[1] But in sport, quantities of money meant the ability to govern the games that could be played. Although ultra-rich Americans did not dictate institutionalized sport among other classes, they made possible the emergence of certain sports that required large outlays of money for facilities and their maintenance. Most important in the interplay of varying attitudes about sport in the early twentieth century, the ultra-rich—the Vanderbilts, the Harrimans, and others—embodied an alternative sensibility about sport.[2] They conducted it as a mode of consumption and as a fashion; and what regeneration they were likely to experience through sport flowed from its social outlets. That the remnant of the gentility, such as Roosevelt and Lodge, might have harbored such sentiments at an unconscious level is possible; but that they could have pursued them deliberately is nearly inconceivable. In this difference lay the curious contribution of the ultra-rich toward attitudes about sport.

It is debatable whether America's sporting life was ever truly democratic, and the question itself hinges largely on matters of definition; but it is certain that democracy of nearly any description had no place in the world of the very rich. Using their sports as badges of social status, the ultra-rich generally confined themselves to pursuits whose cost put them out of reach of ordinary

Reprinted, by permission, from D. Mrozek, 1983, *Sport and American Mentality*, 1880-1910 (Knoxville, TN: The University of Tennessee Press).

Americans. Yachting, polo, fox-hunting, tennis, and golf—these were the characteristic sports of the American rich. Indeed, their penchant to use sport as a means of establishing social exclusiveness and prestige showed itself not only in the activities that they favored but in their departure from various sports that they could not control. Baseball, for example, had been strongly favored by the New York Knickerbockers, widely considered the earliest baseball club and composed of players from the economically advantaged class. Despite baseball's subsequent reputation as a sport of the American masses, it thus found early encouragement among the rich. As the control of baseball came to be concentrated largely in the hands of middling men of commerce, however, the interest that the rich and socially distinguished showed in the sport fell off sharply. Although it was not necessary for them to avoid all contact with baseball or those who played it, it did seem important to mark out some other sports as their distinctive realm.

In this passion for exclusiveness, the very rich, who sought means of certifying their worth, often made the criticisms of Thorstein Veblen seem a miracle of understatement. In the words of Price Collier, they were "a widely advertised, though fortunately small, class, diligent in making themselves conspicuous, who, having been recently poor, are trying to appear anciently rich." In a 1911 volume predicting their passing, Frederick Townsend Martin called them the "idle rich." He thought it a pity and a disgrace that high society in the United States had come to be confused with a small minority who had grafted their quest for outrageous display onto the more conservative system that had preceded them. Martin derided the very rich as imitators of the gauche and vulgar excesses of the underworld, which they merely brought to new levels of extravagance. Expense was the only standard by which to judge their activities; and it was a criterion that Martin deplored as bad sense and bad taste. Moreover, it was a criterion that differed fundamentally from the standards of duty and dedication to the public interest which held such deep appeal for middle- and upper- middle-class Americans. Yet the new ultra-rich were accorded a peculiar publicity; and, while excluding those of an inferior economic class from the scenes of their sport, they nonetheless assumed a certain paradoxical visibility, through which they became the embodiment of the quest for pleasure and self-gratification.[3]

Simultaneously a source of personal amusement and a component of an exclusionary social system, the sports of the very rich industrial magnates and financiers were thus special in kind, special in place, and special in function. The characteristic sportive activities of the rich took place in distinctive environments shaped for their pursuit—whether a country club or even a whole compound such as at Newport, Rhode Island. Sport further served as a device for governing their etiquette and signifying their status. Ironically, the rich found their own way of giving meaning to Grantland Rice's maxim that what mattered was "how you played the game"; and social manners frequently predominated over athletic prowess in determining who really won or lost. Yet, for this reason, sport itself seemed all the more real, as it was tied to the very core of one's social goals and aspirations. Sport thus gained an added constituency that perceived it to have value, fastening on it as a nonproductive amusement and an instrument of display.

The Exclusionary Sports of the Rich

By the very sporting ventures they chose, the American rich set patterns of behavior that distinguished them from the masses and even from much of the respectable middle class. Infected with a desire to set fashion and keep pace with its mercurial changes, the wealthy elite often opted for the customs of the British upper classes—a phenomenon that showed itself in the sudden vogue of tennis and golf and invited satire in the rise of fox-hunting. A key means of distinguishing fashionable sport from common amusement was the price tag. Those requiring expensive and well-maintained facilities had a special appeal for the rich, who affected a lack of interest in the cost of their undertakings while glorying in their ability to pay it. It was the attitude of J. Pierpont Morgan who, when asked how much it cost to maintain his yacht, replied that anyone who had to ask could not afford one. Thus, the difference in dollars segregated the very rich from the majority of Americans, even if temperament might not always have done so. Indeed, it was less a division of the sheep from the goats than a segregation of the sheep from the wolves—an economically predatory group that now feigned purity and breeding and rode to hounds.

Armed with the money to realize virtually any whim, the new rich sometimes experimented with frivolous variations on established sports, at the same time revealing a fascination with mechanical and other novelties that added to the pace of fashion and drawing strength from a somewhat perverse appropriation of the idea of progress. In 1906, for example, the machine made a bumpy and bizarre entrance into the garden of the well-to-do when a Professor J.F. Draughon of Nashville, Tennessee, became an ardent exponent of "Fox Hunting in an Automobile"; and word of his exploits circulated among the curious. Uniting two oddities—one old and the other new—Draughon's short-lived fad suggested, at the level of ideas, a somewhat egoistic desire to amplify personal control over the natural components in sport. This same tendency showed itself in the growing vogue of defying the seasons by traveling to a climate more hospitable to one's favorite sports. Midwinter horse racing in New Orleans gained a following scattered around the country, and midwinter golf tournaments at Pinehurst and elsewhere lured devotees of the links and of country club life. Thus, either modifications of a sport or the gathering at a distant venue might lend social distinction to one's pursuits; and they did so in a way that placed maximum importance on the pleasuring of the individual sportsman taken as a consumer, albeit a wealthy one, and on gratification as a suitable goal in his life.[4]

Reports of costly sporting endeavors mingled with social notices and advertisements for expensive consumer items in the pages of magazines catering to the country club set and to elements within the middle class. *The Illustrated Sporting*

News exemplified this tendency in its lavish issue for Christmas 1906. Included were articles devoted to "Hunting Big Game in Africa," "Automobile Touring in the Rocky Mountains," and "The Phantom Fox." To illustrate an article on fishing, the editors chose a man who could hardly be considered an angler of average social status or personal influence—William Loeb, Jr., the personal secretary to President Theodore Roosevelt. Adding to the impression that sport was a part of fashion and distinction (and hence a fusion of services and commodities to be consumed), advertisements for champagne, luxurious automobiles, banks, and stockbrokers were freely interspersed among announcements of kennels specializing in Dalmatians, Pomeranians, and English and French bulldogs.[5] To someone imbued with the values of the traditional gentility, all of this seemed a dissipation that threatened to become the serpent in the private Eden of the rich. Among the very wealthy, however, it signified the dominance of material things and pleasurable experiences over philosophical sentiment.

Americans who enjoyed wealth and cultivated social distinctions, rather predictably, shied away from various more popular sports that pretended to egalitarianism and suited the means of the more modest consumer. Baseball and cycling thus appealed less to the rich than to others, largely because of the broad interest that the "middling sort" and the working class showed in them. Moreover, the rich demonstrated less commitment to the disciplined development of their abilities in such sports, partly because of their tendency to move restlessly from one diversion to another and also due to their greater sense of sport as leisure. Professional baseball player Roy A. Thomas, who coached at the fashionable Hill School in Pottstown, Pennsylvania, complained that boys born to the upper class pursued too many sports and had little interest in the "national game." By contrast, boys from modest and average backgrounds played the game compulsively, devoted all their play hours to it. "They study it," Thomas added, "look at it from all of its phases, and they naturally become adept at it." For his part, Thomas preferred the schoolboys to the scions of the wealthy, whose lack of enthusiasm for his game suggested their social distance.[6] Yet one must temper Thomas's criticism with a recognition that, as a professional, he carried the spirit and the code of work into his pursuit of a game; and, while the rich surely allowed sport and games a role in their lives, they were no more likely to confuse sport with work than to carry the precepts of play into the world of business and finance.

The rich sportsmen came to compose something of a nationwide network, their customs setting them off as a group from lesser economic classes despite the differences they often had among themselves. Yet the wealthy shied away from that national inclusiveness which cut across social class, ethnic origin, and economic condition and which the likes of Lodge and Roosevelt claimed to want. In *America's National Game*, published in 1911, Albert Spalding asserted: "The genius of our institutions is democratic; Base Ball is a democratic game." Notwithstanding the disingenuity of their coming from a corporate magnate of considerable means, such remarks marked baseball off from the political sympathies and social instincts of the rich, for whom sharing in popular sport would have been a rank eccentricity. In the afterglow of Roosevelt's presidency, Spalding sought to use the mantle of democratic egalitarianism to cover social and economic differences. "The son of a President of the United States," he insisted, "would as soon play ball with Patsy Flannigan as with Lawrence Lionel Livingstone, provided only that Patsy could put up the right article. Whether Patsy's dad was a banker or a boiler-maker," he added, "would never enter the mind of the White House lad."[7] Spalding glossed over the fact that Patsy's chances of playing with a Roosevelt greatly increased if he attended Groton and Harvard; but his overoptimistic, perhaps even self-deceptive, assertion of a classless cosmopolitanism in the great American pastime epitomized what the Vanderbilts and their kind were in the process of avoiding.

Cycling, too, had become virtually a national mania in America by the turn of the century; but the upper classes did not take it up as a regular feature of their sporting regimen. According to Elizabeth Barney, an acute observer of sporting behavior, cycling was "the amusement *par excellence* of the people"; and, in this case, she meant the great middle classes, including smaller shopkeepers, tradesmen, mechanics, and clerks. She conceded that it would be "absurd" to deny that some few members of the upper class had taken up the wheel. But only a small number would thus risk seeming to consort with their presumptive inferiors. So unfashionable did this middle-class participation make cycling that, according to Barney, those few women of the upper stratum who deigned to cycle at all were "not apt to use their wheels in public." The implication was that they would ride within the privacy of their estates. So, too, wealthy women disdained the new "rational costume," such as the bloomers that advocates of dress reform promoted, and thus cycling became more difficult for a very practical reason. The rich showed reluctance, then, to join in "the cycling set," as Barney called them, since the group was not very discriminating and since it was both too large and too established for the wealthier sort to take over its control.[8]

Although many advocates of pure amateurism from varying economic backgrounds were concerned to avoid excessive attention from journalists and sports fans lest it lead to commercialism and subversion of gentlemanly values, the desire for privacy harbored among the rich was another matter entirely. The seclusion of the country club, for example, halted not the corruption of American life but the dilution of upper-class society. Yet, while seeking privacy at one level, the rich invited public attention at another, partly because their exclusionary measures provoked idle curiosity and also because the magnificence of their display could hardly have escaped notice under nearly any circumstances. The first American country club, Brookline, opened in 1882 as a center for Boston's elite in polo, racing, and the hunt. Soon it added golf links, making available to its aristocratic membership yet another sport whose expense barred it from the common citizen. The Newport Country Club, spearheaded by sugar magnate Theodore A. Havemeyer, attracted founding members from the moneyed class such as Cornelius Vanderbilt, Perry Belmont, and John Jacob Astor. Similarly, men of wealth took the spotlight when they joined in 1908 to promote tournament play through the National Golf Links of America; and the roster of promoters included the fashionable names of William K. Vanderbilt, Harry Payne Whitney, J. Borden Harriman, Elbert H. Gary, W.D. Sloane, and Henry Clay Frick.[9] The amateurism preserved by such a group was not much more than a test of wealth or, at best, a yielding of governance of the sport to the wealthy. Less publicized separate competitions were staged among the club "pros," who were more talented but socially beyond the pale. Thus, the structure of the tournament system as well as the identity of the players served the rich in their quest for exclusiveness.

Sportsmen in the socially elite classes did not usually identify themselves as exclusionary and undemocratic. Yet their periodic claims that sports which they favored were open to all Americans form something of a farce in the literature of sports promotion at the turn of the century. For the word "popular" did not really include all Americans when it was used by a member of the upper economic class. The yachtsman Duncan Curry, for example, showed no irony when he wrote of "Yachting as a Sport for the People" in a 1904 article. Curry dismissed as erroneous the widespread belief that yachting belonged exclusively to "kings and millionaires." He freely conceded that the grand steam-yachts such as the *Valiant* cost $1 million and that the syndicate owning the America's Cup contender *Reliance* spent half a million dollars to beat the *Shamrock III*. Ignoring the difference between catfish and caviar, Curry asserted: "Nowadays, when a man can buy a good, serviceable sailing dory for from $35 to $50, or purchase a small power launch from $175 to $250, there is no reason for him to envy a Vanderbilt or an Iselin…" In fact, not only could most of "the people" not afford a yacht comparable to Henry Walter's 224-foot *Narada;* they could not have spent $175 or even $35. In 1890, the average daily wage of the urban industrial worker came to only $1.69. The poorest classes averaged a mere $150 income for the year, and the average family income in the United States was only $500. Per capita income in 1900 reached only $236; and, in 1910, only 4 percent of the population of working families earned more than $2,000, the line that analysts said divided "families enjoying at least modest comfort from families that can scarcely be called well to do."[10]

Curry's assertion of the almost universal accessibility of yachting foundered on his own interpretation of class, status, and exclusivity. As a frame of reference, he used not the national population but the New York Yacht Club and the Royal Yacht Squadron. In their earlier years, Curry admitted, these societies had discouraged the building of small boats by refusing to register craft under certain tonnages. He may have thought the New York club more democratic than the Royal Squadron for having based its restrictions on the indiscriminate standard of wealth, while even so prosperous a businessman as Sir Thomas Lipton was barred from the Royal Squadron for lack of aristocratic pedigree and involvement in mere trade. But the inclusiveness of the sport, if not among the New Yorkers, purportedly showed itself when other clubs "sprang up in response to a demand by people of limited means who were fond of water" but lacked the uncommon wealth of the Vanderbilts. Like *popular, limited* had meaning only in context; and Curry's sense of economic modesty formed in the shadow of millionaires. The average industrial worker would have been sufficiently awed by the $1,400 price tag of a Herreshoff & Gardner raceabout and quite uncomprehending of Curry's buoyant conclusion: "...there is really no excuse for anyone who seriously thinks of going into yachting being stopped by the expense, for it is a sport that is open to practically everyone."[11] What Curry meant was everyone of the better sort.

The new clubs to which Curry referred included the Corinthian clubs, whose genesis belied the simple democracy that the yachtsman imagined in his comfortable world. Influential members of the major yacht clubs observed with deep concern the rising importance of the "sandbaggers," shallow-draft vessels of broad beam that were often owned by men of no social distinction and even by the denizens of taverns in harbor towns. Emerging in the years before the Civil War, the "sandbagger" phenomenon represented a challenge to the integrity of the gentility or the "old stock" in America, since young men who came from good families but lacked money could sail with persons of lesser birth on one of these strange, unstable craft. Even more, it challenged the ability of the superrich to regulate the behavior of young offspring of the gentility and thus to strengthen their claims to legitimacy in social leadership. The Corinthian clubs provided for shared ownership of boats, and even for common ownership that allowed men wellborn socially, but of lesser economic means, to confine their social life to people of their own sort. No longer would they be inclined to consort with longshoremen in a waterfront saloon. Curry's history of the development of yachting, then, failed to note that the "people of limited means" for whom the new clubs provided access to boating did not include the preponderance of Americans and certainly not the working class.

Among wealthy women, the same bias against workers and the common middle class appeared as among men. Anne O'Hagan's "Athletic Girl," described in *Munsey's Magazine* for August, 1901, had little truck with the common working woman. Even for O'Hagan, some gymnasiums seemed to set unreasonably steep and exclusionary fees. "There is one gymnasium," she reported, "with pillowed couches about the room, soft, lovely lights, and walls that rest weary eyes; where a crisp capped maid brings the exerciser a cup of milk during her rest upon the divan, where her boots are laced or buttoned by deft fingers other than her own." These amenities cost her a hundred dollars a year. Other clubs whose appointments were "less Sybaritic" charged membership dues on the order of forty dollars per year. O'Hagan rather blithely noted that, "if one has the distinction of being a working woman," ten dollars would suffice to obtain gymnastic instruction. Although O'Hagan found ten dollars an inconsiderable amount of money, the working girl for whom this represented a week's pay may have thought differently.[12] Among many Americans, bodily exercise was still essentially a private matter; and the inaccessibility of gymnasiums on economic grounds meant the exclusion of large numbers of Americans from the kinds of activities that took place there. Only the gradual provision of facilities through public funding and private voluntary action would remedy this deficiency, and that movement was still only in its early stages in the last decades of the nineteenth century. As a result, glib pronouncements about the availability of gymnasiums with pillowed couches and well-trained maids said "Let them eat cake" to people who struggled for bread.

Elizabeth C. Barney provided readers of the *Fortnightly Review* of August 1894 further evidence of the social myopia of the upper classes, as well as insensitivity to the economic pressures that the working classes faced. In "The American Sportswoman," Barney claimed that tennis had become "a favourite with rich and poor," observing that New York's Central Park included tennis courts where anyone could play for a fee and ignoring the issue of relative levels of disposable income. Her judgment that riding "follows hard upon tennis in popular favour" also exposed her economic and social bias, for even she admitted that hundreds of girls could afford to ride only infrequently. Barney's audience and the object of her concern was the wellborn element of society that considered riding in New York City *de rigueur* and used the term with no hint of parody. The thread of fashion tied together the patchwork of Barney's vision of women's sport; and she spoke of tennis clubs as "fashionable institutions," certified riding as part of "the usual round of social events," and praised the social events attendant upon fox-hunting as "among the *debutantes'* most cherished aspirations." Only in this context did Elizabeth Barney escape self-conscious irony when she pronounced tennis a sport that "all can play without cost."[13] *All* was a term that excluded the humbler classes.

Women of upper-class instincts and means thus tended to isolate themselves from the preponderance of Americans of their sex. Welcoming greater interest in sports and games, they nonetheless used it — perhaps unconsciously—in ways that only sharpened their distinctiveness from men and from working women. Females did exchange muscular for "nervous" strength, and their conscious cultivation of bodily health through sport gave evidence of a "delight in action" that brought them into step with the American male. But they remained three paces behind in the variety of sports available, in their control, and in public sentiment concerning their purpose. No longer a "pallid hothouse flower"— which the working woman had never had a chance to be in the first place—the American sportswoman indulged with most enthusiasm and greatest approval in sports such as tennis, riding, boating, and walking.

Suggestive of the importance of class distinction, the desirability of tennis for women evidently stemmed from its social effects as much as from its hygienic benefits. According to Elizabeth C. Barney, writing in the August 1894 *Fortnightly Review,* the enjoyment of tennis revolved around the "social intercourse" at the club house. The game strengthened and unified the community by drawing together the young people who played and the matrons who watched, while talking over "servants and babies on the club piazzas." Barney praised tennis, therefore, as a "strong, centralising influence," asserting that "the girl who does not play tennis feels that she has missed something out of her life."[14] This sporting scene served as a common ground upon which women could develop social values, much as the sporting options open to men enabled them to realize their own ideals; but the codes for women differed from those of the men.

For Elizabeth Barney and others of her station, tennis served to organize polite society and to put a healthy flush in its cheeks.

The flow of fashion which illuminated the wealthy woman's sporting habits extended into the physical trappings that surrounded them, such as clothing styles and accessories. In a society that prized conspicuous consumption and wasteful dress, the realm of sport had the advantage of adding a whole new set of activities for which special costumes could be devised and socially mandated. Moreover, the criteria of taste and acceptability could be changed from season to season. In 1904, Marion Burton indicated the need for careful judgment so as to conform to prevailing norms. She warned against the "promiscuous wearing of handsome jeweled rings when arrayed in sporting apparel," observing that only "mannish' rings of seal or Roman gold" were suitable for the woman on the links or courts. Other columnists simply played sport as another area in which the twins fashion and waste could be developed. "Originality of design and diversity of style are so marked in the newest spring apparel," one article read, "that a well-groomed sportswoman, who does not wish to come a sartorial cropper, must needs exercise a nicety of discrimination and a keen sense of the eternal fitness of things in the selection of her outing garments." The author went on to provide the latest advice: whips were "in" and riding crops most assuredly "out"; the pleated front had made a strong comeback; and the ankle-length tennis outfit would be all the rage.[15] Such commentators promoted the wasteful and unproductive behavior that Thorstein Veblen termed conspicuous consumption, emphasizing the value of certain sports—often marginal sports, one might add, such as croquet and fencing—in enhancing the worth of woman as an object of pecuniary display.

The conduct of sports themselves became an object of fashion, and social grace competed—successfully—against athletic ability in the design and management of tournaments. In woman's events as in men's, strict control was exerted over admission to play in ostensibly national events. Elizabeth Barney, for example, reported that upper-class women were able to contribute "beautiful form" to the mixed doubles matches in tennis that did so much to enliven weekends at the country club; and they carried the same spirit over into tournament play. The *crème de la crème*, Barney noted, made their way, in 1894, to the Ladies' National Championship at the Philadelphia Country Club, which ranked with "the foremost in tone and social standing, and everything that it does is in the best of style." The tournament operated on rules that ensured protection of the women competitors from contact with their social inferiors. Matches were determined by invitation only, in a way that openly violated the supposedly democratic quality of modern sport, and only those of "assured social position" would think to submit their names for screening.[16]

Much of the "sports" coverage designed to appeal to rich women readers confirmed the view that social pedigree interested them more than athletic achievement. In the regular column "The Sportswoman" in the February 6, 1904, issue of *The Illustrated Sporting News*, word was published of the establishment of the York Athletic Club, composed exclusively of women, with membership limited to 500. Aimed primarily at "women of athletic tastes," it would also provide "accommodations for those who may wish to join simply for the sake of the social privileges afforded." The club's Committee on Organization included women from well-known and well-placed families, such as Mrs. J.J. Astor, Mrs. J. Borden Harriman, Miss A.T. Morgan, Mrs. William G. Rockefeller, Mrs. Harry Payne Whitney, Mrs. Robert Sturgis, and Mrs. Walter Damrosch. To be sure, Irish need not apply.[17] The same issue carried a story about "The Only Pack of Hounds Hunted by Women," a theme pursued the following year by Richard Strong in "Great Britain's Famous Women of the Hunt." Strong insisted that the modern sportswoman took chances equal with men; but he apparently had only a limited equality in mind. For example, "The modern woman not only controls her own fishing-kit, but unhesitatingly gaffs her own salmon." Yet gaffing a salmon hardly constituted equality. Strong himself added a hint that discrimination lay heavily in assigning sports according to sex, and he specifically cited "a few little courtesies of the field which the stronger still show to the weaker sex."[18] It was the sheerest fantasy to suggest that many of the better sort of Americans could compete, whether in sport or in society, with the "women masters of hounds": Miss Isa McClintock of the Tynan and Armagh Harriers; Mrs. T.H.R. Hughes, Master of the Neuadd-Fawr Fox-hounds; Master Edith Somerville of the West Carberry Hunt; and Mrs. H.P. Wardell of the Hawkstone Otter Hounds. Perhaps the highest marriage of society and genteel sport received notice in "Dogs of High Degree and Their Titled Mistresses," which provided women with rare and superfluous models. Queen Alexandra of England was featured with her Chinese spaniel, Little Billie, and the Princess Beatrice posed with her pugs "President Faure," "Dumas," and "King of Siam."[19]

The enthusiastic and influential physical educator Dudley A. Sargent observed, in an article published in 1901, that fashion actually accounted for the rise and fall of many sports themselves, rather than merely the costumes for their pursuit. Archery and fencing, for example, would be pursued as "fads and be rushed for a few seasons, and then become obsolete." Obedient to society's edicts, the *beau monde* took up even serious sports as "the proper thing" and dropped them with equal unintelligence when style changed, substituting social caprice for scientific assessment of their hygienic value. Sargent did not confine his analysis to women, although they were more likely to succumb to the specific voguish sports he mentioned. He feared that the serious sports which could bring great physical benefits would fall before fashion just as marginal activities did, blurring the difference between the substantial and the trivial.[20] The physical educators—whether male or female—wished to avoid turning sport into a secular religion to which scientific hygiene would be sacrificed. But the social elites, who shared the educators' revulsion toward excessive competitiveness, remained deaf to their protests against frivolity. For many socially luxurious sportsmen and sportswomen, moderation was a polite term for laziness, as the real, social competition was played with relentless zeal. An educator such as Dudley Sargent might choose his sports for hygienic reasons, but the rich selected theirs against the criterion of social esteem and fashion.

Special Places for Special Sportsmen

Although there was a strong current in America toward sharing certain sports which were national in sweep and were usually conducted in public places, the new rich bucked the trend and created a more specialized environment for sports. The country club was their most repeated form, and lavish clubhouses designed by leading architectural firms served as centers of social interchange as well as focal points of golf and tennis. Since social aims permeated country club life, one cannot see this institution as unambiguous proof of the rise of athletic sport to respectability; but the relative place of sport in the social world, as compared to the place of business in it, suggests something else. Separated and distinct from work, sport had become an autonomous focal point in the life of the rich. Unlike middle-class Americans who claimed that sport ingrained in players those qualities that empowered them to do life's work, the rich favored sport for its inutility. Their country clubs, then, became symbols of a quite different, pleasure-oriented ethic, which was to make a major contribution to the American notion of leisure.

The physical segregation of sporting activities in a special place for their pursuit, which was an intrinsic feature of the country club, had equivocal implications. On the one hand, it suggested the isolation of play, as ritualized in the games at the club, from work. On the other hand, it made a comprehensive and interactive, if separated, system out of the activities which were conducted there. The gathering of several sports under a single administration at a central facility constituted a limited form of "horizontal integration," as if a corporate structure had been applied to sportive behavior.[21] In short, the sporting life of the rich thus assumed an institutional shape, one which affirmed the viability of sport as an autonomous enterprise and one whose very comprehensiveness helped to provide foundation for the belief that a man might even pursue sport as a calling and an independent source of meaning in one's life.

The fact of physical segregation of the sporting rich and, certainly, its degree were substantial departures from the traditional pattern in the use of resorts. One of the key features of the earlier American resorts, notably the spas and baths that were to be found in many of the original states, was that they were accessible to patrons of no more than ordinary means. Foreign travelers were astonished to find great diversity in the social and economic background of the clientele at the watering places. In theory, such accessibility illustrated both democracy and gentility—democracy in that no rigid social system barred a potential paying customer, and gentility in that the grace of the social interchange was presumed to flow from the gentlemanly decency of visitors and not from lavish facilities and some variant of a caste system. The spas thus showed signs, in corporate terms, of both vertical and horizontal integration; for they included Americans and foreigners of varying economic and social levels, even as they sought to offer a range of amusements and entertainments.[22]

Moreover, earlier resorts were more likely to be diverse in their social roles, as well as in their clientele. For the men operating the great hotels, it was a business venture, as it might well be for those seeking to monopolize public transportation to the facilities. For the natives, there were service-related jobs. The promotion of gambling at various of the resorts added a related but separate industry. So, then, the focus of the earlier American vacation-places was somewhat diffuse. By the end of the century, however, when the ultra-rich established their compound at Newport, Rhode Island, these characteristics were all but eradicated. The wealthy families did not rely on public hotels but on their own "cottages" of as many as seventy rooms; and they maintained permanent staffs to tend the grounds and keep the houses in order, supplemented by a company of personal servants during the brief summer season. As a result, many of the business features that had appeared in the earlier resorts were absent at Newport. Gambling went private and even the admission of spectators to competitions in sports such as tennis was restricted on social grounds. Although the aim was to create an isolated playground for the rich in which social distinction exceeded athletic ability in the pursuit of diversion, the effect was also to lay the groundwork for the concept of the "destination resort," which, while complex in its economic base, was devoted to nothing but the pursuit of pleasure. Newport lent itself, in effect, to the horizontal integration of the high rung of the leisure class, but it also helped in defining the terms of leisure as it was soon to be pursued by Americans of lesser means.

A comparison of Newport with its forerunner in fashion, Saratoga Springs, New York, makes the distinction in the type of resort somewhat sharper. The reputation of Saratoga Springs as a sporting resort originated around the time of the Civil War; and, despite early associations with men of wealth and social prominence, the town soon became more significant for its links to racing and to the emergence of intercollegiate sport than for its catering to the rich. After decades as a popular watering place, the New York resort moved into the business of sport in 1863, when John Morissey opened its first horse-track. Born in Ireland, Morissey came to America in 1834 at the age of three. He later worked as a bouncer in a brothel, entered politics as a ward heeler, was an American heavyweight champion under the London Prize Ring Rules, and emerged as the boss of New York City's lucrative gambling houses. In all, his record invited wicked curiosity but discouraged the close friendship of the social elite. Nonetheless, eager for acceptance among the more reputable classes, Morissey evidently hoped to curry their favor by catering to their desire for amusement. He built lavish facilities at Saratoga which pampered his guests while adding to his own wealth; but he soon identified a restiveness among the patrons, who seemed to crave more elaborate, exciting, and active entertainments. He succeeded in enlisting the advice of the prominent New York stockbroker William R. Travers, whose ideas contributed much to the quality of the early racing seasons.

Whatever the motives of Travers, who was to become a leading figure in the social life of Newport, Morissey's interests in sport grew principally from his growing need to keep Saratoga a commercial success; and even his desire for social acceptance could not possibly be fulfilled unless he continued to attract the rich and wellborn as guests. Moreover, Morissey—as well as other hotelkeepers at Saratoga—did not make the same nice distinctions that some of his guests did; and so he was willing to hazard supporting attractions that might ultimately alienate the self-flattering superrich. Thus, when James Gordon Bennett, publisher of the *New York Herald* and an ardent sports fan, proposed Saratoga as the site of the annual regatta of the newly established Rowing Association of American Colleges in 1874, the hotel operators responded enthusiastically. Yet, by identifying themselves with the generality of college men, by encouraging average citizens in the region to come out to view the events, and by permitting an unseemly amount of betting on amateur events, the proprietors actually made Saratoga ineligible to serve as the true capital of America's wealthy elite. That role fell to Newport, Rhode Island, where sport was by no means the servant of commerce.[23]

The enclosure and definition of space, whether public or private, give it cultural and even ceremonial meaning.[24] In the late nineteenth century, this process exemplified the passion for discipline and order in life that pervaded middle-class society; and it enhanced the sense of importance shown toward the activities pursued within it. With the establishment of the grand compound of the rich at Newport, there came upon the American scene such a defined and enclosed space that was devoted exclusively to leisure; and, although sport was not the only entertainment or amusement pursued within its confines, it occupied a major place and thus became integrated into the concept of leisure itself. Although this latter phenomenon prevailed only within a rarified community at the time, namely the very rich, it lent credence to an interpretation of the worth and respectability of sport that was quite different from what was encouraged by the middle class and the remnant of the gentility. In such a view, sport no longer needed to be a "healthful amusement" that readied one for work; it could become an end in itself, to be sought only as a means of diversion and pleasure.

The concentration of summer houses for the rich at Newport came largely during the last third of the nineteenth century, although it continued much later. In a process that began in 1859, Newport emerged as the summer social center of the "great American families," who had previously been scattered about in resorts of their own choosing. The gravitation toward Newport suggested a certain nationalization, or centralization, of America's rich upper crust; and this, in turn, was to lend itself to a standardization of behavior and amusements among the wealthy. As early as the Civil War years, fashion-setting men of leisure, led by Ward McAllister whose picnics and outings on the coastal beaches became famous, began to move to the attractive bluffs and hills near the old colonial town. Even then, it was a refuge from the world and its troubles, or, somewhat more exactly, a world unto itself with its own cares and concerns. In a sense, even the absorption into the social rounds that became a staple of Newport's image and self-image furthered the sense of insulation from the practical affairs of business and politics, sharpening the sense of protective enclosure.[25]

In at least one regard, the life of the rich at Newport shared in the temperament often seen among other Americans. The summer colony was said to be characterized by a "restlessness" that showed itself in the constant round of parties, yachting trips, rides, social visits, and sporting events.[26] Although the wealthy might choose somewhat different ways of expressing it, a love of action and events predominated. Simply being in Newport was not quite enough. One also needed to be doing things there. This interest in a social life that included activity helped to make the elite of Newport a more eligible model for imitation by those of far lesser means and saved them from complete irrelevance.

Nonetheless, the annual renewal of social ties at Newport itself became a kind of competition, in which sporting events and social occasions became devices for the definition and measurement of status, as had not been the case before, except perhaps in the colonial Tidewater. This relationship applied within the social elite and also between wealthy society as a whole and the rest of America. In the great bulk of cases, the actual performance of athletic feats was less important than the grace and style with which people performed them; and instances in which competitive excellence was prized—notably in yachting—themselves hinged partly on the purchase of expensive, specially designed vessels and on the maintenance of a substantial crew and staff. Even in yachting, however, a social note obtained; and extravagant expenditures conspired with contempt for "new money" to govern participation in competition on the waters off Newport. The dedicated British yachtsman Sir Thomas Lipton was snubbed widely at Newport since he had made his money in trade, and much too recently at that.[27] At least a generation or two was needed to separate the glamour of wealth from the tawdriness of its sources; and so the names of Oliver Belmont, Pierre Lorillard, Cornelius Vanderbilt, and E.J. Berwind loomed high over that of a mere British baronet. As rigid as they could be with outsiders, so were the sportsmen of Newport competitive among themselves, always seeking to put forward the best image and the most stylish display as a substitute for pedigree and as a proof of wealth.[28]

The tendency of the rich at Newport to use sport as part of a whole system of leisure showed itself in their disdain for games that needed no more than an open field and a ball. Instead, they lavished their attention on pastimes that demanded much time, special facilities, expensive equipment, and, sometimes, extensive travel. Although the enthusiasm for yachting, lawn tennis, fox-hunting, and the like was often genuine, so was their social role. As J.P. Morgan put it succinctly, "You can do business with anyone, but you can go sailing only with a gentleman."[29] The devotion of resources to sport and other aspects of leisure thus became more than an emblem of wealth, although it was assuredly that; it also became a means of delineating leisure as an institution whose complexity invited members of the wealthiest classes to pursue it as if it were life's very purpose.

This kernel of difference helps to account for the interest of the American rich in the sporting life of the British upper class. It has been suggested that American sport was largely an imitative extension of British sport. Around the nation as a whole, the claim is rather exaggerated; but among the very rich the imitation ascended toward parody. The wealthy Americans aped what they thought to be the sporting traditions of the British upper class in an effort to stay in international fashion and to act convincingly as an American aristocracy by re-creating the behavior of a confessedly leisured society. Although the imitation often stumbled on bad taste, it encouraged the setting of spatial and temporal boundaries for the life of leisure. Polo ponies were kept in lavish stables, sleeping on monogrammed linen sheets. (Oliver Belmont housed his ponies on the lower level of his own house because he could not bear to treat them as if they were not members of the family.) Pink-coated riders pursued the fox across the fields of disgruntled Rhode Island farmers, who eventually banded together to put an end to the trampling of the crops. Comparing them to plants, Maud Elliott called such sports "exotics"; and their impertinence to American life was taken as a virtue, for it gave the promise of endlessly pursued social distinction.[30]

From another vantage, however, even the "exotic" sports that gradually withered on American soil helped to set the boundaries of leisure as an idea; and they affected the sense that rich and ordinary Americans as well would have of the less flamboyant sports which the wealthy managed to control. The passion for things British, for example, encouraged the rich to show interest in lawn tennis, although the game's survival also depended on its suitability to the needs of the American rich. First brought to New York by Mary Outerbridge after a vacation in Bermuda, where she had observed the game played by British officers, tennis soon became a fixture of Newport's summer season. Partly because it brought the well-dressed spectators together at the Casino, Tennis Week—the informal name for the National Lawn Tennis Tournament—emerged as the most estimable sporting event of the season. The very choice of a grass

Some of the rich and famous exiting a polo match.
Photo courtesy of Library of Congress. LC-B2-ggbain-16308.

surface gave it an air of greater style, since it required much more careful and costly maintenance than hard-packed clay. Players in the tournament, which was initiated in 1881, came from the ranks of social fashion; and professionals were unheard of. Clad in knickers, blazers, and caps, they competed in a mild game, paced by "the genteel pat of the ball against languid strings."[31] Richard D. "Dicky" Sears, who won the first championship match and held the title for eight consecutive years, came from a reputable Boston family; and he held a certain charm for the spectators who gathered behind ropes on camp-stools, watching him play with his tongue lapping out of his mouth somewhat like a napping dog's. Not until 1890 was a grandstand installed, nor were invitations to compete allowed by the Casino's board of governors to players outside the Newport social set until the turn of the century. As with the rest of Newport's summer activities, tennis was as much a matter of style as one of athletics.

Yet one should not miss the fact that this sense of sport—this definition of sport in terms of style, manners, and expression—allowed it a certain space as an autonomous variable and a separately observable force within the life of the rich. Special costume, special facilities, special identity among the players, special limits among spectators—all became a part of the landscape of sport as an independent branch of leisure. In the process of seeking to use sport to define themselves as a special aristocratic class, the American rich thus also did much to confirm the institutional status of sport itself, as an enterprise with facilities, rules, demands, and, above all, purposes of its own.

The Special Role of Sport for the Ultra-Rich

Although the ultra-rich pursued sport as a fashion, it was still something that could be a calling. In this regard, they veered sharply from the gentility who, as Stow Persons has noted, tended to disdain fashion and regard it, in Emerson's phrase, as "virtue gone to seed." Although the thought that "fashionable society was a caricature of the gentry" may have been declining, traditionalists such as Roosevelt found little to approve in the antics of the ultra-rich. Roosevelt never condoned the use of sport for purely personal purposes, arguing that it was a means through which one prepared for societal tasks. Yet, among the very rich, ever more elaborate trappings were forged in service of selfish goals, seeking to use material splendor as proof of personal importance. At the same time, however, the likes of Roosevelt also objected to the implications of the physical separation of the very rich from the great majority of Americans. They were hiving themselves off, apart from the national stream; and they risked firming up a class structure that would threaten national unity. Hence, the very process of physical exclusion that showed itself in the growth of country clubs and in the development of the wealthy colony at Newport ran afoul of the gentility and the middle class, even as it made the undiluted pursuit of a sporting life a more credible and creditable option among the rich themselves. It has been suggested that the instinct of the traditional gentility was to "dignify a humble occupation by a noble purpose."[32]

For the very rich, however, the dignity of sport inhered in the lavishness of circumstance and in the impertinence of its pursuit. Truly, the ultra-rich were pioneers of sport as a leisure activity which required no justification. Precisely this, which so alienated and disgusted the traditional gentility because it seemed to debase sport by subordinating it to motives that were trivial because they were merely personal, constituted the major contribution of the turn-of-the-century rich to the development of twentieth-century attitudes toward sport.

If not uniquely, at least specially, the ultra-rich came to their sport partly from the vantage of excess "spare" time. Although the mere existence of "nonwork" time did not require that sport be used to fill it, "nonwork" did have the potential to become an individual and a social problem if it surpassed a certain magnitude and extensiveness. Admittedly, it is significant that non-work time was appearing during the nineteenth century; and, especially with the alienation of labor from the household and removal from the farms increasing, the very fact of identifiable nonwork time became easier to recognize. On the other hand, the magnitude of nonwork and its pervasiveness in the society must not be exaggerated. For the industrial worker who saw little of the light of day, such "spare" time was hardly a problem requiring a managed solution through sport or anything else. So, too, the dissipation of energies in unsupervised play loomed as a problem only with the reduction of child labor and similar measures. In short, despite the fears of middle-class managers and upper-class industrialists, excessive indulgence in uncontrolled leisure was more a fancied than a real problem among vast numbers of Americans in the late decades of the nineteenth century.

Among the very rich, however, the problem was much more tangible and convincing. Because of its reliance on fashion and its imitation of supposedly British patterns, this small, influential economic stratum wished to seem above and beyond work of virtually any sort; and, in fairness, the rich often showed a genuine desire for a change of pace. J. Pierpont Morgan showed symptoms of this tendency toward leisure when he noted that, although he could do twelve months' work in nine months, he could not do twelve months' work in twelve. A certain restlessness overtook him, and he would be off to Egypt supervising the excavations for the Metropolitan Museum of Art or out on his 302-foot yacht, *Corsair III.*[33] In an age that equated activity with life itself, it seemed senseless and unacceptable to fall into total indolence or passivity. It was in this context of the general need for the sensation of action and the specific need for the impression of economic inutility that the very rich helped to create the American sense of leisure. Contrary to Marx's sense that it was simply uncommitted spare time or rest, the wealthy American capitalist made leisure a rather exhausting round of organized amusements and consumer activities. Transcending or even just ignoring the traditionalists' focus on duty and service, the ultra-rich thus developed a sense of leisure and leisure time that was permeated by activities and suffused with an underlying conviction of the primacy of experience. It was insufficient to have free time, unless you showed it.

Nor was leisure convincing without material expression. Even as the common sense of what constituted the sports hero came to center on the primacy of deeds over virtues, so did the more general sense of a hero of culture center on action over character. In at least one of their guises, the rich thus did much to create the concept of the "sportsman." The very rich could establish influence—other than their manifest economic power—only by accumulating objects and by establishing a record of elitist activities. The absence of usefulness in sport was more than charming, then; for it made sport a superb instrument for the creation of leisure. Ironically, the wealthy Americans' emphasis on the intertwined goals of self-gratification, identity, relief from the tedium of a stultifying structured life, and expressive display resembled the supposed preferences of the laboring class more closely than those of the economic and social middle. In this way, the very rich helped to advance notions about sport and its role in purposeless leisure which would simultaneously compete with the middle class's concentration on the work-ethic and service and encourage the working class to see sport as a part of the American Dream. Like the very rich, the workers could prove their achievement of leisure only by expressing this fact through action, as deeds increasingly assumed greater eloquence than words in the formulation of American ideas. Sport had become a fixture among the idle rich; and Americans who cherished a belief in upward material mobility were prone to follow the reigning models of the culture.

It is not necessary to repeat the criticisms that the gentility, the military, and various elements of the middle class aimed at the rich because of their emphasis on luxury; but it is useful to appreciate that the rich, in their pursuit of luxury and leisure, implicitly asserted that there was such a thing as surplus. In David Potter's term, abundance appeared, even if still more an image than a reality; and the diversity and inefficiency of America's sports system owed much to the fact that a gradually growing surplus encouraged complexity and tolerated waste. In modern times, the new industrial and financial rich were the first to sense this fact and to exploit it. Thus, despite the rarified atmosphere of wealth in which they lived, the rich tended to anticipate trends that would extend throughout America in the twentieth century with progresssively less reference to economic level. Sport became one of several important means for consuming surplus and for persuading Americans that they were indeed sharing in the nation's abundance.[34]

Since the ultra-rich on the one hand and the middle-class and the gentility on the other each considered themselves the guardians of amateurism, an analysis of their respective concerns in this matter helps to clarify their differing understandings of the role and impact of sport and so also to cast light on the conceptual contribution that was developing among the rich. As has been noted earlier, the great captains of industrial wealth, rather paradoxically, did not generally apply the precepts and values of industrial life to their sport. As a consequence, they adopted a relatively narrow and simple test of amateur status. Did the athlete live on money acquired in direct payment for his performance in a sport, whether in competition or as a professional instructor? This simple construction focused on the distinction between work and leisure as it applied in the individual case, and it associated amateurism with the idea of leisure. To their periodic embarrassment, the middle class and the gentility had much more complex notions with far more confusing implications.

Fearful of the supposedly corrupting effect of luxury on character, the respectable middle class and the gentility identified excessive concentration on sport as a form of luxury in itself, thus opposing themselves to the concept of the sportsman as it was emerging among the very rich. Though important to the whole man, sport remained only a part for the likes of Theodore Roosevelt or Dudley Sargent; and the exaggeration of sport thus threatened basic social values. Roosevelt said bluntly that the one-tracked athlete "becomes a bore, if nothing else." Writing in 1901, the perceptive historian and analyst of the athletic movement Henry D. Sheldon decried the fact that spectators and the press had debased sport by giving it more than its appropriate attention. As a result, undue interest in winning had been encouraged; and, with it, team captains and managers developed a cycle of lavish outfitting of players, special foods for them, the hiring of coaches, and the thorough distortion of the college experience for many athletes. Since some players were training four or five hours each day, Sheldon observed, they soon became unsuited to "anything more than nominal participation in the intellectual life of the college."[35]

At Harvard, the effort to stamp out professionalism centered on overseeing the membership on teams to ensure that only students in good standing were permitted to play and on resisting the hiring of coaches paid only for their training of athletes. Yet, in its 1897 report, Harvard's Committee on Physical Training, Athletic Sports, and Sanitary Condition of Buildings—which included Augustus Hemenway, Theodore Roosevelt, and Charles Francis Adams, Jr., among its members—acknowledged that players were provided all athletic equipment and clothing, received better food than other students without additional cost, and generally were accorded special treatment. On the other hand, the Committee urged that spectators, especially at football games, "be limited so far as possible to college men, and that the games be played only on college grounds," all with the aim of discouraging an unbalanced view of the place of athletics in one's life. In order to undercut a natural "tendency to extravagance," the Committee urged that no surplus of funds be allowed to accumulate, recommending that gate receipts in excess of operating expenses be channeled into the maintenance of athletic grounds and buildings.[36]

It is not lacking in irony, however, that Harvard alumni simultaneously pursued victory as a goal of ever greater desirability and importance. Undercutting the genteel critique of the rich, some 500 alumni gathered at Sanders Theater on January 26, 1898, to establish a new Graduate Athletic Association that would include members from all major segments of the university community and would give centralized governance to the athletic programs.[37] Regardless of the reasons for which they focused on the value of victory, the Graduate Athletic Association accorded institutional sanction to a more comprehensive and, arguably, excessive emphasis on sport. In the process, both the Association and the Hemenway Committee came perilously close to the practical policies of the ultra-rich—bar those who made their living through athletics, develop lavish facilities, and reinvest money into the physical plant of the sports programs. Even middle-class and genteel proponents of reform in collegiate athletics unknowingly flirted with the creed of the rich, as when E.L. Godkin protested Yale's playing a football game in New York City. Writing in 1893, Godkin warned that the choice of this venue made the "gambling fraternity and the prostitutes" among the most prominent of those in attendance and turned the event into "a spectacle for the multitudes." In one sense, such criticism aligned itself with the growing effort of college faculties and administrators to exert control over their students' sport; but it also showed similarity to the spirit of exclusiveness that characterized the sport of the rich.[38]

In its actual operations, the collegiate system was riddled much more with equivocation on the matter of amateurism, contamination by outsiders, and the role of sport than was the sporting behavior of the very rich. After all the noble pronouncements and the committee work, only financial sleight of hand permitted Harvard alumni to continue to think of themselves as guardians of the amateur spirit during the 1903-1904 collegiate sporting season. In one of the more imaginative examples of specious reasoning, they decided that their rowing coach F.D. Colson, who had been brought from Cornell for the season in order to share his winning ways, was "not technically to receive any remuneration for his services as a coach." But the Athletic Committee also said that it must "make good to him any loss of income incurred by the temporary surrender of his work at Cornell, as well as any extra expense involved in the trip" to the Boston area. The members of the Committee insisted that this arrangement was consistent with amateurism on the grounds that it gave Colson no official gain over his previous employment and because he professed a secondary interest in studying the methods of instruction at Harvard's law school. Nonetheless, Edwin H. Hall, who had already created a minor flurry with a letter to *The Nation* challenging the utility of a categorical ban on the receipt of money by amateurs for athletic performance, gave implicit support for Colson in the *Harvard Graduates' Magazine* of June, 1904. Hall insisted that the exchange of money was not really the problem. Instead, he returned to the conventional middle-class and genteel concerns over admitting "low morals, low intelligence, low aims, foul speech, bad manners, and trickiness" into collegiate sport by allowing persons other than regular candidates for a degree to play.[39] Seeking to have it both ways, the middle class and the gentility risked having neither.

Harvard was not alone in these problems, nor was the difficulty confined to the colleges. Fearing the evils of professionalism, Princeton and the University of Pennsylvania terminated the employment of their paid baseball coaches in 1906, with Harvard soon following their example. In *The Illustrated Outdoor News*, commentator Edward R. Bushnell showed more enthusiasm than insight in calling the move "a real innovation," since so-called graduates, or alumni, had often served as coaches during the late decades of the nineteenth century; yet his remark reflected the gnawing concern over the possible corruption of sport. Soon, however, this limited reform was imperiled when the three schools, along with

Yale, Cornell, and Columbia, faltered in competition with Georgetown, Amherst, Dartmouth, and Brown—none of which had agreed to abide by the ruling against paid coaches. Georgetown's own record was spotty enough, particularly due to a scandal in 1904 over the school's decision to retain its star pitcher Crumley, who had earlier played four games for the Indianapolis team of the Western League. Officials at Georgetown had focused on intent, saying that Crumley had played merely "for the fun of it" and not for pay. Meanwhile, Harvard kept players out of games if they had competed in an "open" format that mixed amateurs and professionals. Columbia University was forced to dismiss its football coach, R.P. Wilson, around the same time as the Crumley affair, for having included a "ringer" on the school's team. Seeking to clean up the athletic program, the University of Wisconsin experimented in 1904 with a special athletic society composed of varsity players who showed the pure amateur spirit. At Brown University, in the same year, a squabble took place between the Brown Corporation and the school's Athletic Board over the issue of including players who had been paid for summer games within the University Athletic Brotherhood.[40]

Among the urban clubs as well, there was confusion over the meaning of terms such as *amateur, commercial, professional,* and *spectator;* and efforts to agree upon definitions usually failed miserably. As Samuel Crowther, Jr., observed retrospectively in 1905, the separation of the amateur from the "petty professional" was a tricky business; for, in fact, amateurism in the sense that Crowther meant it was largely a creation of the late nineteenth century. Without regulation of competitors in rowing, Crowther warned, the professionals would "drive every gentleman out of the sport"; and true amateur rowing would cease to exist. Yet the efforts of groups such as the National Association of Amateur Oarsmen, founded in 1872, normally met with limited success. Despite chiding of "masquerading amateurs," actual professionals continued to row; and the confusion of interests among oarsmen led many clubs into a long decline from 1885 into the twentieth century. Among the middle class and the gentility, where motivations were many and complex, the struggle to develop workable rules to govern and strengthen amateur competition was endless. Sportswriter J. Parmly Paret, commenting in 1906 on the Amateur Hockey League's ruling that five Canadian players were being paid by the Brooklyn Skating Club and hence must be barred from competition, summarized the sense of frustration and the suggestion of despair: "The greed of graft is a different kind in ice-hockey from that which has undermined the morals of most basketball players and many track athletes. The managers of the teams are much more at fault than the players themselves, and it is they who hold out the golden apple of temptation..." It was not merely a problem of a few bad individuals; the system itself seemed at fault.[41]

The very clarity of the sporting system among the rich made it possible for them to avoid the ambivalence, ambiguity, and occasional sophistry that plagued the exponents of middle class and genteel virtues. Wealth—not virtue—was its own reward; and it was association with wealth that kept a sport worthy of further interest. At the same time, wealth served to guard and insulate a sport so that it remained not only limited in clientele but rarified in its social role. The rear-guard action of the rich in fending off the "sandbaggers" and preserving social distinction in yachting stands as an example of their successful defensive action. Whatever social benefit the very rich saw in sport was "social" only in the small sense, serving to sharpen lines of status.[42] But the effects of sport in individual gratification, in what Veblen called a renewed "clannishness," and in activity-oriented leisure were numerous and systemic. Untroubled by issues of moral purpose, the rich thus established the prototype of the sportsman as an unrestricted consumer.

What the defenders of the older tradition criticized as "monomania" in sport, whether among the rich or among the professionals, passed as a form of virtue among the ultra-rich. The wealthy Americans luxuriated in expensive yachts, "Sybaritic" clubs, and costly holidays. Yet the middle class and the gentility proved ineffective in stamping out their influence. In part, this may have been due to self-contradiction, as when Theodore Roosevelt expressed his belief that most men lived within forty-eight hours of a wilderness area and need only choose a companion to set out for a month in the wild. His glib prescription and its presupposition that the man could afford both the trip and any attendant loss of income suggest the limits of democratic thought and opportunity among the middle class and the gentility. At least the very rich made the best of it, turning a rather vulgar instinct for display into a form of candor. Thus impervious to the internally flawed arguments of their critics, the rich stood as a significant point of gravitation within the realm of sport and so also as a constituency lending sport an aura of legitimacy. It is an enduring irony that, given their privileged and powerful position, they had a largely radical effect, which finally touched the mass of Americans just as deeply as did the self-appointed protectors of American values.

Notes

1. Hofstadter, *Social Darwinism in American Thought* states the concept of status anxiety. Bannister, *Social Darwinism* is its sharpest and best critique. Persons, *The Decline of American Gentility* remains useful. The pertinent point here is not how much socioeconomic difference there was among groups nor how uniformly they divided along class lines or family background, but rather that there were differences in sensibility—obvious in behavior and the literature about it—which appeared inside class lines and across them. In short, the structure of society is less the issue there than the patterns of mentality; and , although often related, they are not always so. Nor are they identical.

2. Boyle, *Sport—Mirror of American Life* recognizes the role of the very rich in advancing certain sports. Significantly, he doubts that his readers will believe him.

3. Veblen, *The Theory of the Leisure Class,* especially 255-72. Also see Collier, *England and the English from an American Point of View,* 288; Martin, *The Passing of the Idle Rich,* 6.

4. "Fox Hunting in an Automobile," 10.

5. *Illustrated Outdoor News* 1 (Dec. 1906).

6. Thomas, "Teaching Baseball," 7.

7. Spalding, *American's National Game,* 6.

8. Barney, "The American Sportswoman," 276.

9. Macdonald, *Scotland's Gift.*

10. Curry, "Yachting as a Sport for the People," 10-11. Also see Spahr, *An Essay on the Present Distribution of Wealth;* King et al., *The Wealth and Income of the People of the United States.* In 1904, when Curry called yachting universal, bacon cost 18 cents per pound, butter 28 cents, sugar 30 cents, and a five-pound sack of flour sold for 16 cents. In short, the industrial worker of 1904 could buy and use a small power launch if he ceased eating, spent nothing on shelter, had no medical expenses, and used the boat rarely enough to keep his fuel bill low.

11. Curry, "Yachting as a Sport for the People," 10-11.

12. O'Hagan, "The Athletic Girl," 734-35.

13. Barney, "The American Sportswoman," 268, 269-73, passim.

14. Ibid., 265-66.

15. Burton, "Hats and Boots for the Sportswoman," 18-19; "Modish Raiment for the Sportswoman," 16.

16. Barney, "The American Sportswoman," 266.

17. "The Sportswoman," 16.

18. Strong, "Great Britain's Famous Women of the Hunt," 8-9.

19. "Dogs of High Degree and Their Titled Mistresses," 8-9.

20. Sargent, "Ideals in Physical Education," 223.

21. See Chandler, *Strategy and Structure* for a consideration of vertical and horizontal integration in context of American business.

22. I am indebted to David D. Wiggins for references to the accounts of nineteenth-century travelers in America.

23. See Bradley, *Such Was Saratoga* for its role as a resort.

24. Bledstein, *The Culture of Professionalism* discusses the concept of enclosure in "Space and Words," 46-79. Bledstein specifically refers to sporting spaces, such as stadiums and country clubs, 6off.

25. Van Rensselaer, *Newport,* provides much information on life during the fashionable summer seasons.

26. Ibid., passim.

27. Even the Prince of Wales was unable to arrange for Sir Thomas's admission into the Royal Yacht Squadron.

28. "Scenes from Sporting Life," in O'Connor, *The Golden Summers* is valuable.

29. Morgan is quoted in O'Connor, *The Golden Summer,* 131.

30. Elliott is quoted in ibid., 135.

31. The phrase comes from an obituary of tennis champion "Dicky" Sears, quoted in ibid., 146.

32. See Persons, *The Decline of American Gentility,* 43, 50, 65.

33. Allen, *The Great Pierpont Morgan,* 188-94; Satterlee, *J. Pierpont Morgan.* A useful and engaging study suggesting the social role of leisure and sport in Hoyt, *The Vanderbilts and Their Fortunes.*

34. Potter, *People of Plenty* deserves attention as a way of modifying Frederic Paxson's application of the concept of the "safety valve" to sport. Much as Potter suggests that the contours of American character were formed with respect to abundance, one may profitably assess how abundance has shaped American sport.

35. Sheldon, *Student Life and Customs,* 232-35, 237-38. Also see Roosevelt, "'Professionalism' in Sports," 187, 190-91.

36. Hemenway et al., "Important Suggestions in Athletics," 191-96.

37. Gardiner, "The Graduate Athletic Association," 344-51. Also see Sargent, "Ideals in Physical Education," 221-23.

38. Godkin, "'The Atlantic Monthly," 422-23.

39. See "Rowing," a subsection in the "Athletics" column, *Harvard Graduates' Magazine* 12 (March 1904) 449; Hall, "The Money Rule in Athletics"; Hall, "The Pitfall of Athletics."

40. Bushness, "With the College Athletes," 14.

41. Crowther and Ruhl, *Rowing and Track Athletics,* 161-62, 164, 169ff, 178ff. The extended quotation is from Paret, "Importing Canadian Professionals for Ice Hockey," 8.

42. Roosevelt, "'Professionalism' in Sports," 188-89.

CHAPTER 7

CREATING AMERICA'S WINTER GOLFING MECCA AT PINEHURST, NORTH CAROLINA

National Marketing and Local Control

■ *Larry R. Youngs* ■

In early November of 1900, at the beginning of the winter resort season, *The Pinehurst Outlook* proclaimed that "the popularity of golf still continues in the ascendant, rolling over the country like a great tidal wave and gaining power as it advances, and [a] high water mark seems farther away than ever." The resort weekly alerted potential visitors to the fact that Pinehurst's gentle, winter climate and "well-kept" golf courses "afford ideal conditions for indulging in this fascinating game."[1] Reflecting golf's increasing popularity, in early April of 1901, the winter colony in Pinehurst held its first annual golf tournament for the United South and North Championship. Organizers scheduled the competition to mark the end of the resort's winter season.[2] Pinehurst regular Henry Haynie "invented" the tournament and, in support of the event, Pinehurst owner James Tufts "gave eight beautiful prizes in the finest silver, and five or six other prizes." Sixteen men and fourteen women competed, with George Dutton of Boston winning the men's title and Mrs. Harry G. Parker of Philadelphia taking first prize for the women's event. Males and females competed together in other "skill" contests, with a man winning the long-driving event and women taking the honors in the approaching and putting competitions. Believing the resort weekly's assertion that "large numbers of golfers make an annual pilgrimage to the Southern States for the sole purpose of enjoying their favorite game," Tufts began to make every effort to accommodate such people.[3]

Article appears by permission of the *Journal of Sport History*.

Like so many aspects of the south Atlantic states' winter-resort industry during the late nineteenth and early twentieth centuries, golf evolved according to the continual interactions between developers and their guests—producers and consumers. This assertion places my analysis of the winter resorts within the continuing scholarly investigation of the commercialization of leisure. Historians have analyzed this ongoing process on a national scale, largely focusing on what Richard Butsch calls questions of "power, domination, and resistance" in terms of "mass culture, popular culture, and working-class culture."[4] A handful of historians have turned their attention to the analysis of leisure and recreation among the upper classes, however, especially in terms of elite Americans frequenting the nation's spas, mineral springs, and seaside and mountain retreats.[5] And though scholars continue to contribute insightful, new perspectives on summer vacationing, regional tourism, the development of specific resorts, and the activities of certain entrepreneurs in the resort industry, inadequate attention has been given to the nexus between the advertising and marketing of elite sports and the emergence and development of tourism in the south Atlantic states.[6]

The premier winter resorts in Florida, Georgia, and the Carolinas offer clear examples of how wealthy, white Northerners responded to resort owners' entrepreneurial efforts to use sport in shaping their elite clientele's leisure activities. At no place was this truer than at Pinehurst, North Carolina. There, the Tufts family cultivated an ideal environment for golfers that, in turn, attracted Northern tourists and commuters interested particularly in playing the game. As more golfers congregated at Pinehurst, first James Tufts and, subsequently, his son Leonard and grandson Richard increasingly catered to the golfers' tastes in terms of what constituted the ideal resort. Unlike the typical country club that drew its membership exclusively from a local population, Pinehurst attracted golfers from across the nation and from eastern Canada. In effect, the Tufts family developed Pinehurst into a nationally recognized public arena where golfers acted out their ideals about the game and, in the process, created a winter colony with golf as its core.

At Pinehurst, as well as at other premier winter resorts in the south Atlantic states, golf gradually took on greater cultural significance than being just another sport or recreational pastime. Resorters and, especially, Northern commuters increasingly used the game to shape their social patterns, their everyday practices, and the evolving "sense of place" that they cultivated while at their favorite retreat and at winter resorts in general.[7] Indirectly, John R. Stilgoe's investigation of New England "borderlands" furnishes a theoretical framework that helps place the winter resorts within a trans-regional context. A key to Stilgoe's work concerns his novel use of the idea of commuting. By defining commute as "to mitigate or to lessen," Stilgoe argues persuasively that for a variety of city dwellers the act of commuting was a "spatial means of grappling with and lessening the difficulties of urbanization and, especially, urbanization based on industrial and corporate capitalism." Similarly, I argue that certain men and women frequented winter resorts in an effort to extend geographically and augment temporally the practice of "mitigating or lessening" the negative aspects they associated with living in industrial America. Thus, seasonal retreats became an enduring method of coping with modernization.[8]

Unlike typical tourists interested in novel locales that could produce fleeting encounters of the picturesque, the curious, and even the exciting, those who traveled to the South as commuters valued more predictable experiences and environs that evoked a familiar sense of place. At such Southern borderlands, resort developers and their Northern guests joined together in cultivating an ambience that preserved delicate balances between urban and rural, private and social, traditional and modern. Although many efforts were made, few winter resort communities ever realized these ideal criteria, and fewer still maintained such standards for extended periods of time. In a handful of southern locales, however, places like Thomasville, Georgia, Aiken, South Carolina, Palm Beach, Florida, and Pinehurst, North Carolina, affluent, white commuters joined idyllic seasonal colonies, or more accurately, "lifestyle enclaves." According to sociologist Robert N. Bellah, the concept of lifestyle "is linked most closely to leisure and consumption...It brings together those who are socially, economically, or culturally similar, and one of its chief aims is the enjoyment of being with those who 'share one's lifestyle.'" A lifestyle enclave is distinct from a traditional community, explains Bellah, in that, "whereas a community attempts to be an inclusive whole, celebrating the interdependence of public and private life and of different callings of all, lifestyles are fundamentally segmental and celebrate the narcissism of similarity."[9] By applying Bellah's definitions to the analysis of the winter resorts, I propose a more nuanced method for understanding one segment of society's reactions to modernization. Specifically, I will use the golfing lifestyle that resorters and their hosts cultivated at Pinehurst, North Carolina, as an example of how and, perhaps why, people formed such enclaves.

Because the vast majority of golf courses built in the United States before World War II were created by the members of private country clubs, understandably, contemporary observers and scholars have treated the rise of American golf as synonymous with the emergence and proliferation of these clubs. In 1900, social critic E.S. Martin wrote in *Harper's Weekly* that "country clubs are the result of the centralization of population, the increase of wealth, and the discovery of America by the game of golf." He explained that, originally as a pragmatic reflection of the British nobility's country estates, elite city dwellers in America formed country clubs around their interest in outdoor recreation, especially equestrian sports such as fox hunting, polo, and coaching. Because these activities were so expensive, claimed Martin, such country clubs "never would have sprung up everywhere, and established themselves as social institutions. What was needed was a sport for all ages of men and some ages of women that would attract, amuse, and refresh and afford a new object in country life. Then came golf."[10] Two years after Martin's article appeared, Frank Arnett concurred with his colleague explaining that "golf, while not the initial cause of the birth of the country club, has been the strongest individual factor in its growth."[11]

Historians have also viewed the game in terms of the country club, under-standing golf in a geographically narrow manner and as developing essentially as a private enterprise. Typically, scholars have characterized golfers as local elites who used the game merely for purposes of enhancing their social status, displaying their wealth through conspicuous consumption, and excluding the masses.[12] Such explanations provide accurate insights into power relations based on class, race, and, to a lesser extent, gender and heritage, but fail to treat golfers on their own terms—as sport enthusiasts, ardent competitors, and impressionable consumers.[13] Steven Riess acknowledges that country club "members got not only peace of mind but also a strong sense of identity, of belonging, and of stability."[14] Richard J. Moss offers a welcome analysis of the game's history in *Golf and the American Country Club*, where he offers the keen insight that "golf and the country clubs where it was played involved much more than a struggle between open, equal access and the personal freedom to exclude undesirables from a private institution."[15] Likewise, James M. Mayo has broadened our understanding of the game's development in the United States by analyzing three entwined factors in golf's growing popularity among upper-class city dwellers: the emergence of country living at nearby summer resorts, the gradual acceptance of certain appropriate sports such as golf, and the technological advances that helped make suburban living so popular. For Mayo, these factors culminated in the proliferation of privately financed, local country clubs.[16]

By the 1920s, estimates indicate that nearly two million male and female golfers supported a thriving, multi-million dollar industry. Such enthusiasm for the game suggests motives beyond mere emulation, social posturing, and pecuniary wastefulness. What contemporary observers largely ignored—like most urban and sport historians—was the symbiotic relationship between the rise of American golf and the emergence and development of the winter resorts.[17] This correlation helps explain the game's growth within a trans-regional context. Spatially, golf played at the winter resorts loosened the game's dependence on city and suburb. Temporally, playing winter golf in southern climates allowed enthusiasts to enjoy the game year round. And culturally, the winter resorts provided public arenas at which men and women from across the country par-ticipated in socially constructing a North American "community" of golfers, as well as using the game to form elite golfing enclaves.

During the 1890s, golf enthusiasts and developers laid out crude, nine-hole golf courses in Southern resort towns such as Thomasville, Aiken, and St. Augustine, Florida, as well as at such independent and self-contained resorts as Jekyll Island, Georgia, Palm Beach, and Pinehurst. Over the next three decades, entrepreneurs worked to generate interest in winter golf by expanding most existing courses from nine to eighteen holes, building additional courses, and continually improving course conditions and golfing facilities.[18]

Less than a decade before the game appeared at the winter resorts, no officially recognized golf course existed in the United States. John Reid, a Scottish busi-nessman who settled in Yonkers, New York, distinguished himself by gaining recognition as the first to transplant the ancient game successfully to American soil. In 1888, Reid recruited four of his friends, later to be known as the "Old Apple Tree Gang," and named his newly organized club, St. Andrews Golf Club. According to golf historian H.B. Martin, Reid had reasoned that "the famous old St. Andrews Club was the cradle of golf in Scotland and its namesake in America might well serve the same purpose."[19] Reid could never have anticipated the swiftness and extent with which his example would be duplicated. By 1895, in what one observer described as the "Yonkers movement," novice American golfers had established seventy-four golf courses in nineteen states. Then, during the last three years of the nineteenth century, as the American economy rebounded from the depression that began in 1893, the number of golf courses and players sky rocketed as Americans formed clubs throughout the nation. By 1900, according to Geoffrey Cornish and Ronald Whitten, "the number of golf courses multiplied to 982, with at least one course in all forty-five states." By the mid 1930s, one of the country's leading golf magazines, *Golf Illustrated*, boasted that the number of American golf clubs had soared to 3,900 by 1923 and 5,300 by 1933.[20]

Of course, no one could have predicted that Tufts's North Carolina village in the Southern pines would develop into one of the nation's leading golf resorts. H.B. Martin contended that "the story of Pinehurst and how, by accident more than by planning, it grew to become the [M]ecca of golf in the Southland reads like a romance."[21] It was a romance, however, that unfolded according to myriad decisions acted upon by a complex array of real people. Initially, the resort's founder, James Tufts, knew nothing of golf. Before Pinehurst's third season (1897-1898), however, he allowed his son Leonard, a novice of the game, and Dr. Leroy Culver, a supposed "expert" from New York City, to lay out the resort's first, primitive nine-hole course on sixty acres located within easy walking distance of the village green.[22]

From the start, the game attracted much attention among the resort's visitors. During the following summer, Tufts acted upon his instinctive business acumen and "thoroughly overhauled" the golf course, built a simple clubhouse to accommodate players and spectators, and hired a golf professional from Scotland, John Dunn Tucker, to manage the golf course and facilities. In November of 1900, *The Pinehurst Outlook* commented that after all the improvements Tufts had made the previous season, from the golfers' point of view, "it would seem that nothing more could be desired." But the resort weekly also pointed out that "golf was undoubtedly the most popular pastime in the village last winter, and every pleasant day found the grounds thronged with enthusiastic players."[23] Tufts sensed that he had stumbled onto a means of enhancing Pinehurst's reputation as a popular winter resort, and he was not about to rest on his laurels. During the remaining few years of his life, Tufts continued to develop Pinehurst in ways calculated to appeal to America's golf enthusiasts. As an indirect incentive to America's golfers, for example, he constructed the resort's fourth hotel, The Carolina, which *The Pinehurst Outlook* described as "the state's largest and most modern hotel." Originally, Tufts had built the Holly Inn, several boarding houses, and numerous cottages to offer modest and affordable accommodations to the mostly middle-class teachers, preachers, and businessmen he targeted as his potential clientele. The Carolina's luxurious amenities and charges of four dollars per day and "upwards" better suited the resort's increasing number of upper-class customers, including the affluent members of exclusive country clubs in the North who wanted to play golf during the winter.[24] In a more direct manner, Tufts took several actions designed to entice such golfers. First, he remodeled Pinehurst's clubhouse. He added separate dressing rooms for men and women, constructed wide piazzas around the building's lower level, enclosed the second-story observation room for players and spectators, and built a separate structure for the caddies. He extended the original nine-hole course to eighteen holes that stretched over one hundred fifty acres of "hill and dale." In the summer of 1900, he hired a new Scottish professional, Donald J. Ross, to rebuild the existing course and to layout a second "championship" course, beginning with nine holes. He also commissioned craftsmen to create numerous cups and trophies to be awarded to the victors in a series of regularly scheduled tournaments for both men and women.[25] Finally, in consultation with advertising agent, Frank Presbrey, he initiated a national campaign that promoted Pinehurst as a golf resort. For example, using prominent illustrations and one bold headline that announced the resort's "two splendid golf courses," Tufts had Presbrey place an advertisement in *Scribner's Magazine* that signified the transformation at work in Tufts's vision of the ideal resort. Increasingly, Tufts depended on the patronage of golfers who, apparently, shifted his attention away from the less affluent New Englanders he originally intended to help recuperate. In pursuing this new strategy, Tufts increasingly relied on Ross for advice about developing the resort's golf facilities and Presbrey concerning promotional policies. These two men would spend the remainder of their lives helping the Tufts family carefully craft a reputation for Pinehurst as *the* winter haven for America's golfers.

At the turn of the twentieth century, however, Tufts faced stiff competition from other developers vying for the patronage of Northern golfers. Numerous winter resorts had begun offering golf several years before Pinehurst, which put Tufts at a seeming disadvantage.[26] In 1900, Scottish golfer John Duncan Dunn ignored Pinehurst in an article he wrote for *Outing* that chronicled his tour of golf courses from Virginia to Florida; a journey that included visits to such winter resorts as Aiken, Thomasville, and Palm Beach.[27] Later in the same season, however, Tufts enticed British golfer, Harry Vardon—arguably the world's most famous champion of the time—to make an appearance at Pinehurst for purposes of publicity. While on his own tour of America's Eastern golf courses, Vardon accepted Tufts's invitation to play several exhibition rounds at Pinehurst. Although it would be his only visit to the North Carolina Sandhills, Vardon's fame brought national exposure to the resort's little-known golf course. Shortly after his appearance, he wrote a brief letter of thanks to his host that Tufts printed in *The Pinehurst Outlook*. Vardon complimented Pinehurst's course for being "very sporty," having "excellent" distances, and "well-placed" hazards. He also predicted that "by next season, when the new ground becomes thoroughly hardened and the present growth of turf becomes more firmly set, you will have 18 holes which it will be a great pleasure to any golfer to play over, and in my judgment [sic] on which will compare very favorably with any of the Eastern courses."[28] Such a seemingly generous and timely endorsement surely influenced Northern golfers to give Pinehurst a try which, in turn, encouraged Tufts to pursue his plan of making Pinehurst into what a 1901 observer, Harry Redan, called "a golfer's paradise."[29]

James Tufts's emerging vision about his resort's future ultimately came to fruition after his death. In February of 1902, his son Leonard inherited all of Pinehurst but did not take direct control of the resort until 1906. During the intervening years, he pursued his career as a mechanical engineer at the American Soda Fountain Company while salaried superintendents managed Pinehurst each season. With the continued support and expertise of Ross and Presbrey, however, Leonard Tufts gradually committed himself to his father's strategy of tying the resort's success to golf. Over the next quarter century, he developed Pinehurst into a world-renowned haven for golfers that surpassed everyone's expectations.[30] As early as 1910, boasting of three golf courses, *The Pinehurst Outlook* stated that "golf and Pinehurst are synonymous wherever the game is known." As increasing numbers of golfers—recreational and competitive, amateur and professional, male and female—congregated at the resort each winter, certain commuters formed a lifestyle enclave that shaped the resort's standards of taste according to their own values and practices. The resort weekly explained that "when we have pressed home the fact that Pinehurst is not all competitive golf, that its players are not all experts, that golf is even the favorite diversion of those who do not play and the Country Club the rendezvous of the entire Village, you have the whole story."[31] This depiction may have been accurate, but it did not explain the factors that coalesced in making it true. How and why did golf take such firm root and flourish at this isolated resort in the Sandhills of North Carolina?

To begin with, it was pure serendipity that James Tufts chose to develop his health resort in a location that proved so naturally suited for golf. Many years later, having earned fame and fortune as the "dean" of American golf course architecture, Donald Ross stated that in deciding upon an appropriate locale to build a golf course, "soil conditions should be of very first importance." He went on to explain that "a sandy loam is by far the very best golfing soil. It provides good drainage and ideal conditions for strong, enduring growth of desirable grasses. It likewise furnishes the exact conditions necessary for the proper playing conditions of golf strokes."[32] Not until Tufts brought the young Scot to Pinehurst did anyone fully realize how perfect the locale's conditions were for golf. From the first season that Ross worked for Tufts, the two men developed a mutually beneficial strategy for realizing the game's potential in Pinehurst. With Tufts's philanthropic sense and the resources to support his endeavors, he provided the setting and circumstances that inspired Ross's artistry and leadership within the American golf movement for the next fifty years. Although each man valued North Carolina's Sandhills for distinctive reasons, their goals and methods complimented one another. Tufts never lost sight of his original intent of providing for over-worked Northerners an opportunity to recuperate in the bucolic setting he created at Pinehurst. While cultivating his belief in the therapeutic value of outdoor activities, Tufts welcomed the addition of golf as one more dignified and health-giving pastime that his guests could enjoy. Ross's approach to the game meshed well with Tufts's tactic of using moderate levels of exercise to rehabilitate people suffering from the physical and mental stresses of modern living. To aid such people in regaining their fitness and vitality, Ross advocated playing golf at a brisk pace, over hilly terrain, and in all types of weather, but he also believed that a properly designed golf course "exercised" a player's "mental control." For nearly fifty years, Ross applied his creative genius toward designing Pinehurst's golf courses in ways that would meet the needs of every type of golfer.[33]

As religious men opposed to alcohol and gambling, Tufts and Ross agreed that Pinehurst should serve a "morally-sound" and "socially-respectable" clientele. While Tufts trusted in the recommendations of local clergymen and community leaders, Ross placed his faith in the natural instincts of people attracted to golf. Ross insisted that since "the game does more to bring out the finer points in a man's character than any other sport….[A] country which gets golf-minded need not worry about the honor, the integrity and the honesty of its people." Ross appreciated Tufts's New England-style village as an ideal environment in which to convert right-minded Americans to the benefits of golf, and Tufts became convinced that the game of golf, as conceived by Ross, seemed a perfect outdoor activity for attracting the right kind of people to the resort. The contributions each man brought to Pinehurst promised significant dividends for themselves and their clientele. But the two men worked together for only three seasons, hardly enough time to establish Pinehurst's reputation as a Mecca for golfers.[34]

Rather, the resort's great success would emanate from the collaborative energies of Ross and Leonard Tufts. Similar in age, these men shared a conservative approach to business, a common-sense attitude about life, and a fervent work ethic that

Donald Ross was one of golf's most famous architects. He designed some 400 courses, including Pinehurst's Legendary No. 2.

Photo courtesy of Tufts Archives, Pinehurst, NC.

enabled them to transform Pinehurst into one of America's favorite winter playgrounds. Perhaps most importantly, however, they shared a passion for golf. For Tufts and Ross, the game became more than a metaphor for life; in a very real sense, golf literally fashioned their careers and defined their seasonal lifestyles.[35]

As an astute businessman, however, Tufts knew better than to rely exclusively on golf to ensure the retreat's continued success. Like his father, he developed Pinehurst as a winter resort that served a variety of peoples' recreational interests. Frank Presbrey took a leading role in crafting this strategy. Working from his offices on Park Avenue in New York City, he orchestrated Pinehurst's national advertising campaign by emphasizing the resort's wide range of recreational amenities. One slogan he developed read: "The Center of Winter Out-of-Door Life in the Middle South." His advertisements always emphasized golf as the resort's premier attraction, but they also mentioned Pinehurst's climate, accommodations, and other sporting facilities such as the private shooting preserve, skeet range, livery stable, and tennis courts. In a 1920 memorandum that summarized the preceding year's promotional budget—more than seventy-thousand dollars—Presbrey divided Pinehurst's account into six sections: booklets and circulars (16.4%), prizes and trophies (15.1%), newspaper publicity (12.3%), advertising in magazines and newspapers (15.1%), exhibitions and entertainments (37.1%), and a miscellaneous category (2.7%) that "includ[ed] special correspondence." A breakdown of advertising mediums included such magazines as *Vogue, Life, Town and Country,* and *Vanity Fair,* several travel magazines, general sporting magazines, publications from Harvard and Yale Universities, and six golf magazines. The listing of newspapers included the leading dailies from most major cities in the Northeast and Midwest. This extensive and complex campaign indicates Tufts's monetary commitment toward promoting Pinehurst on a trans-regional scale. The campaign also reflected the competitive nature of the sport and leisure industry during the early decades of the twentieth century.[36]

To back up the resort's promotional promises, Tufts invested heavily in developing Pinehurst into a haven for a certain segment of America's sporting enthusiasts—those with the necessary time, disposable wealth, and proper heritage.[37] As the advertisements indicated, Pinehurst offered those welcomed as guests a wide range of outdoor activities. Hunters could enjoy a private, forty-thousand-acre game preserve with guides and dogs available to ensure a successful outing. Tufts accommodated trap shooters with a large and well-equipped range, skeet tournaments, and expert instruction. Between 1914 and 1922, Annie Oakley, the famous sharpshooter, gave exhibitions and taught shooting and hunting, while her husband Frank Butler managed the skeet range. To entice enthusiasts of equestrian sports, Pinehurst offered a complete livery stable, a network of bridle paths for horseback riding, three manicured polo grounds, a track for thoroughbred and harness racing, and frequent drags and fox hunts. Tennis fans could enjoy playing a friendly match on the resort's clay courts, entering any number of regularly-scheduled tournaments, and watching exhibitions between many of the nation's finest competitors. Still, the

Ross-designed golf courses and the resort's annual golf tournaments remained Pinehurst's premier attractions.[38]

In terms of Pinehurst's development, a crucial distinction between Leonard Tufts and his father was that Leonard was a golfer. For him, the game would serve as more than just another pastime for Pinehurst's visitors. As a golf enthusiast himself, the younger Tufts agreed with Ross that the best strategy for creating their ideal resort involved gaining the loyalty of golfers like themselves. Within five years of his father's death, Tufts made three decisions that placed golf at the pinnacle of Pinehurst's sporting hierarchy and that enhanced the prestige of those commuters who embraced the game. Even before the younger Tufts had decided to make the development of Pinehurst his life's work, he formalized golf at the resort. In October of 1903 at his office in Boston, Tufts, Harry B. Emery, his brother-in-law, and Donald Ross, officially organized the Pinehurst Golf Club. Their stated purpose was "the promotion and advancement of the game of golf and the maintenance of the links at Pinehurst." The club charter provided for regular and associate memberships depending on the duration of the golfer's stay in Pinehurst. Regular members were those commuters who wintered at the resort and who paid seasonal dues, while associate members visited the resort for only part of the season and paid lesser dues. Only the regular members could hold office in the club or vote on matters concerning the governance of play, rules, handicaps, and maintenance of the courses.[39]

To encourage club members to winter in Pinehurst for its entire season—from mid November until late April—in 1905, Tufts broke with his father's precedent by selling a lot and cottage to one of the annual commuters. Over the next two decades, he selectively sold numerous properties to those he believed fit into the seasonal enclave. Ross and Presbrey both became homeowners in Pinehurst as did many of the golf club's regular members.[40] In a letter of support for Tufts's recommendation to increase golf dues for associate members but not for regular members, Ross stated that "it is a good policy to encourage those who think well enough of Pinehurst to come for the whole season and we ought to encourage people who are likely to buy homes."[41] As business associates, Tufts and Ross continued to profit from the tourist trade, but as avid sportsmen they increasingly embraced their golfing lifestyle.[42]

Tufts's third decision gave Pinehurst's golfing commuters an institutional framework for strengthening their hegemony within the seasonal enclave. In 1907, Tufts and his fellow officers in the Pinehurst Golf Club inaugurated what they called the "Pinehurst System." They adopted this new set of rules to regulate tournament entries and their handicaps—issues of fairness and integrity. One section of the Pinehurst System read: "Should any entrant not be a member of any regularly organized Golf Club, be will he classified at the discretion of the Committee." The effect of this provision was to encourage certain types of golfers to participate in Pinehurst's numerous tournaments while discouraging others. The system enhanced an obvious class distinction between players who could afford to belong to a private club and those who could not. More was at stake, however, than mere wealth and social status. The committee members charged with interpreting and enforcing the rules used their authority to restrict Pinehurst's tournaments to only those people they considered authentic golfers—that is, players who seemed equally committed to perpetuating what the committee members perceived as the integrity of the game. With Tufts as the Golf Club's president, Ross as a charter member, and Presbrey serving on the Board of Governors, these "producers" joined together with the resort's "consumers" in forming Pinehurst's distinctive lifestyle enclave. Tufts, Ross, Presbrey, and their fellow club members entwined issues of character, camaraderie, and competition as they participated in cultivating their community of golfers.[43]

During the 1910s and 1920s, tournament play dominated the golfing scene at the winter resorts. As competitors and spectators, many resorters expressed keen interest in formal competitions and developers responded by scheduling a series of tournaments for men and women, experts and novices, amateurs and professionals. The resort weeklies facilitated the process by printing tournament schedules in advance, identifying all players entering each competition, specifying the types of prizes to be awarded, and covering the actual tournaments by listing all scores or match results depending on the format of the event. Featured matches received even greater scrutiny in the form of hole-by-hole accounts printed in the resort weeklies and, sometimes, photographs of the contestants playing before attentive spectators. A key component of this process seemed to be the publication of players' names, usually accompanied by mention of their Northern affiliation. Early on this meant their hometown, but as more resorters became devotees of the game, players were more commonly identified as members of a specific country club. Thus, by competing in a resort tournament as a representative of their golf club, men and women gained public recognition as authentic golfers.

Operating simultaneously on local, regional, and national levels, competitive golf shaped the game's cultural meaning in the early part of the twentieth century. First, the barrage of articles published about golf tournaments helped disseminate the language of golf. For example, to follow the description of a typical match, readers needed to understand the names and functions of the different clubs each player used. That is, one had to know that a deck was used for lengthy approaches to the greens and a mashie for shorter shots, while a putter was used to roll the ball into the hole once on the green. The golfers' language included scoring terms such as bogey, birdie, and par; competitive formats such as four-ball, match play, and medal play; and elements of etiquette such as honors, playing through, and being away. To gain entry into the golfer's world, even as a spectator, it was necessary to become fluent in the game's terminology; it was not sufficient, however, to make one a golfer. That also required proficiency in hitting the ball, observing the proper etiquette, following the rules and, even, dressing the part.

For both developers and many visitors, tournaments at the winter resorts were seen as public arenas where men and women congregated with their peers to demonstrate their ability to "stand the gaff." In essence, one competed as a display of camaraderie and, in the process, each player supposedly revealed their character. Imagine the scene. As fifty or sixty fashionably-dressed spectators silently watched, a young, African-American caddy wearing shoes, a coat, and hat scooped out a handful of sand from a bucket positioned next to the wooden-framed box of hard-packed earth that served as the first tee. The caddy formed a small pyramid with the sand and gently placed the player's golf ball on top. Immediately following this ritual, the appropriately garbed golfer stepped onto the tee box—much like stepping onto a stage—and hit his or her first drive. The entire match would be played under the scrutiny of other players, the caddies, spectators, and perhaps, a reporter or two. Whether playing poorly or one's best, winning or losing a match, supposedly, the test of the real golfer was being able to perform with dignity and decorum.[44]

During the early years of the twentieth century, upper-class men and women enjoyed few such opportunities to publicly display their athleticism. The game did not demand feats of strength or undignified physical exertion, but players walked several miles, hit the ball between seventy and one hundred fifty times in eighteen holes, and a typical match took at least three hours to complete. By simply participating in a tournament, one earned a minimal amount of recognition as an authentic golfer. Playing according to the rules and following the proper etiquette gained one even greater respect. And to compete with skill, to defeat an opponent, or to win a tournament merited admiration from one's fellow golfers and, perhaps, earned the player a sterling cup or silver medal to prove one's prowess to friends and club members back home.

By organizing tournaments into divisions where players with comparable skills competed against one another, or by using handicaps to balance scoring between different caliber players, resort developers enhanced their guests' opportunities to win. During Pinehurst's 1910-1911 season, for example, Tufts sponsored twelve tournaments. In late November, the season opened with six prizes awarded to men competing in The Seventh Annual Autumn Tournament. At mid season, women competed for nine prizes in the Fifth Annual St. Valentine's Tournament for Women, while the men took away twenty-one awards in the Eighth Annual Midwinter Tournament. Two "open" tournaments allowed professionals to compete for three cash prizes respectively. Toward the end of the season, the resort held its premier event, the Eleventh Annual North and South Amateur Championship where again, male competitors captured twenty-one different awards. Throughout that season, hundreds of men and women competed for no less than one hundred thirty three sterling cups, gold and silver medals, and cash awards.[45] The ample opportunities to compete and win prizes attracted players with few skills, as well as the country's best male and female amateurs and professionals.[46] In particular, the three North and South championships—the women's, the men's amateur, and the open—gained prominence on the American golfing scene. By the 1920s, H.B. Martin stated that the two amateur events "have acquired importance and dignity with the years," and the North and South Open "has always been considered the most important of all the winter open events."[47] Tufts justified promoting these prestigious annual tournaments as the best means of serving Pinehurst's clientele and, at the same time, generating valuable publicity for the resort.

His business strategies sometimes compromised his ideals about golf, however, which subsequently undermined the consensus that generally prevailed between him and Pinehurst's annual commuters. Throughout the first three decades of the twentieth century, Tufts competed with other resort developers by manipulating the resort's tournament schedule. One tactic involved scheduling tournaments to extend Pinehurst's season. In a letter to Ross and three other business associates, Tufts ruminated that:

> The North and South Golf Tournament is placed as nearly as possible at the end of the season. For twenty odd years it has been used to lengthen the season and especially to get publicity for the few remaining weeks that we are open. It is a question in my mind as to whether it has always operated in that way and whether it hasn't possibly been considered as our final gasp for business—and when people say that the North and South is to be on a certain date they say that is the time everybody leaves Pinehurst. If the original idea is a success in lengthening the season we should give very careful thought to what we do with the prominent players for, of course, the more prominent the contestants the greater publicity we will get.

In a related strategy, he and his management team scheduled matches between star players at such times that they believed would benefit the resort most financially. For example, Ross wrote to Tufts that, "I would appreciate your advising me what time of season you think the special pros would be of most value to us." In an apparent effort to keep the resort's guests entertained constantly, Ross suggested, "[W]e could land a good pair the first week in November, then possibly the middle of December, before the January tournament and before the February tournament. We certainly do not want them during any tournament week." For Tufts and Ross, the players, spectators and the integrity of the matches were important but, still, secondary to business considerations.[48]

To lure expert players to compete at specific times or in particular tournaments, Tufts used the common but ethically questionable practice of paying them appearance fees or providing them with free accommodations. Problems arose when it became necessary to bend certain rules such as the strict standards on a golfer's amateur status enforced by the United States Golf Association. For Tufts, and others in the business of golf, the perceived benefits outweighed the ethical indiscretions. Once Tufts received commitments from a pair of famous golfers—the strategy was to generate interest in a competitive match—the resort would get free publicity from the nation's network of sport writers who kept their readers abreast of golf matches between the leading amateurs and professionals. Also, having the best golfers at Pinehurst supposedly attracted visitors interested in associating with celebrities. Tufts and Ross often conferred about the benefits of these strategies. In one letter, Ross spelled out why he supported the continuation of recruiting star players:

> I noticed throughout Florida there seems to be a tendency each year on the part of the substantial clubs to make less of an effort to induce the star players to participate in their tournaments. It is true that in the real estate developments where golf plays an important part, every inducement is made to procure the best in

amateur and professional golf. This is done purely for advertising purposes but I have doubts as to its value.

We are in rather a different category from a Country Club or real estate development. Pinehurst is recognized as the outstanding golf resort, so I think we are obliged to do everything we can to get the very best players to come here and any reasonable inducement which we could offer them would be, I think, good business.....[T]he advertising we get out of them is very valuable.

Clearly, he recognized Pinehurst's chief competitors and the resort's position within the business world of golf. In the same letter, however, he indicated an awareness that, "of course, there is always a lot of guests who do not care to have the courses crowded with tournament players."[49]

Just after James Tufts's death, a group of men and women—many who became local property owners and Pinehurst's most devoted commuters—began contesting Leonard Tufts's escalating emphasis on nationally promoted tournaments. Both as avid golfers and as members of the resort's seasonal community they worried about issues of character, camaraderie, and the meaning of competition. Uninterested in the stress inherent in competing with the nation's best players or participating in the social spectacle often associated with official tournaments, a group of ardent, male golfers decided they preferred playing casual matches among themselves. In 1904, they formed their own private club calling themselves the Tin Whistles.[50] In style and content, the organization's constitution and by-laws were suggestive of its members' attitudes about Tufts's tournaments and those who competed in them. One rather irreverent section of the by-laws read: "It shall be the duty of each member to suppress the incipient conceit of any fellow member who thinks he is in line for the North and South Championship."[51] Charter-member Edgar A. Guest wrote a poem, "To the Pinehurst Tin Whistles," that articulated the members' philosophy of golf.[52] In the author's opening lines he indicated that the club members were by nature men of honor:

> If you're a Tin Whistle, old pal, and I reckon you are,
> Your character, day in and day out, must be rated at par.

Later in the poem's first stanza, Guest pronounced that maintaining one's integrity while competing was more important than winning:

> Your game may be bad, but your word must be good,
> You must take a defeat when it's right that you should.
> You may come home a failure and no one will care,
> May start with high hopes and come down in despair,
> But you must return at the end of the day
> The man that you were when you started to play.

The second stanza reinforced Guest's resolve that his fellow club members' character would remain steady under the pressures of competition. The author's apparent apprehension about playing golf for prizes echoed with the sound of experience. He presumed that competitive golf revealed the player's character— a revelation that was not always positive:

If you're a Tin Whistle, the love of the game
Must mean more to you than the prize you may claim.
You must choose with a smile to go down to defeat
Rather than finish the day as a cheat.
It may be that never a medal you'll wear,
Nor claim the game's silver, but no one will care.
You may struggle to win just as hard as you can,
But failing, you must still come in as a man.

The poem's final stanza made clear that the Tin Whistles placed greater value on camaraderie than on competition. For this group, the pleasure in golf was playing with and competing against others who shared the same lifestyle and values:

If you're a Tin Whistle, your worth isn't told
By the money you own or the station you hold.
You have risen above the base standards of earth
And have come to a higher conception of worth.
You can stand an example to eager-eyed youth
Of the life that is lived in the sunlight of truth,
And whenever you play you must hold to the plan
That the Tin Whistle button's the badge of a man.

With good-humored self-righteousness, Guest and his fellow Tin Whistles believed that only men like themselves—wealthy, white, Christian "gentlemen"—could truly understand and appreciate the game of golf. Those who came to Pinehurst determined to win cups and medals at any cost in one of Tufts's many tournaments, reasoned Guest, failed to understand golf and how the game revealed character and fostered camaraderie. Such visitors to Pinehurst remained just that—visitors. They may have been critical to the resort's financial success, but they seldom gained entry into the resort's premiere lifestyle enclave.

As some of the resort's most loyal commuters, the Tin Whistles refused to allow Pinehurst's management or the resort's general population of visitors to control their everyday activities or disturb their possessiveness about Pinehurst's sense of place. In their daily matches, they refused to play with non-members—those less committed to a golfing lifestyle. An example of their desire to exercise a certain level of autonomy concerned their insistence on perpetuating a particular golfing tradition from Scotland that defied the wishes of the Tufts family, Donald Ross, and many of the resort's other guests. The original club members actually carried small tin whistles. One bit of lore claims that members could blow their whistle on designated golf holes and someone would appear from the pines to supply the player with a drink of Scotch whiskey—a practice James Tufts had forbidden in Pinehurst. Also, the members allegedly smuggled their favorite drink into their hotel rooms and cottages. Supposedly, such practices stimulated their camaraderie and good fellowship. *The Pinehurst Outlook* reported that victors in the Tin Whistles' private competitions won prizes "that wouldn't keep."[53] This coded phrase for bottles of whiskey suggested that the club's practices were well known among Pinehurst's seasonal population.

Such notoriety only enhanced the club members' *espirit de corps* and the club's reputation among other like-minded golfers. The Tin Whistles served as a model for similar clubs, such as The Old Guard Society in Palm Beach and the Stone Crabs at the Belleair resort on the west coast of Florida. In a sense, each club was created in response to the growing popularity of golf. For example, Pinehurst's many tournaments not only caused crowding on the golf courses, but golfers were no longer able to determine with whom they would associate while playing the game. As the national community of golfers continued to grow, particularly among local country clubs, certain resort commuters—who were themselves members of country clubs scattered from across North America—formed selective winter-resort enclaves that distinguished the members as golf purists. Wearing the Tin Whistles' lapel pin identified each club member as one of the game's elite—an authentic golfer recognized by his peers as personifying the game's cherished values.[54]

As representatives of a lifestyle that revolved around golf the all-male Tin Whistles, Old Guard Society, and Stone Crabs exerted ample influence at their respective resorts, but their hegemony did not go unchallenged. In 1909 at Pinehurst, for example, a select contingent of female golf enthusiasts established their own exclusive club: The Silver Foils. The organization's carefully chosen name illustrated the members' resentment for being treated as second-class golfers and being excluded from their male counterparts' club. Silver symbolized a metal more precious than tin and foil declared the women's intentions toward the males' assumed dominance over the affairs of golfers at Pinehurst. In Article II of their constitution, the all-female membership declared that "the object of 'The Silver Foils' is to promote a golfing fellowship begun at Pinehurst, and to maintain there a neutral zone for a choice and chosen few from outside organizations, to which it will be pleasant to return year after year." As members of country clubs from throughout the Northern and Midwestern states and eastern Canada, these women had developed as golfers a sense of camaraderie equally powerful to their male counterparts. Stating that "the eternal headquarters of 'The Silver Foils' shall be at Pinehurst, North Carolina," Article III illustrated the group's emphatic sense of place about Tufts's village in the pines. The club's by-laws, like those of the men's clubs, demonstrated the female members' intentions to establish autonomy over their golfing affairs, including the selection of members and the governance of their competitions.[55]

In a 1920 letter to the Pinehurst Golf Club's (all male) Board of Governors, The Silver Foils expressed their determination to be treated equally as golfers. Apparently, the board had restricted to male players only the resort's premier golf course, Number 2. By "unanimous resolution," the Silver Foils entreated the governors to be allowed to play the Women's North and South Championship how and where they decided. The letter justified their demands on the most practical grounds—money. In part the letter read: "The attention of the Governors is respectfully called to the fact that the women at Pinehurst are under equal expense with the men for their golfing privileges. On consideration of this fact, they feel justified in requesting the use of the Number 2 course for this their one important event each year." The Silver Foils won their battle against the Board of Governors and, although they were forced to continue fighting the war for full equality, they persisted as participants in defining Pinehurst's seasonal community. In one final comparison between this private club of female golfers and their male counterparts, the women acted as the resort's self-proclaimed leaders among all women golfers.[56]

The four private golf clubs at Pinehurst, Palm Beach, and Belleair required that potential members must have wintered at their respective resort for several consecutive years. The Old Guard Society accepted nominations for individuals spending their fourth season in Palm Beach, while the Tin Whistles and Silver Foils demanded that applicants had resided in Pinehurst for the previous five seasons.[57] For the members of these golf clubs the game signified more than simply a sport or recreational pastime. By the early decades of the twentieth century, golf served as the common bond for their distinctive lifestyle. Often the first resorters to arrive in the fall and the last to depart in the spring, the various club members helped establish a sense of continuity at their respective winter resorts. And for those able and willing to play the game year round, joining resort communities like Pinehurst and Palm Beach further solidified their individual and group identities. At Pinehurst, in particular, the golfers who belonged to the Tin Whistles and Silver Foils exemplified certain social patterns, everyday practices, and a sense of place that not only defined their local enclave, they helped establish standards of taste and behavior for a national community of golfers.

In turn, the club members' expectations—even demands—for Pinehurst's owners to provide them a milieu of familiarity on the courses and in the village, provided a continual challenge for Leonard Tufts and, subsequently, his son Richard. Like developers of all the premier resorts, the Tufts family nurtured an environment that depended on attracting new visitors each season while maintaining the loyalty of their annual clientele. They succeeded in this ongoing balancing act only by surrounding themselves with a complex network of employees willing—often even dedicated—to fulfilling the desires of various factions of visitors. By the 1920s, based on a national marketing scheme that was shaped by the continual negotiations between tourists, commuters, and management, Pinehurst developed into America's winter golfing Mecca.

Notes

1. *The Pinehurst Outlook,* 7 November 1900.

2. Around the turn of the twentieth century, the premiere winter resorts in the south Atlantic states welcomed guests only during the winter months. Each resort had its distinct opening and closing dates. Some remained open only from Christmas to Easter, while others welcomed guests from early November until mid May.

3. *The Pinehurst Outlook,* 5 April 1901.

4. Richard Butsch, ed., *For Fun and Profit: The Transformation of Leisure into Consumption* (Philadelphia: Temple University Press, 1990), 4. See also David Nasaw, *Going Out: The Rise and Fall of Public Amusements* (New York: Harper Collins, 1993); John F. Kasson, *Amusing the Millions: Coney Island at the Turn of the Century* (New York: Hill & Wang, 1978); Catherine Cocks, *Doing the Town: The Rise*

of Urban Tourism in the United States, 1850-1915 (Berkeley: University of California Press, 2001), 106-142; Peter Blodgett, "Selling the Scenery: Advertising and the National Parks, 1916-1933," in *Seeing and Being Seen: Tourism in the American West*, eds. David M. Wrobel and Patrick L. Long (Lawrence: University of Kansas Press, 2001), 271-298; and Glenn Uminowicz, "Recreation in a Christian America: Ocean Grove and Asbury Park, New Jersey, 1869-1914," in *Hard at Play: Leisure in America, 1840-1940*, ed. Kathryn Grover (Amherst: University of Massachusetts Press, 1992), 8-38.

5. On upper-class travelers' visits to elite resorts and spas see, for example, Charlene M. Boyer Lewis, *Ladies and Gentlemen on Display: Planter Society at the Virginia Springs, 1790-1860* (Charlottesville: University Press of Virginia, 2001); Joseph Wechsberg, *The Lost World of the Great Spas* (New York: Harper & Row, 1979), 161-182; Maud Howe Elliott, *This Was My Newport* (New York: Arno Press, 1979); and Cleveland Amory, *The Last Resorts* (New York: Harper, 1952).

6. In *Working at Play: A History of Vacationing in the United States* (New York: Oxford University Press, 1999), Cindy S. Aron offers a trans-regional perspective of middle-class vacationing in America, but she largely ignores the importance of winter travel and Southern tourism in her otherwise excellent analysis. For examples of studies on regional travel and tourism, see Charles E. Funnell, *By the Beautiful Sea: The Rise and High Times of That Great American Resort, Atlantic City* (New York: Alfred A. Knopf, 1975); Dona Brown, *Inventing New England Regional Tourism in the Nineteenth Century* (Washington, D.C.: Smithsonian Institution Press, 1995); and Theodore Corbett, *The Making of American Resorts: Saratoga, Ballston Spa, and Lake George* (New Brunswick, N.J.: Rutgers University Press, 2001). On specific resorts, see Bruce E. Johnson, *Built for the Ages. A History of the Grove Park Inn* (Asheville, NC.: Grove Park Inn and Country Club, 1991); and William Barton McCash and June Hall McCash, *The Jekyll Island Club: Southern Haven for America's Millionaires* (Athens: University of Georgia Press, 1989). On resort developers, see Donald W. Curl, *Mizner's Florida: American Resort Architecture* (Cambridge, Mass.: MIT Press, 1984). Also, several articles and biographies have been published about Henry Flagler, including Paul S. George, "Passage to the New Eden: Tourism its Miami From Flagler through Everest G. Sewell," *Florida Historical Quarterly* 59 (1981): 440-463; Sidney Walter Martin, *Florida's Flagler* (Athens: University of Georgia Press, 1949); David Leon Chandler, *Henry Flagler, The Astonishing Life and Times of the Visionary Robber Baron Who Founded Florida* (New York: Macmillan, 1986); and Edward N. Akin, *Flagler: Rockefeller's Partner and Florida Baron* (Kent, Ohio: Kent State University Press, 1988). For a general discussion of Northern tourists in the Reconstruction South, see Nina Silbei; *The Romance of Reunion: Northerners and the South, 1865-1900* (New York: Vintage Books, 1990), 3-26.

7. I borrow the term "resorters" from H.B. Martin's chapter, "Famous Golf Resorts," in *Fifty Years of American Golf* (New York: Argosy-Antiquarian, 1966), 292-307. The term also appears in Donald W. Curl, *Palm Beach County: An Illustrated History* (Northridge, Calif.: Windsor Press, 1986), 31. For my purposes, while tourists were casual or occasional visitors, resorters saw their annual pilgrimages into the south Atlantic states as an integral part of their lifestyle. Concerning the idea of a "sense of place," see Tony Hiss, *The Experience of Place: A New Way of Looking at and Dealing without Radically Changing Cities and Countryside* (New York: Vintage Books, 1990), 3-26.

8. John R. Stilgoe, *Borderland: Origins of the American Suburb, 1820-1939* (New Haven, Conn.: Yale University Press, 1988), 5-9.

9. Robert N. Bellah et al., *Habits of the Heart: Individualism and Commitment in American Life* (Berkeley: University of California Press, 1985), 66-86.

10. E.S. Martin, "The Rise of the Country Clubs," *Harper's Weekly*, 8 September 1900, p. 843.

11. Frank S. Arnett, "American Country Clubs," *Munsey's Magazine*, July 1902, p. 486.

12. For examples of urban and sport historians analyzing golf in terms of class, see Kenneth T. Jackson, *Crabgrass Frontier: The Suburbanization of the United States* (New York: Oxford University Press, 1985), 97-99; Steven Riess, *City Games: The Evolution of American Urban Society and the Rise of Sports* (Urbana: University of Illinois Press, 1991), 59-62; Benjamin Rader, *American Sports: From the Age of Folk Games to the Age of Spectators* (Englewood Cliffs, N.J.: Prentice Hall, 1983), 63-67; Foster Rhea Dulles, *America Learns to Play: A History of Popular Recreation, 1607-1940* (Gloucester, Mass.: Peter Smith, 1963), 241-243; Robert Fishman, *Bourgeois Utopias: The Rise and Fall of Suburbia* (New York: Basic Books, 1987), 144-148; and Stephen Hardy, *How Boston Played: Sport, Recreation, and Community, 1865-1915* (Boston: Northeastern University Press, 1982), 59, 140-142, 144, 180-184. For two examples of traditional histories of golf, see Robert Browning, *A History of Golf: The Royal*

and Ancient Game (New York: F. P. Dutton, 1955); and Dale Concannon, *Golf The Early Days* (New York: Salamander, 1995).

13. In "The Sensual and Intellectual Pleasures of Rowing: Pierre de Coubertain's Ideal for Modern Sport," *Sport History Review* 30 (1999): 95, Douglas Brown argues persuasively that in spite of the "compelling analyses" scholars have recently made about nineteenth-century rowing, "the athletes who rowed during this era seem to be represented as passive objects of class, gender, and ethnic discourses. Their sporting instinct and erotic pleasure is supplanted with abstract references to power relations and the unequal distribution of economic capital." Brown's critique of the scholarship on rowing parallels my view about the scholarly tradition in understanding American golf.

14. Riess, *City Games*, 59.

15. Richard J. Moss, *Golf and the American Country Club* (Urbana: University of Illinois Press, 2001), 3.

16. James M. Mayo, *The American Country Club: Its Origins and Development* (New Brunswick, N. J.: Rutgers University Press, 1998), 7-60.

17. In *Golf and the American Country Club,* Moss acknowledges the existence of the "colony' club serving the needs of a temporary population escaping the city's summer heat or winter cold," but he pays little attention to the role of golf at the winter resorts (p. 43).

18. Early on, golfers "laid out" golf courses simply by walking a piece of land and placing sticks in the ground to mark the location of each teeing area and each green. The courses followed existing terrain and natural conditions. Gradually, the practice of laying out golf courses evolved into a special branch of landscape architecture in which golf course architects constructed courses using increasingly sophisticated design principles, the science of agronomy, and such technological innovations as watering systems and mechanical earth-moving equipment. On the importance of golf course architecture, see Moss, *Golf and the American County Club,* 85-92; and Geoffrey S. Cornish and Ronald F. Whitten, *The Golf Course* (New York: Rutledge Press, 1987).

19. Along with many others, in *Fifty Years of American Golf,* H.B. Martin credited Reid as the "father of American golf." Martin explained that Reid and his four friends used an old apple tree as a makeshift "clubhouse" at the site of their original golf course, thus earning their nickname. The commonly accepted fact that St. Andrews Golf Club was the first officially established golf club in the United States was challenged by Peter Andrews in his undocumented article, "Links With History," *American Heritage* 42 (1991): 52-63. Andrews claims the Dorsett Field Club in Vermont, purportedly established in 1886, deserves the honor of being the first golf club in continuous use in the United States. In *The Golf Course,* Cornish and Whitten state simply that although "St. Andrews has persisted in calling itself the oldest golf club in the United States, the claim…, is disputed by many [other clubs]" (p. 44). In any case, golf did not take root in the United States until at least the mid 1880s.

20. *Golf Illustrated* 28 (1934): 14. According to the Club Managers Association of America, "[T]here were 1000 country clubs in 1915 and 5500 in 1927; there was a total membership of 740,000 in 1915 and 2,700,000 in 1927." Horace G. Duncan, *The First Fifty Years, 1927-1977* (Bassett, Virginia: Bassett Printing, 1977), 27.

21. Martin *Fifty Years of American Golf,* 293.

22. *The Pinehurst Outlook* referred to Culver as an "expert," as did Richard Tufts in *The Scottish Invasion* (Pinehurst, NC,: Pinehurst Publishers, 1962), 17-18, although Cornish and Whitten fail to even mention Culver in their comprehensive study of American golf course architects, *The Golf Course.* More than likely, the Tufts deferred to Culver's "expertise" because of his playing experience. *The Pinehurst Outlook,* 7 November 1900.

23. *The Pinehurst Outlook,* 7 November 1900, 16 November 1900.

24. *The Pinehurst Outlook,* 1 January 1901.

25. Tufts, *The Scottish Invasion,* 18-28; Martin, *Fifty Years of American Golf* 256-260, 294-295.

26. As early as 1898, as part of a national advertising campaign, Flagler tempted the nation's golfers by offering memberships in the Florida East Coast Golf Club, which gave members the privilege of playing courses at each of his five resorts.

27. John Duncan Dunn, "Winter Golf in Southern Sunshine," *Outing* 36 (1900): 486-497.

28. *The Pinehurst Outlook*, 7 November 1900.

29. Harry Redan, "Pinehurst of Today," *New England Magazine*, 19 October 1901, p. 264.

30. Khristine Januzik, comp., "The Pinehurst Story," pp. 75-77, Tufts Archives, Pinehurst, N. C.

31. *The Pinehurst Outlook*, 10 December 1910.

32. Donald J. Ross, *Golf Has Never Failed Me: The Lost Commentaries of Legendary Golf Architect Donald J. Ross* (Chelsea, Mich.: Sleeping Bear Press, 1996), 16.

33. A native of Dornoch, Scotland, Ross became a carpenter after leaving school. While a member of the local golf club, he allowed his fellow golfers to convince him that he should undertake the necessary training to become Dornoch's resident professional. Ross agreed and served his apprenticeship at the Royal and Ancient Club of St. Andrews under the direction of "Old" Tom Morris, the world's leading authority on golf at the time. Ross then applied his training in club making, design work, greens keeping (i.e., horticultural duties) and as an instructor at two courses before settling down in Dornoch. At twenty-five, he met Harvard Professor Robert Wilson who invited him to come to the United States. The following year, 1898, Ross sailed to America in hopes of taking advantage of the game's surging popularity. While employed at the Oakley Country Club near Boston, he met James Tufts who suggested that Ross might supplement his income by working at Pinehurst during the winter. This unlikely chain of events culminated in Ross's continued service as Pinehurst's head professional until his death in 1948. Ross, *Golf Has Never Failed Me*, 9-11.

34. Ross, *Golf Has Never Failed Me*, 38; Tufts, *The Scottish Invasion*, 23-26; Cornish, *The Golf Course*, 240-241. Early on, Tufts required that all his guests submit written recommendations from a clergyman and a leader in their community. Even as the number of visitors to Pinehurst escalated, Tufts maintained his policy. In *The Pinehurst Outlook*, 16 November 1900, an advertisement for available cottages read: "Desirable parties, giving satisfactory references, can secure these attractive winter homes at reasonable rental." Tufts's emphasis on the "good character" and "community standing" of his guests was also reflected in the testimonials printed in the resort's weekly. For example, see *The Pinehurst Outlook*, 3 December 1897, 15 October 1900.

35. In *Leonard Tufts 1870-1945*, E.M. Gray, writes that "Leonard's outstanding mental characteristics were order and reasonableness. He had the orderly analytical and inquiring mind of a scientist. He did not jump to conclusions. A decision was reached by the study of the logic of the case as he could discover it." Facsimile in Januzik, comp., "The Pinehurst Story," 75.

36. Frank Presbrey Papers, DF 23.00, Tufts Archives.

37. As was common in American tourism generally during the second half of the nineteenth and early decades of the twentieth centuries, Jews faced increasing levels of anti-Semitism. Pinehurst's management made a concerted effort to ban all Jews from visiting the resort. On the increasing levels of anti-Semitism in the United States, see Leonard Dinnerstein, *Antisemitism in America* (New York: Oxford University Press, 1994); Steven Riess, "Sports and the American Jew," in *Sports and the American Jew*, ed. Steven Riess (Syracuse, N.Y: Syracuse University Press, 1998), 1-59; and Cindy Aron, *Working at Play*, 2 16-218.

38. Januzik, comp., "The Pinehurst Story." 78-83, 102-105, 109-111; Annie Oakley Papers, DF 81.00, Tufts Archives.

39. Januzik, comp., "The Pinehurst Story," 60; Tufts, *The Scottish Invasion*, 18.

40. Donald Ross, Newton Centre, Mass., to Leonard Tufts, Pinehurst, N.C., 31 May 1924, Donald Ross Papers, DF 138.00, Tufts Archives.

41. Khristine E. Januzik, *A Walking Tour of Historic Pinehurst* (Pinehurst, NC: The Pinehurst Civic Group, 1999), 13-64.

42. In many ways Pinehurst's early development reflected that of local country estates as described by James Mayo in *The American Country Club*, 116-133, except that Tufts and associates catered to a national audience and promoted their seasonal golfing community as opposed to developers interested in attracting urban dwellers to nearby suburbs.

43. In the December 17, 1910 issue of *The Pinehurst Outlook,* an article listed all of the season's scheduled tournaments with information about each one's format and prizes. As a reminder, the resort weekly also included—in fine print—the rules that made up the Pinehurst System.

44. The description of a typical tournament setting around the turn of the century is based on a composite of numerous articles published in *The Pinehurst Outlook* and *Palm Beach Lift*.

45. These numbers were gleaned from the "Tournament Schedule" printed in *The Pinehurst Outlook*, 17 December 1910.

46. Of the winter resorts, Pinehurst offered the most extensive schedule of tournaments, although Palm Beach, Miami, and the Belleair resort near Tampa Bay each held several annual events. For example, during the 1910-1911 season, six annual tournaments were played in Palm Beach.

47. Martin, *Fifty Years of American Golf*, 295.

48. Leonard Tufts, Pinehurst, N.C., to Donald Ross, Pinehurst, N.C., 3 February 1926, Donald Ross, Newton Centre, Mass., to Leonard Tufts, Pinehurst, N.C., 22 August 1925, Ross Papers.

49. Donald Ross, Pinehurst, N.C., to Leonard Tufts, Pinehurst, N.C., 9 February 1926, Ross Papers.

50. Founding member F.W. Kenyon of New York suggested the club's name. He supposedly borrowed the idea from a novel he read, Alfred Henry Lewis' *The Boss*. In the novel, Lewis nicknamed a gang of toughs "the tin whistles." Martin, *Fifty Years of American Golf*, 296.

51. Tufts, *The Scottish Invasion*, 101.

52. Edgar A. Guest, "To the Pinehurst Tin Whistles," a facsimile appears in Martin, *Fifty Years of American Golf*, 298.

53. *The Pinehurst Outlook*, 9 January 1910.

54. Tufts, *The Scottish Invasion*, 100-102; Martin, *Fifty Years of American Golf*, 295-298.

55. Silver Foils Papers, DF 173.00, Tufts Archives.

56. May B. Howard, Pinehurst, N.C., to Board of Governors, Pinehurst Golf Club, Pinehurst, N.C., 27 March 1920, Cottage Owners File, DF 86.00, Tufts Archives.

57. Martin, *Fifty Years of American Golf*, 298-300.

CHAPTER 8

THE FATHER OF AMERICAN FOOTBALL

▪ *Michael Oriard* ▪

Walter Camp was never an All-American but for thirty-seven years the maker of All-Americans, never a paid coach but the "coach of coaches," never a ruler but the preeminent creator of rules.[1] The son of a middle-class school teacher in New Haven, Camp was a star running back at Yale for six years and part of a seventh (1876-82), first as an undergraduate, then as a medical student (the limitation on seasons of eligibility came later, after years of wrangling among the rule makers). More important, after he left medicine and Yale for a career in business, first with the Manhattan Watch Company, then for four decades with the New Haven Clock Company (eventually becoming president and board chairman), Camp continued as graduate adviser to Yale captains for nearly thirty years, serving "as Yale's unofficial, unpaid, unquestioned chief mentor and arbiter."[2] Richard Harding Davis wrote in 1893, "There is only one man in New Haven of more importance than Walter Camp, and I have forgotten his name. I think he is the president of the university."[3] Outside New Haven, among football men he was the game's preeminent spokesman and authority, routinely identified in newspapers and magazines with such epithets as "the leading foot-ball expert in the country" or the "father of football at Yale"; on occasion, with touches of gentle irony, as "the King of American football" or "the great high priest of the grid-iron arena."[4]

Many of the captains and players Camp advised became coaches elsewhere, carrying with them their mentor's methods and ideas. Most important, from 1878 to his death in 1925, Camp served continuously on football's rules committees, for twenty-eight years as secretary. His views dominated the early committees in particular. The scrimmage rule of 1880, assigning possession to one team at a time, was his idea, as was the five-yard rule of 1882 (years later, Camp wrote that this rule initially "had no adherents save the man who proposed it").[5] He proposed eleven players on a side, instead of fifteen, and devised the point-scoring scale, approved in 1883, that with more tinkering became the basis of our modern system. Ironically, though a most gentlemanly sportsman himself, Camp also proposed the legalization of low tackling in 1888, then through the 1890s fought legislation to eliminate the resulting mass momentum plays that critics blamed for football's shocking brutality. Losing that battle, Camp then resisted legalizing the forward pass in 1906, the ultimate shift from "mass" to "open" play. But if he yielded reluctantly to the later stages of development (motivated privately by Yale's self-interest and publicly by a consistent vision that football was preeminently a team game, not an individual sport), it remains true that American football was to a considerable degree Walter Camp's creation.

Camp also wrote voluminously: nearly thirty books, over 200 magazine articles, countless newspaper commentaries. Included in these writings are his reports on the All-American teams he personally selected from 1889 until his death; beginning in 1898 these were an annual feature in *Colliers' Weekly*. Also included, though less well remembered, are numerous treatises on the emerging game, sometimes directed toward would be coaches and players, sometimes meant to teach an awakening public what they were witnessing on the field and, more important, what lay behind the visible action. These writings provide an invaluable detailed record of Camp's understanding of football's deeper meanings and significance, his own reading of football's cultural text. Appearing in major periodicals (*Century, Collier's, Harper's Weekly, Outing, Outlook, Independent*), in the most popular juvenile magazines (St. *Nicholas, Youth's Companion, Boys' Magazine*), in the major New York daily newspapers, and in books by major publishers, Camp's ideas, enhanced by his peerless reputation, had to have a powerful influence on the public's understanding.

Camp's writings reveal no attempt to develop football toward greater narrativity, nor even a conscious understanding that such a quality had unintentionally resulted. Yet his writings also reveal that by the late 1880s Camp himself recognized that football, both its brief history and the games on the field, was a cultural text whose meaning he wished to interpret for its growing audience. Beginning with his earliest essays in *Harper's Weekly* (the era's major middle-class periodical) and *Outing* (its chief monthly devoted to sport and recreation), Camps own narrative of football's development had a distinct plot: the rationalization and tactical development of the game's action, driven by the object of winning, developed in young men the character and experiences essential for success in America. Camp's master metaphor for football in all of his writings was the hierarchically structured, efficiently run industrial corporation, no doubt linked in his own mind with the New Haven Clock Company. That is, in dozens of essays and four major treatises written during football's formative years, Camp consistently interpreted the game's meaning and significance from what is essentially a managerial and technocratic perspective.

This perspective might seem merely self-serving: for Walter Camp, a former three-time captain, then Yale's unofficial coach for a quarter-century, football was a game of tactics and leadership rather than physical achievement. Self-serving or not, Camp expressed a view that continues to distinguish American sports—basketball and baseball, as well as football—from the same or similar games elsewhere. In American basketball and baseball, the games are orchestrated from the sidelines, their outcomes frequently attributed to the winning team's superior "bench coach" or "field manager." When Indiana plays North Carolina in college basketball, it's Bobby Knight vs. Dean Smith; in the World Series it's Billy Martin vs. Tommy Lasorda, Tony LaRussa vs. Roger Craig. The tendency is less strong in professional than in college basketball, in baseball than in football; but in relation to European sport the American emphasis on the coaches is striking. And this emphasis is most pronounced in football, where the importance of teamwork is greatest and the players are drilled to execute, with little improvisation, a game plan devised by the coaching staff. Baseball commentators speak of "the book," the unwritten but universally known traditions that dictate most managers' decisions. There is no "book" in football; tactical styles vary from coach to coach, and at least once a decade some coach's innovation has truly expanded the possibilities in the game. From the original "V trick" and "flying wedge" of the 1890s, to the single wing and double wing and split-T, to the wishbone and shotgun and run-and-shoot, football coaches have repeatedly reconceived the way their game is played.

Initially, coaching during games was forbidden by the rules taken over from the Rugby Union; once the contest began, all decisions were made by the captain on the field. Moreover, the early coaches were unofficial and unpaid, usually graduates returning to the university to advise the captain and help train the new eleven. Through its system of volunteer graduate coaches, Yale had dominated the Harvards and Princetons that continued to depend on student leadership. In addition, as more and more schools and athletic clubs took up the game, they needed coaches from outside because they lacked graduates with football experience (Yale initially provided most of these outside coaches). The professional coach originated at western colleges such as Minnesota and Chicago (where Amos Alonzo Stagg was hired in 1891 with a professor's salary). Not by intention but by necessity, the paid coach emerged as a fixture by the early twentieth century, but only after much agonizing and debate over the intrusion of "professionalism" into amateur sport. The success of the great tacticians of the 1890s and early 1900s, men like Stagg at Chicago, George Woodruff at Pennsylvania, and Henry L. Williams at Minnesota, made the value of professional coaches apparent to everyone. Harvard rarely beat Yale until, against internal resistance at even this late date, it hired its first professional coach in 1905. After several unaccustomed losses to Percy Haughton's teams at Harvard, Yale followed suit a decade later.[6] Having taught the football world the benefits of coaching, Yale accepted the professional coach with great reluctance.

As paid coaches emerged inevitably with the growing importance of winning for the university's prestige, the rule makers did not willingly surrender the game to coaches. Coaches were expected to help the captains organize their teams, train them, and develop strategy; once the games began, the players were to take over, the coaches to become mere interested spectators. A member of Harvard's faculty athletic committee in 1902 spoke for all advocates of amateur purity when he classed "side line coaching" among the "shady practices" that violated true sport. "When eleven young men appear on the football field," he wrote, "it is commonly understood that they are going to win or lose on their own merits, and not with the assistance of someone on the side lines." But he also acknowledged that, unfortunately, sideline coaching was a common practice, difficult for rule makers to prevent.[7]

They tried. American collegians began with a ban on coaching, as was traditional in English sport, but as always they immediately began to circumvent it. A rule in 1892 directed the umpire to prevent coaching from the sideline; another in 1900 forbade coaching during the game by substitutes or anyone else not actually playing; another in 1914 prohibited all persons from walking up and down the side lines. No doubt the most difficult rule to enforce, instituted in 1917, said that substitutes could not communicate with other members of the team until after the first play (thus preventing them from bringing in instructions from the coach). After the offensive huddle became common, beginning in 1921 when it was introduced by the Illinois team coached by Bob Zuppke, the referee joined the huddle as substitutes entered the game, to assure their silence. Sideline coaching was not officially sanctioned until 1967.[8]

The early restrictions proved to be minor obstacles in the march toward coaching dominance, however. Substitution rules, one of the chief mechanisms by which coaching strategy could be expanded or contracted, changed thirty times in college football's first one hundred years. The current intercollegiate rules allowing unlimited substitution (initially permitted in 1941, then restricted in 1953, then restored in two stages, in 1964 and 1973) have brought football coaches' control to new extremes: not just the two-platoon football first made possible in 1941, then again in 1964, but players shuffled in and out of the game to meet increasingly specialized needs determined by huge coaching staffs with their computer-generated strategies. The quarterback who calls his own plays in either college or professional football has become increasingly rare; the computerized efficiency of the Dallas Cowboys under Tom Landry in the 1970s and the "genius" of the San Francisco 49ers' Bill Walsh in the 1980s are recent contrasts in coaching control. How strange it must seem to Americans watching World Cup soccer matches to see that coaching is still not allowed during the contest.[9]

One of the narratives we read in football today, then, concerns a contest between what are seemingly rival corporations, and we can look to Walter Camp for the roots of this narrative—but also for the competing narrative that most directly challenges it. In the 1980s, sportswriters debated whether the Super Bowl victories of the 49ers belonged chiefly to Bill Walsh or to quarterback Joe Montana. When writers argued whether Montana was programmed by Walsh, then plugged into an unbeatable system, or made the system unbeatable himself, they restated competing narratives nearly as old as the game. At the same time that Camp was repeatedly explaining the development of

American football in terms of rational efficiency, he was annually celebrating the eleven best football players in the land, not the coaches and captains who devised the tactics but the individual heroes who executed and sometimes transcended them. These dual perspectives and differing purposes point to what Camp explicitly described as distinct audiences and desires: the knowing few intimately involved with the teams, and the rapidly expanding audience of casual fans who came to the games for excitement and spectacle. From its infancy, in short, even in the mind of its principal author, football's cultural text has had competing interpretations.

Throughout his published writings Camp's account of football's development consistently evoked a cluster of ideas: unbound by tradition (alternately a lack or a freedom in Camp's view), and unaided by experienced rugby players who could interpret the rules, the American collegian "took the English rules for a starting-point, and almost immediately proceeded to add and subtract, according to what seemed his pressing needs." The most pressing initial need, according to Camp, was simply for order. The creation of the scrimmage in 1880 meant the elimination of chance (the random exit of the ball from the rugby scrummage) and opened up possibilities for greater "skill in the development of brilliant plays and carefully planned maneuvers." In turn, this initial act led naturally to further rationalizing, the division of labor according to distinct positions. "The same man did not always snap the ball back as he does now," Camp explained in 1891, "but any one of the rushers would do it upon occasion. The men did not preserve their relative positions in the line, and any one of the men behind the line would act as a quarter back [the man who received the ball from the snap-back]. Such a condition of affairs could not, however, last long where intercollegiate rivalry proved such an incentive to the perfection of play, and the positions of center-rush or snap-back and quarter-back became the most distinctive of any upon the field."[10]

Linking "intercollegiate rivalry" to "the perfection of play" suggests not only that winning mattered more than enjoyment, but also that it contributed to an advance in American achievement. Camp viewed English rugby as chaotic play; he envisioned American football as purposeful work. That is, the model of "perfection" for Camp in late nineteenth-century America was the rationalized, bureaucratic, specialized corporate work force. Rugby distinguished only between rushers and backs. In his writings Camp explained in detail the emergence of end-rushers, tackles, guards, and snap-backs, as well as quarterbacks, halfbacks, and fullbacks, with each position demanding certain skills or qualities: relative degrees of speed, size, strength, agility, and intelligence. And a hierarchy emerged among the positions, a clearly demarcate structure and chain of authority derived from the exigencies of football action, but those exigencies were considerably determined by rules he himself proposed that rewarded organization and tactical skill.

All of the quotations above are from Camp's first book, *American Football* (1891), the first important primer on the new game, but they could as easily have come from his magazine articles earlier and later, or from his other major treatises *Walter Camp's Book of College Sports* (1893); *Football* (1896), coauthored with Harvard's famous tactician, Lorin F. Deland; and *The Book of Football* (1910)—through which Camp reiterated his fundamental ideas about the development and current qualities of the American game. Camp consistently interpreted football's brief history in terms of an evolution from chaos and primitive physicality (the "nondescript running and kicking" of rugby) toward reason and order (a "scientific contest"),[11] and he cast the current manner of playing the game as the endpoint of that evolution, a reflection of the modern corporate organization. Even in his occasional inconsistency Camp was consistent. Reviewing the season of 1887 for *Outing* magazine, for example, Camp decried the illegal practice of interference (destined "to make great trouble and leave an ugly mark on the American game"), only to embrace it three years later in the same magazine (as "a truly American feature" of the sport) and again the following year (as the essence of team play).[12] Similarly, as interference led to mass-momentum plays, Camp defended them against charges of brutality for some twenty years, then in 1912 casually dismissed mass play as a "serious menace to the sport."[13] Such revisions in detail always served the larger claims of a consistent narrative. Camp belatedly embraced interference because it enhanced team play and increased the coach's tactical options. He defended mass-momentum plays initially because they epitomized highly developed teamwork; as they gave way to "line plunging," the chance of injury was reduced without these options being restricted, so that he could later disdain mass play without sacrificing what he valued most. Football for Camp remained always a game of teamwork and coaching strategy.

On occasion Camp compared football to war, with references to "the foot-ball army" and "the kicking or artillery work," and with long discussions of "generalship"—seemingly different qualities from those required for corporate success.[14] *Football* (1896) is particularly laden with such rhetoric, although coauthor Deland is likely its chief source (he developed the king of the mass-momentum plays, the flying wedge, after studying Napoleon's campaigns). In any case, football for Camp was not the *moral* but the *tactical* equivalent of war. Camp's interest in the military lay not in the physical and psychological demands on soldiers, but in its lessons for command and strategy; "generalship" (on-the-field leadership, as opposed to pregame strategy) was a different quality altogether from Purple Heart courage. Saluting the first Army-Navy football contest in 1890, Camp made the point that football most closely mimics "the art of war"—*art* not struggle.[15] Whether writing for himself or with Deland, Camp always placed intellectual above physical requirements. Writing at a time when the brutality resulting from mass-momentum plays was provoking outcries against the game from many directions, Camp's explanation of football tactics—pounding the weak point in the opponent's line, winning by endurance and attrition whenever possible—was peculiarly bloodless. Camp emphasized the tactical advantage of mass play, not what was to his mind the incidental brutality. Football's "great lesson," Camp wrote in the book with Deland, "may be put into a single line: *it teaches that brains will always win over muscle!*"[16]

"Brains" did not have to be evenly distributed throughout the team, of course. Those with brains served the important managerial functions; those without them translated ideas into physical action. As "director of the game" on the field,[17] the quarterback had to have brains, as did the captain, who in the era before paid coaches became common was principally responsible for selecting, training, and directing the team. Camp also reserved a special place for the "graduate adviser," the unpaid coach who met regularly with the captain to develop training methods and game strategy (as Camp himself did with Yale captains from 1882 to roughly 1910). For Camp, football was fundamentally the strategists' and organizers' game, valuable to the players for its lessons in team-work. In accounts ranging over almost twenty years, Camp repeatedly defined football's past as an era of individualism, its present as the era of team play; the game, that is, always having recently evolved away from a more primitive past into the modern era. In 1891, Camp predicted that the new season would be marked by "the progress of the game through the medium of qualified teachers and coaches." In 1897, he claimed that "team play has more or less replaced individual superiority." In 1909, he contrasted the "probably unequaled style of team play" of Yale's team in 1900 to "the individual brilliancy, and beyond that the individual independence and football initiative" of the team in 1891. In a contest between the two, the 1900 squad would win.[18]

First and last, then, football for Camp was a coach's game, whether the coach was a volunteer alumnus or a hired expert.[19] In *The Book of Football* (1910), Camp's fourth and final major account of the game's history and present state, he summed up the role of the coach most succinctly, as both an inevitable part of football's evolution and an expression of the American spirit:

> But where did the coach come from and why did he come? He was developed by the exigencies of the case, and he came because team play began to take the place of ineffective individual effort. The American loves to plan. It is that trait that has been at the base of his talents for organization. As soon as the American took up Rugby foot-ball he was dissatisfied because the ball would pop out of the scrummage at random. It was too much luck and chance as to where or when it came out, and what man favored by Dame Fortune would get it. So he developed a scrimmage of his own, a center-rusher, or snap-back, a quarter-back, and soon a system of signals. One could no more prevent the American college youth from thus advancing than he could stop their elders with their more important and gigantic enterprises. But all these things led to team play, at the sacrifice, perhaps, of individual brilliancy, but with far greater effectiveness of the eleven men in what for them was the principal affair of the moment—the securing of goals and touch-downs.[20]

This passage bristles with loaded phrases: "ineffective individual effort," the American's "talents for organization," the elders' "more important and gigantic enterprises," "the sacrifice…of individual brilliancy" for the sake of the team's "greater effectiveness." For Camp, football was a mirror of the corporation, a preparation for corporate success, and itself a corporate activity. Football was work, not play; Camp used such phrases as "the work of the tackle" and "the play of the guard" interchangeably, always to mean the same thing: effort in behalf of a collective purpose, "the principal affair," as he put it, to be "the securing of goals and touch-downs." That goals and touchdowns should be the objective is not self-evident; playing in order to demonstrate one's fitness to assume social and political power granted by birthright is one obvious alternative (this was a primary function of the rugby matches played at British public schools and at Oxford and Cambridge). Or playing for the simple joy of playing, a possibility Camp explicitly rejected in two essays in *Outing* in 1912 and 1913.[21]

These essays were late affirmations of a position Camp had held for more than two decades. He made explicit the relationship between football and modern business civilization as early as 1891, in the opening sentence of an essay in *Harper's Weekly* titled "Team Play in Football": "If ever a sport offered inducements to the man of executive ability, to the man who can plan, fore-see, and manage, it is certainly the modern American foot-ball."[22] The closest contemporary analogue to football as Camp understood it was not war but the "scientific management" promoted by Frederick Winslow Taylor, whose time-and-motion studies revolutionized American manufacturing. In fact, the parallels between Camp's advocacy of "team work, strategy, and tactics" and of "scientific planning,"[23] and Taylor's "principles of scientific management" are strikingly specific. In a famous paper from this period Taylor identified the four elements of scientific management as Science, Harmony, Cooperation, and Maximum Output. Scientific managers, that is, do four things:

> *First.* They develop a science for each element of a man's work, which replaces the old rule-of thumb method.
>
> *Second.* They scientifically select and then train, teach, and develop the workman, whereas in the past he chose his own work and trained himself as best he could.
>
> *Third.* They heartily cooperate with the men so as to insure all of the work being done in accordance with the principles of the science which has been developed.
>
> *Fourth.* There is an almost equal division of the work and the responsibility between management and the workmen. The management take over all work for which they are better fitted than the workmen, while in the past almost all of the work and the greater part of the responsibility were thrown upon the men.[24]

Camp's version of scientific management could be summarized in a parallel list: the devising of plays; the training of players for the positions that suit them; the cooperation of coach, captain, and quarterback with the rest of the players so as to assure common purpose; and the distribution of responsibilities according to position and ability. Taylor made a science of organizing physical labor; so did Camp. Taylor distinguished the needs for brain and for brawn, and assigned them accordingly; so did Camp. In one example Taylor explained that stupid-ity was necessary for the man handling pig iron in a steel plant; in *The Book of Football,* Camp noted that in the positions of guard and center, football provided "an opportunity not afforded in any other sport for the big, overgrown fat boy."[25] Ultimately, Taylor and Camp shared a common vision for the American future.

Camp's condescension toward fat boys was not a careless remark. Later in *The Book of Football,* in the chapter on "General Strategy," he warned captains and coaches that "oftentime it is entirely inadvisable to let the players know what the final outcome of some of the plays is intended to be." As "the material" to be developed by coach and captain, the players as Camp discussed them seem more like equipment than personnel. "The object must be to use each man to the full extent of his capacity without exhausting any. To do this scientifically involves placing the men in such position on the field that each may perform the work for which he is best fitted, and yet not be forced to do any of the work toward which his qualifications and training do not point."[26] Nowhere in the book is there any suggestion that the players might take over the game themselves. Managers assure productivity; coaches and captains win football games.

The Book of Football includes several accounts of victories by Yale due to the graduate adviser's tactical brilliance. Two decades earlier, in the chapter "Foot-ball in America" from *Walter Camp's Book of College Sports* (1893), Camp illustrated the meaning of "pluck" as the key to football success, with the story of "two little chaps" who once played for Yale, at 125 pounds apiece, "together a little over the weight of the varsity snap back." Realizing that the team that year was overconfident and undertrained, the two players took it upon themselves to mold the scrub team into a force that would challenge the varsity men out of their complacency. Without consulting the captain they began organizing and drilling the scrubs, until they were actually outplaying the "overfed, underworked university players." "These two boys began to show them the way to make use of brains against weight and strength" so successfully that the varsity "speedily developed under this experience into one of Yale's strongest teams." The most telling moment in this anecdote just precedes that triumphant line: "How those two ever got such work out of the rabble they had to handle, no one knows to this day." There were two lessons here: the primary principle that "brains will beat brute strength every time if you give them fair play," but also the secondary one that ingenious management can turn "rabble" into an effective work force.[27]

"Rabble" is a remarkable word. Camp's view of the coach–player relationship was always autocratic, as when, in an 1897 essay, he insisted that "no team will keep always extending itself save under the whip and spur of continual, and many times extremely severe, criticism."[28] The coach, as Camp repeatedly portrayed him, viewed the players from a distance, his outlook shaped by his larger vision and graver responsibilities. As Camp suggested in a 1912 essay, the players in fact constituted the coach's heaviest burden: "I doubt if any really conscientious, capable coach ever reached the end of the second week of fall practice without being pretty well convinced that every big man on his squad was slow and awkward and all the rest were featherweights or too stupid to get a signal even if it were repeated to them twice." As the players develop, credit goes not to them but to the coach: "Meantime the candidates themselves are, if the coaching is good, improving daily in the detail of the work."[29] "Rabble" goes beyond such suggestions of underdevelopment. The members of Yale's scrub team undoubtedly had the same sort of Anglo-Saxon and northern European genealogies as the members of the varsity; yet "rabble" during this period

Walter Camp revolutionized football with his many rules changes and became famous, among other things, for his annual selection of an All-American team.

Photo courtesy of Library of Congress. LC-B2-555-7[P&P].

usually referred to the growing urban underclass—Irish, Italian, Jewish, black. At its harshest, then, Camp's interpretation of football's cultural text makes the sport seem a model of social control. More typically, Camp seems conscientiously paternalistic: the players are boys, not men, to be molded by their experienced elders. In either case, success in football depends more on coaches than players.

Yet Camp was also the creator of All Americans, the man who selected the season's best players for special recognition. Particularly once *Collier's Weekly* showcased the All-American team as an annual feature, selection by Camp was the highest accolade to be won in college football. And as the game acquired its own history, Camp periodically measured present heroes against the "giants" of the past, selecting from the annual lists those names deserving of the highest Olympian honor. In the opening paragraph of "Heroes of the Gridiron," written for *Outing* in 1909, Camp's admiration of the game's great players, both past and present, seems obvious. "Were there really giants in those old football days?" Camp asked rhetorically. "To tell the truth, as one looks back, it certainly seems as if some of those moleskin warriors of other days were indeed veritable Goliaths, not only in prowess but in physique as well. Then as in comparison one comes down the long line of memorable players, the men of the later days loom large and one begins to think that perhaps there are just as many prodigies in the present decade as in those that have preceded it."[30]

The interpreter of football in terms of managers and workers was also the troubadour of individual heroes. But not without some uneasiness. Although his early selections reveal no reservations, over time Camp became strikingly self-conscious, even defensive, about singling out individual players for praise. The explanation may be simple: the greater the distance from his own youth and playing days, and the longer his involvement in various aspects of coaching, the less appropriate may have seemed the conferring of greatness on a handful of twenty-year olds. But All-Americans also presented a more serious challenge to Camp's advocacy of teamwork and managerial control. Camp's awareness of this challenge is apparent in a variety of ways. In selecting his All Americans of 1897, for example, he explicitly rewarded those players who illustrated his own values: placing the steady and reliable players on the first team, the more individually brilliant but erratic ones on the second.[31] In this same spirit the essay "Heroes of the Gridiron" concludes by praising "the man who can sacrifice self for the team." Such comments notwithstanding, a contradiction not only emerges from the very notion of All-Americans but also haunts Camp's writings generally. Its source was simply the game itself: for all its tactical possibilities, football also depended then as now on players who executed the game plan and sometimes exceeded its intentions.

This contradiction is played out most fully in Camp's last full-scale account of the sport, *The Book of Football,* in the collisions between its separate chapters (some of which first appeared as essays in *Century* magazine). In "General Strategy," Camp reasserted his fundamental values: "But while in American intercollegiate foot-ball, the development of players is of great interest, still more appealing to those who enjoy the sport for its strategical possibilities is the study and development of plays."[32] The chapter opens with a long anecdote of Yale's season in 1900, in which "the graduate" (Camp himself) persuades the captain to adopt a set of plays that he admits will provoke objections among the players and skepticism among observers, but whose success will show by the big games at the end of the season. Indeed, the graduate proves his point: despite a rocky beginning, strategy, together with the players' faith and hard work, ultimately results in lopsided victories over Columbia, Princeton, and Harvard.

The hero of the story, of course, is the brilliant "graduate." But in other chapters Camp concedes more power to the players, singling out numerous star athletes throughout the game's already rich history. In the chapter "Personality in Football," Camp notes that before 1876 popular interest in the new sport was slight. "Up to that time few besides the players and would-be candidates manifested any desire to witness the games; but in the next decade public interest increased amazingly." Camp's explanation: "The game took on organized methods, individual players became known for their prowess, and the beginnings of marked 'hero-worship' of prominent players could be noted."[33] The simple comma elides the fact that "organized methods" and individual "prowess" refer to radically different accounts of football's meaning. Camp's discussion of star players in this essay is full of defensiveness and reluctant concessions. Athletic heroism is less celebrated than defended, on the grounds that it is not as pernicious as it seems. "So, on the whole, it is not entirely bad that there should be these stars in athletics," Camp wrote, "for most of them acquire their shining qualities through a clean life, practical self-denial, discipline, obedience, unmurmuring pluck, and a good deal of patience."[34] Camp was equally defensive in the book's final chapter, "All-Time, All-America Teams":

> To be chosen a member of the All-America team in foot-ball falls to the lot of few men who have not practised certain virtues, and practised them for several seasons. To their elders it may seem a foolish casting of the lime-light upon boys whom, in their maturer view of things, they regard as unable to stand the flattering notice. But if these elders could only know these young men as they are known among their intimates, they would speedily be disabused of the delusion that the boys are in danger of being spoiled in any such fashion. Year after year a boy sees the class

ahead of him go out into the world and knuckle bravely down to hard knocks and hard work, sees his own turn coming, and gets a fairer perspective of the relation of things than his timorous elders give him credit for.[35]

Camp's defensiveness is striking. This concluding chapter on All-Americans immediately follows "The Captain and the Coach," where he characteristically approves the sacrifice of "individual brilliancy" for the sake of the "far greater effectiveness of the eleven men" working together as a team. Rationality, efficiency, and the importance of winning: these, according to Walter Camp, made American football a valuable sport. Yet the public cared more about "individual brilliancy." "The Captain and the Coach" is Camp's penultimate chapter; whether by design or not, he gave the final word to the All-Americans.

Camp thus seems an author who lost control of his text. Besides the primary force behind rule making and the organization of intercollegiate football, Camp was the game's tireless proselytizer and publicity agent. But his success in these roles meant a different kind of failure. "Fifteen years ago," Camp wrote in the *Century* in 1894, "when some of the American colleges were endeavoring against great odds to establish the sport of foot-ball, I undertook the then extremely unpleasant task of begging for space in daily papers, weekly periodicals, and magazines in which to exploit the advantages of the sport. It was hard and thankless work, for the real devotees of the game were few in number, and gibes were many. It took the most zealous efforts of those of us who really cared for the sport to persuade editors occasionally to allow a game to be written up by an actual player." Unfortunately, in Camp's view, the discovery by "parents and the general public…that the game was not barbarous, brutal, or demoralizing" had an unintended impact on the game: "During the last two or three years it has become over-popular with the public, and this craze has led it to assume an importance and prominence wholly unsought."[36]

Although the occasion for Camp's essay was the widespread criticism of football's brutality, the larger issue concerned the relationship of the game to its popular audience. Camp envisioned football as the ideal training ground for a managerial elite, and for this he campaigned fervently. He wanted the game to become popular, so that its benefits could be widely shared, but without the inevitable consequences of popularity. The more popular the game became, the more its control by a northeastern elite—the students and graduates of Yale, Harvard, and Princeton—eroded. As football became the object of harsh criticism—for brutality, "professionalism," distorted university priorities, financial excess—Camp repeatedly defended the elite universities that initiated intercollegiate competition, casting blame elsewhere. In this spirit he wrote in 1897, during yet another crisis over brutality on the field, "It is the utter disregard of the interests of the sport itself exhibited by athletic-club teams and some of the mere remote college teams [in the Midwest, that is] that keeps up the agitation against football, and furnishes ammunition for those who enjoy a shot at anything prominent in the public eye."[37] The game Camp created, his vision of its place in American life, kept slipping away from him. Having promoted football to an indifferent public, Camp had to come to terms with public desires far from his own. Having once begged for space in the daily papers, Camp came to rue the manner in which the daily papers transformed individual players into celebrities and melodramatized football violence. And having repeatedly insisted that football was a game of teamwork, Camp had to confront the fact that the great majority of spectators cared considerably more about feats of individual prowess.

An ambivalent quarrel with his audience runs through Camp's writings. Without spectators, football could not survive; with spectators, football took a different course from the one Camp envisioned. Through hindsight this course seems inevitable. Once American collegians broke with rugby rules over the random way in which the ball was put in play from the scrum, football developed in the direction of increasing rationalization—toward "scientific" football. What this meant by the early 1890s was flying wedges and other forms of mass-momentum play: by intention, the epitome of "scientific" strategy (the surest way to gain five yards in three downs with minimal risk of fumbling); by accident, the cause of countless injuries. Moreover, though fascinating to the strategist who devised or at least understood the methods for focusing the greatest offensive force on the weakest part of the defense, mass play was uninteresting to anyone lacking "inside" knowledge of the game. In essays such as "A Plea for the Wedge in Football," Camp continued to champion mass-momentum plays because they rewarded the teams with the most brilliant tacticians and the most disciplined training. At the same time the press, claiming to represent the public, called for their abolition because they were both brutal and boring. Boredom seemed the chief threat in 1891, as Camp wrote: "A long run behind a cleverly-moved wedge is by no means unattractive, and it is a play easily understood and appreciated. But close mass work in the centre, crowding down two or three yards at a time, while it may, and sometimes does, entail just as much skill and combined team work, will never appeal in the least to the spectator, and certainly would, if carried to an extreme, disgust him with the game. And the spectator—that is the spectator who has some technical knowledge of the game—is the man whose opinions are likely in the long run to prevail."[38] By 1893 Camp was acknowledging that brutality had become an additional issue: "The public, as represented by the press, agree with the faculties in desiring the elimination of plays wherein the danger is or may become great, and in addition the public desires the open style of play—the more open the better. Spectators wish to see exactly what is being done, and in kicks and individual runs therefore lies their principal interest." Camp grudgingly conceded in this case that momentum plays should be altered, though not banned entirely: "That the spectator wishes them abolished does not of itself prove that such action should be taken, although the college spectator ought to be considered next to the player."[39]

The crux of Camp's quarrel with the public was his desire for control: control of the games' outcomes through a style of offensive play that minimized the risk of losing the ball and maximized intelligence and generalship, control of football's place in the university and in the larger society, control in interpreting the sport's meaning. Football in all these aspects escaped his control—not quite

Frankenstein's monster berserk in the countryside, but certainly a creation grown more powerful than its creator. The spectators' desire for open play won out, if only after several years of wrangling. The advantages of sheer weight became increasingly obvious, despite Camp's repeated insistence that brains would win over brawn.[40] Hero-worship prevailed with the greater public, despite Camp's repeated insistence on the value of teamwork. And popularity fed unwelcome "extravagance" and distorted priorities in a variety of other ways. "We want the sport within reasonable bounds," Camp wrote in 1895, "—we want it clean, honest and vigorous, but not spectacular or extravagant."[41] Yet spectacular and extravagant it was. Even the great Thanksgiving Day football games in New York between Yale and Princeton in the 1880s and early 1890s became something very different from what had been intended. Writing in 1894, when these games seemed to have gotten out of hand (enormous crowds, huge gate receipts, the postgame riotous behavior of students in the Bowery theaters), Camp claimed that the colleges had first chosen Thanksgiving simply for the convenience of students on holiday, New York because it was "the place *par excellence* for a neutral ground and a fair field." That the Thanksgiving Day game in the city became considerably more than an extracurricular activity for the players and their classmates was not the fault of the colleges: "The public have come to regard the game as one of the important 'sporting events' of the year, and have attached to it many attributes in themselves undesirable."[42]

Not always, but often enough, "the public" becomes openly the enemy in Camp's writings on football. In early articles, while still needing to play the promoter, Camp more simply and enthusiastically called attention to the game's growing popularity, and he approved all changes that contributed to "the pleasure of the spectators."[43] But as popularity itself began to change the game, Camp developed a more ambivalent attitude. In a 1910 essay he could invoke the spectators as a "moral force" operating for football's good. But in 1913 he bluntly stated: "With the wave of popularity that has seized upon all forms of athletic sport, the spectator has become a great problem."[44]

Camp's loss of control over football's cultural meanings was thus part of a larger loss of control over the game itself. In relation to the questions of power raised by cultural theory, the example of Walter Camp challenges any simple model of manipulation from above. Football experienced no simple populist takeover, of course; in calling the spectator the "great problem." Camp failed to name the entrepreneurs and media that developed and profited from football spectatorship. But once constituted as spectators, ordinary people did in fact exert some control over the sport's development, and even more over its meanings. Spectators became a constituency whose desires had to be accommodated, and an audience that read the game according to its own interests.

Camp's writings also remind us that the power of cultural narratives is not shared, whether equally or unequally, by "authors" and "readers" alone; some of it resides in the text itself. That is, at revealing moments in Camp's writings the game of football itself challenges the meanings that he would impose on it. The best example of this is Camp's account of the 1885 Yale–Princeton game, published initially in the popular children's magazine *St Nicholas* in 1889, then incorporated into *Walter Camp's Book of College Sports* (1893)—a rare tended anecdote in what is primarily a treatise on football with the usual Campian themes. The story opens in this way: "One of the most magnificent dashes ever made on an American foot-ball field was the run made by Lamar, of Princeton, in the game with Yale which was played upon the Yale field, November 21, 1885." Princeton reputedly had the stronger team that season, but the managerial genius of Peters, the Yale captain who "had done wonders with his recruits," was immediately apparent as the game opened. Stunning Princeton with an early goal, Yale continued to hold its lead well into the second forty-five-minute half and seemed "certain of victory" as the clock wound down, confirming Camp's belief that tactics would defeat mere physical superiority. Camp even uncharacteristically interjected a little novelistic coloring at this point, as he described Princeton's plight: "The sun was low in the horizon, nearly forty minutes of the second half were gone, and no one dared to hope such failing fortunes could be retrieved in the few remaining minutes." But then, with Yale in possession of the ball, Peters faced a crucial decision: he could "continue with the running game and thus make scoring against him impossible and victory certain," or he could "send the ball by a kick down in front of his enemy's goal and trust to a fumble to increase his score." Electing to kick, Peters implicitly defied some sixty previous pages of Camp's advice on proper tactics for achieving victory; but Camp now as storyteller offered no criticism, and he even made what was for him a startling comment: "A kick was surely the more generous play in the eyes of the crowd." Yale's kick was "perfect," but "Lamar, with the true instinct of the born runner," brilliantly eluded two "inexperienced tacklers," broke into the open field, and raced toward the goal line just beyond the grasp of "Peters, a strong, untiring, thoroughly trained runner" and "the captain of a team which but a moment before had been sure of victory." Building dramatic intensity with all of the novelist's devices (rare in his usually flat, prosaic writing), Camp concluded this way:

> How he ran! But Lamar—did he not too know full well what the beat of those footsteps behind him meant? The white five yard lines fairly flew under his feet; past the broad twenty-five-yard line he goes, still with three or four yards to spare. Now he throws his head back with that familiar motion of the sprinter who is almost to the tape, and who will run his heart out in the last few strides, and, almost before one can breathe, he is over the white goal-line and panting on the ground, with the ball under him, a touch-down made, from which a goal was kicked, and the day saved for Princeton. Poor Lamar! He was drowned a few years after graduation, but no name will be better remembered among the football players of that day than will his.[45]

There are elements in this remarkable tale that reinforced Camp's managerial master narrative: captain Peters's early success and the vulnerability of inexperienced tacklers most obviously. But what is the reader to make of Lamar's "instinct of the born runner," with its implication of innate physical superiority rather than "pluck" or "brains"? The better team triumphed, not by brains over brawn, but by "instinct," individual brilliance, and the opponent's unwise decision to kick. And what, finally, of Lamar's untimely death, so unexpectedly appended to his moment of heroics? The motif is a familiar one: the fleetingness of fame, the bizarre twists of fate, the athlete dying young. Familiar ideas, but alien to Camp's usually detached, pragmatic analysis of football. Both Lamar's last-second touchdown dash and his shocking death give a romantic conclusion to what began as a lesson in technical efficiency and ingenious leadership.

The contradiction in the essay runs deep. Camp's master narrative of football made a hero of the corporate manager by wedding an older ideal of individual prowess to the requirements of the modern corporation. Camp's exemplary captains and coaches were not bloodless intellectuals but charismatic leaders. In the narrative of the Yale–Princeton game that composite heroic figure is separated into Peters and Lamar—the modern and the antimodern, the corporate manager and the swashbuckling hero—as if the game itself could not sustain the narrative Camp imposed on it by locating all of the necessary virtues in a single figure. Camp complicated matters further when he called Peters's decision to kick a "generous" one. The captain's goal, as reiterated throughout the book's earlier discussion of training and tactics, was to *win*. The wise captain exploited every opportunity, took every advantage—attacking the defense, for example, at its weakest point. Camp's was a *democratic* sporting ethic that presupposed success would go to those who earned it. For the "generous" captain, on the other hand, winning was less important than the thrill of competition, the satisfaction of playing well, the high principle of sportsmanship. The lineage of the "generous" captain would go back through aristocrats' sons on English public-school playing fields to Renaissance gentlemen for whom style was all-important. Those aristocratic gentlemen did not need to win because they had already "won" at life by virtue of their birth; *how* they played mattered most because the correct manner demonstrated a proper use of their birthright. The "generous" captain in Camp's tale, then, ceases to be the managerial hero, the figure of "pluck," becoming instead a companion to Lamar from a premodern, aristocratic past.

The chief author of American football produced conflicting narratives, apparently without intention. Not just the public audience but the game itself exerted pressure on Camp's narrative of managerial control. Lamar's run became legendary, an event evoked frequently by football reporters in the 1890s and early 1900s as the benchmark against which other great runs were measured. It was remembered not just because of spectators' preference for individual prowess but because of the game's capacity to make the heroic possible. The arrangement of the concluding chapters of *The Book of Football* that I noted earlier— "The Captain and the Coach" followed by "All-Time, All-America Teams"—is ultimately appropriate, then. By juxtaposing the managerial and the heroic aspects of football, Camp touched on a dialectic that informed the game from its beginnings. By assigning the final pages to the exploits of football's greatest heroes, intentionally or not he acknowledged the course football would follow into the future. The culture of celebrity, in sport the singling out of individual heroes from their teammates or mass of competitors, would become conspicuous by the 1920s. The irony of this development, toward which Camp's writings point, should not be lost on us. The hunger for heroes in the modern world is a powerful *antimodern* impulse, but one fed by the most advanced technologies of the mass media and the techniques of promotion they make possible. Camp's writings also lead to another conclusion: even the most powerful authors of cultural narratives have limited control over their texts.

Notes

1. On Camp's importance to football, see Martin, "Walter Camp and His Gridiron Game," pp. 50-55, 77 81; Ronald A. Smith's profile in Porter, *Biographical Dictionary of American Sports*, pp. 85- 87; and Smith, *Sports and Freedom*, pp. 83-88.
2. Martin, "Walter Camp and His Gridiron Game," p. 54.
3. Davis, "A Day with the Yale Team," p. 1110.
4. See *Independent*, March 22, 1900, p. 715; *New York Times*, November 20, 1897, p. 3; and *World*, November 30, 1893, p 1.
5. Camp, "Methods and Development in Tactics and Play," p. 173.
6. See chap. 11 of Smith, *Sports and Freedom*.
7. Hollis, "Intercollegiate Athletics," pp. 538-39.
8. See Davis, "Evolution of American College Football," in Walsh, *Intercollegiate Football*, pp. 477 79; and Waldorf, *NCAA Football Rules Committee*.
9. As I write, the dominance of coaches may be waning, for basic economic reasons. In professional sport, the rise in players' salaries now means that most coaches and managers earn considerably less than the star players they are to control. Even in professional football, where this increase in players' salary has been smaller and slower, we now have teams such as the Miami Dolphins paying the star quarterback Dan Marino $5 million a year and the coach, Don Shula, $1 million. In college sports, the lure of these huge salaries has increasingly led undergraduates to leave college for the pros before their eligibility expires, with the result that the players' and the coaches' interests at that level are more obviously at odds.
10. Camp, *American Football* (1891), pp. 9-11. Camp had been making the same points since at least 1888 in popular magazines. See, for example, "American Game of Foot-ball," p. 858; and "Game and Laws of American Football," pp. 68-76.
11. Camp, "American Game of Foot-ball," p. 858.
12. Walter Camp, letter to the "Editor's Open Window," pp. 379-81; "Football of 1891," pp. 153-57; and "'Interference' in Football," p. 1115.
13. Camp, "New Football," *Outlook* (1912), p. 174.
14. Camp, *Walter Camp's Book of College Sports*, pp. 99, 117ff.
15. Camp, "Football of 1891," p. 155. Similarly, Deland was a chess master; for him as well as Camp, war and football were both contests of strategy.
16. Camp and Deland, *Football*, p. iv.
17. Camp, *American Football*, p. 81.
18. Camp, "Football of 1891"; "Football at the Colleges," p. 1161; and "Great Teams of the Past," p. 281.
19. See, for example, Camp, "College Football," *Outing*, pp. 384-90; and "Football Season," p. 1090.
20. Camp, *Book of Football*, pp. 333-34.
21. See Camp, "Making a Football Team," pp. 131-43; and "What Are Athletics Good For?," pp. 259-72.
22. Camp, "Team Play in Foot-ball," p. 845.
23. Camp, *Book of Football*, pp. 20, 33.
24. Taylor, *Principles of Scientific Management*, pp. 36-37.

25. Ibid., p. 60; Camp, *Book of Football*, p. 88.

26. Camp, *Book of Football*, pp. 196, 202, 212-13.

27. Camp, *Walter Camp's Book of College Sports*, pp. 139-41.

28. Camp, "College Football," *Harper's Weekly*, pp. 1185-86.

29. Camp, "Making a Football Team," p. 141.

30. Camp, "Heroes of the Gridiron," p. 131.

31. Camp, "Review of College Football," pp. 1233-34.

32. Camp, *Book of Football*, p. 192.

33. Ibid., pp. 137-38.

34. Ibid., p. 140.

35. Ibid., p. 344.

36. Camp, "Current Criticism of Foot-ball," p. 633.

37. Camp, "Football Notes," p. 1210.

38. Camp, "Football of 1891," p. 154.

39. Camp, "Football of 1893," p. 117.

40. See, for example, Camp, "Football. Review of the Season of 1896," pp. 26-29; and "Football of '97," pp. 133-36.

41. Camp, "Football of '95," p. 176. See also "Athletic Extravagance," pp. 81-84; and "Some Abuses in Athletics," pp. 714-17.

42. Camp, "Current Criticism of Foot ball," pp. 633-34.

43. Camp, "American Game of Foot-ball," p. 858.

44. Camp, "New Football," *Outing*, p. 17; and "What Are Athletics Good For?," p. 270.

45. Camp, *Walter Camp's Book of College Sports*, pp. 142-46.

PART IV

SPORT, THE GREAT DEPRESSION, AND TWO WORLD WARS, 1915-1950

The tumultuous changes that took place between 1915 and 1950 greatly affected American sport. The Great Depression, two World Wars, the rise of a consumer culture, women's suffrage, and the Northern migration of Southern African Americans had a decided influence on sport among various individuals and groups at all levels of organization extending from Little League baseball to professional boxing. This period witnessed, among other things, expansion of all-black sporting organizations, an increase in public recreation programs, building of elaborate athletic facilities and sports arenas, growth of less expensive mass sport, increased involvement of women in sport, and the rise of sport heroes.

During World War I sport played a significant role in the American military. The armed services organized and promoted a variety of individual and team sports for enlisted men both at training camps in the United States and behind the front lines in France. According to Steve Pope in chapter 9, "The World War I American Military Sporting Experience," intentionally connecting sport with military preparedness was a "newly invented early-twentieth-century tradition" and served a variety of purposes and objectives. It was, in Pope's words, "the most efficient means to cultivate national vitality, citizenship, and the martial spirit." It also had the added value of infusing soldiers with such values as obedience and citizenship while at once helping "restore class schism, social order, unity, and patriotism to the nation."

Certainly one of the greatest athletes of the first half of the twentieth century was the African American boxer Joe Louis. The second black heavyweight champion of the world (the first was the controversial Jack Johnson, who held the title from 1908 to 1915), Louis realized hero status of arguably unparalleled proportions in the African American community because of his ring triumphs and the manner in which he lived his life and carried himself in public. So great was his fame that African American children jumped rope to rhymes about Louis; Richard Wright, Maya Angelou, and other African American intellectuals penned literally thousands of words indicating Louis's enormous influence on them and others in the African American community; and some 43 songs in honor of Louis were created by musicians in such genres as jazz, gospel, ballad, and blues. In chapter 10, "In Sports the Best Man Wins: How Joe Louis Whupped Jim Crow," Theresa E. Runstedtler provides an insightful account of Louis's hero status and what he came to represent to African Americans. Using an array of primary and secondary sources, Runstedtler places Louis in the context of the New Negro era and argues that not only was the great heavyweight champion of symbolic importance, but he "challenged the masculine foundations of white supremacy." He was the "preeminent 1930s race man," an extraordinary black athlete of great dignity and strength who stood for the collective assertion of black manhood by conquering white men in the ring.

Perhaps no Olympic event has attracted as much attention from scholars and popular writers alike as the 1936 Games in Berlin. The intersection of race, politics, world conflict, and great athletic performances created enormous international interest in the "Nazi Olympics." This interest has been kept alive by a plethora of articles and books as well as Leni Riefenstahl's now-famous documentary film *Olympia.* Recently, however, more academicians have paid an increasing amount of attention to the 1932 Los Angeles Olympic Games, recognizing that the Games in the City of Angels during the middle of the Great Depression was an extremely important mega-event characterized by a highly effective promotional and publicity campaign and outstanding athletic achievements. One of those academicians is Sean Dinces, who provides a fascinating look at the Games in chapter 11, "Padres on Mount Olympus: Los Angeles and the Production of the 1932 Olympic Mega-Event." Dinces provides details about how Los Angeles' commercial elite relied on "regionally specific notions of space and history" to organize and promote the 1932 Olympic Games. Specifically, the commercial elite reinforced the notion of Los Angeles as an unparalleled Olympic site by using promotional strategies that focused on the uniqueness of the southern California lifestyle, the glamour of the Games in relation to Hollywood, and the façade that the host city was a haven of multiculturalism.

Just one year after the Los Angeles Olympic Games, Wendell Smith, the respected African American sportswriter of the *Pittsburgh Courier,* began his campaign to convince the owners in Major League Baseball to sign African

American players. While much is known about the efforts of Smith and other African American sportswriters (such as Sam Lacy and Joe Bostic) to reintegrate Major League Baseball, we know less about the role Jewish Americans played in the campaign to include African Americans in the sport. Stephen H. Norwood and Harold Brackman help rectify that limitation in chapter 12, "Going to Bat for Jackie Robinson: The Jewish Role in Breaking Baseball's Color Line." Norwood and Brackman point out that members of the Jewish community played an important role in the campaign to desegregate the national pastime and this role was part of the general Jewish support for African American civil rights. The key individuals in this campaign were such well-known Jewish Americans as Boston city councilman and civil rights activist Isadore Muchnick and journalists Lester Rodney, Walter Winchell, and Shirley Povich. These men, undoubtedly motivated by idealism and moral standards and "shaped by Jewish values," brought national attention to the campaign to reintegrate Major League Baseball by denouncing the sport's color line while at once pricking the consciousness of white owners and upper-level administrators.

Suggested Readings

Alexander, Charles C. *Breaking the Slump: Baseball in the Depression Era*. New York: Columbia University Press, 2002.

Altherr, Thomas L. "Mallards and Messerschmitts: American Hunting Magazines and the Image of American Hunting During World War II." *Journal of Sport History*, 14(1987): 151-163.

Austin, Brad. "Protecting Athletics and the American Way: Defenses of Intercollegiate Athletics at Ohio State and Across the Big Ten During the Great Depression." *Journal of Sport History*, 27(2000): 247-270.

Baker, William J. *Jesse Owens: An American Life*. Urbana, IL: University of Illinois Press, 2006.

Bennett, Bruce L. "Physical Education and Sport at Its Best – The Naval Aviation V-5 Pre-Flight Program." *Canadian Journal of History of Sport*, 21(1990): 57-69.

Benson, Peter. *Battling Siki: A Tale of Ring Fixes, Race and Murder in the 1920s*. Fayetteville, AR: University of Arkansas Press, 2006.

Bullock, Steven R. "Playing for Their Nation: The American Military and Baseball During World War II." *Journal of Sport History*, 27(2000): 67-89.

Bullock, Steven R. *Playing for Their Nation: Baseball and the American Military During World War II*. Lincoln, NE: University of Nebraska Press, 2004.

Capeci, Dominic J. and Wilkerson, Martha. "Multifarious Hero: Joe Louis, American Society and Race Relations During World Crisis, 1935-1945." *Journal of Sport History*, 10(1983): 5-25.

Carroll, John M. *Fritz Pollard: Pioneer in Racial Advancement*. Urbana, IL: University of Illinois Press, 1992.

Carroll, John M. *Red Grange and the Rise of Modern Football*. Urbana, IL: University of Illinois Press, 2004.

Cavello, Dominick. "Social Reform and the Movement to Organize Children's Play During the Progressive Era." *History of Childhood Quarterly*, 3(1976): 509-522.

Chadwick, Bruce. *When the Game Was Black and White: The Illustrated History of Baseball's Negro Leagues.* New York: Abbeville Press, 1992.

Couturier, Lynn E. "Play With Us, Not Against Us: The Debate About Play Days in the Regulation of Women's Sport." *The International Journal of the History of Sport,* 25(2008): 421-442.

Crepeau, Richard. *Baseball: America's Diamond Mind, 1919-1941.* Gainesville: University Press of Florida, 1980.

Davidson, Judith. "Sport for the People: New York State and Work Relief 1930s Style." *Canadian Journal of History of Sport,* 19(1988): 40-51.

Dyreson, Mark. "American Ideas About Race and Olympic Races from the 1890s to the 1950s: Shattering Myths or Reinforcing Scientific Racism?" *Journal of Sport History,* 28(2001): 173-215.

Dyreson, Mark. "Mapping an Empire of Baseball: American Visions of National Pastimes and Global Influences, 1919-1941." In *Baseball in America and America in Baseball.* Donald Kyle, Robert R. Fairbanks, and Benjamin G. Rader (eds.), pp. 142-188. College Station, TX: Texas A&M University Press, 2008.

Dyreson, Mark. "The Emergence of Consumer Culture and the Transformation of Physical Culture: American Sport in the 1920s." *Journal of Sport History,* 16(1989): 261-281.

Englemann, Larry. *The Goddess and the American Girl: The Story of Suzanne Lenglen and Helen Wills.* New York: Oxford University Press, 1988.

Erenberg, Lewis. *The Greatest Fight of Our Generation: Louis vs. Schmeling.* New York: Oxford University Press, 2006.

Fetter, Henry D. "The Party Line and the Color Line: The American Communist Party, the Daily Worker, and Jackie Robinson." *Journal of Sport History,* 28(2001): 375-402.

Gems, Gerald R. *Windy City Wars: Labor, Leisure, and Sport in the Making of Chicago.* Lanham, MD: Scarecrow Press, 1997.

Gerber, Ellen. "The Controlled Development of Collegiate Sport for Women, 1923-1936." *Journal of Sport History,* 2(1975): 1-28.

Gerlach, Larry. "Baseball's Other 'Great Experiment': Eddie Klep and the Integration of the Negro Leagues." *Journal of Sport History,* 25(1998): 453-481.

Gorn, Elliott J. "The Manassa Mauler and the Fighting Marine: An Interpretation of the Dempsey-Tunney Fights." *Journal of American Studies,* 19(1985): 27-47.

Hietala, Thomas R. *The Fight of the Century: Jack Johnson, Joe Louis and the Struggle for Racial Equality.* Armonk, NY: M.E. Sharpe, 2004.

Howell, Colin D. "Borderlands, Baselines, and Bearhunters: Conceptualizing the Northeast as a Sporting Region in the Interwar Period." *Journal of Sport History,* 29(2002): 251-270.

Kaye, Andrew M. *The Pussycat of Prizefighting: Tiger Flowers and the Politics of Black Celebrity.* Athens, GA: University of Georgia Press, 2004.

Keys, Barbara. "Spreading Peace, Democracy, and Coca Cola: Sport and American Cultural Expansion in the 1930s." *Diplomatic History,* 28(2004): 165-196.

Kimball, Richard I. *Sports in Zion: Mormon Recreation, 1890-1940.* Urbana, IL: University of Illinois Press, 2003.

Lanctot, Neil. *Negro League Baseball: the Rise and Ruin of a Black Institution.* Philadelphia: University of Pennsylvania Press, 2004.

Lester, Robin. *Stagg's University: The Rise, Decline, and Fall of Big-Time Football at Chicago.* Urbana, IL: University of Illinois Press, 1995.

Lewis, Guy. "World War I and the Emergence of Sport for the Masses." *Maryland Historian,* 4(1973): 109-122.

Liberti, Rita. " 'We Were Ladies, We Just Played Basketball Like Boys': African American Womanhood and Competitive Basketball at Bennett College, 1928-1942." *Journal of Sport History,* 26(1999): 567-584.

Lowe, Stephen R. "Change, Continuity, and Golf's Battle of the Century." *Journal of Sport History,* 26(1999): 521-543.

Lucas, John A. "The Unholy Experiment—Professional Baseball's Struggle Against Pennsylvania Sunday Blue Laws, 1926-1934." *Pennsylvania History,* 38(1971): 163-175.

Margolick, David. *Beyond Glory: Joe Louis vs. Max Schmeling, and a World on the Brink.* New York: Alfred A Knopf, 2005.

Marvin, Carolyn. "Avery Brundage and American Participation in the 1936 Olympic Games." *Journal of American Studies,* 16(1982): 81-105.

Mennell, James. "The Service Football Program of World War I: Its Impact on the Popularity of the Game." *Journal of Sport History,* 16(1989): 248-260.

Miller, Patrick B. "To Bring the Race Along Rapidly: Sport, Student Culture, and Educational Mission at Historically Black Colleges During the Interim Years." *History of Education Quarterly,* 25(1995): 111-133.

Mormino, Gary Ross. "The Playing Fields of St. Louis: Italian Immigrants and Sports, 1925-1941." *Journal of Sport History,* 9(1982): 5-19.

Nathan, Daniel A. *Saying It's So: A Cultural History of the Black Sox Scandal.* Urbana, IL: University of Illinois Press, 2003.

O'Hanlon, Timothy P. "School Sports as Social Training: The Case of Athletics and the Crisis of World War I." *Journal of Sport History,* 9(1982): 5-29.

Oriard, Michael. *King Football: Sport & Spectacle in the Golden Age of Radio & Newsreels, Movies & Magazines, The Weekly and The Daily Press.* Chapel Hill, NC: University of North Carolina Press, 2001.

Osbourne, John. "To Keep the Life of the Nation on the Old Lines: The Athletic News and the First World War." *Journal of Sport History,* 14(1987): 137-150.

Park, Roberta J. "Sport and Recreation Among Chinese American Communities of the Pacific Coast From Time of Arrival to the 'Quiet Decade' of the 1950s." *Journal of Sport History,* 27(2000): 445-480.

Regalado, Samuel O. "Sport and Community in California's Japanese American Yamato Colony, 1920-1945." *Journal of Sport History,* 19(1992): 130-143.

Riess, Steven A. "Professional Baseball and Social Mobility." *Journal of Interdisciplinary History,* 11(1980): 235-250.

Riess, Steven A. *Touching Base: Professional Baseball and American Culture in the Progressive Era.* Urbana IL: University of Illinois Press, 1999.

Roberts, Randy. *Jack Dempsey, The Manassa Mauler.* Baton Rouge: Louisiana State University Press, 1979.

Rominger, Donald, Jr. "From Playing Field to Battleground: The United States Navy V-5 Pre-Flight Program in World War II." *Journal of Sport History,* 12(1985): 252-264.

Ruck, Rob. *Sandlot Seasons: Sport in Black Pittsburgh.* Urbana, IL: University of Illinois Press, 1987.

Schmidt, Raymond. "Lords of the Prairie: Haskell Indian School Football, 1919-1930." *Journal of Sport History,* 28(2001): 403-426.

Schmidt, Raymond. *Shaping College Football: The Transformation of an American Sport, 1919-1930.* Syracuse, New York: Syracuse University Press, 2007.

Schultz, Jaime. " 'A Wager Concerning a Diplomatic Pig': A Crooked Reading of the Floyd of Rosedale Narrative." *Journal of Sport History* 32(2005): 1-21.

Seymour, Harold. *Baseball: The People's Game.* New York: Oxford University Press, 1990.

Silber, Irwin. *Press Box Red: The Story of Lester Rodney, The Communist Who Helped Break the Color Line in American Sports.* Philadelphia: Temple University Press, 2003.

Smith, Thomas G. "Outside the Pale: The Exclusion of Blacks from the National Football League, 1934-1946." *Journal of Sport History,* 15(1988): 255-281.

Tygiel, Jules. *Baseball's Great Experiment: Jackie Robinson and His Legacy.* New York: Oxford University Press, 2008.

Wenn, Stephen R. "A Suitable Policy of Neutrality? FDR and the Question of American Participation in the 1936 Olympics." *The International Journal of the History of Sport,* 8(1991): 319-335.

Wenn, Stephen R. "George S. Messermith and Charles H. Sherrill on Proposed American Participation in the Berlin Olympics." *Journal of Sport History,* 16(1989): 27-43.

Wiggins, David K. "Wendell Smith, the Pittsburg Courier-Journal and the Campaign to Include Blacks in Organized Baseball, 1933-1945." *Journal of Sport History,* 10(1982): 5-29.

Zieff, Susan G. "From Badminton to the Bolero: Sport and Recreation in San Francisco's Chinatown, 1895-1950." *Journal of Sport History,* 27(2000): 1-29.

Zingg, Paul J. "The Phoenix at Fenway: The 1915 World Series and the Collegiate Connection to the Major League." *Journal of Sport History,* 17(1990): 21-43.

CHAPTER 9

THE WORLD WAR I AMERICAN MILITARY SPORTING EXPERIENCE

◼ *S.W. Pope* ◼

Between 1917 and 1919, the armed services made sports and athletic training a central component of military life. Millions of enlisted men participated in organized sports at domestic training camps and behind the front lines in France. On playing fields at home and in Europe, "narrow-chested clerks made three-base hits on the same ball teams with college athletes and lean-visaged philosophers learned how to use their fists," boasted *Scientific American.*[1] At Camp Devens, one could see Walter R. Agard, a former Amherst College Greek instructor, spar with light-heavyweight champion "Battling" Levinsky (aka Barney Lebrowitz). "Uncle Sam has created not only an army of soldiers," one writer observed, but "an army of athletes."[2] Sportswriter Albert Britt suggested that every high school and college construct memorial lists alongside the playing fields—these would bear the names of the soldier athletes who had made the ultimate sacrifice. "Let their memory be an inspiration," Britt declared, "to bodily fitness and clean, hard sportsmanship for every boy who comes after."[3]

This vision linking sports and the military was a newly invented early-twentieth-century tradition. The goals, ideology, and organization of the modern American military were profoundly transformed by the Spanish–American War experience. A younger, reformist generation of uniformed officers assumed a moral commitment to the soldiers' welfare and used sport initially to combat desertion, alcohol use, and the lure of prostitution. Immediately after the Spanish–American War, the Navy pursued, as one of its central departmental policies, "all proper means to preserve the health of the ship's crews."[4] As one officer explained, this new orientation represented more than merely a growing awareness of physical fitness, but the knowledge of how to achieve it: "There

Reprinted form S.W. Pope, 1997, The World War I military experience. In *Patriotic games: Sporting traditions in the American imagination* (Oxford, UK: Oxford University Press), 139-155. By permission of Oxford University Press, Inc.

is no better way to make a good sailor," he explained, "and at the same time a loyal and true man to ship and country, than [through] these athletic contests."[5] Maintaining close intellectual and political ties with other preparedness advocates, civilian military officials embraced sport as the most efficient means to cultivate national vitality, citizenship, and the martial spirit. Military training, infused with a heavy dose of sports would not only train American men in the soldierly values of obedience, citizenship, and combat, but would also usefully restore class schisms, social order, unity, and patriotism to the nation. In fact, military sport, historian Donald Mrozek observes, reaffirmed the Victorian concept of manliness by adding a supportive "encrusting" set of rhetoric, rituals, and symbols.[6]

Despite its relative brevity, the war was the most intense conflict the nation had ever fought. Between the declaration of war and the November 1918 armistice, the United States drafted nearly three million men, transported two million of them to Europe, and lost over 100,000 in combat. By 1918, the cost per soldier was almost seven times that of the Civil War in constant dollars. The war prompted the first significant use of the corporate form of organization by Washington, and the first use of direct federal aid to state and local governments—driving a vigorous fiscal–military process of government centralization and growth consonant with an increasingly complex American society and economy. The federal government regulated industry, imposed price controls, and intervened in labor disputes. Adjusted for inflation, annual per-capita spending during the war was nearly twice as high as in either the Civil War or World War II. Indeed, federal outlays soared from $713 million in 1916 to $1.95 billion in 1917; $12.7 billion in 1918 and $18.5 billion in 1919—a 2500 percent increase in less than three years.[7]

The success of military sport during World War I surpassed all expectations—the war experience accelerated the development of a national sports culture. As a visible, respected state institution, the military was ideally suited for popularizing the causes of physical vitality and the American sporting spirit. Millions of men were introduced to sports for the first time and became converts to the cult of strenuosity. Contrary to many prewar speculations, the war did not destroy America's sporting spirit, but, to the contrary, did much to legitimize it in the public mind, both at home and abroad.[8] Shortly after the war, all West Point cadets were obligated not only to engage in major sports, but also learn how to teach them. The mission of spreading American sport throughout Europe culminated dramatically in the Inter-Allied Games of 1919. Never before had so much information about a sports event reached so many publications in so many countries. The War Camp Community Service recreation programs, initiated during the war, multiplied thereafter, and focused national attention on government-funded sports for the masses. The war experience brought sports into high-school and college curriculums. Between 1919 and 1921, 17 states passed physical-education legislation. More important, the military legitimized boxing (illegal in most states before the war) and football (restricted primarily to the collegiate scene) as bona-fide American spectator sports.[9]

Nineteenth-Century Views
of Sport and Military Preparedness

The American armed forces had traditionally tolerated sports as useful diversions from the rigors of military life. In 1777, George Washington urged his officers to promote exercise and vigorous amusements among the troops. As an heir to Protestant suspicions of play, as a believer in republican self-restraint, and as a leader of the revolutionary struggle, Washington insisted that recreations be *useful*. During the Civil War, soldiers, on holiday reprieves, competed in baseball, boxing, wrestling, horse racing, shooting matches, and foot races.[10] Some battalions held gala sports days. Troops embraced the young game of baseball with particular enthusiasm, playing both previously arranged and pickup games. According to baseball lore, a game between two New York infantry squads at Hilton Head, South Carolina, supposedly attracted 40,000 spectators, but in truth, the game's attendance figures were probably closer to several thousand. Nevertheless, the game, and many other such exhibitions, popularized the New York game, sparking a postwar explosion which made the sport the national pastime.[11]

Camp and field programs rewarded toughness, punished squeamishness, and created working conditions that freed up distinct periods of leisure time. Boxing became the other sport of choice. In 1861, American men rushed to war with vivid memories of the Thomas Sayers–John Heenan prizefight, and, within a military context, began to make explicit connections between boxing and warfare.[12] Elliott Gorn astutely captures the ring's symbolism behind Civil War battle lines. "Just as the ring brought momentary symbolic order to the chaos of working-class streets," Gorn writes, "so the drama of fist fighting between equals presented a poignant if fleeting alternative to the ghastliness of battle."[13] Sports like boxing became more than just the "moral equivalent to war"—they supplanted it because, according to Gorn, "the violence of play offered meaning denied by the anarchy of war."[14]

The young, inexperienced U.S. military establishment, in the years immediately following the Civil War, did not embrace sports and amusements in any serious way until the 1890s. During these years, the military was fighting the Indian wars in the West. Men stationed at remote posts relaxed through improvised amusements such as conversation, card playing, and drinking. The diary entries of Private B.C. Goodin (C Troop, First Cavalry), stationed at Fort Grant, Arizona, illuminate how he was on a mounted pass for half a day, and spent the rest of his off duty time reading in his quarters, strolling, playing cribbage, singing and dancing, attending an entertainment in the post chapel, and playing jokes on his comrades in the barracks. But daily mounted drills, saber exercises, revolver practice, and line skirmishes exacted a heavy physical toll on the enlisted men. Most cavalrymen were avid horse racers and often staged competitions against rival companies, civilians, and Indians. In regions where wild game was plentiful, the men sometimes went on extended hunting trips, and a few were ardent anglers. In some companies, athletically minded officers organized baseball games, track-and-field contests, and boxing matches. But, as the historian of the nineteenth-century U.S. regular Army explains, "few post commanders were personally interested in promoting an athletic program"; without any sort of servicewide athletic policy, "organized sports were engaged in as much as a method of gambling as for the enjoyment of the game."[15]

During the 1890s, attitudes toward sports shifted from a toleration of them as diversions to tentative experimentation, as the fledgling American military integrated athletics into the daily regimen of soldiers and sailors to bolster military fitness.[16] As the new century neared, military-sports advocates turned to the strenuous lifestyle. In 1890, Lieutenant C.D. Parkhurst began a series of essays on "The Practical Education of the Soldier," claiming that physical training should precede all specifically military activities, with the exception of battle itself. Parkhurst argued that exercise in the gymnasium and on the playing fields, fusing vitality, traditional deference, and republican virtue, would bring the soldier to a level of "quick and unthinking obedience to orders."[17] Lieutenant Colonel A.A. Woodhull claimed that the James Corbett–John L. Sullivan prizefight demonstrated the importance of speed and agility, and suggested that boxing elevated "primitive force" that harnessed athleticism to military ends.[18] Like their progressive physical-educator peers, military officials believed that cutting-edge physical-fitness programs would achieve specific, desirable results, underscoring, in the words of Mrozek, sport's "entry into the duty-day and into the obligation of 'service' of the American soldier."[19]

The growth of military sports was closely tied to its introduction into the military academies during the 1890s.[20] Prior to 1890, athletics at American military academies were obstructed by stringent restrictions, dismissive official attitudes, and a fundamental lack of functional organization. During these dark ages, for instance, tennis had to be played by cadets in dress coats, and a cadet was punished for having two buttons of his coat unbuttoned while he was playing baseball! The first Army–Navy football game, played on December 1, 1890, was the important watershed in military athletic history. On that memorable day, an impromptu gridiron was roped off on the West Point quadrangle. The Midshipmen's quarterback used nautical terms for signals, like "clear deck for action," while the Cadets employed military commands such as "right front into double line."[21] By 1895, the military academy's sports program had become competitive with established eastern colleges like Harvard, Yale, and Brown. Renowned sports authority Caspar Whitney proclaimed his unabashed admiration for the West Point and Annapolis football programs, just six years after their initiation, when he wrote that "no other institution in the United States more thoroughly demonstrates the *mens sana in corpore sano* in college sport than these two." Army Captain Richmond Davis received letters—from Alaska, Cuba, Puerto Rico, and the Philippines—about the annual Army–Navy game, which elevated the brotherhood of both services to a fuller appreciation of the good old song: "May the services united ne'er sever; But hold to their colors so true; The Army and Navy forever; Three cheers for the Red, White, and Blue."

Several years later, sportswriter Arthur Ruhl commended the Army–Navy game as a pleasant occasion, when "these strong and eager young men might meet and receive this greeting of each other's courage and resource and pluck, and not have to wait for it until those sterner games when they shall have to fight together."[22]

The military academy's sports program was buttressed by a mandatory system of physical training conceived by Lieutenant H.J. Koehler, physical director at West Point for 17 years. Koehler's program developed muscular fitness, and, more important, produced a heroic spirit. For 45 minutes each day, cadets systematically performed a battery of stretching and strengthening exercises. In all, by the turn of the century, just a decade after the legitimization of sports at the service academies, one-half of the cadets took active part in at least one sport; and the other half were enthusiastic spectators and rooters. In 1902 the *Army and Navy Journal* asserted that companies that excelled in athletics would also excel in military duty. Cavalry officer Edward L. King cited the "marvelous results" that the Eleventh Cavalry Regiment obtained when officers added athletics to military instruction. Recruits changed, according to King, from being "soft and awkward" into men who were "rugged, hardy, active, and tough as nails."[23]

The popularity of military baseball, between the Spanish War and World War I, owed much to the deepening inroads of the game at West Point, where the basic attitude apropos of baseball had changed from one in which authorities regarded games as an amusement, in which the outcome mattered little, to one in which a "must-win spirit" was instilled.[24] As the battle fleet continued to expand, so, too did baseball at the Naval Academy. Under the aegis of the Navy Athletic Association, the academy fielded a varsity baseball team along with teams in fencing, football, and rowing. Beginning in 1901, the highlight of each baseball season at Annapolis was the final game with West Point (staged, alternatively, at each academy)—the series was dominated by the Annapolis team. Under the tutelage of professional coaches, Annapolis not only won most of its games with West Point; it also proved its mettle against leading college teams.[25]

Military veterans sometimes worked to spread their newfound sporting gospel and combative exercise programs in civilian society. During the 1890s, for instance, General George A. Wingate promoted military training in New York City's public schools—an effort which culminated in the creation of the New York Public Schools Athletic League in the early years of the twentieth century.[26] With 100,000 members, the league claimed to be the "largest athletic body in the world." The league's transformation of Wingate's military-training program won it more recruits when musket swinging, marching, and fencing were supplanted by running, jumping, basketball, and a wide range of other athletic activities. *The Illustrated Sporting News* speculated that "the patriotic idea will not be in the least minimized" by such a change.[27] Through athletics, the students would acquire basic combative virtues; and the influence of the military would intermix with civilian leadership.

During the first decade of the twentieth century, the American armed forces moved from tentative experimentation with sports to an unqualified acceptance of them as essential elements of a soldier's responsibility. A new generation of West Point and Annapolis graduates chafed at the prospect of suppressing labor disputes and fighting Indians, and campaigned for a modern, national military. Despite its brevity, the Spanish–American War established the United States as an imperial power, whose newly acquired colonies in the Philippines, Guam, Puerto Rico, and Cuba prompted ambitious political and military leaders to double the size of the American armed forces.[28] The new military professionals worked to combat the endemic rate of desertions, and widespread vice among enlisted troops; and, in general, to make military life more attractive. Organized sports were central components in this mission.

Military officials assured doubters that sports and fitness activities made good military sense in developing needed physical endurance.[29] Early-twentieth-century discussions of military sports stressed the importance of building physical manhood. A writer for *Harper's Weekly* maintained that governmental sports sponsorship was designed to "turn sergeants and privates into all-round men," and that the spirit of military sports "meant more than merely improving the physique of the soldier."[30] The writer suggested that "Uncle Sam has not encouraged athletics for amusement," but for the way in which it produced the esprit de corps among both officers and enlisted men—a "rebuilding process which begins when the soldier puts on the blue or khaki."[31]

Despite the growing importance of physical fitness in military circles, its spread was highly erratic. Major R.L. Bullard, superintendent of athletics at Fort Snelling, estimated that the military's use of athletics and physical training in 1905 was "unsystematic, irregular and uncertain in the extreme."[32] Standards varied from post to post, and were dependent on initiatives of particular officers; spectatorship overshadowed mass participation. Lieutenant Colonel Charles Richard thought that physical training should be systematized throughout the year. According to him, officers needed to arrange monthly schedules as their "tastes dictate or their stations afford."[33] Lieutenant Edmund L. Butts, the leading advocate of military sports prior to World War I, declared that athletics "should not be made a fad, but a part of [a] soldier's training, and should be properly subordinated to the more important and practical duties of a soldier's life."[34]

World War I and the Maturation of Military Sport

The military moved to systematic application of sports during the 1916 border crisis sparked by the Mexican Revolution. Anticipating a full-scale war, the United States twice invaded Mexico, and twice more mobilized the National Guard along the border.[35] Without recreational facilities, there was nothing to compete with the saloons and red-light districts patronized by the 100,000 American troops. When reports of widespread venereal disease reached Washington, D.C., early in 1917, War Secretary Newton Baker sent Raymond Fosdick, of the Rockefeller Foundation, to investigate the situation.[36] Fosdick's report confirmed the brass's worst suspicions. Promptly thereafter, he was appointed head of the War Department's Commission of Training Camp Activities, which coordinated activities of other welfare organizations, such as the YMCA, the Knights of Columbus, and the Jewish Welfare Board, to ensure a wholesome environment for the enlisted men. Secretary Baker later admitted that military athletics were "an attempt to occupy the minds of the soldiers and to keep their bodies busy with wholesome, healthful, and attractive things,...to free [the body] from temptations which come to those who are idle."[37]

Shortly after the April 6, 1917 declaration of war, General John J. Pershing summoned YMCA experts for managing Army cantonments. The YMCA combated vices with sports and leisure activities.[38] A YMCA worker noted that "whether men found themselves in populous cantonments or in lonely guard posts, in [a] city or in [a] forest lumber camp," the Y's "right to service was unquestioned."[39] About 75 percent of American troops spent time in one of 32 training camps managed by the YMCA. The Y's war efforts were organized by Dr. John McCurdy, of the YMCA College at Springfield, a leader in the field of physical education, who had been chairman of the National Commission on Secondary Education and was a former editor of the *American Physical Education Review*.[40] As the official representative, in France, of the War Department's Commission on Training Camp Activities, McCurdy also undertook, in September 1917, the duties of YMCA athletic director for the American Expeditionary Forces (AEF). Shortly thereafter, McCurdy hired Dr. James Naismith, a Kansas University physical educator, the inventor of basketball, and a former National Guard chaplain, to head the Y's Hygiene Department. Naismith prepared literature and lectures, infused with Christian principles, on the importance of clean living, social hygiene, fighting efficiency, and the sporting spirit. National organizations, like the American Library Association and the Recreation Association of America, along with churches, social clubs, and fraternal lodges, supported the Y's mission with patriotic fervor.[41]

The YMCA assigned physical-fitness directors to each of the 32 military camps to coordinate the Y's sports mission. The directors sought to develop the abilities of average soldiers, rather than polishing the skills of star athletes.[42] Comprehensive sporting programs were established, featuring intercompany and barracks baseball and basketball leagues. YMCA sponsorship of athletic programs emphasized activities of military significance, including cross-country runs, obstacle races, and military dispatch relays—all done in military uniform.[43] According to an official spokesman, the first important promotional event for military mass athletics was a pentathlon held on Memorial Day in 1917, at an officers' training camp at Fort Niagara; 25 men from each company—375 in all—competed in the standing broad jump, relay races, medicine-ball throwing, 100-yard dashes, and a tug-of-war. This spectacle awakened thousands of mostly college men to the value of mass athletics. The Y's muscular Christian mission was enthusiastically endorsed by the military brass and a host of sports commentators as well.[44]

Many observers feared that U.S. involvement in the European war would wreak disaster on the American sports scene. Collegiate and professional athletics, the argument ran, would fall into entropy, as promising stars would be

Basketball team USMC. League Island Navy Yard, Philadelphia, Pennsylvania, 1923.
From YMCA of the USA Archives.

whisked off to the European front to fight the Huns. Such doomsday prognoses ultimately foundered after the successful incorporation of sports in the military. During the summer of 1917, War Secretary Baker publicized his support of military sports in numerous newspaper and magazine articles. When approached by Verne Lacy, chairman of the Western Association of the AAU, regarding the track- and-field championships scheduled for St. Louis in August 1917, Baker demonstrated his support by granting furlough privileges to athletes participating in an event whose proceeds went to the Red Cross.[45] In October, the War Department and the YMCA radioed the result of the World Series, between Chicago and New York, to the enlisted men in Honolulu, Manila, the Panama Canal zone, Paris, Koblenz, Vladivostok, and Constantinople—an endeavor repeated in 1918 and 1919.[46] Baker, like many other contemporaries, understood the vital connections between sport and Americanism.

The official actions of the military brass were bolstered by confident appeals in the popular media. When some colleges and universities considered discontinuing athletics, due to the War, Washington and Jefferson College football coach Sol Metzger presented evidence that indicated that not only did athletes exceed the regular student body in military enlistments, but that athletic programs usefully trained students for the war effort. Metzger wrote in the *New York Times*, "I regard participating in athletics now the patriotic duty of the student, in that training and preparation make him of far greater value to the country than if he did not have them."[47] Optimistic predictions by sports insiders, like Princeton professor Dr. Joseph Raycroft, did much to bolster public confidence in the compatibility of sports and military involvement. Quoted in *The Sporting Goods Trade Journal*, Raycroft estimated that "there will be more real and widespread athletic activity in this country during the next twelve months [1917-18] than ever before in our lifetime."[48]

Equally assuring to the American sports public were the efforts of Walter Camp. The dean of American football believed strongly in the complementary value of sport in military preparation, a belief that underlay his Naval Training Station athletic program, designed to teach sailors discipline, teamwork, fellowship, leadership, physical fitness, and toughness.[49] Standardized rules for boxing and wrestling were central components of Camp's naval-training regimen. A *New York Times* sportswriter noted that "Uncle Sam's army of stay-at-homes is behind the army of gone-to-war and has organized a system of athletics which is far better systematized than the athletics of the leading eastern universities since the date of the war's beginning."[50] Moreover, in addition to organizing a physical-fitness program for President Wilson's cabinet, which Camp supervised behind the Treasury building every morning, the single most popular event of Camp's wartime sporting activism was the development of his "daily dozen" exercise routine for all Americans concerned about keeping physically fit.[51]

In early March of 1918, two weeks before Germany's mighty spring offensive, the idea of sports for improving fighting efficiency had made sufficient progress, among officers and enlisted men, to warrant a comprehensive proposal written by the commander in chief of U.S. forces, regarding compulsory mass athletics in the Army. Mass athletics were designed to raise the physical efficiency of troops who could neither jump over six-foot-wide trenches, nor run 220 yards in 30 seconds; and who led the commander to assert that "such men could neither catch a Hun nor get away from one."[52] Clearly, an army of athletes had to be made. Led by Luther Gulick, a spirited campaign recruited 1,600 men, who were subsequently trained at the YMCA Training Schools at Springfield and Chicago; and by September, 300 new physical directors had sailed to France.[53] To improve physical efficiency among enlisted men, the YMCA appropriated over $300,000 worth of athletic goods.[54] In a short time, the Y had created an athletic structure which catered to the exigencies of various military regions. Ports of entry, SOS areas, aviation camps, training camps, combat zones, convalescent camps, and leave areas featured mass games, calisthenics, competitive sports, and boxing instruction.[55]

Organized athletic activities were designed to train enlisted men in the survival skills needed for life on the front. Combative exercises, particularly wrestling maneuvers, trained recruits for hand-to-hand combat. Baseball-throwing fundamentals were emphasized in grenade-tossing exercises. Scaling, balancing, jumping, and vaulting exercises incorporated gymnastic skills into daily trench maneuvers and basic survival skills for frontline combat. The greatest attention, however, was given to boxing as training for bayonet fighting.[56] Prior to 1917, boxing was mostly illegal in the United States; and "then came the war to dwarf the miniature battles of the squared circle," wrote *Outing* correspondent Thomas Foster. The result, he contended, was that "the duels of the fighters and their promoters became absurdly small alongside the greater duel and four-ounce gloves were puny weapons as compared with bayonets."[57] Before the American military intervened in Europe, a U.S. sergeant had been teaching Canadian recruits the use of the bayonet, and discovered that the essential movements of feet and hands in bayonet fighting are the same as those of boxing. After 1917, according to Foster, "Uncle Sam dragged the padded gloves out of discard and hastied them on the hands of boys that they may better cope with the Boche when they meet him with steel against steel."[58] For this effort, the military quickly assigned professional boxers, like Mike Gibbons, Johnny Kilbane, Benny Leonard, Packy McFarland, and "Battling" Levinsky, as instructors at training camps, under the direction of the Commission on Training Camp Activities. Boxing not only trained soldiers in hand-to-hand combat; it effectively relieved the monotony of military drilling. American soldiers learned to use the steel and, at the same time, became avid converts to what would become a principal spectator sport at home after the war.[59]

Official integration of sport into military training sparked a wave of team-athletic competition. Not surprisingly, the principal organized sports were baseball, football, and basketball—the big three American sports on the domestic front. Baseball, the national pastime, caught on like wildfire in every place where American troops were stationed on the French front. The *New York Times* marveled that the widespread enthusiasm for baseball in the military marked "a Utopia in athletic endeavor that pioneers in physical education have dreamed of, but never believed would be realized"—particularly, the way in which "every bare space behind the battle lines in France will be converted into a baseball diamond." In early March, the *New York Times* announced the spring training for "Uncle Sam's League"—"greater by far than all the major and minor leagues, together with the semiprofessional and amateur baseball organizations" in the United States, this baseball league was "vaster than any athletic movement in the history of sport," numbering over two million players.[60]

Equally impressive strides were made on the football field. Initially bypassed because of the considerable expenses needed for outfitting teams with pads and helmets, football was quickly recognized as a popular sport among soldiers and sailors, many of whom were former collegiate players and coaches. Service football found favorable opportunities for colleges and intracamp teams to battle in major stadiums. The game quickly proved an unexpected success during the 1917 season, when training-camp teams proved competitive with college football teams. *Outing* magazine noted that never before had so many American men played football. "In every army cantonment," the editor wrote, "footballs were as thick as pumpkins in an autumn cornfield."[61] Sport historian James Mennell suggests that service football popularized the collegiate game significantly. For those athletically inclined, service football was more accessible than the select collegiate game. And the nonplaying soldiers experienced the music, color, drama, and spirit of the game, previously limited to the collegiate crowd.[62] By the war's end, a *New York Times* sports journalist was confident that "football owes more to the war in the way of the spread of the spirit of the game than it does to ten or twenty years of development in the period before the war."[63]

Between February 1918 and June 1919, American soldiers followed service sports through the pages of *Stars and Stripes*, a weekly newspaper whose circulation grew from 30,000 to more than 526,000. Created as an internal organ of propaganda "to stimulate a healthy morale among troops of the AEF by giving them the news of the War and of America attractively and interestingly presented," *Stars and Stripes* became the best-known army newspaper in history.[64] Next to *Stars and Stripes*, the *Sporting News* was the most popular publication among the AEF. Its editor, Taylor Spink, persuaded baseball's American League to buy copies at a reduced rate and send them to the troops at the league's expense. Moreover, the U.S. postmaster allowed civilian readers to merely put a one-cent stamp on their copies if they wanted the paper delivered to overseas soldiers.[65] *Stars and Stripes* accepted the fact that any worthy American newspaper must have a respectable sports page. The editors soon realized that the American sporting experience could help the soldier relate to the war pressures. As an early editorial claimed, "the 'game of war' should hold no terrors for the average American soldier already trained in sports—the familiar experience of the playing field was a framework for war experiences."[66]

Occasionally, *Stars and Stripes* contributors waxed poetic on the nationalistic character of American sport. During the spring-training season of 1918, a soldier penned the following doggerel:

> He's tossed the horsehide far away to plug the hand grenade
> What matter if on muddy grounds this game of war is played?
> He'll last through extra innings and he'll hit as well as pitch
> His smoking Texas Leaguers'll make the Fritzies seek the ditch![67]

With less poetic, but equally assured, conviction, Walter Camp assessed the importance of athletics in American military preparation:

> Our boxing was made the basis of bayonet fighting and our baseball arms were adept in learning to throw the grenade. The men who had gone into the opposing football line when their signal came went "over the top" with that same abandon. Those who had made a stand on the last five-yard line in the grim determination of the gridiron field faced the scrimmage of war with the same do-or-die fortitude. Those who had raced on the cinder track and thrown their last efforts into the sprint at the finish were just as "game" when the pathway was a Flanders field or a Chateau Thierry line. The man who took the big chance on the motor track took the greater chances in the air with the same spirit. The man whose nerves had been tested with "two men on," "one out," and "a run to tie and two to win," stood smiling when the line was thin.[68]

Just as Camp praised athletics for preparing American soldiers for victories on foreign soil, other commentators, like Frank Kleeberger, of the University of California–Berkeley, interpreted German "brutality and unsportsmanlike conduct" as a function of a deficient national system of physical training.

Postwar Developments

Shortly after the armistice, the U.S. military converted Europeans to the athletic cause, which bolstered a maturing national sporting tradition. Although a vibrant sporting scene had existed in Europe for many centuries, American sports had steadily won the hearts and minds of Europeans during the war. United States military personnel saw themselves as international missionaries of the American sporting life. "Thanks to the American doughboy, and his confreres, the marine and the blue jacket, sport, the world over, is about to have its greatest revival," wrote sportswriter Edwin A. Goewey, early in 1919.[69] Noting that baseball had always "followed the flag" to places in Latin America and the Far East, Goewey surmised that it took "the big war" to introduce the game throughout Europe. The widespread popularity of American sport in Europe, accordingly, signaled "a new era for sport," reflecting the "increased interest and general feeling of good will toward the people of this country."[70] The lesson for postwar America, according to Goewey, was that, if subsidized and promoted by government, sport "would greatly improve in general health, and more splendid, more contented, and more democratic citizenship. Nothing does more for true democracy than sport, in which men of all ranks mingle and become brothers in effort and interest."[71]

Fletcher Brockman, a YMCA spokesman, made the case in even more explicit political terms. Speaking to the Physical Directors' Society in Detroit, Brockman said that "to teach half a billion people the true meaning of democracy and train them in its wise use" was the "supreme and urgent task before the world today." Under the able tutelage of Western capitalist societies, particularly the United States, Eastern European and Far Eastern countries could successfully be brought within the respectable, democratic fold, through YMCA-sponsored athletic programs. As an antidote to the wave of "radical democracy" emanating from Petrograd like a "cloud of poisonous gas," association athletics provided the "practical outworking of some of the most difficult problems in democracy."[72]

At no point were the American athletic missionaries' efforts more dramatically successful at converting the unbelievers to sports than during the Inter-Allied Games. The games were designed to provide "constructive and interesting bodily activity" for soldiers who were awaiting return to the States.[73] Military and YMCA officials feared that peace would provoke "moral temptations" and "disorderly physical expressions" among enlisted men.[74] A grand, military Olympiad would be a safety valve and a reinforcement of the military sporting message.

The YMCA handled the logistical details. Led by Elwood Brown, who capably pioneered the Far Eastern Games (designed to promote better relations among Chinese, Japanese, and Filipinos),[75] the Y procured huge amounts of athletic gear; prepared rule books and other printed material; secured pageantry specialists, grounds and prizes; and organized the elimination-contest schedules. With the full cooperation of the YMCA, the Army invited the military commanders of 29 nations, colonies, and dependencies to participate in "keen rivalry, a free field, and fair play"—the ends for which the Allied forces had fought the war. American Olympic gold-medal winner Jim Thorpe described the Games as "one of the most worthwhile experiments the world had ever seen"; he praised Brown as one ideally suited to lead the way, saying Brown was "equipped with a knowledge of the reaction of various races in athletic competition, as perhaps no other man."[76] The YMCA agreed to build a monumental structure, the Pershing Stadium, which would accommodate 40,000 spectators, and would be presented to the French people as a token of American goodwill. Situated in the Bois de Vincennes (on the outskirts of Paris), where French knights, since the time of Henry of Navarre, had contended, the site, donated by the French government was ideally located. The YMCA appropriated one million francs for the preparation of the site and for general operating expenses. On June 22, the stadium was officially dedicated by distinguished guests from all the Allied nations, military delegations, and numerous eloquent speakers who promoted the cause of international sport. Before a standing-room-only crowd of 90,000, Edward G. Carter, the YMCA's chief secretary, proclaimed that the larger meaning of the AEF championships at the Inter-Allied Games "lies not in a few hundred final competitors, but in the hundreds of thousands of soldiers of average skill who unconsciously have established play for play's sake, and sport as the possession of all."[77]

The democratic rhetoric of international sports was not entirely invented, for, in fact, the AEF elimination contests, held between January and June 1919—in football, basketball, boxing, wrestling, baseball, golf, shooting, soccer, swimming, tennis, and track and field—constituted the most extensive athletic program hitherto executed under one management.[78] The AEF championships in football and boxing were a huge success. According to a YMCA spokesman, "no season in the history of sport ever developed better matched teams or more exciting contests" than the preliminary American football games held to decide the supremacy of the Second Army. The finals, won by the Seventh Division, were watched by the Army with all the interest ever called forth by a Yale–Harvard game or a world's championship series—75,000 officers and other personnel participated in football. Thousands of enlisted men competed in the boxing elimination bouts. The majority of the finalists had been professionals before the war. "To witness or take part in a boxing match was, next to a good feed and baseball, the most enjoyment in the Army," Frederick Harris observed, citing the total of more than six million spectators as evidence enough for his assertion. Much of the credit for the success of the boxing contests derived from the active involvement of American welfare organizations, like the Knights of Columbus, the Jewish Welfare Board, and the Red Cross.[79]

American athletes took the Games very seriously. During the rainy French spring, soldier–athletes trained in 150 airplane hangars. The 400′x 150′ facilities were ample enough for football scrimmages, a dozen simultaneous basketball games, and about twice that number for volleyball practice.[80] American and European newspapers dutifully popularized the forthcoming Games. During the week preceding the Games, for instance, the *New York Herald* published 31 items on them, for a total of more than 19,000 words; the *Chicago Tribune* printed 90 items consisting of over 26,000 words; and the *London Daily Mail* featured 69 articles containing over 10,000 words. French newspapers followed suit. Once the Games began, the U.S. government's Committee on Public Information headed the effort to transmit news daily, by wireless, to the United States, Great Britain, Czechoslovakia, and to places throughout the Balkans.[81]

On opening day, 30,000 spectators rose to their feet during the military parade, which was headed by the Garde Republicaine Band, and followed by representatives of the most famous fighting contingents of the war. Tattered regimental flags, many stained with the blood of battles long antedating those of the Great War; national ensigns of all participating nations; uniforms, for example, of the Chasseurs Alpins, Zouaves, Tirailleurs, Italians, Serbians; and the presence of thousands of spectators in uniform—all these were reminders of the worldwide character of the long and bitter struggle now brought to a victorious close. Pershing Stadium was presented by the YMCA, in the name of the Army, to the French people. Commemorating the event, a bronze inscription outside the stadium expressed the hope that "the cherished bonds of friendship between France and America, forged anew on the common field of battle may be tempered and made enduring on the friendly field of sport."[82] Indeed, the partisan Games Committee interpreted the contests in unmistakably ideological terms—namely, to show how "wholeheartedly the nations that had striven shoulder to shoulder on the battlefield could turn to friendly rivalry in the stadium," one advocate claimed.[83] The Games effectively spread the cause of the sporting life to countries that "came into being in the travail of world war and which in the future will take part in the improvement of athletics."[84]

Throughout the two weeks of athletic festivities, nearly 1,500 athletes representing 18 Allied nations or dominions participated in the Games. The United States was the least handicapped of the nations competing, since most of the best American athletes had remained alive after the war and could therefore compete. The U.S. squad laid claim to 12 firsts and 7 seconds in the 24 separate events. The AEF proudly excelled in the rifle and pistol competitions, and took firsts in baseball, basketball, boxing, equestrian contests, swimming, the tug-of-war, and catch-as-catch-can wrestling. American F.C. Thompson, a former baseball player, surpassed all other competitors with a remarkable 246-foot grenade toss.[85]

Between September 1919 and April 1922, the spirit of sports among American enlisted men was kept alive among the American forces in Germany (AFG). This history was documented by a YMCA publication, *Athletic Bulletin*, of which 37 issues were published. *The Bulletin* reported that more than three million men saw or participated in sports at Koblenz. Soldiers participated in baseball, boxing, basketball, football, soccer, rugby, golf, track and field, swimming, tennis, and mass games.[86]

One November day in 1921, the cultural bonds established between France and the United States during the Allied war effort took ritualistic form. The fusion of sport, nationalism, and the military found dramatic expression for

75,000 spectators who flocked to New Haven, Connecticut, to watch Yale host Princeton in football. "For the first time in the history of Big Three football," the *New York Times* reported, "the greatest acclaim of the day was not for the hero of the game," but for another hero of "other and distant battlefields." Just before the opening kickoff, Marshal Ferdinand Foch, commander of the Allied forces in World War I, gallantly strolled into the stadium and then across the gridiron, while a roaring crowd greeted him. Foch's appearance was no less than a "triumphal procession," according to one journalist, who compared it to Lafayette's tour of America.[87] Foch's visit coincided with an elaborate melting-pot pageantry in New York, amid front-page rumors of Bolshevist demonstrations in America. Athletics, Americanization, and the brotherhood of Western democracies proved potent antidotes for a nation in the throes of economic and social transformation.

Summary

The American sporting tradition was profoundly transformed by the military's widespread incorporation of sports into the war effort. The testimonies of militant preparedness advocates were validated: World War I revealed the utility of physical education to the armed services, and to the masses of Americans—many of whom had never been adequately exposed to athletic activity. "We should hang our heads in shame," because of the ill-prepared state of the nation's prewar citizenry, claimed Dr. Thomas Storey, head of the United States Interdepartmental Social Hygiene Board.[88] Citing statistics that revealed that one-third of military recruits were physically "unfit," and that even larger numbers of people were ignorant of protective hygiene, Storey applauded the war effort for heightening national consciousness about physical education. Physical education that begins in infancy and continues throughout life, Storey maintained, constituted the "necessary preparation for citizenship, whether that citizenship serves in peace or in war."[89] Riding the postwar patriotic fervor, many physical educators linked mass athletic activity with the democratic ideal. Thousands of schools nationwide were converted to the cult of strenuosity, and during the 1920s, municipalities increased expenditures sixfold. The war effort also powerfully legitimized the cause of college athletics, which, though national in scope, were not without lingering, trenchant critics—many of whom suggested abolishing collegiate sports. An *Outing* editor reviewed the role of college athletes in the war cause to suggest that the "problem" was not one of "too much athletics, but too little," convincing many former critics to "turn right about face."[90] Certainly, on one level at least, the sporting experience was becoming more widely accessible to the American public.

Some sports fared particularly well after the war. Boxing was the most widely publicized postwar sport. Before the war, boxing had had limited public appeal, due to the fact that it remained illegal in many states; but by 1920, state legislatures began to reverse the sport's prohibition. Although the battle for Sunday baseball probably garnered more newspaper space during 1919, the baseball controversy was only a skirmish as compared to the fight against the rising popularity of boxing. The rebuke by the religious establishment and influential groups of middle-class respectability were met by fierce resistance from the Army, the Navy, the American Legion, and the civilian board of boxing. Even conservative newspapers like the *New York Times* weighed in on the side of boxing by characterizing the opponents of boxing as a "half a century behind the times."[91] Thus, boxing became a huge commercial success during the 1920s, and New York regained its position as the national center of boxing—major bouts staged in Madison Square Garden became big social events that attracted celebrities, politicians, and thousands of avid women boxing spectators.[92]

In sum, the period between the Spanish–American War and World War I proved to be a ripe context for the invention and perfection of a distinctly American sporting tradition. Indeed, the two conflicts marked fundamental watersheds in the development of a sports-oriented military establishment. Several contemporary intellectuals explained the importance of war in modern society: "War is the health of the State," Randolph Bourne declared in 1919.[93] A wartime nation attains "a uniformity of feeling, a hierarchy of values culminating at the undisputed apex of the State ideal," and to such depths that, according to Bourne, distinctions between society and the individual are all but eliminated.[94] War and military service became powerful mechanisms, Eric Hobsbawm writes, for "inculcating proper civic behavior, and, not least, for turning the inhabitant of a village into the patriotic citizen of a nation."[95]

These civics lessons were not lost on the majority of Americans, who overwhelmingly acknowledged the legitimacy of military institutions. For them, the military's enthusiasm for organized sports was cause enough for popular acceptance and appreciation. For the unconverted ones, powerful commentaries emphasized the way in which military athletics transformed the morality of modern sports. Respected Protestant sports advocates like Luther Gulick acknowledged that physical prowess and competitiveness, which were previously associated with "lower-class immorality and crass professionalism," had been recently harnessed by the military for "more powerful social devotions" and patriotic ends.[96] Such views were popularized by a bevy of respected journalists and social commentators. A feature writer for *National Geographic* concurred: Noting the paradox that the "maddest" war ever fought had "turn[ed] the world to simple, wholesome play," the writer characterized sports as forming a "gazetteer of the habits and histories of their peoples." Writing from the Allied vantage point, he concluded that countries adopted national pastimes and modified them so as "to foster and fortify the peoples who play them."[97] Sports both "fortified" American participants and enabled the U.S. military to create an "army of athletes."

Notes

1. "How Uncle Sam Has Created an Army of Athletes." *Scientific American* 126 (1919), 114-15.
2. Ibid.
3. Albert Britt, "From Playing Field to Battle Field," *Outing* 73 (1919), 3. See William Haynes, "In Fighting Trim: Canada Teaching Her Soldiers to Play in Order to Fit Them for Fighting," Outing

69 (1916), 277-88, for a comparative example north of the border. Frederick Harris recorded 75 million "participations" in military sports between 1917 and 1919, in *Service With Fighting Men: An Account of the Work of the American Young Men's Christian Association in the World War* (New York, 1922), vol. 1, 320.

4. *New York Times*, March 8, 1903, 11.

5. Ibid.

6. Donald J. Mrozek, "The Habit of Victory: The American Military and the Cult of Manliness," in J. A. Mangan and James Walvin, eds., *Manliness and Morality: Middle Class Masculinity in Britain and America, 1800-1940* (New York, 1987), 222.

7. Bruce D. Porter, *War and the Rise of the State: The Military Foundations of Modern Politics* (New York, 1994), 269.

8. Mack Whelan, "Will the War Kill Athletics?: Ways in Which Army Life is Making Physical Fitness Faster Than Fighting Destroys It," *Outing* 68 (1916), 278-88. Guy Lewis was the first sports historian to argue that World War I led to widespread national sports interest in the 1920s, in "World War I and the Emergence of Sport for the Masses," *Maryland Historian* 2 (1973), 109-22. Timothy O'Hanlon took Lewis's thesis a step further by suggesting that the wartime emphasis on sports in military training stimulated postwar high-school sports and fitness programs—"School Sports as Social Training: The Case of Athletics and the Crisis of World War I," *Journal of Sport History* 9 (1982), 1-24.

9. Newton Fuessle, "America's Boss-Ridden Athletics," *Outlook* 130 (1922), 643.

10. John R. Betts, "Home Front, Battlefield and Sport During the Civil War," *Research Quarterly* 42 (1971), 113-32. Lawrence W. Fielding has ably documented this episode in American sports history, in three journal articles derived from his doctoral dissertation (Maryland, 1974): "Reflections From the Sport Mirror: Selected Treatments of Civil War Sport," *Journal of Sport History* 2 (1975), 132-44; "War and Trifles: Sport in the Shadow of Civil War Army Life," *Journal of Sport History* 4 (1977), 151-68; and "Gay and Happy Still: Holiday Sport in the Army of the Potomac," *Maryland Historian* 7 (1976), 19-32. Harold Seymour documents the place of baseball among Union troops, in *Baseball: The People's Game* (New York, 1991), 291-309.

11. Benjamin G. Rader, *Baseball: A History of America's Game* (Urbana, 1992), 13.

12. For an excellent, well-documented history of the nineteenth-century Army, see Edward M. Coffman's *The Old Army: A Portrait of the American Army in Peacetime, 1784-1898* (New York, 1986), esp. 215-86, 328-99; Elliott J. Gorn, *The Manly Art: Bare-Knuckle Prize Fighting in America* (Ithaca, N.Y., 1986), 160.

13. Gorn, *The Manly Art*, 164. For early, representative comments on the relationship between sports and militarism see *Wilke's Spirit*, August 17, 1861; *New York Herald*, July 27, 1859; and *New York Times*, March 9, 1862.

14. Gorn, *The Manly Art*, 164.

15. Cited in Don Rickey, Jr., *Forty Miles a Day on Beans and Hay: The Enlisted Soldier Fighting the Indian Wars* (Norman, Okla., 1963), 186-88. This work is a thorough portrait of the U.S. regular Army on the frontier during the second half of the nineteenth century—particularly, in regard to the life of enlisted men.

16. Coffman, *The Old Army*, 359. Donald Mrozek sketches a cogent summary of the initial establishment of military sports during the late nineteenth century, in "Sport and the American Military: Diversion and Duty," *Research Quarterly* (Centennial Issue), 1985, 38-45.

17. C.D. Parkhurst, "The Practical Education of the Soldier," *Journal of the Military Service Institution of the United States* (1890), 946.

18. Quoted in Mrozek, *Sport and American Mentality*, 56.

19. Mrozek cites the War Department's Special Regulation no. 23: "Field Physical Training of the Soldier," (Washington, D.C., 1917), 7-10. See also, R.D. Evans, "Why Athletics Should be Fostered in the Navy," *The Illustrated Sporting News* 5 (1905), 5.

20. Nobody promoted this new approach more passionately than Edmund L. "Billy" Butts, the best all-around athlete in West Point's class of 1888; after graduation, he published articles in the *Journal of the Military Service, Outing,* and the *Army and Navy Journal,* wherein he maintained that athletic training would transform fighting men into "hardened veterans, upon whom the safety

of the nation could depend." Such provocative sporting bombast earned him the respect of the Army, who dispatched Butts in the mid-1890s to various posts to initiate athletics and physical-training programs. See Seymour, *Baseball*, 29 7-98.

21. Fuessle, "America's Boss-Ridden Athletics," 642-43. Early football practices were limited. Only about 2 hours per week were allotted, during Cadets' "liberty time," for preseason practice. Typically, only 9 hours of actual preseason work preceded the first game; and only a total of 56 practice hours were spent during the entire football season. See Captain Richmond P. Davis, "Athletics at the United States Military Academy," *Outing* 39 (1901-02), 384-85; and H. Irving Hancock, *Life at West Point: The Making of the American Army Officer: His Studies, Discipline, and Amusements* (New York, 1902), 135-36.

22. Arthur Ruhl, "The Army-Navy Game," *Outing* 49 (1907), 314.

23. Davis, "Athletics at the United States Military Academy," 390-91; Hancock, *Life at West Point*, 77-81; 85-95; and King, quoted in Seymour, *Baseball*, 315-16. Military sports were not the sole preserve of the Army—naval ships were furnished with a wide variety of sporting goods; there were frequent summertime baseball games between naval teams. Further, regattas, swim meets, and boxing were immensely popular on Sunday evenings after the parade. Football men relished the opportunity of having their ship dock at New York during the fall. See, for instance, Martin E. Trench, "Athletics Among Enlisted Men in the Navy," *Outing* 39 (1902), 436-41. The early support for football in the Navy is cited in Park Benjamin, "Public Football vs. Naval Education: In Defense of the Naval Academy," *The Independent* 55 (1903), 2777-80.

24. Seymour, *Baseball*, 321.

25. Ibid., 314-15.

26. Luther H. Gulick is credited with founding the New York Public Schools Athletic League. As one of the pioneers of American athletics, he collaborated with James Naismith in devising basketball; headed the child-hygiene department at the Russell Sage Foundation; served on the American Olympic Committee and with the American Physical Education Association; and was called by the National War Council to make a survey of the American Expeditionary Forces and to write a report on proposals for physical training. See *Dictionary of American Biography*, vol. 8, 4 7-48; and *American Physical Education Review*, October 1918.

27. Quoted in Mrozek, *Sport and American Mentality*, 61.

28. Graham Cosmas, "Military Reform after the Spanish-American War: The Army Reorganization Fight of 1898—1899," *Military Affairs* 35 (1971), 12-17. In addition to the growth of regular forces, from 28,000 to nearly 60,000, the War Department also recruited more than 200,000 volunteers. Elihu Root, the secretary of war, encouraged Congress to create a permanent regular army— a decision enacted into law in the Reorganization Act of February 2, 1901. For an overview of the pivotal role played almost single handedly by Root during the first few years, see Russell F. Weigley, *History of the United States Army* (Bloomington, 1984), 314-26. A useful contemporary assessment of Root's contributions can be found in William Harding Carter, "Elihu Root: His Services as Secretary of War," *North American Review* 178 (1908), 110-21.

29. Harrod, *Manning the New Navy*, 198; Lt. A. B. Donworth, "Gymnasium Training in the Army," *Journal of the Military Service Institution of the United States* 21(1897), 508-14.

30. Day Allen Willey, "The Spirit of Sport in the Army," *Harper's Weekly* 50 (1906), 1100-1.

31. Ibid.

32. R. L. Bullard, "Athletics in the Army," *Journal of the Military Service Institutions of the United States* 38 (1905), 399-404.

33. Charles Richard, "Suggestions for the Physical Training of Officers on the Active List of the Army," *JMSI* 44 (1909), 73-78.

34. Butts, quoted in Seymour, *Baseball*, 316.

35. See Karl Schmitt, *Mexico and the United States, 1821—1973* (New York, 1974).

36. See C.M. Cramer, *Newton D. Baker: A Biography* (New York, 1961); and M.J. Exner, "Prostitution in Its Relation to the Army on the Mexican Border," *Social Hygiene* 3 (1917).

37. Baker quoted in Seymour, *Baseball*, 331. Ronald Schaffer surveys the social purity crusades which arose in this context and which proliferated throughout the War Camp Community Service as well as behind the lines in France in his *America in the Great War: The Rise of the Welfare State* (New York, 1991), 98-108.

38. For an overview of early YMCA work see William J. Baker, "To Pray or to Play?: The YMCA Question in the United Kingdom and the United States, 1850—1900," *International Journal of the History of Sport* 11(1994), 42-62.

39. Harris, *Service With Fighting Men*, 197-212.

40. Between June 1918 and April 1919, the YMCA handled in France alone over two million cigarettes, 32 million candy bars, 18 million cans of smoking tobacco, 50 million cigars, 60 million cans of jam, and 29 million packages of chewing gum. The Y distributed five million bound volumes of reading material, four million pieces of religious literature, two million magazines, 10 million newspapers, and 1 million copies of an approved songbook. Between August 1917 and April 1919, 90,000 movies were shown to audiences totaling 50 million men. And, between 1918 and 1919, the Y provided 2.25 million athletic items. See George W. Perkins, "Report on Activities of the Y.M.C.A. with the A.E.F.," 1919.

41. Edward Frank Allen, *Keeping Our Fighters Fit For War and After* (New York, 1918); a concise version of Allen's first chapter was published as "Athletics for the Army," in *Century* 96 (1918), 367-74.

42. Montrose J. Moses, "Training Soldiers to Play," *St. Nicholas* 45 (1918), 448-5 3.

43. George J. Fisher, "Physical Training in the Army," *American Physical Education Review* 23 (1918), 65-76.

44. Harris, *Service With Fighting Men*, vol. 1, 320-24.

45. "Baker Supports Games," *New York Times*, August 17, 1917, 10.

46. Ibid.; Edwin A. Goewey, "Flashing the Series to Our Boys in Uniform," *Baseball Magazine*, November 1919.

47. Sol Metzger, "Regards Athletics as Patriotic Duty," *New York Times*, July 22, 1917, sec. III, 4.

48. "Great Year Ahead in Army Athletics," *New York Times*, August 26, 1917, sec. III, 4.

49. Walter Camp, *Athletics All: Training, Organization and Play* (New York, 1927), 16, 67.

50. "Sport Flourishing in Naval Stations," and "Walter Camp Has Systematized Athletic Activities of the Nation's Soldiers," *New York Times*, February 3, 1918, sec. III, 8.

51. Camp, "Our Government Plant," *Outlook* 117 (1917), 12-13; and "Review of the Football Service and the All-America Team," *Collier's* 63 (1919), 13.

52. "Keeping the Nation Fit," *The Independent* 96 (1918), 400-1; and "What I Am Trying to Do," *World's Work* 46 (1923), 600-4.

53. Harris, vol. 2, 34-37.

54. Ibid., 30-32.

55. Katherine Mayo, *'That Damn Y': A Record of Overseas Service* (Boston, 1920), 256.

56. Retired University of Wisconsin professor Walter Agard, who served as an athletics and recreation noncom, told Edward Coffman that boxing was the only sport readily comprehended by most soldiers—many of whom had never competed in organized team sports; hence the "game" concept was novel. I wish to thank Coffman, who shared this insight with me in a letter (in my possession). For a representative how-to guide on military sports drills, see F. L. Kleeberger, "War Sports Embracing Grenade Throwing, Boxing, and Athletic Drills, Arranged in Accord with Military Procedure," *American Physical Education Review* 23 (1918), 383-98. Luther Gulick could not emphasize the tactical importance of bayonet fighting enough in a speech delivered to the American Physical Education Association, shortly after his return from the French front. Lamenting the lack of effective training, Gulick recommended that one hour a day be appropriated for bayonet practice. See his "Physical Fitness in the Fighting *Armies*," *American Physical Education Review* 24 (1919), 341-54, esp. 342-46.

57. Thomas Foster, "Why Our Soldiers Learn to Box," *Outing* 72 (1918), 114-16.

58. Ibid.

59. Ibid.

60. "2,000,000 Men Join Uncle Sam's League," *New York Times*, March 11, 1918, 8.

61. *Outing* 71 (1918), 279.

62. James Mennell, "The Service Football Program of World War I: Its Impact on the Popularity of the Game," *Journal of Sport History* 16 (1989), 259.

63. "War Football," *New York Times*, November 23, 1919, III, 1.

64. Alfred E. Cornebise, *The Stars and Stripes: Doughboy Journalism in World War I* (Westport, Conn., 1984), 3-6.

65. Seymour, *Baseball*, 333.

66. Cornebise, *The Stars and Stripes*. For a transatlantic discussion of British military-sports journalism, see John M. Osborne, "To Keep the Life of the Nation on the Old Line': The Athletic News and the First World War," *Journal of Sport History* 14 (1987), 137-50.

67. Cornebise, *The Stars and Stripes*, 139-40.

68. Camp, "Industrial Athletics: How the Sports For Soldiers and Sailors Are Developing into Civilian Athletics," *Outlook* 122 (1919), 253.

69. Edwin A. Goewey, "Fewer Fans and More Athletes," *Leslie's Weekly*, February 1, 1919, 168; and for a complementary statement on the spread of American sports in Europe, due to the military efforts and the Inter-Allied Games in particular, see "Europe Welcomes American Athletes," *Leslie's Weekly*, September 6, 1919, 372.

70. Goewey, "Fewer Fans."

71. Ibid.

72. Fletcher S. Brockman, "Association Athletics as a Training in Democracy," *Physical Training* 17 (1919), 7 1-76. Special efforts were made to promote sports among the Asiatic and African troops serving in the Allied forces. The Chinese Labor Corps; the Indian troops serving the British Army; the Arabs; the Senegalese; the Tunisians; and other Indo-Chinese soldiers within the French troops—all these encountered Western team sports. For information about the spread of baseball in postwar Europe, see Seymour, *Baseball*, 346-63.

73. Major G. Wythe, Captain Joseph Mills Hanson, Captain C. V. Burger, eds., *The Inter-Allied Games, Paris, 22nd June to 6th July1919* (Paris, 1919), 17-19.

74. Ibid. For additional information on the advent of the Inter-Allied Games, see Frederick W. Cozens and Florence Scovil Strumpf, *Sports in American Life* (Chicago, 1953), 198-203; and Dixon Wecter, *When Johnny Comes Marching Home* (Boston, 1944), 58 7-9.

75. For a partisan interpretation of the Far Eastern Games, as well as the internationalist role of the Y.M.C.A., see Elwood S. Brown, "Teaching the World to Play," *Outlook* 121 (1921), 689-93.

76. *Jim Thorpe's History of the Olympics*, 229-30.

77. Harris, *Service With Fighting Men*, v.2, 39-49.

78. Thorpe, 230. Harris calculated the participation "in all sports for the first five months of 1919" as over 31 million, in his *Service With Fighting Men*, v.2, 44.

79. Ibid., 46-7. For several months after the signing of the Armistice, the YMCA staged weekly bouts at the Cirque de Paris, which accommodated a standing crowd of 8,000, where pro boxers like Carpentier, Jeannette, McVey, battled and soldiers were admitted free of charge.

80. Edwin A. Goewey, "The Doughboys' Great Olympics," *Leslie's Weekly*, April 5, 1919, 487, 496.

81. *The Inter-Allied Games*, 154.

82. Ibid., 159-60. See also, W. D. Ball, "The Greatest Athletic Event in History," *Association Men*, March 1919, 536-37.

83. Ibid.

84. Ibid.

85. *The Inter-Allied Games*, 177.

86. See the final issue of *Athletic Bulletin*, May 1, 1922, 2.

87. *New York Times*, November 13, 1921, sec. VIII, 1; sec. VII, 2; sec. I, 23.

88. Thomas A. Storey, "War-Time Revelations in Physical Education," *American Physical Education Review* 25 (1920), 1-5, quote, 5.

89. Ibid.

90. "Field Sports," *Outing* 72 (1918), 54.

91. *New York Times*, May 28, 1919, 13.

92. See Jeffrey T. Sammons, *Beyond the Ring: The Role of Boxing in American Society* (Urbana, 1988); Gorn, "The Manassa Mauler and the Fighting Marine: An Interpretation of the Dempsey-Tunney Fights," *Journal of American Studies* 19 (1985), 20-42; Riess, *City Games: The Evolution of American Urban Society and the Rise of Sports* (Urbana, 1989), 175-80, 206-8.

93. Randolph Bourne, "War as the Health of the State," in James Oppenheim, ed., *Untimely Papers,* reprinted in *The Annals of America* (Chicago, 1968), vol. 14, 135-39.

94. Ibid.

95. Hobsbawm, *The Age of Empire,* 304-305.

96. Gulick, "Physical Fitness for the Fighting Armies," 350-51, 348-49.

97. J. R. Hildebrand, "The Geography of Games: How the Sports of Nations Form a Gazetteer of the Habits and Histories of Their Peoples," *National Geographic* 36 (1919), 89-144; quotes are on 89 and 91.

CHAPTER 10

IN SPORTS THE BEST MAN WINS

How Joe Louis Whupped Jim Crow

■ *Theresa E. Runstedtler* ■

A single column cannot begin to describe the feeling of the man
of color who watches a brown-skinned boy like Joe Louis, from
Alabama, the most backward State in the Union, fight his way up
from the coal mine and the cotton field through strength
of his body and mind.

—Ted Benson, Sunday Worker, reprinted in *Pittsburgh Courier*, February 29, 1936

American Hero or Race Man?

On June 22, 1938, when Joe Louis, the Brown Bomber, won a decisive, first-round knockout in his revenge match against Nazi-promoted Max Schmeling, white America embraced the black heavyweight champion as a national hero. Amid increasing reports of Hitler's imperialistic aggression and persecution of the Jews, the mainstream white press highlighted the bout's worldwide implications, claiming Louis's triumph as an American victory in the larger fight against fascism. As Heywood Broun of the *New York World-Telegram* mused, "One hundred years from now some historian may theorize, in a footnote at least, that the decline of Nazi prestige began with the left hook of a former unskilled autoworker."[1] Inspiring more than just a mere footnote, Louis's 1938 win expanded into a celebrated epic of American patriotism and democracy. Brimming with postwar confidence in 1947, Louis's close friend, Frank Sinatra, declared: "If I were the government official responsible for the job of making the rest of the world understand our national character and the ideals that motivate us, I would certainly make use of the case history of Joe Louis."[2]

Amy Bass, In *The Game*, published 2005, Palgrave Macmillan, reproduced by permission of Palgrave Macmillan.

However well-known the narrative of Louis as the quintessential U.S. citizen became, another story, one that white America and history have overlooked, meant more to African Americans in the 1930s: Joe Louis as Race Man. That Louis earned the customary title of "Race Man" was a mark of high distinction, since this phrase had long been reserved for men who best exemplified racial progress and leadership in areas like business, academics, and politics.[3] Writing for the *New Masses* in 1938, a skeptical Richard Wright derided the Louis–Schmeling fight as "a colorful puppet show, one of the greatest dramas of make-believe ever witnessed in America."[4] For Wright, the real significance of Louis lay not in his dubious status as a national hero, but in his ability to inspire the black masses. Three years earlier, in September 1935, when Louis garnered a swift victory over Jewish American Max Baer in front of 90,000 fans at Yankee Stadium, Wright described the "religious feeling in the air" on Chicago's South Side, where over twenty thousand "Negroes poured out of beer taverns, pool rooms, barber shops, rooming houses and dingy flats and flooded the streets." With Louis's win over Baer "*something* had ripped loose, exploded," claimed Wright, allowing "four centuries of oppression, of frustrated hopes, of black bitterness" to rise to the surface. Louis was "a consciously-felt symbol…the concentrated essence of black triumph over white."[5]

Wright was certainly not alone in recognizing Louis's influence as the period's iconic New Negro. African Americans' limited access to legal and political channels of protest meant that sports, and in particular boxing, became one of the preeminent mass media through which they articulated their conflict with the racial status quo. Until 1947, when Jackie Robinson joined baseball's Major League, boxing was the only professional sport that allowed whites and blacks to compete in the same arena. Moreover, in this individual sport of hand-to-hand combat, fighters emerged as contested symbols of race, manhood, and nation among the American masses. By 1933 Louis was already a fixture in the black press, supplying African Americans with the cultural ammunition to critique their persistent lack of democratic rights and dignity. Louis graced the front page of the *Chicago Defender* more times than any other black figure during the Depression, including Ethiopian emperor Haile Selassie.[6] Not only did his life story become the focal point of sports and human-interest sections in various weekly newspapers, but his pugilistic exploits sparked larger debates about black representation as editorialists evaluated his role in racial advancement.

As the dawn of the New Negro era symbolized the race's passage into "the sunlight of real manhood," Louis's well-documented whupping of Jim Crow provided a public outlet for diverse expressions of black struggle across the socioeconomic and political spectrum.[7] The term "New Negro," meaning a progressive, politically savvy African American, initially emerged from the turn-of-the-century writings of Booker T. Washington.[8] However, black participation in World War I in tandem with the Great Migration of African Americans to northern cities like New York and Chicago had a radicalizing effect, infusing the New Negro movement with a heightened sense of militancy, urgency, and racial pride. In revisiting the Harlem Renaissance, historians have begun to expand on its traditional interpretation as a middle-class, bourgeois literary movement to uncover the various facets of New Negro activism from black theater companies to leftist internationalism.[9] The sport of boxing offered yet another arena in which New Negroes could express their racial militancy, albeit vicariously, through the hard punches and prosperous lifestyle of men like Joe Louis. Indeed, the rising figure of Joe Louis gave the masculine New Negro ideal unprecedented, mass appeal.

A detailed analysis of Louis's coming of age in his first major professional fight against Mussolini's darling, Primo Carnera, on the eve of the 1935 Italo–Ethiopian conflict, capped off with a suggestive re-reading of his well-known loss to Max Schmeling in 1936, not only uncovers how discussions of black manhood dominated both domestic and diasporic resistance strategies, but also helps to explain the historical emergence of the male sports celebrity as an integral symbol of black success in the twentieth century.[10] The Louis–Carnera match takes center stage, since most accounts have tended to downplay its significance as a matter of coincidental timing in which foreign affairs over-lapped with box-office promotion. However, a close examination of the riotous celebrations Louis inspired, along with his mass representation in the black and leftist presses, photographs, fight films, and blues songs, reveals that African Americans actively fashioned him as a Race Man, using him to fight racism and fascism on two fronts—at home and abroad.[11] Taken from this vantage point, the Louis story obliges historians to expand their understandings of the New Negro's popular dimensions as a cultural conduit through which African Americans of the 1930s continued to address the interlocking questions of race, gender, nation, and class.

Biography of a Race

Triumphant tales of the young boxer's rise to fistic fame filled the pages of black and young communist publications, along with mass-circulated biographies. Even though each had a differing agenda, they all spun his life story into a kind of utopian biography of the race. While the sympathetic white writer Edward Van Every engaged in hyperbole when he claimed the boxer's life made "story book tales of fight heroes seem tame," the popular depictions of Louis's struggles from southern sharecropper to northern migrant to industrial worker to suc-cessful boxer must have resonated with the experiences of many of his African American fans.[12] Providing a mythical link that connected an oppressive black rural "past" with the promise of a prosperous urban future, the young boxer's personal story defied regional, class, and even generational boundaries to offer an accessible, yet decidedly masculine vision of collective progress.

According to the composite story that emerged in the black press, Joe Louis Barrow was born on May 13, 1914, in Lafayette, Alabama, the seventh of eight children in a sharecropping family. In 1926, Louis and his kin joined the Great Migration to the North, settling in one of Detroit's black ghettos. Soon after their

Joe Louis, heavyweight champion of the world.

Photo courtesy of Library of Congress. LC-USZ62-35334.

arrival, twelve-year-old Louis developed his young muscles in a part-time job delivering ice to the city's wealthier citizens. Trained in cabinetry at the Bronson Vocational School, Louis later worked at the Ford plant right up until he joined the ranks of professional boxing.[13] As the papers revealed, Louis had honed his fighting skills at Detroit's Brewster Recreation Center during his teenage years. By the time he won the national Amateur Athletic Union light heavyweight championship in April 1934, the youthful pugilist had participated in fifty-four bouts, winning forty-three of them by knockout, thereby garnering the support of the African American management team of John Roxborough, Julian Black, and Jack Blackburn. Writers bragged that at twenty-one, Louis was already two hundred pounds, standing six feet, one and a half inches tall, with fifteen-inch biceps.[14] Showcasing his muscular physique, groomed hair, and boyish smile, the black press helped mold him into a statue of strength and charm that appealed to men, women, and children.

Even the *Young Worker,* an interracial communist organ, included frequent reports on Louis that tended to cast him as an exemplary African American worker. As one journalist related, "He was born in the slums of Birmingham, Ala. When only a mere lad, he carried cakes of ice to eke out a living. He worked in King Henry Ford's plant in Detroit. Always on the fringe of starvation, he learned how to struggle for self-preservation." Imbuing Louis with a black labor consciousness, the writer continued, "He can see that as a worker, he will end up just where he started from, in the slums, because of the widespread discrimination that is practiced against his race."[15] Portraying him as an everyday man with "a chance to cash in on his skillful dukes," the *Young Worker* used Louis to not only advance a positive image of African Americans to white youth, but also to show black workers that they did not have to give up their race heroes to join the communist ranks. White and black laborers both could rally around this male protagonist.

By the time Louis entered the ring against Primo Carnera in June 1935, his humble beginnings and subsequent climb to international success had taken on an epic quality, as sympathetic journalists fashioned his biography into the ultimate story of racial and economic uplift. In an era when images of bumbling Sambos, feminized male minstrels, and confused primitives still held currency, Louis's public personification of forcefulness and fairness, virility and respectability, stylishness and responsibility, resonated with popular understandings of manhood, civilization, and modernity. Thus, from the footnotes of the well-known narrative of Louis as American hero emerges not only the buried history of a black diasporic icon, but also a larger story about the intersection of gender and resistance in America's race wars.

From Uncle Tom to New Negro

Writing in the *New York Amsterdam News*, editorialist Theophilus Lewis dubbed Joe Louis a "Boxing Business Man." Lewis praised him as a model of mature focus, telling readers, "Joe Louis prefers to be Joe Louis and not what white people think Joe Louis should be. Professional boxing is his chosen road to success." As Lewis continued, "A man's success is not a playful matter—it is a serious business. He refuses to pretend it is a pastime, a sort of youthful prelude to mature living."[16] Despite the obvious passion and respect with which Louis's African American contemporaries followed his career, sports historiography, much like popular memory, has tended to overlook black representations of Louis. For the most part, scholars' focus on mainstream daily newspaper accounts has skewed their assessments of him as a moderate and even ineffectual figure of white cooptation.[17] While several historians challenge this "Uncle Tom" critique, most still emphasize Louis's contributions as a crossover American hero, without deconstructing whites' and blacks' differing perceptions of his cultural and political importance.[18] Overall, these approaches obscure the reality that various segments of black America acknowledged and even lauded Louis's accomplishments, fashioning him as a gendered expression of public resistance.

Louis's folk hero status relied, in large part, on his masculine embodiment of the period's shifting constructions of black identity and advancement. Just ten years earlier, in the opening essay of *The New Negro*, scholar Alain Locke had declared that "Uncle Tom and Sambo have passed on," and now the "American mind must reckon with a fundamentally changed Negro." According to Locke, despite African Americans' continued exclusion from the rights of full citizenship, they could still "celebrate the attainment of a significant…phase of group development, and with it a spiritual Coming of Age."[19] As Louis rose in the ranks of professional boxing alongside this collective rite of passage, racial progress became increasingly conflated with the redemption of black manhood.

African Americans had long deployed masculine constructions of powerful blackness to confront what historian Gail Bederman describes as the Progressives' tradition of weaving race and gender into a web of white male supremacy. According to popular, early-twentieth-century thought, one could determine a group's civilization based on their extent of sexual differentiation. In keeping with this pseudoscientific doctrine, black men and women were supposedly identical, while the patriarchal organization of the "civilized" white race signified that they were not only the furthest along in the Darwinist chain of evolution, but also uniquely capable of wielding political authority and exercising the rights of citizenship.[20] According to historian Barbara Melosh, the economic difficulties of the Depression helped to reify this overall paradigm of white male supremacy. Concerns over family stability and conflicts over female labor led to the retrenchment of white patriarchy after the gender subversions of the 1920s such as the passing of the 19th Amendment for women's suffrage, the rise of the assertive New Woman, and the racy culture of the flapper.[21] Not surprisingly, as whites continued to articulate their racial supremacy through an assertion of male control, many African Americans attempted to prove their equality using resistance strategies that embraced male dominance.

Even though the African American political and intellectual movements of the 1930s shared a common focus on promoting the legitimacy of black manhood, New Negro activists, by no means, agreed on a standardized definition of its cultural, political, and economic terms. Instead, they harnessed and shaped gendered discourses to suit not only their differing philosophical and tactical aims, but also their varied constituents. While established organizations like the National Association for the Advancement of Colored People (NAACP) and Marcus Garvey's pan-Africanist Universal Negro Improvement Association (UNIA) had long appropriated the white Victorian principles of patriarchy, propriety, industry, and thrift as the foundation for black advancement, Harlem's up-and-coming cadre of New Negro writers and poets began to challenge these rigid ideals by exploring homosocial bonds and masculine pursuits beyond the realm of bourgeois domesticity.[22] In turn, the public assertion of militant black manhood became a rallying cry for the emerging politics of collective race and class protest led by groups like the Brotherhood of Sleeping Car Porters (BSCP) and the Communist Party.[23] Whether they worked within the framework of American democratic ideals, or rejected their hypocrisy, African American activists of the 1930s used manhood as a mobilizing force.

As different sectors of black society claimed Louis as one of their own, his public representation came to embody the class and generational tensions surrounding Depression-era articulations of black manhood. On the one hand, the period's constructions of black manliness incorporated the contradictory ideals of savagery and civilization, as metaphors of battle and physical prowess existed alongside discussions of intelligence, artistry, and respectability. On the other hand, the New Negro movement also signaled a nascent shift toward a more modern sense of masculinity grounded less in middle-class notions of gentility, and expressed through recreational pursuits, the conspicuous consumption of mass-marketed commodities, and the open display of bodily might and sexual virility.[24] The popular celebration of Louis as Race Man connected these gendered imaginings of blackness with the spirit of the masses. This was not a solo performance on the part of Louis, but rather a collective spectacle involving a complex process of negotiation among his body of black supporters.

However, even as one uncovers Louis's significance as *the* quintessential New Negro of the 1930s, the inherent dangers of a masculinist critique of racism inevitably rise to the surface. Trapped in a paradox, Louis, his black fans, and members of the black press challenged white superiority by engaging the same constructions of patriarchal authority that were simultaneously confirming their racial inferiority. Not only did they ultimately legitimize existing power relations, but their male-centered modes of resistance also pushed black women to the periphery of the struggle.

Boxing's New Negro Comes of Age

When Louis celebrated his twenty-first birthday on May 13, 1935, the black press urged his African American fans to pay tribute to his work as "a sterling young fighter, a gentleman and sportsman." In calling Louis "the finest type of *American manhood*," they granted him two labels that blackness did not usually allow.[25] On the front-page of the *Pittsburgh Courier* sports section, one writer declared, "Joe Louis, you are a man now.... [O]nly a step across the threshold of boyhood, the hopes of a race and the best wishes of a nation are with you." Recognizing Louis's importance as an emblematic figure through which gender and race coalesced in a narrative of black progress, the writer warned the young fighter to "live a clean, honest life…and always remember that your very qualities of modesty and manliness are the things which bring thousands of people to see you fight."[26] In emphasizing Louis's own coming of age as a man, black journalists exposed the collective focus on questions of black manhood.

In the buildup to his bout against Primo Carnera, the black press promoted Louis's redemptive and unifying mission in what some were dubbing the "battle of the century." With bold optimism, one writer in the *Pittsburgh Courier* maintained that Louis would defend successfully "the ardent hopes of more than twelve million Americans" when he stepped into the ring at Yankee Stadium. Another pre-fight feature in the *Chicago Defender* named Louis the most "outstanding Race athlete of the past 30 years," citing his unprecedented ability to draw black fans to the box office. In the month preceding the fight, Harlem buzzed with expectant energy as African Americans of all ages kept Louis as their favorite topic. The *New York Age* even noted that "women from all walks of life, some who had never taken any interest in fights," prayed for a race victory in the ring.[27]

As widespread interest in the Louis–Carnera match cut across racial lines, many African Americans relished the fact that the black fighter's rise was revitalizing the entire boxing industry after years of sparse ticket sales.[28] In a bid to bring Louis closer to a title bout, his African American managers, Roxborough and Black, had formed a pragmatic alliance with Mike Jacobs, an influential Jewish American promoter. Jacobs held a virtual monopoly of the industry, organizing major heavyweight events in conjunction with the Hearst Milk Fund for Babies, a New York charity run by the wife of publishing magnate William Randolph Hearst.[29]

Even though Louis was already a superstar in the black press, Jacobs "introduced" the young fighter to white America. A public relations mastermind, he hired press agents like black journalist Russell Cowans to crank out daily media releases for white and black newspapers all over the country. These reports

carefully constructed Louis as the epitome of white middle-class respectability.[30] While this centralized communications scheme ensured that overlapping
portrayals of the "official" Louis appeared in both presses, a comparison of
white and black sources reveals that writers reinterpreted and reshaped the
Louis image along racial lines, often using manhood as a metalanguage for race.

While most journalists in the mainstream press certainly favored Louis to
win, they were not ready to count out Carnera, even though a streak of fixed
fights and messy dealings with the mob underworld soiled the veteran boxer's
seven-year record.[31] Despite their high praise of Louis's technical abilities and
well-mannered conduct, many white writers held reservations about his physical
and mental toughness. Invoking the emasculating stereo type of black cowardice,
infantilism, and emotionality, they charged that Louis's encounter with Carnera
would determine if this "beardless" boy could hold his own against boxing's
big men. After all, in addition to being eight years Louis's senior, Carnera stood
nearly half a foot taller and outweighed Louis by almost 70 pounds. As one
writer in the *Macon Telegraph* observed, the question of "Can he take it?" was the
"one predominant note of skepticism" among the white, fight-going public.[32]
Nationally syndicated sports columnist Grantland Rice agreed that if Louis
failed to score an early knockout, the "rugged" Carnera would "outmaul" the
boy to win by decision. Moreover, Rice and many of his colleagues questioned
whether the young fighter would remain poised in the midst of the "terrific ballyhoo" of what promised to be one of the biggest fight crowds in many years.[33]
Casting Louis as the "dusky David" to Carnera's "Goliath," white journalists
wondered whether the youthful, black technician possessed the gritty manhood
to defeat the roughhousing Italian Giant.[34]

As Louis's rite of passage to boxing manhood, the fight also became a litmus
test for the strength and maturity of the race. However unconvinced the white
press was, black writers supported Louis with great resolve, predicting an easy
knockout in two to five rounds.[35] The question of whether or not Louis could
"take it" reportedly drew a loud chuckle from Manager Roxborough, who
bragged that the young fighter had already prevailed in the face of knockdowns,
a fractured knuckle, and even punches to the jaw.[36] Louis's manly battle against
Carnera not only had "colored America looking to redeem its honors in the fistic
world," but it took on greater implication as a proxy for larger racial conflicts
at home and abroad.[37]

Enlisted for Ethiopia

While Louis prepared for his conquest of Carnera, another race war threatened
to erupt across the Atlantic. Benito Mussolini's imperialistic designs on Haile
Selassie's Abyssinia weighed on the minds of many African Americans. From the
Courier to the *Crisis*, articles in the black press kept readers apprised of the latest
news on the impending Italo-Ethiopian conflict during the spring and summer
of 1935. While mainstream publications tended to bury the reports of Abyssinia,

the black press featured them prominently, often as front-page news. They carried not only current, but historical accounts of Ethiopia, along with human-interest stories on Selassie, his family, and the plight of the Abyssinian soldiers.

Ethiopia was the last independent nation on the African continent and its potential takeover had grave implications for struggles of black autonomy and equality throughout the world. In particular the perception of a parallel between Italian fascism and United States racism served to provoke strong, public African American reactions to the looming invasion.[38] Moreover, when the League of Nations failed to come to the aid of the African country, it further emphasized the racial dimensions of the conflict, as self-interested, white governments turned a deaf ear to the pleas of their colored counterpart.[39] Given the depressed economic conditions in northern black communities like Harlem and the continued terror of Jim Crow in the South, African Americans recognized the close connections between their plight and that of their Ethiopian brothers. As poet Langston Hughes declared:

Ethiopia, Lift your night-dark face,
Abyssinian Son of Sheba's Race!
…

May all Africa arise
With blazing eyes and night-dark face
In answer to the call of Sheba's race:
Ethiopia's free!
Be like me,
All of Africa,
Arise and be free![40]

Out of the crucible of modern colonialism and fascism emerged a growing sense of black diasporic consciousness.

Many black fans saw the upcoming Louis–Carnera fight as an apt microcosm of the pending matchup between Il Duce and Selassie. In the major black weeklies, stories and photos of Louis's training regimen, his victory, and the subsequent celebrations ran side-by-side with reports of the Abyssinian crisis and pictures of the Ethiopian emperor. Arguably, even African Americans who did not read the papers must have picked up on the obvious analogy. Enthusiastic discussions of the Louis–Carnera bout, from street corners and front porches to local barbershops and beauty salons, surely touched on the boxer's symbolic role as he went fist-to-fist with Mussolini's Darling. Not only had Louis become a ubiquitous folk hero by 1935, but as historian William R. Scott argues, Italy's imminent invasion stimulated an unprecedented period of black American militancy and group protest. From Los Angeles to New York, the black masses organized Abyssinian-defense loans, acts of civil disobedience, huge rallies that attracted thousands of participants, economic boycotts, and even the recruitment of volunteer combat troops.[41]

Complementing the efforts of grassroots activists, Louis became a popular outlet for articulations of nascent black nationalism, along with radical international critiques of racism. He offered a public embodiment of the intellectual discussions of the conflict that graced the pages of periodicals like the *Crisis, Opportunity,* and Marcus Garvey's *Black Man.* Various black groups even met with Louis during his training camp to underscore the importance of his upcoming fight for black people on the world stage. Louis recalled, "Now, not only did I have to beat the man, but I had to beat him for a cause."[42] Enlisted as a fistic soldier in the fight against fascism, he promised to enact Abyssinia's struggle for black autonomy in a way that his legions of African American fans could grasp with a sense of visceral immediacy. In the spectacle of the ring, Louis's body would perform a utopian vision of not only the black American body politic, but also that of the Ethiopian homeland.

Beyond just the basic fact that Louis, a black man, would wage hand-to-hand combat against an Italian fighter, there were a number of physical and metaphorical parallels between the real and ring conflicts enabling African Americans to engage in a gendered critique of domestic racism and foreign fascism.[43] In particular, contemporary black American discourses of African redemption were suffused with the language of manly battle, independence, and honor. To black writers and political figures of the New Negro era, the colonized continent represented black womanhood, while the autonomous Abyssinian nation was a decidedly male construct. Writing to the *Negro World,* a Garveyite publication, in the lead-up to the annual UNIA convention in 1924, Irene Gaskin exhorted, "Our flag boys [the African tricolor of red, black, and green]…means loyalty to our country and the protection of our women in our motherland Africa."[44] Labeling colonized Africa the "motherland," she placed men at the head of both nation-building and the defense of black womanhood. Since white imperial justifications often connected a society's ability to self-govern with its degree of patriarchal order, it is not surprising that African American commentators infused both these battles for racial nationalism with an overwhelmingly masculine bent.

The conflict between Italy and Ethiopia became anthropomorphized into a duel between Mussolini and Selassie, as the black press portrayed Abyssinia's struggle to remain autonomous as a test of the tiny country's racial manhood. At a time when a boxer's moniker usually had ethnic overtones, Louis, dubbed the Brown Bomber, the Ethiopian Exploder, and the African Avenger, became a natural stand-in for the Abyssinian emperor, and by extension, black nationhood.[45] African American cartoonist Jay Jackson encapsulated this connection in a clever drawing that showed a much smaller Louis boxing against a bestial caricature of Carnera in front of Ethiopian and Italian fans, while a seat reserved for the League of Nations remained empty in the foreground.[46]

As the celebrated "Crown Prince of Fistiania," Louis was, in many ways, the ultimate "Abyssinian Son of Sheba's Race."[47] While some white journalists and intellectuals questioned the racial heritage of the light-skinned Louis and Selassie, writers in the black press embraced both men as strong Race heroes. White biographer Edward Van Every's attempts to connect Louis's athletic prowess with his tri-racial "blood strain" resonated with numerous reports in the mainstream dailies that sought to deemphasize the boxer's African roots. Although the biographer acknowledged that Louis "insists…the Negro predominates in his blood," Van Every stressed the possibility that Louis was "a good part white and more Indian than African."[48]

Flying in the face of such efforts to undermine Louis's role as Race Man, African American writers positioned him as the "Black Hope," arguing that Louis was a "badge of racial prestige...in man's most honored sphere of endeavor—the noble art of self-defense."[49] Similarly, the black press showed impressive pictures of the emperor Selassie in his full regalia, underscoring his links to the ancient kingdom of Cush and claiming him as the "King of all Negroes everywhere." One editorial in the *Baltimore Afro-American* even maintained that "one glance at...[Selassie's] hair" surely proved that Ethiopia was a black nation.[50] Louis and Selassie's shared African roots became a reservoir of strength, and thus, their victories in manly battle would be victories for the race on both a national and international scale.

Just as reports conflated Louis with Ethiopia's emperor, Carnera became the Italian dictator's sporting deputy. With ethnic epithets like Mussolini's Darling, the Ambling Alp, and the Vast Venetian, Carnera served as a popular platform for the fascist leader's chest-beating propaganda. Just five years earlier in July 1930, when Carnera's criminal associations had caught up with him, Il Duce had personally intervened to prevent the fighter's deportation from the United States. Moreover, when Carnera won the world heavyweight title against Jack Sharkey in 1933, Mussolini ordered a uniform of the black shirt fascisti for his boxing champion and posed with Carnera in photos that he sent to newspapers throughout the world. The fighter even addressed his leader with the fascist salute.[51]

Paralleling the Louis–Carnera pre-fight publicity, white Americans wondered whether the tiny Ethiopian nation would survive the onslaught of Il Duce's larger, more modernized forces. Despite Italy's clear military advantages, an editorial in the *Crisis* challenged Mussolini's bravado, claiming that the "last gobble of Africa" would prove to be a "bloody swallow." It charged that Il Duce and his army would have to navigate the country's treacherous terrain while facing the unpredictable guerrilla strikes of Selassie's courageous and cunning men.[52]

In the ring, Louis would have to practice and then engage a similar guerrilla strategy in order to compensate for the gigantic proportions and long reach of Mussolini's Darling. Mapped out by trainer Blackburn and perfected by Louis, the ingenious battle plan involved breaking down the Italian's defensive stance with punishing body shots, and then moving in to attack Carnera's head. While Marcus Garvey urged his pan-Africanist brothers to "act manly, courageously, [and] thoughtfully" in mobilizing for the crisis that would come with Mussolini's invasion, the black press highlighted Louis's strict training regimen as another confirmation that he would prevail. Although Garvey lamented that Abyssinia's lack of preparation would only permit a "passionate, enthusiastic, and emotional" response to Italy's attack, the calm and conscientious Louis appeared well-equipped to conquer Carnera as he slashed his way through a host of gargantuan sparring mates.[53] Intelligence and rational discipline became integral to Louis's performance of black nationhood.

Many African American journalists and politicos connected the Louis–Carnera fight to the gendered debates of savagery versus civilization in the

Italo–Ethiopian conflict. Although Mussolini declared that he sought to bring progress to the supposedly backward nation of Abyssinia, black intellectuals like James Weldon Johnson questioned the dictator's rhetoric, arguing that Italy was simply after African loot. Critiquing Mussolini's violent designs, Johnson questioned the conventional, Western definition of civilization, arguing that even though Ethiopians lacked a modern infrastructure, they were at least civilized in character, with "courage, honesty, and consideration for the needs of others."[54] Drawing on similar tropes, *Pittsburgh Courier* commentator J.A. Rogers compared "Selassie, The Gentleman, And Mussolini, The Braggart." Not surprisingly, Rogers used heavyweight boxing as a metaphor for this larger battle of savagery against nobility, emphasizing Mussolini's baseness by equating his "gesturing" and "clowning" to that of the irreverent black fighter Jack Johnson.[55] In this racial and gendered reversal, Mussolini became the minstrel, as Rogers not only claimed Ethiopia as a civilized nation, but also referenced Louis's concurrent role in bringing racial progress to the boxing ring.

Playing on the brutish appearance of Mussolini's Darling, along with his reputation for illegal wrestling and holding, the black newspapers' drawings and photos of the Italian Giant made Carnera appear more beast than man, while their renderings of Louis retained a lifelike appearance. Although white journalists and cartoonists certainly portrayed Louis in more humane ways than his predecessor, Jack Johnson, some still tended to depict him using Sambo stereotypes. Paul Gallico's fight-day column in the *New York Daily News* included a thick-lipped, hairy depiction of Louis chasing after Carnera. Even though Gallico predicted that Carnera would face a "shy, easily upset man mellow," the writer also suggested that the animalistic Louis could "go berserk" at any time.[56]

In contrast, the black press steered away from caricatures of Louis and quoted him using full sentences. Moreover, while boasting of his strength, black journalists also emphasized his kindness and generosity to his mother and family. In mid-April 1935, many black writers celebrated Louis's display of patriarchal responsibility when the fighter used one of his purses to purchase a fully furnished home for his mother.[57] Whereas the Italian Giant embodied everything that was barbaric and violent about white racism and fascism, Louis came to exemplify an exalted form of civilized black manhood, grounded in a mix of physical prowess and force of character.[58] By more than just a case of coincidental timing, Louis became a gendered metaphor of black militancy and nationalism that drew on the rhetorical power of prevailing discourses of manliness and civilization. Even if Selassie had little chance of preventing an Italian takeover, Louis would defend black honor.

The Manly Art of Self-Defense

As Louis fought for Ethiopian independence, he also fought for the dignity and citizenship rights of African Americans at home. In addition to his symbolic connections to more radical, transnational black activism, he became the focus of an interrelated debate over questions of black American manhood and the state of the race. This discursive battle in the popular media was an equally significant race war being waged on the African American home front. While he prepared for his match, black journalists shaped many of the same gendered critiques associated with the international dimensions of his fight into a domestic narrative of black progress.

Black Americans' disproportionate suffering during the Great Depression only served to highlight their continued alienation and second-class citizenship. In the South, Jim Crow segregationists still ruled by legal and extralegal means, as struggling black sharecroppers and laborers sought to combat economic exploitation, widespread disfranchisement, and the terror of lynching.[59] Many African Americans left the South in search of safety and opportunity in the North, but even the Black Mecca of Harlem experienced police brutality and high unemployment. On March 22, 1935, the famed New York neighborhood erupted into violence after rumors circulated that the white manager of a local store had beaten and killed a Puerto Rican boy. Even though several hours later the rumors were discounted, Harlem's first-ever race riot continued into the night, as African Americans expressed their frustrations through mass destruction.[60]

Against this oppressive backdrop, Louis's success became the most conspicuous argument against the continued exclusion of African Americans from the benefits of full national citizenship. Black journalists inscribed his body with the ideals of black manliness and masculinity, and they sculpted his persona into a cultural vessel in which they poured their hopes and dreams. As an editorial in *Opportunity* described, "[t]he picture of a young Negro boy working in the Ford plant at $5.00 per day…who literally forces his way to a place where he can command a half million dollars within a single year" appealed to African Americans from "every walk of life."[61] While establishment uplifters could still embrace Louis for his respectability and productivity, a younger generation of New Negroes lionized him for his style and virility. To them, Louis was not exceptional; rather he represented what black America could do with the chance to compete on level ground. As he climbed his way from the dirt of the cotton fields to the bright lights of the boxing ring, he linked African Americans from different classes and vocations in a story of collective progress.

As musicologist Paul Oliver argues, Louis's heroic climb from the cotton fields of Alabama to boxing fame encapsulated the appealing drama and seeming invincibility of traditional African American ballad heroes like John Henry. Indeed, Louis was the only Depression-era athlete that popular blues artists commemorated in recorded songs.[62] As a man who faced the prospect of punishment alone in the ring, he enacted through sport the same kinds of struggles confronting many of his fans. Houston singer Joe Pullman's recording, entitled "Joe Louis is the Man," was the first song to honor Louis's toppling of Carnera. Although Oliver describes Pullman's creation as a "naïve piece of folk poetry," it captured the essence of Louis as the archetypal New Negro. While revering the Bomber as "a battlin' man," it also noted that he was "not a bad dressed guy," and that even though he was "makin' real good money," it failed to "swell his head." Just as Pullman celebrated "powerful Joe" in his performance, the husky-voiced Memphis Minnie McCoy of Chicago recorded "He's in the Ring (Doin' the Same Old Thing)" as a tribute to Louis's two-fisted "dynamite." The mix of Memphis Minnie's throaty lyrics, her guitar, and Black Bob's pounding piano emphasized the indestructibility of Louis, who knocked out his opponents with remarkable consistency to the delight of his poor and working-class fans:

> When your people's goin' out tonight,
> Jes' goin' to see Joe Louis fight,
> An' if you ain't got no money gotta go tomorrow night,
> 'Cause he's in the ring doin' the same ol' thing.[63]

As a rallying point for black communities across the nation, the figure of Louis served to unite the ethereal realm of diasporic politics with the everyday troubles of African Americans.

Louis received a hero's welcome from the black community at Grand Central Station in New York City in the middle of May 1935. As the black press included photos of Louis in chic suits enjoying the finer things in life like driving brand-new cars, he moved beyond his station as prizefighter to become both celebrity and socialite.[64] His bodily display of impeccable fashion was one of the most integral aspects of his gendered performance of black pride, since it allowed him to transgress racial norms, moving beyond the ubiquitous black identity of poor worker to showcase his wealth and individuality. One black correspondent praised Louis for looking the part of fistic champion in "his street togs," while another carefully itemized the boxer's wardrobe of a "dozen suits, nine pairs of shoes, two dozen shirts, 100 neckties, ten hats, six coats and countless sweaters, zippercoats, [and] suits of underwear and pyjamas."[65] Likewise, newspaper ads for Murray's Pomade, a popular hair straightener, reinforced Louis's reputation for being not only a great fighter but also "one of the best dressed men in America." As the text of the advertisement claimed, Louis strived to be "well-groomed" both in and out of the ring. The company encouraged the reader to support Louis and to buy their product, since doing both would enable a man to take on the young boxer's power and panache in his everyday life.[66] As the consummate New Negro, Louis reinforced his manhood through his prodigious consumption and street-hip style, offering an optimistic vision of the possibilities of black urban America.

Part politician, part pop idol, and part philanthropist, Louis spent a busy week in the Big Apple meeting with civic leaders like Mayor Fiorella LaGuardia, shaking hands with boxing legends like Jack Dempsey, and attending a series of charity benefits. Trading in his trousers for workout gear four times a day, Louis also starred in a promotional, vaudeville show at the Harlem Opera House, scoring one of the biggest draws in the history of the theater. With a kick-line of pretty dancing girls in the background, he sparred, skipped, and punched the heavy bag to the delight of packed houses. However, the respite was short-lived. With only a month left before the Carnera fight, Louis left for his training camp in Pompton Lakes, New Jersey.[67]

Black correspondents painted an idyllic picture of the countryside estate where Louis prepared for battle, emphasizing its connections to old American gentility, while also touting its modern conveniences. Celebrating Louis's role as the temporary master of the "Big House," they cloaked him in a mantle of both bourgeois respectability and technological efficiency.[68] According to local lore, George Washington had slept there, and black writers claimed that Louis now occupied the same room where the first president had stayed. Reputedly "one of the most famous fistic training grounds in the world," the camp was "[n]estled in a nature-scooped nook of the Ramapo Mountains," yet close enough to the city of Patterson to offer all of the amenities of rural and urban life combined. Although Louis spent most of his days working out, in his few moments of leisure time he supposedly enjoyed freshwater fishing, boating, golfing, and even horseback riding.[69] The training camp itself became an expression of not only Louis's nobility and modernity, but also the dignity and advancement of his people.

As the first fighter to ever rent the entire grounds for the exclusive use of his training camp, Louis ruled as lord of the estate. He retained a sixteen-man, African American entourage that included an eighteen-year-old, personal valet and the "expert dietician" Frank Sutton, a former restaurateur. In particular, Sutton, who had once served Booker T. Washington, became a popular figure in the black press reports from Pompton Lakes. Referencing the "nutritionist," black writers presented detailed accounts of Louis's disciplined, "two-meal-a-day diet," countering white reports of the fighter's supposed penchant for ice cream and tendency to overeat.[70]

Editorials in the black press insisted that African American fighters no longer needed to seek out white assistance to get ahead. Louis reputedly rejected the possibility of white patronage, saying that he would "hang up the gloves for good" if Roxborough and Black sold any part of his earnings. By this time Jacobs certainly provided much of Louis's financial backing, but black reports tended to downplay the white promoter's role, while emphasizing the influence of his black managers. Roxborough, Black, and Blackburn's tactical abilities at the negotiating table and at ringside formed an important plotline in the story of Louis's success. In true New Negro form, Louis and his black "Board of Strategy" were beating white men at their own enterprise.[71]

A steady stream of cars and pedestrians traveled to the estate to see Louis in action. In this seemingly apolitical space, showing support for Louis enabled his black supporters to publicly express their own status and worth and to gain vicariously the strength of his fists. By the middle of June, his sparring workouts had already attracted around 3,200 visitors, and as the fight drew nearer writers predicted crowds of 1,000 per workout of mostly African American fans from all along the East Coast.[72] Alongside regular folk, professionals and celebrities made appearances. Black newspapers like the *New York Age* and the *Baltimore Afro-American* provided weekly lists of the VIP spectators—judges, sportsmen, entertainers, entrepreneurs, orchestra leaders, morticians, and politicians—who ranged from local to national elites. Many of those who saw Louis in the flesh achieved their own form of celebrity as they returned home to trumpet his prowess on the street corners and in the bars of their urban communities.[73] Attending the Louis camp became, for spectators, an expression of pride and promise.

As Louis toppled his sparring mates, his African American fans celebrated him as a polished, physical specimen of black virility. Louis embodied an undeniable, yet understated sexuality that appealed to the younger generation of New Negroes without upsetting the traditional conventions of respectability. Even though the Louis team's "official" position was that the fighter did not associate with women, black fans still celebrated his bodily perfection. As public school teacher Helen Harden recounted in a letter to the *New York Age*, many spectators visited the camp "with one purpose," and that was "to gaze on the Detroit Bomber." Harden gushed that he was simply "lovely to look at. Not a blemish on his saffron hued skin." Another black female fan refused to believe the official reports that claimed Louis would keep women out of his life until he won the world title, arguing that "Joe is a real man, after all."[74]

Although the young boxer obviously appealed to women, many articles in the white press twisted the Louis party line to unsex and infantilize the black fighter, claiming that "iceberg" Louis had "no time for women" and that his only "sweetheart" was his mother.[75] Challenging these images, the black press fashioned him as an idol of masculinity, showing suggestive photos of Louis washing himself in the shower and gazing at the camera partially disrobed. While black writers did acknowledge that Louis had no serious plans for marriage, they also reported that camp intimates swore he was a "lady-killer."[76] However, concerned with dissociating their fighter from the negative legacy of Jack Johnson, Louis's handlers kept the young man's sexual escapades with white women, along with his love of speeding cars and frivolous spending, out of the press.[77] In an era when black male sexuality connoted rape and recklessness, Louis's carefully constructed balance of physicality and decency offered a positive model of virile black manhood.

Despite the more daringly masculine aspects of his persona, Louis still stood as a paragon of manly productivity in the face of racist, white reports of his laziness. Even a sympathetic white writer like Van Every betrayed his prejudice when he claimed that Louis's trainer had to "force Joe…to cut out his dissipation…even if it infringed on his sleep."[78] In refuting these types of disparaging comments, one journalist in the *New York Amsterdam News* declared that "[n]o fighter during the past twenty years has trained with more earnestness than this Detroit boy."[79]

Following the conventions of contemporary boxing manuals, the black press provided detailed descriptions of Louis's routine, arguing that his abilities were not just "natural," but cultivated.[80] With scientific precision and utmost discipline, Louis arose at six in the morning to run in the mountains, followed by a demanding afternoon of sparring matches, bag punching, rope skipping, and bending exercises. So important was it to counter notions of black indolence that one sportswriter even maintained that Louis was a model of efficiency when he slept, taking "it as seriously as he does his fighting. No faking, no lost motion."[81] In this way, Louis's persona combined the traditional watermarks of gentlemanly respectability with the rising tide of New Negro masculinity. He became not only *the* Race Man, but also an Everyman for the race.

The New Negro and His New Crowd

Just days before the fight-date, the impending Italian invasion of Ethiopia permeated local politics as the Hearst Milk Fund contemplated canceling the Louis–Carnera bout for fear that it would inspire race riots. The Hearst announcement marked the high point in a month-long racial debate over the potential for black–Italian violence at the match. Pointing to the rioting of Harlem's black population in March 1935 and the ongoing furor over the Abyssinian crisis, white sportswriters Westbrook Pegler and Arthur Brisbane warned that a boxing match pitting a black American against an Italian fighter would furnish the fuel for racial unrest in both the stands and streets. Pegler deemed the bout a "new high in stupid judgment," while Brisbane worried that it might inspire "a fight bigger than the scheduled fight."[82]

Given Pegler and Brisbane's predictions, it became clear that not just Louis's manhood was on the line in the upcoming match, but also the collective manhood of his African American spectators. The black press responded with vehemence. Al Monroe of the *Chicago Defender* recognized white America's unease with the sudden rise of the Race Man Louis, whose burgeoning popularity was "moving 'out of control.'" He dismissed the warnings of violence, claiming that his Nordic counterparts had no intention of writing "the real facts."[83] In turn, while the *New York Amsterdam News* claimed that "Negroes today are unlikely to riot over anything less than deep-seated social injustice and economic exclusion," they also warned that "Negroes ARE likely to be forced to defend themselves against attack by whites who have been stirred by repeated comment on the possibilities of rioting."[84]

In late June, when a front-page editorial in the white *Newark Ledger* called for a boycott of the fight, the black press upped its ante. The *Baltimore Afro-American* claimed that this was a deliberate move to prevent Louis from advancing to the heavyweight championship, reporting that blacks and Italians in Newark's "hill" sections had responded with their own boycott of the *Ledger*. Linking it to larger political questions, the *Chicago Defender* placed the ultimate blame in Mussolini's lap, declaring that the dictator's shameless use of the Louis–Carnera fight as fodder for race hatred in the Italian American press had provoked the *Ledger* boycott.[85] Just as Louis's individual victory would prove his boxing manhood, so too would his black fans have a communal chance to prove their maturity and respectability as spectators. Characteristic of the period's wider questioning of the merits of bourgeois respectability alongside the rise of popular strains of more aggressive, mass politics, class tensions surfaced in this aspect of the pre-fight publicity. Recalling the controversy over Harlem's first-ever race riot in March, black journalists understood that much was at stake. Their arguments were not just defensive, but prescriptive. While Louis's win would certainly be cause for celebration, it had to remain civilized. Otherwise, his ultimate strength would remain locked in his fists, unable to transfer its impact to the larger struggle against racism and fascism at home and abroad.[86]

On the morning of June 25, 1935, the Brown Bomber and Mussolini's Darling readied themselves "to clash for the synthetic championship of two continents."[87] Despite the reassurances of the black press, the Hearst Milk Fund was taking no chances with the possibility of violence, and for the first time in New York City's boxing history, a troop of armed police would surround the ringside at Yankee Stadium as Louis and Carnera fought. Over 1,000 patrolmen and detectives would also be stationed at strategic points throughout the arena.[88]

Since the major radio networks of NBC and CBS refused to air the match for fear of potential bloodshed across the country, the 100 ticket sellers in the stadium box office had their hands full with a last-minute rush of spectators.[89] For weeks before the fight, several black newspapers had advertised organized bus trips to the event, along with special railroad rates and flights that welcomed both men and women.[90]

Under a sunny, steamy New York sky, most of the nearly 15,000 African Americans on hand to see Louis arrived long before the white spectators with ringside seats. They congregated in the right- and left-field bleachers as soon as the Yankee Stadium gates opened at five o'clock, singing, cheering, and performing ad hoc speeches during their two-hour wait for the preliminary fights. A journalist for the *New York Age* spoke with one man who had traveled with his wife all the way from Leland, Mississippi. The writer could only interpret this cotton buyer and Fisk University graduate's dedication as an example of "the spirit of enthusiasm and race pride that urged him and thousands of others from Chillicothe, Kinder Lots and many other hidden hamlets" across the country to attend the fight.[91] In addition to the lively crowds in the bleachers, black America's royalty, from politicians to professionals, and from sportsmen to entertainers like Bill "Bojangles" Robinson and Lena Horne sat closer to the ring.[92] By the time of the main event, over 60,000 spectators of all races packed the stadium, with gate receipts totaling nearly $350,000, a new high for a nontitular match.[93]

As ring announcer Hugh Balogh urged, "in the name of American sportsmanship…[R]egardless of race, creed, or color, let us all say, may the better man emerge victorious."[94] As the fighters approached each other, Carnera looked like a massive beast alongside the young David. Yet, it was Louis, expressionless and calm, who commanded the center of the ring, while Mussolini's Darling danced around him. By the end of the first round, Louis had already drawn blood, cutting the Italian Giant's lip with a smashing right to the mouth. Louis continued to explode with hard body shots, followed by rights and lefts that bruised Carnera's face. Toward the end of the fifth, Mussolini's Darling looked ready to collapse, with blood streaming down his face, but Louis, still fresh-legged, blasted him with more head and body combinations. Louis rocked Carnera with a series of hard rights in the sixth round, sending Mussolini's Darling to the canvas three times. As Carnera staggered to his feet Referee Arthur Donovan called off the fight as Louis hit his target with a cannonade of punches. The crowd burst into cheers as Louis won by technical knockout, with not a mark on his face.

Even without the benefit of a radio broadcast, news of Louis's win traveled quickly. Not too far from the stadium, a phone call conveyed the result to the estimated 20,000 fans who gathered at the Savoy Ballroom in Harlem. As the *Pittsburgh Courier* reported, floods of African Americans poured into the streets from Seventh to Lenox and 125th to 145th with a carnival spirit "reminiscent of Marcus Garvey's best days." The ravages of the Depression seemed momentarily suspended as celebrants in the taverns offered up toasts to Louis, while cars with plates from as far away as the District of Columbia, Illinois, Maryland, Tennessee, Georgia, and Canada crawled and honked their way down Seventh Avenue.[95]

As the black press pointed to the relative order of the post-fight festivities as confirmation that African Americans were not as uncivilized as Pegler and Brisbane had thought, the behavior of Louis's fans became another mark of resistance. As a correspondent for the *Journal and Guide* asserted, "Contrary to unfounded anxiety expressed in some quarters, there was no sign of disorder before, during or after the fight."[96] Yet, the glowing descriptions in the black press appear to have obscured the multiple ways in which African Americans from different walks of life expressed their support of Louis.

Articles in the white dailies presented a much more raucous picture of the post-fight revelry. By reading their accounts intertextually with the black press reports, one can draw a more nuanced portrait of the vigorous celebration without much regard to hallowed respectability. One elderly, black orator named Gill Holton reputedly declared, "It [wa]s the greatest night Harlem…had since the riot." Officers on foot and horseback, along with those driving motorcycles and radio cars, monitored the thousands of fans that surrounded the packed Savoy Ballroom. Mounted police had to intervene when members of the crowd stormed the entrance, breaking down one of the doors and injuring a half-dozen people. When the community's honorary mayor, entertainer Bill "Bojangles" Robinson, arrived in a limousine, he made a cursory speech cautioning the throngs of fans to remain calm, but minutes later he, too, joined in the shouting as he moved down the street. Belligerent youths postured on the hoods of moving cars, yelling at the tops of their lungs, while children who should have been in bed pounded ashcans on the streets and compared their flexed biceps.[97] Even if Louis's managers advised him against expressing his jubilation in the ring, the Brown Bomber's victory gave his fans an opportunity to aggressively assert their racial pride en masse, in a way that defied conventional racial norms.

The events surrounding the Jersey City Riots of August 1935 paint an even clearer picture of this sense of militancy. According to a report in the *New York Age,* around 100 black and Italian men armed with knives, baseballs, stones, and other blunt objects engaged in a "free for all" of street fighting on August 11. A verbal dispute over the impending Italo–Ethiopian conflict and the related Louis–Carnera bout had apparently sparked a fistfight that exploded into a massive brawl, leaving four wounded and leading to eleven arrests. An emergency squad consisting of radio cars, along with police on foot with tear gas bombs, managed to quell the unrest. African Americans claimed that Louis's recent victories had heightened white aggression in the district. Yet, according to the whites involved, black youths had been taunting passers-by, demanding that everyone acknowledge Louis's superiority. After the initial clash, the hostilities almost resurfaced the next day, as two bands of white males totaling around ninety exchanged verbal challenges with a group of African American men.[98] More than just an inspiration for the writings of New Negro elites, Louis's decisive win sparked an already smoldering sense of militant consciousness among the African American masses, bringing strong expressions of black pride to the surface that defied the combined strictures of white racism and elite decency.

Brown Moses?

In addition to energizing the masses, Louis's conquering of Carnera ignited a passionate debate in the black press regarding the proper representation of the race and what constituted legitimate forms of black progress. His victory gave writers and intellectuals a symbolic slate on which they attempted to negotiate and navigate their struggle for manhood rights. For the most part, black writers never questioned whether Louis had "sold out" to the white establishment or had shirked his duties to black America.[99] Rather, they argued over whether Louis, as boxer, was a suitable male figurehead for the future of the race, both nationally and internationally. After all, with his success in the corporal realm of pugilism, Louis presented somewhat of a dilemma to the traditional politics of bourgeois uplift. Many black elites struggled to come to terms with the fact that this popular hero was gaining unprecedented notoriety and wealth through muscular achievement, rather than education and erudition. As African Americans endeavored to escape the reductionist stereotypes of black physicality that consigned most to menial labor, Louis emerged as a gendered wild card with multiple possibilities in the changing game of racial construction.

Some commentators expressed their utter joy over Louis's manly victory as a source of racial pride and progress. Dan Burley of the *Baltimore Afro-American* dubbed Louis the "Brown Moses of the Prize Ring," claiming that through his win over Carnera, Louis had become a national leader in the way that Moses brought the Israelites out of bondage. Citing the fact that Texas was now competing for a chance to host a Louis fight, along with Missouri's decision to lift its ban of interracial matches, Burley maintained that Louis was literally knocking out Jim Crow, with his wins being every bit "as good as electing a Congressman to represent us in Washington."[100]

In some respects, Louis could exert physical force and command white attention in a way that escaped his black political and intellectual counterparts. Only in the ring could a black man actually harm a white man without being arrested or lynched. Because of the ostensibly apolitical nature of Louis's triumph, many black writers, conscious of its larger symbolic implications, could celebrate it in detail without fear of reprisal. Extensive photo layouts of the Italian Giant's boxing demise splashed across the pages of many black newspapers, presenting multiple pictures of Louis standing over his conquered foe.[101]

Even though some African American journalists highlighted Louis's mix of muscular prowess and mental acuity, contending that "his cunning brain work[ed] in accordance with fast and deadly fists," others cautioned black Americans not to place their hopes in the individual, physical triumph of Louis.[102] While the *Crisis* understood his importance to the "rank-and-file," they advised black America not "to hitch its wagon to a boxer; or base its judgments of achievement on the size of a black man's biceps or the speed and power of his left hook."[103] Moreover, another editorial in the *Baltimore Afro-American* claimed that the contributions of intellectual Race Men like Carter G. Woodson and W.E.B. Du Bois, along with the legal advances in the anti-lynching campaign, were "worth a dozen successes in the prize ring."[104] Regardless of its cathartic value, Louis's win had not altered the structures of oppression in America, nor had it blazed any new paths for racial progress. Placing more weight in the potential of academic and political tactics for achieving manhood rights, they questioned the significance of sporting victories.

Falling between these two extremes, some editorialists believed that even if Louis did not bring institutional changes, he was still an appropriate role model of racial uplift, especially for young boys. While not inclined to view Louis as "a Moses of the race or as an Economic Hope," one writer for the *Journal and Guide* maintained that the Bomber's "moderation, temperance, [and] modesty" offered the "real moral in his victory, the most important thing to be proud of."[105] A few weeks after the Louis–Carnera bout, the *New York Amsterdam News* attempted to put these ideals into action, founding and sponsoring a "Joe Louis Boys Club" that encouraged youngsters to follow in the footsteps of "America's model young man." According to its advertisement, the club's main purpose was to instill the young men of the community with Louis's discipline and competitive spirit.[106] Yet, however much adults wished that young boys would emulate Louis's respectability, the teen generation had different reasons for idolizing the boxer. According to the fieldwork of sociologist E. Franklin Frazier, black youths from all classes in the 1930s admired Louis for his conspicuous wealth and hip style and drew vicarious satisfaction from his brutalizing of white opponents.[107] To them, Louis was less about uplift and more about black pride and militancy.

Ultimately, even if the heavyweight emerged as a contested symbol with little concrete effect on the realities of long breadlines and Mussolini's imperial designs, his win over Carnera still served to shine a critical spotlight on the struggles and ironies of black life. Both journalists and cartoonists in the African American press used the gendered images of boxing to formulate political critiques that drew explicit connections between foreign fascism and domestic racism. The focal point of the *Chicago Defender's* picture page showed a battered Carnera on the mat with a caption that read, "I'd rather be in Ethiopia."[108] In another particularly poignant, post- fight drawing, a boxer resembling Louis became a proxy for the Brotherhood of Sleeping Car Porters, standing victorious over a dazed Carnera look-alike that had "Pullman Company, Unionism" written across his chest.[109] As a figure that embodied the deep connections between diasporic and domestic politics, Louis's victory in the ring had underlined the hypocrisy and unfairness of not only Mussolini and the League of Nations, but also white America.

Pointing to the sheer absurdity of it all, another *Afro-American* editorialist wondered what "secret of mass psychology" turned white humanity in one part of the nation into a murderous mob, while in another "they cheer to the echo a little brown boy who pummels the gore out of a big white man mountain?"[110] Louis's victory over Carnera had exposed the many-headed beast of white supremacy, while also subjecting it to a cultural barrage of strong black manhood.

Schmeling Takes Sampson

Following the Carnera fight, many journalists in the white dailies suddenly became repositories of advice for Louis, offering cautionary tales of what could happen if the young fighter let amusement and overconfidence get in the way of his boxing. Bill Corum of the *New York Evening-Journal* warned Louis to stick to his "Ma" and to steer clear of the jazzy night life in Harlem. In a patronizing, almost race-baiting fashion, the writer counseled: "Don't get big headed.... Behave yourself." Above all, Corum reminded Louis that he was not only a fighter, but a symbol to his race.[111]

On May 16, 1936, in Lakewood, New Jersey, Louis celebrated his twenty-second birthday, along with the official opening of his training camp for the first of his two bouts against Germany's Max Schmeling. Boxing's dignitaries, from Nat Fleischer of *Ring Magazine* to World Heavyweight Champion Jim J. Braddock, honored the young fighter for his spectacular achievements over the last year.[112] However with his next match only a month away, one of the most popular questions in the white mainstream press was whether or not Louis "could take" the pressures of his newfound fame. As yet another test of his mettle as Race Man, Louis's skirmish with Schmeling would once again become a stand-in for larger racial conflicts at home and abroad.

As Louis began his preparations, Corum's foreshadowing of the young boxer's potential downfall seemed to be coming true. Over ten pounds heavier and reputedly more interested in improving his golf game than his fighting skills, Louis appeared disinterested and sluggish during his initial practices. Even though Louis was the younger and more talented boxer, journalists from both presses wondered if his apparent smugness would cause him to falter. As Lloyd Lewis of the *Chicago Daily News* contended, "Joe Louis is the only man who can whip Joe Louis."[113]

While some writers in the white dailies continued to infer that Louis's listlessness confirmed that blacks could not handle positions above their usual station, the African American press responded with continued faith in the abilities and ambition of their New Negro of the manly art. Although one journalist in the

New York American argued that "success and plenty" were spoiling the former "canebrake baby" turned "million-dollar corporation, most reports in the black press tended to take on a more positive view of Louis's training efforts by the beginning of June.[114]

Outside the ring, African American writers celebrated Louis's new role as husband and provider for his sophisticated beautiful bride, Marva Trotter, thereby appropriating the gender roles of white bourgeois society. After their wedding in September 1935, the black press seized on the opportunity to refute the popular racist image of Louis as a "Mammy's boy," promoting the young couple as black America's first family. Freed from the responsibilities of her secretarial job, Mrs. Louis pursued charity work, practiced the piano, visited the beauty salon, and attended parties of New York's black society. While Marva soon gained her own form of celebrity, admired by black women for her poise, charm, and fashion sense, she assured her fans that "Joe's the boss of our family and he's always going to be so."[115] Even though economic imperatives prevented most African Americans from fulfilling these patriarchal ideals, journalists shaped Louis and his wife into a public display of healthy black American family life.

Yet, an underlying critique of Louis's decision to marry before obtaining the heavyweight title would later come back to haunt Marva after her husband's loss to Schmeling. Even before their nuptials, many of Louis's black fans made it clear that they thought his managers needed to shield him from the corrupting influences of women to protect his strength. As one editorialist in the *Baltimore Afro-American* argued, "An athlete who marries is usually no good for a year, trainers say. And this is the reason managers of Joe Louis will be shooing sweet girls away from their charge until he is champion." The temptations of female sexuality were apparently a dangerous distraction in the field of manly battle, and the editorialist went on to warn Louis' handlers not to take any chances "with some Delilah who might snear [sic] their Sampson."[116]

In addition to this sexualized, domestic plotline, the Louis–Schmeling match up became a metaphorical battle in which African Americans could combat the theory of Aryan supremacy that stripped the Jews of their rights in Nazi Germany and kept blacks from achieving equality in the United States. The African American press had already been reporting the Nazi's persecution of the Jews and its links to American racism as early as 1933.[117] Arguably, the Jewish question did not acquire the same kind of popular resonance in the black press in comparison to the Abyssinian crisis, which still continued as a featured news item even in the summer of 1936. However, it was clear that, for some sectors of the black population, the Louis–Schmeling match had both international and national implications for the race. Although the suave Schmeling did not have the same savage appeal as Carnera, the black press still invited their readers to make ethnic comparisons, offering side-by-side photos of the fighters' physical weapons, along with listings of their measurements.[118]

In contrast, white sportswriters generally ignored the international implications of the fight, since Hitler's persecution of the Jews had not yet become an issue in the mainstream daily press. Even the Nazis had little interest in promoting their ties to the match, since they assumed that Schmeling would lose.[119] In the weeks before the bout, many white American dailies appeared to put aside their national allegiances to promote the German in articles and pictures. While the text of the *Atlanta Constitution* grudgingly argued for Louis's inevitable victory over Schmeling, the southern paper's absence of Louis pictures versus its numerous, handsome photos of the German heavyweight spoke volumes about who they wanted to win.[120] Other white sportswriters were more transparent with their allegiances to Schmeling, like Pat Rosa of the *New York Post* who claimed that the prideful and industrious German would certainly give Louis the "Drifter" a run for his money. For Rosa, this test of "mind…over matter" would favor the talents of Schmeling.[121] Louis was not the American hero that he would later become in his rematch against the German in 1938. For many white fans, the upcoming bout was decidedly racial rather than nationalistic.

Already delayed one day because of rain, the fight took place at Yankee Stadium on the overcast evening of June 19, 1936. The poor weather coupled with a Jewish boycott of the fight made for a relatively small crowd of 45,000 spectators. Unlike the cool, lean panther of just a year ago, Louis looked thicker around the waist, while Schmeling possessed the best physique of his career. In pre-fight interviews, Schmeling revealed that he had discovered a weakness in Louis's supposedly impenetrable defense, and he intended to exploit it. Throughout the bout as Louis consistently dropped his left guard when throwing his right, Schmeling hit him with stiff counterpunches to the jaw. In the fourth round, the German fighter rocked Louis with a hard right, sending him reeling. Although Louis managed to stand his ground in the face of many punishing blows, in round twelve Schmeling smashed him with a right, sending him to his knees against the ropes. As Louis rose to his feet on the count of four, Schmeling finished him off with another stiff right. Louis dropped to the canvas and lay prostrate as if sleeping.[122]

A shell-shocked black America went into mourning. African American fans all across the country hung their heads in gloom. Their Race Man had fallen to the representative of Aryan supremacy. As one report from Louis's home base of Detroit described, "It was like a sudden death in the family."[123] With black America grieving, the white press quickly threw their support behind Schmeling, arguing that the so-called Nazi boxer had proved "[he]was too smart for the Negro." While Grantland Rice exaggerated when he deemed the fight the "most severe beating in ring history," the *New York Post* presented a pitiful picture of the fallen Louis on his backside, accompanied by a headline that reduced him to "Just a Scared and Beaten Boy."[124] Louis's loss seemed to confirm black America's inferiority.

African American fans did not know what to make of their "Superman's" fall from grace. Rumors of doping quickly hit the black press. Another particularly vicious example of the post-fight gossip pointed the finger of blame at Marva, charging that she had distracted Louis before the match by showing him a recent love letter from her former boyfriend. In the *Black Man*, Marcus

Garvey maintained that Louis had simply married too early, reasoning that the young boxer would have won against Schmeling if he were still a single man. For Garvey and many of Louis's black fans, the tragic defeat appeared to prove the liability of women in the war of the races. Their male-centered conceptions of the fight for racial equality seemed to leave little room for the meaningful participation of women. Ultimately, Garvey hoped that Louis had "learned a lesson from the fight, that when a white man enters the ring in a premier bout with a black man, he realizes that he has in his hands the destiny of the white race." Apparently Louis had not taken his role as Race Man seriously enough.[125]

On the other hand, many black fans remained supportive of Louis, pointing to his integrity and respectability even in the face of defeat. In a letter to the *New York Amsterdam News*, Sam J. Jones of Brooklyn argued that Louis had proved his manhood by showing that he could withstand prolonged physical punishment. Moreover, Jones suggested that black America take its lead from Louis in the midst of this crisis because the young fighter's denial of the rumors, along with his willingness to take responsibility for his mistakes, illustrated his true sportsmanship and dignity.[126]

While their pillars of racial manhood toppled one by one, with the Italian conquest of Ethiopia and the continuing problems of the Great Depression, some journalists in the black press worried about the future progress of the race. As one post-fight headline in the *Chicago Defender* asked, "Haile Selassie First, Now Louis; Who Next?" Louis's loss against the German fighter had managed to bring things full circle, intensifying black Americans' fears about the implications of the Abyssinian defeat at the hands of Mussolini. Depicting the instability of racial uplift in the form of a "Stool of Achievement" lying on its side with two broken legs labeled "Louis" and "Selassie," one cartoonist argued, "It can still be repaired."[127] In the wake of the Brown Bomber's defeat, Race Men across the nation called upon each other to stand up and take charge.

By the time white America embraced Louis as a national hero with his famous knockout win in his 1938 rematch against Max Schmeling, black fans, even outside the United States, had long lauded the boxer as the epitome of black pride and success. In the heart of the Nazi nation, a young Afro-German man could barely contain his excitement over Louis's pummeling of Schmeling, as he sat surrounded by white patrons in a public bar. When asked what he thought of the fight, the Louis fan responded, "In sports, the best man wins."[128] This subtle, but smug reply incensed someone to throw an iron chair at his head. Louis's victory was more than just the symbolic overthrow of Nazi fascism; it challenged the masculine foundations of white supremacy. For the young Afro-German, it was not just an American triumph, but the triumph of a fellow black man connected to him through a cultural and political identity forged in the transnational crucible of racist and fascist oppression.

Undoubtedly, Louis was neither an uncomplicated hero of American democracy nor a simple figure of racial cooptation, for the real moral of his success stands as one of the most important cultural legacies of the New Negro era. His rise as the preeminent 1930s Race Man points to the period's larger trend toward the engendering of blackness as a male construct. Despite various class and generational tensions, conceptions of black dignity, black strength, black resistance, and even the imagined black nation remained intimately connected to the imagined status of black manhood. From popular culture to academics to political organizations, the "crisis of black masculinity" moved to the forefront of discussions on racial progress, with increasingly visible and vocal calls for the "proper affirmation of black male authority."[129] While political, economic, and social equality remained elusive, the fantastic successes of African American athletes with the racial integration of U.S. professional leagues in the following decades meant that sports emerged as the ultimate, public stage for this collective project in the assertion of black manhood. Moreover, calls for black male athletes to conform to the bourgeois, patriarchal standards of respectability and productivity as "role models" for young African American men, continues to pervade current discourse on the social significance and responsibility of black athletes.

Even though the U.S. Army would soon use the figure of Joe Louis to inspire tolerance among white G.I.'s, African Americans had already laid claim to him as Race Man and budding patriarch. His model of black masculinity—one that vanquished white men, while leading black women—stayed with African Americans as they left home to fight Hitler and later returned to take on Jim Crow again.

Notes

Parts of this article were presented at the 2003 Harvard University Graduate Conference on "Performing Ethnicity" and at the 2003 Annual Meeting of the Association for the Study of African American Life and History. The author would like to thank all of those who graciously helped this piece to evolve over multiple drafts, including Glenda Gilmore, Seth Fein, Paul Gilroy, Matthew Jacobson, Amy Bass, Jeffrey Sammons, Pamela Grundy, and the members of the Spring 2002 Yale Research Seminar in American History.

1. Heywood Broun, *New York World-Telegram*, 1938, qtd. in Chris Mead, *Joe Louis: Black Hero in White America* (New York: Charles Scribner's Sons, 1985), 159.

2. Frank Sinatra, "Foreword," in Neil Scott, Joe *Louis: A Picture Story of his Life* (New York: Greenberg, 1947).

3. St. Clair Drake and Horace Cayton offer a sociological account of the "Race Man" concept in *Black Metropolis: A Study of Life in a Northern City* (New York: Harcourt and Brace, 1945). They argue that this social type developed as a means for black Americans to resist their second-class status by pointing to black superiority in particular areas of expertise. In other words, the success of the Race Man became a metaphor for the success of all African Americans (390-392). In examining the various facets of Louis's popular construction as a 1930s Race Man, this article builds on the gendered critique of twentieth-century black politics in Hazel V. Carby, *Race Men* (Cambridge, MA: Harvard University, 1998). Black feminist scholars like Carby argue against the popular practice of equating the redemption of black patriarchal manhood with racial progress, since using the Race Man as the dominant metaphor for black success tends to render black women's roles and struggles, along with the relationship between racism and sexism, largely invisible. Moreover, this association of patriarchy with progress has often foreclosed a united front against the related oppressions of white supremacy and gender inequality. Please note that I use the terms African American and black or black American interchangeably throughout this article.

4. Richard Wright, "High Tide in Harlem," *New Masses*, July 1938.

5. Richard Wright, "Joe Louis Uncovers Dynamite," New *Masses*, Oct. 8, 1935, 18-19.

6. Drake and Cayton, *Black Metropolis,* qtd. in Mead, *Joe Louis: Black Hero in White America,* 92.

7. Chicago *Whip* qtd. in David Levering Lewis, *When Harlem was in Vogue* (New York: Penguin, 1979, reprinted 1997), 24.

8. See Booker T. Washington, *A New Negro for a New Century: An Up-to-Date Record of the Upward Struggles of the Negro Race* (Chicago: American Publishing House, 1900).

9. On the Harlem Renaissance as a literary movement see Lewis, *When Harlem Was In Vogue;* and Cary Wintz, *Black Culture and the Harlem Renaissance* (Houston: Rice University Press, 1988). For research that expands the scope of the New Negro movement see David Krasner, *A Beautiful Pageant: African American Theatre, Drama, and Performance in the Harlem Renaissance, 1910-1927* (New York: Paigrave Macmillan, 2002); Mark Schneider, *We Return Fighting: The Civil Rights Movement in the Jazz Age* (Boston: Northeastern University Press, 2002); and Brent Hayes Edwards, *The Practice of Diaspora: Literature, Translation, and the Rise of Black Internationalism* (Cambridge, MA.: Harvard University Press, 2003).

10. I ground my definition of resistance in the theory of political scientist Jim C. Scott. See *Domination and the Art of Resistance: Hidden Transcripts* (New Haven, CT: Yale University Press, 1990), 8-9, 41. Louis's victories offered moments when African Americans' "hidden transcripts" of grievances could be brought into public view. Moreover, my discursive deconstruction of the variety of covert ways that African Americans articulated their notions of black representation and resistance through Louis's persona and accomplishments employs Scott's overall conception of "infrapolitics" (19).

11. My analysis draws on historian Penny Von Eschen's discussion of black diasporic activism in the 1930s. See Penny Von Eschen, *Race Against Empire: Black Americans and Anti-Colonialism, 1937-1957* (Ithaca, NY: Cornell University Press, 1997). Louis's matches against Carnera and Schmeling further demonstrate the extent to which antifascism and anticolonialism informed public debates over black identity and politics during the Depression.

12. Edward Van Every, *Joe Louis, Man and Super-fighter* (New York: Frederick A. Stokes Co., 1936): book cover. Van Every was the white sports journalist who gave Louis his first feature break in the daily press. Black newspapers like the *Chicago Defender* carried advertisements for Every's biography (see June 13, 1936, 13).

13. Fans could read about Louis in the 1935 *Pittsburgh Courier* series, "The Life Story of Joe Louis, as told to Chester Washington and William G. Nunn." Other major black press organs also included regular updates about the boxer's life outside of the ring. Also see Van Every, 34, 36, 46.

14. "Here are Details on Weight and Size of Joe Louis," *Pittsburgh Courier,* June 8, 1935, section 2, 4.

15. B. Weinstein, "Joe Louis Comes to Town," *Young Worker,* June 25, 1935. Also see "The Real Joe Louis, by his sister Eunice Barrow," *Young Worker,* December 24, 1935, 1.

16. Theophilus Lewis, "Boxing Business Man," *New York Amsterdam News,* July 6, 1935.

17. Much of the literature depicts Louis as a docile "Uncle Tom" who functioned as a "race ambassador" to white America. In these treatments, the quiet, gentlemanly Louis pales in comparison to supposedly less conventional boxers like the flamboyant Jack Johnson and draft resistor Muhammad Ali. See Othello Harris, "Muhammad Ali and the Revolt of the Black Athlete," in *Muhammad Ali: The People's Champ,* ed. Elliott Gorn (Chicago: University of Illinois Press, 1995): 56. Also see Harry Edwards, *The Revolt of the Black Athlete* (New York: Free Press, 1969); Bill Hawkins, "The White Supremacy Continuum of Images on Black Men," *Journal of African American Men* 3, no. 3 (Winter 1998): 7-18; Othello Harris, "The Role of Sports in the Black Community," in *African Americans in Sport,* ed. Gary A. Sailes (New Brunswick, NJ: Transaction Publishers, 1998), 3-14; David K. Wiggins, "The Notion of Double Consciousness and the Involvement of Black Athletes in American Sport," in *Ethnicity and Sport in North American History and Culture,* eds. George Eisen and David K. Wiggins (Westport, CT: Greenwood Press, 1994) 133-156; and Gorn, ed. *Muhammad Ali.* See Ken Burns, "Unforgivable Blackness: The Rise and Fall of Jack Johnson." USA: PBS, 2005; Gail Bederman, *Manliness and Civilization: A Cultural History of Gender and Race in the United States, 1880-1917* (Chicago: University of Chicago Press, 1995), 8-10; and Randy Roberts, *Papa Jack: Jack Johnson and the Era of White Hopes* (New York: The Free Press, 1983). In particular Ken Burns' documentary for PBS has brought the Jack Johnson story to a mass audience on PBS. This biographical film traces Johnson's public exploits and the heated controversies they created within the context of Jim Crow America. In particular, it details Johnson's well-publicized

marriages to white women, his unapologetic enjoyment of material riches from clothes to cars, and his notorious taunting of white opponents while beating them in the ring.

18. Mead, 156-157. While Mead champions Louis's contributions to the struggle for racial integration, his project investigates Louis through the eyes of white sources. For a discussion of state-sanctioned constructions of Joe Louis in wartime propaganda, see Lauren Rebecca Sklaroff, "Constructing G.I. Joe Louis: Cultural Solutions to the 'Negro Problem' during World War II," *Journal of American History* 89, no.3 (December 2002): 958-983. Also see Jeffrey Sammons, *Beyond the Ring: The Role of Boxing in American Society* (Chicago: University of Illinois Press, 1988): 97-129; Gerald Astor, *"And a Credit to His Race": The Hard Life and Times of Joseph Louis Barrow, a.k.a. Joe Louis* (New York: E. Dutton, 1974); Jill M. Dupont, "The Self in the Ring, the Self in Society': Boxing and American Culture from Jack Johnson to Joe Louis," Ph.D. diss. (Chicago: University of Chicago, 2000); Art Evans, "Joe Louis as Key Functionary: White Reaction Toward a Black Champion," *Journal of Black Studies* 16, no. 1 (September 1985): 95-111; William H. Wiggins, "Boxing's Sambo Twins: Racial Stereotypes in Jack Johnson and Joe Louis Newspaper Cartoons, 1908-1938," *Journal of Sport History* 15, no. 3 (Winter 1988): 242-254; and Dominic J. Capeci, Jr. and Martha Wilkerson, "Multifarious Hero: Joe Louis, American Society, and Race Relations During World Crisis, 1935-1945," *Journal of Sport History* 10, no. 3 (Winter 1983): 5-25. Even though several valuable works examine Louis's black folk hero status, they still tend to overlook key questions of gender. See A.O. Edmonds, *Joe Louis* (Grand Rapids: Wm. B. Eerdmans Publishing Company, 1973); Lawrence Levine, *Black Culture and Black Consciousness: Afro-American Folk Thought from Slavery to Freedom* (New York: Oxford University Press, 1977); Wilson J. Moses, *Black Messiahs and Uncle Toms: Social and Literary Manipulations of a Religious Myth* (University Park: Pennsylvania State University Press, 1982); Richard Bak, *Joe Louis: The Great Black Hope* (Dallas: Taylor Publishing Company, 1996); Donald McRae, *In Black & White: The Untold Story of Joe Louis and Jesse Owens* (London: Scribner, 2002); and Thomas Hietala, *Fight of the Century: Jack Johnson, Joe Louis, and the Struggle for Racial Equality* (New York: M. E. Sharpe, 2002).

19. Alain Locke, ed., *The New Negro: Voices of the Harlem Renaissance* (New York: MacMillan, 1925, reprinted 1992): 5, 8, 16.

20. Bederman, *Manliness and Civilization*, 5, 25.

21. In analyzing New Deal public art and theater, Melosh illustrates the period's preference for constructions of rugged, white manhood in opposition to the detested, feminine images of weakness and over-refinement. See Barbara Melosh, *Engendering Culture: Manhood and Womanhood in New Deal Public Art and Theater* (Washington: Smithsonian Press, 1991): 43.

22. See Kevin Gaines, *Uplifting the Race: Black Leadership, Politics, and Culture in the Twentieth Century* (Chapel Hill: University of North Carolina Press, 1996), 12-13; and Martin A. Summers, *Manliness and its Discontents: The Black Middle Class and the Transformation of Masculinity, 1900-1930* (Chapel Hill: University of North Carolina Press, 2004), 8-9.

23. See Beth Tompkins Bates, *Pullman Porters and the Rise of Protest Politics in Black America, 1925-1945* (Chapel Hill: University of North Carolina Press, 2001), 7-12; Robin D.G. Kelley, *Race Rebels: Culture, Politics, and the Black Working Class* (New York: Maxwell Macmillan, 1994), 112-114. Bates's analysis of A. Philip Randolph's BSCP places the trade union's increasingly strident demands for the "manhood rights" of full citizenship within context of the larger shift from a "politics of civility" and white patronage to the aggressive "new-crowd" demonstrations of the 1930s and 1940s. Moreover, as Kelley contends, the Communist International's 1928 Black Belt thesis of self-determination offered black radicals a racial platform from which to participate in the Party's masculine vision of militant, international revolution.

24. Summers, *Manliness and its Discontents*, 151-153.

25. Emphasis added, "Joe Louis Needs Boosters, Not Knockers," *Pittsburgh Courier*, May 11, 1935.

26. "Joe Louis is 'Three Times Seven,'" *Pittsburgh Courier*, May 18, 1935, section 2,4.

27. "Joe Louis—Primo Carnera Fight Holds Spotlight," *Pittsburgh Courier*, June 22, 1935, section 2, 4; "Rise of Joe Louis is Biggest Sensation in Sports History, *Chicago Defender*, May 4, 1935; and Lewis E. Dial, "The Sports Dial," *New York Age*, July 6, 1935, 8.

28. In the early 1930s, the sport of boxing was on shaky ground, experiencing its own kind of depression. With the title changing hands almost yearly in the first part of the decade, public interest waned. Quickly becoming the sport's biggest drawing card, Louis ushered in what some contemporary authors termed the pugilistic New Deal. See Alexander Johnson, *Ten—And Out! The Complete Story of the Prize Ring in America* (New York: Ives Washburn, 1936): 245.

29. For a discussion of Jacobs' monopoly of fight promotion in the 1930s, see Richard Bak, *Joe Louis: The Great Black Hope,* 82-87. Also see Daniel M. Daniel, *The Mike Jacobs Story* (New York: Ring Book Shop, Inc., 1949). Although historian Jeffrey Sammons casts Louis's affiliation with Jacobs as an unfortunate loss for Louis and black America, it was necessary for them to align themselves with Jacobs because the promoter's influence insured that Louis would have a chance to challenge for the world title *(Beyond the Ring,* 98).

30. Mead, 53.

31. Although Carnera was a former world heavyweight champion, by 1935 his shady associations with gangsters like Al Capone, along with his participation in what many believed were fixed fights, was common knowledge in the boxing world. Moreover, his early days as a carnival side-show act, in addition to his freakish size and frequent clumsiness in the ring, made him a kind of laughing-stock of the profession. For more biographical information on Carnera see Astor chapter 7. Also see Clifford Lewis, *The Life and Times of Primo Carnera* (London: Athletic Publications, 1932). Lewis, in conjunction with Carnera's French manager Leon See, wrote this biography in defense of Carnera's already tarnished image.

32. "Joe Louis, Training for Carnera Match, Decides to Become First Beardless Heavyweight Champion," *Macon Telegraph,* June 17, 1935; Van Every, 119, 123. For a contemporary discussion of the common stereotypes of black fighters as "cowardly and unwilling to face punishment," see Robert Scott McFee, "The Rise of the Dark Stars," *Vanity Fair,* July 1935, 57.

33. "Rice Says 'Terrific Ballyhoo' Puts Big Burden on Joe Louis," *Baltimore Sun,* June 25, 1935. Also see Joe Williams, "Negro Star on the Spot, Louis by Early Kayo, Or—Carnera will Outmaul Him," *New York-World Telegram,* June 25, 1935; and Hugh Bradley, "Louis Picked to Win But He Must Start First to Stop Primo," June 25, 1935.

34. Sid Mercer, "50,000 to See Fight Tonight," *New York American,* June 25, 1935.

35. See Al Monroe, "Fight May Even End in Two if Detroiter Starts Early," *Chicago Defender,* June 22, 1935; Bill Gibson, "Brown Bomber Should Win before 6th Round," *Baltimore Afro-American,* June 15, 1935, 21; Russell J. Cowans, "Louis in Great Shape, Battle Predicted," *Pittsburgh Courier,* June 22, 1935, section 2, 4; and "Louis's Spar Mate, Six and One-Half Feet Tall, Gives Carnera 5 Rounds," *California Eagle,* June 21, 1935.

36. "Joe Louis Can Take It; His Manager Tells Why," *Chicago Defender,* June 22, 1935.

37. "New York Likes Joe Louis," Claude Barnett Papers, Part I, Series A, Reel 10, May 20, 1935, 16.

38. William R. Scott, *Sons of Shebas Race: African-Americans and the Italo–Ethiopian War, 1935-1941* (Bloomington: Indiana University Press, 1993): 9. Also see Brenda Gail Plummer, *Rising Wind: Black Americans and U.S. Foreign Policy, 1935-1960* (Chapel Hill: University of North Carolina Press, 1996); Von Eschen, *Race Against .Empire;* Joseph E. Harris, *African American Reactions to War in Ethiopia* (Baton Rouge: Louisiana State University Press, 1994); J. Diggins, *Mussolini and Fascism: The View from America* (Princeton, NJ: Princeton University Press, 1972); William R. Scott, "Black Nationalism and the Italo–Ethiopian Conflict, 1934-1936," *Journal of Negro History* 63, no. 2 (April 1978): 118—. For contemporary explanations of the conflict and its implications for African Americans see J. A. Rogers, "Italy over Abyssinia," *Crisis,* February 1935, 38-39, 50; Makonnen Haile, "Last Gobble of Africa," *Crisis,* March 1935, 70-71, 90; and George Padmore, "Ethiopia and World Politics," *Crisis,* May 1935, 138-139, 156-157; and Charles H. Wesley, "The Significance of the Italo–Abyssinian Question," *Opportunity,* May 1935, 148; Marcus Garvey, "Barbarism in America," *Black Man,* October 1935, 8. The Abyssinian crisis was arguably the most talked-about story of foreign fascism for African Americans, as reports on the conflict continued to appear on the front pages of black newspapers well into 1936.

39. See cartoon entitled "Maybe He Bribed the Guard," *Chicago Defender,* March 9, 1935. This cartoon shows an Italian burglar robbing an Ethiopian storehouse of natural resources as a League of Nations security guard looks the other way. Also see "The League of Nations," *Chicago Defender,* March 2, 1935, editorial page; "See Mussolini Forcing a War with Ethiopia: France, England Join Plot Against Africa," *Chicago Defender,* May 25, 1935, 2.

40. Langston Hughes, "Call of Ethiopia," *Opportunity,* September 1935, 276.

41. Scott, *Sons of Sheba's Race,* 9, 59. For more detailed descriptions of popular black activism during the Abyssinian crisis, see Scott's chapters entitled "Grass-Roots Activism" and "Harlem Mobilization." For a southern perspective, see Kelley, "Afric's Sons with Banner Red" and "This Ain't Ethiopia, But It'll Do" in *Race Rebels.*

42. Joe Louis, with Edna and Art Rust, Jr., *Joe Louis: My Life* (New York: Harcourt Brace Jovanovich, 1978): 58.

43. Although journalists in the white, mainstream press also played on the international implications of the Louis–Carnera fight, they characterized the impending invasion as a wholly foreign affair with no real links to contemporary, domestic forms of racist fascism in the United States. In their reports, Louis did not function as a representative of American democracy, but rather, he took on the role of an Ethiopian auxiliary defending Abyssinia from the ravages of Italian fascism. See Westbrook Pegler, "Emperor Goes in Training for His 'Big Boy Peterson': Mussolini Takes Leaf Out of Carnera's Science of Warfare By Selecting Setup For His First Battle," *Birmingham Post,* February 16, 1935; "Police Squads to Guard Louis," *Baltimore Sun,* June 25, 1935; and John Lardner, "Can't Help Being King, Says Louis: Wins First Real Skirmish Between Men of Italy and Ethiopia," *Evening Bulletin Philadelphia,* June 26, 1935.

44. Irene Gaskin, "Boys Salute the Flag, the Red, Black, Green," *Negro World,* July 5, 1924, 10, qtd. in Summers, 100. On the male-inflected language and performance of African redemption in Garvey's UNIA, see Summers, "A Spirit of Manliness," in *Manliness and its Discontents,* 66-110. In Garveyite rhetoric, the physical space of Africa and the process of redemption both presented ideal sites for the assertion of black manhood as men took on a militaristic function while women played supporting roles. For the African Americans' gendered imaginings of Haiti, see Mary A. Renda, *Taking Haiti: Military Occupation and the Culture of U.S. Imperialism, 1915-1940* (Chapel Hill: University of North Carolina Press, 2001), 261-288. New Negro artists' rehabilitation of Haiti as "America's Africa" involved a re-reading of the Haitian Revolution as a triumphant narrative of black manhood and black pride through figures like Toussaint L'Ouverture.

45. For a list of Louis's popular nicknames see Lenwood G. Davis, *Joe Louis: A Bibliography* (Westport, CT: Greenwood Press, 1983), 202-203. Also see Mead, 50-51.

46. Jay Jackson, "Ethiopia Shall Stretch Forth—(Modern Version: His Fist)," *Chicago Defender,* May 25, 1935, editorial page.

47. Chester Washington, "Sez Ches," *Pittsburgh Courier,* June 1, 1935, section 2, 4; Hughes, "Call of Ethiopia."

48. Van Every, 24, 26, 27. One pre-fight cartoon even played up the Asian characteristics of Louis's face, touting him as "more Mongolian than Senegambian." See Burns Jenkins, Jr., "Brown Study," *New York Evening Journal,* June 6, 1935.

49. Dan Burley, "Louis Ready for Baer," *Baltimore Afro-American,* April 20, 1935, 21.

50. "Just let Italy Try it!" *Chicago Defender,* June 15, 1935; "One Look at His Hair," *Baltimore Afro-American,* April 6, 1935, 4.

51. *New York Times,* November 28, 1930, 31; Astor, 95; and *The Kings of the Rings,* produced by Jean Labib and T. Celal for HBO Home Video, 1995.

52. "No Snap," *Crisis,* March 1935, 81. Also see "Ethiopia Defiant as Italy Plans to Grab Africa," *Chicago Defender,* February 16, 1935; "Ethiopia Has 500,000 Mei, for Conflict," *Chicago Defender,* June 22, 1935, 1-2; "Ethiopia in Stern Reply to Mussolini," *Chicago Defender,* May 11, 1935, 1; and "Look Out, Italy," *Chicago Defender,* June 15, 1935, 1.

53. Compare Marcus Garvey's treatise on the value of preparedness with respect to the Abyssinian crisis in "Lest We Forget," *Black Man,* Oct. 1935, 4, with Louis's various training updates in the black press such as "Couldn't Take it, Ace Clark Deserts," *Pittsburgh Courier,* June 15, 1935; Russell Cowans, "Louis in Great Shape, Battle is Predicted," *Pittsburgh Courier,* June 22, 1935, section 2, 4; and Dan Burley, "Louis In Tip-Top Form on Eve of Carnera Bout," *Baltimore Afro-American,* June 22, 1935, 20.

54. Thomas O'Halloran, "Forced Civilization Hit By Educator in Talk on Ethiopia," *New Jersey Post,* October 30, 1935, James Weldon Johnson Scrapbooks, Box 7, Beinecke Library, Yale University, New Haven, CT. For other examples of the savage versus civilized debate, see Rev. E.A. Abbott, Letter to the Editor, "Mussolini and Ethiopia," *New York Age,* July 20, 1935; and "Civilizing,' Ethiopia," *New York Age,* August 3, 1935, 6.

55. J. A. Rogers, "Selassie, the Gentleman, and Mussolini, the Braggart, Compared: J. A. Rogers Gives Graphic Comparison of Italian and Ethiopian Tactics," *Pittsburgh Courier,* August 3, 1935, section 2, 2. Garvey also concurred with Johnson's assessment of the Italian aggression, critiquing Mussolini's plans to bomb and gas innocent women and children and labeling the dictator, "the

arch-barbarian of our present age." See Marcus Garvey, "The War," *Black Man*, October 1935, 1. Also see Garvey's poems, "The Beast of Rome," *Black Man*, October 1935, 4, and "Il Duce—The Brute," *Black Man*, July-August 1936, 6.

56. Paul Gallico, "At it Again," *New York Daily News*, June 25, 1935. The white dailies' infantilized, Sambo portrayals of Louis continued even after his defeat of Carnera. See Hoff, "Ink Pot-Pourri," *St. Paul Pioneer Press*, July 21, 1935; Ed Hughes, "Another Case of 'Bad Hands," *Brooklyn Daily Eagle*, August 17, 1935. For a more thorough discussion of Sambo depictions of black boxers, see Wiggins, "Boxing's Sambo Twins."

57. See "Joe Louis Purchases Home for his Mother in Detroit," *Chicago Defender*, April 13, 1935, 7; and Julia B. Jones, "How does it feel to be the Mother of the Next Heavyweight Champ?" *Pittsburgh Courier*, April 27, 1935, section 1, 11.

58. See "The Stage is Set," *New York Amsterdam News*, June 22, 1935, 14. In a stark inversion of the traditional savage-civilized dichotomy, a picture of the clean-cut Louis in his defensive crouch stands alongside an enlarged photo of Carnera's scowling, teeth-baring mug. For examples of cartoons that follow these conventions see George Lee, "Spotting Around," *Chicago Defender*, May 18, 1935, 15; and *Chicago Defender*, June 1, 1935, 13.

59. For comprehensive treatments of black activism for economic and citizenship rights in the South see Robin Kelley, *Hammer and Hoe: Alabama Communists During the Great Depression* (Chapel Hill: University of North Carolina Press, 1990); Patricia Sullivan, *Days of Hope: Race and Democracy in the New Deal Era* (Chapel Hill: University of North Carolina Press, 1996).

60. Jervis Anderson, *This was Harlem: A Cultural Portrait, 1900-1950* (New York: Farrar Straus Giroux, 1982): 242-244. For contemporary descriptions of the Harlem Riot, see "Machine Guns Set Up," *Baltimore Afro-American*, March 23, 1935, 1-2; "Harlem Race Riot," *Pittsburgh Courier*, March 23, 1935, 1-2; "Blame Radicals for Spreading False Rumors," *Chicago Defender*, March 23, 1935, 1-2.

61. "Joseph Louis Barrow," *Opportunity*, October 1935, 295.

62. Paul Oliver, *Aspects of the Blues Tradition* (New York: Oak Publications, 1970): 149-50.

63. Lyrics qtd. in Oliver, 152-53.

64. See "New Buick Brings Smile to Joe Louis," *Pittsburgh Courier*, May 11, 1935. For the most part, the white dailies only included pictures of a shirtless Louis in his fighting gear. In comparison to the black press, mainstream white papers did not print as many photographs of Louis. Even though writers often made him the centerpiece of their articles, pictures of Louis often failed to accompany their words. Instead, the white press tended to showcase more pictures of Louis's white opponents, even if they were foreigners and underdogs like Carnera.

65. Al White, "New York Likes Joe Louis," Claude Barnett Papers, Part I, Series A, Reel 10, May 20, 1935, 16; and "Louis Called Best-Dressed Heavyweight," *Baltimore Afro-American*, June 15, 1935, 1.

66. *Chicago Defender*, June 22, 1935, 16. This same ad also appeared in several other black newspapers. Although some may argue that Louis's endorsement of Murrays Pomade is representative of his willingness to ape white culture, historians like Robin Kelley view "the conk as part of a larger process by which blacks appropriated, transformed, and reinscribed coded oppositional means onto styles derived from the dominant culture" (Kelley, *Race Rebels*, 168).

67. Al White, "New York Likes Joe Louis," Claude Barnett Papers, Part I, Series A, Reel 10, May 20, 1935, 16; "Defender Cameraman Follows Joe Louis Around in N.Y.," *Chicago Defender*, May 25, 1935, 17; "Joe Louis Captures New York," *New York Age*, May 25, 1935, 15. For a description of the vaudeville show, see Louis, *Joe Louis: My Life*, 54.

68. William G. Nunn, "Courier Writer Paints Word-Picture of Trip to Pompton Lakes Camp," June 8, 1935.

69. Bill Gibson, "Hear me talkin' to ya," *Baltimore Afro-American*, June 15, 1935, 20. Also see Russell Cowans, "Room Said to Have Been Used by Geo. Washington Now Used by Joe Louis," *Baltimore Afro-American*, June 8, 1935, 21; Jersey Jones, "Joe Louis's Training Camp is One of Most Modern and Ideal Spots in the Metropolitan District," *New York Age*, June 8, 1935, 8; *Baltimore Afro-American*, June 8, 1935, picture page; Lewis E. Dial, "The Sports Dial," *New York Age*, June 22, 1935.

70. See Jones, "Joe Louis's Training Camp," 8; "Sutton, Who Helped Johnson Before Title Fight, To Be Dietician In Joe Louis Camp," *Pittsburgh Courier*, April 6, 1935, section 2, 5; Chester Washington, "Visiting the Joe Louis Training Camp," *Pittsburgh Courier*, June 8, 1935; "Joe Louis Going Great

on 2-Meal Diet—Sutton," *Pittsburgh Courier,* June 15, 1935; and William G. Nunn, "Courier Writer Paints Word-Picture of Trip to Pompton Lakes Camp," *Pittsburgh Courier,* June 8, 1935. For descriptions of Louis's poor eating habits in contemporary white sources, see Charles Heckelmann, "Eat and Sleep Pastimes for Bomber Louis," *Brooklyn Daily Eagle,* July 17, 1935; and Van Every, 56-57.

71. For articles on Jack Blackburn's skills as a "mastermind" trainer see "Joe Louis Going Great as He Trains for Big Bout with 'Da Preem'," *Pittsburgh Courier,* June 8, 1935; and "Joe and Jack—The Perfect Combination," *Pittsburgh Courier,* July 20, 1935, section 2, 4. For discussions of Roxborough and Black's business smarts see "Joe Louis and His Board of Strategy," *Pittsburgh Courier,* March 23, 1935, section 2, 5; "No White Managers," *Baltimore Afro-American,* June 22, 1935, editorial page; and "Joe Louis Wins," *Chicago Defender,* June 29, 1935, editorial page. According to Summers, young, black radicals of the 1930s spoke out against the traditional avenues of white patronage, even as they accepted white funds, in order to dissociate themselves from the prevailing feminized image of the dependent black man *(Manliness and its Discontents,* 234-240).

72. Van Every, 127-129.

73. Lewis E. Dial, "The Sports Dial," *New York Age,* June 8, 1935, 8; "Many Visitors at Joe Louis's Camp," *Baltimore Afro-American,* June 8, 1935, 16; and "Johnny Dundee, Claude Hopkins Visit Louis Camp," *Baltimore Afro-American,* June 15, 1935, 20; Joseph Mitchell, "Harlem Argues Itself to Sleep About Joe Louis and How He'll Tear the Stadium to Pieces Tonight," *New York World-Telegram,* June 25, 1935.

74. Harden letter qtd. in Lewis E. Dial, "The Sports Dial," *New York Age,* June 22, 1935; Julia B. Jones, "How Does it Feel to Be the Mother of the Next Heavyweight Champ?" *Pittsburgh Courier,* April 27, 1935, section 1, 11.

75. Wilbur Wood, "Louis Iceberg in Ring or Out: Bomber Abhors Flattery and Flatterers and Girls Don't Interest Him," *New York Sun,* August 12, 1935; "Mother is Louis's Only Sweetheart," *Buffalo Evening News,* July 16, 1935; Jack Miley, "Naw, I ain't got no girl 'cause I ain't got no time for women," *San Francisco Chronicle,* June 27, 1935.

76. "Famed Bomber Ready," *New York Amsterdam News,* June 22, 1935, 14; "Hear me talkin' to ya," Bill Gibson, *Baltimore Afro-American,* June 15, 1935, 20; Doc Morris, "Following Joe Louis," *Chicago Defender,* June 15, 35; and "Live Clean Life, Louis Advises Ring Hopefuls," *Baltimore Afro-American,* June 15, 1935.

77. Most biographers have pointed to an apocryphal list of Roxborough's rules of etiquette for the young fighter printed in many white and black papers to demonstrate Louis's dissociation from Johnson. According to the list, the Bomber was never to have his picture taken with white women; he was never to go to a nightclub alone; he would not participate in soft or fixed fights; he was never to gloat over his opponents; he was to keep "deadpan" in front of the cameras; and he was to live and fight clean (Mead, 52; Sammons, 98). Yet, as Louis himself admitted in his various autobiographies, he often did things that were in direct violation of Roxborough's "list." However, the Jacobs publicity machine kept these aspects of his character out of the public eye.

78. Van Every, 56-57. After the fight, many articles continued to describe Louis as lazy and sleepy. See John Lardner, "Joe Louis Sleeps and Sleeps But He's Happy, Family Says So," *New York Post,* June 27, 1935; Margaret Garrahan, "Fame Doesn't Bother Giant Killer Louis: Joe Just Sleeps and Eats as Rest of World is Agog Over Win," *Birmingham News,* June 28, 1935; Henry McLemore, "Joe Louis May be a Whirlwind Killer Inside Ring Ropes, but Out of Them He is World's Laziest Man," *Wilkesbarre Times-Leader,* July 2, 1935; and Charles Heckelmann, "Eat and Sleep Pastimes for Bomber Louis," *Brooklyn Daily Eagle,* July 17, 1935.

79. "Famed Brown Bomber Ready," *New York Amsterdam News,* June 22, 1935, 14.

80. For examples of contemporary boxing manuals see Nat Fleischer, *Scientific Blocking and Hitting and Other Methods of Defense* (New York: C. J. O'Brien, 1935); *Boxing: A Guide to the Manly Art of Self Defense* (New York: American Sports Publishing Company, 1929); and Tommy Burns, *Scientific Boxing and Self Defense* (London: Athletic Publications, 1927). These books teach the reader how to be a skillful boxer rather than a brutish brawler.

81. Russell Cowans, "News from the Joe Louis Camp," *Pittsburgh Courier,* June 1, 1935, section 2, 4; Lewis E. Dial, "The Sports Dial," *New York Age,* June 8, 1935, 8; Gibson, "Hear me talkin' to ya," 20; and "Live Clean Life." In addition to these articles, many photos showed Louis in various stages of his training day. See "Joe Louis at Work," *Chicago Defender,* June 1, 1935, 15; and "Defender Scribe Does Road Work with Louis," *Chicago Defender,* June 15, 1935.

82. Westbrook Pegler "Fair Enough: Plan to Stage Italian–Negro Prizefight at Very Door of Embittered Harlem is Called New High in Stupid Judgment," *New York Sun*, 1935. Brisbane article qtd. in Mead 58.

83. Al Monroe, "Speaking of Sports," *Chicago Defender*, May 25, 1935, 15. Also see "Pegler Inspires Race Riot," *Chicago Defender*, May 25, 1935; "Do They Want Trouble?" *New York Amsterdam News*, June 15, 1935; and "Columnist Spoofs Rumor of Trouble at Louis–Camera Go," *Journal and Guide*, June 1, 1935, 14.

84. "Do They Want Trouble?" *New York Amsterdam News*, June 15, 1935.

85. "Louis–Carnera Fight Boycott is Sought by Daily," *Baltimore Afro-American*, June 22, 1935, 1; and "Uses Papers to Separate Groups Here," *Chicago De fender* June 22, 1935, 1.

86. The Harlem Riot had exposed an existing class divide in terms of appropriate race representation and activism. In the aftermath, establishment uplifters expressed their disapproval of the riot and attempted to distance themselves from "the mob." The editors of *Opportunity* claimed that "the mob does not and cannot reason," and that it drew its sanction from the underworld of the "irresponsible soap box orator and the street corner agitator." Thus, more civilized black leadership needed to "direct the aspirations of the Negro into peaceful channels" of protest. See "The Harlem Riot," *Opportunity*, April 193 5, 102. For a general discussion of these political tensions, see Gaines, *Uplifting the Race*, 246-251.

87. Chester Washington, "Louis Favored to Win by Knockout," *Pittsburgh Courier*, June 22, 1935.

88. Jack Miley, "Riot Guns Ready at Primo-Louis Fight," *New York Daily News*, June 26, 1935.

89. The box-office stat is from Miley, "Riot Guns Ready at Primo-Louis Fight." Also see "Prejudice Kept Joe Louis–Carnera Fight Off the Air," *Indianapolis Crusader*, July 6, 1935. This was the first major fight in years that had failed to get national airplay, and the *Indianapolis Crusader* argued that networks' actions exposed their racial prejudice. Bowing to popular demand, the Michigan Network comprised of several stations managed to put the fight on air, aided by the sponsorship of Detroit's Stroh Brewery. A couple other Detroit stations also aired telegraphic reports of the fight.

90. For advertisements for organized trips see the *Chicago Defender*, June 8 and June 22, 1935; and the *Baltimore Afro-American*, June 8, 1935.

91. "Distinguished Gathering Throngs Stadium for Heavyweight Battle," *New York Times*, June 26, 1935, 24; Dan Parker, "Fans on Hand Early," *New York Daily Mirror*, June 26, 1935; "Singing, Happy Negroes Jam Bleachers To See Ring Idol Continue Win String," *Boston Herald*, June 26, 1935; and "Louis–Carnera fight drew sport fans from all over country; Gross receipts were $328,655.44," *New York Age*, July 6, 1935.

92. "Stars of Stage, Screen, Mingle with the Masses," *Pittsburgh Courier*, June 29, 1935, section 1, 4; and "List of Those at Big Bout Amazes," *Pittsburgh Courier*, June 29, 1935, section 1, 4.

93. "Louis–Carnera fight drew sport fans from all over country." The fight also broke the record for newspaper coverage, with hundreds of journalists from both presses on hand.

94. Mead, 59. The following description of the fight is based on my viewing of the fight film acquired from private collector Ken Noltheimer of Ringwise, Inc., along with contemporary white and black press reports, and secondary sources. See *New York Daily Mirror*, June 26, 1935; "Al Monroe in Vivid Story of Big Fight," *Chicago Defender*, June 29, 1935, 14; and "Ches' Gives The Courier Readers Ringside Story," *Pittsburgh Courier*, June 29, 1935, section 1, 4.; and Mead, 59-61.

95. Floyd J. Calvin, "Harlem Goes 'Mad With Joy' as Joe Louis Chops Down Giant Opponent," *Pittsburgh Courier*, June 29, 1935, 1; and Astor, 102. Similar scenes played out across the country. In Macon, Georgia, a throng of 6,000, with an estimated 3,500 blacks, congregated in front of the press offices of the *Telegraph* to hear regular updates of the fight. In Detroit, thousands of supporters reportedly converged on the Joe Louis headquarters at St. Antoine and Beacon Streets, and in Chicago, around 10,000 fans blocked traffic out-side the offices of the *Chicago Defender* until the wee hours of the morning. See Bobby Norris, "White or Black—He's Dynamite," *Macon Telegraph*, June 27, 1935; "Detroit Fans Believe Baer Gave up Title to Evade Joe Louis," *Journal and Guide*, June 29, 1935, 14; and "10,000 Hear Defender Broadcast of Fight," *Chicago Defender*, June 29, 1935, 1.

96. Bernard Young, Jr., "Conquest of Italian Foe is Complete," *Journal and Guide*, June 29, 1935, 2. Also see "Brisbane and Pegler" *Chicago Defender*, July 6, 1935.

97. Joseph Mitchell, "Harlem is Wild About Joe Louis, Don't Folks Here Sleep? He Asks," *New York World-Telegram*, June 27, 1935; Archer Winsten, "There's only Joy in Harlem as Joe Louis is Acclaimed"; Joseph Harrington, "Many Injured Celebrating Victory"; and "Harlem Celebrates," *Chicago Daily Tribune*, June 27, 1935. This scene is also supported by pictures and descriptions contained in the documentary *I Remember Harlem*, Schomburg Center for Black Culture, New York Public Library, Audiovisual Division, New York, NY.

98. "Race Riot Quelled in Jersey City," *New York Age*, August 17, 1935, 1, 11.

99. There is one article that warned Louis "not to get too broad in [his] sympathies" and therefore, neglect the special needs of his people and his special obligation to black America. However, this piece was the exception, rather than the rule. See Gordon B. Hancock, "A Letter to Joe Louis," *Journal and Guide*, July 13, 1935, 6.

100. Dan Burley, "Calls Joe Louis Worth Vice President or Congressman," *Baltimore Afro-American*, July 6, 1935, 16.

101. See "How Louis Smashed Primo's Defense," Pittsburgh Courier, July 6, 1935; "The Scene as Joe Louis Smashed his Way to Victory Over Giant Carnera," Pittsburgh Courier, June 29, 1935, picture page; "Through the Magic of the Speed Carnera the Guide Gives you a Louis–Carnera Ringside Seat," Journal and Guide, July 4, 1935, 14; and "David Anoints Goliath' with Barrage of Bruising Leather," Chicago Defender, July 6, 1935, 14.

102. Bill Nunn, "Perfect Fighting Machine," *Pittsburgh Courier*, June 29, 1935. Also see "Celebrities Praise Louis for Victory," *Chicago Defender*, June 29, 1935, 7.

103. "Joe Louis and Jesse Owens," *Crisis*, August 1935, 241.

104. "How Proud Should We Be of Joe Louis's Victory?" *Baltimore Afro-American*, July 6, 1935, 4. Also see "Three of a Kind," *New York Amsterdam News*, July 6, 1935, editorial page.

105. "The Moral in Joe Louis' Victory," *Journal and Guide*, July 13, 1935, 6.

106. "Joe Louis Boys Club," *New York Amsterdam News*, July 14, 1935, 4.

107. E. Franklin Frazier, *Negro Youth at the Crossways* (New York: Schocken Books, 1940, 1967), 174-185.

108. "Graphic Story of Louis–Carnera Fight Told in Pictures," *Chicago Defender*, June 29, 1935, 13.

109. Chase, "Another Joe Louis," *New York Amsterdam News*, July 13, 1935, 12. Also see "Front Page," *Chicago Defender*, July 6, 1935. In this cartoon, the artist has a black man with the words "you and me" on his back reading a number of front page headlines like "Joe Louis Wins," "Jesse Owens Sets New Records," "Haile Selassie Defies Italy," while gruesome caricatures of the Brain Truster, Huey Long, Mussolini, and Hitler complain that the black men have stolen their space. Once again, race progress, and even the racial subject is male.

110. William N. Jones, "Day by Day," *Baltimore Afro-American*, July 6, 1935, 4; and Ralph Matthews, "Watching the Big Parade," *Baltimore Afro-American*, July 6, 1935, 4.

111. Bill Corum, "Stick to your 'Ma,' Joe," *New York Evening-Journal*, June 27, 1935. Also see "Risko Warns Louis Against Overconfidence with Max," *New York American*, June 16, 1936.

112. Fred Van Ness, "Louis Celebrates 22nd Birthday; Cuts Cake and Gets Gold Belt," *New York Times*, May 14, 1936.

113. Lloyd Lewis, *Chicago Daily News*, June 17, 1936. For other examples from the white press that discuss Louis's poor showing at Lakewood, see "Louis Listless in Sparring with Mates," *New York American*, May 27, 1936; and Hype Igoe, "Bomber Can't Resist Lure of Golf Course," *New York Evening Journal*, June 4, 1936. For examples in the black press, see Al Monroe, "Bomber Fails to Slay 'Em in Workouts, *Chicago Defender*, May 30, 1936; and Ralph Matthews, "Joe's Camp Upset," *Baltimore Afro-American*, June 6, 1936.

114. James Cannon, "Fame and Riches May Bring About Louis' Downfall," *New York American*, June 2, 1936. For examples of positive reports in the black press, see "Brown Bomber Back in his Stride," *Chicago Defender*, June 6, 1936; "Joe Louis Impressive in Camp Workout Sunday," *Baltimore Afro-American*, June 13, 1936.

115. Thelma Berlack-Boozer, "Joe's Always To Be the Boss of the Family," *New York Amsterdam News*, June 20, 1936. For examples of Marva's exposure in the black press, see "Sunday Workout Shows Look Like Social Affair," *Pittsburgh Courier*, June 6, 1936, section 1, 9; "Harlem Elite Deluge Marva Louis with Favor!" *Pittsburgh Courier*, June 20, 1936, section 1, 9; "The Bomber's Bride," *New York Times*, June 19, 1936. For examples of white press reports that depicted Louis as a young boy under the disciplinary control of his "Mammy," see the series of articles that ran in the *New York*

Daily Mirror in the early part of July 1935: "Joe's Mammy Sees Lesson in Poverty," July 6, 1935; "Joe's Behavior Mother's Care," July 7, 1935; "Joe in Church Sunday Under Mother's Care," July 8, 1935; "Mother Warns Joe of Sugar-Mouths," July 8, 1935; "Joe's Mother O.K's Fights," July 12, 1935; and "Mother Confident Joe Will Be Champ," July 13, 1935.

116. "Keeping the Girls Away from Joe," *Baltimore Afro-American,* July 13, 1935. For descriptions of Louis's appeal with the ladies see the series of articles in the *Baltimore Afro-American* from July 13 to August 24, 1935, that described his fan mail and the various incidents in which mobs of women rushed him for his autograph.

117. Several secondary sources offer general analyses of the connections between Jim Crow in the South and Nazi Germany. See Glenda Gilmore, "An Ethiop Among the Aryans: African Americans and Fascism, 1930 to 1939," unpublished manuscript; Stefan Kouhl, *The Nazi Connection: Eugenics, American Racism, and German National Socialism* (New York: Oxford University Press, 1994); and Seth Forman, *Blacks in the Jewish Mind: A Crisis of Liberalism* (New York, New York University Press, 1998). For some contemporary discussion of the connections see Rabbi Stephen S. Wise, "Parallel Between Hitlerism and the Persecution of the Negroes in America," *Crisis,* May 1934, 127-129; Jacob J. Weinstein, "The Jew and the Negro," *Crisis,* June 1934, 178-179 (part 2 in July 1934 issue); "Stop Lynching Negroes is Nazi Retort to American Critics," *Pittsburgh Courier,* August 10, 1935, section 1, 3; and "American Nazis Quite as Bestial as Their German Brothers," *Baltimore Afro-American,* August 24, 1935, 6.

118. See "Powerhouses of Heavyweights Compared," and "Fighting Eyes Show Determination of Heavyweight Fighters," *Pittsburgh Courier,* June 20, 1936.

119. Mead, 92. See "Schmeling's Departure for the U.S. Practically Ignored in Ger many, *New York Times,* April 16, 1936; and "Hitler Still Frowns on Max Fighting Joe Louis in U.S.," *New York American,* May 19, 1936.

120. See "It's All Part of Day's Work—In Busy Schmeling's Camp," *Atlanta Consti tution* June 14, 1936; "Can He Stop the Bomber?" *Atlanta Constitution,* June 18, 1936; "Mapping Out Maxie's Battle Plans," *Atlanta Constitution,* June 19, 1936. This same trend was characteristic of other papers like the *St. Louis Daily Globe Democrat* and the *New York Daily News.*

121. Pat Rosa, "Stolid Uhian's Pride and Ideals May Halt Joe Louis the 'Drifter'," *New York Post,* June 13, 1936. Several reports also praised Schmeling for his hard work at training camp. See Bill Farnsworth, "Industrious Max Changes Style for Louis Bout," *New York Evening Journal,* May 13, 1936; Mary Knight, "Girl Reporter Discovers Civilized Fight Camp," *Dayton Herald,* June 13, 1936.

122. I base the above description of the fight on my viewing of the fight film acquired from private collector Ken Noltheimer of Ringwise, Inc., along with contemporary white and black press reports.

123. "Detroit, Harlem in Gloom as Idol Collapses," *Detroit Evening Times,* June 20, 1936.

124. Fred Digby, "Max in Sensational Win!" *New Orleans Morning Tribute,* June 20, 1936; "Just a Scared and Beaten Boy," *New York Post,* June 20, 1936; "Schmeling Knocks Out Louis in Twelfth Round; Most Severe Beating in Ring History, Says Rice," *Atlanta Constitution,* June 20, 1936, 1.

125. See "Continued Probe of Rumors That Bomber was Doped," *Chicago De fender* June 20, 1936, 1; "Louis Not Doped; Love Rift Spiked," *Baltimore Afro-American,* June 27, 1936; and Marcus Garvey, "The World As It Is," *Black Man,* July/August 1936, 19-20.

126. Sam J. Jones, "He Can Take It," *New York Amsterdam News,* June 27, 1936, 12.

127. *Chicago Defender,* June 27, 1936, 19.

128. Interview with Gupha Voss recalling her father's story of the second Louis Schmeling fight qtd. in Clarence Lusane, *Hitler's Black Victims: The Historical Experiences of Afro-Germans, European Blacks, Africans, and African Americans in the Nazi Era* (New York: Routledge, 2002), 215. There are other examples of international attention *from* people of color. See "What the People Think," *Pittsburgh Courier,* December 28, 1935, section 2, 4, for a congratulatory letter from "the colored young people of Costa Rica." For a reference to purported fan mail from India, see "Fans Advise Joe Louis on Marriage," *Baltimore Afro-American,* July 20, 1935, 2. Also see "Joe Louis Beats Braddock and Is World Champion," *The Bantu World,* South Africa, June 26, 1937, 1.

129. Philip Brian Harper, *Are We Not Men? Masculine Anxiety and the Problem of African American Identity* (New York: Oxford University Press, 1996), x.

CHAPTER 11

PADRES ON MOUNT OLYMPUS

Los Angeles and the Production of the 1932 Olympic Mega-Event

■ *Sean Dinces* ■

An Unheralded Success

In the summer of 1932 Evelyn Hall Adams and other members of the American female track team made their way by train from Chicago to the Games of the Tenth Olympiad in Los Angeles. Adams later recalled that, despite the excitement of the impending competition, larger issues consumed her and her fellow athletes. "In 1932, we were in the throes of the Depression….No one can fully realize how hard those times were and how they affected the athletes. I had five dollars in my purse and that was a real sacrifice."[1] The dwindling economy spelled doom for an Olympics on the West Coast of the United States. Those awaiting the 1932 games wondered how nations would fund their teams' travel and participation expenses and how Los Angeles would handle the impending financial strain and infrastructural demands. The *New York Times*, only two months before the opening ceremonies, reported that, due to the American Olympic Committee's insufficient funding, "full American participation" seemed "quite unlikely."[2] To make matters worse, the Olympic movement was struggling to maintain international legitimacy. Four years earlier in Amsterdam, the games had proved mediocre at best. Attendance was less than spectacular, as was coverage of the event in many nations outside of Holland. The upcoming Los Angeles games seemed primed for disaster.[3]

The disaster, however, never came, and as explained by *Time* magazine, those expecting the Depression to dim the Olympic torch "were vastly disappointed."[4]

Article appears by permission of the *Journal of Sport History*.

Dubbed by the *Los Angeles Times* as the "greatest in all history," the 1932 Olympic games quieted skeptics, not only by drawing more than 105,000 spectators (over 75,000 more than Amsterdam in 1928), but also by turning a profit for the host city for the first time ever.[5] Despite the drastic turnaround, scholarly interest in the Los Angeles games has been largely overshadowed by the 1936 Berlin Olympics, in which Hitler and the National Socialists transformed them into a nationalistic display of "mass pageantry" and Fascist propaganda.[6] Understandably, the events of the Berlin games sparked—and continue to spark—a torrent of monographs, articles, and other literature dealing with the "Nazi Olympics."[7] While these works facilitate a better understanding of the social and political significance of the Fascist annexation of the Olympic movement, they also reflect an undue consideration of the Berlin games as the holy grail of the movement's development into a legitimate global spectacle and enterprise—what sociologist Maurice Roche has termed the Olympic "mega-event."[8]

Much of the relatively limited amount of scholarship dealing with the 1932 games has contextualized the event's significance in national terms—for good reason. Mark Dyreson, in his work on the 1932 games and American culture, argues convincingly that the first Los Angeles Olympics "provided a crucible in which to cast a world-beating citizenry [out of] the American republic."[9] In many ways, the games proved an American project, and their significance must be understood—at least partially—in the context of national culture and identity during the early 1930s. Historian David Welky, through a detailed analysis of American newspapers, has shown how the 1932 games proved but one component of a larger movement by conservative American elites that aimed at imposing "traditional cultural values" upon society as a whole.[10] What these accounts fail to highlight, however, is the degree to which the site of Los Angeles—and more generally of Southern California—provided those charged with promoting the games with a level of rhetorical power that far outstripped any previous Olympic promotional campaign. The one exception to this trend within the existing scholarship is the work of environmental design scholar Jeremy White. White provides ample evidence to suggest that not only were the 1932 games a thoroughly commercial venture but that they also embodied a style of urban boosterism that he aptly dubs the "Los Angeles way of doing things."[11] Although he does a superb job of revealing how the games constituted a tourist attraction first and an athletic event second for Los Angeles' elites, White's focus on the Olympic Village leads to a relatively narrow understanding of the rhetorical project pursued by the promoters. While the Village was one of the most defining aspects of the promotion of the Los Angeles games, boosters' efforts were often more wide ranging and subtle than might be inferred from White's analysis. To gain both a more comprehensive and more nuanced awareness of the first Los Angeles Olympics and the strategies of those who staged them, it is necessary to consider in more detail how Southern California provided a uniquely persuasive rhetorical stage for the event. This involves moving beyond the confines of the Olympic Village, in addition to paying closer attention to the diversity of promotional efforts leading up to and during the games.

The organization, promotion, and execution of the 1932 Olympic games by Los Angeles' commercial elite, which depended heavily upon regionally specific notions of space and history, played a critical role in transforming the modern Olympic games from a sideshow into an internationally recognized site of cultural production.[12] The ingenuity and preexisting promotional strategies of Los Angeles' boosters allowed them to plan and present the event in a way that no other city could have in 1932. The games of 1932 not only marked a prelude to those that took place four years later but also established a general template for success in staging an ideologically and commercially successful Olympics. The locality and timing of the Games of the Xth Olympiad—much like that of the Berlin games—had everything to do with its success. The effectiveness of the boosters' rhetoric emerged from its focus on the uniqueness of Los Angeles and generated widespread appeal based on its ambiguous relationship to and flexible usage of the notions of modernity and localism—both of which Roche identifies as critical to the staging of a mega-event.[13] Well before the 1932 Olympics, promoters of Los Angeles highlighted what they described as the progress of Anglo-American modernization above and beyond the region's Mexican, Spanish, and Native American history. They also portrayed Southern California as a place that was undoubtedly American but at the same time unlike anywhere else the nation could offer—what historian and activist Carey McWilliams has described as an "island on the land."[14]

Roche's approach to the analysis of mega-events and their relationship to the concepts identified above depends upon a multi-perspective analysis that considers both temporal and ideological contexts. Within his framework, the temporal breakdown of such an event is simple—it consists of the planning and organization leading up to the event, the actual execution and presentation of the event as well as the long-term impact (and seminal causes) of the event.[15] A focused study of the first two of these temporal categories reveals that, in planning and executing the games, boosters skillfully recycled and reinvented aspects of Southern California's "fantasy past," facilitated certain historical erasures, and highlighted the role of the games as an antidote for the hardships of the Depression.[16] This involved the production of a barrage of pamphlets and other promotional literature that perpetuated notions of the event as a modern spectacle with historically romantic appeal, a global spectacle dependent upon local organization and resources, and an unprecedented chapter in Olympic history. The actual staging and presentation of the event included the dramatization of the Olympic Village, the glamorization of the games in relation to Hollywood, and the portrayal of the host city as a haven of multiculturalism. Official reports and print media coverage reveal how these endeavors created a remarkably durable façade of interethnic and international harmony in Southern California in conjunction with the games and reinforced the notion of Los Angeles as an unparalleled host city.

Planning and Promoting the 1932 Olympic Games: Fantasy, Erasure, and Opportunism

In 1920 William May Garland, a Los Angeles attorney and real estate mogul, attended the Olympic games at Antwerp. It was there that Garland, future president of both the California Olympiad Commission and Organizing Committee of the Games of the Xth Olympiad, first sowed the seeds of bringing the games to Los Angeles for 1932. Granted an audience in front of the International Olympic Committee during his visit, Garland "made special mention of the charms of California and Los Angeles; that [the] State was sometimes called the 'Italy of America'...and that every country in the world had had a share in the development of [this] beautiful metropolis."[17] According to historian Barbara Keys, Garland and other members of the Los Angeles elite who wanted to land the games for Southern California "were less interested in sport than in what they presciently recognized as an 'advertising' opportunity a means to raise the profile both at home and abroad of America's fastest growing city"[18] In the years and months leading up to 1932, they coordinated a massive promotional campaign relying heavily upon descriptions of the region's "fantasy past" and the portrayal of the event as an antidote for the Depression. Promotional literature and photographic material reveal how these components of the planning phase—which often went to great lengths to obscure the less friendly side of Southern California—generated an appeal for the 1932 games based on the portrayal of Los Angeles as an unmatched host city.

McWilliams explains that Garland and his fellow boosters—local professionals, businessmen, politicians, and intellectuals—were part of the fraternity of West Coast elites who, at the close of the nineteenth century "began to organize Southern California as one of the greatest promotions the world has ever known."[19] This booster network demands close attention because, according to Roche, "urban mega-events are typically conceived and produced by powerful elite groups with little democratic input to the policy-making process by local citizens."[20]

In ratcheting up promotional efforts for the games, promoters unleashed a flood of pamphlets, many of which played specifically on the mission myth and "Spanish fantasy past"—a trademark of Southern California's image since the nineteenth century. A pamphlet entitled "Shell's 3-Flag Tour"—a pitch for using Shell gasoline on the way to and from the games in Los Angeles, as well as for using the games as an opportunity to take a road trip spanning Mexico, the U.S., and Canada—assured readers that by driving to the games, they would retrace the "footsteps of the padres." The pamphlet's juxtaposition of the impending games with the "charming" and "venerable" aspects of California's "twenty-one mouldering [sic] missions" creates an indirect, yet ironic form of deception when viewed through the lens of such critics as McWilliams.[21]

McWilliams asserts that the "heroic view of the padres and their efforts at conversion divorced them from any causal relationship with the genocide of California Indians."[22] Moreover, private advertisers like Shell were not the only ones to exploit the fantasy past theme. A promotional map issued for the games by the Los Angeles Chamber of Commerce asserted that "the romance and glamour attached to the early history of California is retained in the crumbling ruins and interesting old landmarks scattered" throughout Los Angeles.[23] Boosters had few qualms about wedding the supposedly peace-ridden Olympics to invented histories steeped in forgetting past injustices. Part of the boosters' ingenuity—however distasteful—came from their ability to co-opt the games within preexisting models of promoting Southern California's fantasy past. In this context, they defined the impending international competition on a local basis that appeared historically and geographically unique.

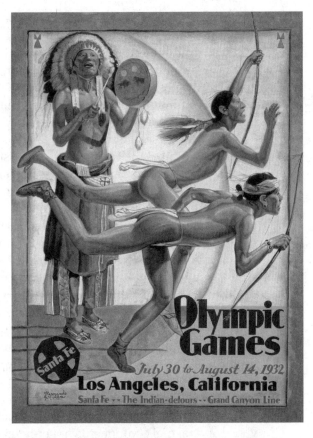

This poster of the 1932 Olympic Games was done by well-known Los Angeles artist and illustrator Hernando Gonzallo Villa. The intent was to entice travelers on their way to the Olympic Games to visit Indian reservations in the southwest.

Reprinted with permission from BNSF Railway.

Boosters, in promoting the Olympics via the mission myth, also revealed their project's useful ambiguity with respect to the notion of modernity. The Olympics—a symbol of athletic and cultural achievement as well as an exhibition of capitalist potential—became linked to idealized notions of Southern California's past that celebrated peoples and cultures that by 1932 had long been marginalized politically, economically, and religiously by American Anglos.[24] This dialectic dominates the Shell pamphlet, as the automobile and road trip—symbols of the technological sophistication and spatial freedom of the twentieth-century—appear superimposed upon an intensely romantic fantasy past during which padres and explorers traversed dirt trails along Southern California's coastline. Photographs from event venues in Los Angeles reinforce the spatial aspect of this modern/non-modern duality. In pictures of the Long Beach Marine Stadium, the site of the rowing events in 1932, the skyline appears as a veritable forest of oil derricks rising out of the "pastoral" California landscape. Their overwhelming presence suggests notions of techno rationalism and capitalism highlighted by Roche as characteristic of the modern aspect of mega-events.[25] At the same time, they occupy a landscape promoted as an idyllic and sparsely populated Spanish paradise—a conceived environment far removed from clouds of automobile exhaust. Promotional literature for the 1932 games depended upon blurring the incongruities between the mission myth and Los Angeles' rapid urbanization. It generated a peaceful and harmonious temporal continuum between Southern California's fantasy past and the promise of the Olympic games in solidifying Los Angeles' evolving present and future.

One of the best illustrations of this continuum emerges from a pamphlet entitled "See All of the Fiesta State," published by the Los Angeles Chamber of Commerce—a group of Los Angeles business elites closely tied to, and sometimes overlapping with, the Organizing Committee presided over by Garland.[26] The selection of the term "fiesta" suggests a celebration of something Spanish and brings to mind Anglo appropriation of the fiesta concept through the La Fiesta Parades organized in Southern California around the turn of the century. Historian Bill Deverell asserts that during the celebrations, "as legions of military escorts suggested, ethnic flavor and indulgence in non-Anglo Saxon behavior could easily be controlled. Flags were everywhere, observers remarked, as if to insist that the event's ethnic or non-American background was simple play."[27]

This sense of control emanated not only from the use of the term "fiesta" but also from the juxtaposition of the pamphlet's image—an illustration of a sombrero-wearing guitar player serenading a woman in Spanish-style dress—with the phrase: "A unified expression of optimism and prosperity arranged and co-ordinated [sic] by the California State Chamber of Commerce and the California Newspaper Publishers' Association."[28] The interplay between the visual and textual components not only reinforced the blending of the modern and pre-modern within boosters' promotional efforts, it also pointed to the promoters' self-valuation relative to the fantasy past. In the context of Deverell's critique of the Fiesta Parades, the "simple play" aspect of the non-American parts of the pamphlet offers a critique in which the host city considered itself to occupy a "significantly more powerful role" than guest nations or, in this case, the Spanish who remained so essential to boosters' efforts to paint Los Angeles and the 1932 Olympics as a haven for potential tourists.[29] One advertisement from the Texaco Gasoline Company echoed this notion of modern Anglo-American supremacy, encouraging Olympic tourists to visit the "great Western Empire."[30]

By carefully limiting their use of the Spanish fantasy past to overtly romantic and pre-modern portrayals, promoters not only suggested that Los Angeles' role in the Olympic movement represented contemporary ideals of progress but also that it coincided with something different from—and essentially superior to—the pre-modern and non-white aspect of Southern California's past. Whether conveyed in the Shell pamphlet's description of "cloistered tranquility" of the California missions' "crumbling walls," or the cartoon-like containment of Spanish and Mexican culture by the Chamber of Commerce, the message remained that Los Angeles' non-Anglo heritage was best seen in its comparative testament to WASP progress since the turn of the century.[31] In the eyes of the games' promoters, participants in the Los Angeles Olympics—both athletes and spectators—would help to assert the superiority of modern Southern California and of the modern nation at large.[32]

Not only did the term "Olympics" appear solely in the title of some of the promotional materials, some of them contained neither images of athletes nor the event venues. In the promotional context of the Los Angeles games, boosters sometimes focused exclusively on Southern California's historical allure and thus on the "particularity of place" that Roche sees as so critical to many mega-events.[33] Another Chamber of Commerce pamphlet promoting an "Olympic Games Boy's Tour" managed a visual reference to an athletic endeavor with an illustration of a hurdler on the cover, but the text inside appears divorced from the significance of the games as a sporting event. Summarily describing the games as the "greatest athletic event ever held in America," the pamphlet proceeded to tempt young males to enter a contest for a trip to the Olympics by touting a visit to a movie studio in Hollywood, a tour of the "orange country;" and an exclusive "inspection trip" to see the Pacific Fleet. Notably, the arm of the Chamber of Commerce in charge of orchestrating the Boy's Tour preferred to tout the romantic California fantasy past rather than the obvious attraction of young male and female athletes. Rather than offering biographies of and potential meetings with competitors, the piece shows a picture of "Charlie Natchez, famous Apache Scout."[34] Ultimately, the draw of Olympic sport played second fiddle to the advertising power contained in booster rhetoric surrounding the juxtaposition of idyllic missions and modern highways.

One can explain partially the disjunction within the promotional literature between references to the games themselves and the tourist attractions of Southern California by the direct relationship between the entertainment opportunities offered by Los Angeles and the appeal of traveling to the 1932 Olympic games. However, this does not account adequately for what appears to be a surprisingly superficial treatment of the games in many of the pamphlets, inserts, and other advertisements urging Americans from around the country to make the trip. One could easily miss the relatively small print reading "Tenth Olympiad—Los Angeles 1932" at the bottom of a poster created by the International Federation for Housing and Town Planning. The poster conveys greetings from California's governor as well as its "counties, cities, legislatures, consular representatives and civic bodies in extending…a cordial invitation to meet at Los Angeles."[35] The illustrated background does show an element of physical culture—a few pioneer cowboys accompanying a wagon train west—but the diminutive print at the bottom is the sole reference to the impending games.

In prioritizing the promotion of place over the athletic components of the Olympics, organizers in Los Angeles realized that the site of a sporting event was more important than athletic components for its success as a spectacle. As illustrated by sports geographer John Bale, the spatial particularity of a sporting venue can serve as the primary factor in spectators' decision to attend and to spend considerable time and money in doing so.[36] In this way, Los Angeles' promoters carefully refocused the rhetoric of the impending Olympic games in a way that pushed the athletic ideology of Pierre de Coubertin and his follow-ers into the background. While Southern California's boosters did pay heed to the historical and athletic significance of the games in much of their published literature, they correctly anticipated the promotional precedence of regional specificity in transforming the modern Olympic movement into what historians can now retrospectively refer to as a "mega-event."[37]

The promotional ambiguities fostered by the boosters, while often dominated by regional themes such as the mission myth, also emerged from rhetorical links between staging the modern games in Los Angeles and the ancient Olympic movement. Boosters contrived geographical and climatic comparisons between Los Angeles and ancient Greece—what sociologist Richard Gruneau refers to as "positive classicism"—in order to bolster the appeal and legitimacy of Los Angeles as a host city.[38] Robert Sproul, the president of the University of California, captured this promotional theme in his speech during the opening ceremonies. In comparing the physical environment of Los Angeles to that of Greece, he explained that "with the changes of season our hill[s] and valley[s] mark the death and re-birth of vegetation as they do in Greece."[39] Sproul was certainly not alone in making such a comparison. *Time* magazine agreed, not only pointing to similarities of the "brilliant skies," "bright landscapes," and "blue waves" of Greece and California but also by calling attention to the "Spartan pride in physical perfection" and "Athenian confidence in their own Golden Age" exhibited by Californians.[40]

The likening of the Pacific Ocean to the Aegean Sea fits nicely into what McWilliams describes as the "invention" of the "miraculous qualities of the [Southern California] climate," much of which revolved around a comparison with that of the Mediterranean.[41] Furthermore, boosters did so despite the fact that the "Mediterranean paradise" analogy became seriously threatened as early as the 1920s due to the region's exponential rate of urban expansion.[42] The specter of the Olympics allowed boosters such as Sproul to bypass this threat effectively, invoking the Mediterranean reference without fear of creat-ing ideological friction with the areas increasing urbanity. The reference to the ancient games allowed for an obvious and seemingly appropriate comparison of Los Angeles in the 1930s with Mediterranean localities that hosted pre-modern games. Such a comparison sent a clear message that Southern California offered an ideal locale for staging an Olympic event—perhaps even more ideal than ancient Greece, as Sproul went so far as to point out that "our valleys sink deeper…and our mountains rise higher…than those of Greece."[43]

As highlighted by White, the place of the Los Angeles Olympics within the larger booster project in Southern California indicates that the festival main-tained serious, if unofficial, ties to the commercial interests of the city's business elites—the games offered the potential to draw an unprecedented number of tourists within a remarkably short span of time.[44] Despite the transparency of this connection—apparent from images like that of an Standard Oil advertise-ment—the Organizing Committee went to great lengths in its *Official Report* to reassure readers that the event distanced itself entirely from any semblance of commercialism.[45] The report reiterates the claim that "not a single note of commercialism was allowed to permeate the consummation of this task," asserting that "protective control" over concessions helped keep the "organization of the Games on a true Olympic basis devoid of professional activities and commercialism." It reassured readers that the Organizing Committee "endeavored at all times to keep the element of commercialism out of the Games."[46]

Outside the confines of the *Official Report,* the city's commercial elite sometimes made little effort to conceal its priorities, as was the case when Harry Harper, the president of the Citizens' Olympic Committee, described the games as "a most necessary contribution to aid a revival of business conditions here."[47] The *Los Angeles Times* reported that Garland "did express the opinion that the advertising feature would be worth $10,000,000 to this city and vicinity."[48] While it's difficult to imagine that the assurances of the *Official Report* convinced most Angelinos that their city had staged such a massive event purely in the name of civic altruism and the Olympic spirit, it remains important for historians of the 1932 Olympics to place the rhetoric of anti-commercialism of the Organizing Committee within the context of a more general project of manipulating ideas about the city's past and present.

Boosters' attempts to cloak commercial aspirations bolstered the larger project of diverting attention from the American Depression. The American press touted the games as a "Depression-buster," and the games certainly offered a rare opportunity for certain contingents of the public to forget temporarily their hardships by partaking in such an event.[49] Roche explains the general function of a mega-event in this context, noting that "for the masses of spectators who attend [mega-events], they can be understood to represent...the bringing of an order to an otherwise disorderly world."[50] The June 1932 issue of *Literary Digest* confirmed that the public viewed the games very much in this context, explaining the 1932 Olympics would offer "a good-sized contribution from sportdom to the cause of normalcy."[51] In portraying the event as a means of combating the Depression, boosters recognized its representational and functional potential for aiding the economic revival of Los Angeles. They took advantage of an otherwise desperate situation to magnify the role of the 1932 games not only as a seminal moment in the history of the modern Olympics but also as a turning point in the economic history of Los Angeles and the United States.

Highlighting the link between the games and the Depression allowed organizers to describe tourism at the event not only as a privilege but also as what William May Garland referred to as a "sacred duty" that went toward the cause of rehabilitating the economy and enhancing of the image of Southern California and the U.S. at large.[52] The headline in the Organizing Committee's first issue of *Olympic*, "Eager to do its Share," demonstrated California's willingness to accept the enormous challenge of hosting the Olympics and reminded its citizens—as well as Americans in general—that "our opportunity is great, let us make the most of it."[53] Thus, even if the games were an elitist commercial venture at heart, organizers assured skeptics that the venture had the best interests of average Angelinos in mind. And even if the games depended upon the particularity of place offered by Los Angeles, their benefit could be contextualized on a national level.[54] The occasional distance placed between the Olympics and Los Angeles business by organizers' rhetoric, as well as the "Depression-buster" label, corresponded to the central role of the games in bringing legitimacy to the host city and its leaders, not entirely unlike the function of the Olympics in 1936.[55]

The 1932 Games as Theatre: Hollywood, the Village, and the So-called Melting Pot

When American javelin thrower Malcolm Metcalf arrived at the Olympic Village in Baldwin Hills—the first Olympic Village in the history of the games—he discovered that his luggage had been lost. Fortunately for him, his stint at the Village—hailed by the press as "the talk of several continents because of its model management, almost unbelievable efficiency of operation and general charm"—quickly took a turn for the better when he bumped into Hollywood movie star Will Rogers.[56] Rogers, upon learning of Metcalf's problem, walked to the administration building and "straightened it out" for him.[57] Where else but in Los Angeles could an Olympic athlete receive such service from a world famous movie star? In cleverly manipulating the rhetoric surrounding the Olympic Village, the presence of big-name stars like Will Rogers, and the ethnic diversity in Los Angeles, boosters aggressively reinforced the primary theme of their promotional literature—that nowhere other than in Los Angeles could such an event be staged so successfully.

Jeremy White confirms the Olympic Village's dramatic function in asserting that it "was above all a tourist attraction."[58] This function emerged in part from the Village's various references to the Spanish fantasy past, of which the most obvious took the form of mission-style architecture. Originally, the Los Angeles Organizing Committee floated ideas to construct the small cottage-size houses at the Village according to an "aesthetic [Spanish] regionalism" that White regards as a "messy concoction of race, nationality, and geography."[59] Though organizers scrapped this plan in favor of cheaper "undecorated boxes," they held on to the mission look for the administration building, which not only stood as the largest structure in the Village but also served as a nerve-center in which athletes mingled with one another, the press, and visitors.[60]

The administration building stood as the lone, token vestige of Spanish history among modernized rows of pre-fabricated cottages. The physical presence of the administration building remained nearly as contained as the fantasy past it represented. The two flags—one U.S. and one Olympic—flown above it underscored this containment and its ambiguous relationship to the theme of modernity The preeminent position of the flags added to the more modern, less Spanish surroundings and provided a subtly symbolic suggestion of the superiority of the modern present over a pre-modern Spanish past. Different from the illustrations in the pamphlets, the Village offered a tangible appropriation of the fantasy past by an Olympic venue. However, the rhetorical message remained the same—the idyllic mission myth suggested the distinctiveness of the Southern California setting and at the same time amplified the event's modern overtones by providing the fantasy past as a comparative backdrop.

The presence of rodeo cowboys employed to "patrol" the confines of the Village— they actually served more as entertainers than security guards— embodied the region's invented history in a different way.[61] The cowboys stood as animate, interactive reminders of their respective fantasy past, while the Spanish styling of the administration building remained entirely passive—no photographs or written accounts cited herein indicate the presence of any Spanish or Mexican actors posing as *padres* or *rancheros*. This says something about the type of bodies that the organizers preferred for symbolizing the region's history within the confines of the Village.[62] For the boosters who organized the Village, it was all right to include celebrations of the region's fantasy past, as long as the non-Anglo—and hence non-modern—elements remained enclosed in inert and romanticized references.

Boosters' description of the international, interracial, and interclass character of the Village, considered in the context of Los Angeles' social history, suggests tensions between the themes conveyed dramatically by Olympic spaces and the city's identity as an urban hotbed of discrimination. Described in the *Official Report* as a "miniature world set up by itself, rigidly protected from the world outside," the planners of the games advertised the secluded tract of land in Baldwin Hills as an insulated space where Olympic internationalism could thrive.[63] While the Village excluded female athletes, male athletes of all nationalities, races, and ethnicities had access and permission to stay there. The tangible mixing of demographics at the Village allowed boosters and the press to drive home the rhetoric of the games as a place where differences disappeared because all the competitors resembled one another in having "teeth, eyes, ears, arms, legs, hearts, lungs and the requisites of normal human beings."[64] The reflections of Olympic athletes corroborated the press and promotional accounts. Charles H. McCallister, a member of the American water polo team, recalled that the Village "was carefully built and the accommodations were very good…and the camaraderie was terrific. People of the various countries, although they could say only 'hello,' were all friends."[65]

The fairytale image of the Village evaporates when juxtaposed against concurrent attempts by minorities to find housing in Los Angeles. Since the First World War, restrictive covenants insulated Los Angeles' upper- and middle-class white residents from African Americans and other minorities—"every foray by Black homebuyers into an outside residential area was met by the immediate wealth of white homeowners."[66] Boosters did not concern themselves, before or after the games, with bringing this sort of equality to the city as a whole. Even so, it seems difficult to label the Village as outright "deceitful"—or even "misleading"—as it did fulfill its role as a "meeting ground for male athletes from around the world."[67] *Los Angeles Times* columnist Irving Eckhoff was quick to point out that the Village—and the games as a whole—erased normal social tensions, as "bricklayers beat lawyers, taxi drivers trounced doctors, and chain-store grocery clerks vied for Olympic championships."[68] As echoed in Eckhoff's editorial and water poloist McCallister's testimonial, athletes and the press perceived the space just as the organizers had intended—a forum predicated on horizontal equality where national differences served as reason for celebration rather than tension. The Village stood as a full-fledged theatrical production and effectively obscured the frictional nature of the city's multiethnic makeup.

Jeremy White has already pointed out that while the peaceful multiculturalism of the Village probably constituted one of the only legitimate spaces of interethnic harmony in 1930s Los Angeles, the Organizing Committee had no qualms about projecting its aura upon the city as a whole. In *Olympic*, the committee noted that "much of the total population [of Los Angeles] is made up of people from all nations. This fact has contributed to the great interest in the coming celebrations of the Games."[69] In this particular case, diversity normally perceived by the city's elite as a hindrance received a positive spin so that the games could gel easily with the advertised image of the region. Not surprisingly, the committee also invoked California's multicultural history as justification for Los Angeles' selection as host, making sure to highlight that the "history of California is linked so inseparably with that of so many nations" that the choice proved only "fitting and proper."[70] Nevertheless, the line taken by the committee in *Olympic* did not necessarily represent a consensus amongst the promoters of the games. The *Official Report* agreed that the Village satisfied its function as an enclave of peace and goodwill, but in averring that it consisted of a "miniature world...rigidly protected from the world outside," it revealed less confidence in the characterization of greater Los Angeles as a multiracial Eden.[71] Not surprisingly, none of the promotional material acknowledged the city's poor race relations. However, the promoters' inability to devise a streamlined rhetoric around the cosmopolitan implications of the games suggests that the projection of the Village's aura upon the whole of Southern California proved problematic even for those who invented it.

The Organizing Committee also cited the excitement of having foreign-born celebrities visit their countrymen at the games. Japanese actor and occasional Hollywood resident Sessue Hayakawa was quoted as saying, "I wish to convey greetings to the athletes of Japan who will participate in these sports.....I wish you good luck as a fellow countryman."[72] That the blurb comes from a well-known Japanese Angelino implies that the city already enjoyed a sense of peaceful diversity prior to the games. The organizers of the games invited foreign athletes to take in their city—enjoy the sights and frequent the local establishments—at the same time that, as historians such as Mike Davis and Norman Klein explain, they authored plans to marginalize the permanent populations of many of those athletes' countrymen.[73] The local press reinforced the welcome offered to Japanese athletes by Los Angeles' Japanese Americans, citing various "Japanese events...staged in their honor."[74] By displacing the entrenched discrimination of Los Angeles with a focus on the temporary egalitarianism of the Olympic environment, boosters reminded visitors that Los Angeles' supposed ethnic diversity made it an especially hospitable locale in which to play host to athletes and tourists from around the globe.

The multicultural façade the Village provided for the games and the city did not fool everyone. The perceived hypocrisy of the event incited some instances of dramatic resistance against organizers' rhetorical hegemony. On the final day of the games, a group of five men and two women stormed onto the field at the Olympic Coliseum, with banners reading "Free Tom Mooney."[75] The demonstration protested the alleged framing of Tom Mooney, a prominent West Coast socialist and labor organizer, for a bombing at the 1916 San Francisco Parade. In flyers advertising boycotts and alternative athletic events in Chicago, the group responsible for the protest—the National Counter-Olympic Committee and its sponsor, the American Communist Party—pointed out that the "Olympics claim they discriminate against no one. This is a rank lie! The National Provisional Counter Olympic Committee states that south of the Mason-Dixon line, Negro athletes are openly Jim-Crowed."[76] The flyers also took a direct shot at the boosters, noting that "many of those who are organizing and supporting the Olympics are the same magnates and politicians who helped to grab Tom Mooney and are now trying to keep him there."[77] The Mooney protest represented only a portion of the Counter-Olympic Committee's effort, which included the staging of the Chicago Counter-Olympics of 1932—officially named the International Workers Athletic Meet—from July 28 to August 1. Unfortunately for the organizers of the Counter-Olympics, the event, according to sports historian William Baker, was "largely ignored, then quickly forgotten."[78]

Despite the failure of the Counter-Olympic Committee to garner the level of national attention it sought, its efforts coincide with Roche's contention that mega-events, in fostering ambiguous and hypocritical messages, "create opportunities for the development of…'resistant' responses by members of the public."[79] Other isolated instances of resistance also emerged. The *Christian Century*, a Chicago-based magazine, openly chastised the hypocrisy of the games's rhetoric of international peace during a time of impending war. Its tongue-in-cheek criticism suggested that "perhaps…the good will dispensers of the Los Angeles ham and eggs breakfast club can manage the peace until this latest 'contribution to international peace is over.'" It even poked fun at the boosters' rhetoric regarding the host city's particularity of place and the popular prediction that it would help American athletes triumph, explaining that "under the inspiration of the Southern California climate and the promised presence of practically the entire feminine population of Hollywood, the Americans are expected to clean up."[80]

The efforts of resisters such as the Counter-Olympic Committee and *The Christian Century* were dismissed by boosters and their press outlets as aberrations. The *Los Angeles Times* reported that the crowd cheered as police arrested the Mooney "demonstrators" while the stadium band "started playing the 'Star Spangled Banner'…in an effort to cover the confusion."[81] The aggressive response to the protestors, especially in light of the use of the anthem as a diversionary tactic, speaks to another aspect of the event's conditional conception of cultural citizenship. Participating in the drama of the event was encouraged by boosters but only as long as it adhered to narrow conceptions of modernity and, in this particular case, nationalism. While racial groups that normally experienced marginalization in Los Angeles might find a fleeting haven in the Village or Coliseum, political radicals could not hope for the same leniency in the name of Olympism.

Part of the promoters' success in suppressing various critics emanated from the adoption by minority press outlets of their rhetoric about the transcendence of cultural difference by the games. In a *Los Angeles Times* article emblematic of the coverage of many foreign competitors and teams, the columnist asserts that "California's welcome to [Japanese athletes] is the most pleasant thing about their visit here, they wish it known."[82] The paper even noted the flattering words issued by Douglas Fairbanks to the leader of the Japanese Olympic delegation. Fairbanks reportedly told the representative, "I want to compliment you on your fine boys. I'm sure you're going to make a fine showing."[83] Sport historian Mark Dyreson reveals that the *Los Angeles Times's* description of this welcome was overstated, pointing to coverage in both the *Japan Times* and *New York Times* about offense taken by Japanese athletes over several instances in which they were met with the notice "Mexicans are not admitted" when they attempted to enter various establishments in Los Angeles. The coverage by the *Japan Times* went on to assert that worse than the discrimination itself was the complacence of Southern California's Japanese population, and its failure to respond adequately to anti-Japanese sentiment in Los Angeles.[84]

Coverage by *Rafu Shimpo*, the leading Japanese-American newspaper in Los Angeles, reflected the lack of resistance among the Japanese-American community that was the subject of the *Japan Times's* condemnation. Most of the articles dealing with the games discuss the various receptions, picnics, and other events attended by the athletes and repeatedly stress the classiness of Japanese Americans in welcoming their countrymen. A rare example of critical coverage only goes so far as to request politely that the mainstream press discontinue its usage of the term "Jap" in reference to Japanese athletes.[85] This critique from *Rafu Shimpo* implicitly acknowledges the city's otherwise acceptable performance as the Olympic host. In addition to welcoming Japanese athletes, many articles went to great lengths to celebrate the success of the games in their "purpose of instilling international friendship."[86] As pointed out by literary scholar Eriko Yamamoto, the 1932 Olympics "offered the chance to redefine marginality as a cosmopolitan quality that could coexist with white culture and contribute to American Society."[87] One editorial even went so far as to describe the games as a racial leveler, explaining that the games "brought a new angle on racial problems. When [Eddie] Tolan won the sprints for the United States, what Southerner did not get up and cheer. When [Shoichiro] Takenaka stepped over two lanes [in the 5000-meter race] to let Hill and Lehtinen fight it out, the crowd that cheered him was not made up only of Nipponese."[88]

The obvious exaggeration behind the "Southerner" comment aside, *Rafu Shimpo's* coverage suggests that some local minority groups embraced, in large part, Anglo booster rhetoric surrounding the games. That ethnic groups in Los Angeles would want to appropriate the games to solidify notions of their belonging in Los Angeles does not come as a surprise, yet the consensus between Anglo and Japanese-American press outlets in the city still offers striking evidence of the local hegemony of booster ideology.[89] The local nature of this hegemony must be stressed. Undoubtedly, minority press outlets in Los Angeles reflected a higher degree of cultural inclusion in the 1932 games than those in other parts of the United States or abroad. Not only were Japanese competitors invited to Southern California to compete, Japanese Angelinos were invited by boosters to prove to the world the multiculturalism of their city. Yamamoto explains that, not surprisingly, the location of the Olympics in Los Angeles—the city with the largest Japanese-American population in 1932—"encouraged the surge of collective ethnic sentiments that transcended divisions of age, group affiliations, or strategies for acceptance."[90] In this context, the interpretation and valuation of the 1932 games became a function of welcomed spectatorship and participation of minorities on a local level, but of institutional racism and discrimination on a national one.

This dynamic of cultural inclusion and resistance also emerged in the coverage of the games by African-American media sources. David Welky's thorough survey of American journalistic coverage of the games confirms that the minority press "provides an interesting contrast to the mainstream papers and suggests that different groups could interpret the Olympics in varying ways that appealed to their own agendas."[91] Welky notes that the *Chicago Defender* "decried the 'lily-whiteism' of the Games, and noted that the only black employee at the vaunted Olympic Village was a shoeshiner."[92] Other biting, broadly-aimed criticisms emerged from the pages of the *Defender*. A caption showing Ralph Metcalfe, a black member of the men's track team and the favorite to win the 100-meter dash, reads, "Uncle Sam, who is showing plenty of prejudice in the selection of his athletes for the games, is counting on this boy to bring in two first places."[93] Here, the *Defender* reminds the reader of the ironic place of African Americans in the games, in which the U.S. simultaneously marginalized them and depended upon them to prove American athletic supremacy. As Dyreson explains, "Gold medals won by black Olympians confirmed to most white Americans the superiority of the American system."[94] The critical attitude towards the games by Chicago's black press suggests that many African Americans looking at Los Angeles from the outside in 1932 had few illusions about the event's multicultural fantasy present. While black athletes certainly received praise in the pages of the *Defender*, articles focused more on their individual prowess and achievements than on the humanitarian aspect of the games as described by Los Angeles print media. Similar to *Rafu Shimpo*'s divergence from the critical coverage of the *Japan Times*, the African-American press in Los Angeles deviated significantly from the approach taken by black journalists in Chicago. The sports sections from the *California Eagle*, a prominent African-American paper in Los Angeles, did report on racism surrounding the games—a few articles decry the exclusion of two black female athletes from an American relay team because of what it suspected to be racial discrimination.[95] The *Eagle* acknowledged that the games were not "devoid of the usual and natural difficulties and unpleasant happenings" associated with day-to-day racism. At the same time, however, it carefully avoided the *Defender's* structural critique of the games as an Anglo-centric project. The paper assured Los Angeles' African-American community that the "gorgon head" of "segregation and color prejudice" did not rear itself to the degree that local minority communities had originally expected, but also that the instances in which it did represented isolated incidents rather than any sort of structural discrimination.[96] The paper's simultaneous recognition of racism and its deference towards the Anglo Olympic bureaucracy effectively separated the two, suggesting that racism at the games consisted of isolated incidents outside the control of the organizers. The *Eagle* reveals a more specific form of this separation in an article regarding how Clarence Muse, an African-American entertainer who had been booked to perform at the Olympic Village, received notice that he could not perform due to the decision by a Village official (not a member of the Organizing Committee) that blacks should not serve as official entertainers. The story chastises the official, yet exonerates the leadership of the Los Angeles Organizing Committee by claiming that "[General Secretary Zack] Farmer himself had nothing to do with the slight intended for Mr. Muse" and describes the Organizing Committee itself as administrating "with the bright star of fairness, tolerance, and impartiality."[97]

Such passive condemnation of racism at the games suggests that local African-American news coverage, like its Japanese-American counterpart, interpreted the games more sympathetically than did outsiders, mostly because they had a uniquely local investment in the event. If they aggressively attacked the social implications of the games, Los Angeles' minority groups would have lessened the perceived legitimacy of their place in the city and the role of minority athletes in the games. In opting not to challenge directly the booster narrative of multiculturalism and social equality surrounding the Olympics, the city's minority news sources had to embrace the rhetoric concerning Los Angeles' purported interethnic harmony. Ultimately, the failure of the local minority press to highlight structural forms of racism in their coverage of the games points to the supremacy of booster rhetoric in Los Angeles and the limited elbow room for dissent and protest. In fostering this seemingly united front within the city, boosters appropriated the energies of groups normally marginalized by Los Angeles' elite in order to appeal to as diverse an audience as possible and further legitimate their rhetoric on the grounds that the two-week event marked an apex of cultural inclusion. This insight complicates the work of historians like Welky and Dyreson on the racial dynamics of press coverage of the 1932 games—while some minority press coverage did prove critical, the appealing rhetoric of boosters often divided the loyalties of the nation's non-white spectators based upon their relationship to the locality of Los Angeles.[98]

In addition to the region's minority print media, boosters used ethnic attractions like Olvera Street to appropriate the efforts of Los Angeles' non-white population. According to historian Phoebe Kropp, Olvera Street—the invention of white "society matron" Christine Sterling a few years before the games—was a "sophisticated statement of the fantasy past," revealing a carefully crafted mélange of "Indian primitivism" and "Spanish romance." The street embodied many of the same rhetorical tensions apparent in the pamphlets discussed previously, namely that between the historically "exotic" elements of the fantasy past and the "celebration" of the security promised by the modern conquest of America.[99] With these tensions in mind, it is not surprising that Olvera Street also became linked directly to Los Angeles' role as an ethnically diverse metropolis uniquely equipped to host the games. A photograph in a program for the Hostesses' Ball of the Tenth Olympiad offers a welcome to spectators from around the world from Consuelo Castillo De Bonzo. De Bonzo owned a well-known Mexican restaurant on Olvera Street and, according to Kropp, "employed her resulting stature on the Street to establish an independent agenda there…using her café as the focus for Mexican organization and culture."[100] Kropp's description of the restaurantrice as a patron of Mexican culture suggests that she wanted to reach out to visitors of the games, especially those of Mexican descent. However, the target audience of the program—a group of predominantly Anglo hostesses—suggests that the Olvera Street advertisement spoke almost exclusively to a white contingent. The advertisement, in this context, illustrates perfectly how boosters co-opted Mexican Americans within the project of covering up the city's less than admirable record of urban discrimination. Even De Bonzo, a community leader and someone who probably witnessed violent repatriation efforts that took place on and around Olvera Street, became a symbol of the city's cultural appeal and interethnic harmony during the games.

Hollywood's connection to the 1932 games constituted a part of the event's dramatic aspect very different from, yet no less important than, the presentation of supposed multiculturalism fostered by the Village and print media. Dyreson astutely notes that the proximity of Hollywood to the host city in 1932 allowed the games to develop as an "ideal venue in the west coast capitol of culture production."[101] By incorporating the glamour and name recognition of the motion picture industry into the production of the games, boosters added considerably to the event's one-of-a-kind dramatic atmosphere.

Hollywood's involvement spanned a broad range of activities. Movie mogul Louis Mayer participated in booster activities, actors became the personal tour guides and entertainers for the athletes, and movie cameras shot footage of each day's competitions for newsreels.[102] Malcolm Metcalf, the javelin thrower who found his luggage with Will Rogers' help, recalled the invitation he received from the screen star to attend a luncheon at the Fox Studio. "The most exciting thing that I remember was sitting across the table from Ginger Rogers…then, Will invited several of us to go out and watch him play polo at the Riviera Country Club. We…spent the afternoon watching him perform on horseback."[103] Metcalf and his fellow athletes thus received lessons from movie personalities on how to entertain. They actually became spectators, rather than performers, of sport, as Will Rogers displayed the importance of supplementing athletic performance with lavish entertainment.

Newspaper coverage amplified the concept of athletes as entertainers.[104] A lengthy column in the *Los Angeles Times* dealt specifically with Douglas Fairbanks' predictions for the outcome of various events. The article noted that Fairbanks, after meeting with athletes in the Village, remarked, "What a thrill this is! Meeting all these athletes. Wonderful fellows, you won't find better any place."[105] The accolades offered by Fairbanks create an image of the athletes as super-celebrities—entertainers admired by even the most famous actors in Hollywood. The *Los Angeles Times,* independent of Fairbanks, recognized the athletes' dramatic abilities in an article explaining the ease of transitioning between sports and the movies. According to the piece, "if you can swim, bat, dive, box, run, wrestle, golf, lift weights or play tennis better than most anyone else in the world, the door is wide open to you."[106] Pointing to a number of former Olympic athletes—Nat Pendleton, Harvey Perry, Johnny Weissmuller, Clarence "Buster" Crabbe and others—who entered the acting business, it clarifies Hollywood's interpretation of the games as an audition for the big screen.

Sometimes the depiction of athletes as larger-than-life assumed proportions absurd enough that only Hollywood's fantastical setting could contain them, as suggested by a picture from the *Los Angeles Examiner* of Georgia Coleman, a member of the American women's diving team. The photo shows Coleman in a swimsuit operating a steam shovel while sporting a giant grin. Superimposed above the shovel is an artist's rendering of the Los Angeles Swimming Stadium, thus placing Coleman in the role of the builder of the complex. It suggests that athletes shouldered the responsibility of creating the Olympic city. The same paper also ran a photo with a group of seven white male athletes in their athletic apparel as they all wield hammers in what was supposed to be their effort to construct one of the bungalows for the Olympic Village. The photo is undoubtedly posed like the Coleman image, and the significance proves similar. When boosters did choose to use athletes within their larger promotional project, they often employed a dramatic style that did not require a sporting context but rather depended upon an almost mythical portrayal of the competitors' role in endowing Los Angeles with an unprecedented Olympic venue. In this way, organizers and the mainstream press blurred the divide between athletes and movie stars and thus tied the 1932 games to aspects of popular culture that probably interested many who would have otherwise ignored the games. The fantasy present engendered by this linkage—the imagined seamlessness between world-class athletes and world-class movie stars—helped to popularize the allure and accessibility of the games beyond a niche audience.

The physical and rhetorical juxtaposition of Hollywood's movie industry—a technologically advanced and evolving field—with the Olympic games helped boosters legitimate the festival as a "modern cultural event." In Roche's words, such an event does its best to "represent and display a substantial range and mix of types of cultural phenomena."[107] Not only did a trip to the 1932 games promise visitors the opportunity to watch top-flight athletic events but also the chance to rub elbows with media celebrities, explore the mission ruins, and travel along scenic expanses of California highway. The Hollywood component—perhaps the most regionally specific of the event's dramatic aspects—allowed boosters to simultaneously stress the event's local particularity and make it consumable on a global level. Newsreels using technologies and techniques perfected in Hollywood allowed for worldwide viewing of certain events and thus functioned as global disseminators of the games. Ultimately, the tension created between the concentration of the film industry in Los Angeles and its role as a source of global culture embodied the creation of the 1932 games as a distinctly local project capable of captivating an international audience.

Conclusion

Carl Diem, secretary of Germany's Committee for Sport and Recreation, was one of the most important spectators among the throngs of people attending the 1932 Olympics, but he went largely unrecognized during his two-week visit to Los Angeles. Heading up Germany's efforts to organize the 1936 games in Berlin, he copiously studied the planning and execution of the games by Los Angeles and amassed an impressive library of notebooks and photographs. His interaction with organizers and designers in Los Angeles provided him with vital input on everything from timing technologies to athletes' dietary preferences.[108] According to Roche, the success of Diem and other German organizers at streamlining the Berlin games's "organization and staging...far outstripped all previous Olympic events, including the preceding Los Angeles Games in 1932 in spite of that event's Hollywood flamboyance."[109]

While Roche's statement is not necessarily inaccurate, it gives short shrift to the importance of 1932 within the overall development of the Olympic movement and reifies the tendency of Olympic historiography to minimize the role of the Los Angeles games in the movement's maturation into a mega-event. Diem himself recognized the importance of Los Angeles as an influence on the 1936 games, noting that his surveillance of the 1932 Olympics convinced him "that the 1936 Games will have an international appeal which will put all other events in the shade." He learned from Los Angeles the fact that a successful Olympics depended largely upon effective mediation between the host city's particularity and its universal appeal and offered the assurance that the "1936 Games must be both an international and a great German festival."[110]

Diem's words remind us that Olympic scholars may benefit from broadening their conception of the emergence of the Olympic mega-event by paying closer attention to what happened before 1936. While the Berlin games did surpass its predecessor in certain respects, the strategies implemented by Los Angeles boosters in planning and staging the event provided a streamlined example of how to create a viable and almost universally appealing sports mega-event within a distinct locale. Their success emerged not so much from their ability to promote Olympic sport but rather from their ability to convincingly sell the viability of the host city. Furthermore, this promotion proved more complex and far-reaching than the idea for the first Olympic Village. In skillfully weaving

Southern California's fantasy past and the economic significance of the event into their promotional campaign, the commercial elite of Los Angeles drew record crowds to the Coliseum and other venues. While scholars need not look at 1932 as the singular turning point in the emergence of the Olympic mega-event, they should devote more attention to Los Angeles as a critical marker in the maturation of the modern Olympic movement into a legitimate site of commercial and cultural enterprise.

Even though the narrative of the 1932 games as a site of athletic and cultural production is a story of success, it is also one of failure. Boosters and other Los Angeles' elites created a spectacle that effectively obscured the hypocrisy of the city—as well as that of the games—with regard to issues of race, commercialism, and historical perspective. These obfuscations helped to streamline the Olympic project so that it encountered a minimal amount of resistance from local and non-local communities. In this way, the 1932 Olympics offered a lurid and—as was to be seen four years later in Berlin—dangerous example of the power of local propaganda in conjunction with the games. By offering a textbook model for popularizing the Olympics, they revealed the irony of the modern Olympic experiment and its many internal contradictions.

Notes

1. 'Evelyn Hall Adams, interview by George Hodak, October, 1987, transcript, An Olympian's Oral History Collection, Amateur Athletic Foundation Library, Los Angeles, California (hereafter AAFLA).

2. "Brundage Orders Team Reductions," *New York Times*, 27 May 1932, p. 29.

3. On the inconsistent international coverage in 1928, see Allen Guttmann, *The Olympics: A History of the Modern Games* (Urbana: University of Illinois Press, 1992), 48. On the Amsterdam games in general, see John Findling and Kimberly Pelle, eds., *The Historical Dictionary of the Modern Olympic Movement* (Westport, Conn.: Greenwood Press, 1996), s.v. "Amsterdam, 1928," by Edward S. Goldstein; and Alfred Senn, *Power, Politics, and the Olympic Games* (Champaign, Ill.: Human Kinetics, 1999).

4. "Xth Olympiad," *Time*, 15 August 1932, p. 18.

5. Braven Dyer, "Marvelous Cast of Performers Made 1932 Olympic Games Greatest in All History," *Los Angeles Times*, 14 August 1932, sec. E, p. 7.

6. Richard Mandell, *The Nazi Olympics* (Urbana: University of Illinois Press, 1971), xii.

7. On the 1936 games, see Mandell, *Nazi Olympics,* John Hoberman, *Sport and Political Ideology* (London: Heinemann, 1984); Pierre Arnaud and James Riordan, eds., *Sport and International Politics: The Impact of Fascism and Communism on Sport* (London: Routledge, 1998); Guttmann, *The Olympics*; David Kanin, *A Political History of the Olympic Games* (Boulder, Col.: Windview Press, 1981); John A. Lucas, *The Modern Olympic Games* (New York: A.S. Barnes & Co., 1980); Arnd Kruger and William Murray, eds., *The Nazi Olympics: Sport, Politics, and Appeasement in the 1930s* (Urbana: University of Illinois Press, 2003); Wendy Gray, "Devotion to Whom? German-American Loyalty on the Issue of Participation in the 1936 Olympic Games," *Journal of Sport History* 17 (1990): 214-231; William Murray, "France, Coubertin, and the Nazi Olympics: The Response," *Olympika: The International Journal of Olympic Studies* 1 (1992): 46-69; George Eisen, "The Voices of Sanity: American Diplomatic Reports from the 1936 Berlin Olympiad ," *Journal of Sport History* 11(1984): 56-78; and David Kass, "The Issue of Racism at the 1936 Olympics," *Journal of Sport History* 23 (1996): 223-235.

8. Roche defines mega-events as "large-scale cultural (including commercial and sporting) events which have a dramatic character, mass popular appeal and international significance." See Maurice Roche, *Mega-Events and Modernity: Olympics and the Expos in the Growth of Global Culture* (London: Routledge, 2000), 1.

9. Mark Dyreson, "Marketing National Identity: The Olympic Games of 1932 and American Culture," *Olympika: The International Journal of Olympic Studies* 4 (1995): 23-48.

10. David B. Welky, "Viking Girls, Mermaids, and Little Brown Men: U.S. Journalism and the 1932 Olympics," *Journal of Sport History* 24 (1997): 24-49.

11. Jeremy White, "The Los Angeles Way of Doing Things: The Olympic Village and the Practice of Boosterism in 1932," *Olympika* 11(2000): 79-116.

12. On the 1932 games as a site of cultural production, see Dyreson, "Marketing National Identity"; Welky, "Viking Girls"; White, "The Los Angeles Way"; Barbara Keys, "Spreading Peace, Democracy, and Coca-Cola: Sport and American Cultural Expression in the 1930s," *Diplomatic History* 28 (2004): 165-196; Eriko Yamamoto, "Cheers for Japanese Athletes: The 1932 Japanese Olympics and the Japanese American Community," *Pacific Historical Review* 69 (2000): 399-430.

13. Roche suggests that these categories prove to be critical to the functionality of mega-events' ambiguity.

14. Carey McWilliams, *Southern California: An Island on the Land* (Salt Lake City, Utah: Gibbs Smith, 1994).

15. Roche refers to the dramatic phase as the "event-core/dramatological zone," the planning phase as the "intermediate/contextual zone," and the long-term phase as the "event-horizon." See Roche, *Mega-Events and Modernity,* 11-14.

16. The label "fantasy past," as it relates to Southern California, comes from McWilliams, *Southern California*. He uses it to refer to historical constructions that significantly romanticize, erase, or otherwise distort the past. On California and popular memory, see the work of Kevin Starr, *Inventing the Dream: California Through the Progressive Era* (New York: Oxford University Press, 1985) and *Endangered Dreams: The Great Depression in California* (New York: Oxford University Press, 1996); Clark Davis, "From Oasis to Metropolis," *Pacific Historical Review* 61(1992): 357-386; Norman Klein, *The History of Forgetting: Los Angeles and the Erasure of Memory* (New York: Verso, 1997); Phoebe Kropp, "All Our Yesterdays: The Spanish Fantasy Past and the Politics of Public Memory in Southern California, 1884-1939" (Ph.D. diss., University of California at San Diego, 1999); idem, "Citizens of the Past? Olvera Street and the Construction of Race and Memory in 1930s Los Angeles," *Radical History Review* 81(2001): 35-60; and Bill Deverell, *Whitewashed Adobe: The Rise of Los Angeles and the Remaking of its Mexican Past* (Berkeley: University of California Press, 2004).

17. William May Garland, "Story of the Origin of the Xth Olympiad Held in Los Angeles, California, in 1932, as Written by William May Garland," undated, Olympic Collection, AAFLA.

18. Keys, "Spreading Peace," 169.

19. McWilliams, *Southern California,* 157.

20. Roche, *Mega-Events and Modernity,* 126.

21. "Shell 3-Flag Tour," pamphlet, ephemeral material from the Los Angeles 1932 Olympic Games, Olympic Collection, AAFLA.

22. Kropp, "All Our Yesterdays," 32.

23. Los Angeles Chamber of Commerce, pamphlet map showing locations of Olympic events, ephemeral material from the Los Angeles 1932 Olympic Games, Olympic Collection, AAFLA.

24. On conquest and racial diversity in California before the twentieth century, see Douglas Monroy, *Thrown Among Strangers: The Making of Mexican Culture in Frontier California* (Berkeley: University of California Press, 1990).

25. See Roche, *Mega-Events and Modernity,* 1-30. The techno-rational and capitalistic tendencies Roche refers to include "predictability and control over time, over the pace and direction of change, in a world where social, technological, and ecological changes can often appear "out of control" (pp. 7-8).

26. Kropp, "All Our Yesterdays," xv.

27. Deverell, *Whitewashed Adobe,* 77.

28. Los Angeles Chamber of Commerce, "See All of the Fiesta State," pamphlet, ephemeral material from the Los Angeles 1932 Olympic Games, Olympic Collection, AAFLA.

29. Roche, *Mega-Events and Modernity,* 9.

30. Unidentified newsprint, scrapbook, 1932 Olympic Games Collection, folder 15, box 1, Special Collections, University of California, Los Angeles (UCLA).

31. "Shell 3-Flag Tour."

32. It is noteworthy that the rhetorical project evident from this pamphlet coincides remarkably well with Roche's description of the power of "otherness" in promoting world expositions around the turn of the century, specifically with their exhibits of "pre-modern" societies. Roche explains, "The overall effect of these human displays, by creating images of 'otherness' and 'primitive' and 'savage', and thus, by implication and comparison, images of 'us' and who 'we' were as 'modern,' were probably as inclusionary for the host population…as they were profoundly exclusionary for the people displayed" (Roche, *Mega-Events and Modernity*, 85).

33. Roche, *Mega-Events and Modernity*, 10.

34. *Pittsburgh Post Gazette*, "*Pittsburgh Post Gazette* Boys' Tour," pamphlet, ephemeral material from the Los Angeles 1932 Olympic Games, Olympic Collection, AAFLA. The promotional scheme behind this tour, which was promoted by a number of major newspapers throughout the U.S. via the Los Angeles Chamber of Commerce, is touched on in the Los Angeles Chamber of Commerce Board Meeting Minutes, 31 September 1931, University of Southern California Western Regional Library, Department of Special Collections, University of Southern California, Los Angeles (USC). The minutes discuss the "benefits of the tremendous amount of free publicity and paid advertising which the participating newspapers would give to the Olympic Games and other benefits to be derived there from."

35. Photo N-002-653, Security Pacific Photo Collection, Los Angeles Public Library, Los Angeles.

36. See John Bale, *Sports, Space, and the City* (Caldwell, NJ.: The Blackburn Press, 2001).

37. In a letter to William May Garland in the October following the 1932 games, Pierre de Coubertin included his thoughts on some of the critical components of the Olympic publicity campaign outside of the U.S. Interestingly, he listed four major categories, of which "The Olympic Games" was the last. The first three listed are "the work of nature," "the work of men" (Coubertin cites the "Spanish missions" as an example here), and "the city." Pierre de Coubertin, to William May Garland, 29 October 1932, Olympic Collection, AAFLA.

38. Richard Gruneau, "The Critique of Sport in Modernity: Theorising Power, Culture, and the Politics of the Body," in *The Sports Process: A Comparative and Developmental Approach*, eds. Eric G. Dunning, Joseph A. Maguire, and Robert E. Pearton (Champaign, Ill.: Human Kinetics, 1993), 85-110. Gruneau generalizes the significance of the linkages drawn between modern and ancient sport. He explains, "[D]raping the Olympics in positive symbols from the past proved a convenient way to differentiate modern socially improving sport from other popular physical recreations. In this version of positive classicism the most important signifiers of socially improving sport had to be Greek" (p. 89).

39. Quoted in "Los Angeles—1932——The Games are Open," *Olympic Review*, nos. 66-67 (1973): 186.

40. "Xth Olympiad," *Time*, 8 August 1932, p.25.

41. McWilliams, *Southern California*, 98.

42. On the Mediterranean comparison, see Clark Davis, "From Oasis to Metropolis."

43. Quoted in "Los Angeles—932—The Games are Open," 186. Boosters' promotion of the event may have been more blatantly manipulative of historical memory than creatively deceptive descriptions of the region's "fantasy past." in *Olympic: The Official Publication of the Organizing Committee of the Games of the Xth Olympiad*, Hollywood movie stars such as Douglas Fairbanks and Mary Pickford offer brief quotations expressing their excitement regarding the impending Olympic games. Charlie Chaplin offering reads: "I am gratified to join with all my confreres in the motion picture industry and the people of Southern California in welcoming the athletes of the world to the [Games of the] first Olympiad in history in the United States of America." Chaplin knew much more about acting than he did about modern Olympic history. The United States hosted the Olympic games prior to 1932—at St. Louis in 1904. See "Cinema Stars Will Welcome Olympic Participants," *Olympic: Official Publication of the Organizing Committee of the Games of the Xth Olympiad*, October 1931, Olympic Collection, AATLA [emphasis added]. This publication was the official, printed promotional arm of the Organizing Committee by such prominent Angelino members as William May Garland and Zack Farmer. Issues were printed and distributed biannually, from May of 1930 to May of 1932 (five issues total).

Chaplin's error proved far from isolated—the description of the 1932 games as the first Olympic competition held in the U.S. occurs repeatedly in the promotional literature. The aforementioned Chamber of Commerce pamphlet map (see endnote 23) stares, "[T]he Los Angeles Games will mark the first time that this great international sports event has ever been held in the United States." The *3-Flag Tour* brochure (see endnote 21) asserts, "[I]f these pages help to keep fresh the memory of the first Olympic Games to be held on New World soil…they will have fulfilled their service." The same assertion appears in numerous other pamphlets, programs, and official publications. If intentional, this *refusal* to acknowledge the games of the St. Louis Olympiad may correspond to boosters' belief that, in order for the event to become a success, they had to portray it as a legitimate and unprecedented "turning point" in the history of the Olympics. Roche explains that this sort of attitude often emerges from mega-event planners, as they "often like to present themselves as 'makers of history', or at least 'makers of historic/memorable events." Roche, *Mega-Events and Modernity*, 230.

The boosters wanted to set their project apart, and by associating the Xth Olympiad with the 1904 games—or any of the previous games for that matter—they would have implicated their own project in a less than illustrious history. Divorcing the Los Angeles games from the legacy of St. Louis amplified the regional specificity of the event—implying that Southern California superseded American cities in the East and Midwest.

The argument that boosters intentionally erased the legacy of St. Louis is speculative and impossible to confirm with the sources cited herein. It seems plausible that those in charge of printing the literature—especially if not connected officially to the Organizing Committee as in the case of the commercial pamphlets—were ignorant of 1904. However, with regard to publications tied directly to the Organizing Committee such as *Olympic,* it would surprise this author to find that those in charge had no knowledge of the St. Louis games. Members of the committee, especially Garland, had extensive contact with Pierre de Coubertin and the International Olympic Committee in the years leading up to the Los Angeles games. While they were probably not personally editing *Olympic,* it also seems plausible that those charged with that task were aware of 1904. Another possibility is that the reputation of the 1904 games as a distortion of the proper Olympic format led Los Angeles organizers to disregard it altogether. On the failure of the St. Louis games to meet the standards of Coubertin and the International Olympic Committee, see Mark Dyreson, *Making the American Team: Sport Culture, and the Olympic Experience* (Urbana: University of Illinois Press, 1998); Findling and Pelle, eds., *Historical Dictionary of the Modern Olympic Games,* s.v. "St. Louis 1904," by C. Robert Barnett. One might suggest that the 1904 games did not constitute a "genuine" Olympic event because they occurred in conjunction with the World's Fair in St. Louis. However, none of the archival material cited herein suggests that organizers made this general distinction.

44. On the games as a tourist attraction, see White, "The Los Angeles Way"; Keys, "Spreading Peace."

45. The transparency of this connection is also evident from the overlap between the Los Angeles' business elite and the membership of the Organizing Committee. Members included the aforementioned Garland (an established real estate mogul), Harry Bauer (president of Southern California Edison), William Humphrey (president of the Associated Oil Company), Paul Shoup (president of the Southern Pacific Railroad Company), and a long list of other publishers, professionals, and industrialists. For a full list and specific details on members of the Organizing Committee, see Xth Olympiad Committee, "In the Matter of the Funds Realized from the Olympic Games Held in California in 1932," submitted by the Xth Olympiade Committee of the Games of Los Angeles to the United States Treasury Department and the Bureau of Internal Revenue, 1935, Olympic Collection, AAFLA. See also Steve Riess, "Power without Authority: Los Angeles' Elites and the Construction of the Coliseum," *Journal of Sports History* 8 (1981): 50-65; and White, "The Los Angeles Way."

46. Xth Olympiade Committee, *The Games of the Xth Olympiad Los Angeles L932-Official Report,* pp. 30, 180, 225, Olympic Collection, AAFLA.

47. Harry Harper quoted in Los Angeles Chamber of Commerce Bulletin, 21 March 1932, Regional History Collection, USC. Papers from the Los Angeles Chamber of Commerce at USC's Regional History Collection are replete with comments from its members regarding the Olympics as a commercial boon.

48. "Olympiad Seen as Aid to State," *Los Angeles Times,* 17 September 1924, sec. A, p. 1.

49. See Dyreson, "Marketing National Identity," 26. Eriko Yamamoto's work on the 1932 Olympics reveals that minority press outlets—specifically Japanese-American ones—also portrayed the upcoming games as a probable source of economic resuscitation for their respective communities. See Yamamoto, "Cheers for Japanese Athletes," 426.

50. Roche, *Mega-Events and Modernity*, 225.

51. "Olympic Games as a Depression-Buster," *Literary Digest*, 18 June 1932, pp. 28-30.

52. Garland quoted in *Olympic News*, October-November 1930, issued by the American Olympic Association, Olympic Collection, AAFLA. The American Olympic Association was the precursor to the United States Olympic Committee (USOC). The aforementioned Harry Harper (see endnote 47) also described supporting the event as a "civic duty" for the citizens of Los Angeles.

53. *Olympic: Official Publication of the Organizing Committee of the Games of the Xth Olympiad*, May 1930, Olympic Collection, AAFLA. See endnote 43 for a discussion of this publication.

54. White provides an excellent discussion of the translation of local appeal into national appeal within the larger booster project. See White, "The Los Angeles Way."

55. Mandell, *Nazi Olympics*, xxv. Mandell explains, "[T]he world drew lessons from the Berlin Olympics. The effectiveness of the festive arrangements proved to many skeptics who had been incredulous in 1933 that the group of wild men in charge of Germany was administratively capable and would stay that way."

56. Jean Bosquet, "Olympiad Focuses Eyes of World on Southland; Magnitude of International Event, and Its Significance, So Great as to Baffle Description," *Los Angeles Times*, 24 July 1932, sec. A, p. 1.

57. Malcolm Metcalf, interview by George Hodak, February 1988, An Olympian's Oral History Collection, AAFLA.

58. White, "The Los Angeles Way," 79.

59. Ibid, 91.

60. The *Official Report's* description of the administration building is worth noting here: "Arts characteristic of the American Southwest struck the prevailing note in the furnishings of this spacious room. It was colorful with Navajo Indian rugs, and the Mission furniture, while modern in origin, was based on Spanish-Colonial models used by the Franciscan fathers and other early California pioneers." See Xth Olympiade Committee, *Official Report*, 281.

61. On the cowboys, see White, "The Los Angeles Way," 96.

62. Security Pacific Photo Collection.

63. Xth Olympiad Committee, *Official Report*, 235.

64. Mel Wharton, "Olympic Village: The Answer to an Athlete's Prayer," *Hygeia*, August 1932, p. 722.

65. Charles H. McCallister, interview by George Hodak, February, 1988, transcript, An Olympians Oral History Collection, AAFLA.

66. Mike Davis, *City of Quartz. Excavating the Future in Los Angeles* (New York: Vintage, 1990), 161.

67. White, "The Los Angeles Way," 81.

68. Irving Eckhoff, "Laborers and Lords Collide," *Los Angeles Times*, 14 August 1932, sec. E, p.3.

69. "Many Los Angeles People are of Foreign Birth of Descent: All Are Looking Forward to Greeting Fellow Countrymen," *Olympic: Official Publication of the Organizing Committee of the Games of the Xth Olympiad*, May 1930, Olympic Collection, AAFLA.

70. "California History Interests Visitors," *Olympic: Official Publication of the Organizing Committee of the Games of the Xth Olympiad*, September 1930, Olympic Collection, AAFLA.

71. *The Games of the Xth Olympiad Los Angeles 1932-Official Report*, 236. The same lack of confidence might be inferred from the promotional pamphlet distributed by Union Pacific Railroad Company, which claimed that "Los Angeles will undoubtedly be one of the most cosmopolitan cities in the world during the two weeks while the Olympic Games are in progress." The wording of this claim could suggest that the multiethnic makeup of Southern California was being celebrated, but only temporarily. That is, the games provided temporary relief to an otherwise racist metropolis. See "Go Union Pacific to Los Angeles," pamphlet, ephemeral material from the Los Angeles 1932 Olympic Games, Olympic Collection, AAFLA.

72. "Cinema Stars Will Welcome Fellow Countrymen," *Olympic*, October 1931, found in Olympic Collection, AAFLA.

73. On ethnic and racial diversity in Los Angeles in the twentieth century, see Davis, *City of Quartz;* and Klein, *The History of Forgetting.*

74. "Japanese Laud Welcome Here," *Los Angeles Times,* 12 June 1932, sec. A, p. 1.

75. The exact number of participants is not consistently reported by primary and secondary sources. This is what the *Los Angeles Times* reported. The participants were later sentenced to six months in prison for their actions. See "STUNT FOR MOONEY JEERED: Finale of Olympiad Marked by Demonstration; Crowd Cheers Arrest of Participants," *Los Angeles Times,* 15 August 1932, sec. A, p. 1.

76. "National Counter-Olympic Committee, Boycott The Olympics! Forward to The International Workers Athletic Meet, July 29, 30, 31 and August 1, Chicago, Illinois," [1932], flyer, Olympic Collection, AAFLA.

77. Ibid.

78. William J. Baker, "Muscular Marxism and the Chicago Counter-Olympics of 1932," *International Journal of the History of Sport* 9 (1992): 397-410.

79. Roche, *Mega-Events and Modernity,* 102.

80. "Well, Let's Hope For the Best," *The Christian Century,* 3 August 1932, p. 949.

81. "STUNT FOR MOONEY JEERED."

82. "Japanese Laud Welcome Here"

83. Ralph Huston, "Win or Lose, They're for Doug Fairbanks," *Los Angeles Times,* 30 July 1932, p. 11.

84. Dyreson, "Marketing National Identity," 37. Dyreson found the reference to the *Japan Times* editorial in Hugh Byas, "Japan's Athletes Tell Impressions," *New York Times,* 9 October 1932, sec. E, p. 7.

85. Roku Sugahara, "Nipping the Nipponese, Look What You Done to Me," *Rafu Shimpo,* 26 July 1932, p. 2. The articles cited herein from *Rafu Shimpo* all come from the English language section of the paper.

86. "Impressions: Sportsman," *Rafu Shimpo,* 21 August 1932, p. [illegible].

87. Eriko Yamamoto, "Cheers for Japanese Athletes," 403.

88. "Impressions: Sportsman." Eddie Tolan was an African-American sprinter from the University of Michigan who won gold in both the 100- and 200-meter dashes at the 1932 games. Shoichiro Takenaka was a Japanese competitor in the 5000-meter race, in which the Finn Lauri Lehtinen committed a technical foul against Ralph Hill of England. In a controversial decision, the race judges refused to disqualify Lehtinen. See Gurtmann, *The Olympics,* 50-51.

89. See Roche, *Mega-Events and Modernity,* 72. In the context of Roche's analysis, the effort by minority groups to embrace the games on a rhetorical basis must be viewed as fundamentally ironic. Speaking of the dynamic of cultural inclusion surrounding the Olympics that took place prior to World War II, Roche explains that "as movements in popular culture," they "were profoundly and ideologically exclusionary" with respect to race, class, and gender.

90. Yamamoto, "Cheers for Japanese Athletes," 403.

91. Welky "Viking Girls," 37.

92. Ibid, 38.

93. "Metcalfe Goes Hunting for a Records," *Chicago Defender,* 30 July 1932, cover page of sports section.

94. Dyreson, "Marketing National Identity," 40.

95. "Tidye Pickett and Louise Stokes Were on First U.S. Track Team," *California Eagle,* 19 August 1932, p. 1; "White Press Raves When Colored Girls are Barred From Olympic Relays," *California Eagle,* 19 August 1932, P. 1; "The Close of the Olympics and a Hint of Prejudice," *California Eagle,* 12 August 1932, editorial section. This episode involved the last minute replacement of two black athletes, Tidye Pickett and Louise Stokes, by two white athletes on one of the female relay teams. Rumors circulated among the black press that female superstar Babe Didrikson had lobbied for their replacement.

96. "The Close of the Olympics and a Hint of Prejudice," *California Eagle,* 12 August 1932.

97. "White Stars Stick with Muse," *California Eagle,* 5 August 1932, p. 1.

98. *La Opinion,* the major Spanish-language newspaper in Los Angeles in 1932, covered the games extensively and offers valuable insight into the Latin-American community's reaction to the

event. However, this author did not encounter and is not aware of any other Spanish-language media source in the U.S. that offered comparable coverage. As this article's discussion of minority press coverage revolves around a comparison of local and non-local newspapers, an analysis of the articles from *La Opinion* is beyond the immediate scope of this paper. For those interested in potential areas of further research, *La Opinion's* various discussions of the disadvantages faced by Mexican athletes by virtue of their home country's struggle to keep up with the modernization of nations such as the United States and Japan would certainly provide key insight into inquiries surrounding the relationship between notions of ethnicity and modernity at the games. Issues of *La Opinion* from 1932 are available at the Young Research Library, UCLA.

99. Kropp, 'All Our Yesterdays," 429.

100. Ibid, 531-532.

101. Dyreson, "Marketing National Identity," 23.

102. Ibid, 24.

103. Metcalf interview.

104. Keys, "Spreading Peace," 171.

105. Ralph Buston, "Win or Lose, They're for Doug Fairbanks," *Los Angeles Times,* 30 July 1932, p.11. Fairbanks and Pickford were familiar with the Olympic games prior to 1932. At the 1924 games in Paris, they had attended in support of the American sprinter Charles Paddock, who took silver in the 200-meter dash. See Mark Dyreson, "Scripting the American Olympic Story-Telling Formula: The 1924 Paris Olympic Games and the American Media," *Olympika: The International Journal of Olympic Studies* 5 (1996): 45-80.

106. Erskine Johnson and Victor Sidler, "The Quickest Way Into the Movies," *Los Angeles Times,* 2 October 1932, p. 51.

107. Roche, *Mega-Events and Modernity,* 9.

108. Mandell, *Nazi Olympics,* 44.

109. Roche, *Mega-Events and Modernity,* 113.

110. Carl Diem, "Olympic Days of Wandering, Teaching, and Learning," in *The Olympic Idea: Discourses and Essays,* ed. Carl-Diem Institut (Stuttgart: Hofmann, 1970), 62-63.

CHAPTER 12

GOING TO BAT FOR JACKIE ROBINSON

The Jewish Role in Breaking Baseball's Color Line

Stephen H. Norwood and Harold Brackman

We live in an age of second thoughts about civil rights progress and black Jewish cooperation. Jackie Robinson's desegregation of major league baseball recalls a time of surer moral compass and strong mutual support between African Americans and Jews. The encouragement Robinson received at a critical point in his rookie year of 1947 from Jewish slugger Hank Greenberg highlighted the solid backing of the Jewish community for his major civil rights advance. Nor was this support an isolated incident.

Headlines of the day, suggesting strong parallels between the African American and Jewish struggles, offer reasons for the mutual support. Expectations for greater tolerance after the Allied victory in World War II were quickly dashed. In the United States, racial segregation and denial of African American voting rights, and discrimination against blacks and Jews in housing, education, and employment, continued after the defeat of Nazism. Blacks in the United States and Jews in Europe were each subjected to renewed violent attacks. Fifty-six African Americans died in racially motivated killings between June 1945 and September 1946, and few, if any, of the perpetrators were punished. In Aiken, South Carolina, policemen gouged out the eyes of Isaac Woodard only three hours after his discharge from the army, having arrested him on a false charge of disorderly conduct. In May 1947, early in Jackie Robinson's rookie season, the press reported that an all-white jury in Greenville, South Carolina, had acquitted 28 "confessed lynch murderers" charged with torturing a black man to death.[1] American Jews, many of whose relatives had been slaughtered by the

---

Article appears by permission of the *Journal of Sport History*.

Nazis and their accomplices, recoiled in horror once again upon learning that pogromists in Kielce, Poland, had on July 4, 1946, annihilated 41 of the 200 Jews in the town who had survived the Holocaust. Kielce had had a prewar Jewish population of 18,000. By mid-1947, the Jewish death toll in Poland's postwar pogroms had surpassed 1,500.[2]

Jews fleeing the postwar pogroms found no peace. In May1947, a British destroyer rammed the Haganah ship *Hatikvah,* carrying 1,500 Holocaust survivors to Palestine. British sailors boarded the ship and attacked the Jews with tear gas and fire hoses. The British then shipped the Jews to a detention camp in Cyprus. Reflecting strong black support for the creation of Israel, the African American Chicago newspaper *Defender* condemned both the British government and the U.S. State Department for their "unbelievably shameful double-crossing" of the Jews.[3]

The prominent role of Jews in the struggle to break major league baseball's color line has been almost entirely overlooked, although the African American press emphasized it at the time. The writing of the history of baseball's desegregation shows signs of the same revisionism discernible in recent accounts of Jewish participation in the civil rights movement. Clayborne Carson, for example, has treated the Jewishness of Jewish civil rights workers as accidental or irrelevant, ostensibly because their involvement was not narrowly rooted in a religious identification. David Levering Lewis claims, moreover, that "opportunism underlay the Afro-American–Jewish coalition," and that African American collaboration with Jews proved to be "minimally beneficial to the Afro-Americans."[4] The evidence of the importance of Jewish ethnic heritage in predisposing young people toward civil rights involvement is ignored. At the same time, the ethno-religious identity of Jewish merchants, criticized as black ghetto exploiters, goes unquestioned. Emerging from the crucible of this historical alchemy, the civil rights martyrs Michael Schwerner and Andrew Goodman cease to be Jewish—but mercantile Blumstein's on 125th Street in Harlem remains as Jewish as ever.

Strong support for the desegregation of baseball reflected a long-standing Jewish commitment to promoting African American civil rights that dated back to the Progressive era. Jews provided far more emotional commitment and organizational and financial support to the black civil rights movement and the advancement of black education than any other white group. Martin Luther King, Jr. declared that "It would be impossible to record the contribution that Jewish people have made toward the Negro's struggle for freedom, it has been so great."[5]

During the early twentieth century, many Jewish philanthropists, most notably Julius Rosenwald, contributed heavily to African American education. Rosenwald's donations helped build over 5,000 black schools and colleges. He donated half the funds to a new school for blacks to any Southern community that raised the other half. Rosenwald would not donate to Southern white schools. By 1932, 25 to 40 percent of all African American children attending school in the South were educated in Rosenwald schools.[6] African American sociologist Horace Mann Bond discovered Southern blacks' deep appreciation for Rosenwald's philanthropy in an encounter on a rural Alabama road in the 1930s, after his car became stuck in the mud. Two black men with a mule suddenly appeared and pulled Bond's car from the rut. When Bond mentioned that he worked for the Rosenwald Fund, the men exclaimed excitedly, "You work for Cap'n Julius!" and refused to accept payment for their service.[7] Jewish philanthropists Jacob Schiff, Felix Warburg, Paul Warburg, Jacob Billikopf, and Julian Mack also made very large financial contributions to support black education.[8]

Rosenwald and other Jews provided strong backing for Booker T. Washington's Tuskegee Institute. During the early twentieth century Jews comprised the majority of whites at Tuskegee's commencement exercises.[9]

The black–Jewish alliance was institutionalized when the National Association for the Advancement of Colored People (NAACP) was established in 1909, the most important organization for the advancement of black rights of the next half century.[10] Jews provided a substantial part of the NAACP's original financing and emergency aid when the association almost went broke during the Depression. The NAACP's first successful event, a 1910 national conference on the disenfranchisement of African Americans in the South, was organized by Henry Moskowitz, a Rumanian-born Jewish social worker and garment industry arbitrator, and Hungarian-born rabbi Stephen Wise. Three of the NAACP's presidents were Jews: Joel Spingarn, who in 1912 joined with Henry Moskowitz and Jane Addams in an unsuccessful attempt to introduce a civil rights plank at the Progressive Party convention; Arthur Spingarn; and Kivie Kaplan. In 1917, Joel Spingarn was instrumental in convincing the U.S. Army to commission hundreds of black officers. In 1940, W.E.B. Du Bois paid tribute to Joel Spingarn's contribution to black civil rights, a year after his death, by dedicating his autobiography to his memory, describing him as a "Scholar and Knight"—"one of those vivid, enthusiastic but clear thinking idealists which from age to age the Jewish race has given the world." Jews constituted nearly half the NAACP's legal staff through the 1930s.[11]

Jews were also prominent in supporting the National Urban League (NUL), formed in 1911 to assist African Americans who had migrated from the South to northern cities. Columbia University economics professor E.R.A. Seligman served as the NUL's first chairman, and its board included a significant number of both religious and secular Jews.[12]

During the 1930s, Jews rallied behind the Scottsboro boys, nine African American youths falsely accused of rape in Alabama and put on trial there for their lives. Jewish attorneys Samuel Leibowitz and Joseph Brodsky served as their defense counsel, putting their own lives at risk. The Yiddish and English-language Jewish press solidly backed the defendants. In his summation, prosecutor Wade Wright condemned Leibowitz and Brodsky and the masses of Jews who agitated for the defendants' release, shouting to the jury, "Show them that Alabama justice cannot be bought and sold with Jew money from New York."[13]

The two principal Jewish trade unions, the International Ladies Garment Workers Union (ILGWU) and the Amalgamated Clothing Workers Union

(ACW), sharply criticized the refusal of many American unions to admit or organize African American workers, and welcomed blacks into their own ranks.[14] That the ILGWTJ and ACW were socialist-led does not explain their pro-black orientation, since non-Jewish socialist unions, like the United Brewery Workers, showed little interest in African American workers.[15]

There may have been an element of self-interest in Jews' strong backing for African American civil rights, since ending racial discrimination might also result in Jews gaining equal access to jobs, housing, and education. But Jewish support for the black cause was motivated largely by Jews' ability to identify with another oppressed people, and by idealism and moral conviction shaped by Jewish values. Like blacks, Jews during the 1940s continued to be barred from many colleges and professional schools by discriminatory quotas, and from many neighborhoods by restrictive housing covenants. Many job advertisements stipulated that the employer would consider only Christian applicants.[16] But Jews also risked intensifying anti-Semitism by embracing the cause of the nation's most despised minority.

Anti-Semitism is the world's longest hatred, and Jews, descended from a people who had been slaves in Egypt, saw many similarities between their historical experience and that of African Americans. Every year at Passover, Jews remembered their people's suffering in slavery and their exodus from Egypt, reinforcing their identity as a people in bondage who had struggled for freedom. This underscored the commonality of their historical experience with that of the blacks. For Jews, philanthropy was theologically rooted in the Hebrew Bible and the Talmud, which "made charity not only a virtue, but a duty."[17] Mario Cuomo has noted that American Jews were "the most generous people in the world that I've seen," giving heavily "not just to Jewish causes—to hospitals of all kinds, to education of all kinds. They marched in the civil rights campaign…"[18]

Both the Yiddish and English-language Jewish press in America devoted considerable attention to exposing anti-black racism, and drew parallels between the oppression of African Americans and Jews in Europe. These newspapers compared American anti-black riots to European anti-Semitic pogroms, and Southern lynchings to autos-da-fé, the public burnings of Jews during the Spanish Inquisition. The *Forward*, for example, editorialized: "Kishiniev and [East] St. Louis—the same soil, the same people. It is a distance of four and a half thousand miles between these two cities, and yet they are so close and similar."[19]

The important Jewish role in agitating for the desegregation of the National Pastime was part of this decades-long, intense Jewish support for African American civil rights. But the Jewish contribution to breaking baseball's color line has been obscured, hidden in tributes to "progressive whites" and celebrations of the civil rights efforts of American Communists. Considerable attention has recently been devoted to the crusade waged against baseball's color line by Lester Rodney as sports editor of *The Daily Worker*, the Communist Party (CP) newspaper, yet the fact that Rodney and most of his reporters were Jewish is almost never mentioned.[20] By contrast, mainstream Jews who were critical players—on the field, in the press box, in the front office, in the stands, and in American society—in the struggle to integrate baseball have become invisible, their contribution retrospectively erased.[21]

Among American Communists, Jews were disproportionately involved in the campaign to desegregate baseball, and after the growing threat of fascism led the Comintern to initiate the Popular Front in 1935, they were increasingly identified as Jews. Lester Rodney noted that it was Hitler's rise that propelled him into a "kind of Jewish consciousness."[22] Jews constituted a substantial percentage of the pickets in the CP and Bronx American Labor Party demonstrations against baseball's color line at Yankee Stadium.[23] The logic of the Popular Front led the CP to make a concerted appeal to Jews, who, as the Nazis' primary targets, were a critical component of any anti-fascist coalition, and the Party promoted a "progressive Jewish identity."Jewish Communists' ethnic consciousness was further strengthened during World War II, as the Allies struggled to defeat Nazism, and in the late 1940s, when the CP supported the creation of the state of Israel.[24]

From 1935 through the late 1940s, Jews in the CP gave significant attention to combating anti- Semitism, which they linked to anti-black racism. In fact, the Party gave considerable emphasis to the importance of the "Negro–Jewish alliance," implying that a special bond existed between the two oppressed peoples. Jews were heavily represented in the CP's Harlem branch; most of the white Communist teachers and relief workers in Harlem were Jewish.[25]

The even more important mainstream Jewish support for the desegregation of baseball and for Jackie Robinson himself was greatly influenced by the central role of the major Jewish organizations—most prominently, the American Jewish Committee, the American Jewish Congress, the Anti-Defamation League (ADL), the Jewish Labor Committee, and the Union of American Hebrew Congregations—in the intergroup relations movement, which emerged and attained its peak influence in the years immediately following World War II. This movement embraced the "theory of the unitary character of prejudice," in which all forms of bigotry, including both anti-Semitism and racism, were seen as "inseparable parts of the same phenomenon."[26] This perception was rooted both in the common barriers American Jews and African Americans confronted in gaining access to housing, universities and professional schools, hotels and resorts, and employment in many fields, and in a deepening insecurity among Jews after the Holocaust. Both Jewish community centers and synagogues and African American churches suffered dynamite bombings by hate groups in the postwar period.[27]

Anti-Semitism had never been more intense in the United States than immediately before and during World War II, and Jewish organizations feared it would become even more widespread in the postwar period. Many predicted another cataclysmic depression in which demobilized veterans accustomed to violence and angry about unemployment might take out their resentment on Jews and other minorities, as had been the case in central Europe after World War I. In March 1938 an Opinion Research Corporation (ORC) poll showed that a majority of Americans believed that Nazi Germany's persecution of Jews was "wholly or partly" the Jews' fault.[28] In the month of D-Day, June 1944, ORC found that 24% of Americans considered Jews in this country a "menace to America," up from 17% in August 1940, while only 6% viewed the Germans in the United States in that way. Even in February 1946, only months after Allied troops had entered the annihilation camps, fully one-fifth of the American population continued to believe Jews were a menace to the country; by comparison, the figure for Germans was only 1%. Moreover, that same month another ORC poll revealed that a substantial majority of the American population would not be influenced to vote against a congressional candidate because he had declared himself to be anti-Semitic, and "almost a quarter declared they would find him more attractive for being so."[29]

Jewish organizations also feared that a massive increase in hate propaganda might follow the lifting of wartime censorship. Jews had become greatly alarmed during the 1930s about the proliferation of domestic fascist groups like the Silver Shirts, the Black Legion, and the German-American Bund, which spewed hatred of both Jews and African Americans, and the increasingly strident anti-Semitism of the popular radio priest Charles Coughlin.[30]

Additional developments immediately after World War II reinforced Jews' belief that they and African Americans faced a common threat. A resurgent Ku Klux Klan (KKK), anti-black and anti-Semitic, claimed a membership of 20,000, and newly formed neo-Nazi groups like the Columbians demanded the deportation from the United States of both Jews and African Americans. The 1946 *American Jewish Yearbook* considered "the most significant anti-Semitic [threat] of the year" to be "the reemergence of the KKK." Jewish observers at KKK rallies reported that anti-Semitic remarks produced tumultuous applause. Segregationists, in fact, saw Jews "as the brains—and the money—behind black attacks on segregation." Segregationists in Congress, like Senator James Eastland of Mississippi, alarmed many Jews by their prominence among those calling for the immediate reindustrialization of Germany as an anti-Soviet bulwark. Jewish World War II combat veterans returned in 1945 to Miami to see the familiar signs "No Jews Wanted, Christians Only" along the beach. "Restricted Clientele" notices barring Jews from housing and hotels were displayed in many Florida communities where Jackie Robinson was denied accommodations during spring training. Jewish organizations failed in their effort after the Holocaust to pass displaced persons legislation that would modify the national origins quota system on which U.S. immigration policy was based, and which was highly discriminatory against Jews.[31]

The major Jewish organizations joined with the principal African American civil rights groups in aggressively lobbying for fair employment, fair education, and open housing legislation in the immediate post-World War II period. The Jews gave the strongest support among whites for the bill, establishing the Fair Employment Practices Commission. In the late 1940s, the major Jewish organizations produced a vast assortment of posters, pamphlets, and films that condemned all forms of racial, ethnic, and religious intolerance and presented positive images of minorities. In 1947, the American Jewish Committee endorsed federal anti-lynching and anti-poll tax legislation, with no dissent from its southern members, and called for the creation of a permanent federal commission on civil rights.[32]

During the late 1940s, the African American press highlighted Jews' dispro-portionate support for the civil rights cause, emphasizing that blacks and Jews were joined in a common struggle against bigotry. Black newspapers praised Jewish journalists like Walter Winchell and Shirley Povich of the *Washington Post* for their prominent role in the campaign to desegregate baseball.[33]

Because few whites covering sports criticized baseball's color line, Jewish sportswriters were especially important in presenting the case for desegrega-tion to a mainstream readership and radio audience. Although he exaggerated somewhat, Branch Rickey had warned Jackie Robinson when he signed him to a contract in October 1945 that "virtually nobody" supported their challenge to organized baseball's color line: "No owners, no umpires, very few newspaper-men."[34] Rickey claimed in 1948 that his fellow major league club owners, sup-ported by National League president Ford Frick, had unanimously denounced his signing of Jackie Robinson in a secret report presented at a 1946 meeting. But a member of New York mayor LaGuardia's Committee on Unity noted that what Rickey most feared was "the venom of some of the sportswriters."[35] St. Louis Cardinals owner Fred Saigh, who fiercely opposed desegregation, compared Midwestern sportswriters favorably with the "Jewish boys" writing for eastern newspapers, whom he described as "very minority-minded."[36]

Jewish sportswriters and journalists of the era were prominent among the practitioners of a new big-city style whose hard-boiled edge was softened by sympathy for the underdog. Saigh was accurate in highlighting the commitment of many Jewish sportswriters and journalists to desegregating baseball. Walter Winchell, the most prominent newspaper columnist and radio newscaster in the United States during the 1940s, long an outspoken champion of civil rights, gave high priority in his commentary to denouncing baseball's color line. He provided valuable emotional support for Jackie Robinson during his critical rookie year. Winchell's views had considerable impact, since his column was syndicated in more than 2,000 newspapers. Fifty million people read the column or listened to his weekly Sunday night radio broadcast.[37]

Although he was not observant, Winchell's "Judaism ran deep," accord-ing to his biographer. The son of a shirtmaker and grandson of a cantor, he was raised in East Harlem by Russian Jewish immigrant parents and spoke Yiddish fluently. Winchell possessed a "radar—like sensitivity to…anti-Sem-itism," which drew him into the struggle against all forms of bigotry. Almost immediately after the Nazis came to power in Germany, Winchell was being called "the most rabid anti-Hitlerite in America."[38] His attacks on anti-Semitic groups like the Silver Shirts during the 1930s and the KKK after World War II were a major focus of his columns and broadcasts. Winchell became one of the Federal Bureau of Investigation's primary sources of information on pro-Nazi groups operating in the United States. He worked closely with the ADL, which supplied him with research material on anti-Semitism and racism.[39] As a result of his campaign against hate groups, Winchell was "inundated" with anti-Semitic mail, and segregationist Congressman John Rankin of Mississippi denounced him on the floor of the U.S. House of Representatives as a "little communistic kike." By contrast, the Anti-Defamation League praised Winchell in January 1947 for his "excellent campaign to eradicate [the] use of distorted stereotypes of all minorities." During the late 1940s, Winchell was also a very vocal and passionate Zionist.[40]

Winchell, who conspicuously accompanied African American boxing great Sugar Ray Robinson around Miami when its hotels still posted signs "No Negroes, Jews, or dogs allowed," became one of Jackie Robinson's strongest and most visible supporters.[41] Robinson's wife, Rachel, recalled that Winchell invited Jackie and her, along with Sugar Ray Robinson and his wife, to be his guests at a "white" Miami Beach nightclub. She remembered the tension as Winchell "literally led the way, parted the waters," as the two African American couples "followed him like sheep to his table." In May 1947, Winchell joined Jackie Robinson at a "Negro Freedom Rally" at New York's Madison Square Garden.[42] That same month the Chicago *Defender* praised Winchell for "blast[ing] the St. Louis Cardinals' 'Klansmen' who had planned to strike rather than play against Jackie Robinson." Winchell declared on his weekly radio broadcast of May 11, 1947: "Ball players who don't want to be in the same ball park with Robinson, don't belong in the same country with him."[43]

Shirley Povich, sports editor of the *Washington Post*, was among the most prominent critics of the color line in baseball and other sports, even before the United States entered World War II. Povich was raised as an orthodox Jew by Russian immigrant parents in a large family where "there was always one boy preparing for a Bar Mitzvah." Povich's opposition to discrimination against African Americans was undoubtedly shaped by what he had learned as a child about the persecution of Jews in Russia. The person he called his "Malamud," his Hebrew teacher, whom Povich idolized, had "a big saber wound across [his] cheek" as a result of resisting induction into the army of Russia, the world's leading anti-Semitic country at the time. Povich's grandfather had had his friends put out one of his eyes to evade the czar's military service.[44]

Covering spring training in 1941 for the *Washington Post*, Povich wrote that many players in the Negro leagues were as good or better than current major league stars, and that by maintaining a color line, the major leagues were missing out on "a couple of million dollars worth of talent."[45] Povich continued to press the baseball establishment to accelerate the pace of desegregation after Robinson's entry into the major leagues, writing a 15-part feature for the *Washington Post* in 1953 on the African American contribution to baseball and the fall of the color line, for which he received racist hate mail. Povich also regularly denounced George Preston Marshall for refusing to recruit African American players for his "burgundy, gold, and caucasian" Washington Redskins.[46]

Sam Lacy, sports editor of the Baltimore *Afro-American*, recalled that Jewish sportswriters had come to his support when he was excluded from ballparks.

Dick Young of the New York *Daily News* perched with him in protest on the roof of a New Orleans stadium press box during spring training, and Milton Richman of United Press "jumped all over" the Yankee functionary who tried to bar him from Yankee Stadium at World Series time.[47]

Roger Kahn, who joined the New York *Herald Tribune* as a sportswriter in 1947, was among the most outspoken critics of racism in organized baseball during the late 1940s and 1950s. Kahn saw the anti-Semitic prejudice he experienced studying at New York University's uptown campus, where there were no Jews on the faculty as part of a "loathsome" racism that "ruled America" in the 1940s. He claimed that his biology professor, a consultant to Nazi industry in the late 1930s, deliberately gave Jewish students lower grades than they deserved to prevent their admission to medical school. Kahn, who identified strongly as a Jew, later wrote a book on the subject of "What it Means to be a Jew in America," entitled *The Passionate People*.[48]

According to Kahn, insensitivity to the condition of blacks pervaded baseball writing through the 1950s, and he encountered considerable opposition in his efforts to expose baseball's racist practices. His editor at the *Herald-Tribune* after 1948, Bob Cooke, opposed the desegregation of baseball, and his deputy "maintained a Gatling-gun chatter of prejudice," taunting Kahn for being pro-black. Cooke resisted Kahn's efforts to describe the abuse Jackie Robinson suffered, and the "slothlike" pace of the major leagues' desegregation. The *Herald-Tribune* refused to print an article Kahn wrote that strongly criticized the big league clubs for using a St. Louis hotel that barred Jackie Robinson and the other early black players. Kahn's editor told him he was being paid to write about sports, not race relations. Kahn's repeated denunciations of the rampant racism in baseball led Jackie Robinson to ask him to help him set up an African American magazine called *Our Sports*.[49]

To be sure, there were some Jewish sportswriters, most notably Dick Young of the New York *Daily News,* who agreed with mainstream sportswriters that Jackie Robinson as a veteran player had become too strident and abrasive. Initially very supportive of Robinson, Young came to prefer the Dodgers' more soft-spoken African American catcher Roy Campanella. But Young nonetheless declared after Robinson's retirement that no African American player could have handled the role of breaking the color line as well as Robinson. Young, who as a Jew was restricted from staying at some hotels, was angered that the Dodgers had trouble finding lodging for Robinson in St. Louis and Cincinnati. In 1949, the year Robinson won National League Most Valuable Player honors, Young remarked, "He leads the league in everything but hotel reservations." Robinson himself, looking back on his career in 1968, stated that he had respected Dick Young.[50]

A Jewish city councilman in Boston, civil rights activist Isadore Muchnick influenced Branch Rickey's decision to desegregate baseball by pressuring the Boston Red Sox to arrange a tryout in April 1945 for Jackie Robinson and two other African American players, Sam Jethroe and Marvin Williams. The tryout attracted Rickey's attention and probably contributed to his choosing

Robinson as the player to break the color line. In 1944 Muchnick introduced a motion to revoke the privilege to play Sunday baseball that the city council had granted to Boston's two major league teams, the Red Sox and the Braves, if they did not desegregate. Muchnick declared, "I cannot understand how baseball, which claims to be the national sport and which...receives special favors and dispensations from the Federal Government because of alleged morale value, can continue a pre-Civil War attitude toward American citizens because of the color of their skins." Immediately after Muchnick made his motion, he received a letter from Red Sox general manager Eddie Collins, informing him that no blacks wanted to play in the major leagues. When Muchnick made Collins's letter public, he was contacted by African American sportswriter Wendell Smith of the *Pittsburgh Courier,* who offered to supply black players for a tryout.[51]

The ethnic identity of Isadore Muchnick, representing the so-called "Jewish Ward 14" (consisting of part of Dorchester and part of Mattapan) from 1942 to 1947, was hardly incidental to his human rights activism. Muchnick called himself a Jew of "deep religious convictions" and had originally planned to become a rabbi. He was prominently involved in Jewish causes, serving as secretary of the New England region of the Zionist Organization of America, and with the Common Jewish Appeal.[52] In 1943 and 1944, Muchnick had introduced resolutions in the city council favoring the creation of an educational program in the Boston public schools to combat racial discrimination, but they had been blocked by Irish-American councilmen, who comprised a majority. Muchnick pressed for school desegregation a decade or more before the issue became fashionable among liberals. As chairman of the Boston School Committee during the early 1950s, the first Jew to hold a citywide office in Boston, Muchnick favored banning an essay contest on good citizenship sponsored by the Daughters of the American Revolution (DAR) because the DAR had refused to allow the great African American contralto Marian Anderson to sing at Constitution Hall in 1939.[53]

Scholars and sportswriters have always implied that Councilman Muchnick's push to desegregate Boston baseball was calculated to appeal to black votes in his district. This reflects the increasingly widespread revisionist view that Jewish activism on behalf of African American civil rights was motivated only by self-interest. This explanation for Muchnick's call for an end to baseball's color bar originated with Wendell Smith, who told interviewer Jerome Holtzmann in the early 1970s that he was the initiator of the call to revoke the Sunday baseball privilege in Boston: "I saw this little piece in the paper where [Muchnick] was running for reelection in a predominantly Negro area and was having quite a time getting reelected...I telephoned him...and told him 'If you want some Negro votes, why don't you stand up in the City Council and vote against Sunday baseball?'...He said he would." Smith told Shirley Povich that Muchnick had represented a "heavily Negro district" when Povich interviewed him in 1953 for his feature on African Americans and baseball for the *Washington Post.* Jules Tygiel, author of the principal scholarly study of the desegregation of baseball, identifies Muchnick as "a white politician representing a predominantly black district." David K. Wiggins, another leading sport historian, in an article on Wendell Smith, which discussed the April 1945 tryout, states that Muchnick "represented a largely black district." Arnold Rampersad, in the most recent Jackie Robinson biography, similarly writes that Muchnick's district had shifted from Jewish to "mainly black"[54]

Yet the assumption that Councilman Muchnick's challenge to baseball's color bar was primarily motivated by his desire to win supposedly much-needed African American votes for reelection is entirely without foundation. His district was 99.69 percent white in 1940, and 99 percent white in 1950, with only 439 nonwhites among 51,170 residents. And Muchnick won reelection twice without opposition. There was no significant African American migration into Muchnicks old district until the 1960s.[55] Moreover, in discussing the April 1945 tryout in 1947, Wendell Smith made no mention of Muchnick's representing "a predominantly Negro area," nor of any difficult reelection prospects, and did not suggest that Muchnick was merely responding to an initiative from Smith.[56]

Although the Red Sox showed little interest in the African American players when they showed up at Fenway Park, treating them like "freaks from a strange and distant world," Robinson deeply appreciated Muchnick's efforts, and the two became good friends. Muchnick called the Boston Braves front office the next day to request a tryout for the black players, but was turned down. Wendell Smith noted that when Jackie Robinson joined the Brooklyn Dodgers two years later, one of the first letters he received was from Muchnick, a message of strong support in which the councilman declared, "I have every confidence you will make the grade." Robinson inscribed a copy of Carl Rowan's 1960 biography of him to Muchnick: "I hope you enjoy *Wait Till Next Year.* Much of it was inspired by your attitude and beliefs."[57]

It is also quite possible that two Jews, Ike Levy and his brother Leon Levy, wealthy Philadelphia businessmen, had planned to desegregate major league baseball in the early 1940s, before Branch Rickey. The Levys intended to purchase the financially ailing Philadelphia Phillies from Gerry Nugent, and to hire as their general manager Eddie Gottlieb, a Jew and leading promoter of African American sports in Philadelphia. It was believed that Gottlieb might recruit Negro League stars for the Phillies. But National League president Ford Frick made it clear that "he wanted neither Jews nor blacks in the majors."[58]

Branch Rickey himself identified Jewish professor Frank Tannenbaum, a scholar of comparative slavery and race relations at Columbia University and immigrant from Austria-Hungary, as a major influence on his decision to break baseball's color line. Tannenbaum was prominent in organizations that assisted European Jewish refugees to escape Nazi persecution. Rickey noted in 1956 that he had worried that placing a black player on a major league club "would be a repeat of…the 18th Amendment," an experiment that "would over-leap itself" and thus "set back rather than solve the negro problem in this country." To determine whether desegregating baseball was feasible, he had consulted several scholarly works on slavery and race. According to Rickey, it was Tannenbaum's *Slave & Citizen*, published in 1946, that gave him the "'spine' to make the move." He informed Tannenbaum's publisher, Alfred A. Knopf that *Slave & Citizen* was "the one book that gave me a set conviction that I was doing the right thing and that the consequences would be favorable."[59]

Rickey was particularly impressed with Tannenbaum's argument that increased contacts between blacks and whites would undermine "all seemingly absolute systems of values and prejudices." Tannenbaum emphasized that American society was "essentially dynamic" and predicted that "future generations [would] look back upon the record of [racial] strife with wonder and incredulity." Rickey urged Tannenbaum's publisher to issue *Slave & Citizen* in a cheap paperback edition, since it "furnishes the reasoning that will solve the negro problem…with rapidity," and announced that he had given away six dozen copies of the book.[60]

As a result of Rickey's reading of *Slave & Citizen*, he and Tannenbaum became friends. Tannenbaum, who had always been disappointed that professors "wrote learned books which few people read and which had little influence," was very pleased to hear from Rickey that his work had influenced him in his decision to bring Jackie Robinson to the major leagues. He thanked Rickey for giving him "a sense of moral justification for the kind of academic career that I have pursued." Rickey invited Tannenbaum to watch a Dodgers game with him at his box in Ebbets Field, and personally introduced him to Jackie Robinson. Robinson and Tannenbaum corresponded until the latter's death in 1969.[61]

American Jews as a whole viewed Jackie Robinson as a surrogate whose successes were as much Jewish as African American triumphs, having already been drawn in the 1930s to African American boxing great Joe Louis, who became for them a dramatic symbol of their opposition to fascism. American Jews had devoted increasing attention to sports in the 1930s, horrified that the Nazis used sports to advance their cause. Jews had spearheaded a vigorous, although ultimately unsuccessful, campaign for a United States boycott of the 1936 Olympic games in Berlin. These games provided the Nazis with an opportunity to score a major propaganda triumph for fascism over the allegedly decadent western democracies.[62] Jews were ecstatic when Joe Louis demolished German heavyweight Max Schmeling, embraced by the Nazi regime as a symbol of Aryan supremacy, in a dramatic one-round knockout in 1938—the year of the *Kristallnacht*, when the Nazis declared open season on Germany's Jews. President Roosevelt himself had highlighted Joe Louis's importance as an anti-fascist symbol when he invited Louis to the White House, asked to feel his muscles, and announced, "Joe, we need muscles like yours to defeat Germany."[63]

Jews were the only white ethnic group that shared with African Americans the experience of being regularly subjected to physical beatings during childhood and adolescence because they were a despised minority. This led Jews to become disproportionately involved in boxing, as a means of promoting self-defense and enhancing self-esteem. By 1928, Jews had more contenders in the eight weight divisions than any other ethnic group. Most of the major Jewish fighters during the 1930s considered themselves symbols of Jewish resistance to anti-Semitism and fascism. Barney Ross, holder of the world welterweight, junior welterweight, and lightweight titles, told a friend, "The news from Germany made me feel I was…fighting for all my people." His antifascist convictions led him to enlist in the Marine Corps immediately after the attack on Pearl Harbor. Demanding a bout with Max Schmeling, Kingfish Levinsky declared, "I'll take on Hitler the same night after I've brushed Schmeling out of the ring." Max Baer, who wore the Star of David on his trunks for the first time in defeating Schmeling in 1933, hoped to deliver another blow against Nazism by facing him again, and even offered to fight him in Germany. Baer openly baited the Nazis by proclaiming, "Every punch in the eye I give Schmeling is one for Adolf Hitler." But Hitler would not permit Schmeling to fight a Jew again.[64]

For the innumerable Jews whose most searing memory of childhood was being beaten and taunted as "Christ Killers," Joe Louis—the African American scorned and ridiculed by the Nazis, who had humiliated Max Schmeling—was *their* avenger, just like the Jewish boxer with the Star of David on his trunks, who pummeled the gentile fighter as the opposing cornermen desperately cried out for their man to "Kill the Jew Bastard!"[65]

As with Joe Louis, Jews were strongly drawn to Jackie Robinson, who displayed incredible courage and dignity in facing horrible verbal and physical abuse, and even death threats against himself and his family—and in so doing delivered major blows against the forces of bigotry that threatened all minority groups. Jack Greenberg, who became director of the NAACP Legal Defense and Education Fund, recalled that he and the Jewish youth he grew up with viewed Robinson as a "surrogate hero," explaining, "He was the way we saw ourselves triumphing against the forces of bigotry and ignorance."[66] In 1948, when the *American Hebrew* claimed that "America's unrealized ideal of equality is becoming a reality in the sports world," it barely mentioned Jews who had achieved mobility through sports, and instead focused almost exclusively on blacks personified by Jackie Robinson. This identification inspired Robinson's enshrinement as iconic hero even in the recent spate of novels—Alan Lelchuk's *Brooklyn Boy* (1990), Mark Lapin's *Pledge of Allegiance* (1991), and Pete Hamill's *Snow in August* (1997)—in which first- and second-generation Jewish protagonists enter the mainstream of American culture through their love of baseball. For many Brooklyn Jews, "Wait till Next Year!" replaced "Next Year, in Jerusalem."[67]

Jews could more easily empathize with Jackie Robinson because the few Jews who played in the major leagues had been regularly subjected to anti-Semitic taunts from opposing players and fans. Hank Greenberg, who played in the major leagues from 1933 to 1947, with a four-year interruption for military service during World War II, recalled that he was constantly baited: "How the hell could you get up to home plate every day and have some son of a bitch call you a Jew bastard and a kike and a sheenie…without feeling the pressure. If the ballplayers weren't doing it, the fans were."[68]

During the 1935 World Series, the Chicago Cubs hurled such vicious anti-Semitic epithets at Hank Greenberg, playing for the Detroit Tigers, that plate umpire George Moriarty walked over to the Cubs dugout and warned some players he would throw them out of the game if they continued to use those insults. But because umpire Moriarty used profanity in warning the Cubs, Commissioner Landis fined him, without fining any of the Cubs. When Greenberg told the press he was upset by Landis's action, the Commissioner sent him a long formal letter expressing his outrage at Greenberg's comments. During the Series the Cubs also shouted "Christ Killer" at Jewish umpire Dolly Stark.[69]

Unlike Jackie Robinson, who was ordered by Brooklyn management not to respond to racist taunts, Greenberg and other Jewish players warned the bigots that they would physically retaliate. Andy Cohen, who played for the New York Giants in the 1920s when he was in the minor leagues, had to endure a fan yelling "Christ Killer" at him throughout a game. Cohen finally marched over to the grandstand with a bat and called out to the fan, "Come down here and I'll kill you too."[70]

Once when bench jockeys hurled anti-Semitic epithets, Hank Greenberg charged the New York Yankees dugout, challenging the entire team to a fight. Jewish sportswriter Haskell Cohen gleefully noted that during the 1947 season a teammate of the 6' 4", 215-pound Greenberg, then finishing out his career with the Pittsburgh Pirates, and playing with painful elbow chips, sneered, "For a Jew playing as lousy ball as you are, that's certainly a lot of money you're getting." Greenberg told him to keep his mouth shut, and when he continued his taunts Hank promptly knocked him down with a punch to the jaw. Cohen also recalled an earlier incident when a Detroit Tiger teammate of Greenberg's made an insulting remark about his Jewishness. Greenberg picked up a bat and walked up to the player with a wicked glint in his eye. "You Southern —," Hank muttered. "If you so much as peep once again, I'll bring this bat across your thick skull." Needless to say, the bigot beat a hasty retreat.[71]

Strongly identifying with the Jewish struggle against fascism, Greenberg said that he came "to feel that if I, as a Jew, hit a home run, I was hitting one against Hitler." He was the first major leaguer to enlist in the army in World War II. Unlike many other players who became athletic directors in the service, Greenberg volunteered for combat. He served as captain of a B-29 bomber squadron in the China-Burma-India theater, and participated in the first land-based bombing raids of the Japanese home islands. Along with his four home run titles, he won four battle stars.[72]

But Greenberg said that the only time he really felt like a hero was the day he sat out a game late in the 1934 season to attend synagogue on Yom Kippur and received a standing ovation from the congregation. With Greenberg, a major leaguer's observance of Jewish holidays became the subject of widespread public attention for the first time in the nation's history. Greenberg's not playing on Yom Kippur was an important affirmation of Jewish identity in a period that witnessed an alarming intensification of anti-Semitism. On Rosh Hashanah in 1934, the front page of the Detroit *Free Press* carried a headline in Yiddish, and over it the English translation, "Happy New Year, Hank!"[73]

Greenberg's experience was hardly unique; anti-Semitism, while not as pervasive as anti-black prejudice, was common in major league baseball at least until the 1960s. Don Newcombe, Brooklyn's pitching ace and the third African

American to become a permanent member of the club, recalled that white teammates during the 1950s frequently made anti-Semitic comments about the Dodgers' two Jewish players, Cal Abrams and Sandy Koufax, within earshot of the black players in the locker room and on the field. Hearing players spouting epithets like "Jew son of a bitch" was as objectionable to Newcombe as listening to their racist, anti-black comments. In fact, the Dodgers' African American players, including Robinson, Newcombe, and Roy Campanella, provided support for the Jewish players as they experienced this harassment.[74] Abrams himself maintained that his playing time was reduced because of Brooklyn manager Chuck Dressen's anti-Semitism, and Koufax stated that Walter Alston, who succeeded Dressen as manager, delayed making him a starter because he was Jewish. Abrams's son claimed that there were times when his father, because he was a Jew, was told that there was no room for him on the team bus, and that he had to ride instead in a station wagon with the equipment man.[75] In 1949 bench jockeys targeted Jewish outfielder Sid Gordon of the New York Giants with such vicious anti-Semitic epithets that the Anti-Defamation League asked all sixteen major league clubs whether they had any regulations prohibiting prejudiced conduct by players A *New York Post* editorial condemned the St. Louis Cardinals for "their personal comments on Sid Gordon's religion."[76] When Cardinal infielder Solly Hemus would get a scratch hit in the 1950s off Warren Spahn or Lew Burdette of the Braves, the all-star pitchers, believing mistakenly that he was Jewish, screamed at him, "Hemus, that's a goddamn cheap Jew hit and you're a goddamn Jew hitter!"[77]

Anti-Semitic taunts precipitated physical confrontations on the diamond into the 1950s. Cleveland slugger Al Rosen responded combatively to such insults on numerous occasions during that decade, challenging an opposing player who had "slurred [his] religion" to fight him under the stands. When a Red Sox catcher called Rosen anti-Semitic names, he called time and "started toward him, to take him on." Hank Greenberg recalled that Rosen "want[ed] to go into the stands and murder" fans who hurled anti-Semitic insults at him. Rosen, who grew up in a Miami neighborhood where Gentile youth called out to him, "Lookit the Jewboy. Go home and eat yuh matzos, sheeny," had taken boxing lessons to defend himself. His "Jewish education was measured in jabs and hooks."[78]

Even Jews wealthy enough to purchase a major league club suffered anti-Semitic abuse from the other owners, who viewed them as socially unacceptable. Nate Dolin, part of the group that bought the Cleveland Indians in 1949, recalled, "We were just about the first Jewish owners in baseball." (Andrew Freedman and Barney Dreyfuss, both of German Jewish background, had owned major league clubs in the early twentieth century). Dolin emphasized that fellow owners subjected his group to "a lot of anti-Semitism." The Cleveland group was barred from the other owners' private clubs, where important meetings were held, and sometimes were excluded from their hotels. Mary Jo DeCicco, who later married Hank Greenberg, recalled that New York Yankees owners Dan Topping and Del Webb, and their general manager George Weiss, made an impression by uttering anti-Semitic comments when she and her first husband were their guests at the 1955 World Series.[79]

Jews rallied behind Jackie Robinson during his rookie season in 1947, when he suffered unprecedented abuse from opposing players and fans and hostility from many of his teammates. Bill Veeck, owner of the Cleveland Indians, the first American League club to desegregate, noted that Brooklyn was the "ideal place" in which to break baseball's color line because it was more hospitable to African Americans than any other city. Not coincidentally, Jews constituted about 40 percent of Brooklyn's population, the highest proportion of any place with a major league club. As Robinson's most recent biographer, Arnold Rampersad, observes, "Jews were…far more ready than any other major group…to identify with the fight against Jim Crow." When the Philadelphia Phillies visited Brooklyn in late April, their manager Ben Chapman, an Alabaman, ordered his players to harass Robinson with a barrage of racial insults so venomous that he came close to a nervous breakdown. Robinson recalled that the Phillies hurled at him "the worst garbage I ever heard in my whole life, counting the streets, counting the army."[80]

The response of Jews in the press was strikingly different from that of non-Jewish editors and reporters, who generally responded with what Roger Kahn described as "belligerent neutrality." The *Sporting News,* for example, accepted Chapman's explanation that aggressive bench jockeying was routine in the major leagues, and that Robinson had been treated no differently from any opposing player. It reported that the Phillies had been inundated with "an avalanche of letters and telephone calls…commending Chapman for his fair stand toward Robinson."[81] But when Walter Winchell learned of the Phillies' conduct, he announced at the Stork Club that he would "use [his] column to get Chapman out of baseball," and that "I'll nail him on my radio show too." He vowed to "make a *big hit* on that *bigot.*"[82] Robinson himself believed that Winchell's immediate denunciation of Chapman on his radio broadcast and in his syndicated newspaper column had strongly influenced Commissioner Happy Chandler's decision to warn the Phillies not to use racial epithets against him in future bench jockeying.[83]

Jewish newspapers quickly exposed the connection between Chapman's racism and anti-Semitism. As a New York Yankee player in the 1930s, Chapman earned a reputation for shouting anti-Semitic insults at Jewish fans, holding his hand over his nose to indicate Jews. He nearly sparked a riot in 1933 when he slid into the Washington Senator's Jewish second baseman Buddy Myer and, according to Shirley Povich, "cut a swastika with his spikes on Myer's thigh." Soon after Chapman ordered the attack on Robinson, the Philadelphia *Jewish Exponent* noted that he had hurled anti-Semitic insults at the Polo Grounds at a Jewish GI who had lost a leg in combat.[84]

The most dramatic display of Jewish solidarity with Jackie Robinson came from Hank Greenberg. The legendary Detroit Tiger slugger who hit 58 home runs in 1938, then with the Pittsburgh Pirates in his last season, was the first opposing player to offer Robinson encouragement. Probably no major leaguer before Robinson had been more abused by opposing players and fans than Greenberg, who was continually taunted for being Jewish.

On May 15, 1947, in a game between the Pirates and the Dodgers, Robinson laid down a perfect bunt and streaked down the line to first. The pitcher's throw pulled first baseman Greenberg off the bag. Reaching for the throw, he collided with Robinson, who was able to get up and reach second. The next inning Greenberg walked, and asked Robinson, who was playing first base, if he had been hurt in the collision. Assured by Robinson that he hadn't been, Greenberg said to him, "Don't pay any attention to these guys who are trying to make it hard for you. Stick in there….I hope you and I can get together for a talk. There are a few things I've learned down through the years that might help you and make it easier."[85]

Greenberg's support deeply moved Robinson and was widely praised in the African American press. Jackie told the *New York Times*, "Class tells. It sticks out all over Mr. Greenberg."[86] Although Robinson suffered harassment unparalleled in baseball history, he recognized a kinship with what he called the "racial trouble" that Greenberg had also experienced.[87] The Pittsburgh *Courier* reported that the Jewish slugger, who "many times…had [had] to close his ears when they hurled racial epithets at him from the opposing bench," definitely "understands Jackie's problems." The Baltimore *Afro-American* informed its readers that Greenberg, as "a Jew," was well-qualified to advise Robinson: "The more pressure you're under, the better ball player you'll become—I know."[88]

African American sportswriter Wendell Smith suggested that, had the collision involved a player other than Greenberg, it might have sparked a riot. One has to remember the unprovoked spiking attacks on Robinson by Cardinals Joe Medwick and Enos Slaughter during the 1947 season, and the apoplectic reaction a few years later when Robinson, for sliding into a Giant to retaliate for a beanball, was called "a Hitler" by shortstop Alvin Dark.[89] Playing first base that rookie season, Robinson probably developed "the quickest

Hank Greenberg in a rare photograph of him in his Pittsburgh Pirates uniform.

National Baseball Hall of Fame Library Cooperstown, N.Y.

foot in the history of baseball," being well aware that he had to remove it immediately after tagging the bag to avoid spikings.[90]

In his autobiography, Greenberg emphasized his strong admiration for Robinson, coupled with disgust at the racist behavior of his teammates: "Here were our guys, a bunch of ignorant, stupid Southerners who couldn't speak properly...and all they could do was make jokes about Jackie. They couldn't recognize that they had a special person in front of them." Greenberg also recognized differences as well as similarities between his experience and Robinson's: "Jackie had it tough, tougher than any player who ever lived. I identified with Jackie Robinson. I had feelings for him because they had treated me the same way. Not as bad, but they made remarks about my being a sheenie and a Jew all the time."[91]

The strong encouragement and support from Hank Greenberg came at a particularly important time for Jackie Robinson. On May 9, six days before, Stan Woodward, sports editor of the New York *Herald Tribune,* had broken the story that the St. Louis Cardinals, acting in collusion with two Brooklyn players, had planned to strike rather than play against a Dodgers team that included Robinson.[92] The same day Brooklyn management informed the press about several death threats Robinson had received in the mail directed both at him and his wife, along with threats to kidnap his infant son Jackie, Jr. As a result, two police department detectives were accompanying him home each day.[93] To make matters worse, several of the Philadelphia Phillies, whom the Dodgers played May 9-11, sat in their dugout during the games pointing bats at Robinson, to simulate guns and remind him of the death threats, and made machine gun-like noises. Chapman had also informed his pitchers that he would fine them $50 if they had two strikes on Robinson early in the count and did not throw at him. The Benjamin Franklin Hotel, where the Dodgers had stayed for several years when playing in Philadelphia, refused to admit Robinson, and he was forced to find other quarters. And on May 13 in Cincinnati, the Crosley Field organist had openly mocked Robinson by playing "Bye, Bye, Blackbird" at the end of the Dodgers–Reds game, as the players walked off the field. Robinson was only just beginning to pull out of a slump that had dropped his batting average to .238 on May 9.[94]

Robinson's sister, Willa Mae Robinson Walker, recalled the horror Robinson and his family experienced during that time in an interview with journalist Maury Allen, and said that Jackie "talked about quitting": "In those early days in Brooklyn he got so much hate mail and so many threats on his life....and we worried all the time about him....The phone would ring and we would be afraid to pick it up. We used to think it would be a call from somebody saying Jackie was dead."[95] Nor was Robinson receiving much emotional support from his teammates. Jimmy Cannon of the *New York Post* noted: "In the clubhouse Robinson is a stranger...it is obvious he is isolated by those with whom he plays...Robinson never is part of the jovial and aimless banter of the locker room. He is the loneliest man I have ever seen in sports."[96] It is obvious, then, how important, and how moving, it was for Robinson when Hank Greenberg reached out to him and offered such warm words of encouragement.

Surprisingly, this highly important conversation in Pittsburgh between Greenberg and Robinson has been almost entirely ignored by Robinson's biographers and other scholars of the desegregation of baseball. Only Jackie Robinson and Hank Greenberg give it significant attention—Robinson in his 1948 autobiography written with Wendell Smith, and Greenberg in his autobiography, edited by Ira Berkow and published in 1989 after his death. Carl Rowan's 1960 biography of Robinson does not mention the encounter. David Falkner's very brief description in his 1995 biography says only that Greenberg had "endured his own trials"; it does not explicitly mention anti-Semitism, nor the impact Greenberg's support had on Robinson. Jules Tygiel, in his *Baseball's Great Experiment: Jackie Robinson and his Legacy* (1983), a highly valuable study of baseball's desegregation process, states only that Robinson "publicly thanked opposing players, like Hank Greenberg and Frank Gustine, who welcomed him into the league."[97] This fails to convey the significance of Greenberg's contribution in helping Robinson, or to note that Jackie recognized similarities between African American and Jewish suffering. Robinson did say in his 1948 autobiography, after all, that "I felt sure that he understood my problems." And Gustine's "welcome" was hardly as important as Greenberg's; he merely told Robinson that Pirate hurler Fritz Ostermueller, who hit Jackie with a pitch, had not done so deliberately.[98]

Greenberg noted that Robinson and he "always were friends" after their May 15, 1947, encounter at first base, even though their contacts were necessarily reduced when Greenberg moved back to the American League to become general manager of the Cleveland Indians following his retirement as a player after the 1947 season. The Cleveland press frequently criticized Greenberg during his years as general manager (1949-57) for placing too many blacks on the Indians, more than any other American League team. Greenberg also desegregated the Texas League in 1952, when he assigned an African American player to Cleveland's Dallas farm club. His determination in the front office to promote desegregation was undoubtedly influenced by the anti-Semitism he experienced in baseball. Prejudiced against both African Americans and Jews, Cleveland's sportswriters denounced Greenberg for replacing "nice Catholic boy[s]" Bob Kennedy and Kenny Keltner with Harry Simpson, a black, and Al Rosen, a Jew; even though the latter two were the superior ballplayers, the fans "rode [Greenberg] terribly." Having experienced exclusion himself, Greenberg instructed Cleveland's traveling secretary to inform hotels that had refused to admit the team's African American players that they would have to take all the Indians' players, or none at all. Even as Cleveland's general manager, Greenberg had been denied admittance in Phoenix to the hotel where American League clubs were staying for their winter meetings, because he was Jewish.[99]

Jackie Robinson throughout his playing career, and after his retirement, enjoyed the strong support and friendship of many Jews, and he deeply appreciated Jews' important contributions to the civil rights movement. Roger Kahn recalled that most sportswriters during the 1950s considered Robinson "uppity" because "he exuded an air of complete independence," which "was not acceptable in a Negro." But Kahn shared Robinson's outrage at the sports-writers' complaints, and the two men became "fast friends," who joined in denouncing baseball's slow pace of desegregation. Robinson also developed a close friendship and working association with Jewish sportswriter Milton Gross of the *New York Post*. Gross assisted Robinson in writing an article entitled "Why Can't I Manage in the Majors?" directly challenging a color bar the major leagues maintained long after they admitted African Americans as players. In his *Post* column, Gross also urged the Dodgers to hire Robinson as a television announcer after his retirement.[100]

Robinson's biographer Arnold Rampersad notes that "the Robinsons found Jews far more ready than other whites to accept them socially." The Robinsons' closest friends in Montreal during the critical year of 1946, when Jackie first broke into organized baseball, were a Jewish couple, sportswriter Sam Maltin and his wife Belle. Another Jewish couple, the Satlows, welcomed the Robinsons to Flatbush in 1948, and became lifelong friends. The Robinsons were also close to many other Jews, including Dodgers broadcaster Andre Baruch and his wife Bea, broadcaster Howard Cosell and his family, and Frank Schiffman, whose Apollo Theater in Harlem became for Robinson during his retirement "almost his private uptown office." Grossinger's became the Robinsons' favorite family resort during the 1950s.[101]

Robinson also received important assistance from Jewish businessmen. When the Robinsons decided to move to Connecticut in the mid-1950s, they discovered that the banks were "dead set against" providing them with a loan to build a house; they finally obtained one from a bank operated by two Jewish brothers. Robinson forged close relationships with Jewish businessmen who supported the Freedom National Bank, of which he was chairman of the board—an African American owned and operated commercial bank that tried to stimulate economic development in Harlem—and the Jackie Robinson Construction Company, which built low-cost housing.[102]

Just as Jews had been in the front lines for him when he broke baseball's color line, Robinson, who became an important civil rights activist after his retirement as a player gave considerable support to Jewish causes, while urging African American civil rights groups to join Jewish organizations in a coalition similar to that promoted by the intergroup relations movement of the late 1940s. Robinson's widow recalled in her recently published book *Jackie Robinson: An Intimate Portrait* that "Jack believed that positive relations between blacks and Jews were critical to both." Robinson gave his support to the United Jewish Appeal and raised money for the state of Israel.[103] When Kivie Kaplan, a Jew, became president of the NAACP in 1966, Robinson told him, "No man deserves [the office] more."[104] Even as a player, Robinson became highly interested in the Anti Defamation League's campaign against anti-Semitism, and was determined to apply its techniques in combating anti-black racism. He sought out ADL leader Arnold Forster, and "asked [him] searching questions about fighting anti-Semitism." Forster recalled that in the ensuing years, Robinson "helped intensify [the ADL's] cooperative relationship with black civil rights groups."[105]

Robinson's breaking of baseball's color line in 1947, one of the most important civil rights advances of the first half of the twentieth century, benefited very significantly from such Jewish cooperation and support.

Notes

1. Martin Duberman, *Paul Robeson* (New York: Alfred A. Knopf, 1988), p. 305; Robert J. Donovan, *Conflict and Crisis: The Presidency of Harry S. Truman, 1945-1948* (New York: W. W. Norton, 1977), p. 244; "Greenville Jurors Allow Twenty-Eight Confessed Lynch Murderers to Go Free; Trial Judge Displays His Disgust," New York *Age,* May 31, 1947 (quote).

2. Bernard Wasserstein, *Vanishing Diaspora: The Jews in Europe Since 1945* (Cambridge, Mass.: Harvard University Press, 1996), p. 24.

3. "British Ram Runner; 1500 Jews Aboard," New York *Herald Tribune,* May 18, 1947; Editorial," Chicago *Defender,* May 24, 1947.

4. Clayborne Carson, "Blacks and Jews in the Civil Rights Movement" in Joseph R. Washington, Jr., ed., *Jews in Black Perspectives* (Teaneck, N.J.: Fairleigh Dickinson University Press, 1984), pp. 113-17 and Carson, "Blacks and Jews in the Civil Rights Movement: The Case of SNCC" in Jack Salzman et al., eds., *Bridges and Boundaries: African Americans and American Jews* (New York: George Braziller and The Jewish Museum, 1992), pp. 36-39; David Levering Lewis, "Shortcuts to the Mainstream: Afro-American and Jewish Notables in the 1920s and 1930s" in Washington, ed., *Jews in Black Perspectives,* p. 84; Murray Friedman, *What Went Wrong?: The Creation and Collapse of the Black-Jewish Alliance* (New York: The Free Press, 1995), p.8.

5. Leonard Dinnerstein, *Anti-Semitism in America* (New York: Oxford University Press, 1994), p. 208.

6. Howard M. Sachar, *A History of the Jews in America* (New York: Vintage Books, 1993), p. 802; Hasia Diner, *In The Almost Promised Land: American Jews and Blacks, 1915-1935* (Baltimore: The Johns Hopkins University Press, 1995), pp. 168, 175.

7. Julian Bond, "Forward" in Adam Fairclough, ed., *The Star Creek Papers* (Athens: University of Georgia Press, 1997), pp. viii-ix.

8. Diner, *In The Almost Promised Land,* p. 168.

9. Murray Friedman, *What Went Wrong?,* p. 43.

10. Ibid., p. 45.

11. Ibid., p. 48; Nancy Weiss, "Long Distance Runners of the Civil Rights Movement: The Contribution of Jews to the NAACP and the National Urban League in the Early Twentieth Century" in Jack Salzman and Cornel West, eds., *Struggles in the Promised Land: Toward A History of Black-Jewish Relations in the United States* (New York: Oxford University Press, 1997), pp. 132 (quotes), 135-37; Diner, *Promised Land,* pp. 125, 127, 133; B. Joyce Ross, *J.E. Spingarn and the Rise of the NAACP 1911-1939* (New York: Atheneum, 1972), pp. 85-97.

12. Nancy Weiss, *The National Urban League, 1910-1940* (New York: Oxford University Press, 1974), pp. 53-54; Diner, *Promised Land,* p. 185; Sachar, *Jews in America,* p. 803; Friedman, *What Went Wrong?,* p. 48.

13. Friedman, *What Went Wrong?,* pp. 99-100; Diner, *Promised Land,* pp. 42, 98; Dan Carter, *Scottsboro: A Tragedy of the American South* (Baton Rouge: Louisiana State University Press, 1979), p. 235 (quote).

14. Friedman, *What Went Wrong?,* p. 59.

15. Diner, *Promised Land,* pp. 199-202.

16. Friedman, *What Went Wrong?,* p. 131; Dinnerstein, *Anti-Semitism,* p. 158; Diner, *Promised Land,* p. 229.

17. Letty Cottin Pogrebin, *Deborah, Golda, and Me: Being Female and Jewish in America* (New York: Anchor Books, 1992), pp. 112-13; Diner, *Promised Land,* p. 125 (quote).

18. Jack Newfield, "An Interview With Mario Cuomo," *Tikkun,* May/June 1998, pp. 21-22.

19. Diner, *Promised Land,* pp. 43, 75; Lewis, "Shortcuts to the Mainstream" in Washington, ed., *Jews in Black Perspectives,* p. 84 (quote).

20. See, for example, Jules Tygiel, *Baseball's Great Experiment: Jackie Robinson and His Legacy* (New York: Vintage Books, 1984), pp. 36-37; Mark Naison, "Lefties and Righties: The Communist Party

and Sports During the Great Depression" in Donald Spivey, ed., *Sport in America: New Historical Perspectives* (Westport, Conn.: Greenwood Press, 1985), pp. 129-44; Kelly Elaine Rusinack, "Baseball on the Radical Agenda: The *Daily* and *Sunday Worker* on the Desegregation of Major League Baseball, 1933 to 1947," MA, thesis, Clemson University, 1995.

21. Tygiel's *Baseball's Great Experiment*, for example, the principal scholarly study of the desegregation of baseball, devotes considerable attention to the campaign of African-American sportswriters and the Communist Party (although not Jews in it) against baseball's color line, but ignores the Jewish role in desegregating baseball. The principal biographies of Jackie Robinson, Carl Rowan's *Wait Till Next Year. The Life Story of Jackie Robinson* (New York: Random House, 1960); David Falkner's *Great Time Coming: The Life of Jackie Robinson From Baseball to Birmingham* (New York: Simon & Schuster, 1995); and Arnold Rampersad's *Jackie Robinson: A Biography* (New York: Alfred A. Knopf 1997), also give little or no attention to the Jewish role, although Rampersad does discuss the importance of Robinson's friendships and business contacts with Jews.

22. Paul Buhle and Michael Femanowsky, "Baseball and Social Conscience: An Interview with Lester Rodney," 1981, pp. 3-4, UCLA Oral History Program, University of California at Los Angeles Library.

23. Joe Gerstein, "Anti-Semitism in Baseball," *Jewish Life*, July 1952, p. 22.

24. Mark Naison, *Communists in Harlem During the Depression* (Urbana: University of Illinois Press, 1983), pp. 322-24.

25. Ibid., pp. 322-24 (quote p. 324). Jewish Communists sometimes deferred their own political aspirations to advance black empowerment. In 1943, Adam Clayton Powell's election to Congress would have left the New York City Council without black representation. To prevent this, Carl Brodsky withdrew as a candidate in favor of Ben Davis, Jr., because, "As a member of the Jewish people I can appreciate what it means not to have the great Negro minority represented." Gerald Horne, "Black, White, and Red: Jewish [sic] and African Americans in the Communist Party" in Marla Brettschneider, ed., *The Narrow Bridge: Jewish Views on Multiculturalism* (New Brunswick, N. J.: Rutgers University Press, 1996), p. 127.

26. Stuart Svonkin, *Jews Against Prejudice: American Jews and the Fight for Civil Liberties* (New York: Columbia University Press, 1997), p. 18.

27. Dinnerstein, *Anti-Semitism in America*, pp. 84-93; Deborah Dash Moore, *To the Golden Cities: Pursuing the American Jewish Dream in Miami and LA.* (Cambridge, Mass.: Harvard University Press, 1994), pp. 154, 163-64, 308.

28. Ellen H. Posner, "Anti-Jewish Agitation' in *American Jewish Yearbook* (Philadelphia Jewish Publication Society of America, 1946), p. 172; Charles Herbert Stember and Others, *Jews in the Mind of America* (New York: Basic Books, 1966), p. 9; Glen Jeansonne, *Gerald L.K. Smith: Minister of Hate* (New Haven, Ct.: Yale University Press, 1988), p. 94.

29. Posner, "Anti-Jewish Agitation," *American Jewish Yearbook*, p. 128 (first quote), p. 133 (second quote), p. 134.

30. Posner, "Anti-Jewish Agitation," *American Jewish Yearbook* (1946), pp. 172-73; Svonkin, *Jews Against Prejudice*, pp. 13-14; Jonathan Kaufman, *Broken Alliance: The Turbulent Times Between Black and Jews in America* (New York: New American Library, 1988), p. 89.

31. Posner, "Anti-Jewish Agitation," American *Jewish Yearbook* (1946), p. 191 (first quote); Moore, *To The Golden Cities*, pp. 154, 177 (second quote); Arnold Forster, *Square One* (New York: Donald I. Fine, 1988), p. 97; Melissa Fay Greene, *The Temple Bombing* (Reading, Mass.: Addison Wesley, 1996), pp. 33-34; "Another Mississippi Statesman," *Washington News Letter*, Washington, D.C. office, Anti-Defamation League, [hereafter ADL] Papers, American Jewish Archives, Cincinnati, Ohio; Sachar, *A History of the Jews*, p. 621.

32. Svonkin, *Jews Against Prejudice*, pp. 43, 48, 88-90; Lawrence H. Fuchs, *The Political Behavior of American Jews* (Giencoe, Ill.: The Free Press, 1956), p. 108; Naomi W. Cohen, *Not Free to Desist: The American Jewish Committee, 1906-1966* (Philadelphia The Jewish Publication Society of America, 1972), pp. 385-87.

33. See, for example, Pittsburgh *Courier*, May 17, 1947; Chicago *Defender*, May 17, 1947; "Wendell Smith" in Jerome Holtzman, ed., *No Cheering in the Press Box* (New York Henry Holt, 1995), p. 317.

34. Tygiel, *Baseball's Great Experiment* p. 36; Jackie Robinson as told to Alfred Duckett, *I Never Had It Made: An Autobiography* (Hopewell, N. J.: The Ecco Press, 1995 [1972]), p. 32 (quotes).

35. Tygiel, *Baseball's Great Experiment*, p. 80; Dan W. Dodson, "The Integration of Negroes in Baseball" in Jules Tygiel, ed., *The Jackie Robinson Reader* (New York: Dutton, 1997), p. 158 (quote).

36. Tygiel, *Baseball's Great Experiment* p. 286.

37. David Q. Voigt, "From Chadwick to the Chipmunks," *Journal of American Culture* 7 (Fall 1984): pp.31-37 Forster, *Square One*, pp. 57,94-95; Neal Gabler, *Winchell: Gossip, Power, and the Culture of Celebrity* (New York: Alfred A. Knopf 1994), pp. xi, 377.

38. Gabler, *Winchell*, pp.3, 9-10, 195 (first and second quotes), 196 (third quote).

39. See, for example, *ADL Press Digest*, January 13 and July 16,1947, reel 2774, ADL Papers; Gabler, *Winchell*, pp. 196-97, 294; Forster, *Square One*, pp. 58, 95.

40. Gabler, *Winchell*, pp. 296 (first quote), 333 (second quote), 385; *ADL Press Digest*, January, 1947, reel 2774, ADL Papers (third quote). Mississippi Senator Theodore Bilbo chimed in with a letter to Winchell calling him a "limicolous liar and notorious scandalizing hike." Edward Shapiro, "Anti-Semitism Mississippi Style" in David A. Gerber, ed., *Anti-Semitism in American History* (Urbana: University of Illinois Press, 1986), p. 143.

41. Gabler, *Winchell*, p. 409.

42. Rampersad, Jackie Robinson, p. 266 (first three quotes); "Negro Freedom Rally," *New York Age*, May 17, 1947.

43. "Terry Moore, Marty Marion and Two Dodgers Accused," Chicago *Defender*, May 17, 1947.

44. Holtzman, ed., *No Cheering*, pp. 114, 116, 117 (quotes).

45. James C. Kaufman, "Shirley Povich" in Richard Orodenker, ed., *Dictionary of Literary Biography—Volume 171, Twentieth Century American Sportswriters* (Detroit and Washington, D.C.: Bruccoli Clark Layman, 1996), pp. 277-78.

46. Shirley Povich, *All These Mornings* (Englewood Cliffs, N.J.: Prentice-Hall, 1969), pp. 88 (quote), 128, 133.

47. Ron Fimrite, "Sam Lacy: Black Crusader," *Sports Illustrated*, October 10, 1990, p. 93; "Sam Lacy" in Orodenker, ed., *Twentieth Century Sportswriters*, p. 177.

48. Roger Kahn, *Memories of Summer: When Baseball Was an Art, and Writing About it a Game* (New York: Hyperion, 1997), pp. 35, 40 (quotes); Roger Kahn, *The Passionate People. What It Means to be a Jew in America* (New York: William Morrow & Co, 1968).

49. Kahn, *Memories*, pp. 98 (first quote), 147, 207 (second quote).

50. Rampersad, *Jackie Robinson*, p. 271; Tygiel, *Baseball's Great Experiment*, pp. 208, 327; Roger Kahn, *The Era, 1947-1957: When the Yankees, the Giants, and the Dodgers Ruled the World* (New York: Ticknor & Fields, 1993), p. 206 (quote); Roger Kahn, *The Boys of Summer* (New York: Harper & Row, 1971), p. 400.

51. Clif Keane, "Robinson's Day With Sox Told: Muchnick Recounts Tryout Arrangement," *Boston Globe*, April 29, 1959; Glenn Stout and Dick Johnson, eds., *Jackie Robinson: Between the Baselines* (San Francisco: Woodford Press, nd.), p. 38 (quote).

52. Isadore Muchnick, Obituary, *Boston Globe*, September 16, 1963; Jordan Muchnick (nephew of Isadore Muchnick), telephone interview June 5, 1997; "Isadore Harry Yaver Muchnick" in *25th Anniversary Class Report, Harvard College Class of 1928* (1953), p. 772 (quote) in Pusey Library, Harvard University Cambridge, Mass. On "Jewish Ward 14" see Charles H. Trout, *Boston: The Great Depression and the New Deal* (New York: Oxford University Press, 1977), pp. 41, 47, 299.

53. Jordan Muchnick, telephone interview; David Muchnick (son of Isadore Muchnick), telephone interview, June 4, 1997.

54. Holtzman, *No Cheering*, p. 318 (first quote); Povich, *All These Mornings*, p. 132 (second quote); Shirley Povich, telephone interview, June 5, 1997; Tygiel, *Baseball's Great Experiment*, p. 43 (third quote); David K. Wiggins, "Wendell Smith, The Pittsburgh *Courier-Journal* and the Campaign to Include Blacks in Organized Baseball, 1933-1945," *Journal of Sport History* 10 (Summer 1983): 25 (fourth quote); Rampersad, *Jackie Robinson*, p. 119 (fifth quote). Smith's inaccurate account continues to be repeated by sportswriters. See, for example, Larry Whiteside, "They Tried, But Had No Chance," *Boston Globe*, March 28, 1997.

55. "Total and Non-White Population of Boston's Ward 14 as of 1950 by Census Tract," 1950 U.S. Census of Population, Boston, Mass. Census Tracts, Bureau of the Census, U.S. Department of Commerce; David Muchnick, telephone interview; "Isadore Harry Yaver Muchnick" in *25th*

Anniversary Class Report, Harvard College Class of 1928, p. 772; Yona Ginsberg, *Jews in a Changing Neighborhood: The Study of Mattapan* (New York: The Free Press, 1975), p. 29; Hillel Levine and Lawrence Harmon, *The Death of an American Jewish Community: A Tragedy of Good Intentions* (New York: The Free Press, 1992), pp. 194-224.

56. Wendell Smith, "The Sports Beat," Pittsburgh *Courier,* April 26, 1947.

57. Ibid. (quote); Keane, "Robinson's Day With Sox Told," *Boston Globe,* April 29, 1959; David Muchnick, telephone interview. Autobiographical inscription from copy in possession of Isadore Muchnick's daughter, Fran Muchnick Goldstein. Isadore Muchnick later said about the tryout, "You never saw anyone hit the wall the way Robinson did that day." Stout and Johnson, eds., *Jackie Robinson: Between the Baselines,* p. 40.

58. Bruce Kuklick, *To Every Thing A Season: Shibe Park and Urban Philadelphia* (Princeton, N.J.: Princeton University Press, 1991), p. 146 (quote); Povich, *All These Mornings,* pp. 129-30.

59. Branch Rickey to Alfred A. Knopf May 9, 1956, box 14, Frank Tannenbaum Papers, Rare Book and Manuscript Library, Columbia University, New York, N.Y. (quotes); Obituary of Frank Tannenbaum, *New York Times,* June 2, 1969, and death notices, June 3, 1969.

60. Frank Tannenbaum, *Slave & Citizen* (New York: Vintage Books, 1946), pp. 127-28 (first three quotes); Rickey to Knopf May 9, 1956 (fourth quote), Branch Rickey to Frank Tannenbaum, January 23, 1963, box 14, Tannenbaum Papers.

61. "A Story and a Question: II," *Adirondack Enterprise* (Saranac Lake, N.Y.), June 6, 1969 (first quote); Frank Tannenbaum to Branch Rickey, May 18, 1956 (second quote); Jackie Robinson to Frank Tannenbaum, May 31, 1961; and Alice H. Maier to Jackie Robinson, July 18, 1969, box 14, Tannenbaum Papers.

62. On the campaign to boycott the 1936 Olympics see Richard D. Mandell, *The Nazi Olympics* (Urbana: University of Illinois Press, 1987), pp. 69-82 and Peter Levine, *From Ellis Island to Ebbets Field: Sport and the American Jewish Experience* (New York: Oxford University Press, 1992), pp. 185, 219-21. The Nazis used the medal results to claim the superiority of fascism over democracy. Germany accumulated more points than the United States, Italy more than France, and Japan far more than Britain. Mandell, *Nazi Olympics,* p. 280.

63. Chris Mead, *Champion. Joe Louis, Black Hero in White America* (New York: Charles Scribner's Sons, 1985), pp. 133-34.

64. Levine, *Ellis Island to Ebbets Field,* pp. 177-81 (first quote from p. 178, second from p. 180); Jeffrey Sammons, *Beyond the Ring: The Role of Boxing in American Society* (Urbana: University of Illinois Press, 1988), p. 106 (third quote). Max Baer, the son of a Jewish father and a non-Jewish mother, identified strongly as a Jew. The public, boxing promoters, and the press, including the Jewish press, considered him a Jew. Baer resented charges that he was not a Jew, pointing out that Adolf Hitler and the Nazi party viewed him as Jewish. Baer claimed to be "the first *bona fide* heavyweight champion of the Hebrew race." He is included in the *Encyclopedia Judaica*. Levine, *Ellis Island to Ebbets Field,* p. 182 (quote); Sammons, *Beyond the Ring,* p. 91; "Max Baer," *Encyclopedia Judaica,* Volume 4 (Jerusalem, Israel: Kerr Publishing House, Ltd., 1973), p. 79.

65. Turner Lippe, sparring partner and friend of Jewish boxing great Abe Attell, world featherweight champion from 1901 to 1912, recalled opposing cornermen at Attell's fights frequently yelling for their fighter to "Kill the Jew bastard!" Telephone interview, December 1986. On the Jewish boxer as avenger of American Jews beaten and taunted by anti-Semites, see Ken Blady, *The Jewish Boxers' Hall of Fame* (New York: Shapolsky Publishers, 1988), pp. 29-30, 52-53, 111-13.

66. Kaufman, *Broken Alliance,* pp. 83-84.

67. Levine, *Ellis Island to Ebbets Field,* pp. 240-41 (first quote); Eric Solomon, "Jews and Baseball: A Cultural Love Story" in George Eisen and David K. Wiggins, eds., *Ethnicity and Sport in North American History and Culture* (Westport, Conn.: Praeger, 1995), pp. 75-101; Carl Prince, *Brooklyn's Dodgers: The Bums, the Borough, and the Best of Baseball* (New York: Oxford University Press, 1996), pp. 42-44; Eric J. Greenberg, "From Prague to Park Slope," *Jewish Week,* May 9, 1997; Irv Saposnik, "To Brooklyn: Again and Again," *Jewish Currents,* January 1993, pp. 9-10 (second quote).

68. Hank Greenberg, *The Story of My Life,* ed. by Ira Berkow (New York: Times Books, 1989), p. 116.

69. Ibid., pp. 82-84; Tygiel, *Baseball's Great Experiment,* p. 182.

70. Ira Berkow, "Introduction," Greenberg, *Story of My Life,* p. xv.

71. Greenberg, *Story of My Life*, p. 104; Haskell Cohen, "In Sports," *Jewish Exponent* [Philadelphia], October 3, 1947 (quotes).

72. Greenberg, *Story of My Life*, p 117 (Quote); William M. Simons, "The Athlete As Jewish Standard Bearer: Media Images of Hank Greenberg," *Jewish Social Studies* (Spring 1982): 107; Ralph Kiner, "Unforgettable Hank Greenberg," *Reader's Digest*, October 1988, p.85.

73. Levine, *Ellis Island to Ebbets Field*, pp. 135-37; Kiner, "Unforgettable," *Reader's Digest*, p. 85; Aviva Kempner, "The Game Came Second," *Washington Post*, September 18, 1994; Greenberg, *Story of My Life*, p. 57.

74. Don Newcombe, telephone interview, June 5, 1997. In his autobiography Sandy Koufax describes Newcombe as good-natured and helpful to him during his difficult years as a "bonus baby" in Brooklyn. Sandy Koufax with Ed Linn, *Koufax* (New York: The Viking Press, 1966), p. 89.

75. Elli Wohlgeterneter, "Interview: Calvin R. Abrams and May Abrams," *American Jewish History* 83 (March 1995): pp. 114-15; Peter Golenbock, *Bums: An Oral History of the Brooklyn Dodgers* (New York: G. P. Putnam's Sons, 1984), pp. 263, 266-67; Harvey Araton, "A Dodger Who Faced Barriers, Too," *New York Times*, March 1, 1997; Kahn, *The Era*, pp. 327-28.

76. Arnold Forster, *A Measure of Freedom* (Garden City, N.Y.: Doubleday, 1950), pp. 168-69.

77. David Halberstam, *October 1964* (New York: Villard Books, 1994), p. 110. Even as late as 1977 Reggie Jackson witnessed Yankee manager Billy Martin and several Yankee players, including stars Thurman Munson, Sparky Lyle, and Graig Nettles hurling anti-Semitic insults at teammate Ken Holtzman; in his autobiography Jackson quotes Nettles publicly denouncing a reporter as a "Jew cocksucker." Stephen H. Norwood, "My Son the Slugger: Sport and the American Jew," *Reviews in American History* 21 (September 1993): p. 470.

78. Harold U. Ribalow and Meir Z. Ribalow, *The Jew in American Sports* (New York: Hippocrene Books, 1966), p. 44 (first quote); Roger Kahn, *How the Weather Was* (New York: Harper & Row, 1973), pp. 75, 76 (fourth and fifth quotes), 78 (second quote); Greenberg, *Story of My Life*, p 218 (third quote).

79. Greenberg, *Story of My Life*, p 208 (quotes), 254; David A. Rausch, *Friends, Colleagues, and Neighbors: Jewish Contributions to American History* (Grand Rapids, Mich.: Baker Books, 1996), p. 116.

80. Bill Veeck with Ed Linn, *Veeck As In Wreck: The Autobiography of Bill Veeck* (New York: Simon and Schuster, 1962), p. 175 (first quote); Rampersad, *Jackie Robinson*, pp. 220-21 (second quote); Tygiel, *Baseball's Great Experiment*, pp. 182-83; Haskell Cohen, "In Sports," *Jewish Exponent*, June 20, 1947; Roger Kahn, "We Doan Need No Niggers Here" in Richard Orodenker, ed., *The Phillies Reader* (Philadelphia: Temple University Press, 1996), p. 58 (third quote); Percentage of Jews in Brooklyn's population is calculated from Isaac Landman, ed., *The Universal Jewish Encyclopedia in Ten Volumes* (New York: Universal Jewish Encyclopedia Corp., 1948), Vol. 2, p. 544; *American Jewish Yearbook* (1955), and Population Division of the U.S. Census Bureau, 1940 and 1950.

81. Kahn, "We Doan" in Oroderker, ed., *Phillies Reader*, pp. 59 (first quote), 60; Tygiel, *Baseball's Great Experiment*, p. 183 (second quote).

82. Kahn, "We Doan" in Orodender, ed., *Phillies Reader*, p. 62.

83. Jackie Robinson as told to Wendell Smith, *Jackie Robinson: My Own Story* (New York: Greenberg, 1948), p. 145.

84. Tygiel, *Baseball's Great Experiment*, p. 182; Povich, *All These Mornings*, p. 55 (quote); Haskell Cohen, "In Sports," *Jewish Exponent*, June 20, 1947.

85. Wendell Smith, "The Sports Beat," Pittsburgh *Courier*, May 24, 1947; Robinson, *Jackie Robinson: My Own Story*, pp. 146-47 (quote).

86. Ibid., p. 147; "Hank Greenberg A Hero to Dodgers' Negro Star," *New York Times*, May 18, 1947 (quote).

87. Robinson, *Jackie Robinson: My Own story*, p. 147.

88. Smith, "The Sports Beat," Pittsburgh *Courier*, May 24, 1947; "From A to Z," Baltimore *Afro-American*, May 17, 1947. See also Dan Burley, "Major League Dozens' Playing," *Amsterdam News*, June 25, 1947.

89. Smith, "The Sports Beat," Pittsburgh *Courier*, May 24, 1947; Tygiel, *Baseball's Great Experiment*, pp. 202-03; Falkner, *Great Time Coming*, p. 239 (quote).

90. Michael Berenbaum, "Jackie and Campy: Ethnicity in the 1950s," *Los Angeles Jewish Journal*, April 18-24, 1997, p. 29.

91. Greenberg, *Story of My Life,* pp. 189-91 (first quote p. 190, second pp. 190-91).

92. Tygiel, *Baseball's Great Experiment,* pp. 185-88; "Terry Moore, Marty Marion And Two Dodgers Accused," Chicago *Defender,* May 17, 1947. Robinson included an entire chapter titled "Strike!" in his 1948 autobiography.

93. Cardinal Strike Plot Thwarted; Robbie Gets Threatening Mail," New York *Age,* May 17, 1947; Rowan, *Wait Till Next Year,* p. 185; William Nack, "The Breakthrough," *Sports Illustrated,* May 5, 1997, p. 61.

94. Tygiel, *Baseball's Great Experiment,"* p. 185 Nack, "The Breakthrough," pp. 62, 65; Pittsburgh *Courier,* May 24, 1947.

95. Maury Allen, "Pepper Street, Pasadena" in Tygiel, *Jackie Robinson Reader,* p. 24.

96. Nack, "The Breakthrough," p. 61.

97. Rowan, *Wait Till Next Year,* Falkner, *Great Time Coming,* pp. 172-73; Tygiel, *Baseball's Great Experiment,* p. 192.

98. Robinson, *Jackie Robinson: My Own Story,* p. 147; Smith, "The Sports Beat," Pittsburgh *Courier,* May 24, 1947.

99. Greenberg, *Story of My Life,* pp. 191 (first quote), 207-08, 212 (second quote), 213, 217 (third quote); Gerstein, "Anti-Semitism in Baseball," *Jewish Life,* p. 22. See also the recollections of Al Smith, one of Cleveland's early black players, in Lee Heiman, Dave Weiner, and Bill Gutman, eds. *When the Cheering Stops...Former Major Leaguers Talk About Their Game & Their Lives* (New York: MacMillian, 1990), p. 77.

100. Kahn, *Memories of Summer,* pp. 67-68 (quotes), Rampersad, *Jackie Robinson,* pp. 254, 286, 300.

101. Ibid., pp. 152, 221 (quotes), 313; Robinson, *I Never Had It Made,* Rachel Robinson *Jackie Robinson: An Intimate Portrait* (New York: Harry N. Abrams, 1996), pp. 88, 124-27.

102. Roger Kahn, "The Lion at Dusk" in Tygiel, *The Jackie Robinson Reader,* p. 268 (quote) Rachel Robinson, *Intimate Portrait,* pp. 190-92, 208; Robinson, *I Never Had it Made,* p. 195.

103. Robinson, *An Intimate Portrait,* p 162 "Beyond the Box Score: Jackie Robinson, Civil Rights Crusader," *Negro History Bulletin,* October-December 1995, p. 19.

104. Jackie Robinson to Kivie Kaplan, Kivie Kaplan Papers, American Jewish Archives.

105. Rampersad, *Jackie Robinson,* p. 220.

PART V

SPORT IN THE AGE OF TELEVISION, DISCORD, AND PERSONAL FULFILLMENT, 1950-1985

Between 1950 and 1985, sport grew at an unprecedented rate. Such factors as post–World War II technological advancements, increased wealth of larger segments of the population, the G.I. Bill, civil rights legislation, and the women's movement made sport more accessible to a larger and more diverse population and contributed to its rise as a multibillion-dollar industry that greatly influenced all of America's social institutions. This period witnessed the reintegration of both amateur and professional sport, increased involvement of women in organized sport, creation of lucrative television sports contracts, establishment of players' unions, international sporting contests between the East and West, and increased interest in health and fitness through promotion of physical activity and sport. Coinciding with the aforementioned transformations in sport were disruptive yet often beneficial events such as the protests lodged by black college athletes against racial discrimination, player strikes in professional sport, passage of proposition 48 (intended to improve the academic performances of Division I college athletics), filing of dozens of lawsuits by girls protesting gender discrimination in Little League baseball, passing of the

Amateur Sports Act (which established the United States Olympic Committee as the central governing body of amateur sport), and the dissolving of the Association for Intercollegiate Athletics for Women (which allowed the NCAA to take over women's sports).

The tensions of the Vietnam era were played out at all levels of sport in this country. Some athletes, influenced by the popular culture of rock and roll and moved to action by both the antiwar and civil rights movements, were increasingly critical of sport's very ideals and fully challenged coaches and others in position of authority. Other athletes, maintaining a more conservative and traditional attitude and approach, continued to work hard, adhered to the belief in the character-building qualities of sport, and followed the dictates of coaches and others in positions of authority. David W. Zang makes these dichotomies clear in chapter 13, "Toil and Trouble: A Parable of Hard Work and Fun." Zang, in a rare scholarly analysis of contemporary wrestling, provides a view of the contrasting lifestyles and careers of college and Olympic wrestlers Dan Gable and Rick Sanders. Avoiding simplistic explanations and shunning broad generalizations, Zang recounts Gable's fabled story as an extraordinarily hard-working and zealously driven wrestler from Iowa State who capped his competitive career with a gold medal in the 1972 Munich Olympic Games. Unwilling to give into pain and exhaustion, Gable with his grueling regimen and discipline gave hope to many Americans who believed the county was quickly becoming decadent and heading to ruin during the tumultuous decade of the 1960s. Sanders, on the other hand, was in many ways the antithesis of Gable: an outstanding wrestler from Portland State who grew his hair long, adopted the counterculture's love of marijuana and free love, and could frequently be impudent in his approach to friends and foes alike. Sadly, Sanders had to settle, partly a result of his loose and carefree lifestyle, for a silver rather than a gold medal in Munich. About a month after the close of the Games, he died in an automobile accident in Yugoslavia.

Far more famous than Gable and Sanders, and perhaps any other athlete in history for that matter, was the once-controversial and now-beloved heavyweight boxing champion Muhammad Ali. A native of Louisville, Kentucky, Ali seemingly realized only admiration and avoided any controversy early in his career as he swept through Golden Gloves matches and captured the gold medal in the light heavyweight division at the 1960 Olympic Games in Rome. That all changed after his 1964 title victory over Sonny Liston, when he announced that he was a member of the Nation of Islam and was changing his name from Cassius Clay to Muhammad Ali. This announcement and Ali's frequent involvement with the Nation of Islam are the focus of chapter 14, "Victory for Allah: Muhammad Ali, the Nation of Islam, and American Society." In this essay, Wiggins recounts, among other things, the relationship between Ali and the Nation of Islam's leader Elijah Muhammad and most famous member Malcolm X, Ali's legal problems with the U.S. government resulting from his refusal to enter military service because of his membership in the Nation of Islam, and how Ali and his many followers would be affected by the Nation of Islam's eventual transformation into a more orthodox Islamic religion. Wiggins also recounts Ali's role in the Nation of Islam and how his Muslim faith and heavyweight championship combined to bring unprecedented attention to himself while serving as an uplifting force in much of the African American community.

In 1972, just one year after the Supreme Court unanimously voted against indicting Muhammad Ali for draft evasion, the U.S. Congress passed Title IX of the Educational Amendments. This new law was supposed to allow female athletes the same opportunities as their male counterparts. Unfortunately, female athletes did not realize equal opportunities immediately after the passage of Title IX and are still struggling to this day to ensure their equitable treatment. Perhaps nowhere has this struggle been more evident and pronounced than in the sport of basketball. In chapter 15, "The Fight for Title IX," Pamela Grundy and Susan Shackelford point out the battles fought by players, coaches, and administrators to guarantee that women's basketball was provided the same financial resources and facilities that men had enjoyed for many years. Key individuals in these battles were familiar coaches in women's college basketball such as Tennessee's Pat Summitt, Stanford's Tara VanDerveer, Delta State's Margaret Wade, and Maryland's Chris Weller.

Suggested Readings

Bale, John. *Roger Bannister and the Four-Minute Mile.* New York: Routledge, 2004.

Bale, John. *The Brain Drain: Foreign Student-Athletes in American Universities.* Urbana, IL: University of Illinois Press, 1991.

Bascomb, Neal. *The Perfect Mile: Three Athletes. One goal. And Less than Four Minutes to Achieve It.* New York: Houghton Mifflin, 2004.

Bass, Amy. *Not the Triumph But the Struggle: The 1968 Olympics and the Making of the Black Athlete.* Minneapolis, MN: University of Minnesota Press, 2002.

Berryman, Jack W. and Roberta J. Park (eds.) *Sport and Exercise Medicine: Essays in the History of Sports Medicine.* Urbana, IL: University of Illinois Press, 1992.

Chandler, Joan. *Television and National Sport: The United States and Britain.* Urbana, IL: University of Illinois Press, 1988.

Ciotola, Nicholas P. "Spignesi, Sinatra, and the Pittsburgh Steelers: Franco's Italian Army as an Expression of Ethnic Identity, 1972-1977." *Journal of Sport History,* 27(2000): 271-289.

Coenen, Craig. *From Sandlots to the Super Bowl: The National Football League, 1920-1967.* Knoxville, TN: University of Tennessee Press, 2005.

Davis, Jack E. "Baseball's Reluctant Challenge: Desegregating Major League Spring Training Sites, 1961-1964," *Journal of Sport History,* 19(1992): 144-162.

Elcombe, Tim. "The Oberlin Experiment: The Limits of Jack Scott's Athletic Revolution in Post 1960s America." *The International Journal of the History of Sport,* 22(2005): 1036-1059.

Festle, Mary Jo. *Playing Nice: Politics, and Apologies in Women's Sports.* New York: Columbia University Press, 1996.

Fields, Sarah K. "Hoover V. Meiklejohn: The Equal Protection Clause, Girls and Soccer." *Journal of Sport History*, 20(2003): 309-321.

Fitzpatrick, Frank. *And the Walls Came Tumbling Down: The Basketball Game That Changed American Sports.* Lincoln, NE: University of Nebraska Press, 2000.

George, Nelson. *Elevating the Game: The History & Aesthetics of Black Men in Basketball.* New York: Simon & Schuster, 1992.

Gorn, Elliott J. (ed.) *Muhammad Ali: The People's Champ.* Urbana, IL: University of Illinois Press, 1995.

Goudsouzian, Aram. "The House that Russell Built: Bill Russell, the University of San Francisco, and the Winning Streak that Changed College Basketball." *California History*, 84(2007): 4-25.

Guttmann, Allen. *A Whole New Ball Game: An Interpretation of American Sports.* Chapel Hill, NC: University of North Carolina Press, 1988.

Guttmann, Allen. *From Ritual to Record: The Nature of Modern Sports.* New York: Columbia University Press, 1978.

Guttmann, Allen. *The Games Must Go On: Avery Brundage and the Olympic Movement.* New York: Columbia University Press, 1984.

Hartmann, Douglas. *Race, Culture, and the Revolt of the Black Athlete: The 1968 Olympic Protests and their Aftermath.* Chicago: University of Chicago Press, 2003.

Hunt, Thomas M. "Countering the Soviet Threat in the Olympic Medals Race: The Amateur Sports Act of 1978 and American Athletics Policy Reform." *The International Journal of the History of Sport*, 24(2007): 786-818.

Kashatus, William C. *September Swoon: Richie Allen, The 64 Phillies, and Racial Integration.* University Park, PA: Penn State University Press, 2004.

Korr, Charles P. *The End of Baseball As We Know It: The Players Union*, 1960-1981. Urbana, IL: University of Illinois Press, 2002.

Lansbury, Jennifer H. "'The Tuskegee Flash and the Slender Harlem Stroker': Black Women Athletes on the Margin." *Journal of Sport History*, 28(2001): 233-252.

Lomax, Michael E. "'Detrimental to the League': Gambling and the Governance of Professional Football 1946-1963." *Journal of Sport History*, 29(2002): 289-311.

MacCambridge, Michael. *The Franchise: A History of Sports Illustrated Magazine.* New York: Hyperion, 1997.

Paino, Troy D. "Hoosiers in a Different Light: Forces of Change v. the Power of Nostalgia." *Journal of Sport History*, 28(2001): 63-80.

Rader, Benjamin G. *In Its Own Image: How Television Has Transformed Sports.* New York: The Free Press, 1984.

Rader, Benjamin G. "The Quest for Self-Sufficiency and the New Strenuosity: Reflections on the Strenuous Life of the 1970s and 1980s." *Journal of Sport History*, 18(1991): 255-266.

Robertson, Robert J. *Fair Ways: How Six Black Golfers Won Civil Rights in Beaumont Texas.* College Station, TX: Texas A&M University Press, 2005.

Smith, Thomas G. "Civil Rights on the Gridiron: The Kennedy Administration and the Washington Redskins." *Journal of Sport History*, 14(1987): 189-208.

Snyder, Brad. *A Well-Paid Slave: Curt Flood's Fight for Free Agency in Professional Sports.* New York: Penguin, 2006.

Sullivan, Neil J. *The Dodgers Move West*. New York: Oxford University Press, 1987.

Todd, Terry. "Anabolic Steroids: The Gremlins of Sport." *Journal of Sport History*, 14(1987): 87-107.

Wenn, Stephen R. "A Turning Point for IOC Television Policy: U.S. Television Rights Negotiations and the 1980 Lake Placid and Moscow Olympic Festivals." *Journal of Sport History*, 25(1998): 87-118.

CHAPTER 13

TOIL AND TROUBLE

A Parable of Hard Work and Fun

■ *David W. Zang* ■

> Gable trains as if he's going to row stroke on a slave galley.
>
> —Leo Davis, *The Oregonian*, 1972

> I'd bang on the wall many times at night in no uncertain terms, telling Rick to get his ass to bed, shut that music off. He had the girls in there and they were—I'm pretty sure—smoking dope.
>
> —Wayne Wells, 1972 U.S. Olympic wrestling team captain

Even in 1972, at the height of his powers, Dan Gable offered slight evidence of his physical prowess. Just 150 pounds, with black rimmed glasses, slightly rounded shoulders, and sandy red hair—already thinning at age twenty-six—he had a bookish appearance that hid his stature as the most indomitable athlete in the nation's history. A wrestler from wrestling-mad Iowa, Gable's cumulative high school and college record had been 181-1. There had been no one in his Iowa State workout room, including a 420-pound national heavyweight champion, that he feared. In 1971 he had become one of the few American wrestlers to have ever won a world championship. Now, as he prepared for the Olympic Games in Munich, Gable was just one gold medal from immortality.

Rick Sanders was Gable's Olympic teammate, older by nine months. A jaunty 125-pound bantam from Oregon, Sanders had a body that more than a decade of wrestling had sculpted into an odd but functional shape, with forearms that had little taper between elbow and wrist, and squat legs that provided ballast for a head with the one-size-too-large look of caricature. Sanders, too, had won like winning was going out of style. His high school record had been 80-1, with three state championships. He was 103-2 at Portland State, with national collegiate championships in the NAIA, NCAA College Division, and NCAA University Division. He tacked on five national AAU championships, a Pan Am Games gold, and the first world championship ever won by an American. In 1969, the year he won an Olympic silver medal, he served as the sport's mascot, peering like an innocent choirboy in tights from the cover of the NCAA Wrestling Guide. Now, as he prepared for what would become his final competition in Munich, he had dumped the choirboy look. Sporting long hair, a beard, and a necklace of hand-carved wooden beads, Sanders, too, was just one medal away from immortality, one silver medal from being forever remembered as a slack-ass hippie.

The divisive fury of the Vietnam era put the two wrestlers in a tough spot. While pop culture enticed baby boomers with endless seductions to a life of ease, the nation's elders looked to young athletes for sober assurance that an entire generation had not been lost to hallucinogens, loud music, and an Asian jungle. For those disposed to carrying easy lessons from the tough times, the possibilities attending Gable and Sanders translated to obvious parable.

Gable was deaf to the sirens of pleasure. In the final match of his college career, for yet another national title in 1970, Gable had been upset in a 13-11 thriller by Larry Owings, a brash upstart from the University of Washington who had gone out of his way to compete in Gable's weight class. The following morning's *Des Moines Register* headlined, simply and cruelly: TITLE TO CYCLONES—GABLE FAILS! Stunned by the solitary blemish on his high school and college record, Gable began a seven-hours-a-day, seven-days-a-week regimen that made his body, in the words of writer John Irving, "no more pretty than an axhead,... no more elaborate than a hammer."[1] He beat Owings in a rematch, claimed his world championship in 1971, and set his sights on the Munich Olympics.

As Gable was following the unswerving path mapped by his conviction, Sanders was moving through life like mercury on a tabletop. "He could wrestle as hard and fast as anybody who ever lived," Hall of Famer Wayne Baughman told a writer a few years ago. But he also could live as hard and fast as anybody. "Everything looked good to Rick," says '72 Olympic coach Bill Farrell.[2] In a previous era such a hearty appetite might have passed as rakish virtue. In the manly environs of the locker room, wine, women, and song had been winking material for decades; now, however, in the late '60s, to the thinking of many, the new parallels—sex, drugs, and rock 'n' roll—were irredeemable and dangerous components of a worthless youth culture.

Sanders took his fill of all three. His long hair and beard alone caused many to label him "hippie." Ronald Reagan, as California governor, had in 1966 described a hippie as someone who "dresses like Tarzan, has hair like Jane, and smells like Cheetah." Notre Dame football coach Ara Parseghian was more succinct, once referring to hippies simply as "scum."[3]

To anyone looking to choose sides, the nature of wrestling tilted in Gable's favor. The sport is as old and merciless as the human race. Matches feature barely dressed bodies entangled too intimately for some, and a pageant of disfigurement—crippled knees, crooked noses, and cauliflower ears—that mark it as coarse and vulgar to others. Indeed, wrestling's vocabulary is just a roll call of body parts and hints of what can be done to them: ankle picks, chicken wings, headlocks, bar arms, tight waists, high crotches, cradles, pancakes, and can openers.

The ring is a line painted on a sea of compressed foam; it offers no escape, no ropes to slump against. Matches last six to eight endless minutes (in the '60s and early '70s, international matches went nine). Though rules mute the sport's primitive aspects, a wrestling loss is a humiliating lesson in applied Darwinism. A wrestler who gives in to exhaustion and pain, or has his arms turn suddenly to spaghetti, will be taken apart, his opponent compounding the torture by exposing him as weak, a quitter.

Even ancient and seemingly immutable pastimes, however, were vulnerable to the shifting currents of the sixties, and, for some, the tide of social change carried a measure of approbation for Rick Sanders. The '60s brought two visions—self-sacrifice and self-realization (concepts whose opposition the noted historian and social observer Warren Susman has tracked back to the start of the twentieth century)[4] into notable collision. Whether or not the youth backlash against sacrificial effort lay in subtle pop culture enticements of the '50s and early '60s (Disney's Seven Dwarves, whose happy message was that even work was supposed to be fun; the baby boom television icon Peter Pan, who said sprinkling good thoughts with pixie dust could send one soaring to Neverland—a fancy that may have translated into acceptance of the transportive powers of hallucinogens; the pop music of the Beach Boys, who touted California teen life as "Fun, Fun, Fun"), it is hard to deny that the feel-good slogans of the counterculture—"It's Your Own Thing, Do What You Wanna Do," "If It Feels Good, Do It," and "Make Love, Not War"—owed as much to pleasure-seeking as they did to political philosophy.

One would be hard pressed to create a social profile for predicting one's embrace—or rejection—of the counterculture. Many of its most radical members were collegians from America's affluent suburbs; some, like those who gravitated toward San Francisco's Haight-Ashbury District, were from broken blue-collar homes. Historian Allen Matusow observed, "hippies were only a spectacular exaggeration of tendencies transforming the larger society."[5] Exaggeration or not, conservatives portrayed counterculture members as spoiled and unmotivated, the products of a consumer culture that encouraged immediate self-gratification in an atmosphere of slackening discipline, child rearing, and educational standards.[6] Neither Gable nor Sanders were any more or less a candidate, by virtue of upbringing or demographics, for the counterculture than anyone else. Nonetheless, both would be judged by a society awash in issues brought to the fore by the emergence of the hippie.

Gable was born in 1945, on the cusp of the baby boom, and his childhood in Waterloo, Iowa, was not one of ease or indulgence. Though his parents,

Dan Gable in his Iowa State University wrestling uniform.

Iowa State University Library/Special Collections Department.

Mack and Katie, oversaw a clean, well-ordered, middle-class household, they drank to the point of fistfighting now and again. In the father's estimation, Dan was the "meanest, ornierest kid alive," and his tendencies were tempered by corporal punishment—Katie occasionally breaking a yardstick over his head, Mack rapping his noggin with a heavy ring.[7] The family dynamics—and Dan's life—changed dramatically in 1964 when his nineteen-year-old sister was raped and murdered in the family home. Mack and Katie wanted to move. Dan insisted they stay, and he took over his sister's room. Thereafter, he poured all of his energies, rage, and attention into wrestling.

Gable's aversion to losing and his capacity for hard work were well established by the time he finished high school. The summer before he enrolled at Iowa State, Gable wrestled a former two-time Big Eight champ on the basement mat of the Gable home. "He beat me so bad that I cried," Gable told *Sports Illustrated*. "Right then I set a goal that I'd work out at *least* once every day." Six years later he was still honoring the pledge.[8]

As Gable's fame began snowballing in the late '60s, media reports scarcely noted his skill or intelligence on the mat. Despite his kinesthetic genius (an *Esquire* profile by Irving noted, "When Dan Gable lays his hands on you, you are in touch with grace"),[9] most accounts focused on one thing: his over-the-top effort. There were rumors that he'd practiced so hard that he had to be removed from the Iowa State wrestling room on a stretcher. A writer asked him about this in recent years and discovered it to be unfounded. Gable's goal had merely been to end a workout unable to get to his feet. "A couple of times I was so exhausted that I would start crawling towards the door," he said. "Then I'd be good enough to get to my feet. So I never really did do it, but that was my goal."[10]

Even stories aimed at something else eventually circled back to his ceaseless effort. In Ames, Iowa, in the spring of 1972 Gable was arrested for standing outside a keg party with a quarter inch of beer left in a paper cup. When a teammate was also jailed shortly thereafter, he arrived to find Gable using his brief hours in the poky doing pull-ups from a ceiling pipe.[11] In a culture gravitating toward personality, gratification, and fun, it was understandable that many baby boomers saw little point to Gable's dedication. But others did, and to them, both young and old, who believed that America was following the Roman Empire's road to ruin, Gable's regimen looked like exactly the sort of heroic sacrifice needed to put the nation back on track.

Rick Sanders had little pulling him in the direction of heroism. His father, Melvin, a millworker, had an affinity for hard drinking that matched Mack Gable's, but an approach to big dreams that more closely echoed those of Disney's Jiminy Cricket, who told baby boomers that dreams were theirs for a "wish upon a star." Melvin Sanders shot for the stars in an endless succession of implausible schemes that too often ran through the local taverns and eventually led his wife, Anita, to take Rick and older sister Patricia from south central Oregon to Portland.[12] Thereafter, Melvin wandered fitfully through Rick's life, but his big dreams left a lasting impression.

"Peanut" Sanders dreamed of attention and glory. Boys who enter high school weighing less than a hundred pounds know athletics are an unlikely place to find either. Still, for the combative, needy, or gifted—or all three—wrestling can provide entrée to the varsity club. For a rare few, such as Sanders, it becomes more. Wrestling "was in his soul," his sister says. It became, confirms Bobby Douglas, a close friend and now coach at Iowa State, a place where Sanders "had an opportunity to compete and be someone."[13]

With each win over another ninety-eight-pound schoolboy Sanders became more cocksure on the mat, and by the time he took his third high school state title, he was flashing an insouciance rooted in change and unpredictability. During a 1963 nine-match tour of Japan with other Oregon prep stars, Sanders drew his host's attention as the American team's best, but also its most dangerous: when he asked to stay a little longer in the country, the Japanese told him, "no, go home." Preparing to stage the '64 Olympics in Tokyo, they sensed in Sanders an intrepid spirit—"nothing malicious," assures tour coach Delance Duncan—that alarmed them.[14] They were not specific in their rejection, but the implication was remarkable: they saw the elfin eighteen-year-old as a threat to their meticulous and rigid planning. To Sanders, already cultivating a disdain for tradition, the Japanese attitude was confirmation of what he'd written a few days earlier to a friend. Some of Japan's customs, he'd decided, "are not very practical now days. To put it mildly the Japanese are very resistant to change."[15]

Sanders embraced change. "He was fearless," says Douglas, and during the long hours spent in the wrestling room, Sanders put himself into precarious positions that begged for new approaches.[16] Gable did the same, determined to never find himself surprised on the mat. Surprise delighted Sanders. He learned not just to squirm out of trouble, but to turn it into stunning reversals of fortune. He concocted imaginative, unprovable theories. Don Behm, later one of Sanders's fiercest rivals but closest friends, remembers in particular Sanders's "expansion and contraction theory," a belief Sanders had that his hips worked in tandem through a countervailing tendency to shrink and enlarge.[17]

An Olympic teammate once spotted Sanders running with one foot on the sidewalk and one foot in the gutter. "Why are you running like that?" he asked. "To give my hips more flexibility," Sanders told him. In the years afterward, the teammate asked exercise physiologists about the credibility of Sanders's theory. Nothing to it, they assured him. Nonetheless, Sanders believed, and each new hypothesis stirred him to enthusiastic proclamations. "He'd babble on and on—like little kids will do," remembers Behm. "You couldn't get a word in."[18]

The inventive curiosity pleased Howard Westcott, Sanders's coach at Portland State College. A mathematician with a doctorate from Columbia, Westcott was constantly searching for the angles, balance points, and forces that would tip an opponent. His wrestling room was his laboratory, and he exulted when Sanders began thinking along with him, then started to imagine and refine showstopping moves of his own. "He developed moves never tried before," said Westcott. "He'd accidentally do something, think it was good, and the next thing you know he'd be doing it [regularly]."[19]

Sanders's need to move constantly, to engage an opponent, to put himself at risk was exhilarating to watch. Following a trip to England and Finland as part of the U.S. world team in 1965, Sanders received a letter from the coach, Bill Smith. "Your way of wrestling gives ulcers to people watching," Smith wrote, "but I enjoyed every second of it."[20] In short, Sanders's act had become one of a kind and all that wrestling was ordinarily not—creative, entertaining…fun.

Along with teammates and friends Masaru Yatabe and Chuck Seal, Sanders made Portland State a little giant, placing fifth at the 1967 major college tourney. Sanders lost the first match of his college career, ran off 103 straight victories, then—like Gable—dropped the very last—the finals for yet another national championship. Spun down headfirst early in the match, he continued to wrestle, without use of his numbed right hand. He lost 4-2 while attempting to take down his opponent with ten seconds left. One of his detractors says that the truth is somewhat fuller, claiming that Sanders stayed out all night before the match, drinking.[21]

For most athletes this would be a damning accusation. With Sanders it was impossible to gauge the effect because he had by then already folded into the sport all his other interests—food, sex, good times—like pecans into a cake batter. Said Behm: "I watched him take eight ounces of straight rum one day." Sanders's reasoning? Another theory: "It's only eight ounces of weight," he told his friend. "By the time I sober up, I will have lost the six pounds and I won't feel any pain while I'm doing it."[22]

Pulling weight was nearly always a pain. During the '66 trip abroad Sanders was twelve pounds above his limit less than twenty-four hours before competition. A pair of wrestlers from the upper weight classes, annoyed at his irresponsibility, locked him in a sauna while they went to a movie. When Sanders was freed hours later, he crawled from the box limp as a dishrag. Still naked, but armed with a butter knife, he eventually patrolled the hotel hallway in search of the two. The next morning he refused to walk the six blocks to weigh-in;

teammates put him in a laundry basket and carried him to the scales, where he refused to stand up. He then went out and nearly upset the world champion. Perhaps the only time that paring weight was tolerable came when he wore a sweat-inducing rubber suit during bouts of lovemaking.[23]

While Sanders managed to stay small, Gable grew into the middleweight classes. Only once, while Gable was still a high school phenom, had the two found themselves the same size. It was a moment just long enough for one memorable encounter. Before meeting in the finals of a tournament, Sanders approached Gable with some advice: "Bring a baseball bat with you." When Gable asked why, Sanders told him, "You've got me next; you're going to need it." Sanders won, 6-0. As Gable recalls, "I basically needed the bat." By the late '60s they were separated by too many pounds to make a direct rivalry possible. Still, Sanders, aware of Gable's rising fame, kept the needle in. One summer he stopped at Gable's home. Finding the clean-living prodigy out of town, he grabbed Gable's dad, Mack, and went drinking. Then he spent the night in Gable's bed.[24]

Though he'd won their only head-to-head contest, though he'd returned from the '68 Olympics in Mexico City with a silver medal, and though he'd followed that with America's first world championship the following year, Sanders was in Gable's shadow at the end of the decade.

In the next few years leading to Munich, Gable's competitive insularity did little to mute media praise and attention. ABC sent a camera crew to Iowa to record his efforts for what would become a seven minute up-close-and-personal piece to air during the Games. A *Sports Illustrated* feature noted that the Soviets were so impressed with him that they had begun scouring the vast expanse of their republics for a single wrestler who could upend him in the Olympics. Their search, he says, was "the spark that set me on fire again."[25] He continued to drive himself relentlessly; at one point he brought John and Ben Peterson, brothers with Olympic hopes, to work out—and live—for several months in the Gable home.

As Gable eclipsed him, Sanders found new attention by transforming himself into what the press called the "wrestling hippie." Former acquaintances do not agree on how it happened, or on whether Sanders grasped the full implications of his provocation. Some maintain that he never changed from the day they met him. "He was always himself," claims Yatabe. Others say they could sense a new direction. Both camps are probably right: he may not have changed much, but then again he was already equipped by nature to run headlong into the arms of the youth counterculture. Says Behm, "In a way he was a young kid…and the things he did were attention-getting devices."[26] They were the kind that would make him a lightning rod in the era's cultural storms.

Amid the splash of large political gestures—an Olympic black power salute, a heavyweight champion's draft resistance, a basketball floor set ablaze to protest university policy—the mere immoderations of a wrestler seem inconsequential. The truth, however, is that the smaller acts of insubordination—a few minutes of curfew tested, sideburns an inch too long, a blazer not worn for a bus trip—committed in the thousands, were just as damaging to sport's ideological foundation. Whether Sanders would have fit everyone's definition of "hippie" or not, the fact is that there were damn few athletes, and virtually none of world-class caliber, who could simultaneously meet the demands of both sport and the surging fun crusades of the counterculture. Sanders gave it a try.

If he hadn't partaken of all of pop culture's enticements to pleasure in his early years, Sanders had, after moving to Portland, smelled what was in the wind. "He drew fascinating people to him," his sister recalls. Some of them, sensing his free spirit and good humor, led him into easy alliance with sex, drugs, and rock 'n' roll.[27] On his own after leaving Portland State, without coach or team to mollify, he exercised his freedom to do as he pleased until it became an addiction—an open invitation to excess as enervating as any narcotic.

Almost overnight, Sanders went from precocious peanut to *enfant terrible*. It would be futile to try to track turning points. One of the lures of hippie existence was its enticement to changing identity so thoroughly and quickly—Janis Joplin, high school ugly duckling turning up at her first reunion as sexy blues queen. You could arise one morning, rinse the Brylcreem out of your hair, comb it with a towel, and climb into a pair of bell bottoms: ready to live life as Someone Else. "Rick was living the life," assures his friend and Olympic teammate Sergio Gonzalez. Appeasing Dionysus, Sanders took his fill of grass, drink, and women. His oversized gym bag became a magician's hat. "We affectionately called him 'Snipe'," remembers '72 Olympic captain Wayne Wells. "He loved that name. There wasn't anything that he couldn't dig out of that damned ol' bag: sugarless ketchup, wrestling gear, whiskey bottles, marijuana joints." Long before boom boxes appeared on shoulders coast to coast, Sanders began lugging a portable stereo everywhere. Folk rocker John Prine's eponymous first album was a favorite, and Sanders listened over and over to "Illegal Smile," a song whose title was widely interpreted as a reference to marijuana and whose chorus mocked its opponents: "Won't you please tell the man I didn't kill anyone/ no, I'm just tryin' to have me some fun."[28]

Fun gave hives to the sport's traditionalists, who regarded good times in the wrestling world the way a cattle rancher regards a plateful of sushi. Gable represented the side of wrestling favored by nearly all of those involved in the sport: the ascetic discipline that punished bodies and denied the pleasures of flesh against flesh. Sanders exalted the sport's hidden delights, the indulgence of tactile sensations. On the mat, he literally embodied fun, a tactic that allowed his ability to be wrongly tainted by the perception that he wasn't trying that hard. This was a cardinal sin at a time when many Americans associated the nation's sudden, humiliating impotence in Vietnam with hippie influence on our soldiers: dope, loud music, but most of all, lack of effort.

Sanders was complicit in promoting the illusion of effortlessness. "Rick always tried to give the impression that he didn't train very hard," says Gonzalez, though he says it was all just "part of his mind games." Baughman, after watching apparently drunk Sanders appear to guzzle bottle after bottle of beer at a party, caught him—sober as a nun—secretly pouring out the contents on the ground. "I've got to maintain my image," he told Baughman. "You won't tell anyone will you?" John Peterson, one of Gable's training partners, adds: "I think Rick did train hard. He liked the attention he got from acting a little strange… [but] there were times when I saw him working out harder than anybody else." Assistant Olympic coach Jim Peckham recalls a day in training camp when the coaches had scheduled a run of the stadium steps: "Ricky Sanders did nothing but complain and moan and groan and whine and bitch." But, when the team finished, everyone came down to the field except Sanders and Gonzalez. "Picky and Sergio did them again," says Peckham. "Then Sergio dropped out and Sanders did them again."[29]

Those who knew how hard Sanders had worked to become a world champion were puzzled at his wish to have people believe otherwise. Once banished from a camp run by the Christian group Athletes in Action for bringing women and booze into the dorm, Sanders began the 1970s with a series of more public offenses. Following the 1970 World Games in Toronto, he was arrested and fined for marijuana possession. On his way to a dual meet with the Soviets the following year he began running in a plane aisle to lose weight. Asked to stop, he turned belligerent, challenging the stewardesses to throw him off the flight. Though all ended well, with the understanding stews piling blankets on him, the incident earned him another black mark with the sport's higher-ups.[30]

Good thing they didn't know that he had that same year returned West from a tournament on a trip with Gonzalez that would have stood them well with Ken Kesey's Merry Pranksters. During stops Sanders ran barefoot through snowdrifts, perched on top of the sign marking the Continental Divide, rummaged trash cans for empty soda bottles to buy ice cream, walked through four states on his hands at the famous Four Corners landmark, and then dropped peyote buttons at the Grand Canyon. When he found a beaver-gnawed log near a stream, he insisted on finding it a spot in the car and taking it all the way home to Oregon.[31]

Not that he needed to do anything more than have his picture taken to raise the ire of conservative coaches and critics. Wrestling officials in the United States had safeguarded the sport against the insidious encroachment of hippiedom by banning

A long haired and bearded Rick Sanders in 1972.

Photo courtesy of John Hoke.

(beginning in 1968) long hair, beards, and moustaches under the guise of hygiene. In 1971 high school referees began carrying into prematch locker rooms rulers to diagnose the afflicted and scissors to effect the cure. International wrestling had no such standards, and in the early '70s Sanders let his beard and hair grow until they wreathed his head with the full size and grandeur of a lion's mane. To keep his anxious hands busy, he carved wooden beads, then strung them together into a necklace. From its center he hung a hand-wrought wooden hash pipe.

Finally, in August of '71, he stepped across the line in the sand when Pennsylvania troopers picked him up hitchhiking along the state turnpike. He was stark naked. Placed in the back of the squad car, Sanders crawled over the seat, got behind the wheel, and began to drive away. But he did it ever so slowly, like a nervous teen inching down the driveway for the first time. The police caught him on foot. He told them that someone had slipped LSD into his coffee. The incident caused him to arrive in Annapolis, Maryland, too late for the tryouts for the 1971 world team. He responded by filing an affidavit that accused the coaches and officials of "arbitrarily" eliminating him from consideration.[32]

The incident saddened America's Olympic coach, Bill Farrell, who was assembling what would become the country's best-ever team. A flexible, compassionate man, Farrell liked Sanders, but he had no tolerance for drug use and little understanding of what seemed to be driving Sanders in such an untoward direction at such a crucial time. Exasperated by the second arrest, in September he wrote Sanders a long, heartfelt plea to do whatever was necessary to remain eligible for the '72 Games. "Some in the Federation do not want you to wrestle again because of the influence on the young wrestler," he wrote. Farrell made it clear he would stand up for Sanders, providing the wrestler curbed himself. In a paragraph of escalating urgency he pleaded: "By changing your ways I mean this. You must stop creating such a bad image. If you want to drink a little, drink in private. Don't tell everyone. If you want to smoke pot, do so in private, don't tell everyone. Stay out of trouble. If you have just one incident between now and June, 1972, there will not be one vote to let you wrestle. Not one. Rick, you have got to stop trying to 'shock' everyone. You must stop trying to convince people that you don't care what they think or what they do. You must stop trying to let everyone know that you fight the establishment (whatever that means). Can't you use your good sense and stay clean until the Olympics? I guarantee you, just one more incident, and you will be out."[33]

Sobered, perhaps, by his mother's death in January of '72, Sanders turned down the heat just enough to get by. That spring Farrell mailed all potential Olympians an Athletic Motivation Survey. Sanders didn't send his back and never responded to his invitation to the Olympic camp. When he finally arrived at the team gathering he seemed distant to longtime friend Bob Douglas. "Something was different, something had changed," Douglas says. "I couldn't put my finger on it, but I knew it wasn't the same Rick Sanders that I was very close to."[34]

Gable presented no such mysteries. If anything had changed it was that his zest for work had, impossibly, accelerated. He and the Petersons were insatiable, frustrating a coaching staff that would have preferred they back off a little. "If we had two practices, they'd sneak off and have three," says head coach Farrell. "They'd go off someplace and I couldn't find them." When the U.S. Olympians gathered at the White House for a presidential reception before departing for Germany, Gable and the brothers decided to stay instead in their motel room. There they shoved the beds and mattresses aside and spent the time wrestling on the floor.[35]

Sanders, theretofore "actively disinterested" in politics, according to friend and former professor Earle MacCannell, attended the reception wearing a "Ban the Bomb" button. Behm has vague recall that Sanders also gave Tricia Nixon a brief but impassioned scolding for her father's Vietnam War policy, though this, he says, could be a product of later mythmaking.[36]

When the U.S. squad landed in Munich, Sanders was in full flight, clearly having the time of his life. He railed in interviews about the stifling effect on sport of Olympic-related publicity and politics and scoffed at an *L.A. Times* reporter who asked about his schedule. "A schedule? I don't have any schedule with what I do with my life…Wrestling is my recreation. I get kicks out of seeing what I can do with myself." Asked by another reporter if he checked his appetite for women during competition, he responded similarly. "I don't put them on a schedule," he said, ogling a passing pair of breasts.[37]

Though the coaches and wrestlers drew plaudits for their unity and discipline, Sanders was relentless in his search for kicks. He spent hours in the city's beer gardens, at least once sharing dope with a large gathering of strangers—new friends all. In the Olympic Village, Sanders, Gonzalez, and Behm, who'd gone along as a workout partner, crowded into a small room that quickly became, according to Behm, "a pig sty." Overrun at times with friends and hangers-on—one man spent three days there before it was discovered he was unknown to all three—the partying there had no end. Team captain Wayne Wells, next door, says that Sanders was living out his commitment to sex, drugs, and drink.[38]

When assistant coach Peckham entered Sanders's room a few days before the first competition, he found empty beer bottles littering the floor and Sanders in bed with two women. "Ricky, don't cross me on this," Peckham scolded. "I want those two women out of here now." When he returned the next day, he found that Sanders had followed orders exactly. "If I hadn't seen it, I don't know if I'd believe it," Peckham says, his head still wagging in disbelief twenty-five years later. "He was in bed with two more." Behm and Gonzalez agree that while the tale may be apocryphal, its spirit was pure Sanders.[39]

No small wonder, then, that Farrell says Sanders was, on the eve of the Games, "the center of controversy and discussion." His impudent approach offended some of the others, particularly the Petersons, devout Christians who would end up winning gold and silver medals. "Off the mat, Rick lost," Ben says. "He was a troubled man in the midst of America's hippie movement. Rick was lost in the middle of that. He had no moorings for his life. I wanted to obey God in the scriptures. So when I saw anyone else that didn't…there might be tension involved." But, he said, "we were trying to find a way to be in agreement with each other." Most of the time, anyway. Behm says that Sanders's choice of songs during practices struck Ben as "the devil's music" or what brother John later referred to as "wild music." Ben and Sanders battled over the stereo one day, alternately dialing the volume up and down. With each turn Sanders escalated his high-pitched, squeaky needling. "What's the matter—can't take it, can ya, Ben? Can't ya turn the other cheek, Ben?" Peterson's answer was to kick the box across the room, breaking it and ending the devil's work for the day.[40]

If Sanders was the center of the team's attention, it was Gable, the Petersons, Wells, and Taylor, the 420-pound heavyweight, who were drawing the bulk of media interest. The last best hope for Sanders to grab his share would be on the mat. When the past wrestling experience of ABC's head of sports Roone Arledge created the rarity of wrestling matches televised in prime time, Sanders was ready. Announcers Ken Kraft and Frank Gifford loved his act, and their commentary amplified his swaggering reputation. Chuckling, Gifford called Sanders "one of the more interesting characters we have ever seen, and certainly a brilliant wrestler. He's kept everyone around here alert—laughing, checking the crowd out, putting the referee on."[41]

Dominating his first three opponents stoked Sanders's enthusiasm for showy performance. In Westcott's memory, Sanders wore his necklace of beads to mat's edge, removing them only upon the referee's demand and only long enough to wrestle.[42] Current Portland State coach Marlin Grahn, then an enamored spectator, remembers that each time the bantamweight was called to wrestle, the fans in the Ringerhalle scrambled excitedly to claim new seats near his mat.[43] Sanders rewarded them with scintillating wrestling. Against the Italian, Maggiolo, he worked a spectacular cow catcher cradle, inching almost imperceptibly from a position of disadvantage beneath Maggiolo to purchase an instant of possibility. Then, impossibly to the untrained eye, he levered Maggiolo suddenly and irreversibly to his back, folding his opponent's head and rear end together until they nearly touched, the Italian's body rendered as motionless as if it had been dipped in quick-drying cement.

His confidence running high, Sanders commented freely and unflatteringly on Gable. "Gable isn't as relaxed as I am," he told the *Oregonian*. "He wrestles the same way I used to in college—balls out, trying to overpower people. He'll learn, though, and if he stays around, he'll be great." Moving to matters of personality, he chirped, "Sure, our lifestyles are different; so are our wrestling styles. Most Americans don't have style. Me, I'm a cosmopolite, I can wrestle like a Japanese, a Rumanian, or a Russian." Then he added the killing touch: "I used to work hard all the time. But as you get older, you don't work as hard."[44]

Gable may have lacked style in Sanders's eyes, but his first-round bout had brought him his own cachet and lent his quest for gold a new sense of drama.

What would finally make 1972 the best showing by an American team in Olympic history was its challenge to the longstanding supremacy of the Soviet Union. For two decades the Soviets had dominated on the mats and in the sport's inner circle. They had undue influence both with FILA (Federational Internationale de Lutte Amateur) and with the satellite nations of the Communist bloc. Farrell had warned his wrestlers beforehand: "Just be ready to get screwed and wrestle through it."[45] As American viewers got their first look at Gable, the warning was reified. Handling his Yugoslavian opponent with ease, Gable was suddenly head butted midway through the match. As blood spurted from a gash above the American's eye, the German referee called time. As a FILA doctor (the only authority for stopping the match on medical grounds) from an Iron Curtain nation advanced toward the mat, Gable's teammates set up a blockade while Farrell wound yards of white gauze round his wrestler's head. The blood momentarily stanched, the doctor bid Gable continue. A short time later, with the blood seeking to ooze through his bandages, Gable pinned the Yugoslav, dispatching the only threat he would have for days. In winning his first five matches Gable allowed not a single point.

Sanders was trying to keep up. Apprising his fourth-round match with favored Hideaki Yanagida, he predicted victory. His confidence stemmed, he explained, from the fact that the Japanese "haven't seen the new offense I have developed." But the Japanese, according to Douglas, "were very much aware of Rick's style," and Yanagida thwarted the Americans aggressiveness with caution and speed in the same way that Shigeo Nakata had while beating Sanders for the gold at Mexico City.[46] Yanagida won, 4-2. The gold was gone.

Sanders's subsequent matches gave no hint that he considered it a grievous loss. He pinned an Indian, decisioned a Bulgarian, and then, with the silver medal at stake, pinned Laszlo Klinga of Hungary. Against Klinga, Sanders ran the score to 9-4 in the first period, an exhibition of such effortless invention that Gifford observed, "He's just havin' himself a lot of fun at this point." At 16-5, Gifford empathized with Klinga, telling the audience that the Hungarian was "in with a long-haired buzzsaw."[47]

A few minutes later it became obvious that Sanders's fun had turned to boredom. In the center of the mat he went into an exaggerated "sugar-foot" stance, his right leg hung out on its own, inviting Klinga to grab hold of it. Such baiting was not unusual. Asked about the Maggiolo match in which he had similarly ceded his leg, Sanders had told a reporter, "He didn't have my leg. I had his arm." Now, he lost interest in the leg and in Klinga. His gaze went elsewhere, and Gifford, laughing uneasily, asked Kraft, "What was he looking at?" Peckham, sitting in the corner, knew the answer and it infuriated him: Sanders was watching a match on another mat. Peckham lit into him between periods. "Jesus Kee-rist," he seethed. Worried that embarrassing a Communist bloc wrestler could lead to collusion that might damage the chances of other Americans, Peckham lectured: "You have no right to shame him, Ricky." Sanders, nonplussed, asked the coach what he wanted him to do—pin the Hungarian?

Wrestle him in earnest, Peckham said. Sanders returned to the mat and pinned Klinga. He had his second silver.[48]

Still focused on gold, Gable had just one obstacle left. The Soviet search for someone to whip him had settled on Ruslan Ashuraliev. "They went up a weight class and found somebody that they thought was mentally tough enough to pull the weight and be a factor," Gable says.[49] They thought wrong. Though Gable wrestled tentatively, Ashuraliev had no more success than anyone else. The Iowan had simply stored too much away in seven years of training to be undone in nine minutes. Finishing the Olympic tourney unscored upon, Gable won 3-0 for the expected gold. Teammates put him on their shoulders and carried him from the mat, eventually setting him down in a hallway. There, alone with assistant coach Peckham, the universe's hardest working athlete finally revealed the barest hint of what the years of hard work had cost. "Geez, am I tired," he said. "That's OK, Dan," Peckham whispered back. "I won't tell anybody."[50]

The inability to reach the top step alongside three of his teammates hurt Sanders more than he let on. Privately, he approached first the Petersons and then Gable with an amazing and humbled proposal: "I want to hang out with you," he told them. The morning after his final match, Gable arose early for his workout—"I wasn't about to change my habits just because I'd won a gold medal"—and, taking Sanders at his word, went to collect his new partner. Sanders looked, says Gable, "like he'd just got in." Gazing up bleary-eyed from his bed, Sanders rolled over, telling the new god of all wrestling, "I think I'll start tomorrow." It was the last time Gable ever saw Sanders.[51]

Shortly after the freestyle competition ended, Gable headed for home. "I'll see sights for a couple of days," he told a reporter, "but there isn't much here for me. I can watch Jim Ryun on television."[52] Waterloo, Iowa's hardest working athlete had just buzzed through the world's peak competition untouched. He would be going home a hero.

Sanders was reminded that he would probably be returning as something less. A friend warned him that folks back home were "going to say you didn't train properly and didn't have the right attitude." To which Behm says, "I don't think Rick cared—he never did before."[53] Nonetheless, whether struck by wanderlust or regret, Sanders decided to stay abroad.

Unbeknownst to Gonzalez, after nearly a month in Europe Sanders set out to catch up to his friend, who was by then in Greece. Traveling with the fiancée of Buck Deadrich, another friend and fellow free spirit from the Greco-Roman team, Sanders hitched a ride in Yugoslavia. On a winding road in bad weather, the driver ran headlong into a bus. Rick Sanders and Deadrich's fiancée were killed instantly.

Friends went to Portland to await the body and a funeral. When neither came in timely fashion, old acquaintances read the delay as a personal affront to Sanders and started to stew. Westcott was particularly upset, and former Olympic wrestler Henry Wittenberg railed at the insensitivity of the U.S. Olympic Committee for not intervening.[54] Sanders's stepbrother, Dave Stockner, says—and documents back him up—that the delay owed primarily to the difficulties of dealing with an obtuse Yugoslavian bureaucracy and its demand for cash in exchange for the body. Finally, donations from coaches and wrestlers enabled Portland State to have the remains returned—on a commercial flight, no special honors—and interred near Eagle Creek, Oregon.

Sanders died with $7.50 in his pocket and little of tangible worth in his backpack: parts of his Olympic parade uniform, his wooden beads, a tiny chess set. Eventually, the silver medal, at first thought to be lost, arrived in a diplomatic pouch. It was the only item to which the Yugoslavian government had been unable to assign a value. It merited a simple appraisal: "inestimable."[55]

In an era when the young seemed to be gleefully watching the ethics of hard work, frugality, self-control, and postponed gratification swirl down the drain, it was easy to see Sanders and Gable as symbols. It was impossible to disregard Gable's work in assessing his ascendancy. And it was impossible—even for Sanders himself—to ignore the connection between his dissolution and his disappointment. What do the pair look like in retrospect?

Easier to say in Gable's case. He is, after all, still with us. He spent a quarter century after Munich grinding out countless more wins as a coach at the University of Iowa. In all, he won fifteen national titles and twenty-five consecutive Big Ten championships, so many that they blended together until their impact was just as a dull thud: victory was always expected; no crisis ever surprised or debilitated Gable's Hawkeyes.

The years on the mat have had some tangible costs. He has been pained and hobbled by many operations (including two hip replacements). He remained socially insular for many years. "As a competitor," he admits, "whether as an athlete or coach, I always had this way of focusing that kept me from getting close to a lot of people." The emotional suppression kept him from accepting his 1970 loss to Larry Owings. "There was just too much pain there," he admits. Finally, in 1997 he offered sincere compliments to Owings for the first time.[56]

He has, however, had a fulfilling family life. He married and raised four daughters. And he was never an outcast. Despite our tendency to recall the Vietnam era in terms of its zeitgeist of upheaval, it is important to remember that Dan Gable, as much as Sanders, was a child of the sixties—a prototype of and model for those oft forgotten ones: those who embraced most of the old virtues, who went in silence to the jungles of southeast Asia, who watched contemptuously as Abbie Hoffman tried to levitate the Pentagon, and kept their hair close cropped so as not to ruin the family portrait. Philip Slater's *The Pursuit of Loneliness* (1970) maintained that those feelings people worked hardest to suppress and spoke loudest to condemn in the '60s were likely those that lay closest to the surface of their own desires. If so, then despite the barriers they built, Gable and Sanders—as well as their supporters and detractors—were just inches apart.

Even years after his death, Sanders continues to yield flamboyant memories. "Rick Sanders stories?" muses Wells. "You could tell 'em forever."[57] In June of

1997, when the remaining wrestlers of 1972 (heavyweight Chris Taylor also died, in 1979) gathered for their first reunion at the Wrestling Hall of Fame induction banquet in Stillwater, Oklahoma, Rick Sanders stories continued to surprise. One told how, after the massacre of Israeli athletes, Sanders had been one of the few wrestlers to attend the stadium memorial. When he found an angry Jim Peckham fuming about man's inhumanity to man, Sanders put his arm around him, kissed him gently on the shoulder, and told him: "Coach, you shouldn't talk like that; it's not good for the soul." John Peterson said that in 1984, while doing Christ's work in eastern Europe, he had run into the Hungarian wrestling coach, the same man that Sanders had pinned in 1972. Peterson asked him if he had a Bible. "Yes, I have one," he replied. "Well, where did you get it?" Peterson asked. "Rick Sanders gave it to me at the '72 Olympics," Klinga told him. Even the unflappable Gable continues to be surprised by Sanders. Read a quote from the *L.A. Times* of 1972, one in which Sanders named him as the only wrestler he wouldn't want to face again, Gable sighed softly. "I was kind of always intimidated by Sanders," he said. "I learned something new today."[58]

He might be more surprised still to know that his attachment to Sanders runs even deeper. In 1968 Gable's future nemesis, Owings, had left a freestyle tournament in Portland triumphant but broke. He'd won his class but had no money to get to Ames, Iowa, for that year's Olympic trials, a crucial stepping-stone toward becoming the kind of wrestler who might one day make an NCAA finals. A fellow wrestler—no doubt scraping by himself—recognized Owings's potential and stepped forward with the cash to send him to Iowa: Rick Sanders.[59]

Perhaps the least surprising thing about Sanders was his death. Many who knew him reflect on the inevitability of an early passing, and so they wonder as well about what a longer life might have brought. "He couldn't have coached," muses Behm, "and he'd have kept wrestling—but there are no wrestling bums."[60] That dilemma makes it nearly impossible to imagine Rick Sanders as senior citizen. When he died, his youth—no...his being—was trapped forever in the '60s, a tie-dyed bug caught in time's amber. Just as well. It's best we don't see him—in sandals and long, graying ponytail—limping on ruined knees through Portland's Saturday morning bazaar, eating tofu burritos and grooving with the other fifty-something stoners. How should he be remembered, then?

There are many who believe he got what he deserved: two silver medals. Sanders needed fifteen years to gain election to the sport's Hall of Fame in Stillwater, Oklahoma. If he knocked on the doors of the nation's wrestling rooms today, including some in his hometown, more than a few would stay closed.

"There is a kind of cosmic connection between wrestling and life itself," says Iowa State coach Bob Douglas. "You wrestle out of the womb, you struggle when you're dying. Everyday is somewhat of a wrestling match in one way or another."[61] Both Sanders and Gable intuited the connection, even if life itself sometimes appeared to each as a different proposition.

Gable remains confident about the value of hard work. Responding to the decline of collegiate wrestling programs in the 1990s, he has said, "America needs wrestling to survive. I don't mean wrestling, I mean work ethic. We're taking some very important values and letting them slide."[62] It is hard to argue his point when you find that not a single wrestler—not even Gable—made it onto ESPN's list of the twentieth century's top one hundred athletes. Coaches still preach hard work, and many athletes live it, but the byword is talent. Look at highly paid stars who don't run out ground balls, quit on their teammates when the final play is drawn up for someone else, rob fans by failing to fulfill their potential, and you will know Gable's meaning.

Sanders, too, however, had lessons for American sport. At a point in time when fun was seemingly everywhere in youth culture except in organized sports, he was fresh air. Few would concede then or now that the sliver of glory separating silver from gold is really everything. How much virtue was there in the 1996 Nike ad campaign that was contemptuous of Olympic losers (one billboard proclaiming "You Don't Win Silver, You Lose Gold")? We demand more. We suspect a leaden spirit beneath the gold currently gilding our arenas. While too many of our athletes don't seem to be overly committed, we suspect they're not having much fun either.

The people who knew Sanders best, including some he beat, bedeviled, and befuddled, are convinced of his worth. Farrell, who entered the Hall of Fame with Sanders, calls him "the most selfless person I've ever known." Peckham likewise remembers him with affection. Behm, Douglas, Gonzalez, and Yatabe—all of whom command respect in the sport's inner circles—have never wavered in their love.[63]

At Sanders's services, though most of his fellow Olympians did not attend, a large crowd filled Portland's largest funeral home, necessitating loudspeakers for those left outside on the sidewalk. Two women, each believing themselves to be the love of Sanders's life, stepped forward to place a rose on the Olympic flag covering his coffin.

Notes

1. Nolan Zavoral, *A Season on the Mat: Dan Gable and the Pursuit of Perfection* (New York: Simon and Schuster, 1998), 10; John Irving, "Gorgeous Dan," *Esquire 79* (April 1973): 109.

2. Mike Gerald, "Sanders Set Standard as U.S. First World Champ," *Amateur Wrestling News* (7 November 1997): 33; Bill Farrell, Personal Interview, 2 December 1997.

3. Todd Gitlin, *The Sixties*, 217; Underwood, "The Desperate Coach" (1 September 1969): 22.

4. Warren Susman, "'Personality' and the Making of Twentieth-Century Culture," in *Culture as History*, ed. Warren I. Susman (New York: Pantheon, 1984), 216-17.

5. Matusow, *The Unraveling of America: A History of Liberalism in the 1960s* (New York: Harper and Row, 1984), 306.

6. Clecak, *America's Quest for the Ideal Self: Dissent and Fulfillment in the '60's and 70's*, 26-27.

7. Herman Weiskopf "A Kid Who Doesn't Kid Around," *Sports Illustrated* 36 (19 June 1972): 38; Zavoral, *A Season on the Mat*, 63-64.

8. Weiskopf, "A Kid Who Doesn't Kid Around," 38.

9. Irving, "Gorgeous Dan," 221.

10. Zavoral, *A Season on the Mat*, 10.

11. Irving, "Gorgeous Dan," 220.
12. David Stockner, Personal interview, October 1998.
13. Bobby Douglas, Personal Interview, 19 November, 1998.
14. Delance Duncan, Personal Interview, 9 October, 1998.
15. Rick Sanders to "People—and Georgie," in "Rick Sanders Scrapbook," property of David Stockner, Eagle Creek, Oreg.
16. Douglas, Personal Interview.
17. Don Behm, Personal Interview, 22 October 1998.
18. John Peterson, Personal Interview, 25 November 1997; Behm, Personal Interview.
19. From obituary from untitled, undated newspaper article in "Rick Sanders Scrapbook"; also the *Oregonian*, 20 October 1972, 3M.
20. Bill Smith to Rick Sanders (n.d.) in "Rick Sanders Scrapbook."
21. Personal Interview, interviewee anonymity requested.
22. Behm, Personal Interview.
23. Wayne Baughman, *Wrestling—On and Off the Mat* (Colorado Springs: Wayne Baughman, 1987), 31-32; Larry Kristoff, Personal Interview, 21 October 1998; Masaru Yatabe, Personal Interview, 30 November 1998.
24. Dan Gable, Personal Interview, 22 January 1998.
25. Ibid.
26. Yatabe, Behm, Personal Interviews.
27. Patricia Rogers, Personal Interview, 16 October 1998.
28. Sergio Gonzalez, Personal Interview, 27 August 1997; Wayne Wells, Personal Interview, 14 January 1998.
29. Gonzalez, John Peterson, Personal Interviews; Jim Peckham, Personal Interview, 26 November 1997; Baughman, *Wrestling—On and Off the Mat*, 32.
30. Newspaper article, n.d., in "Rick Sanders Scrapbook."
31. Gonzalez, Personal Interview.
32. Ibid.; "Request for Criminal Record Check," Pennsylvania State Police, 28 April 1999; Affidavit copy in "Rick Sanders Scrapbook."
33. Bill Farrell to Rick Sanders, "Rick Sanders Scrapbook."
34. Douglas, Personal Interview.
35. Bill Farrell, John Peterson, Personal Interviews.
36. Earle MacCannell, Personal Interview, 14 November 1998; Behm, Personal Interview.
37. *Washington Post*, quoting Dwight Chapin of *Los Angeles Times*, 30 August 1972; Leo Davis, *Oregonian*, n.d., from "Rick Sanders Scrapbook."
38. Behm, Wells, Personal Interviews.
39. Peckham, Personal Interview.
40. Farrell, Personal Interview; Ben Peterson, Personal Interview, 22 January 1998; John Peterson, Personal Interview; Behm, Personal Interview.
41. ABC videotape of Olympic wrestling competition, 1972.
42. *Oregonian*, 29 October 1972, 9.
43. Marlin Grahn, Personal Interview, 14 November 1998.
44. Leo Davis, *Oregonian*, 30 August 1972, from "Rick Sanders Scrapbook.
45. Wells, Personal Interview.
46. Davis, *Oregonian*, 30 August 1972, from "Rick Sanders Scrapbook"; Douglas, Personal Interview.
47. ABC videotape.
48. ABC videotape; Peckham, Personal Interview.
49. Gable, Personal Interview.
50. Peckham, Personal Interview.
51. Gable, Personal Interview.

52. Maury White, "Golden Day for Gable, Peterson," *Des Moines Register,* n.d., clipping in Iowa State University Sports Information file,

53. Gonzalez, Behm, Personal Interviews.

54. Marty Twersky, article in *New York Times,* reprinted in *Oregonian,* 29 October 1972, 3M, 9M.

55. "Inventory of Effects," included in letter from Thomas R. Hudson, U.S. Embassy, Yugoslavia, to David Stockner in "Rick Sanders Scrapbook."

56. Gable, Personal Interview.

57. Wells, Personal Interview.

58. Peckham; Peterson, John; Gable, Personal Interviews.

59. Michael Gerald, *Owings! A Decade of Immortality* (Medford, Oreg.: n.p., 1982), 10-11.

60. Behm, Personal Interview.

61. Douglas, Personal Interview.

62. Gable, Personal Interview.

63. Farrell, Personal Interview.

CHAPTER 14

VICTORY FOR ALLAH

Muhammad Ali, the Nation of Islam, and American Society

David K. Wiggins

"I envy Muhammad Ali," declared Bill Russell, the basketball great, following a well-publicized meeting between the famous boxer and several other prominent black athletes in Cleveland during the summer of 1967. "He has something I have never been able to attain and something very few people I know possess. He has an absolute and sincere faith."[1] Russell's assessment of Ali's religious belief, which came just a month prior to the fighter's conviction for refusing induction into America's armed forces, was entirely accurate; Ali embraced the Nation of Islam with great fervor and has shown unquestioning devotion to Muslim leadership and complete faith in Allah throughout his adult life. Even after being suspended from the movement during the late 1960s, Ali never wavered from his commitment to Allah or to the religious teachings of Elijah and Wallace Muhammad.[2] He willingly submitted to the rigid discipline of a movement designed to control the total behavior of its members.[3] In doing so, he rejected many of the essential values of American society to which other middle-class citizens adhered and set himself apart as perhaps the most influential and significant athlete in history.

Ali's conformity to the dictates of Muslim philosophy was a primary reason for his influence on the black community and the broader American society. Muslim doctrine gave him the faith and single-mindedness necessary to combat injustices in American society. Much of the black community's adulation for Ali stemmed from his refusal to seek a middle ground while he simultaneously pursued athletic success and maintained beliefs that were often antithetical to those found in sport. Ali was not universally endorsed by the black community because he rejected Christianity and talked of racial separation. But he satisfied the wishes of the Muslim leadership by being recognized as an autonomous, proud black man who was not dependent on the heavyweight championship for his sense of self-worth or his livelihood. He became the movement's most important symbol of black masculinity, a man of heroic stature who came to represent the struggle for civil rights in a society torn by racial divisions and by war.

To many in the white community, Ali's membership in the Nation of Islam was both frightening and detestable. His involvement with a group that advocated separation of the races was reprehensible to whites who expected black champions to concentrate on boxing and refrain from speaking out on racial and political issues. Rather than acquiescing to the sport establishment and assuming the subservient role traditionally assigned black athletes, Ali acted "inappropriately" by showing contempt for white authority and values. Instead of being appreciative for his many opportunities, Ali had the audacity to call America an oppressive society and insist on a separate homeland for blacks. Ali was considered a traitor for refusing induction into military service on religious grounds, instead of rallying around the flag.

Ali ultimately attained an honored position among broad segments of American society and won grudging admiration from even the most conservative blacks and whites. The transformation of much of the Nation of Islam into a more orthodox Islamic religion, along with improved race relations, resulted in a growing respect for Ali that transcended race and eventually led to his becoming one of the world's most revered persons. The aging Ali, more appreciated than ever because of his contributions to boxing and his unwillingness to sacrifice his religious principles, endeared himself to a wide audience by abandoning the idea of racial separateness and supporting integration and the democratic process. Ali's changing beliefs, while criticized by Muslims who continued to hold a racialist position, seemed to be natural for a man whose fundamental generosity and racial tolerance was never subsumed by rhetoric about black superiority and white devils. Once feared and despised because of his religious faith, Ali became a beloved figure lionized by people of all races and backgrounds.[4]

Acceptance of Allah and the Nation of Islam

Ali became involved with the Nation of Islam long before it was known to the American public. The young Cassius Clay first heard of Elijah Muhammad and his followers during a Golden Gloves boxing tournament in Chicago in 1959. Two years later in Miami, Clay met a follower of Muhammad named Sam Saxon (now known as Abdul Rahaman) who convinced him to attend a meeting at the local Muslim temple. This meeting, as Clay would later proclaim, was a turning point in his life. Saxon, along with two other Muslim ministers, Jeremiah Shabazz and Ishmael Sabakhan, inculcated Clay with Muslim philosophy and the teachings of Elijah Muhammad. They taught him that Allah was a black man who, in contrast to the white man's Jesus, was a "powerful prayer-answering God" genuinely concerned about the plight of the oppressed black masses. They explained to him that blacks had been brainwashed, led to believe that anything of value was always white rather than black. They told him that Elijah Muhammad was the only black leader in America with enough courage to tell the truth about the white man. And they assured him that the solution to the black man's suffering was separation of the races rather than integration.[5]

Though cautious at first about what he heard, Clay was enthralled by the Muslim doctrines and gradually embraced them with great passion. He seemingly found comfort in the elaborate rules of behavior prescribed by the Nation of Islam. As with members of more orthodox religions, there was a side to Clay that relished leaving decisions to higher authorities who dictated what to eat, how to pray, what clothes to wear, and how to spend free time. He was enamored with the Nation's work ethic. He believed strongly in the group's insistence that its members engage in hard, honest labor, practice thrift and sobriety, refrain from gambling and idleness, and adhere to principles of good nutrition and personal hygiene. Clay also believed in the Nation of Islam's more extreme teachings, which claimed that there was no heaven or hell, that Christianity was a religion organized by the enemies of the black community, and that white civilization was a genetically engineered devil race.[6]

Moreover, Clay was infatuated with Elijah Muhammad, the self-professed Messenger of Allah who assumed leadership of the Nation of Islam in 1934 following the sudden disappearance of his mentor, the spiritual founder of the movement, W.D. Fard.[7] In Muhammad, Clay found a surrogate father, a powerful man who would teach him the ways of the world and nurture his latent sense of social and political responsibility. Clay was awakened, most noticeably, by Muhammad's talk of black pride in the face of white domination. Inspired by Muhammad's dreams of a separate black nation and powers of a glorious African heritage, Clay could now take pride in his own negritude and align himself with other blacks to overcome the effects of white oppression that had lingered since childhood. Like many other blacks at this historical moment, he was outraged by the crimes committed against blacks by white Americans.[8]

Clay initially tried to shield his allegiance to the Nation of Islam from the American public. There was a heavyweight championship in his future, and Clay, aware that many people hated and feared the Nation, believed that knowledge of his ties to the movement would jeopardize his chances for a title fight. He spent the next couple of years quietly entering Muslim meetings through the back door and keeping talks with other believers secret.[9]

Despite his good intentions, Clay's attempts at religious privacy were destined to fail as his star rose in boxing. In the months leading up to his championship fight with Sonny Liston in Miami, newspapers reported Clay's attendance at Muslim rallies across the country and speculated about his level of involvement in the black nationalist movement. As Thomas Hauser noted, Clay's interest in the Nation of Islam first came to public notice in September 1963 when the *Philadelphia Daily News* reported his appearance at a local Muslim gathering. Some five months later, the *New York Herald Tribune* ran a front-page story describing Clay's involvement in a Muslin rally, noting rather prophetically that the young fighter's presence at meetings of the Nation of Islam lent the group immediate prestige. Two weeks after the appearance of the *Herald Tribune* column, the *Louisville Courier-Journal* published an interview in which Clay expressed his agreement with the Muslims' opposition to integration and announced his refusal "to impose myself on people who don't want me."[10]

Any remaining doubts about Clay's religious leanings were laid to rest by activities at the young fighter's training camp in Miami. He was accompanied virtually everywhere by clean-shaven, conservatively dressed Muslims with short-cropped hair, men who looked more like uniformed guards than boxing fans. One black man who stood out from the rest, conspicuous for both his light skin and reddish hair, was Malcolm X, the brilliant and controversial Muslim minister. Malcolm was in town at the request of Clay, who had invited the famous Muslim leader and his family to Miami as a sixth wedding anniversary present. The two men had established a close friendship, which extended back to 1962 when Clay and his brother, Rudolph, journeyed to Detroit to hear a speech by Elijah Muhammad.[11]

Malcolm's stay in Miami was not a typical wedding anniversary celebration. Although attempting to enjoy the excitement surrounding the championship fight, Malcolm found himself embroiled in turmoil and controversy. Recently suspended from the Nation of Islam by Elijah Muhammad, Malcolm X was not welcomed by everyone in Miami. He and his Muslim friends cast a shadow over the whole affair. The fight's promoter, Bill MacDonald, believed that the Muslim presence had alienated the local community and caused sluggish ticket sales. Worried about financial losses, MacDonald, with the help of Harold Conrad, a boxing promoter and friend of Clay's, convinced Malcolm to leave Miami until the day of the fight.[12]

In truth, Malcolm's decision to leave Miami was as much a result of pressure from the Muslim leadership in Chicago as anything else. He showed some vestiges of respect for Elijah Muhammad by disassociating himself publicly from Clay's camp. Muhammad feared that Malcolm's presence in Miami would ultimately be an embarrassment to the Nation of Islam. Muhammad expected Clay to be defeated by the heavily favored Sonny Liston, and any association of Malcolm X or other members of the Nation of Islam with the losing fighter would reflect negatively on the movement. Perhaps the best indication of the Nation of Islam's approach to the fight was the fact that no writers from the organization's official publication, *Muhammad Speaks*, were in Miami to cover the fight.[13]

Malcolm returned to Miami in time to offer Clay encouragement just prior to his battle with Liston on February 25, 1964. He tried to convince Clay of the symbolic importance of the fight, that it was no ordinary heavyweight championship bout between two black gladiators but an encounter pitting the "cross and the crescent" in the prize ring for the first time. "It's a modern Crusades—Christian and a Muslim facing each other with television to beam it off telstar for the whole world to see what happens," Malcolm wrote in his autobiography. "Do you think Allah has brought about all this intending for you to leave the ring as anything but the champion?"[14]

Armed with a belief in his own ability and the power of Allah, Clay made short work of Liston. He made the "Big Bear" look amateurish, pummeling his face and wearing him down until he refused to answer the bell for the seventh round. The real excitement, however, did not take place until the following morning at a Miami Beach press conference. Responding to a question about his rumored membership in the Nation of Islam, Clay explained that he was no longer a Christian but a believer "in Allah and in peace." "I know where I'm going," said Clay, "and I know the truth and I don't have to be what you want me to be. I'm free to be what I want."[15]

At a second press conference the following morning, Clay could not have been more direct about his religious affiliation. He told those in attendance that "Islam is a religion and there are 750 million people all over the world who believe in it, and I'm one of them. I ain't no Christian."[16] That same day, Elijah Muhammad acknowledged Clay as a member of the Nation of Islam. "I'm so glad that Cassius Clay was brave enough to say that he was a Muslim," Muhammad told a cheering crowd at the Nation of Islam's annual convention in Chicago. "I'm happy that he confessed he's a believer. Clay whipped a much tougher man and came through the bout unscarred because he has accepted Muhammad as the messenger of Allah."[17] Several days later, Clay was again seen in the company of Malcolm X, this time in New York touring the United Nations and taking in a film of the championship fight.[18] Finally, on the night of March 6, Elijah Muhammad provided the ultimate affirmation of Clay's status in the Nation of Islam by announcing in a radio broadcast from Chicago that he was giving the fighter the name Muhammad Ali. Muhammad thereby repudiated the champion's "slave name" and bestowed upon him a name that signified his rebirth as a proud black man in racist white America.[19]

The Movement's Leading Symbol of Black Pride

The American public reacted swiftly to Ali's membership in the Nation of Islam. The initial disbelief expressed by many white Americans quickly turned to disdain. Northern liberals, veteran sportswriters, southern conservatives, and ordinary citizens expressed both fear and loathing toward Ali because he had joined a movement that advocated separation of the races, denounced Christianity, celebrated negritude, and accused America of being a racially oppressive society. The new champion provoked trepidation among white Americans because of his membership in a group that was willing to confront civil authority, rebel against social norms, and engage in militant acts of defiance. Ali was a threat because he belonged to a religious organization that challenged white supremacist ideology through a celebration of black intellect, culture, and physical beauty. Perhaps most important, Ali was denounced because he joined a group that challenged the authority associated with the dominant conceptions of the sacred in America. The champion deserved to be vilified, many believed, because he had turned his back on the Christian God and pledged faith in Allah as the source of all power, wisdom, and authority.[20]

Segments of the black community, while sometimes hesitant to speak out too loudly against the new champion for fear that criticism would be construed as racial disloyalty, were disturbed by Ali's membership in the Nation of Islam for many of the same reasons expressed by white Americans. Both Joe Louis and Floyd Patterson were troubled by Ali's rejection of the Christian religion, believing the ties between the heavyweight championship and the black separatist group would ultimately prove fatal to boxing.[21] Perhaps no member of the black community was more appalled by Ali's new religion than his own father, Cassius Marcellus Clay, Sr. The elder Clay despised the Muslims, not so much for their religious beliefs but because he believed they were exerting too much control over his son and had designs on his money. He told the sportswriter Pat Putnam prior to the Liston fight that the Nation of Islam had brainwashed Cassius and his younger brother, Rudolph. "They have ruined my two boys," said Clay senior; "they should run those Black Muslims out of the country before they ruin other fine people."[22]

Negative reactions to Ali's membership in the Nation of Islam were quickly countered by Elijah Muhammad. He realized the symbolic importance of a Muslim heavyweight champion and proceeded to orchestrate a public relations campaign that transformed Ali into the movement's leading example of black pride. He used the controversy surrounding Ali to his own advantage, branding criticism of the heavyweight champion as religious persecution and hatred of Muslims. With Malcolm X now defrocked and discredited within the Nation, Ali could step in as a charismatic leader who would spread the word. He could serve as an example of righteousness for blacks who had been instilled with a false sense of racial inferiority by white Christian Americans. Elijah Muhammad envisioned Ali as the Nation of Islam's model citizen, a beautiful black man who would lend credibility to the movement, embodying Muslim ideals and the Islamic way of life. In one of his first discourses on Ali in *Muhammad Speaks*, Elijah Muhammad declared that America hated the new champion because he had given up the life of a Christian, sought the "hereafter and not the world," courageously elevated himself "to the side of the true god," and had "shaken off the slavermaster's ways." "The heavyweight champion's name," proclaimed Muhammad, "will live forever."[23]

Shortly after receiving Muhammad's blessings, Ali embarked on a trip to Africa. Arranged by Osman Karriem, a close friend of Malcolm X, the month-long tour was ostensibly intended to provide Ali with some rest and remove him from the controversy surrounding his recent religious conversion. In truth, the trip served more as a promotional tour for the Nation of Islam and as an opportunity for Ali to nurture ties with his black brethren and gain a sense of his cultural heritage. *Muhammad Speaks* covered the trip in great detail and was

Muhammad Ali in attendance at a Nation of Islam meeting presided over by Elijah Muhammad.

Photo courtesy of Library of Congress. LC-USZ62-116838.

always careful to mention that the enthusiastic reception of Ali by the African countries indicated their approval of Elijah Muhammad.[24]

Ali's trip was marked by a number of memorable moments, but none of them seemed to affect him so deeply as his chance meeting with Malcolm X in Ghana. After months of quarreling with Elijah Muhammad over a variety of issues, including Muhammad's supposed sexual misbehavior and financial transgressions, Malcolm had embarked in early spring 1964 on a pilgrimage to Mecca. While in the lobby of Ghana's Hotel Ambassador preparing for his return to the United States, Malcolm bumped into Ali, who had just come back from a morning walk around the city. Accounts of the unexpected meeting differ, but observers agree that the encounter was awkward and strained.[25] Having once respected and genuinely admired one another, the two men were now headed in opposite directions, a split caused by their conflicting racial ideologies and religious beliefs.

Malcolm's pilgrimage to Mecca helped to solidify his already changing view of the Nation of Islam by convincing him that true Muslims believed in the brotherhood of all people irrespective of color. His travels through the Muslim world had given him "a new insight into the true religion of Islam" and a better understanding of America's entire racial dilemma.[26]

The change in Malcolm did not stop him from caring for Ali. Distraught at the prospect of losing Ali as a friend, Malcolm claimed he had tried to avoid the encounter at the Hotel Ambassador because it might prove embarrassing for the heavyweight champion, who had undoubtedly been prohibited by the Nation of Islam from associating with him. After his return to the United States, Malcolm sent a telegram to Ali imploring him "to make sure he'd never let his enemies…exploit his reputation."[27] For Malcolm, it was obviously difficult to stop being a spiritual adviser to his former student even if that student had chosen a different path to fulfillment.

Ali, for his part, cemented his strong allegiance to Elijah Muhammad and the Nation of Islam by virtue of his trip to Africa. His sojourns in Ghana and Egypt, in particular, heightened his sense of black separateness and his belief in the righteousness of Muhammad's cause. Unlike Malcolm, Ali did not gain faith in the brotherhood of all men. "In America," Ali explained to a Ghanese audience, "everything is white—Jesus, Moses and the angels. I'm glad to be here with my true people."[28] Osman Karriem perhaps said it best when he noted: "I'll remember that trip to Africa as long as I live, because that was where I saw Cassius Clay become Muhammad Ali."[29]

For Ali, coming face to face with Malcolm meant confronting the Nation of Islam's chief apostate. The heavyweight champion believed that Malcolm had forgotten his degraded past and that Muhammad had transformed him from a hustler and pimp into a proud and committed black man. When asked about Malcolm's telegram warning him of possible exploitation at the hands of his enemies, Ali showed his disgust by commenting to reporters about his former comrade's appearance in Africa: "Did you get a look at Malcolm? Dressed in that funny white robe and wearing a beard and walking with that cane that looked like a prophet's stick? Man he's gone. He's gone so far out he's out completely. Nobody listens to Malcolm anymore."[30]

Ali was right that nobody listened to Malcolm anymore. On February 21, 1965, Malcolm was murdered while delivering a speech at the Audubon Ballroom in New York City.[31] Ali had no public response to the death of one of the most controversial figures in American history. He let Elijah Muhammad and Malcolm's own brothers, Philbert and Wilfred, vilify the slain black leader, whose "foolish teaching brought him to his own end."[32] At the Nation of Islam's annual Savior's Day Convention in Chicago, shortly after Malcolm's death, Ali cheered on Elijah Muhammad as the leader announced: "We didn't want to kill Malcolm and didn't try to kill him. They know I didn't harm Malcolm. They know I loved him."[33]

Ali's much-publicized association with Malcolm tended to overshadow the relationship he had forged with Herbert Muhammad, the third son of Elijah Muhammad. Shortly after capturing the heavyweight title from Sonny Liston in 1964, Ali found himself in the company of Herbert Muhammad, who had been asked by his father to shield the new champion from hangers-on and other people with questionable motives. Elijah Muhammad, who always preferred to stay behind the scenes and who recognized the advantages of working through an intermediary, wanted Herbert to guide Ali so as to protect the interests of the Nation of Islam as well as the champion himself. He did not want people preying on Ali, taking money out of the pockets of the heavyweight champion who was expected to give over a portion of his yearly earnings to the Nation of Islam. Perhaps most important, he wanted to ensure that the public image he was trying to cultivate for Ali was going to be protected and promoted in the appropriate fashion.[34]

Herbert Muhammad, who operated both *Muhammad Speaks* and a small photography studio in Chicago, had journeyed to Africa with Ali and increasingly spent time with him on their return to America. Ali hardly made a move without first consulting Herbert, seeking his advice on everything from legal issues to religious doctrine. The two men became close friends and eventually formed a business partnership (Herbert became Ali's manager) that proved financially beneficial to both of them and, by extension, to the Nation of Islam.[35] "He [Herbert] has made it possible for me to help change the history of manager/ boxer relationships," noted Ali in the acknowledgments to his autobiography, "and is forever encouraging me not only to give the best performance to the people, but to be concerned with the progress of the people and to stand for the principles of peace, justice and equality—to show that in a profession which is mainly known for brutality and blood, a man can have nobility and dignity. It is not only I who owes Herbert Muhammad a debt of gratitude, it is the entire boxing and athletic world."[36]

Testing Ali's Religious Convictions

The alliance between Ali and Herbert Muhammad coincided with the controversy over the champion's opposition to the Vietnam War and his refusal to enter military service. Of all the factors in the debate over Ali's draft status, perhaps the central issue was his membership in the Nation of Islam. In February 1966, Ali created a national furor when he requested deferment from military service due to financial hardship and on various procedural grounds.[37] Once deferment was denied, Ali appealed his 1-A reclassification and fought for exemption from the draft before various boards and courts of justice. He then decided, however, to abandon his original argument for deferment and to seek exemption from military duty based on conscientious objector status. From spring 1966 until his conviction on draft evasion charges on June 20, 1967, Ali went through a number of appeals to overturn his 1-A reclassification, with the central questions usually focusing on his membership in the Nation of Islam: Was Ali's objection to military service based on political and racial considerations rather than on religious grounds? Was the Nation of Islam a true religion?[38]

Ali spelled out his religious convictions and opposition to the war on August 23, 1966, at a special hearing before retired circuit court judge Lawrence Grauman, who was brought in to determine the merits of the heavyweight champion's request and to make a recommendation to the Kentucky Appeal Board. Under oath, Ali testified that he sincerely believed in the teachings of Elijah Muhammad and the Holy Qur'an, which forbade true Muslims from participating in wars "on the side of nonbelievers." He illustrated the depth of his faith by pointing out that he would not have risked losing large sums of endorsement monies nor sacrificed his public image unless he was genuinely committed to the Nation of Islam.[39]

Lawrence Grauman surprised most people by concluding that Ali was sincere in his religious opposition to war and should be granted conscientious objector status. Grauman's recommendation was countered by the Department of Justice, which claimed in a written communiqué to the Appeal Board that Ali's opposition to the war was based on political and racial considerations rather than religious beliefs. The appeal board ultimately sided with the Department of Justice, and Ali's claim for conscientious objector status was rejected.[40] Eight months later, Ali's 1-A classification was upheld by the National Selective Service Presidential Appeal Board. On April 28, 1967, during induction ceremonies in Houston, Ali refused to take the customary one step forward signifying entrance into the army. In a written statement, he rejected induction because he was "a minister of the religion of Islam."[41] Ten days later, Ali was indicted by a Federal Grand Jury in Houston for refusing induction.[42] Finally, on June 20, 1967, he was found guilty of draft evasion by a twelve-person jury that returned its verdict after only twenty minutes of deliberation. Mort Susman, head of the United States Attorney's Office for the Southern District of Texas, expressed the belief of many people when he declared shortly after the verdict had been returned "that he had studied the Muslim order and found it as much political as it is religious."[43]

Susman's beliefs about the Muslim order seemed to strike at the heart of Ali's problems with the United States government. Because he belonged to a movement that was not considered a legitimate religion, Ali found it difficult to convince anyone that he deserved the same status as conscientious objectors who came from the Mennonite Church and other Christian groups. Ali's claim of pacifism was contradicted by the Nation of Islam's blending of radical social and political philosophy with religious doctrine. The Muslim militancy invoked hostile responses from a society that granted legitimacy only to those religions that complied with societal norms such as accommodation and submissiveness. Ali had to convince people of the sincerity of his religious beliefs while belonging to a movement that was overtly political, one that took uncompromising positions on racial issues and insisted on a separate state for black Americans. The burden of proof ultimately rested with Ali since the government would not accord Muslims the same constitutional and legal rights enjoyed by more traditional faiths. Because the Nation of Islam merged religion and politics, Ali was unable to enjoy the benefits granted other faiths and could not avoid the hardships that typically befell members of secular protest movements.[44]

The Nation of Islam took no official position on Ali's draft status and his struggles with the United States government. But it took a keen interest in Ali's fight for conscientious objector status and used the whole affair to help legiti-mize its own goals, stir up an already angry black community, and point out the injustices and hypocrisy of white America. *Muhammad Speaks* ran one article after another reporting the wide-ranging support for Ali from individuals and groups around the world, including the philosopher Bertrand Russell, the civil rights activist Floyd McKissick, and Martin Luther King, Jr. It also began describing Ali's religious commitment in greater detail, referring to him more frequently as a great Muslim minister as well as the heavyweight champion of the world. Though unable to sway the courts directly, the Nation of Islam realized it was essential to portray Ali as a man who performed clerical functions if his fight for conscientious objector status was to be taken seriously. In a March 3, 1967, column titled "World Champion Moves Step Closer to Full-time Task as Muham-mad's Minister," the newspaper announced that Ali "took complete charge" of the Muslim mosque in Houston because the regularly assigned minister was on a temporary leave of absence. "Reaction to the young athlete's assumption of his spiritual duties," noted the newspaper, "was not only highly favorable among the believers, but exclamations of admiration were many among lead-ers of the black community here [Houston]—many of whom jammed into the temple to hear Muhammad Ali expound upon the teachings given him by the Honorable Elijah Muhammad, the Messenger of Allah."[45]

Elijah Muhammad dealt with Ali's military status with uncharacteristic open-ness. Careful not to incriminate himself in any wrongdoing, Elijah Muhammad, who had served time in jail for draft evasion during World War II, nurtured Ali's public identification with the Nation of Islam while maintaining that the fighter's refusal to be inducted into military service was done independently of anyone else. In a rare and carefully orchestrated interview broadcast by the major networks in May 1967, Muhammad announced that Ali's refusal to be inducted into the armed forces was the champion's own decision and an indi-cation that he had learned the truth about himself and the status of blacks in American society. When asked if Ali sought his advice on the draft, Muhammad responded by saying that "every one of my followers is free to make his own choice. I gave him no more advice than I gave the faithful ones who followed me to the penitentiary in 1942." When asked if he thought Ali should be excused from the draft because he was a Muslim minister, Muhammad noted that he himself was a minister when he went to jail and that the United States govern-ment "does not excuse you for righteousness because by nature, it is against righteousness." When questioned as to whether Ali was being mistreated at the hands of the government simply because he was a Muslim, Muhammad replied: "It can't be anything else. Muhammad Ali is harassed to keep the other mentally sleeping so-called Negroes fast asleep to the fact that Islam is a refuge for the so-called Negroes in America."[46]

Notwithstanding these comments, in the late 1960s and early 1970s Muham-mad willingly stepped aside as an ever-increasing number of people began speaking out on behalf of Ali and his right to freedom of religion. Attitudes had changed. The hatred and disdain once directed at Ali gave way to genuine respect as a result of the increasing dissatisfaction with the war, a consensus on civil rights, gradual acceptance of athletes' struggles against racism, and the Nation of Islam's diminishing anti-white rhetoric. In addition, Ali's willingness to suffer the loss of fame and fortune for his ideals had garnered him adherents of all colors and from different strata of society. Sportswriters, entertainers, politicians, Christian leaders, business people, orthodox Muslims, and more conservative black organizations such as the Congress of Racial Equality (CORE) praised Ali's courage. Articles in such major publications as *Christian Century, Newsweek, Sports Illustrated,* and *Esquire* commended him for maintaining his sincerity and dignity in the face of persecution from America's power structure, which unfairly took his title and denied him the right to make a living.[47]

It was in this atmosphere that Ali's battles with the government finally drew to a close. In April 1971 his draft evasion case came up before the United States Supreme Court. During oral argument, Solicitor General Erwin Griswold contended that Ali was not truly a conscientious objector because he had claimed on several occasions that as a member of the Nation of Islam he would not go to war unless it was declared by Allah. Five of the eight justices agreed with Griswold and decided Ali should go to jail. The members of the majority were especially worried that a vote in Ali's favor would result in hordes of blacks joining the Nation of Islam in an effort to avoid military service.[48]

Chief Justice Warren Burger selected Justice John Harlan to write the majority view. In preparing the draft opinion, however, two of Harlan's clerks told him they were convinced that Ali's religious beliefs did qualify him for conscientious objector status. They suggested that Harlan read the *Autobiography of Malcolm X* and Elijah Muhammad's *Message to the Blackman in America* to gain a greater understanding of the Nation of Islam. Harlan took their advice and was transformed by the two books, enough to change his vote and convince him that the government had mistakenly characterized Ali as a racist and distorted the Black Muslim religion. Harlan's change in position put the vote at 4 to 4, but it still meant that Ali would go to jail.[49]

Equally divided decisions by the justices were never accompanied by an opinion, meaning that Ali would go to jail without knowing why his conscientious objector status had been denied. To resolve the stalemate, Justice Potter Stewart suggested that Ali could be set free because of a technical error made by the Justice Department. Stewart noted that the draft appeal board had never indicated the specific reasons for denying Ali conscientious objector status. It was possible, therefore, that the denial contradicted the government's previous acknowledgment before the Supreme Court that Ali's opposition to the war was sincere and based on religious training. A decision based on a technicality would ensure that the ruling in the case would not establish a precedent or expand the classification under which others could assert conscientious objector status. After much debate, the justices agreed to go along with Stewart's compromise and voted unanimously to set Ali free. The decision was announced on June 28, 1971, ending Ali's five-year struggle against the United States government.[50] "I thank Allah," Ali said after hearing about the decision in Chicago, "and I thank the Supreme Court for recognizing the sincerity of the religious teachings that I've accepted."[51]

Suffering the Wrath of Elijah Muhammad

One of the ironies of Ali's struggle against the United States government was that his status within the Nation of Islam had changed dramatically between the time he was found guilty of draft evasion in June 1967 and the point four years later when the Supreme Court finally granted his freedom. In early 1969, Howard Cosell asked Ali during an ABC television interview if he thought he would return to the ring soon. Ali responded, in effect, by telling Cosell he would return to boxing because he needed the money.[52] Ali's comments angered Elijah Muhammad. In an April 4, 1969, column in *Muhammad Speaks,* entitled "We Tell the World We're Not with Muhammad Ali," the Messenger explained that he wanted everyone to know that Ali had "stepped down off the spiritual platform of Islam to go and see if he can make money in the sport world." In stating his intentions to return to boxing, noted Muhammad, Ali had "plainly acted the fool to the whole world," placed "his hopes and trust in the enemy of Allah (God) for survival," and showed his love for "sport and play," which the "Holy Quran teaches him against."[53]

Muhammad continued to blast Ali in the next issue of *Muhammad Speaks* and announced that the champion was "out of the circle of the Brotherhood of the Followers of Islam for one (1) year" and would be referred to as Cassius Clay rather than recognized "under the Holy Name Muhammad Ali." Muhammad showed the extent of his indignation by publishing statements of support for his actions from two of Ali's closest associates, Herbert Muhammad and John Ali. Herbert declared to the world that he was "no longer manager of Muhammad Ali (Cassius Clay)" nor was he "at the service of anyone in the sports world." The Nation of Islam's national secretary, John Ali, in a much lengthier declaration of support for the Messenger, announced that he was "with the Honorable Elijah Muhammad in his defense of Islam against the reckless statements by Muhammad Ali." He noted that the boxer's need to fight in order to pay off debts resulted from the champion's "own ignorance and extravagance." Ali had failed to follow the teachings of Elijah Muhammad, who advised all of his disciples to be prudent in handling their money. "Neither Messenger Muhammad, the Nation of Islam nor the Muslims," stated John Ali, "have taken any money from Muhammad Ali. In fact, we have helped Muhammad Ali. Even Muhammad Ali's sparring partners made better use of their monies than Muhammad Ali who did not follow the wise counsel of Messenger Muhammad in saving himself from waste and extravagance."[54]

Ali's difficulties with the Nation of Islam obviously resulted from a number of interrelated factors. Elijah Muhammad was always suspicious of organized sport, believing it greatly harmed the black community. Like many others, he argued that white America had intentionally encouraged blacks to participate in games in order to divert their attention from the real source of their problems and to keep them from advancing as a civilized people. Sport, and the associated evils of gambling, drunkenness, and crime, was another tool used by white Christian society to keep blacks in a state of confusion and ignorance. In his book *Message to the Blackman in America*, Elijah Muhammad stated that "poor so-called negroes are the worst victims in this world of sport and play because they are trying to learn the white man's games of civilization. Sport and play (games of chance) take away the remembrance of Allah (God) and the doing of good, says the Holy Quran. Think over what I am teaching, my people, and judge according to justice and righteousness."[55]

While Muhammad's feelings about the "white man's games of civilization" seemed genuine, it was not Ali's participation in sport or boxing per se that drew his wrath. Muhammad was troubled more by Ali's departure from the party line as interpreted by himself and articulated by his ministers. Like Malcolm X a number of years earlier, Ali had failed to overcome his own impulses and adhere to the Nation of Islam's exclusive code of behavior. He mistakenly expressed a dependence on white society rather than having faith that Allah would provide him with the material goods and other necessities required for an abundant life. Such attitudes revealed Ali's self-absorption and his lack of complete trust in Muhammad, the Nation of Islam, and its doctrines. It also angered Muhammad since it left the impression that the Nation of Islam had taken advantage of Ali by funneling the heavyweight champion's earnings into its own coffers. Muhammad was troubled by any comments, including those from Ali himself, that might confirm rumors that the Nation of Islam had stolen the champion's money and was not looking out for his best interests.[56]

Muhammad's suspension of Ali, then, was his own attempt to rehabilitate the champion. He wanted to ensure a public image for Ali that fit his own needs as Messenger of Allah and those of the Nation of Islam. He was intent on guaranteeing that Ali mold himself to the requirements of the Nation of Islam and project an image of himself as an autonomous, proud black man. Muhammad ingeniously passed off Ali's success as evidence of black superiority and as a means to pay homage to Allah. At the same time he minimized the importance of the heavyweight title, which whites had once held up as a symbol of racial superiority. Muhammad believed that Ali had to be seen first as a Muslim. Otherwise, Ali would appear to be just the latest in a long line of black heavyweight champions, a mere gladiator serving entertainment-hungry white America.[57]

The severity of Ali's suspension by Elijah Muhammad became evident when he was ignored in *Muhammad Speaks*, the publication that in previous years had filled its pages with literally hundreds of photographs and stories of the champion. The newspaper did not mention anything about Ali for three years, completely ignoring his triumphant return to the ring against Jerry Quarry in 1970 and his initial bout with Joe Frazier one year later. He would not be mentioned in the newspaper again until February 4, 1972, and even then it was apparent he was not back in Elijah Muhammad's good graces. Responding to a series of questions about Ali's status in the Nation of Islam, Muhammad said in that issue that the Muslim fighter was "full of sport and he goes along with sport, too, but I think in his heart he wants to be good. As far as certain duties or posts as he used to hold as teaching the ministry," continued Muhammad, "I do not know when that will take place."[58]

Muhammad's suspension of Ali had obviously evolved into a deep dissatisfaction with the fighter that would never be completely eradicated.[59] Meanwhile, Ali seemed to gravitate toward boxing with greater urgency. He needed the money from boxing to pay off debts and stay abreast of alimony payments, but the sport also provided him with many of those things that had initially attracted him to the Nation of Islam. He was lured by the asceticism and discipline of boxing. He found sustenance in comradeship with his fellow fighters, his entourage, and the boxing world in general. He craved the attention, intense excitement, and respect that boxing brought him. As a fighter he was taken seriously, given a feeling of specialness and an unparalleled degree of adulation. He was enticed by the mystique of the ring, relishing the struggles in the sacred circle against men who were also striving for acclaim and immortality. The ring provided him with unparalleled opportunities for transcendence of self, peak experiences, and emotional "highs."[60]

Ali's status in the Nation of Islam was made most apparent by the kinds of relationships he established during the early 1970s. Although Herbert Muhammad continued to serve as his manager and confidant, Ali was no longer surrounded by Muslims who looked after his every move and protected his interests. Cassius Clay, Sr., became a more visible member of his son's entourage, which was now sprinkled with larger numbers of nonbelievers and attendants. Ali's press conference following his well-publicized return fight against Jerry Quarry was noteworthy in that he shared the podium with Mrs. Martin Luther King, Jr., and the Reverend Ralph Abernathy, "who presented him with the Dr. Martin Luther King Memorial Award for his contributions to human rights and equality."[61] Bundini Brown, whom the Muslims hated for his womanizing, heavy drinking, and other assorted vices, had returned to Ali's camp, reading poetry and clowning with the champ. Ali also chose to relocate his wife and three daughters to Philadelphia after living close to Elijah Muhammad in Chicago for a number of years.[62]

These changes never stopped Ali from openly expressing faith in the Muslim religion. Nor did they hinder the Nation of Islam from eventually breaking its silence on the champion and cashing in on the publicity generated by his success in the ring. Although his relationship with Elijah Muhammad would never be the same, Ali continued to praise the Messenger and Allah at every opportunity. He told inmates at a New York correctional facility during the latter part of 1974 that the only man who could stop blacks from wrongdoing was Elijah Muhammad. "I am a follower of the Honorable Elijah Muhammad.

We are peaceful people. We don't hate nobody. We are just trying to clean up our people and unite."[63]

The Nation of Islam began publicizing Ali's accomplishments more frequently as the 1970s progressed. Elijah Muhammad's deteriorating health resulted in gradual changes in the daily operations of the Nation of Islam, which in turn resulted in a resurrection of sorts for Ali. The champion seemed to resume a more prominent position in the Nation of Islam. He was revitalized as the movement's greatest symbol of black pride by virtue of his ring triumphs and his outspokenness on racial issues. Ali's rehabilitation was best reflected in the extended coverage that *Muhammad Speaks* devoted to his trip to Jamaica following his regaining of the heavyweight championship from George Foreman in 1974. Reminiscent of the coverage he received during his tour of Africa ten years earlier, Ali's every move in Jamaica was detailed by the newspaper. It was another promotional tour for the Nation of Islam, with Ali again the main attraction.[64]

From the Nation of Islam to the World Community of Al-Islam in the West

Ali's involvement with the Nation of Islam changed significantly following his trip to Jamaica. On February 25, 1975, Elijah Muhammad passed away, ending a forty-one-year reign as leader of the Nation of Islam. He was succeeded by his son, Wallace D. Muhammad, who took the organization in an entirely different direction through a series of policy changes and modifications in philosophy. Wallace, who had been suspended from the Nation of Islam by his father on several occasions and had considered Malcolm X one of his good friends, transformed the movement in many ways, including changing its name to the World Community of Al-Islam in the West. He reinterpreted his father's contributions to the organization, acknowledged the positive contributions made by Malcolm X, refuted the notion of black racial superiority, ceased to ask for a separate state for blacks within America, honored the American Constitution, and advocated the adoption of orthodox Islamic practices.[65] In his first official interview, Wallace Muhammad proclaimed that the World Community of Al-Islam in the West would no longer dwell on the past atrocities of white America and would accept people of all races into membership.[66]

The changes made the movement more palatable to an American public that had begun to appreciate both Muslim doctrine and the demands of the black community. For some members of the movement, however, the modifications brought about by their new leader were sacrilegious. The enormous sense of racial pride instilled in black Americans and the many other contributions made by Elijah Muhammad, including his emphasis on self-help and moral uplift, appeared to be cast aside in favor of a program that was focused more on integration than on continuing the fight for justice and freedom of opportunity. Louis Farrakhan, the former professional musician and calypso singer who became one of the Muslim organization's leading ministers, was so troubled by Wallace Muhammad's changes that he eventually mounted a public campaign against the new leader and rebuilt the Nation of Islam based on the early principles of Elijah Muhammad. Believing that blacks had not yet achieved liberation, Farrakhan began promulgating his beliefs through publication of the *Final Call*, taking the name of a newspaper put out by Elijah Muhammad in 1934.[67]

Ali's response to the changes made by Wallace Muhammad were the opposite of Farrakhan's. Instead of resisting, Ali almost immediately expressed his support for the new policies, which were similar to those suggested by Malcolm X some ten years earlier. Nearly everywhere he went, Ali carefully rationalized the practical utility of Elijah Muhammad's old programs while paying homage to Wallace Muhammad and declaring enthusiasm for the new changes in the movement. He now de-emphasized race and exalted the deeds of humankind, stopped talking of a separate black state and praised America as the greatest country in the world, spoke of the bonds of brotherhood in the Muslim faith, and avoided any mention of white devils. A perfect illustration of Ali's changing attitudes was an interview he did on May 2, 1976, on the CBS program "Face the Nation." In the interview, which was published in its entirety in the *Congressional Record*, Ali noted that it was necessary for Elijah Muhammad to speak of white devils because during much of the first half of the twentieth century, black Americans "were being castrated, lynched, deprived of freedom, justice, equality, raped." Because of improved racial conditions in society, continued Ali, "Wallace Muhammad is on time. He's teaching us it's not the color of the physical body that makes a man a devil. God looks at our minds and our actions and our deeds."[68]

Ali had no sooner declared his support for the World Community of Al-Islam in the West when Wallace Muhammad began chiding him for his continued involvement in boxing. Like his father, Wallace was concerned about the image the fighter was projecting. He was particularly alarmed by the unsavory people and temptations associated with boxing. He was troubled by Ali's illicit associations with women because they called to mind his own father's indiscretions and could prove embarrassing to the World Community of Al-Islam in the West.[69] Wallace was saddened, moreover, by the potential tarnishing of Ali's reputation brought on by inferior performances in the ring and worried about the harm the sport was inflicting on his physical well-being. Wallace argued that boxing provided much-needed income for the participants and necessary pleasure and excitement for blacks in this country, but he hated to see Ali struggle against opponents who would have been no match for him earlier in his career.[70]

Other Muslims, as well as millions of fans of both races, would eventually join in calling for Ali's retirement from the ring. People were heartbroken by the champion's diminishing abilities and the punishment he absorbed with each successive fight. As they witnessed the erosion of Ali's physical skills, people who had identified with the champion because of his triumphs and stands against social injustice were reminded of their own frailty. To see Ali flounder in the ring was tragic for his followers because he had touched the hearts of so many. He was much more than an athlete or celebrity or entertainer. He had won respect and adulation because he combined incredible abilities as a boxer with moral courage and a social conscience. Nassar Akbar, an inmate in a Michigan prison, captured the prevailing mood when he asked: "Do you, Brother Ali, wish to bring tears to our eyes, sadness to our hearts by returning to the fight game? Or would you like to see smiles on the faces of your brothers and sisters?"[71]

Ali failed to heed the advice of his supporters and continued to fight without any apparent regard for his physical well-being. He remained addicted to the excitement of the ring, but the fights he entered only damaged him further. The long march to destruction finally ended when Ali retired from boxing following his defeat at the hands of Trevor Berbick in 1981. After more than a quarter century of lacing up the gloves and doing battle in the squared circle, Ali now faced life without boxing.[72]

Ali's retirement from the ring allowed him more time to work on behalf of Wallace Muhammad and the World Community of Al-Islam in the West.[73] He was involved throughout the 1980s in everything from helping to promote the annual Muslim-sponsored Patriotism Day parade, and distributing religious literature on the streets, to being a member of the Muslim Political Action Committee (MPAC) and raising funds for the Sister Clara Muhammad School Educational Fund. Interspersed with these activities was his involvement with several Muslim-related businesses, including the marketing of "Muhammad Ali Ummmee Brand Seafood Sausage."[74] Ali even found time to visit the White House and present Ronald Reagan with a copy of Wallace Muhammad's *Prayer and Al-Islam*.[75]

Further evidence of Ali's commitment to the World Community of Al-Islam in the West came when he took on Louis Farrakhan and the resurrected Nation of Islam. He was appalled by Farrakhan's continued belief in racial superiority and separatism. In 1984, for example, Ali took Farrakhan to task for his derogatory remarks about Jews and made every effort, as did Jesse Jackson, then a presidential candidate, to dissociate himself from the new leader of the Nation of Islam. At an Independence Day celebration in Washington, D.C., Ali chastised Farrakhan for his recent anti-Semitic remarks and misrepresentation of true Islam. "What he teaches is not at all what we believe in," noted Ali when asked to comment about Farrakhan's controversial remarks. "We say he represents the time of our struggle in the dark and a time of confusion in us and we don't want to be associated with that at all."[76]

Ali's dissociation from Farrakhan resulted from his involvement in a religious movement that now stressed a more democratic decision-making process and spiritual fulfillment even while it put less emphasis on controlling the total behavior of individual members. Al-Islam in the West was sympathetic to the capitalistic system, committed to the United States Government, and open to nonblack peoples.

Without the tight reins of control and almost mesmerizing influence of Elijah Muhammad, Ali now exercised more freedom of thought. He had been transformed from a black rebel into a conservative American who favored steady progress for his people within American society. The emphasis Ali once placed on racial separateness and black solidarity had been undermined by the very things they were meant to produce; namely, equal justice and more freedom of opportunity for black Americans. Ali had inspired and helped foster pride among the most deracinated African Americans by spreading the belief in white devils and in the superiority of blacks. He now discarded those notions yet maintained a strong sense of racial consciousness, adhered to the distinctive creed of Islam, and embraced a more disparate group of individuals.[77]

Commitment to Boxing and Faithfulness to the Muslim Religion

The changes in Ali's religious beliefs capped a long spiritual journey marked by steadfast devotion and commitment. Though renowned for his sexual appetite and enjoyment of worldly pleasures, Ali was unwavering in his faithfulness to the Muslim religion and his belief in Allah. He derived strength and a sense of freedom from unquestioning obedience to Muslim leadership and belief in the omnipotence of Allah. His commitment to the Nation of Islam also supported him in his own quest for a sense of identity and racial consciousness. His loyalty to the movement gave him the confidence necessary to express pride in his blackness and the merits of black culture. He shed the humility and accommodating attitude typically associated with black athletes and defiantly rebelled against the limitations imposed by American society.

The Nation of Islam benefited as much from Ali's membership as did the fighter himself. Elijah Muhammad might have preached black separatism, railed against the evils of commercialized sport, and viewed boxing with disdain, but he had recognized the value of having Ali as a member of the Nation of Islam. Muhammad knew that what ultimately set Ali apart from anyone else in history was that he was both a Muslim and the heavyweight champion of the world, a combination that would attract unprecedented attention for the Nation of Islam, act as an uplifting force in America's black community, and cause impassioned responses in a society that placed unremitting faith in the power of sport to break down racial barriers. Ali could be held up as a symbol of unlimited possibilities for black achievement even while he was portrayed as a proud black man who received his basic sustenance from the Muslim religion. He proved invaluable to the Nation of Islam because he encouraged believers to rebel against social oppression and helped to create unity among competing factions.

Ali's importance to the Nation of Islam can be measured to a large extent by his influence on both the black and white communities in this country. His membership in the Nation of Islam, along with the heavyweight championship, elevated him to hero status of almost mythic proportion among many black Americans. Even those blacks who were appalled by the Nation of Islam's extremism and segregationist policies were infused with racial pride because of the champion's boldness in upholding a religion that accused America of everything from crass materialism to racial oppression. By embodying Muslim ideals, triumphing in the ring, and refusing to acquiesce to either the sport establishment or the broader American society, Ali helped invert stereotypes about blacks and inspired members of his race whose daily lives were often filled with drudgery and belittlement. Black Americans of every age group, economic class, political affiliation, and religious denomination were inspired by Ali's refusal to sacrifice his principles when the clash came between individual success in sport and the imperatives of group action.

Although he garnered respect from white Americans for his great boxing skills and even for the courage of his convictions, large segments of the dominant culture were appalled by Ali's membership in a movement that talked of "white devils," scorned Christianity, refused to fight for their country, and believed in black racial superiority. To many whites, Ali was a traitor, pure and simple, an ingrate who had turned his back on America and joined forces with hate-filled blacks who worshiped an unfamiliar god and refused to abide by the guiding principles of this country. They believed that Ali was a misguided soul who had been taken in by manipulative charlatans interested merely in self-aggrandizement rather than true religion. It was inconceivable to many whites that Ali could criticize a country that had provided him with limitless opportunities and the chance to secure wealth beyond that of ordinary citizens.

The transformation of the Nation of Islam following the death of Elijah Muhammad, along with the winding down of the war in Vietnam, the lessening of racial tensions, and other societal changes, would eventually lead to greater admiration of Ali by members of all races. Refusing to join forces with Louis Farrakhan and other blacks who remained loyal to Nation of Islam policy, Ali adhered to the orthodox Islamic religion adopted by Wallace Muhammad and the World Community of Al-Islam in the West. In so doing, Ali assumed an honored place in the public consciousness and became less threatening to many Americans. Like the World Community of Al-Islam in the West, Ali seemingly evolved from a revolutionary who was intent on promulgating social upheaval to a conservative American more concerned with spiritual salvation than racial confrontation.

The discipline, self-help, and strict moral code Ali was expected to observe as a member of the Nation of Islam would be forcefully transmitted into his new religion. Finding himself in an atmosphere more favorable to African Americans and armed with a transformed religiosity, Ali shed his racism to speak of the brotherhood of man and the power of God. His new religious beliefs did not sit well with blacks who continued to worship at the shrine of Elijah Muhammad, but it was a relatively smooth transition for the heavyweight champion, who realized that the promise of freedom in American society served to diminish the belief in racial separatism. Ali had helped to liberate African Americans psychologically. He now involved himself in the uplifting of all people through the promotion of Islam. For Ali, separatism had given way to integration, devils and saints were now members of both races, and Christians were no longer responsible for all the evils in the world.

Notes

I would like to thank Elliott Gorn, Steven Hardy, Steven Riess, and Randy Roberts for their cogent comments and suggestions on an earlier version of this manuscript.

1. Bill Russell with Tex Maule, "I'm Not Worried about Ali," *Sports Illustrated,* June 1, 1967, 19-21. See also *Muhammad Speaks,* June 16, 1967; Muhammad Al with Richard Durham, *The Greatest: My Own Story* (New York: Ballantine, 1975), 208-9.

2. For secondary accounts that touch upon Ali's relationship to the movement, see Jeffrey T. Sammons, *Beyond the Ring: The Role of Boxing in American* Society (Urbana: University of Illinois Press, 1988); Don Atyeo and Felix Dennis, *The Holy Warrior: Muhammad Ali* (London: Bunch Books, 1975); Budd Schulberg, *Loser and Still Champion: Muhammad Ali* (Garden City, N.Y.: Doubleday, 1972); Frederic Cople Jaher, "White America Views Jack Johnson, Joe Louis and Muhammad Ali," in *Sport in America: New Historical Perspectives,* ed. Donald Spivey (Westport, Conn: Greenwood Press, 1985), 145-92; Thomas Hauser, *Muhammad Ali: His Life and Times* (New York: Simon and Schuster, 1991).

3. Still one of the best analyses of Muslim philosophy is C. Eric Lincoln, *The Black Muslims in America* (Boston: Beacon Press, 1973),

4. Jaher, "White America Views Jack Johnson, Joe Louis, and Muhammad All," 145-92; Randy Roberts and James Olson, *Winning Is the Only Thing: Sports in America since 1945* (Baltimore: Johns Hopkins University Press, 1989), 163-88; Sammons, *Beyond the Ring,* 184-223.

5. Hauser, *Muhammad Ali,* 92-93.

6. Ibid., 84-89.

7. *Muhammad Speaks,* May 22, 1964.

8. Ali, *The Greatest,* 35.

9. Hauser, *Muhammad Ali,* 97.

10. Ibid., 83.

11. Ibid., 97-98. Information about Malcolm X's stay in Miami and involvement with Ali prior to the fight can also be gleaned from Malcolm X and Alex Haley, *The Autobiography of Malcolm X* (New York: Ballantine, 1990), 305-8, 407-11; George Plimpton, "Miami Notebook: Cassius Clay and Malcolm X," *Harper's Magazine,* June 1964, 54-61; Robert Lipsyte, "Cassius Clay, Cassius X, Muhammad All," *New York Times Magazine,* October 25, 1964, 29, 135, 140-42; Bruce Perry, *Malcolm: The Life of a Man Who Changed Black America* (New York: Station Hill Press, 1991), 245-50.

12. Hauser, *Muhammad Ali,* 66-67.

13. See Malcolm X and Haley, *Autobiography of Malcolm* X, 306.

14. Ibid., 306-7. The FBI busily charted the meetings between Malcolm X and Clay while the two men were in Miami. See Claybourne Carson, *Malcolm X: The FBI File* (New York: Carroll and Graf, 1991), 71, 248-50, 255.

15. *New York Times,* February 27, 1964.

16. Ibid., February 28, 1964. See also U.S. Congress, Senate, "Civil Rights and Cassius Clay," 88th Congress, 2d Session, *Congressional Record,* February 28, 1964, 4006-10; *Louisville Courier-Journal,* February 27, 1964; *Raleigh News and Courier,* February 28, 1964.

17. *Muhammad Speaks,* March 13, 1964.

18. "Cassius X," *Time,* March 13, 1964, 78; "Cassius X," *Newsweek,* March 16, 1964, 74.

19. *New York Times,* March 7, 1964. One of the ironies is that Ali's "slave name," Cassius Clay, was taken from a famous Kentucky abolitionist who served as Abraham Lincoln's bodyguard for a time and later as his ambassador to Russia. See U.S. Congress, Senate, "Civil Rights and Cassius Clay," 4006-10.

20. Don Atyeo and Felix Dennis, *The Holy Warrior: Muhammad Ali,* 57; John Cottrell, *Man of Destiny: The Story of Muhammad Ali, Formerly Cassius Clay* (London: Frederick Muller, 1967), 154, 180-86.

21. Martin Kane, "The Greatest Meets the Grimmest," *Sports Illustrated,* November 15, 1965, 36-41; *New York Times,* March 8, 1964; *Muhammad Speaks,* December 3, 1965.

22. *Kansas City Call,* February 14, 1964. See also *Baltimore Afro-American,* February 15, 1964; *Miami Herald,* February 7, 1964.

23. *Muhammad Speaks,* April 24, 1964.

24. Ibid, May 8, 1964; June 5, 10, 19, 1964; July 17, 1964. See also "Muhammad Ali in Africa," *Sports Illustrated,* June 1, 1964, 20-25.

25. For details of the chance meeting, see Malcolm X and Haley, *Autobiography of Malcolm X,* 359; Bruce Perry, *Malcolm: The Life of a Man Who Changed Black America,* 270; Peter Goldman, *The Death and Life of Malcolm X* (Urbana: University of Illinois Press, 1979), 178.

26. Malcolm X and Haley, *Autobiography of Malcolm X,* 3 39-40.

27. Perry, *Malcolm,* 271.

28. "Muhammad Ali in Africa," *Sports Illustrated,* June 1, 1964, 20.

29. Hauser, *Muhammad Ali,* 112.

30. Quoted in Perry, *Malcolm,* 271. See *New York Times,* May 18, 1964.

31. Malcolm X and Haley, *Autobiography of Malcolm X,* 434-39.

32. Ibid., 450.

33. Ibid.

34. Hauser, *Muhammad Ali,* 119.

35. Ibid., 150-52.

36. Ali, *The Greatest,* 8.

37. Hauser, *Muhammad Ali,* 144.

38. Ibid., 144-70. See also *Muhammad Speaks,* March 25, 1966; May 5, 19, 1967; June 23, 30, 1967.

39. Hauser, *Muhammad Ali,* 154-55.

40. Ibid., 155,

41. Ibid., 169.

42. Ibid., 173.

43. Ibid., 179.

44. See Oliver Jones, Jr., "The Black Muslim Movement and the American Constitutional System," *Journal of Black Studies* 13 (June 1983): 417-37.

45. *Muhammad Speaks,* March 3, 1967. See also *Muhammad Speaks,* April 14, 28, 1967; October 20, 1967; November 10, 1967.

46. Ibid., May 12, 1967.

47. See Jaher, "White America Views Jack Johnson, Joe Louis, and Muhammad Ali," 175.

48. Bob Woodward and Scott Armstrong, *The Brethren: Inside the Supreme Court* (New York: Simon and Schuster, 1979), 136-39.

49. Ibid.

50. Ibid.

51. See Sammons, *Beyond the Ring,* 216.

52. See Peter Wood, "Return of Muhammad Ali, a/k/a Cassius Marcellus Clay Jr.," *New York Times Magazine,* November 30, 1969, 32-33, 116, 123, 133-32; Robert Lipsyte, "I Don't Have to Be What You Want Me to Be, Says Muhammad Ali," *New York Times Magazine,* March 7, 1971, 24-25, 54-59, 62, 67.

53. *Muhammad Speaks,* April 4, 1969.

54. Ibid., April 11, 1969; see also April 25, 1969.

55. Elijah Muhammad, *Message to the Blackman in America* (Chicago: Muhammad Mosque of Islam No. 2, 1965), 246-47.

56. See Hauser, *Muhammad Ali,* 81-82,

57. *Muhammad Speaks;* April 4, 11, 1969.

58. Ibid., February 4, 1972.

59. Hauser, *Muhammad Ali,* 193.

60. Those closest to Ali frequently discussed the fighter's devotion to boxing. For comments from his trainer, Angelo Dundee, see Hauser, *Muhammad Ali,* 460-6 1.

61. Lipsyte, "I Don't Have to Be What You Want Me to Be," 67.

62. Ibid.

63. *Muhammad Speaks,* January 3, 1975.

64. See, for example, *Muhammad Speaks,* January 17, 24, 1975.

65. For information on changes in the movement, see the *Washington Post,* July 5, 1977; Lawrence H. Mamiya, "From Black Muslim to Bilalian: The Evolution of a Movement," *Journal for the Scientific Study of Religion* 21(1982): 138-52; Zafar Ishaq Ansari, "W.D. Muhammad: The Making of a 'Black Muslim' Leader (1933-1961)," *American Journal of Islamic Social Sciences* 2 (1985): 245-62; Clifton E. Marsh, *From Black Muslims to Muslims: The Transition from Separatism to Islam, 1930-1980* (Metuchen, N.J.: Scarecrow Press, 1984).

66. *Muhammad Speaks,* March 21, 1975.

67. Mamiya, "From Black Muslim to Bilalian," 138-52; Askia Muhammad, "Civil War in Islamic America," *The Nation,* June 11, 1977, 721- 24; David Gates, "The Black Muslims: A Divided Flock," *Newsweek,* April 9 (1984): 15+; "The Farrakhan Formula," *National Review,* November 1, 1985, 19-20; *Washington Post,* July 5, 1984.

68. U.S. Congress, Senate, "Muhammad All Faces the Nation," 94th Congress, 2d Session, *Congressional Record,* May 4, 1976, volume 122, 123 72-75.

69. *Bilalian News,* June 1, 1979.

70. See *Bilalian News,* October 15, 1976; June 1, 1979.

71. *Bilalian News,* April 11, 1980.

72. See Hauser, *Muhammad Ali,* 430.

73. Ibid., 500.

74. *Muslim Journal,* December 4, 1987.

75. Ibid., November 18, 1988.

76. *Washington Post,* July 5, 1984.

77. See Jaher, "White America Views Jack Johnson, Joe Louis, and Muhammad Ali," 145-92; Roberts and Olson, *Winning is the Only Thing,* 163-88; Sammons, *Beyond the Ring,* 184-23 3.

CHAPTER 15

THE FIGHT FOR TITLE IX

■ *Pamela Grundy and Susan Shackelford* ■

Between 1974 and 1976, Stanford University's female basketball players got to know the athletic director's office almost as well as their own locker room. They had plenty to discuss. They wanted out of the women's gym, "so claustrophobic that our 20 fans sat on a single bench between sideline and wall," wrote team member Mariah Burton Nelson. They wanted a paid coach. They wanted real uniforms, rather than the red shorts and white T-shirts over which they tied red P.E. class-style "pinnies."

"We were angry," Burton Nelson noted. "We were persistent. We were, I'm sure, a pain in the neck."[1]

In 1972, the passage of Title IX had promised a revolution in scholastic sports. Under the new law, women were to have the same athletic opportunities as men. For aspiring female athletes such as Burton Nelson, this meant the same teams and uniforms and facilities that men had enjoyed for generations. When Stanford's program fell far short of those expectations, the Stanford players realized it was up to them to make sure those promises became reality. They made a habit of camping out at the office of athletic director Dick DiBiaso, meeting with him more than two dozen times over two years. "We just showed up without an appointment, sat in the lobby until he agreed to see us, then listed our complaints, demands and requests," Burton Nelson said. "We got increasingly persistent. We told him Title IX had passed and that it was his job to start implementing it, that it was unfair to discriminate."

Like many young women of the times, the Stanford players felt entitled to equal treatment and were ready to fight for it. The women's liberation movement was in full swing. Women were taking up new jobs, challenging old assumptions and marching together in rallies to demand rights and respect. In 1972, singer Helen Reddy had reached the top of the pop charts with the unabashedly feminist "I Am Woman." The next year, with much of the nation watching, tennis star Billie Jean King had soundly beaten former Wimbledon champion Bobby Riggs in a highly publicized "Battle of the Sexes," demolishing the claim that women were unable to withstand the pressure of high-stakes athletic contests. Young women watched, listened and expanded their own ambitions.

"In high school, I did a project on the suffragists," Burton Nelson remembered. "One of my male teachers pointed out that women's lib was a derogatory term, and it launched a discussion. Then at Stanford, I took every women's studies class there was. I was personally very empowered, and it affected my sense of entitlement as an athlete."

On a Tennessee farm, future coach Pat Summitt was building similar resolve. "Nobody in the family seemed to regard me as a girl when it came to work or playing basketball," she later wrote. "I fought hard and played hard, and I was expected to hold my own with my brothers, whether we were in the fields or in the hayloft." But she was also keenly aware that such equal opportunity was not the norm. While her brothers went to college on athletic scholarships, there were none for her. Though her mother worked as hard or harder than anyone else, when the family sat down to eat, the men came first. "At the dinner table, when my brothers would finish their tea, they'd hold up their empty glasses and rattle them," she wrote. "They wouldn't say a word. They'd just lift their glasses and shake them, until my mother served them. I can still see those hands, holding up their glasses, rattling the ice. My mother waited on them. And I thought, *That isn't right.*" As she began to plan her future, one thing was clear: "I knew I wanted to make a difference for women."[2]

As Stanford's players quickly learned, building up women's sports programs would prove a demanding task. It was hard enough to challenge long-held ideas about women's physical abilities. Far more effort would be needed to transform institutions that had invested enormous amounts of social, political and financial capital in male sports. "Sharing money is tough," noted Donna Lopiano, who in 1974 became director of women's athletics at the University of Texas. "Opening the door and saying, 'Come on, play', is easier." In Title IX's early years, its supporters would spend as much time in congressional hearings and with college administrators as on the field of play. The country's best teams would come not from wealthy universities but from small schools that drew on persisting pockets of grassroots tradition. The language of Title IX was simple. Turning its promise into reality would require decades of struggle.

When Title IX passed in the spring of 1972, its implications for athletic programs had not been spelled out. The bill's wording was broad, simply stating that neither women nor men could "be excluded from participation in, be denied the benefits of, or be subjected to discrimination under any educational programs or activities." As an extracurricular pursuit, athletics seemed at the margins of the mandate. But that impression did not last long. The bill's implications for athletics quickly became evident, and Christine Grant, the longtime women's athletic director at the University of Iowa, vividly recalled the impact. "All hell broke loose," she said.

As with any federal education law, officials in the Department of Health, Education and Welfare (HEW) were charged with drawing up the regulations that would transform words into reality. As soon as they tackled Title IX, athletics moved to center stage. First, they ruled that athletics would in fact be subject to the law's requirements. They then concluded that the best way to expand opportunity was to create women's teams. "It did not mean girls could try out for boys' teams," explained Jeffrey H. Orleans, one of HEW's civil rights lawyers. "That was not going to produce real equal opportunity, so we had to set up a way of providing separate but equal opportunity."[3]

As soon as those decisions came to light, athletic directors across the country saw the writing on the wall and mobilized for a fight. They knew that unless athletic budgets expanded to accommodate new women's teams, men's programs would get squeezed. The prospects of such increases did not look bright. The early 1970s were tight economic times, with rising oil prices, stagnant employment and spiraling inflation. In addition, the gap in funding between men's and women's sports was staggering. Many universities spent millions on men's athletics and virtually nothing on women's. Making up that disparity through budget hikes alone seemed out of the question. The National Collegiate Athletic Association (NCAA), which regulated men's intercollegiate competition, set aside a $1 million war chest and began lobbying to gut Title IX.[4]

Athletic directors were especially protective of their big-time programs, the so-called "revenue" sports of football and basketball. In the 1950s and 1960s, expanding television coverage had transformed the landscape of American college sports, raising the stakes for success. Schools successful enough to build national reputations, reach bowl games or advance to late rounds in the NCAA basketball tournament reaped the benefits of a national platform, as well as lucrative television revenues. As colleges fought fiercely for a place in this national spotlight, the money spent on recruiting, facilities, coaches' salaries and other athletic perks skyrocketed. NCAA executive director Walter Byers cast the idea of meddling with this formula in apocalyptic terms. Creating equal opportunities for women, he said, would devastate existing men's budgets. The quality of play would plummet, and spectators would lose interest. The result, he gloomily concluded, was the "possible doom of intercollegiate sports."[5]

At first, the Senate agreed. In May 1974, Senator John Tower, a Republican from Texas, proposed that football and other revenue-producing sports be excluded from Title IX coverage. The Tower Amendment promptly passed by voice vote.[6]

But women's organizations fought back. Men's "revenue" sports—mainly football and basketball—had gained their prominence in an era when women were largely barred from college competition. Exempting them from Title IX's standards would lock those old inequalities into place, institutionalizing the idea that women's sports could never be expected to carry the same weight as men's. An exemption would also have ceded authority to the marketplace, allowing money and status to take precedence over equality or education. In practical terms, removing the enormous sums spent on football and basketball from the equity equation would mean far less money for women's programs.

When the Tower Amendment passed, women leaped into action. Physical educators had just formed a new organization, the Association of Intercollegiate Athletics for Women (AIAW). The AIAW hired a tough lawyer Margot Polivy, and launched a wide-reaching grassroots lobbying campaign—AIAW members wrote letters, sent telegrams, visited congressional representatives and testified against the amendment. They were joined by other women's groups—many focusing on sports for the first time. Until the Tower Amendment, most national women's groups had concentrated their efforts on the bread-and-butter issues of health, education and employment. But when Title IX came under attack, women's groups quickly grasped the principle at stake. The central issue was not athletics, but equality. If women settled for second-class status in the powerfully symbolic realm of sports, they would leave the field open to other "exceptions" to full equality.[7]

After months of work, the effort paid off. A joint conference committee eliminated the Tower Amendment. HEW and the congressional committee charged with reviewing the Title IX regulations took a broad view of the issue. "We had some sympathetic ears at HEW," Christine Grant explained. "I think Congress was uneasy about contemplating any kind of exemption because we were talking about educational opportunity." AIAW members rejoiced in the hard-won victory over a far more powerful opponent. "The women in AIAW were very committed to what they were doing," Grant noted. "I'm not just talking about the leadership. I'm talking about the average member. I think our volunteer system was probably the best since the Red Cross."

The final regulations were explicit about the need for athletic equality, stating: "A school must provide equal athletic opportunity for both sexes." A handful of institutions achieved exemptions, among them fraternities, sororities and "scholarships or other aid offered by colleges and universities to participants in single-sex pageants which reward the combination of personal appearance, poise and talent." Football was not among them. In measuring equality of opportunity, the regulations specified, HEW would "consider whether the selection of sports and levels of competition effectively accommodate the interests and abilities of members of both sexes." It would also look at factors that included "facilities, equipment, supplies, game and practice schedules, travel and per diem allowances, coaching (including assignment and compensation of coaches), academic tutoring, housing, dining facilities and publicity." The regulations became final on July 21, 1975, with compliance required by 1978. Women's sports programs, once scattered across a handful of schools, would become a reality across the nation.[8]

As schools began to put together women's teams, aspiring coaches were among the first to benefit. Because most coaching jobs began as part-time positions, linked to jobs in women's physical education departments, most of them went to women. In 1975, South Carolina native Judy Rose was studying for a master's degree in physical education at the University of Tennessee. "There were about thirty of us in grad school at Tennessee…about fifty-fifty male and female," explained Rose, who would go on to become one of the first female athletic directors of a Division I university. "And I remember the guys would walk into class and this is toward the end of the year—and one guy would go: 'Yes! I am the new junior high football coach at such-and-such junior high school!'… One of the girls would walk in and she'd go, 'Guess what, guess what…I'm the new women's tennis coach at the University of North Alabama!'…Now ours was definitely right time, right place."

But while the jobs were easier to get, they were far more challenging to handle. Most novice male coaches were hired to coach established teams or to assist more experienced coaches. Women often started from scratch, with little coaching experience. In 1974, Pat Summitt fell into the head basketball job at the University of Tennessee when the head coach unexpectedly left. "I was a twenty-two-year-old head coach, and I had four players who were twenty-one," she recalled. She dealt with the situation in the best way she knew. "I was hard on them and myself and everyone around me. I thought I had to be. I thought that's how you commanded respect."[9]

The first day of practice revealed the flaws in this single-minded approach. "I worked those prospects up and down the court, at full speed, for two solid hours," she wrote. "At the end of that, I ordered them to run a bunch of conditioning drills. I ran [them] in suicide drill after suicide drill. A group of four young ladies were running together. When they got to the end of the line, they just kept on running. They ran out the door and up the steps, and I never saw them again."

At least Summitt had players to lose. Other coaches were not so lucky. In 1975, Judy Rose was hired as the head women's basketball coach at the University of North Carolina at Charlotte. As she scurried through her new duties—like most early women's basketball coaches she was expected to teach P.E., organize intramurals and coach other sports as well—one of the first things she did was put up signs announcing an organizational meeting for the women's team. "I was so excited," she recalled.

The night of the meeting, however, few showed up. "I remember I went home to my apartment that night, and I was so depressed." One of the women who had hired her "called me at home that night, and she said: 'How did the meeting go?'" Rose continued, "And I said: 'It was awful.' And she said: 'Well, what happened?' I said: 'We only had eight people.' She said: 'That's wonderful!' And I knew I was in trouble."

Rose met with a similar response when she tried to draw spectators to her games. In one promotional effort, she wrote letters to the city's high school and junior high girls' basketball coaches, offering them free tickets to both men's and women's games. "I said: 'If you come to the women's game, I'll let you in the men's game free,'" she explained.

"I kept waiting for the replies," she said. "I never got a reply, never." She stayed perplexed until she ran into one of her supporters. "I said: 'You know I cannot believe that not one person has responded to my letter, not one.' She said: 'Who'd you send them to?' I said: 'Well, I just addressed it to "Women's Basketball Coach."'...And she said: 'Uh, Judy, they don't have women's basketball in the junior high schools or the high schools in Charlotte.' I'm like: 'What?' There's nothing to recruit from. So, I mean, it was a rude awakening."

Judy Rose was far from alone. Outside of places such as Iowa, Texas or Mississippi, female players had few opportunities and limited support. Only the most die-hard players had pressed on. Most of those had never heard of Title IX.

Indiana was a prime example. Indiana boys' high school basketball, with its renowned state tournament, was the stuff of legend. But as in many states, physical educators' pressure had largely eliminated the girls' game. In the late 1950s, when a handful of high school teachers began a cautious revival, they purposely kept a low profile. "What we would do would be to ask a neighboring school to come over to an after-school basketball game," explained Pat Roy, who would later become the director of girls' athletics for the Indiana High School Athletic Association. "We'd have a volleyball game at noon and call the whole thing Sports Day. Really we were there to play basketball."[10]

"Nobody knew about it," she noted. "We weren't sure we wanted anybody to know about it because they probably would have said 'Stop'."

The result was a culture in which young athletic women had to work hard to get respect. Twins Melissa and Melinda Miles learned this firsthand. The boys who played pickup games with them in their family's driveway could join teams as early as elementary school. The twins didn't get to play on one until the fall of 1973, their freshman year at Bloomfield High School. "Nobody thought basketball would amount to anything for us; it was just something to do as kids," Melissa explained. When she asked why boys had teams and girls didn't, her teachers replied, "This is the way it is."

"My dad would also talk about how boys are different, boys are better," she continued. "He was trying to get my goat, but in part he was trying to prepare me, that it's different for boys and girls."

The difference also came clear in the way the Miles's parents reacted to their sporting ambitions, as opposed to their brother's. "I remember asking my mom over dinner one night if I could try out for the high school basketball team," Melissa explained. "She just said, 'We'll see.' She didn't get that it was important to me. It wasn't a big deal. It was like my asking if I could join the Latin Club. But then Bill wanted to play, it was a big deal."

In upstate New York, future coach Tara VanDerveer had run into similar roadblocks. As a young girl, VanDerveer pursued basketball with a determined passion. When local boys left her out of playground pickup games, she saved up her allowance and bought the best basketball she could find. "If the boys wanted to use the ball, they had to take me with it," she noted. But she had little encouragement. "My father couldn't have been a more supportive parent," she wrote, "but even he couldn't see the point of a girl playing basketball." It was hard to blame him, she continued. "It was foolish to think I'd have a future in basketball. How could there be a future when there wasn't a present? There was no girls' basketball team in my junior high school. There was a so-called team in high school that played all of four games but held no practices. There were no women that I knew or had heard of who made their living in the sport."[11]

As soon as they got the chance, however, women showed what they could do. At Bloomfield High, the Miles twins and a handful of their friends spearheaded their team to a 67-2 record over four years, going unbeaten each regular season and winning forty-eight straight games at one point. "Once my parents saw we were good, my mom and dad jumped on the bandwagon," Melissa recalled. "They encouraged us. It was very frustrating that they had not realized how important it was to us to begin with."

Tara VanDerveer, head coach of women's basketball at Stanford, and David Black of the Department of Education participating in the 2007 conference, "Title IX Today, Title IX Tomorrow."

Photo courtesy of Joel Lewenstein.

Bloomfield High won the county title all four years and reached the state championship game in 1976, the first year that Indiana held a state tournament for girls. More than nine thousand fans attended the championship game, where the unbeaten Warsaw Tigers defeated previously unbeaten Bloomfield, 57-52. In 1977, the Miles twins led the team back to the semifinals, and Melissa was named to the Indiana Girls' All-Star Team. But like most high school players at the time, they had never heard of Title IX. Not until they talked to a recruiter from West Point, where they eventually enrolled, did they realize how much women's sport was about to change.

By the mid-1970s, it was clear that change was coming. Still obstacles loomed. As newly hired coaches started to build programs, they had only a handful of government regulations to deploy against decades of habit and tradition. Some women found male allies at their schools. At Cheyney State, for instance, Vivian Stringer developed a fast friendship with men's basketball coach John Chaney. Stringer was hired in 1971, the year that women's college basketball scrapped the six-player women's game in favor of five-player, full-court play. The two young coaches hit it off, and began to work together on plays and strategy. "We had so many lively debates," Stringer recalled. "And so many times the players would come in the gym and we would have been working through a lunch, working with salt and pepper shakers, about 'We need to do this defensively' and 'Here's what I would do offensively,' 'How would you handle this and that?'"

When practice time came, the men's and women's teams mingled on the floor, while Stringer and Chancy took turns lecturing on strategies and fundamentals. "We took the game called basketball as just that," Stringer explained. "Not women's basketball or men's basketball. Because of the way it was presented, the guys had ultimate respect for the women players. And the women broke their necks all the time to keep up."

When Chris Weller became the women's basketball coach at Maryland in 1975, she worked hard to convert Maryland's men's coach, the legendary Lefty Driesell, and succeeded to a point. "Finally, he understood I was just as passionate about my team as he was about his," Weller said. "At press conferences where he went first, he would end by introducing me and saying, 'Now those girls are serious.' I cringed every time he would say 'girls,' but he'd come a long way."

One day, Weller's team was stood up by a group of male players they were supposed to scrimmage in preparation for a big game against Old Dominion. Driesell stepped in, dragging his team managers with him. "'I'll do what you need,'" she recalled him saying. "I told him I needed a tall player on the low block," she continued, "and he said, 'I can do that.' To this day I regret not having a tape of Lefty running up and down the court with his managers playing us."

Most coaches faced far greater resistance. When Tara VanDerveer enrolled in the University of Indiana in the early 1970s, she saw the situation plainly. Indiana had one of the strongest women's programs in the country. But her team's second-class status was palpable.

"It was the whole athletic system that values the men so much more than the women," VanDerveer later wrote. "The men had the gym every day from two until six o'clock, so we didn't practice until evening. There was never a thought that we could split up the prime practice times between us. Basically, it was steak for the men, hot dogs for the women." The disparity, she continued, "struck me as selfish, hoarding all the good things for themselves. I didn't really understand it. I was coming of age during the civil rights movement, and I was passionate about issues of fairness and equality. Why were blacks treated the way they were treated? Why were women treated this way?" But like Melissa Miles, VanDerveer found her complaints fell on unsympathetic ears. "No one had any answers," she concluded. "That's just the way it was."[12]

While Title IX regulations gave women some clout, they did not offer a road map to equality. In addition, the requirement that colleges provide opportunities that "effectively accommodate the interests and abilities of members of both sexes," contained a degree of uncertainty. If only eight women showed up at a basketball organizational meeting, did this mean they had less interest and thus required fewer resources than the men? Reluctant athletic directors, bolstered by the NCAA, seized on every ambiguity as an excuse to drag their feet. Progress was often incremental, and women's coaches carefully weighed their requests. "I didn't go in and ask for things that were outrageous, but I did ask for things," Chris Weller explained. "I wanted the things that counted, like good shoes, good equipment, a place to call home, our own locker room…We didn't even have warm-ups."[13]

Like the Stanford players, Weller also wanted out of the team's second-class gym, which could hold a grand total of two dozen spectators—that was, if everyone stood up. After some stiff negotiation, she won the right to play in Cole Field

House, where the men's team played. "We didn't even have our own locker room, we had to use the visitors' locker room," she said. "But I knew if we just got our foot in the door, that they weren't going to be able to get us out of there."[14]

While they battled for resources, women's coaches also began to shape the guidelines for a distinctive form of competition. Leaders of the AIAW, which governed women's sport the way the NCAA governed men's, were determined to chart a path that departed from the trail men had blazed, avoiding the academic and recruiting scandals that plagued the male athletic model. They were well suited to the task. Women such as Katherine Ley and Carol Eckman were longtime physical educators, strong-willed women who believed in female independence and were accustomed to putting students first. They and others like them made a powerful impression on younger coaches. "These women were so strong," Vivian Stringer recalled of her college mentors at Pennsylvania's Slippery Rock University. "They had doctorate degrees and stood up for their rights. My role models were women for once in my life."As a student at Maryland, Chris Weller noted, "I began to meet a lot of impressive women."

The first set of AIAW regulations, drawn up in 1972, signaled the organization's resolve to put education first. The regulations prohibited scholarships, placed limits on recruiting and emphasized that a female athlete was a student first and an athlete second. "It was the main focus of every delegate assembly," Iowa's Christine Grant recalled of the AIAW annual conventions. "Any proposal for change was always looked at from the educational perspective. I headed a committee on recruiting. The rules said you could watch talent but couldn't talk to the athlete. It worked, and worked well. It protected the student-athlete from harassment."

As they laid down guidelines for programs and recruiting, AIAW members also began to shape the rules for bona fide national championships. Carol Eckman, the women's basketball coach at West Chester State in Philadelphia, had gotten the ball rolling in 1969, when she organized the first national invitational tournament ever held in women's college basketball. The tournament brought together fifteen teams, each of which paid $25 to cover the cost of officials and awards. Competition was only one of the goals. A health and physical education professor, Eckman saw a tournament as a place for the sport's supporters to meet one another and trade information. "This was a time when women's game results were printed on the society page in some newspapers," Tara VanDerveer remembered. "Travel schedules were limited, so most teams had never seen their counterparts from across the country." The host West Chester Ramlettes, starring a future coach named Marian Washington, took the inaugural title. Invitational competitions were held the next two years as well—the 1970 title was won by Cal State Fullerton and the 1971 crown by the Mississippi College for Women, coached by former Nashville Business College star Jill Upton. The AIAW took on tournament duties in 1972, instituting a series of regional playoffs that led to a national tournament.[15]

In contrast to the men's game, which was driven by the deep pockets of major universities, these early women's events had a distinctly small-school flavor. The scholarships, facilities and recruiting budgets that would eventually allow large institutions to dominate play were not yet in place. Rather, success turned on a recruiting base in a region that had retained a tradition of competition and the choice of a coach who could groom homegrown talent into championship material.

The winners of the first AIAW-sponsored championship, the Mighty Macs from Immaculata College, were a perfect example of this combination. With nuns banging buckets in the stands during games, the Catholic women's college was an improbable champion even for that early era. In 1972, Immaculata had no gym—its beloved fieldhouse had burned in 1967, and there had been no money to replace it. Instead, the team practiced in the basement of a convent for novice nuns where the walls came right up to the out-of-bounds lines. Part-time coach Cathy Rush had been hired for the grand sum of $450 a year. But Immaculata was located just outside of Philadelphia, where Catholic institutions had resisted national trends and nurtured a flourishing girls' basketball culture. Immaculata had fielded teams since the 1940s, drawing most of its players from working-class Catholic neighborhoods and developing squads whose tough, aggressive play reflected the hours players had spent competing on Philadelphia's streets and playgrounds, as well as in Catholic Youth Organization leagues.[16]

In 1972, point guard Marianne Crawford could pass and dribble with the best, once dazzling a local sportswriter so completely that he announced: "If there is a better guard in Philadelphia than Marianne Crawford, it's a boy, and if so, I want to see them go one-on-one."[17] Post player Rene Muth was tough under the boards, as was center Theresa Shank. Theresa was "light years ahead of her time," Cathy Rush once noted. "Six feet tall, and if anybody pressed us, she would bring the ball up. She was quick, an excellent athlete. She could jump and shoot. The whole package."[18] Most team members came from working-class families and, like generations of their predecessors, had enrolled in Immaculata because it was nearby, Catholic and cheap. Shank, a high school star, had planned to attend school out of state. But when she was a senior, her family's home burned to the ground. "I was the last one out of the house," Shank later recalled. "All I had left was the pair of yellow pajamas on my back…everyone was devastated. I made the decision to go to Immaculata. It's not what I wanted to do, but what I needed to do."[19]

Cathy Rush, who had been hired in 1970, proved herself more than worthy of such players. Rush was a Baptist, not a Catholic, but she had loved sports all her life. She was also married to an NBA referee, which gave her a front-row view of developments in the men's game. She thoroughly researched opponents and constantly tried out new techniques, molding the Macs into a team marked by a fast-breaking offense and pressure defense.[20]

As with many other women's college teams in the early to mid-1970s, the Mighty Macs had to focus on much more than their play. The players washed their own uniforms at times and carpooled to regular-season games. Leading the caravan, Rush earned the nickname, "Queen of the U-turn" from her players. When the team qualified for the 1972 national tournament, players scrambled to sell pencils and toothbrushes to finance the trip. "I have enough toothbrushes to last for three lifetimes," Sister Marian William Hoben once recalled. "They looked like little kid toothbrushes. They weren't even full-sized." Still, three players had to miss the tournament because of cost, and those who went flew standby to take advantage of half-price fares.[21]

Immaculata had not set its sights on national renown. The team did not even know about the national championship until halfway through the 1971-72 season. Several years later, when staying competitive at a national level began to require a greater investment of time and resources, Immaculata would decide such efforts conflicted with its larger educational mission and would drop from the national scene. But in the early 1970s, a little went a long way. The AIAW had set up regional tournaments that fed into a national tournament draw, and Rush got the team admitted to the mid-Atlantic competition. In the regional finals, Immaculata lost badly to rival West Chester State, 70-38. But the second-place finish won them a bid to the national tournament, in Normal, Illinois. The Mighty Macs regrouped, and Rush reworked her strategy. Immaculata played through to the final and then avenged their loss, beating West Chester, 52-48. The team that had flown standby to Illinois returned to Philadelphia in the first-class section, deplaning to a thunderous reception.[22]

Immaculata ruled women's college basketball for two more years, going undefeated in the 1972-73 season and taking the national title in both 1973 and 1974. In the spring of 1975, however, they finally met their match.

The 1975 national championship in Harrisonburg, Virginia, was a memorable event on several counts, not the least of which was noise. The Mighty Macs had always drawn strength from a large and loyal following, which distinguished itself in the stands by beating galvanized buckets with drumsticks. In 1975, however, the fans of Delta State, from the small town of Cleveland, Mississippi, were not to be outdone. They headed out to local hardware stores, bought wooden blocks and answered the Immaculata challenge with an equally loud rapping. Cheered by the enthusiasm but troubled by the racket, tournament organizers eventually banned all noisemakers. When the air cleared, Delta State had upset Immaculata 90-81 to win the title.[23]

Delta State's victory was especially sweet for the team's coach, Margaret Wade. She had been a member of the Delta State varsity back in 1933, the year that school administrators suddenly decided basketball was "too strenuous for young ladies" and abolished the team. It was a crushing blow. "We cried and burned our uniforms," Wade said, "but there was nothing else we could do." Wade had stuck with her sport, playing two years on a semi-professional men's team before turning to coaching. Mississippi continued to support high school girls' basketball, and Wade became one of the sport's great stars. In more than two decades of coaching, she compiled a record of 453-89-6 and took her teams to three state title games. Most of her victories came at her alma mater Cleveland High, and she became a legendary figure throughout the state.[24]

In 1973, when Delta State president Aubrey Lucas decided to restart the women's basketball program, the first step was obvious. He asked Margaret Wade, who was teaching in the school's physical education department, to coach the team. The sixty-year-old Wade had been retired from coaching for more than a decade, and her health was fragile. She had recovered from both cancer and a nearly fatal car wreck, and she suffered from painful arthritis. But she agreed to get things started.

The other key to Delta State's success lay in an astute recruiting decision. One of the state's top high school players, center Lusia Harris, competed for Amanda Elzy High, just down the road from Cleveland in Greenwood, Mississippi. Like so many great Mississippi players, Harris had grown up on a family farm, building her muscles with her chores and honing her skills in backyard contests with brothers and sisters. Amanda Elzy always fielded top teams and Harris, who stood 6'3", was hard to miss. In the spring of 1973, she recalled, Delta State recruiter Melvin Hemphill made the drive over to Greenwood "and asked me did I want to play basketball in college."

A decade earlier, such a question would have been unthinkable. Lusia Harris was black, and Delta State was a white school. Throughout the 1950s and 1960s, Mississippi had mounted some of the country's fiercest resistance to the civil rights movement. Both Cleveland and Greenwood had been the scene of demonstrations, arrests and violence, as local African Americans began to stand up for their rights. As late as 1963, when the all-white Mississippi State men's basketball team qualified for the NCAA tournament, the staunchly segregationist governor, Ross Barnett, forbade the team to go, because participation would mean taking the court against teams that fielded black players.[25]

By the 1970s, however, blacks and whites across the South were cautiously testing a new racial order, and even Mississippians proved ready for some change. Although Lusia Harris had planned to attend historically black Alcorn State, the school fielded no women's team. Delta State's largely white campus required "a big adjustment," Harris noted, and the school offered no scholarships. But the lure of the game was enough. As she modestly put it, "I went on over and played a little ball at Delta State."

The Delta State team proved a formidable mix of restraint and resolve. Like many teams of the era, they carried on the old tradition of off-setting on-court prowess with off-court charm. According to forward Wanda Hairston, "We tried to go out and prove you could be an athlete and a lady at the same time."[26] Wade was known for her refined demeanor. "She was the type that never raised her voice," Lusia Harris noted. But like many genteel southern women, Wade was tough as nails underneath. She knew what she wanted her players to do and how to get them to do it. During games, Wade always wore a special pin under her suit jacket. "Whenever we played, she would just open that coat up, and it said, 'Give them hell.'" Harris explained. "So, you know, she would never say that, but she would just open her coat up… and the pin had on it, 'Give them hell.' I always remember that."

Harris was equally complex. She was a shy person, a loner who channeled her energy into playing and study. "I wanted to be able to make a living after basketball was over," she explained. "The only thing that I concentrated on was my schoolwork and playing basketball." On the court, however, she was an imposing figure: her 6'3" stature was heightened by a sizeable Afro, and she had the strength to "clean folks out from under that board," as a longtime fan noted.[27] "She could overpower people," a teammate echoed, recalling that despite defenders "hanging on her arms," Harris routinely powered up and hit her shots. Her concentration also helped her to brush off the racist comments encountered by most black athletic pioneers. "Sometimes the fans would say you know, things in the stands," she recalled, "but my focus was to score that basket…And sometimes it got to be pretty rough in the games, you know…. Everybody always said that I did a lot of smiling, but I had a few to say that I was pretty physical under the boards."

Mississippi had a top-notch high school girls' program, and Wade rounded Harris with a stellar cast. In the 1976 tournament, when Harris came down with the flu, point guard Debbie Brock stepped up. Brock stood 4'11" and weighed eighty pounds—"I carry her around in my pocket," Margaret Wade joked. But she was a deft ballhandler as well as a crack shot. Backed by teammates Wanda Hairston, Cornelia Ward and Ramona Von Boeckman, she sparked the team to its second championship, defeating Immaculata once again in the title contest. As usual for Delta State, the five starters played the entire game. The same starting lineup would take the court for Delta State in the 1977 championship, defeating Louisiana State University for a third straight title.[28]

Mississipians responded with enthusiasm. In 1976, a local radio station broadcast the national tournament games to three states. The night that Delta State played a cliff-hanging semifinal, one college official reported, "They took five people to the hospital with heart attacks." After the team returned to Cleveland, students elected Lusia Harris homecoming queen. In 1977, the Lady Statesmen sold out half of their home games and made more money than the men's basketball or football teams. "Wherever we played, we had people from Cleveland and surrounding areas to travel to support the team," Harris said. "And that meant so much…A lot of other places, we had more people than the home team." That same year, the Lady Statesmen received a police escort from northern Mississippi all the way to Minneapolis, where the national championship was held.[29]

As women's competition expanded and rivalries developed, the game began to draw more notice. On January 27, 1975, a game between Immaculata and the University of Maryland was broadcast nationwide, the first nationally televised game in women's college basketball history. A month later, women's basketball made its debut at Madison Square Garden, one of the nation's most venerated basketball facilities. More than 12,000 fans made their way into the storied arena to the strains of "I Am Woman." They were then treated to a "breathtaking game" between two of the nation's top programs—New York's Queens College and Immaculata. "Immaculata would set up and score and Queens would answer, then Immaculata would run a pattern and Queens would steal the ball and score, and so it went, nip and tuck," Queens coach Lucille Kyvallos wrote. In the end, the Mighty Macs triumphed, 65-61. Women's basketball also made another important breakthrough—snagging a long-term corporate sponsor. Throughout the postwar era, as athletic budgets grew, athletic institutions increasingly began to depend not simply on ticket and television revenues, but on corporate funding. In 1975, Kodak agreed to pay $3,000 to sponsor the first All-American women's collegiate basketball team. The next year, Mel Greenberg, a sportswriter at the *Philadelphia Inquire,* started the national women's college basketball poll.[30]

The sport became the focus of national attention, in 1976, when a U.S. women's team competed in the Olympic Games for the first time. After decades of negotiation women's basketball had finally become an Olympic sport—a development that would give the game an international platform and a tremendous boost. Most Americans still paid little attention to women's college basketball. But with national pride on the line, almost any Olympic sport had the chance to catch the public eye.

Internationally, U.S. women faced an uphill battle. Back in the 1950s, when the International Basketball Federation began sponsoring world championship tournaments for women, U.S. squads had won the first two titles triumphing in Chile in 1953 and Brazil in 1957. But then other countries—most notably the Soviet Union—had surged to the fore, pouring resources into national teams even as Cold War conservatism dealt a severe blow to the American women's game. International play became something of an ordeal. International games were always played with full-court rules, and the games were especially physical. "I've often said to get ready for international ball what you ought to do is have people shoot lay-ups and take concrete, fill up a tire, and then hit them with it when they come in—swing it into them," explained Carla Lowry, who played for several national teams in the 1950s and 1960s. "I remember finishing those games and we were just totally exhausted. You had bruises and scratches all over. Nothing like anything we'd ever experienced." In 1967, at the world championships in Prague, the U.S. team went a dismal 1-6, losing by an average of 16 points per game, and coming in dead last out of eleven countries.[31]

The team that took the Olympic court in Montreal, Canada, promised a fresh start. It was full of new faces, a reflection of the changes the sport had undergone in only a few years of college play. During the 1950s and 1960s, U.S. national squads had consisted largely of the AAU's top players, most of whom came from a handful of southern states. But with the rise of college programs and the organization of the United States Olympic Committee (USOC), the AAU had ceased to play a dominant role in top-level national sports and had refocused its efforts on youth programs. The Olympic basketball program was now handled by the USOC, which drew from a vastly expanded pool of talent. More than 250 women from around the country showed up for the 1976 tryouts.

Not only was the starting team racially integrated, it indicated how much the game had grown around the country. The South still held its own, fielding Pat Summitt from Tennessee, Lusia Harris from Mississippi, Cindy Brogdon and Patricia Roberts from Georgia, as well as assistant coach Sue Gunter, a native Mississippian who had pursued her coaching career in Tennessee and Texas. But California was also well represented. Head coach Billie Moore hailed from California, as did two of the players—Nancy Dunkle and rising superstar Ann Meyers. Although the team had only one Midwesterner, Charlotte Lewis from

Illinois, the Northeast made a strong contribution, with Juliene Simpson from New Jersey, Mary Anne O'Connor from Connecticut, Sue Rojcewicz from Massachusetts, and Gail Marquis and Nancy Lieberman from New York.

In the weeks leading up to the Olympics, players trained as they never had before. Billie Moore knew the challenge was formidable. She and Gunter calculated that the team could not match the strength or depth of international powerhouses such as the Soviet Union, and thus focused on conditioning. "I think they thought I was going to kill them, and that was probably true," Moore recalled. She was not far off the mark. Pat Summitt later recalled that Moore was the first woman she ever met who pushed her players to their limits. Practices ran like clockwork. "She could walk into the gym and by simply looking at the clock she could tell what her team was supposed to be doing," Summitt noted. "Coach Moore challenged me every day."[32]

In Montreal, the team quickly learned it still had a long way to go. The United States lost its first game to Japan, 84-71. Against the Soviet Union, Lusia Harris scored 18 points but couldn't stop 7', 280-pound Uljana Semjonova, who camped out under the basket for soft left-handed shots, scoring 32 points in barely more than half a game. The Soviets prevailed, 112-77, and went on to win the gold medal.

Still, the United States surprised observers by defeating Canada, Bulgaria and Czechoslovakia to take second place in the round-robin competition. They got plenty of promotion on ABC's television broadcasts, prompting *Sports Illustrated* correspondent Frank Deford to remark that "it was as if the network was getting ready to replace *Charlie's Angels* with a women's basketball league." Capturing the silver medal in such a high-profile event brought the game welcome notice. "Up until then many people didn't know we had national teams playing in international competition," Juliene Simpson explained. "After the Olympics, that changed quite a bit."[33]

Back home, players and coaches continued to struggle. The NCAA was battling Title IX's requirements at every turn, stonewalling efforts to increase women's funding, continuing to lobby congressional legislators and filing lawsuits aimed at limiting the measures reach. Some college administrations encouraged women's play; others did not. New York's Queens College had one of the best programs in the country in the 1970s. But the pleasure that coach Lucille Kyvallos took in her teams' success was "marred by a small minority of men in the Department of Physical Education who were unhappy with the attention the women's basketball program was receiving." The women's program was far more successful than the men's during those years, Kyvallos later wrote, and the situation did not sit well either with the men's coach or with other faculty members, who consistently worked to limit the women's funding. Kyvallos was far from alone in that experience.[34]

Still, women had also made great strides. By the end of the decade, sports opportunities for girls and women had soared. More than 60,000 women were playing college sports in 1976-77, twice as many as in 1971-72.[35] Basketball had grown dramatically on the high school level as well. In 1973, the year after Title

IX's passage, only eight states sponsored state high school tournaments for girls. By 1977, only New York lacked a state competition. From 1972 to 1981, the number of female high school basketball players would grow more than tenfold, from approximately 400,000 to 4.5 million.[36]

Meanwhile, at Stanford, two years of sitting, talking and pressing had brought athletic director Dick DiBiaso to his female players' side. When the team started practice in the fall of 1976, the women's basketball team had uniforms, a trainer and full-time coaches—all for the first time. Head coach Dotty McCrea had assisted Cathy Rush at Immaculata, and assistant Sue Rojcewicz was fresh from playing on the U.S. Olympic team. The Stanford squad played an expanded schedule and held their home games in the 7,400-seat Maples Pavilion. Though it would still be two more seasons before the first Stanford women basketball players were on athletic scholarship, Mariah Burton Nelson and her teammates had stood up for their rights—not just under Title IX but as women. The victory was sweet. "Mission accomplished," she said.

Notes

1. *Ms.*, December 2002/January 2003, http://www.mariahburtonnelson.com/Articles/WomenSportsMsTitleIX.html (accessed May 2004).

2. Summitt, *Reach for the Summitt*, 21-23.

3. *Chronicle of Higher Education*, 21 June 2002, A38.

4. For expenditure figures, see Cahn, *Coming on Strong*, 250.

5. Festle, *Playing Nice*, 127-28.

6. Ibid., 131.

7. Ibid., 13 1-33.

8. Title IX of the Education Amendments of 1972, 34 Code of Federal Regulations § § 106.1-106.71(1988). (Nondiscrimination on the basis of sex in education programs or activities receiving federal financial assistance). Specifics on athletics are in 106.41. HEW would issue an additional policy interpretation on December 11, 1979.

9. Summitt, *Reach for the Summit*, 11-12.

10. Schwomeyer, *Hoosier HERsteria*, 288.

11. VanDerveer, *Shooting from the Outside*, 31.

12. Ibid., 73.

13. *College Park Magazine*, Summer 2002, http://www.inform.umd.edu/cpmag/summero2/inbounds.html (accessed September 2004).

14. Ibid.

15. VanDerveer, *Shooting from the Outside*, 68 69. Hutchison, "Women's Intercollegiate Basketball," 309-11.

16. For a comprehensive account of basketball at Immaculata, see Byrne, *O God of Players*.

17. Ibid., 184.

18. *Scholastic Coach and Athletic Director*, March 1997, 76.

19. Walters, *Same River Twice*, 212.

20. *New Orleans Times-Picayune*, 6 April 2004; Byrne, *O God of Players*, 194,

21. *New Orleans Times-Picayune*, 6 April 2004.

22. Byrne, *O God of Players*, 174-75.

23. Hutchison, "Women's Intercollegiate Basketball," 314.

24. Trekell and Gershon, "Title IX, AIAW, and Beyond," 405. For an overview of Wade's career, see *Coaching Women's Basketball*, March/April 1997, 14-19.

25. For the civil rights movement in Greenwood, see Payne, *I've Got the Light of Freedom*, 132 79; for the Mississippi State incident, see Henderson, "Mississippi State University Basketball Controversy."

26. *Coaching Women's Basketball*, March/April 1997, 19.

27. O.W. Reily Jr. interview.

28. *Sports Illustrated*, 5 April 1976, 50.

29. Ibid.; *Sports Illustrated*, 4 April 1977, 59.

30. Kyvallos, "Queens College," 361.

31. For an overview of international play, see Ikard, *Just for Fun*, 95-103, 147 53.

32. *Coaching Women's Basketball*, March/April 1997, 22; *Basketball Quarterly*, 2004, http://www.abqmag.com/rnagazine/2004/1stQuarter/w_summit.php (accessed September 2004).

33. *Sports Illustrated*, 18 August 1976, 35; *Coaching Women's Basketball*, March/April 1997, 21.

34. Kyvallos, "Queens College," 365.

35. *Chronicle of Higher Education*, 21 June 2002, sec.A, 38.

36. Lannin, *History of Basketball*, 89; Festle, *Playing Nice*, 249.

PART VI

SPORT DURING THE PERIOD OF CELEBRITY AND GLOBALIZATION, 1985-PRESENT

The recent past has been marked by a significant transformation in American sport. Corporate sponsorships, urban rivalries, specialized media coverage, and improved marketing strategies have contributed to an increased popularity in commercialized sport and made celebrities out of such athletes as Michael Jordan and Tiger Woods. This commercialization has even gone global, as evidenced by the production of sporting goods in underdeveloped countries and athletes' migration to various countries. At the same time, American sport continues to struggle with such age-old issues as the dilemma of race, gender inequality, professionalization of youth sports, gambling, academic performance of high school and college athletes, and performance-enhancing drugs.

During this period, one event that kept many Americans transfixed was Cal Ripken's quest to break Lou Gehrig's streak of 2,120 consecutive games in Major League Baseball. When the great Baltimore Oriole shortstop did break the record in early September 1995, fans lucky enough to be in Camden Yards and even those witnessing the event on their television screens broke out in jubilation. Daniel A. Nathan and Mary G. McDonald address the significance of this event in chapter 16, "Yearning for Yesteryear: Cal Ripken, Jr., The Streak, And the Politics of Nostalgia." Nathan and McDonald contend that the media transformed Ripken and the streak into a narrative "that summoned a highly romanticized version of history and reinforced dominant ideologies of masculinity, race and class." In an era marked by economic problems, "demographic and social instability and change," Ripken "was cast by the media as a heroic model of middle-class virtue and manliness" who "spoke to the longings of many white middle-class Americans (especially men), longing for a mythic time when fathers played catch with sons and the boys of summer reigned."

This notion of manliness lies at the center of chapter 17, "Manhood, Memory, and White Men's Sports in the American South." Ted Ownby sets out by describing "five definitions of manhood that southern white men once claimed as their own." These five are personal independence, honor, racism, paternalism, and what is termed "helluvafella." He then "asks what modern hunting, stock car racing, and college football have come to express about the identities of southern white men and if they continue any of those five traditional meanings of manhood." Ownby concludes that none of these three sports shows "a direct line" to any of the five traditional meanings of manhood. In fact, the traditional southern meanings of manhood in all three sports "have undergone dramatic redefinitions to fit contemporary needs."

One event that also seems to fit contemporary needs is the Super Bowl. An extraordinary national mega-event, the Super Bowl is now America's most-watched television program and is intentionally marketed and promoted to an international audience. Christopher R. Martin and Jimmie L. Reeves take up the topic of the Super Bowl in chapter 18, "The Whole World Isn't Watching (But We Thought They Were): The Super Bowl and U.S. Solipsism." As the title of their essay suggests, Martin and Reeves are primarily concerned with analyzing the Super Bowl as an international phenomenon and pointing out why it "is unlikely to become the favorite sporting event of the rest of the world." Using data from the CNN World News Archives, they make clear that America has overestimated the Super Bowl's "global might."

Suggested Readings

Ashe, Arthur R. *A Hard Road to Glory: A History of the African-American Athlete.* 3 vols. New York: Warner Books, 1988.

Baker, William J. *Playing with God: Religion and Modern Sport.* Cambridge, MA: Harvard University Press, 2007.

Baker, William J. *Sports in the Western World.* Urbana, IL: University of Illinois Press, 1988.

Batchelor, Bob. (ed.) *Basketball in America: From the Playgrounds to Jordan's Game and Beyond.* New York: Haworth Press, 2005.

Djata, Sundiata. *Blacks at the Net: Black Achievement in the History of Tennis.* Vol. 1. Syracuse, NY: Syracuse University Press, 2006.

Djata, Sundiata. *Blacks at the Net: Black Achievement in the History of Tennis.* Vol. 2. Syracuse, NY: Syracuse University Press, 2008.

Fisher, Donald M. *Lacrosse: A History of the Game.* Baltimore, MD: Johns Hopkins University Press, 2002.

Fox, Stephen. *Big Leagues: Professional Baseball, Football and Basketball in National Memory.* New York: William Morrow, 1994.

Guttmann, Allen. *Sports: The First Five Millennia.* Amherst, MA: University of Massachusetts Press, 2004.

Guttmann, Allen. *Women's Sports: A History.* New York: Columbia University Press, 1991.

Higgs, Robert J. and Michael Braswell. *An Unholy Alliance: The Sacred and Modern Sports.* Macon, GA: Mercer University Press, 2004.

Hoberman, John. *Darwin's Athletes: How Sport Has Damaged Black America and Preserved the Myth of Race.* New York: Houghton Mifflin, 1997.

Hoberman, John. *Mortal Engines: The Science of Performance and the Dehumanization of Sport.* New York: The Free Press, 1992.

Jay, Kathryn. *More than Just a Game: Sports in American Life Since 1945.* New York: Columbia University Press, 2004.

Katz, Milton S. *Breaking Through: John B. McLendon, Basketball Legend and Civil Rights Pioneer.* Fayetteville, AR: University of Arkansas Press, 2007.

Lafeber, Walter. *Michael Jordan and the New Global Capitalism.* New York: W.W. Norton, 2000.

Levine, Peter. *Ellis Island to Ebbett's Field: Sport and the American Jewish Experience.* New York: Oxford University Press, 1992.

MacCambridge, Michael. *America's Game: The Epic Story of How Pro Football Captured a Nation.* New York: Random House, 2004.

Miller, Patrick B. "The Anatomy of Scientific Racism: Racialist Responses to Black Athletic Achievement." *Journal of Sport History,* 25(1998): 119-151.

Miller, Patrick B. (ed.) *The Sporting World of the Modern South.* Urbana, IL: University of Illinois Press, 2002.

Miller, Patrick B. and Wiggins, David K. *Sport and the Color Line: Black Athletes and Race Relations in Twentieth-Century America.* New York: Routledge, 2004.

Moore, Kenny. *Bowerman and the Men of Oregon: The Story of Oregon's Legendary Coach and Nike's Co-Founder.* New York: Rodale, 2006.

Oriard, Michael. *Brand Football: Making & Selling America's Favorite Sport.* Chapel Hill, NC: University of North Carolina Press, 2007.

Phillips, Murray G. *Deconstructing Sport History: A Postmodern Analysis.* Albany, NY: State University of New York, 2006.

Pope, S.W. *The New American Sport History: Recent Approaches and Perspectives.* Urbana, IL: University of Illinois Press, 1997.

Rader, Benjamin G. *American Sports: From the Age of Folk Games to the Age of Televised Sports.* 4th edition. Upper Saddle River, NJ: Prentice-Hall, 1999.

Rhoden, William C. *Forty Million Dollar Slaves: The Rise, Fall, and Redemption of the Black Athlete.* New York: Crown, 2006.

Riess, Steven A. *City Games: The Evolution of American Urban Society and the Rise of Sports.* Urbana, IL: University of Illinois Press, 1990.

Riess, Steven A. (ed.) *Major Problems in American Sport History.* Boston: Houghton Mifflin, 1997.

Riess, Steven A. (ed.) *Sports and the American Jew.* Syracuse, NY: Syracuse University Press, 1998.

Roberts, Randy. (ed.) *Pittsburgh Sports: Stories from the Steel City.* Pittsburgh, PA: University of Pittsburgh Press, 2000.

Roberts, Randy (ed.) *The Rock, the Curse, and the Hub: A Random History of American Sports.* Cambridge, MA: Harvard University Press, 2005.

Roberts, Randy and Olson, James. *Winning Is the Only Thing: Sports in America Since 1945.* Baltimore, MD: Johns Hopkins University Press, 1989.

Ross, Charles K. (ed.) *Race and Sport: The Struggle For Equality On and Off the Field.* Jackson, MS: University Press of Mississippi, 2004.

Sammons, Jeffery T. *Beyond the Ring: The Role of Boxing in American Society.* Urbana, IL: University of Illinois Press, 1988.

Shropshire, Kenneth L. *Being Sugar Ray: The Life of Sugar Ray Robinson, America's Greatest Boxer and the First Celebrity Athlete.* New York: Civitas Books, 2007.

Shropshire, Kenneth L. *In Black and White: Race and Sports in America.* New York: New York University Press, 1996.

Shultz, Jaime. "Stuff From Which Legends Are Made: Jack Trice Stadium and the Politics of Memory." *The International Journal of the History of Sport,* 24(2007): 715-748.

Smith, Ronald A. *Play-by-Play: Radio, Television and Big Time College Sport.* Baltimore, MD: Johns Hopkins University Press, 2001.

Suggs, Welch. *A Place on the Team: The Triumph and Tragedy of Title IX.* Princeton, NY: Princeton University Press, 2005.

Vertinsky, Patricia and Captain, Gwendolyn. "More Myth than History: American Culture and Representations of the Black Female's Athletic Ability." *Journal of Sport History,* 25(1998): 532-561.

Wada, Mark Fainaru and Williams, Lance. *Game of Shadows: Barry Bonds, Balco, and the Steroids Scandal that Rocked Professional Sports.* New York: Gotham Books, 2006.

Watterson, John. *The Games Presidents Play: Sports and the Presidency in the Twentieth Century.* Baltimore, MD: Johns Hopkins University Press, 2006.

Wiggins, David K. *Glory Bound: Black Athletes in a White America.* Syracuse, NY: Syracuse University Press, 1997.

Wiggins, David K. (ed.) *Out of the Shadows: A Biographical History of African American Athletes,* Fayetteville, AR: University of Arkansas Press, 2006.

Wiggins, David K. and Miller, Patrick B. *The Unlevel Playing field: A Documentary History of the African American Experience in Sport.* Urbana, IL: University of Illinois Press, 2003.

Wiltse, Jeff. *Contested Waters: A Social History of Swimming Pools in America.* Chapel Hill, NC: University of North Carolina Press, 2007.

CHAPTER 16

YEARNING FOR YESTERYEAR

Cal Ripken, Jr., The Streak, And the Politics of Nostalgia

■ *Daniel A. Nathan and Mary G. McDonald* ■

In early September 1995, when Cal Ripken, Jr., of the Baltimore Orioles played in his 2,131st consecutive baseball game to break Lou Gehrig's 56-year-old record, most of the sports world paid its respects and cheered. Presumably due to his remarkable endurance, the media catapulted Ripken—then 35 years old, a veteran of thirteen major league seasons, and a perennial all-star short-stop—into the national limelight and hailed him as an exemplar of all that was right, and frequently conspicuously absent, in professional sports. He was often portrayed as a "throwback" ballplayer who evoked an earlier era of baseball history. Because Ripken bested a record few thought was approachable, observers described him as a synonym for durability and a symbol of reliability. The media represented Ripken as self-reliant, hard working, responsible, stoic, humble, and family-oriented. It heralded him as someone who could symbolically revitalize sports, and by extension the nation.

Sports Illustrated offered a particularly vivid example of this cultural narrative by memorializing the occasion of Ripken's 2,131st consecutive game with a cover representing Ripken as a Norman Rockwell figure. Critic Carol J. Pierman suggests that the message of this image is: "Down on one knee, bat on his shoulder, the Rockwellian Cal who waits his turn on deck is emblematic of the small-town hero of an earlier generation, a man who must embody the qualities of life we think we have lost."[1]

This essay analyzes how the media constructed Ripken and the streak. More specifically, we interrogate how Ripken and the streak elicited historical parallels and analogies, and how they provided the media with opportunities

Reprinted, by permission, from D.A. Nathan and M.G. McDonald, 2001, "Yearning for yesteryear: Cal Ripken, Jr., The streak, and the politics of nostalgia," *American Studies* 42: 99-123.

to revitalize interest in Major League Baseball by constructing a nostalgic and culturally conservative vision of the past. Put differently, we examine how the media transformed an event into a narrative, one that summoned a highly romanticized version of history and reinforced dominant ideologies of masculinity, race, and class. Although Ripken is an impressive athlete—he was the American League's (AL) Rookie of the Year in 1982, the AL's Most Valuable Player twice (1983 and 1991), has been on seventeen straight all-star teams, and has set numerous major league records for his power hitting and fielding—we are not interested in his accomplishments, per se.[2] Rather, we link the Ripken phenomenon to wider cultural, historical, and political concerns.

By pursuing interconnected themes (such as the politics of representation and nostalgia, and the maintenance of hegemonic masculinity), we describe the media's role in promoting the interests of major league baseball through the construction of Ripken's old-fashioned masculine persona. Of course, the mutually beneficial entanglement between professional sport and the media has a long history dating back to the formation of professional baseball itself. Yet by the beginning of Ripken's baseball career in the early 1980s, professional sport leagues, including major league baseball, were increasingly dependent upon media exposure, rights fees, and advertising revenues for their survival and expansion. Communication studies scholar Sut Jhally suggests that the association among professional sport industries, the media, advertisers, and individual athletes is a mutually beneficial economic relationship known as the sport/media complex.[3] Newspapers and radio and television networks use sport to fill print space and air time while delivering presumably male audiences to advertisers. Mark S. Rosentraub puts it bluntly when he describes sports as the media's "bread and butter." Rosentraub correctly notes that a "never-ending and mutually reinforcing network or linkage exists between sports and the media."[4] This symbiotic relationship is an emotionally powerful union because most Americans experience sport as spectators: the cultural experience of sport is largely a mediated one. Within this relationship, media workers often serve as "the definers of the subculture of sport, the interpreters of its meaning," argues sociologist George Sage.[5]

To illuminate the larger cultural, historical, and ideological implications of the ways in which the media represented the streak, we offer a critical reading of Ripken as a popular icon at a particular moment, *fin de siècle* America.[6] In an era marked by backlash sentiments, nostalgic images such as those connected to Ripken and the streak suggested a return to an era prior to the civil unrest and progressive gains made by the political and cultural movements of late twentieth-century America, including those espousing civil rights for people of color and women. Nostalgic constructions of the past obscure the conflict, violence, and intolerance that have existed throughout U.S. history and continue into the present. While often contradictory, the nostalgic visions linked to Ripken and the streak represented an opportunity to reassert the superiority of a past in which rigid gender role conformity and structured racial segregation were locked firmly in place. Ultimately, then, our essay critiques and contextualizes media representations of Ripken; it argues that they were responses to contemporary cultural anxieties, and that they buttressed the interests of major league baseball and the political status quo. In short, we use Ripken and the streak to engage the politics of nostalgia, and to illustrate how social context contributes to meaning.

Pre-Game Warm-Ups

Understanding Nostalgia

Before we consider the cultural meaning of Cal Ripken's public persona and how representations of the streak evoked a particular version of the past, it is important to outline a few of the presuppositions at work in this essay. First, we acknowledge that there is a politics of representation; that is, regardless of anyone's intentions, the ways in which narrators portray people and events inevitably have ideological subtexts and political and cultural implications. The process of transforming an event into a narrative necessarily requires choices rife with political meanings: on a relatively basic level, for instance, someone must decide who and what to include and exclude. This is not to suggest that all is merely rhetoric or that the past is irretrievably lost (though clearly some pasts are) or that we are advocating some form of radical relativism. Rather, we believe that in the struggle for cultural hegemony, certain images, ideas, and practices appear in media discourses as natural, authentic or inevitable and that this tends to reinforce dominant social relations. Therefore, the narratives that construct social reality need to be read critically *as narratives,* created and written by and for people at specific socio-historical moments.[7]

We also assert that there is a politics of nostalgia. Used here, nostalgia refers to a kind of temporal homesickness, a bittersweet, sentimental way of thinking about or yearning for the past. It is a cultural sensibility, perhaps even a state of consciousness, both private and, more significantly, collective.[8] A variety of critics and historians have considered the nature of nostalgia—a subject which seems to be increasingly recognized by scholars and the media as an influential cultural force—and have informed our understanding of it.[9] Historian and geographer David Lowenthal argues that nostalgia is the current "catchword for looking back," and that it is a way of remembering with the pain removed.[10] In a similar vein, historian Michael Kammen writes, "nostalgia, with its wistful memories, is essentially history without guilt."[11] Put differently, the late cultural critic Christopher Lasch belittled nostalgia as "the abdication of memory," and suggested that it was a way of looking at the "past cut off from the present rather than entwined with it."[12] Cultural critic Michael Eric Dyson further suggests that nostalgia "is colored memory. It is romantic remembering. It recreates as much as it reveals."[13]

But more so than anyone, sociologist Fred Davis has advanced our understanding of nostalgia. In *Yearning For Yesterday: A Sociology of Nostalgia* (1979), which remains the best work on this subject, Davis contends that nostalgia's sources always "reside in the present, regardless of how much the ensuing nostalgic experience may draw its sustenance from our memory of the past"[14] and that "nostalgia tells us more about present moods than about past realities."[15] In this way, Davis continues, nostalgia "occurs in the context of present fears, discontents, anxieties, or uncertainties, even though they may not be in the forefront of awareness," and that it often becomes a way of "holding onto and reaffirming identities which" have "been badly bruised by the turmoil of the times."[16] Often fueled by an underdeveloped sense of history or the fallacy of the innocent past, nostalgia is sometimes contradictory. And although nostalgia has (always?) existed in America, as in many societies, we think that its pull was particularly powerful in America during the 1980s and 1990s, in large part a consequence of demographic, social, economic, and technological transformations that many Americans experienced.[17]

Cultural Contexts

When Cal Ripken, Jr.'s, consecutive-game streak began in 1982, political and cultural conservatives, espousing what they characterized as "traditional" values, had already exerted a powerful—some would argue, dominant—voice in American culture. It was a powerful political and cultural backlash against 1960s- and 1970s-style liberal activism and activists, most notably women and people of color. "The Reagan revolution gave political voice to the mood of reaction and backlash that had gripped middle America in the troubled 1970s," according to historian Paul Boyer. "The individualistic, acquisitive, and socially conservative outlook that Reagan personified influenced America culture no less than American politics."[18] While always challenged and resisted, the Reagan–Bush and Clinton years were a time of zealous patriotism, corporate conspicuous consumption, and scapegoating. New Right initiatives (such as the drive for a constitutional amendment requiring school prayer, the deregulation of big business, an obsession with military spending, and the dismantling of the welfare state) sought to restore a mythic post-World World War II golden age. In the process, some conservatives (and liberals) encouraged nostalgia for a simpler, more innocent time—one when families were seemingly stable and self-reliant, fathers knew best, married women were happy homemakers, class and racial divisions were out of sight and mind, and the United States dominated the world economy. These neoconservative actions and ideals were not only regressive but were also fraught with contradictions and ironies.

Calling for a return to a mythic past of communal harmony and morality, conservatives encouraged policies that further devastated communities and social formations through deregulation, the movement of capital, corporate downsizing, and rollbacks in public spending.[19] The era also witnessed a rapidly globalizing economy, the movement toward an information, service-sector economy, and the beginning of a demographic shift which will (reportedly) eventually make white Americans a numerical minority by the year 2050.[20] These shifts were informed by and intertwined with complex racial, gender, and class dynamics. Deindustrialization resulted in the quest for cheaper labor via the transfer of many well-paying manufacturing jobs from the United States to recently industrializing, economically impoverished countries where labor costs are low. Concurrent assaults by big business on union organizing and the minimum wage were deployed as inevitable and necessary to keep the United States competitive in the global economy. Immigration hysteria encouraged a largely white obsession with the ways in which illegal immigrants allegedly put a strain on public social services and dominate the service sector of the economy.[21] Media representations of Ripken as a traditional masculine hero and a relic from a simpler time reflected and contributed to this conservative world view.

It is important to mention that both American masculinity and major league baseball—which, are intricately bound, although that link is infrequently noted—suffered crises during this period. As many social critics and historians have noted, American masculinity was in crisis for much of the twentieth century.[22] In the late 1960s and 1970s, however, a faltering, de-industrializing economy produced economic insecurity in millions of men. In particular, the status of middle- and working-class men as breadwinners became more tenuous as men's median weekly earnings in the 1990s fell below levels in the 1970s.[23] Moreover, Second Wave feminism and critiques of patriarchy challenged male hegemony.[24] As a result, many American men experienced acute anxiety about their gender identity and the privileges historically associated with masculinity. With continuous challenges to male economic and cultural power and privilege, many men were (and remain) uncertain and anxious about what it meant to be a man.

Similar to the late nineteenth and early twentieth century, when various social commentators decried the feminization of young men and society itself, countless coaches and commentators during the late twentieth century lauded sport as a character building, healthy, and masculine activity. According to sociologist Michael A. Messner, elite sport serves as a site linking men to a more patriarchal past. Via the glorified mass media spectacles of sport, men, regardless of their backgrounds, are encouraged to identify masculine physicality with presumed male cultural and social supremacy. Thus Messner writes, "organized sports have come to serve as a primary institutional means for bolstering a challenged and faltering ideology of male superiority in the 20th century."[25] By extension players like Cal Ripken, Jr., a quietly confident man with a strong work ethic, served as idealized symbols of what it meant to be a man.

While Ripken played his way to 2,131 games, major league baseball was probably most notable for its labor disputes, strikes, threats of strikes, owner collusion scandals, to say nothing of numerous revelations of substance abuse and the lifetime suspension of major league baseball's all-time hit leader Pete Rose for betting on baseball and damaging the integrity of the game.[26] Baseball, however, was resilient. Public relations and image problems notwithstanding, major league baseball remained popular, in part to its historic linkages to heroic masculinity. In 1980, a record 43 million people attended major league baseball games, income from baseball–television contracts accounted for a record 30 percent of the game's $500 million revenue, and television ratings for the World Series had never been higher. During the 1980s and the early 1990s, all of these leading indicators continued to rise. Reflecting on the period, historian Charles C. Alexander observes in *Our Game: An American Baseball History* (1991) that "profits, salaries, attendance, and general excitement over things baseball would be greater than ever, but it would be an unprecedentedly strife-filled period."[27]

One of the ways major league baseball was able, despite its problems, to maintain its hold on the U.S. public was through the use of nostalgia. Of course, baseball has been embedded in nostalgic discourses since the nineteenth century. As cultural critic Gerald Early puts it, baseball is commonly perceived to be "a 'pastoral' sport of innocence and triumphalism in the American mind, a sport of epic romanticism, a sport whose golden age is always associated with childhood."[28] Nonetheless, John Bloom argues in *House of Cards: Baseball Card Collecting and Popular Culture* (1997) that the "decade of the 1980s might be seen as a watershed for baseball nostalgia."[29] Bloom contends that contemporary images of baseball's past provided a social and psychological retreat for those middle-class male "baby boomers" searching for more authoritarian and presumably "authentic" images of (white) masculinity grounded in the patriarchal past. Baseball nostalgia took many forms in the 1980s and early 1990s, from novels like W.P. Kinsella's *Shoeless Joe* (1982) and Eric Rolfe Greenberg's *The Celebrant* (1983), to films like Barry Levinson's *The Natural* (1984) and Phil Alden Robinson's *Field of Dreams* (1989), to ballparks like Oriole Park at Camden Yards in Baltimore (which was completed in 1992) and Jacobs Field in Cleveland (which opened in 1994).

Nostalgic images associated with baseball held particular sway after the 1994-95 Major League Baseball strike—which lasted 232 days and caused the cancellation of 921 regular-season games, not counting the World Series and other postseason games.[30] It was by far the longest, most bitterly contested, and costliest work stoppage in sports history. For much of the public, the work stoppage was insignificant. To many people, however, the strike mattered a great deal. "The players and owners can both go to hell," said one former baseball fan. "I'll find other outlets for my time and money."[31] Others were less concise and more melodramatic. "This most recent stalemate between players and owners suddenly feels as grim and tragic as Verdun—irrational as that seems," wrote journalist Bill Gallo, two months before the strike ended.[32] "Never again will baseball occupy the cherished place in the American imagination that it once held. Never again will we believe. No matter what the loudmouths in Washington proclaim, or how the owners backpedal, or what concessions the players now make, the essential joy of the game is gone." Admittedly hyperbolic, Gallo nonetheless articulated the way numerous baseball fans felt about the labor dispute. Public opinion surveys, lagging ticket sales, and depressed television ratings—not to mention a few acts of protest and civil disobedience—indicated that many fans were deeply resentful about the ways in which they were treated by the owners and the players, and that they were wary of re-investing—financially and emotionally—in the game.[33] The mythic appeal of baseball as pastoral national pastime seemed to be shattered once and for all.

The cancellation of the World Series was another significant source of fan discontent. "For a lot of people," said Bill Giles, the owner of the Philadelphia Phillies, "taking away the World Series was like taking away the American flag."[34] A showcase of American masculinity, the World Series has come to symbolize qualities which baseball and the nation purportedly embody: competition, excellence, fair play, and hard work—in short, democracy and meritocracy. It is an annual event that encourages men to pass along these values to their own children, especially their sons. Many Americans simply found it inconceivable that the owners and the players would tamper with and despoil baseball's most revered event and ritual of masculinity, but they did. At the beginning of the 1995 strike-shortened season, Charles Krauthammer of the *Washington Post* argued that the "great blow to baseball, the crucial alienating event, was the cancellation of the '94 World Series. From that baseball will never recover."[35]

The 1995 baseball season concluded with the World Series. But that alone did not ennoble the season (except perhaps to Atlanta Braves fans). Rather, many observers noted that the 1995 baseball season was given an imprimatur of integrity when Ripken broke Gehrig's consecutive games played record. More than anything else, the media claimed, the streak gave the 1995 season meaning and helped to restore the game's battered image and its link to the past. For as Krauthammer observed in May, many in baseball were "counting on Cal Ripken's consecutive games streak to revive the game, some say, as Babe Ruth did after the 1919 Black Sox scandal."[36]

2,131: A Nation Turns its Eyes to Cal

Conventional wisdom has long maintained that George Herman "Babe" Ruth (1895-1948), with his brilliant power hitting and exuberant and flamboyant life style, rejuvenated—indeed, transformed—baseball after the Black Sox scandal, in which several prominent Chicago White Sox ballplayers allegedly conspired with gamblers to "throw" the 1919 World Series to the Cincinnati Reds.[37] It is commonly held that, having slugged a record-shattering 54 home runs the year that the World Series scandal was revealed, Ruth galvanized popular interest in the game the following season. To the delight of the baseball establishment, argues writer Ken Sobol, it turned out that most fans "were more interested in speculating about what the Babe would do for an encore in 1921 than they were in rehashing the delinquencies of the White Sox."[38] To put it mildly, the public loved Babe Ruth, in part because he represented the realization of the American dream and in part due to his rambunctiousness. While Kenesaw Mountain Landis, a stern jurist and moralist hired as commissioner in 1920 in the wake of the Black Sox scandal, imparted an appearance of rectitude, propriety, and stability, it was Ruth who revitalized professional baseball. "If Landis was the image of its new purity," argues writer Eliot Asinof, "it was Babe Ruth who gave it excitement."[39] Many historians and critics have identified Ruth as a vibrant cultural symbol for his era.[40] According to the late historian Warren Susman, Ruth "was the perfect creation for an increasingly mechanized world that still hungered for the extraordinary personality, that tired of the Model T automobiles and yet was also appreciative of their virtues—wanting only something more, something bigger than life."[41] Ruth was certainly that. Yet in terms of baseball history and mythology, he was (and remains) the game's savior.

By the spring of 1995, Major League Baseball once again desperately needed redemption. It was in obvious disfavor with the public because of the strike. "Yes, there was a certain amount of joy over the return of the game," wrote Tom Verducci of *Sports Illustrated*, after the first week of the season. "But in ballparks all across the country people spit on the flag of baseball. The return of the game was greeted with anger, derision, mockery and—the worst insult of all—indifference."[42] Considering Major League Baseball's public relations problem, as early as spring training some observers were positioning Cal Ripken and his endurance record as the focal point of the upcoming season.[43] The *Washington Post*, for example, wrote that Ripken's "pursuit of Gehrig is *the* story to which baseball people can point these days as a positive while their ravaged sport tries to put the pieces back together following the strike."[44]

Ripken did not eschew media attention, but he was publicly uncomfortable with it. "In some ways, I wish I wouldn't receive so much attention for this," Ripken said. "But I guess I understand what the importance is, and I accept it."[45] As one writer put it, Ripken was "Baseball's Reluctant Messiah."[46] Ripken was cast in the role because he had been in the Orioles' line-up every day since May 30, 1982. For over thirteen years, Ripken slowly but inexorably wound his way toward September 6, 1995. Unassuming and seemingly unflappable, Ripken was a superb candidate for the task at hand. To many, he appeared to be a throwback to an earlier era when baseball players seemed more dignified and humble, and less motivated to perform for financial rewards than for the joy of the game. Veteran observer Heywood Hale Broun mused, "Ripken seems like some figure emerging from a time machine. You half expect him to be wearing a baggy flannel uniform and using a skimpy glove."[47] Of course, the post-strike timing of his final assault on Gehrig's record contributed to the sense that Ripken was a living relic from a more innocent, less contentious bygone age. "At a time when the game is in serious rehab," wrote Curry Kirkpatrick of *Newsweek*, "Ripken stands out as the ideal role model—an anti-[Mickey] Mantle who, rather than abuse his family and body over the span of a distinguished career, has held them aloft as the twin citadels of his success."[48] Unlike so many of his colleagues, Kirkpatrick continued, Ripken is "a quiet, serene hero so gracious that he actually respects the integrity of the sport. He also signs autographs for hours for no charge, and drives and drinks what he endorses (Chevy Suburban, milk)."[49] Hailed by the media nationwide as a paragon of steadiness, hard work, determination, and decency, Ripken was transformed from an All-Star ballplayer into an icon of All-American homespun masculine virtues.

Ripkenmania reached a crescendo on the evening of September 6, 1995, in Baltimore when the Orioles' shortstop officially broke Gehrig's record in the fifth inning of a game against the California Angels.[50] To commemorate the historic moment, play was interrupted, fireworks exploded, and balloons were released. Major League games all over the country stopped so that fans and players alike could watch the celebration.[51] Millions more watched on television in what turned out to be the highest-rated baseball game ever broadcast by ESPN.[52] Back in Baltimore, after more than ten minutes of cheering by the 46,000-plus fans in attendance, Ripken was pushed out of the dugout by his teammates for an impromptu goodwill lap around the ballpark. All told, the game was suspended for 22 minutes. "If there was a more joyful 22 minutes in baseball," wrote sportswriter Tim Kurkjian, "no one could remember it."[53] Applauded wildly throughout the evening, Ripken retained his composure, so much so that he subsequently hit a home run. At the conclusion of the game, the Orioles held an hour-long ceremony to honor Ripken and his achievement. Hall of Fame outfielder Joe DiMaggio offered congratulations: "wherever my former teammate Lou Gehrig is today, I'm sure he's tipping his cap to you, Cal Ripken."[54]

Finally, Ripken spoke. He expressed his gratitude to Baltimore's baseball fans and to fans all over the country for their kindness and support. He honored his

Cal Ripken at bat in Baltimore's Camden Yards during his historic streak.
National Baseball Hall of Fame Library Cooperstown, N.Y.

parents for their guidance and love. He thanked his former teammate Eddie Murray for his example and friendship. And he acknowledged his wife, Kelly, for her advice, support, and for enriching his life. Ripken concluded:

> Tonight I stand here, overwhelmed, as my name is linked with the great and courageous Lou Gehrig. I'm truly humbled to have our names mentioned in the same breath.
>
> Some may think our strongest connection is because we both played many consecutive games. Yet I believe in my heart that our true link is a common motivation—a love of the game of baseball, a passion for our team, and a desire to compete on the very highest level.
>
> I know that if Lou Gehrig is looking down on tonight's activities, he isn't concerned about someone playing one more consecutive game than he did. Instead, he's viewing tonight as just another example of what is good and right about the great American game. Whether your name is Gehrig or Ripken; DiMaggio or Robinson; or that of some youngster who picks up his bat or puts on his glove: You are challenged by the game of baseball to do your very best, day in and day out. And that's all that I've ever tried to do.[55]

Like the man himself, remarked many observers, Ripken's speech was respectful and gracious; it lent dignity to The Streak and to the game itself, which was still suffering from the post-strike doldrums. At the same time, by evoking names from baseball's past like Gehrig, DiMaggio, Robinson, it explicitly tapped into the nostalgia upon which the game thrives.

Immediately after game 2,131, numerous fans, ballplayers, and journalists described the streak as a vehicle to restore interest, respect, and faith in Major League Baseball. At the conclusion of the record-breaking game, for example, one fan held a sign that read: "CAL, THANK YOU FOR SAVING BASEBALL."[56] President Clinton, who usually kept close tabs on popular sentiment and who was at Camden Yards that night, remarked: "I think the games last night and tonight are going to do a lot to help America fall back in love with baseball."[57] Some of Ripken's colleagues concurred. According to the *Baltimore Sun*:

> Fans were angered by the strike, and they've taken out some of their frustration on the players. But, some players say, Ripken and his streak have served as a salve. "With everything that baseball went through last year with the strike, the loss of fans and some of the loss of popularity for the sport, things like this are nice to see," [Orioles catcher Chris] Hoiles said.[58]

Orioles pitcher Mike Mussina observed that, if one were to choose a year to break a major record, "you couldn't have picked a better year, under better circumstances, in a better period of time for baseball."[59] When asked about the streak and its possible salutary effects on the game, first baseman Rafael Palmeiro noted: "We—baseball—really needed this, and Cal came through."[60] Many members of the fourth estate (especially in Baltimore) lauded Ripken and the streak. More than a few connected the streak and the strike. Long-time *Baltimore Sun* sports columnist John Steadman argued that Ripken, "whether he knows it or not, stands as an animated monument to all that's good about America's most revered but too often beleaguered pastime."[61] The *New York Times* sports columnist Murray Chass described Ripken's feat as "the brightest, most dramatic development of a season damaged by an unresolved labor dispute."[62] And Bob Verdi of the *Chicago Tribune* opined: "The Streak was years of hard labor. The Lap was a spontaneous love-in. Cal Ripken did everything Wednesday night but restore peace to his embattled industry. He took a run at it, though. Maybe baseball will take the hint."[63] It did not, for the players and owners took another fourteen months to reach a collective bargaining agreement.[64]

To Ripken's apparent discomfort, some journalists viewed The Streak as a remedy for their strike-induced baseball blues. "If the owners and the players had wanted to invent an antidote to their image problems," columnist E.J. Dionne, Jr. quipped, "they would have invented Cal Ripken."[65] For some, the streak seemed to be a baseball tonic. Indeed, some observers viewed Ripken as a blue-collar healer, as someone who had nursed the wounds baseball sustained during the strike. As Tony Kornheiser of the *Washington Post* put it: "Baseball was ailing, and Cal became its Florence Nightingale."[66] Thanks to his relentless, self-effacing pursuit of excellence, Ripken somehow made a great many people care about baseball again. Still, Kornheiser reflected, Ripken

> couldn't rescue baseball by himself; not even Babe Ruth could after what [baseball commissioner] Bud Selig and [union leader] Donald Fehr did to the game. But Cal saved it from disappearing down a rat hole. Baseball has become passe lately. Football has surpassed it as the national pastime, and basketball has all the younger demographics. But baseball is still the sport of fathers and sons and myth in this country, and it is no small cultural accomplishment that Ripken was its life preserver.[67]

In recognition of Ripken's achievement, *Sports Illustrated* named him Sportsman of the Year for 1995, and the Associated Press selected his consecutive games-played streak as the sports story of the year.[68] Six months later, the streak still going strong, sports columnist Thomas Boswell maintained that Ripken broke baseball's endurance record "with such humility and generosity of spirit that he restored half the good name of his tarnished sport."[69] All of which suggests that, to many people, perhaps especially journalists, Ripken revivified, perhaps even re-ennobled, major league baseball after the strike, somewhat like Babe Ruth did after the Black Sox scandal. As Buster Olney of the *Baltimore Sun* put it: Ripken may have done "more for baseball than any player since Babe Ruth in 1920 and 1921, when the Bambino's awesome power overwhelmed the cynicism created by the 1919 Black Sox scandal."[70] The analogy is not precise, of course. The two men obviously embody radically different (even antithetical) versions of baseball heroism: one appears to be the quintessential self-made man, disciplined and modest, while the other seems to be the ultimate natural man, hedonistic and brash. (In this way Ruth and Ripken illustrate the truism that different historical moments demand and produce different types of heroes.) But Ruth and Ripken both provided the baseball crises of their day with (the appearance) of narrative closure that they so desperately needed. Both ballplayers re-focused popular and media attention on the game itself and projected cultural values that many Americans esteemed and apparently yearned for in themselves. Like Ruth, a fellow Baltimorean, Ripken seemed to provide baseball with redemption when it needed it most.

The streak—a genuinely impressive accomplishment rather than a mere pseudoevent—became a media-created cultural commodity eagerly consumed by hungry fans. One way of illustrating this is to note the myriad products—T-shirts, hats, bumper stickers, posters, videos, "limited edition" collector plates, newspaper and magazine articles, and books, including Ripken's autobiography, *The Only Way I Know* (1997), as well as the actual game broadcast on ESPN—sold to commemorate Ripken's feat before, during, and after the record- setting game. In fact, ESPN's broadcast of Ripken's 2,131st consecutive game articulated many of the themes examined here.[71]

The Cultural Work of Cal Ripken, Jr.

The media's construction of the Ripken persona and the streak evoked romantic remembrances of multiple pasts. Most frequently, the media linked Ripken to sanitized accounts of the 1920s and 1930s (the era of Ruth and Gehrig), Ripken's own Ozzie-and-Harriet-like childhood in the 1960s, and baseball prior to 1970s free agency, collective bargaining, and work stoppages.[72] While each of these "pasts" offered distinctive narratives, the overall representation of Ripken projected an idealized family man from yesteryear.

The mythic pasts Ripken's persona evoked were similar to other nostalgic impulses of the 1980s and 1990s. Through them, mainstream Americans were invited to return to a seemingly more stable, more innocent time. A conspicuous example of this type of nostalgia was found in appeals for a return to so-called "traditional family values." Although never explicitly articulated, "traditional family values" suggested a link between morality and responsibility. It also encouraged Americans to hearken to bygone eras when family life was presumably more wholesome, purer, and the cornerstone of U.S. greatness.[73] The nuclear family of the past—with the breadwinner father, stay-at-home mother, and two children—was thus made to stand as the antithesis of the presumed moral and political decay of the present. Cultural critic John Fiske identifies the coded language and ideological role associated with images of the traditional nuclear family:

> In this ultraconservative but loudly voiced imagination, the traditional family upon which U.S. society apparently depends for its stability is implicitly white, and the threat to it, therefore, is colored. Unsurprisingly, this imagination has made the single Black young mother on welfare stand for everything the all-American family is not.[74]

In this way, the responsibility for wholesale cultural tensions and transitions was diverted from deindustialization, institutional racism, and the gendered division of labor to the backs of individuals and individual families, especially African-American and recent immigrant families. Here nostalgia focused blame for present disruptions on certain sectors of society that have supposedly undermined the coherence of a constructed, sentimental past.

Representations of Ripken's boyhood in the 1960s participated in this portrait of (white) family life as presumably superior to most contemporary families, which were allegedly in a state of crisis. The media often told the story of Ripken's childhood as a tale of family solidarity and male bonding. Cal Ripken, Sr., spent years coaching and managing in the Orioles organization and during Cal, Jr.'s, youth the family moved around the country before ultimately returning to its Aberdeen, Maryland home. Early on, Vi Ripken (Sr.'s wife and Jr.'s mother) took the young children—Cal, Jr., Fred, Billy, and Ellen—to the ballpark to watch Cal, Sr.'s, games. Later, as a teenager, Cal, Jr., accompanied his father to baseball clinics and games and mingled with professional players, like future Hall-of-Famers Brooks Robinson and Jim Palmer. In 1978, Ripken officially became a member of the Orioles "family" when he was selected in the second round of the amateur draft. Thomas Boswell notes, "Cal Ripken was raised by a strict family on the small-town values of rural Maryland. For him, the '60s and '70s might as well have been the '40s and '50s—when America was productive, self-confident, simplistic and not too hip to have heroes."[75] In the words of Ripken biographer, Harvey Rosenfeld:

> very caring and loving parents insisted on discipline and order, courtesy, respect for elders, and hard work. Both mother and father eschewed all vices and strongly recommended that their offspring do the same. They taught their children always to ally themselves with what is right, to value the importance of family life, and to believe in themselves, doing the best in everything they did.[76]

Ripken's wife, Kelly, and children, Rachel and Ryan, were represented similarly, but with a few notable twists. Whereas Cal Ripken, Sr., was often absent due to his baseball responsibilities, Cal Ripken, Jr., was commonly portrayed as a concerned, attentive husband and a doting father determined to maintain a close relationship with his family. Without drawing an explicit contrast to his own father, Ripken, Jr., said it is important to make "the best of whatever situation you have and having a good rapport with your kids and your family and letting them know you'll be there no matter what."[77] The media often represented the Ripken family as blissfully domestic, oftentimes at their sprawling suburban home, a result of Ripken's success as a breadwinner.

Ripken: Cal on Cal (1995), an oversized, fan-friendly, behind-the-scenes book which includes numerous photographs of Ripken's family, is emblematic of this preferred portrait. In addition to depicting Ripken in action on the field, it features pictures of Ripken playing with his children in their pool and shooting basketballs with Kelly in their full-size gymnasium; it also shows Rachel and Ryan taking swings in a batting cage. These images are juxtaposed with text in which Ripken discusses his childhood, his mother's contributions to his development, and his father's meticulous attention to detail, duty, and work. It is clear from the text that Cal, Sr., had a tremendous influence on Cal, Jr.'s, baseball career ("I guess it's not surprising that my approach to baseball comes from being around my father," Ripken explained), but it is also plain that Cal, Sr., passed along desirable masculine traits as a family provider and caretaker.[78] These accounts suggested deference to and reverence for fatherly authority. Ripken put it succinctly, "I thought my dad knew the right way to do everything."[79] When combined with Ripken's image as a baseball throwback, this portrait conveyed an old fashioned kind of masculine icon. The focus on the Ripken families demonstrated that Cal Ripken, Jr., has realized the American dream due to hard work, perseverance, and familial love and support, qualities once commonly passed from father to son, but are now, according to some of those who espouse a return to "traditional family values," increasingly rare.[80]

Media representations of Cal Ripken, Jr., also recalled an era when professional athletes were commonly (and often mistakenly) perceived to be clean-cut role models—rather than over-paid, over-exposed, pampered celebrities—and professional sports teams were respected pillars of the community—instead of cold-blooded, corporate institutions only interested in the bottom line who frequently hold ransom their city with the threat of relocation. Despite a multi-million dollar a year income, Ripken was positioned apart from most contemporary ballplayers, who are often characterized as avaricious mercenaries. Ripken's behavior on and off the field suggests a (romanticized) pre-free agency temperament when baseball players made far less money for playing a child's game and were loyal to the home team (largely because they were forced to because of baseball's reserve clause).[81] In this way Ripken was notable because, as Steve Wulf of *Time* magazine put it, he "has turned down several opportunities to become a free agent, preferring to remain an Oriole and a Baltimorean. He has endorsement deals, to be sure, but his most famous one is for milk."[82] Another journalist described Ripken as "the new 'Iron Horse' because he has lived and played against the sorry trends of this era: laziness, transient loyalty and galloping prima donnaism."[83] Because he seemed to be the antithesis of these trends, Ripken appeared to be an anachronism, out of place in the present.

The previously mentioned Rockwellian portrait of Ripken is an excellent case in point. Here the sordid history of contentious race relations and Jim Crowism in sport and the wider culture is literally whitewashed via a romantic depiction of a benevolent small-town white hero. This portrait ignores the history of white supremacy which has and continues to structure white privilege.[84] As the modest hero of yesteryear, Ripken summons racial innocence, industriousness, and self-assurance. The celebration of these characteristics gained further significance in relation to the negative attributes often assigned to people of color, and it obscured structured inequality and institutional racism. In contrast to representations of whites, people of color (particularly African Americans and Latinos) are more likely to be stereotyped as lazy, self-gratifying, and depraved.[85]

A particularly vivid example of the way Ripken was used to suggest racial dominance was a *Wall Street Journal* editorial which contrasted Ripken to multi-sport star Deion "Prime Time" Sanders, a perennial all-pro defensive back in the National Football League and middling major league outfielder. The *Wall Street*

Journal editorialized, "it's hard to think of two men who are more different—one the flashy 'Prime Time,' the other the no-nonsense 'Iron-man.' Their differences speak volumes about the challenges confronting not only professional sports but society in general."[86] Through coded language and (not so subtle) implication, Sanders was portrayed as the stereotypical egocentric, brash, boastful, and mercenary contemporary African American athlete. Ripken, on the other hand, embodied "old school" athletic sensibilities. "Mr. Ripken has achieved renown for his steady hard work on the diamond, not for off-the-field theatrics," continued the *Wall Street Journal.* "The 'Ironman' never sulks, never boasts, never insults opponents—and he never disdains the small jobs." Although the *Wall Street Journal* never mentioned either man's racial identity, the racial inference it raised is clear. The *Wall Street Journal* concluded on a wistful, cautionary note: "Sports used to be full of Cal Ripkens; now it's full of Deion Sanderses. Can pro sports—or America in general—survive under those conditions?" Nostalgic depictions of Ripken and the past comforted whites and provided a sense of superiority in the wake of an increasingly multicultural (and thus supposedly inferior) America society. In short, Ripken represented the great white hope. Ripken's All-American persona encouraged whites to escape the messy, contentious economic and political struggles resulting from America's transformation from a country "organized around a relatively homogeneous, Eurocentric consensus to a more diverse multicultural social order."[87]

Obviously these renditions were not absolute; they were subject to interpretation and existed with notable contradictions. Roger Aden's observations concerning the polyvocal nostalgia surrounding the baseball documentary *When It Was a Game* (1991) illuminate the complex classspecific character of the Ripken phenomenon.[88] Aden notes that in an era of downsizing, outsourcing, declining blue-collar jobs, and increasing part-time work without benefits, discussions of a baseball icon as emblematic of America's past partially reflected American workers' desire for a time when working-class men presumably "possessed a strong identity and a perceived sense of collective power."[89] Read from this perspective, Ripken, whose salary was $6.3 million in 1995 and who made $4 million more in endorsements, thus became a (surrogate) blue-collar hero, a laborer who has a job (to do).[90] The October 15, 1995 issue of *People* magazine articulated this theme by comparing Ripken's consecutive game streak to the productivity of other working Americans. Or as *People* phrased it: "Eat your heart out, Cal Ripken! These hardworking Americans started their on-the-job streaks before you were even born."[91] The magazine featured six people whose consecutive streak of never missing a work day (save vacations) spans at least 35 years, including proofreader Audrey Stubbart (50 years) and Herb Christiansen, a purchasing agent (59 years). Of course, these durable workers share a common fortuitousness in that their jobs have not (yet) been eliminated by an increasingly global and multinational capitalist economy. In all of these ways, positioning Ripken as a blue-collar hero of a conflict-free past conjured up an emotionally-charged vision in which masculine strength was hailed as essential to the maintenance of the family and national life.

The multiple pasts associated with Ripken participated *in fin de siècle* American popular culture, which was awash with "retro" ideas and images that served as dubious antidotes to the anxiety created by large scale and exasperating cultural changes. Rather than engaging creatively and directly to ease these transitions, nostalgic discourses encouraged a conservative response by focusing attention backward and hailing a decontextualized simplistic past that never existed. Media representations of Cal Ripken, Jr., participated in this process and served to re-make history in a politically regressive way.

The Streak Ends, The Nostalgia Continues

On September 20, 1998, after 2,632 consecutive games, Cal Ripken, Jr., ended the streak by sitting out the final home game of the season. (He had extended the streak by 502 games after eclipsing Lou Gehrig's record.) Although Ripken was concluding a disappointing year, the streak's end came as a surprise to virtually everyone in attendance (and soon thereafter, people nationwide), since he was healthy, he had been playing well of late, and his name was in the lineup before the game. Minutes into the first inning, when it was clear that Ripken would not play, the New York Yankees walked to the top step of the visitors dugout and applauded. Ripken emerged from the Orioles dugout, tipped his hat toward the Yankees, and returned to the bench. Soon thereafter, with the sellout crowd of over 48,000 giving him a standing ovation, Ripken came out again, waved, and took a bow. All told, he made three curtain calls. After the game, the 38-year-old third baseman explained why he pulled himself from the lineup: "The emphasis should be on the team," said Ripken. "There have been times during the streak when the emphasis was on the streak, and I was uncomfortable with that. I reached a point where it was time to change the subject and refocus the attention on the team and move on."[92] (For several years, some observers argued that Ripken would benefit from an occasional day off and that his exalted status due to the streak damaged the team's chemistry and thus success.) Despite the contemporaneous hoopla surrounding the historic home run hitting of Mark McGwire of the St. Louis Cardinals and Sammy Sosa of the Chicago Cubs, when Ripken ended the streak he received a great deal of media attention—much of which reiterated and consequently reinscribed the themes articulated three years earlier when he broke Gehrig's record.

Once again, journalists widely credited and celebrated Ripken as baseball's savior after the work stoppage of 1994-95. Peter Schmuck of the *Baltimore Sun* maintained that when Ripken broke Gehrig's record the major leagues "needed someone to heal its fractured relationship with the fans, and Ripken was in the perfect position to save the image of the sport. He was just a few months shy of breaking a record that previously was considered unassailable, and he was just the kind of squeaky-clean, all-American guy who could move gracefully past Gehrig and deliver Major League Baseball back into the heart of a nation."[93] Reflecting on the streak's end and meaning, Thomas Boswell wrote: "On the night of 2,131, baseball needed Ripken as its standard bearer more than the sport had needed any player at any time since Ruth saved the game with his home runs and his smile in the wake of the Black Sox scandal of 1919."[94] The *New York Times* editorialized that Ripken "helped rescue baseball from its funk after a strike shortened the 1994 season. Interest in the game revived as he began closing in on Lou Gehrig's mark of 2,130 consecutive games, and when he broke that record he inspired a celebration not surpassed until McGwire set a new home run record two weeks ago."[95] On this issue, even baseball commissioner Bud Selig and his arch nemesis Major League Baseball Players Association director Don Fehr could agree. "The recovery was much more difficult than we thought it was going to be," Selig said. "Baseball is forever grateful to Cal Ripken, because that moment played an enormous role in our recovery. We really needed something historical and positive. Sept. 6 was the event that did it."[96] Fehr agreed and suggested that Ripken's accomplishment "had a catalytic effect. It reminded people what this game can provide. Like McGwire's 62nd home run, it was a completely joyful event, something we had not seen in a long time. Something we really needed."[97] Nationwide, commentators declared that, while McGwire and Sosa were bringing people back to Major League ballparks, it was Ripken who had actually rejuvenated interest in the national pastime.

And once again the media constructed and hailed Ripken as the personification of cherished and dominant national ideals and values. Predictably, the most prominent among them was the work ethic. "Cal Ripken Jr. proves a lot," opined sports columnist Douglas S. Looney. "He proves that the work ethic is alive and well."[98] Dan Shaughnessy of the *Boston Globe* added, "We all could use a dose of the Ripken work ethic. You do your job, you do it to the best of your ability and you do it every day."[99] Perhaps sportswriter Tom Verducci best articulated what the streak signified to many Americans: "The Streak wasn't just his identity; it was ours, too. This was America the way we wish it to be—blue-collar, reliable, built on an honest day of work, one day after another."[100] Widely portrayed and understood as a decent, diligent, hard working, humble, responsible, self-reliant, family man, as an athlete given neither to hyperbole nor selfaggrandizement, that is, as an All-American hero and role model, Ripken was used, as Verducci aptly put it, as an "American allegory."[101] Set amidst the McGwire and Sosa home run race which so captured the nation's attention, media representations of the streak's conclusion, like those of the streak itself, promoted a nostalgic, politically conservative vision of American culture, social relations, and history which celebrated hegemonic masculinity and reifed the status quo.[102]

Conclusions

Immediately before and long after Streak week, Ripken's image was ubiquitous. Besides the sportspages, its presence was particularly felt in the advertising world. His endorsements expanded to include deals with Nike, True Value Hardware, Franklin Sports batting gloves, regional milk and Coke distributors,

Esskay meats, Adventure World, PowerAde athletic drink, Starter athletic wear, Wheaties, and Chevrolet Trucks. Virtually all of these advertisements accentuated Ripken's dependability, durability, and wholesomeness.[103] Perhaps the most explicitly nostalgic was a photograph for a popular milk advertising campaign which features celebrities and prominent athletes—like Patrick Ewing, Jeff Gordon, Florence Griffith Joyner, Pete Sampras, and Steve Young, among many others—wearing milk mustaches. Unlike all the other athletes, however, Ripken evoked multiple historical contexts, for he is wearing a batting glove (a relatively recent development) and is attired in a generic old-fashioned uniform (witness the high stirrups), and is holding the type of glass milk bottle Americans used to have delivered to their front doors. This image signified Ripken as a healthy throwback. There was also an implicit morality to the image. After all, milk is nutritious, milk is pure, milk is white.

As we have argued, a similar morality pervaded representations of the streak and Ripken in general. More often than not, the media constructed the streak as a didactic American morality tale: its lesson, with old fashioned hard work, dedication, and a little luck anything is possible. "No other record in sports better exemplifies the most enduring of American values: hard work, steadiness, loyalty," wrote Steven V. Roberts of *U.S. News & World Report.* "There's no flash and dash to Ripken, no swagger, no earrings. He's just there, every day, doing his job."[104] Part of his job, it seems, was to fulfill what historian Benjamin G. Rader refers to as a "compensatory cultural function," that is, the Ripken persona re-affirms and reproduces "traditional values," like rugged individualism and the work ethic, believed to be in decline.[105]

In some ways, the media's representations of Ripken and the streak remind us of historian John W. Ward's representation of Charles Lindbergh's 1927 solo flight across the Atlantic, specifically the kind of attention it received and the nostalgia it generated. As Ward observed in his essay, "The Meaning of Lindbergh's Flight" (1958), Lindbergh's accomplishment "provided an opportunity for the people to project their own emotions into his act and those emotions involved attitudes toward the meaning of their own experiences."[106] Against the backdrop of turbulent, anxiety-producing economic, political, and social change, Ward noted, "Lindbergh's flight was the occasion of a public act of regeneration," it was portrayed and widely understood as an act of heroism and self-reliance in uncertain times.[107] Ward maintained that until the media's glorification of Lindbergh's accomplishments, heroism and self-reliance, two mythic cornerstones of American greatness, appeared to reside entirely in the past.[108] Over sixty-five years later in yet another era distinguished by disconcerting economic, demographic, and social instability and change, for many Americans Ripken seemed to represent who and what they yearned to be. Ripken exhibited skill, stamina, and modesty and was cast by the media as a heroic model of middle-class virtue and manliness. In Ripken and the streak the media constructed and celebrated icons that spoke to the longings of many white, middle-class Americans (especially men), longings for a mythic time when fathers played catch with sons and the boys of summer reigned.

Numerous commentators have unproblematically noted and celebrated the nostalgia associated with Ripken; we have provided critical contexts to illuminate the politics and culture of nostalgia and its relationship to the Ripken phenomenon. In addition to providing an alternative way of understanding Ripken's public persona, the streak, and the values they represented, we think that the media's construction of the Ripken persona and the streak are important for other reasons. First, they illustrate the process of transforming an event and a public figure into a narrative that serve present interests, in this case one that celebrated a mythic national past when American men were (supposedly more) hard-working, responsible, and family-oriented, when major league baseball was a game that stood alone as the national pastime (despite excluding blacks and women), and when the game's labor-management relations were not as openly contentious as they are today. That is, the narratives which constituted the Ripken phenomenon illuminated how a sports hero and an event can be used to deploy specific, if often implicit, political agendas.

The Ripken phenomenon also reminds us that media narratives, perhaps especially those depicting celebrities, tend to be flat and one-dimensional, if not formulaic. Ripken the man is more complicated than Ripken the media-created cultural icon. When speaking about his family, Ripken often gives his mother and wife, not just his late father, a great deal of credit for his success. Moreover, though the media did not make much of it, it was significant that the only ballplayer Ripken thanked by name on the evening he broke the record was longtime teammate and friend Eddie Murray, an African-American first baseman with a reputation for surly relations with the press. Journalists also tend to ignore Ripken's temper, which is most frequently directed toward umpires. Like most people in the public eye, Ripken is infrequently portrayed in all his complexity.

This analysis of Ripken also demonstrates how personal memories—especially those related to childhood—can intertwine with mediated nostalgic discourses. Throughout the streak, the media offered abstracted images of Ripken as a dutiful son and a doting father, thus offering a formula for fans, especially male "baby boomers," to reenact. Reframing Ripken's childhood as idyllic, joyful, and free of conflict encouraged a similar model, perhaps even an invention of fond personal childhood memories among baseball fans. Emotionally charged representations of Ripken's youth encouraged aging "baby boomers" to try to recapture their own youth. They invited people to fantasize and idealize their own childhood and young adulthood, projecting them into the present.

Finally, the ways in which the media constructed Ripken and the streak did not just re-create a mythic national past; they also condition us for the future. Since they constitute a dominant or preferred reading of social reality, they will surely influence how Ripken and the streak will be re-told and remembered in the years to come. And although the writing of history is an inherently revisionist enterprise, and meaning is perpetually re-negotiated, once an event has been wrought as a specific kind of story, it is very difficult (but not impossible) to imagine it differently. In other words, there is inertia to narratives like the streak that is hard to counteract. The media constructions of Ripken we have identified are now securely woven into the national memory. Cultural critic and historian George Lipsitz calls the production and circulation of this kind of mass mediated, sanitized, and decontextualized historical image "memory as managed misappropriation."[109] The Ripken phenomenon demonstrates that historical remembering is always linked to the present and to issues of historical forgetting, that popular memory is always partial and political.

Notes

We want to thank Kathy Frantz, Allan Winkler, Norman Yetman, and two anonymous reviewers for their helpful comments and criticism of this essay.

1. Carol J. Pierman, "Cal Ripken and the Condition of Freedom: Theme and Variation on the American Work Ethic," *Nine: A Journal of Baseball History and Social Policy Perspectives* 7 (Fall 1998): 60.

2. Baseball fans and journalists sometimes debate the significance of the streak in purely baseball, rather than culturally symbolic, terms. For some, Ripken's consecutive game record pales in comparison to other kinds of major league (i.e., necessarily masculine) accomplishments, like Hank Aaron's 755 career home runs, Joe DiMaggio's 56-game hitting streak, and Nolan Ryan's seven career no-hitters, in addition to Ripken's own home run records for a shortstop (his 345 homers, among a career total of 402, is a record for that position) and fielding records (in 1990, he became the first shortstop in major league history to make only three errors in a complete season). As cultural critics, the debate does not interest us, except to the extent that it illuminates the notion that "significance" and "meaning" are always contested and debated, ever fluid and negotiated.

3. Sut Jhally, "Cultural Studies and the Sports/Media Complex," in *Media, Sports & Society* (Newbury Park, Calif., 1989), 77.

4. Mark S. Rosentraub, *Major League Losers: The Real Costs of Sports and Who's Paying For It* (New York, 1997), 50.

5. George Sage, *Power and Ideology in American Sport: A Critical Perspective* (Champaign, 1990), 129.

6. See Mary G. McDonald and Susan Birrell, "Reading Sport Critically: A Methodology for Interrogating Power," *Sociology of Sport Journal* 16 (1999): 283-300.

7. See Hayden White, *The Tropics of Discourse: Essays in Cultural Criticism* (Baltimore, [1978] 1992).

8. It is worth noting that the word was coined in the late seventeenth century and is derived from the Greek *nosos* return to native land, and *algos* = suffering or grief. See Fred Davis, *Yearning For Yesterday: A Sociology of Nostalgia* (New York, 1979), 1-2.

9. See Fred Pfeil, *Another Tale to Tell: Politics and Narrative in Postmodern Culture* (New York, 1990); Christopher Hitchens, *Blood, Class, and Nostalgia: Anglo-American Ironies* (New York, 1990); Paul Starobin, "Politics of the Past," *National Journal*, February 17, 1996, 354-358; Kelly Barron, "P.C. nostalgia," *Forbes*, October 20, 1997, 48; Keith Naughton and Bill Vlasic, "The Nostalgia Boom," *Business Week*, March 23, 1998, 58-64.

10. David Lowenthal, *The Past is a Foreign Country* (Cambridge, [1985] 1990), 4, 8.

11. Kammen adds that there "is nothing necessarily wrong with nostalgia per se, but more often than not the phenomenon does involve a pattern of highly selective memory. Recall the good but repress the unpleasant." Michael Kammen, *Mystic Chords of Memory: The Transformation of Tradition in American Culture* (New York, 1991), 688, 626.

12. Quoted in Jackson Lears, "Looking Backward: In Defense of Nostalgia," *Lingua Franca* (Dec/Jan 1998), 61.

13. Michael Eric Dyson, *Race Rules: Navigating the Color Line* (Reading, 1996), 117.

14. Davis, *Yearning For Yesterday*, 9.

15. Ibid., 10.

16. Ibid., 34, 107.

17. The politics of representation and nostalgia are often intertwined with one another. This is because they are influenced by the same phenomenon: presentism. With regard to representation, presentism is unavoidable. Indeed, it is a precondition of the process of telling a story, for

all storytellers exist in time. They/we cannot escape the limitations of time and place, nor the subjectivities that specific contexts produce. As historian Norman J. Wilson puts it, "we will always interpret the past from a perspective of contemporary knowledge." Obviously we always interpret the present from the perspective of contemporary knowledge and perceptions, too. The politics of nostalgia are likewise affected by presentism, for, as Fred Davis persuasively demonstrates, nostalgia is produced by the ways in which individuals and institutions understand and respond to contemporary situations, events, and relationships. Sometimes nostalgia is "invented" by those who have a vested (though occasionally unconscious) interest in remembering the past in a particular way. Sometimes nostalgia emanates from deep reservoirs of personal and collective memory and emotion. Either way, it is the present that causes those with specific kinds of political sensibilities to wax nostalgic. For those discomfited, frustrated, or threatened by the present, the sentimentally remembered past becomes a refuge. In this way present circumstances ignite self-serving and romantic conceptions of yesterday, rather than critically alert and historicized understandings of it. Norman J. Wilson, *History in Crisis? Recent Directions in Historiography* (Upper Saddle River, NJ, 1999), 9.

18. Paul Boyer, *Promises to Keep: The United States Since World War II* (Lexington, 1995), 444-5.

19. See Haynes Johnson, *Sleepwalking Through History: America in the Reagan Years* (New York, 1991); Walter LaFeber, Richard Polenberg, and Nancy Woloch, *The American Century: A History of the United States Since 1941* (Boston, 1998).

20. Arturo Madrid, "Diversity and its Discontents," *Academe* (November-December 1990): 15-19.

21. John Fiske, *Media Matters: Everyday Culture and Political Change* (Minneapolis, 1994), 35.

22. See Michael A. Messner, *Power at Play: Sports and the Problem of Masculinity* (Boston, 1992); E. Anthony Rotundo, *American Manhood: Transformations in Masculinity from the Revolution to the Modern Era* (New York, 1993); Michael Kimmel, *Manhood in America: A Cultural History* (New York, 1996).

23. Susan Faludi, *Stiffed: The Betrayal of the American Man* (New York, 1999), 153.

24. Sara M. Evans, *Born for Liberty: A History of Women in America* (New York: Free Press, 1989); Susan Faludi, *Backlash: The Undeclared War Against American Women* (New York, 1991).

25. Michael Messner, "Sports and Male Domination: The Female Athlete as Contested Ideological Terrain," *Sociology of Sport Journal* 5 (1988): 198.

26. James Reston, Jr., *Collision at Home Plate: The Lives of Pete Rose and Bart Giamatti* (New York, 1991).

27. Charles C. Alexander, *Our Game: An American Baseball History* (New York, 1991), 311.

28. Gerald Early, 'Performance and Reality: Race, Sports and the Modern World," *The Nation*, August 10/17, 1998, 11.

29. John Bloom, *House of Cards: Baseball Card Collecting and Popular Culture* (Minneapolis, 1997), 4-5.

30. Steve Wuif, "An Unwhole New Ball Game," *Time*, April 17, *1995*, 48.

31. Quoted in *Sports Illustrated*, June 7, 1995, 7.

32. Bill Gallo, "Dead Ball Era," *Icon*, January 26-February 1, 1995, 4.

33. See Robert McG.Thomas, Jr., "Clubs May Just Have to Replace Fans, Too," *New York Times*, February 28, 1995, B9; Tom Verducci, "Anybody Home?" *Sports Illustrated*, May 8, 1995, 18-23; Claire Smith, "Plenty of Good Seats Available, Fans," *New York Times*, May 28, 1995, sec. 8, p. 1; David Greising, "America's Pastime. Yeah, Right," *Business Week*, June 5, 1995, 40.

34. Quoted in Greising, "America's Pastime. Yeah, Right," 40.

35. Charles Krauthammer, "The Trouble With Baseball," *Washington Post*, May 5, 1995, A25.

36. Ibid.

37. See Bill James, *The Bill James Historical Baseball Abstract* (New York, [1985] 1987), 124.

38. Ken Sobol, *Babe Ruth & the American Dream* (New York, 1974), 135.

39. Eliot Asinof, *Eight Men Out: The Black Sox and the 1919 World Series* (New York, [1963] 1987), 275.

40. See Richard C. Crepeau, *Baseball: America's Diamond Mind 1919-1941* (Gainesville, 1980); Benjamin G. Rader, "Compensatory Sport Heroes: Ruth, Grange, and Dempsey," *Journal of Popular Culture* 16 (Spring 1983): 11-22.

41. Warren I. Susman, *Culture as History: The Transformation of American Society in the Twentieth Century* (New York, 1984), 148.

42. Verducci, "Anybody Home?" 20.

43. Mike Lupica, "Let's play two thousand," *Esquire,* April 1995, 48-52.

44. Mark Maske, "Ripken's Streak of Burden," *Washington Post,* April 7, 1995, Cl.

45. Quoted in Ibid., C7.

46. Quoted in Mat Edelson, "Cal on the Verge," in *The Best American Sports Writing 1996* (Boston, 1996), 314.

47. Heywood Hale Broun, "The Twin Symbols of Baseball's Timeless Virtues," *New York Times,* September 3, 1995, sec. 8, P. 13.

48. Mickey Mantle, the iconic former New York Yankees centerfielder who died of cancer a month before Ripken set the record, was an apposite foil for Ripken due to his well-documented carousing. According to sports columnist Ira Berkow, late in his life Mantle discussed "how he could have played beyond age 36 if he had not 'wasted' the talents God had given him. He confessed to being an alcoholic, a poor father and husband, and to a profligacy wrapped in self- absorption." Curry Kirkpatrick, "The Pride of the Orioles," *Newsweek* September 11, 1995, 79; Ira Berkow, "Much More Than Just a Hall of Famer," *New York Times,* August 14, 1995, C4.

49. Ibid.

50. The record was set in the fifth inning, rather than in the first, because by then it had become an official game.

51. In Arlington, Texas, for example, the Texas Rangers and the Chicago White Sox delayed their game to watch a live feed from Baltimore on the stadium's JumboTron screen. *Baltimore Sun,* September 7, 1995, 8C.

52. *Des Moines Register,* September 8, 1995, 2S.

53. Tim Kurkjian, "Touching 'Em All," in *2,131: Cal Ripken, Jr. Stands Alone* (a Special Collector's Edition issue of *Sports Illustrated,* 1995), 15.

54. Quoted in Jerome Holtzman, "2,131—and counting," *Chicago Tribune,* September 7, 1995, sec. 4, p.1.

55. Quoted in the *Baltimore Sun,* September 7, 1995, 6C. The *Robinson* Ripken referred to may have been purposefully vague; it may have referred to Hall-of-Famer and former Brooklyn Dodger Jackie Robinson (1919-1972), who broke the Major League's color line in 1947, Hall of Fame outfielder and former Orioles great Frank Robinson, the first African-American manager in Major League history, or former Orioles third baseman, Hall-of-Famer, and local legend Brooks Robinson. The latter two were in attendance that night. It is also worth noting that Earl Weaver, Ripken's former manager, is reported to have once said, "I want nine guys named Robinson."

56. Kurkjian, "Touching 'Em All," 8.

57. Quoted in the *Baltimore Sun,* September 7, 1995, 1C.

58. Buster Olney, "Players throw support behind streak," *Baltimore Sun,* September 7, 1995, 4D.

59. Quoted in Ibid.

60. Quoted in Harvey Araton, "Great Day For Baseball In the 90's," *New York Times,* September 7, 1995, 1319.

61. John Steadman, "This sentimental journey for the ages," *Baltimore Sun,* September 7, 1995, 1C.

62. Murray Chass, "Orioles' Ripken Goes to Work And Steps Into History Books," *New York Times,* September 7, 1995, 1319.

63. Bob Verdi, "A run for glory puts finishing touch on run for record," *Chicago Tribune,* September 7, 1995, sec. 4, p. 5.

64. See Murray Chass, "Reluctant Baseball Owners Approve Pact With Players," *New York Times,* November 27, 1996, Al.

65. E. J. Dionne, Jr., "Baseball's Ordinary Hero," *Washington Post,* September 5, 1995, Al7.

66. Tony Kornheiser, "Sportsman of the Year: No Contest," *Washington Post,* December 7, 1995, 132.

67. Ibid.

68. *Des Moines Register,* December 27, 1995, 1S.

69. Thomas Boswell, "Quiet Cal Speaks Volumes," *Washington Post,* June 30, 1996, Dl.

70. Buster Olney, "At crossroads, party is over for O's," *Baltimore Sun,* September 10, 1995, 10D.

71. See Ray Schuck, "Everything That is Good About Baseball—Theory of the Subject, ESPN, and Cal Ripken, Jr.," a paper presented at the Diamonds in the Desert International Baseball Conference, March 1998. Schuck observes that the broadcast's play-by-play announcer, Chris Berman, explained before the game that the contest celebrated "much more than just a major record." According to Berman, "We celebrate baseball the way it hasn't been celebrated for quite awhile. And we celebrate it the old-fashioned way—hometown boy playing for his hometown team in front of his hometown fans. We celebrate a work ethic that used to be a staple for baseball and, if you think about it, a work ethic that helped build America—you get up, you put in a hard day's work, and you go home to your family." Schuck argues: "At a time when Americans voiced disillusionment with baseball due to labor disputes and escalating player salaries—as well as at a time when Americans voiced concerns about what they perceived to be a loss of the value of community, a loss of the value of hard work, and a loss of the value of family—ESPN created a text to reaffirm these Americans' hope that their disillusionment could end and their lost values can be found again."

72. Free agency refers to the circumstance in which an athlete, after a period of time stipulated in his or her respective sport's collective bargaining agreement, can sell his or her services to the most attractive bidder. Economist Paul D. Staudohar puts it succinctly: "The players have been the chief beneficiaries from free agency." Paul D. Staudohar, *Playing For Dollars: Labor Relations and the Sports Business* (Ithaca, [1986] 1996), 37.

73. See Stephanie Coontz, *The Way We Never Were: American Families and the Nostalgia Trap* (New York, 1992).

74. Fiske, *Media Matters*, xvii.

75. Thomas Boswell, "Focused on Greatness," *Washington Post Magazine*, March 22, 1992, 30.

76. Harvey Rosenfeld, *Iron Man: The Cal Ripken, Jr. Story* (New York, [1995] 1996.), 4.

77. Mark Maske, "One Man, Many Irons," *Washington Post*, July 6, 1997, D7.

78. Cal Ripken (photographs by Walter boss, Jr., edited by Mark Vancil), *Ripken: Cal on Cal* (Arlington, 1995), 49.

79. Ibid., 64.

80. Cal Ripken, Sr. died of lung cancer on March 25, 1999, at the age of 63. Before retiring in 1992, he had spent 36 years in the Baltimore Orioles organization as a player, scout, coach, and manager. He was eulogized "by his close-knit family and hometown friends as a devoted father and tireless baseball man who would settle for nothing less than what he believed to be the right way of playing the game." William Gildea, "Ripkens, Town Say Goodbye to Cal Sr.," *Washington Post*, March 31, 1999, DI.

81. The reserve clause, a gentlemen's agreement codified in 1879 and overturned by an arbitrator in 1975, bound players to their teams indefinitely by giving the team for which he played exclusive rights to his services. For a useful discussion of the reserve clause's history, see Robert F. Burke, *Never Just A Game: Players, Owners, and American Baseball to 1920* (Chapel Hill, 1994), 62-63.

82. Steve Wulf, "Iron Bird," *Time*, September 3, 1995, 70.

83. Harrison Rainie, "Chasing Lou Gehrig and Immortality," *U.S. News & World Report*, December 26, 1994/January 2, 1995, 87.

84. For us, whiteness is not an essentialized racial identity, but a strategic deployment of power. As the dominant norm, whiteness remains invisible, rarely explicitly interrogated in mainstream accounts. Yet whiteness is omnipresent, almost always constructed in positive terms which seek to maintain the racial status quo. See George Lipsitz, *The Possessive Investment of Whiteness: How White People Profit from Identity Politics* (Philadelphia, 1998).

85. See Philip M. Hoose, *Necessities: Racial Barriers in American Sports* (New York, 1989); Richard Lapchick, *Five Minutes to Midnight: Race and Sport in the 1990s* (Lanhani, 1991); Kenneth L. Shropshire, *In Black and White: Race and Sports in America* (New York, 1996).

86. Max Boot, "Cal, Deion—And Us," *Wall Street Journal*, September 13, 1995, Al 7.

87. Fiske, *Media Matters*, 13.

88. Roger C. Aden, "Nostalgic Communication as Temporal Escape: When It Was a Game's Reconstruction of a Baseball/Work Community," *Western Journal of Communication* 59 (Winter 1995): 20-38.

89. Ibid., 26.

90. Randall Lane and Josh McHugh, "A very green 1995," *Forbes*, December 18, 1995, 219.

91. *People Weekly*, October 16, 1995, 140.

92. Richard Justice, "It's Over: Ripken Sits After 2,632 Games," *Washington Post*, September 21, 1998, All.

93. Peter Schmuck, "Credit him with a big save," *Baltimore Sun*, September 27, 1998, 7S.

94. Thomas Boswell, "For Timeless Player, It Was Time," *Washington Post*, September 21, 1998, Al0.

95. *New York Times*, September 22, 1998, A30.

96. Quoted in Hal Bodley, "One man's integrity restored fans' faith," *USA TODAY*, September 22, 1998, 3C.

97. Quoted in Schmuck, "Credit him with a big save," 7S.

98. Douglas S. Looney, "Baseball's Mr. Reliable and the Virtues of Just Showing Up," *Christian Science Monitor*, September 23, 1998, 3.

99. Dan Shaughnessy, "Iron man streak comes to an end," *Boston Globe*, September 21, 1998, Al.

100. Tom Verducci, "Endgame," *Sports Illustrated*, September 28, 1998, Il.

101. Ibid.

102. McGwire, for example, was constantly hailed as a hard worker (it was frequently noted that he rebuilt his body in the weightroom) and as a family man through his relationship with his father, his son (who sometimes served as the Cardinals' bat boy, and who met his father at home plate after he hit his record-tying 61st home run), and even his ex-wife (who extolled his love and commitment to their son). At the same time, the media clearly marginalized Sosa in comparison to McGwire, arguably because he trailed McGwire in the home run chase for most of the season, and because of his African-Caribbean racial identity and Dominican Republic citizenship. The ways in which McGwire was celebrated for his home run hitting exploits led some to refer to him as the Great White Hope *de jour*.

103. See Jon Morgan, "Marketing Cal Ripken," *Baltimore Sun*, June 24, 1995, D4; Raymond Serafin, "Cal just a short stop from making history," *Advertising Age*, September 4, 1995, 4; Randall Lane, "Nice Guys Finish First," *Forbes*, December 16, 1996, 236-242.

104. Steven V. Roberts, "Remember, baseball is a great game," *U.S. News & World Report*, August 14, 1995, 6.

105. See Benjamin G. Rader, "Compensatory Sport Heroes: Ruth, Grange, and Dempsey," *Journal of Popular Culture* 16 (Spring 1983): 11-22.

106. John W. Ward, "The Meaning of Lindbergh's Flight," *American Quarterly* X (Spring 1958): 15.

107. Ibid., 7.

108. Ibid.

109. George Lipsitz, *Time Passages: Collective Memory and American Popular Culture* (Minneapolis, 1990), 80.

CHAPTER 17

MANHOOD, MEMORY, AND WHITE MEN'S SPORTS IN THE AMERICAN SOUTH

■ *Ted Ownby* ■

In the 1960s, Paul Dietzel, the football coach at Louisiana State University and later the University of South Carolina, loved to read his own poem when he spoke at athletic banquets. He called it "Sissy."

Is it a sissy to be the first guy on the practice field.
Is it a sissy to be the most vicious tackle on the squad.
Is it a sissy to *knock* your opponent on his butt.
Pick him up, and say, "get braced, Buddie, cause
That's how our team does things!"
Is it a sissy to say NO when your buddies ask you to join them in abusing your body by dissipation
And your only excuse that you can say is, "I don't think that'll help me to be a National Champion."
A sissy to teach a Sunday School class like Jerry Stovall, or
A sissy to believe in God.
Yes, it takes a real sissy to be the toughest guy on the field and not a *tough* in the classroom,
A sissy to wear short hair rather than a mop-cut like the rest of the girls,
A sissy believes that the *team* always comes first before any personal glorification,
And only a sissy has courage enough to be a *member* of a team rather than one of the creeps whom every bartender in the area calls by first name.
He's definitely a *sissy* if he respects Mom and Dad and honors their wishes, And he's not only a sissy, but a stupid one too if he "guts it out" even if he doesn't get to play too much rather than joining the *ever growing ranks* of quitters.
And of those who get to play, you'll note that the sissies'll lay it on the line any time the team asks.

Reprinted, by permission, from T. Ownby, 1998, "Manhood memory and white men's sports in the recent American south," *The International Journal of the History of Sport* 15: 103-118. Reprinted by permission of Taylor and Francis. http://www.informaworld.com.

> If that's being a sissy
> Thank God for sissies
> I'm hunting for sissies
> Because sissies, Gentlemen, are the timber
> From which CHAMPIONS are fashioned.[1]

Perhaps the most remarkable thing about this poem is that Dietzel felt that he needed to defend football players from charges of being sissies. Believing that some people considered his players less than manly, Dietzel hoped that irony could show the positive and manly values of football.

Few images of the contemporary American South seem to say as much about the region as the beloved college football coach, the stock car driver, or the lonely deer hunter. This essay offers an interpretation of the relationship between sports, white male identity, and regional memory. Does it mean anything significant to be southern, white, and male after all of the changes that have challenged the traditional meanings of manhood in the American South since the 1940s? And do the meanings of being white and male and southern have any connection to older meanings rooted in southern history? Why would a football coach in the American South have to defend his players against charges of being sissies?

There was a time when sports had little to do with southern identity. Sports hardly appear at all in the classic works from the 1930s through the 1950s in which one white male southern writer after another tried to define what it meant to be southern. Most clearly, in *I'll Take My Stand,* published in 1930, the Vanderbilt Agrarians mentioned sports primarily to say southern culture was better off without them. The Agrarians valued leisure and thought southern history offered modern America an example of a culture given over not to strenuous work and acquisitiveness but to noncompetitive pleasures enjoyed in a community setting. Donald Davidson complained that in industrial society, "The furious pace of our working hours is carried over into our leisure hours, which are feverish and energetic," and he claimed that most modern forms of play are "undertaken as a nervous relief." In his introduction to the volume, John Crowe Ransom included only one sport when he asserted that the best habits of the region's people were the "social arts of dress, conversation, manners, the table, the hunt, politics, oratory, the pulpit. These were the arts of living and not the arts of escape; they were also community arts, in which every class of society could participate after its kind. The South took life easy, which is itself a tolerably comprehensive art."[2]

Eleven years later, in another aggressive attempt to define what it meant to be white, male, and southern, W.J. Cash analyzed the leisure and hunting of southern white men not as part of long communal traditions but as one of the new and defining features of antebellum southern culture. Most white men, separated by slavery, fertile land, and fat hogs from the need to work very hard, felt free to enjoy the pleasures of the frontier. Cash claimed that most antebellum white men hunted not as a continuation of English tradition or within an agrarian sense of identity but out of a hedonistic pursuit of intense, individualistic excitement. When the typical southern white farmer hunted, "It was simply and primarily for the same reason that, in his youth and often into late manhood, he ran spontaneous and unpremeditated foot-races, wrestled, drank Gargantuan quantities of raw whisky; let off wild yells, and hunted the possum; because the thing was already in his mores when he emerged from the backwoods, because on the frontier, it was the obvious thing to do, because he was a hot, stout fellow, full of blood and reared to outdoor activity, because of a primitive and naive zest for the pursuit in hand."[3] Thus, Cash's sportsman is not the Agrarians' hunter who understood his pleasures as part of a folk community; nor, certainly, was he the sportsman of the Teddy Roosevelt age, who sought especially physical pleasures because his work and education allowed him no excitement or exertion. Instead, this was a sportsman with no boundaries and no limits.[4] For both Cash and the Agrarians, hunting was the only sport that mattered in thinking about southern identity, and it was part of a complex of activities not related to sport. Writing at the same time, William Faulkner was creating the most exhaustive portrait of southern life, and he had the same relative inattention to all sports except hunting. He wrote at length about hunting, but his only character who played a modern sport did so outside the knowledge and respect of the various communities of Faulkner's men. In *The Hamlet*, published in 1940, Roy Labove, a teacher and University of Mississippi student, played football, but he had to explain the game to a planter who had never seen it and showed no particular interest in it. The game also held no interest for his own family, who only cared that he brought them back shoes, or even for the students he was teaching, or their parents.[5]

Beyond those books, it becomes almost ridiculous to think about sports as playing a significant role in the works that analyzed southern identity at mid-century. William Alexander Percy's *Lanterns on the Levee*, published in 1941, is the classic statement of what upper-class manhood meant to someone who felt his generation could not live up to that standard. He had a chapter entitled "A Small Boy's Heroes," which if written today almost certainly would include some sports figures. His heroes were men his father knew—amateur philosophers, accomplished talkers. The only sport he mentioned was, again, hunting, which he associated with the self-assurance of his father. But Will Percy himself considered hunting a sport that was "lacerating to the spirit."[6] The other major work of 1941 was *Let Us Now Praise Famous Men*, by James Agee and Walker Evans. The book says not a word about sport, and it is almost impossible to imagine the tenant farmer men of the Ricketts, Woods, and Gudger families as fans of spectator sports—almost as impossible as it is to imagine their contemporary male descendants *not* following sports of some kind.[7]

The final work in that body of literature that searched so hard for the identity of southern white men was C. Vann Woodward's essay "The Search for Southern Identity," published in 1958. Interested less in the values of white southerners than their defining experiences, Woodward said that what made people southern was their shared experience with military defeat, agricultural poverty, and racial conflict and guilt. In a fourth point, Woodward wrote that southerners, black and white, male and female, had learned the importance of the past and a sense of limits in thinking about the future.[8] There was little in those points that one could even try to attach to sports. The experience of limits and the understanding gained from defeat offer little help in understanding contemporary spectator sports, with their emphasis on money, publicity, and devotion to winning.

The belabored point is that when white male writers at mid-century tried to figure out what made white men think of themselves as southerners, they thought of no organized sports and of no sports at all except hunting. They wrote about government and politics, economics and work, certainly race and the Civil War, probably religion, but they did not write about sports. For comparison, one needs only to think of all of the people who have chosen over the years to theorize about why baseball helped define American culture. Up to mid-century, no sport attracted much attention from people trying to define southern culture. In fact, the first writer in that genre who wrote about team sports, Thomas Clark in *The Emerging South,* published in 1961, interpreted them as a sign of how much the South was changing. Discussing high school and college football and basketball, he wrote, "Today most southern communities have developed a local mania over their athletic teams. Even hardened old rednecks who have wandered in from the cotton fields have caught the fever. Fifty years ago they would have regarded these sports as either effeminate or juvenile."[9]

If a similar body of literature in the late 1990s tried to explain what it means to be a southerner, sports would seem far more significant.[10] If no one thought John Heisman helped to define southern identity for white men in his day, many people think Bear Bryant and Richard Petty have helped them define what it means to be a southerner. This should not be surprising. Scholars of southern identity have been saying for some time that as the objective features of southern distinctiveness decline—a concentration on farming, poverty, state-supported racial segregation, a single-party political system—people in the South, especially white people, have been looking to culture for definitions of regional identity.[11] The most celebrated of these scholars, John Shelton Reed, argues that a southern middle class has developed a particular desire for consumer products like magazines, books, T-shirts, and food that can offer an identity in the midst of the seeming placelessness and timelessness of mass culture.[12]

Have modern sports offered part of that identity?[13] If so, have they offered any connections to traditional meanings of manhood in the South? Historians have described at least five definitions of manhood that southern white men once claimed as their own.[14] First was the goal of personal independence. To many southern white men, working for someone else or depending on someone else for one's livelihood seemed to resemble the position of slaves or women, or men with no character.[15] Second was the concept of honor. Men whose sense of esteem came not from themselves but from their communities had an extraordinary sensitivity to challenge and insult and a corresponding desire to prove themselves publicly.[16] A third meaning involved racism—especially the desire white men had long showed for physical power over African American men.[17]

Fourth was the notion of paternalism. That meaning defined fatherly control as the best model for all of society and tended to celebrate the rule and special character of an old upper class.[18] A final meaning, one especially important in discussing sports, is the "helluvafella," a term W.J. Cash used to describe the hedonistic man cut off from past social institutions. According to Cash, the primary interest of the helluvafella was "To stand on his head in a bar, to toss down a pint of raw whiskey in a gulp, to fiddle and dance all night, to bite off the nose or gouge out the eye of a favorite enemy, to fight harder and love harder than the next man."[19] The rest of this essay asks what modern hunting, stock car racing, and college football have come to express about the identities of southern white men and if they continue any of those five traditional meanings of manhood.

Hunting is the one sport with roots deep in southern history. Many people who do not hunt have little idea of how dramatically hunting practices have changed in the past fifty to seventy-five years, but it seems fair to argue that hunting has changed in that period more than it has stayed the same.

In the late 1800s and early 1900s, with large numbers of people living on farmland either as owners or laborers, hunting operated both as a sport and a supplement to family diets.[20] Men pursued a broad range of small animals—squirrels and rabbits most of all, raccoons and opossums, foxes, doves, quail—all of which could help feed the family. Large game such as deer did not thrive in an agricultural system that spread farm people widely on the land; deer lived primarily on uncleared areas around rivers, and the bears and panthers that once roamed substantial parts of the South fared even worse.

Two realities helped encourage the helluvafella pursuit that W.J. Cash described. First, hunters often took small game in large numbers and thus could delight in a kind of binge-killing.[21] Second, general access to land that almost everyone treated as common encouraged most hunters to feel free to pursue and kill any game they found. This freedom encouraged the widespread use of dogs in most forms of hunting, and hunting with dogs encouraged a rushed kind of attack on game. (The important exception to this access to common land were African Americans. Large landowners had tried to restrict their access to hunting since shortly after emancipation, largely because they did not want potential laborers to be able to feed themselves.)[22] But most white hunters had access to most game on most land. To return to my list of definitions of manhood, white men in the late nineteenth and early twentieth century could hunt in ways that combined the notion of personal independence, in putting food on the table, with the notion of the helluvafella, in the freedom to run like crazy over fields and through woods with few worries about limits of any kind.

The best scholarly work on hunting in the modern South, Wiley Prewitt's M.A. thesis on Mississippi, concludes that "Just as slipping out the back gate for a mess of quail symbolized hunting" in the earlier period, "so the drive from town to the rural deer camp symbolized the chase after agricultural mechanization, demographic reorganization and organized wildlife conservation."[23] The most significant change involves the dramatic decline in the number of people who make their living from farming. Most of those people and their descendants now live in towns and in cities, and they do not step out the back gate to help feed their families. Closely connected to that change is the revolution in land use, with the rise of large-scale commercial farming and the dramatic growth of the timber industry. Owners of large expanses of profitable rural land have severely restricted any access hunters may have to it.

With those changes, hunting land is simply not available to many people, or at least not easily accessible or affordable. There is public hunting land, available to anyone with a license and a brightly colored vest, and on certain Saturdays in November public lands are full of orange-clad men with guns. But most people in the South gain access to hunting land either by leasing it, sometimes from timber companies, or by joining all-male hunting clubs for several hundred dollars a year. As hunting becomes a commodity, the poor—increasingly urban and with access to land blocked out by fences, prominently posted "no hunting" signs, and their own lack of income—are more than ever left out of the sport. For most hunters or would-be hunters, the sport has little to do with gaining personal independence.

With the changes in land use, the animals hunted have also changed. Deer thrive in areas with low human populations, so with rural depopulation and with help from state game policy, they have returned in extraordinary numbers. In Mississippi, where deer were rare early in the century outside a few areas of the state, deer and deer hunters thrive in every county. Turkeys, which also need a great deal of space, have likewise increased in number and in popularity as game birds. On the contrary, quail numbers have declined in many parts of the South, and today they thrive primarily on quail preserves kept largely for wealthy hunters and their high-priced dogs. Rabbit hunting and squirrel hunting survive, but certainly not with the popularity they once had.[24]

Hunting with dogs has declined, and with it the helluvafella frontal assault on game has declined as well. Hunting with dogs only made sense when land was treated as common, because of course dogs do not respect property rights. Many hunting clubs have passed rules against hunting with dogs, and some hunting groups are trying to make it illegal. Dogs remain essential in fox hunts and quail hunts, both of which have become primarily upper-class sports on land preserved just for the purpose, and in coon hunting.[25]

Perhaps the greatest change of all is the extraordinary complexity of the rules. Southern legislatures first created game and fish commissions in the early twentieth century, but the complexity and enforcement of the rules has grown dramatically in recent decades. Once the hunter has found a place to hunt, he must think about the season, the number of game, the size, the age, and sometimes the sex of the game, and the legality of his own weapon before proceeding with his sport. Once he hunts, he must then report frequently to a state official to prove he is not breaking the rules.

Most hunters recognize the need for game conservation and in one way or another have led movements for it. However, the larger point is that the modern experience of hunting is an extremely limiting sport. It has limits on space, with the hunting camp as a fenced area beyond which hunting is not acceptable. Men no longer hunt in the natural world, they hunt in what are essentially special sporting arenas with special rules.[26] It has limits on time, both in the seasons in which certain hunting is legal and the time hunters must find away from their nonagricultural employment. It has limits enforced by state officials. And it has limits based on the ability to pay. With all of those limits, hunting is becoming very much like a modern sport—a commodity for the middle and upper classes, enjoyed primarily on weekends, at special places and times, with arcane rules determined by a distant governing body.

There are, to be sure, traditional sides of hunting. Men still take pleasure in escaping everyday behavior into a male world in a natural environment. Young men still learn from older men. Gun ownership and marksmanship are still parts of the definitions of freedom. Nonetheless, the changes are significant enough that it seems fair to conclude that hunting offers few connections to traditional definitions of manhood. Modern hunting does not help men gain independence; it simply represents freedom from the job. Hunting is rarely part of being a helluvafella; with the many limits on hunting, the sense of limitless freedom is a distant memory.

Stock car racing is one of the few professional sports with unmistakable southern origins. As an organized sport, it began in the 1930s in the South, most of the races are held in the South, and virtually all of the drivers and most of the team members and owners are white southerners. The sport's best drivers are some of the most durable and most recognizable white southern heroes—especially working-class heroes—and the striking number of recent drivers who are the sons of older drivers suggests that fans can follow a racing family for their entire lives.

Significantly, stock car racing is one of the few mass sporting events in which white people make up virtually all of the spectators and participants. Perhaps stock racing offers lower-class whites the connection to a regional past that hunting does not allow. Stock car racing seems the clearest example in sport of what bluegrass represents in southern music; that is, something new that seems old and seems to offer connection to the past.[27] In fact, racing has numerous connections with the music of white southerners. Racing figures have drawn the comparisons themselves,[28] and today one can turn on the radio on Saturdays and hear the AC-Delco NASCAR Country Countdown, which calls itself "the fastest two hours on radio."

One could easily construct an argument that would depict stock car racing as a white man's paradise. Even more than hunting, it is an almost exclusively male sport. One prominent mechanic made the point that "'If you get mad at the car and you want to cuss because the damn thing won't run, you shouldn't have to turn around and apologize to some woman."[29] With few exceptions, the women of significance in the sport are waiting in Victory Lane with champagne, kisses, and corporate logos. It is well known—probably too well known—that some of the earliest racers learned to drive fast by bootlegging whiskey in the hills of North Carolina. The term "good ol' boy" was coined to describe the early driving hero Junior Johnson in a memorable article by Tom Wolfe, a starry-eyed New York writer looking for someone who combined folk traditions and resistance to authority.[30] The scholar inclined to think of the sport as a carrier of traditional male identities could make a case that begins with the helluvafella who lives for immediate, hedonistic pleasures like speed, then connects that to the legacy Junior Johnson represented in trying to maintain independence by selling a corn product, and then ties it all together with the southern white man's traditional resistance to the federal government. In those ways, the sport, despite its recent origins, would seem a thoroughly traditional union of the goal of independence with the pleasures of the helluvafella.

But there are serious problems with drawing a straight line from traditional meanings of southern manhood to Winston Cup racing. Writers about stock car racing have almost certainly overstated the significance of the bootlegging origins of the sport.[31] As an organized sport, it began not in the mountains but in Daytona Beach, Florida, a relatively new place, a tourist place, a place for new money, people, and technology. And the sport has numerous corporate elements that have either helped or forced redefinitions of old concepts of manhood.

It seems fair to speculate that stock car racing is particularly appealing to working-class southern white men who are undergoing one of the most significant changes in the region's economic life. Most southern industry has been the kind that moves into a town that offers a package of tax breaks, puts up an inexpensive building, hires some nonunion workers, and then moves onto another town or another part of the world.[32] Workers in those insecure jobs can choose to move repeatedly, but many choose to live in the same place and drive a lot. For workers who drive substantial distances five or six days a week, the time on the road is probably a significant part of the meaning of freedom. It is time away from an unsatisfying job and contemporary uncertainties about family life. When they are on the road, they want to drive fast, and they can for a time feel free from anyone—boss, government, parent, or wife—trying to tell them what to do. In that definition of freedom, they seem connected less to country music, where the road always leads either safely home to a good woman or to sin and sadness,[33] than to the message of 1970s southern rock music that portrayed life on the road as a constant reality and the only place for any real pleasure. It was Lynyrd Skynyrd who sang, "The only time I'm satisfied is when I'm on the road."[34] For people who identify with such a sentiment, stock car racing—driving with no ultimate destination—represents a significant part of the definition of freedom.

By identifying freedom with life on the road, fans of stock car racing also identify themselves with at least part of the corporate side of stock car racing. More important to the experience of racing and race-watching than the corporate sponsors—Tide and Mountain Dew and Spam and the rest—are the ways the cars themselves connect the sport and the fans to Detroit auto-makers. Two myths about the cars tell democratic stories. One asserts that the cars are, in appearance at least, essentially the same as the cars anyone can buy. As the former driver and owner Bud Moore from Spartanburg, South Carolina, said, "we're running the kind of cars that Mr. Tom, Dick and Harry can go down and buy. I mean a replica of that car….This is really what brought stock car racing along, because we raced the cars that the American public drives."[35] The former driver and announcer Ned Jarrett made the same point. "You see cars raced in stock car racing that look like your own car." The second myth is that fans root for stock cars of the same brand as the cars they drive themselves. As Richard Petty said of race fans, "if they drove a Pontiac, they pulled for Pontiac. If they drove a Ford they pulled for Ford." Bud Moore agreed, "If you drive a Ford, you love that Ford to death and you want to see it win."[36]

These are myths. The cars we drive do not go 190 miles per hour, and we do not drive them on specially constructed speedways that allow us to take turns at full speed. But like other myths in sport, these myths help reveal some of the attraction of the sport. The idea that an important part of freedom is the ability to select among consumer choices has a short history in the South. Whereas white men traditionally tied freedom to control over production, this freedom suggests pleasure and identity in consumption—in buying a favorite car.

Thus, the notion of personal independence embodied in stock car racing has taken the old notion of freedom from being controlled and celebrates the relatively few moments that allow that kind of freedom. Obviously, stock car racing, as a mass spectator sport, merely represents and celebrates that freedom for people who feel they do not have much of it in the rest of their lives. If the modern southern white man believes freedom comes with mobility, he is celebrating in stock car racing a form of mobility that goes nowhere except around and around and around.

The ideal of the helluvafella also lives in stock car racing. The sheer emphasis on speed, on barely escaping injury, on running as fast as possible, sounds as much as any modern sport like something W.J. Cash would have recognized. One of the biggest reasons for the popularity of Dale Earnhardt, nicknamed The Intimidator, is that his racing style risked his own safety and the good will of other drivers by trying to drive without limits, most obviously by bumping drivers who got in his way. Richard Petty claimed that such an attitude fueled the early popularity of the sport in the South. When stock car racing was "about as unrespectable as a sport could be," he remembered that "Nobody would give an inch, and if one guy didn't get out of the way, they would run right over him."[37]

But there are complications with trying to see the stock car driver as a helluvafella. Stock car racing, even more than hunting, is an extremely complex sport, with numerous rules that change every year both to protect the drivers and to offer the illusion that the cars do indeed have some qualities of the stock that anyone can buy. Stock car racing is a sport for cheaters—a sport for understanding the limits of what one can do to one's car and going beyond them only slightly. It says something about the sport that the first race sanctioned by NASCAR, at Charlotte in 1949, involved a substantial amount of money (a six-thousand-dollar winner's prize), attracted a surprising crowd (thirteen thousand people), and saw its winner disqualified for cheating.[38] Perhaps part of the appeal lies in feeling that the stock car racer can be a helluvafella within a system dominated by rules and officials. Thus it may be that stock car racing offers dramatizations of the helluvafella and a very limited dramatization of the ideal of personal independence in a spectator sport dominated by technology and corporate power. He is not free from rules; he gains freedom by breaking the rules.

The only sport to rival stock car racing in popularity in the South is college football. College football was a growing sport in the early 1900s, but it did not dominate newspapers, normal conversation, and life on Saturdays on campuses and in campus towns until the post-World War II period. The early proponents of football at southern colleges, as Patrick Miller and Andrew Doyle have shown, tried hard to link the game to regional symbols and to derive regional pride from it,[39] but it took a long time before football came to work in the opposite direction and helped define what it meant to be southern.

Just as changes in hunting illustrate cultural shifts related to changes in agriculture and stock car racing dramatizes changes in how lower-class whites make their living, college football only makes sense in light of changes in the South's upper and middle classes. The most important precondition for the growing popularity of college football lies in the dramatic increase in the number of people in the South who attend colleges and universities. Throughout most of southern history, higher education was reserved for the wealthy. The number of students was on the rise with the building of agricultural and teachers' colleges in the late 1800s and early 1900s, but by far the most dramatic increase has

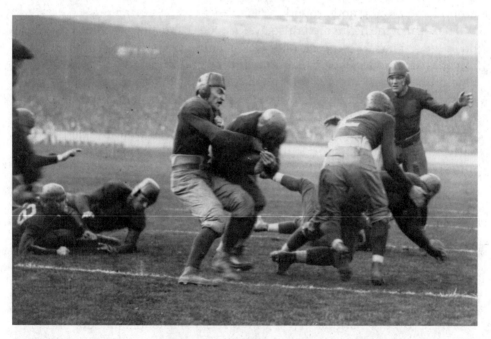

A Georgia Tech running back smashing through the Penn State line in a 1921 contest between the two football powerhouses.

Photo courtesy of Library of Congress. LC-USZ62-99631.

come since World War II. In 1950, 565,000 people in the southern states attended college of some kind. By 1992 there were 4.2 million—a rate of expansion far surpassing the national rate.[40]

In his 1971 autobiography, the University of Mississippi coach Johnny Vaught recalled that football seemed irrelevant to most people in northern Mississippi when he started coaching in the 1940s. The farmers who went to the town square on Saturdays, he said, were not interested in football. "[T]he university had to face the fact that a lot of farmers didn't know or care that 15,000 people were yelling their lungs out a mile away from the square. I suppose many of those who heard the cheers wondered 'what in tarnation' was going on. But times change. Today, they and their children are sitting in the stands at kickoff time."[41] What happened is that the number of those farmers declined dramatically, and the number of people whose livelihoods connected them to the university system increased almost as sharply. The farmers did not have a change of heart and start going to the games; more importantly, their children started going to colleges and universities and developed closer ties to university social life.

Connections between the nature of modern football and college education are clear. Football has become an enormously complicated sport with complexities that mirror the technical, scientific, and especially professional language and expertise demanded by the economic changes of the modern South. Football probably has the fattest rulebook of any sport, and that book changes every year. The sport has a large number of officials on the field to enforce those rules. Not only is the rule book long and complex, the playbook is longer than many university textbooks. Football forces its players to learn a complex technical language that combines a numerical system with idiosyncratic jargon. And players do not simply learn their own language; every week they learn the language of the other team. Football requires considerable memorization in dealing with plays and scouting reports, and it requires constant close scrutiny in dealing with games on film. During the season, some coaches give tests, some of them more than once a week, to make sure players keep up with their own plays, new plays, and plays run by opposing teams.

In his book *Bobby Dodd on Football*, the Georgia Tech coach made a point in 1954 that coaches probably say about each new generation of players. Because of innovations in the game, he wrote, "A player had to be thinking all the time to play at any position on a modern football team and the days of sheer brawn were gone forever." In the first sentence of that book, Dodd celebrated the increasing complexity of the sport, saying, "the game of football has advanced from the roughest of beginnings to one of the most scientific and interesting of all athletic events."[42] With its emphasis on technical language and specialized knowledge, football represented the sport of a society undergoing the kind of professionalization that characterized the northeastern United States much earlier in the twentieth century.[43]

But when football fans, players, and coaches talk about their sport, they rarely emphasize specialized knowledge, idiosyncratic language, and numerical systems. The long-time University of Alabama coach Bear Bryant said he asked parents of potential players, "Listen, does your boy know how to work? Try to teach him to work, to sacrifice, *to fight*."[44] He and most coaches claim that football embodies and teaches essential character traits. Are any of those traits, like the willingness to fight, part of the traditional southern meanings of manhood? There is no sense of the traditional meaning of personal independence in football. Players learn to work within their coach's system, or they do not play. Likewise, there may be some degree of the helluvafella in the headhunting linebacker, but football places so many limits on what players can and cannot do that Cash's ideal type has little role on the team either. Most of the violence within football is carefully coached, and it has little to do with the limitless hedonism Cash imagined.

If football continues any of the traditional definitions of manhood, it would seem to be the old language of honor. Bear Bryant, in a section of his autobiography in which he condemned quitters, recalled, "I've laid it on the line to a lot of boys. I've grabbed 'em, kicked 'em, and embarrassed them in front of the squad. I've got down in the dirt with them, and if they didn't give as well as they took I'd tell them they were insults to their upbringing, and I've cleaned out their lockers for them and piled their clothes out in the hall, thinking I'd make them prove what they had in their veins, blood or spit, one way or the other, and praying they would come through."[45] Bryant's statement brings together several features Bertram Wyatt-Brown described as part of the antebellum concept of honor—the overpowering fear of being shamed within the male community, the need to protect the family name, and the centrality of violence. The notion that a man either had character or did not—either had blood or spit in his veins—also sounds a great deal like the old notion of upholding one's own honor from any challenge.[46]

Bryant's assertion that football echoed an old code of ethics returns to Paul Dietzel and his sissies. Football players, Dietzel said, could not be counter-cultural figures. They do not drink or enjoy "dissipation" and thus could not be a helluvafella. Nor could football players believe strongly in personal independence; they had to think of the team before themselves and be willing to "lay it on the line any time the team asks." Thus, honor came to mean fighting for one's team and, ultimately, serving one's college.

To conclude, none of these three sports offers a direct line to any of the traditional definitions of southern white manhood. Modern hunting offers a faint resemblance of the experience of personal independence, but only in a postagricultural South. Stock car racing offers a drama about the independence of mobility and a vision of the helluvafella in a corporate and consumer age. And college football offers violence within the language of group honor, but in a university setting that stresses technical language, complicated planning, and the crucial significance of the team. People thinking and writing about sports should be wary of making simplistic assertions about regional stereotypes as if any of these sports were part of ages-old folk cultures. In all three sports, the traditional southern meanings of manhood have undergone dramatic redefinition to fit contemporary needs.

Men playing and watching modern sports may be expressing other, newer notions of manhood and newer southern identities. Only new questions can sort out how the racial desegregation of team sports, the growing importance of women's athletics, and the rapid expansion of professional sports may offer new definitions of region and gender. There is no reason to believe that the concept of the South has become meaningless in discussions of sports, but it seems clear that modern sports offer white southern men a sense of regional identity that has little to do with southern history.

Notes

This chapter is reprinted, with minor editorial changes, from *International Journal of the History of Sport* 15 (August 1998): 103-18, with the permission of the editor, J. A. Mangan, and Frank Cass Publishers.

1. Paul F. Dietzel, "Sissy," in *Coaching Football* (New York: Ronald Press, 1971), 7-8.

2. Donald Davidson, "A Mirror for Artists," and John Crowe Ransom, "Reconstructed but Unregenerate," in *I'll Take My Stand: The South and the Agrarian Tradition*, by Twelve Southerners (Baton Rouge: Louisiana State University Press, 1958), 34.

3. W.J. Cash, *The Mind of the South* (New York: Alfred A. Knopf, 1941), 31-32.

4. On physicality and sports among Victorian men, see Steven A. Riess, "Sport and the Redefinition of American Middle-Class Masculinity," *International Journal of the History of Sport* 8 (1991): 5-27.

5. William Faulkner, *The Hamlet* (New York: Random House, 1940), 103-13.

6. William Alexander Percy, *Lanterns on the Levee: Recollections of a Planter's Son* (Baton Rouge: Louisiana State University Press, 1941), 58.

7. James Agee and Walker Evans, *Let Us Now Praise Famous Men* (Boston: Houghton Mifflin, 1941).

8. C. Vann Woodward, "The Search for Southern Identity," *Virginia Quarterly Review* 34 (1958): 321-28.

9. Thomas D. Clark, *The Emerging South* (New York: Oxford University Press, 1961), 162.

10. Near the conclusion of his interpretation of the twentieth-century South, Pete Daniel describes football as very significant, but not as a part of regional identity. A growing middle class, he writes, "laughed at the sitcoms, told racist jokes, belched through football games, sent their children to soccer practice, worried about drugs, read *Southern Living* and *Sports Illustrated*, attended a nearby church (or watched one of the evangelists on television), and lived or died by the victories and defeats of their college alma maters. In other words, they were thoroughly American." Pete Daniel, *Standing at the Crossroads: Southern Life since 1900* (New York: Hill and Wang, 1986), 230.

11. The most prolific proponent of this point is John Shelton Reed. See his works such as *The Enduring South: Subcultural Persistence in Mass Society* (Chapel Hill: University of North Carolina Press, 1972); *One South: An Ethnic Approach to Regional Culture* (Baton Rouge: Louisiana State University Press, 1982); and *"My Tears Spoiled My Aim" and Other Reflections on Southern Culture* (Columbia: University Press of Missouri, 1993).

12. Reed, *One South*, 119-38.

13. For a characterization of modern sports, see Allen Guttmann, *A Whole New Ball Game: An Interpretation of American Sports* (Chapel Hill: University of North Carolina Press, 1988).

14. I have described these meanings in more detail in "Freedom, Manhood, and Male Tradition in 1970s Southern Rock Music," in *Haunted Bodies: Gender and Southern Texts*, ed. Anne Goodwyn Jones and Susan V. Donaldson (Charlottesville: University Press of Virginia, 1998), 369-88, C5. 371.

15. Among the many works discussing the significance of personal independence for men are Lacy K. Ford Jr., *Origins of Southern Radicalism: The South Carolina Upcountry, 1800-1860* (New York: Oxford University Press, 1988); Steven A. Hahn, *The Roots of Southern Populism: Yeoman Farmers and the Transformation of the Georgia Upcountry, 1850-1890* (New York: Oxford University Press, 1983); Joan E. Cashin, *A Family Venture: Men and Women on the Southern Frontier* (New York: Oxford University Press, 1991); and Stephanie McCurry, *Masters of Small Worlds: Yeoman Households, Gender*

Relations, and the Political Culture of the Antebellum South Carolina Low Country (New York: Oxford University Press, 1995).

16. Bertram Wyatt-Brown, *Southern Honor: Ethics and Behavior in the Old South* (New York: Oxford University Press, 1982); Steven M. Stowe, *Intimacy and Power in the Old South: Ritual in the Lives of the Planters* (Baltimore: Johns Hopkins University Press, 1987); Edward L. Ayers, *Vengeance and Justice: Crime and Punishment in the Nineteenth-Century American South* (New York: Oxford University Press, 1984); Kenneth S. Greenberg, *Masters and Statesmen: The Political Culture of American Slavery* (Baltimore: Johns Hopkins University Press, 1985); Kenneth S. Greenberg, *Honor and Slavery: Lies, Duels, Noses, Masks, Dressing as a Woman, Gifts, Strangers, Humanitarianism, Death, Slave Rebellions, the Pro-slavery Argument, Baseball, Hunting, and Gambling in the Old South* (Princeton, N.J.: Princeton University Press, 1996).

17. See, for example, Winthrop D. Jordan, *White over Black: American Attitudes toward the Negro, 1550-1812* (Chapel Hill: University of North Carolina Press, 1968); and Joel Williamson, *The Crucible of Race: Black-White Relations in the American South since Emancipation* (New York: Oxford University Press, 1984).

18. The principal theorist on the significance of paternalism is Eugene D. Genovese. See especially *Roll, Jordan, Roll: The World the Slaves Made* (New York: Vintage Books, 1976). See also Elizabeth Fox-Genovese, *Within the Plantation Household: Black and White Women of the Old South* (Chapel Hill: University of North Carolina Press, 1988).

19. Cash, *Mind of the South*, 52. See also Elliott J. Gorn, "'Gouge and Bite, Pull Hair and Scratch': The Social Significance of Fighting in the Southern Backcountry," *American Historical Review* 90 (February 1985): 18-43; Ted Ownby, *Subduing Satan: Religion, Recreation, and Manhood in the Rural South, 1865-1920* (Chapel Hill: University of North Carolina Press, 1990).

20. The following paragraphs on hunting draw on Wiley Charles Prewitt Jr., "The Best of All Breathing: Hunting and Environmental Change in Mississippi, 1900-1980" (M.A. thesis, University of Mississippi, 1991). The conclusions about the cultural distance of modern from earlier hunting are my own.

21. Ownby, *Subduing Satan*, 21-37.

22. Hahn, *Roots of Southern Populism*; Charles Flynn Jr., *White Land, Black Labor: Caste and Class in Late Nineteenth-Century Georgia* (Baton Rouge: Louisiana State University Press, 1983).

23. Prewitt, "Best of All Breathing," 131.

24. Ibid., 131-53.

25. On fox hunting, see Stuart A. Marks, *Southern Hunting in Black and White: Nature, History, and Ritual in a Carolina Community* (Princeton, N.J.: Princeton University Press, 1991), 93-134; and Wiley Charles Prewitt Jr., "Going Inside: Transformation of Fox Hunting in Mississippi," *Mississippi Folklife* 28 (1995): 26-32. On coon hunting, see Marks, *Southern Hoisting in Black and White*, 231-62.

26. On space and modern sport, see John Bale, *Landscapes of Modern Sport* (Leicester: Leicester University Press, 1994).

27. On the ancient image of a relatively new form of music, see Robert Cantwell, *Bluegrass Breakdown: The Making of the Old Southern Sound* (New York: Da Capo Press, 1992).

28. Ned Jarrett compared stock car drivers to country music figures like Dolly Parton because both hailed from poor backgrounds but remained "down to earth" after they achieved wealth and fame. Sylvia Wilkinson, *Dirt Tracks to Glory: The Early Days of Stock Car Racing as Told by the Participants* (Chapel Hill, N.C.: Algonquin, 1983), 154.

29. Quoted in ibid., 81.

30. Tom Wolfe, "Junior Johnson Is the Last American Hero Yes!" *Esquire* 80 (October 1973): 211.

31. Arguing that previous writers, especially for Hollywood, have placed too much emphasis on bootlegging is Allan Girdler, *Stock Car Racers: The History and Folklore of NASCAR's Premier Series—"Tail Straight Out and Belly to the Ground"* (Osceola, Wis.: Motorbooks Illustrated, 1988), 13.

32. See James C. Cobb, *The Selling of the South: The Southern Crusade for Industrial Development, 1936-1990*, 2d ed. (Urbana: University of Illinois Press, 1993); Linda Flowers, *Throwed Away: Failures of Progress in Eastern North Carolina* (Knoxville: University of Tennessee Press, 1990).

33. Cecilia Tichi, *High Lonesome: The American Culture of Country Music* (Chapel Hill: University of North Carolina Press, 1994).

34. Lynyrd Skynyrd, "Whiskey Rock-a-Roller," *Gold and Platinum,* MCA (MCAD2-6898).

35. Wilkinson, *Dirt Tracks to Glory,* 54. See also Richard Petty with William Neely, *King Richard I: The Autobiography of America's Greatest Auto Racer* (Toronto: Paperjacks, 1986), 64.

36. Girdler, *Stock Car Racers,* 42; Wilkinson, *Dirt Tracks to Glory,* 71. See also Petty, *King Richard I,* 26.

37. Petty, *King Richard I,* 40-45.

38. Girdler, *Stock Car Racers,* 28.

39. Andrew Doyle, "'Causes Won, Not Lost': College Football and the Modernization of the American South," *International Journal of the History of Sport* 11 (August 1994): 231-51; Patrick B. Miller, "The Manly, the Moral, and the Proficient: College Sport in the New South," in this volume.

40. See E.F. Schietinger, *Fact Book on Higher Education in the South, 1965* (Atlanta: Southern Regional Education Board, 1965), 18, for the figures on 1950. See National Center for Education Statistics, *Digest of Education Statistics* (Washington, D.C.: U.S. Department of Health, Education, and Welfare, 1994), 191, for the figures on 1992. On the southern rate of expansion, compared to the national rate, see Michael M. Myers, *Fact Book on Higher Education in the South, 1981 and 1982* (Atlanta: Southern Regional Education Board, 1982), 16.

41. John Vaught, *Rebel Coach: My Football Family* (Memphis: Memphis State University Press, 1971), 36.

42. Robert L. Dodd, *Bobby Dodd on Football* (New York: Prentice-Hall, 1954), 8,1.

43. Still one of the major works on professionalization is Robert Wiebe, *The Search for Order, 1877-1920* (New York: Hill and Wang, 1967).

44. Paul W. Bryant and John Underwood, *Bear: The Hard Life and Good Times of Alabama's Coach Bryant* (Boston: Little, Brown, 1974), 10. The emphasis on fight is Bryant's.

45. Ibid., 11.

46. Wyatt-Brown, *Southern Honor.*

CHAPTER 18

THE WHOLE WORLD ISN'T WATCHING (BUT WE THOUGHT THEY WERE)

The Super Bowl and U.S. Solipsism

Christopher R. Martin and Jimmie L. Reeves

A little more than a decade ago, as the symbolic Berlin Wall was coming down, political leaders in the United States assured their citizens that a New World Order had come to fruition. This new international, political arrangement would bring peace, of course, but more important was that it was implicitly an orderly peace—one which would be administered and maintained by the United States, to the advantage of the United States. In other words, to the winner go the spoils.

Almost as quickly, the New World Order got disorderly. A Gulf War quelled, but did not dislodge Saddam Hussein's regime in Iraq; hundred of thousands died in Rwanda as warring factions engaged in genocide; Pakistan and India rattled sabers with nuclear tests; and the worst act of terrorism visited U.S. soil, performed by a U.S. citizen. Daily NATO bombings of Serbia (including a few that were unfortunately aimed at the Chinese Embassy in Belgrade) failed to quickly halt ethnic cleansings in Kosovo, nor end the rule of the Serbian leader Slobodan Milosevic. And at a mostly white, upper-middle-class high school in Littleton, Colorado, two students turned guns and assorted weaponry on their peers and then themselves, ultimately killing 14 people and seriously injuring many more.

In countless ways U.S. political hegemony has been deflated in this New World Order. Although the U.S. side of the global economy mostly hums along, the problems of ungovernable international leaders, ineffective military inter-ventions, and chronic internal violence make the U.S.'s favorite chant of 'We're Number One' ring a little hollow in the post-cold war era.

Into this tableau enters the Super Bowl. Each year, this supremely nationalistic event—the United States' most-watched television program—is marketed to people in the U.S. by the National Football League (NFL) and the mainstream national news media as an international affair. World-wide audiences of nearly one billion are routinely announced in the pre-game hyperbole, and actively promoted during the broadcast. Many reports proclaim, as a public relations official for the NFL told us, that the Super Bowl 'is the greatest one-day sport-ing event around.'

But, is the Super Bowl the most super and most watched of sporting events in the world? What is the cultural significance of laying claim to being the sporting event with the most television viewers world-wide, especially in the historical conditions of this New World Order?

In a paper related to material in this chapter ('Rewriting the Super Bowl: From Cold War Spectacle to Postmodern Carnival'), we documented and examined transformations in the Super Bowl experience since the 1970s.[1] Over the course of more than 30 years the centrality of the Super Bowl's championship game spectacle has been undermined by a decentralized Super Bowl carnival with multiple narratives. The chief aspects of the post-modern rewriting of the Super Bowl experience include the foregrounding of commercial discourse, the con-spicuous display of promotional discourse, and the hyper-hyping of half-time discourse. These three companion narratives come together with the football championship narrative to form something of a metanarrative—one that cap-tures compelling mutations in the Super Bowl experience, and that accounts for its enormous U.S. television audience and its significant place in U.S. culture.

Another paper ('Re-Reading the Super Bowl'), updated Michael R. Real's influential and widely-read interpretation of football's championship game event as 'mythic spectacle'.[2] Whereas Real's structuralist reading of the 1974 Super Bowl focused on outlining the central features of the NFL's utopian vision of winning at all costs, our post-structuralist re-reading of the 1994 Super Bowl emphasized the struggle to uphold this embattled vision in the increasing fragmentation and declining expectations of post-Fordist television and society.

Our analysis in this paper begins with Real's interpretation of the 1974 Super Bowl. His 'The Super Bowl: Mythic Spectacle' concludes with a summation of the football's structural values: 'American football is an aggressive, strictly regulated team game fought between males who use both violence and technol-ogy to win monopoly control of property for the economic gain of individuals within a nationalistic, entertainment context'.[3] Ultimately, Real makes a relatively convincing argument that the 1974 Super Bowl is best understood as a vehicle for displaying what he terms 'the sexual, racial, and organizational priorities' of U.S. cold war culture.

Of course, the Super Bowl is still a major cultural event that, like the Balinese cockfight, renders 'ordinary, everyday experience comprehensible'.[4] But what happens when a ritual originating in one regime of experience is applied to a very different set of historical conditions? In our re-reading of the Super Bowl we do not set out to negate any of Real's insights. Instead, we use them as a point of departure to explore how the Super Bowl ritual has been transformed by the changing economic, technological, and political realities of deindustrialized, post-modern, Nafta-esque America—a United States in which the cold war values of Vince Lombardi and Richard Nixon have given way to the New World disorder of Monica Lewinsky, war in the Balkans, and the Columbine High School massacre.

This chapter first reviews the origins of the Super Bowl, especially how the event has evolved from a cold war, mythic spectacle to a televised carnival, with multiple—but still U.S.-centric—narratives. Secondly, we analyze the meaning of the Super Bowl as an international phenomenon. Our arguments on its relevance to the rest of the world will be supported with data from the CNN World News Archives and from a close textual reading of an introductory package from the 1995 broadcast of Super Bowl XXIX. Finally, we discuss why the United States' favorite professional sporting event is unlikely to become the favorite sporting event of the rest of the world.

From a Mythic Cold War Battle to the Post-Cold War Carnival

As the subheading suggests, we characterize these transformations as a shift from the mythic to the carnivalesque. We argue that the ritual competition of the actual championship game has steadily declined in cultural relevance—especially in relation to the increasing public fascination with both the advertising discourse and half-time entertainment. In fact, our analysis suggests that the tracing of transformations in the meanings and pleasures generated by the Super Bowl is one way of mapping the cultural deterritorializations and reterritorializations of a fundamental change in the U.S. television experience—the shift from TV I to TV II.[5]

A shorthand term for the broadcasting system that emerged in the U.S. in the 1950s, triumphed in the 1960s, and was slowly displaced in the 1970s, the term 'TV I' refers to what has also been studied as 'network era television'. A period dominated by a three-network oligopoly, TV I played a central, ideological role in promoting the ethic of consumption, naturalizing the nuclear family ideal, selling suburbanization, and sustaining cold war paranoia. Put another way, TV I was one of the chief products and producers of Fordism—a 'rigid' economic order named after Henry Ford that drove the general prosperity of the post-war boom through an expansive manufacturing economy of assembly-line production and mass consumption.[6] And, as an expression of Fordism, television popularity during the 1950s and the 1960s is most properly studied as mass culture oriented toward attracting the largest possible audience. The Super Bowl is, of course, a relic of the 1960s. And, like TV

I, after emerging from the Fordist order it then contributed, actively, to the reproduction of Fordism.

As such, televised professional football is an almost pure expression of values associated with Fordism. Like the Fordist assembly line, football, more than any other popular sport, is marked by a highly differentiated division of labor, with each position on both the offense and the defense carrying with it highly specific responsibilities. It also exhibits Fordist hierarchies of control that reach from the quarterback (often called a 'field general'), through specialty coaches and coordinators, through the head coach, through the managerial elite, to ownership. Furthermore, as an expression of the utopian visions of the Fordist economic order, football is infatuated with discipline, conformity, and winning. After all, under Fordism, the world of work was supremely a masculine domain devoted to the ethic of competition. And the Super Bowl is the ultimate manifestation of this ethic. This competitive ethic was perhaps most clearly stated by the legendary Vince Lombardi (who coached the Green Bay Packers to victory in the first Super Bowl) when he said, 'Winning isn't everything, it's the only thing.' Standing in stark contrast to an older sports ethic ('It doesn't matter if you win or lose, it's how you play the game'), Lombardi's words have been echoed over and over again by people such as the Oakland Raiders owner Al Davis ('Just win, Baby').[7]

Indeed, Real's analysis presents a compelling 'reading'—grounded in the political concerns and interpretive trends of the period—of how the Super Bowl performed as a mechanism of ideological reproduction. But what Real was not able to discern at the time, and what his structuralism was simply not designed to address, is how this same sports ritual can, at one and the same time, operate as a conservative celebration of Fordism's aggressive masculinity while also performing as an instrument of change, a mechanism of ideological transformation that now exhibits all the attributes of a new order of popularity associated with 'post-Fordism' and TV II.

What we refer to as TV II (or 'post-Fordist TV') emerged in the 1970s, triumphed in the 1980s and in the 1990s was being marketed under the alias of the 'information superhighway'. Although TV I's broadcasting distribution system is still an integral part of this new communication order, TV II also incorporates satellite, cable, VCR, and personal computer technologies. To say that these new forces in the marketplace have undermined the dominance of TV I's three-network oligopoly would be an understatement: where once ABC, NBC, and CBS commanded over 90 percent of the prime-time audience, today the major network audience, even with the addition of a fourth national broadcast network, has decreased to less than 60 percent. In this transformation, older notions of popularity would be rewritten as television's mass audience was systematically fragmented into lifestyle sectors and niche markets—and the rigidities of Fordist TV would give way to more flexible programming and scheduling strategies devoted to generating 'quality demographics'.

This rewriting of popularity signaled a shift from mass culture and its unifying influences to something that might best be described as 'cult culture', a system of taste distinctions that has figured prominently in supporting and masking the radical inequalities of our times by segmenting the audience into 'insiders' and 'outsiders'. This re-visioning of the American television experience is most clearly manifested in cult shows of the past dozen years such as 'Twin Peaks', 'Mystery Science Theatre 3000', 'The X-Files', and 'South Park'. Even some of the latest programming trends in U.S. television, which seek to re-establish mass audiences for the major broadcast networks, do so with a post-Fordist twist. The biggest and most copied hit of the 1999-2000 television season, ABC's 'Who Wants to be a Millionaire?', is reminiscent of America's love affair with prime-time game shows during the TV I era of the 1950s, but breaks the traditional proscenium of the glass screen. The show invites home viewers to be contestants by dialing a toll-free telephone number, and collects data on the fans who visit the show's web site to play an on-line version of the game or who complete a marketing survey for ABC in an attempt to win prizes. Other programs, including CBS's 'Survivor' and 'Big Brother', inspired by similar television programs in Europe and 24-hour webcam Internet sites, turn to an unprecedented voyeurism regarding ordinary people's daily lives to attract mass audiences to television and to companion web sites offering live video streaming and free subscription newsletters. Although CBS hopes to gain huge audiences with these programs, the Internet elements of the programming allow the network to distill mass audiences into niche markets and even targeted individuals. The viewers watch programs of surveillance and are themselves tracked by the network during their visits to program Internet sites.[8]

Thus the shift in the culture of U.S. television is apparent in the segmentation of mass audiences via cult television and the Internet, and also through other programming strategies: the hybridization of the police show, the yuppification of the family drama, the tabloidization of the news, and, more to the point of this analysis, the carnivalization of the Super Bowl. Drawing on terms that David Harvey uses to describe the difference between the cold war era of modernity and post-cold war era of postmodernity,[9] we argue that—in the ascendancy of TV II—the authority, permanence, and centrality of the Super Bowl's championship spectacle has been undermined by an eclectic, ephemeral, and decentralized Super Bowl circus with multiple side-shows.

Although our 'Re-writing' paper also considers promotional discourse and half-time entertainment, here we limit the discussion to the most flagrant aspect of the post-modern mutation of the Super Bowl experience: that is, the hyper-hyping of commercial discourse. In fact, we have informally observed that many viewers are now more attuned to the advertising extravaganza than to the actual game. At many Super Bowl gatherings partiers will converse during game time, ignoring the contest in favor of good company, but then will be hushed during the commercial breaks. One can only imagine how Vince Lombardi would respond to such callous indifference to his beloved competition.

At least since Super Bowl III,[10] advertising space on the annual event has attracted widespread attention simply because it is one of the most expensive commercial slots of the broadcast year. A 30-sec commercial for what is now remembered as the first Super Bowl in 1967 would have cost between $37,500 and $42,500. By 1985, 30 sec of Super Bowl time cost an average of $500,000; the price jumped to $1 million by 1995.[11] Because of the continuous decline of audience size for regular network television programs since the early 1980s, the Super Bowl now has no peers in its per-minute advertising price. Thus it is unlikely that we shall ever again see a situation where another special program can command more money than the Super Bowl, as the last episode of 'M*A*S*H' did in February 1984. In that special 2½-hour final episode, CBS charged an average of $450,000 for a 30-sec slot, $50,000 more than NBC charged during Super Bowl 18 months earlier.[12] By 1995 the Super Bowl's $1 million-for-30-sec advertising price was far above the other high rated programs of the same period: a 30-sec slot cost an average $643,500 on the Academy Awards show, $305,000 on the number-one rated 'Home Improvement', and $214,000 on the well-hyped NCAA men's basketball finals. The Super Bowl advertising price continues to increase: the average cost for 30 sec of time in 1999 hit $1.6 million[13] and $2.2 million in 2000.[14]

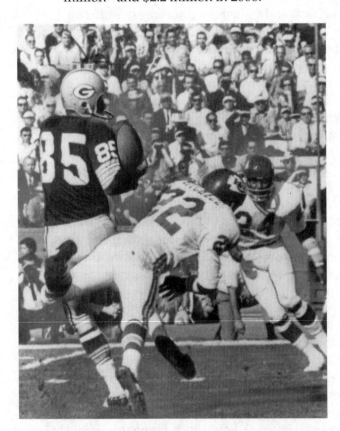

Max Magee of the Green Bay Packers catching a pass against the Kansas City Chiefs in the 1967 Super Bowl at the Los Angeles Coliseum.
Photo Courtesy of Library of Congress. LC-USZ62-121407.

Through the 1970s, mass media (and public) fascination with Super Bowl advertisements was limited to the issue of their relatively exorbitant cost, and the demand to buy them as a sort of indicator of the health and confidence of American business. The content of Super Bowl commercials was not a popular topic of discussion. However, on 22 January 1984 a single 60-sec Super Bowl XVIII advertisement revolutionized the way advertisers would approach the game. The Super Bowl would no longer be a means to reach a large audience, with the same old truck or motor oil commercial, but a way to make a stunning, dramatic, entertaining commercial statement. In the third quarter of the Los Angeles Raiders' blow-out of the Washington Redskins, viewers were confronted with a visually compelling 60-sec advertisement directed by the British filmmaker Ridley Scott (*Blade Runner* and *Alien*) and costing nearly $400,000 to produce—four times the cost of a typical 30-sec advertisement at the time.[15] It ended with the tag line, 'On January 24th, Apple Computer will introduce Macintosh. And you'll see why 1984 won't be like *1984*'. For those who missed the message, the Apple chairman Steve Jobs suggested two days later that the real 'Big Brother' was the computer industry leader IBM. The Macintosh advertisement has attained 'classic' status, and is now part of the advertising industry's Clio Awards Hall of Fame.

But, whereas the Macintosh advertisement is now famous for making the Super Bowl a showcase for innovative advertising and a time for strategic product introductions, a largely forgotten Burger King campaign two years later initiated the practice of advance publicity for Super Bowl advertisements—in other words, advertisements to watch advertisements. The $40 million Burger King promotion began in November 1985 with the search for 'Herb the Nerd', a man who was purportedly the only person in America who had not eaten at a Burger King restaurant. The advertisement-induced excitement over the identity of Herb reached its peak in January 1986, when Burger King promised to reveal his identity to the more than 100 million people watching the Super Bowl. The rather anticlimactic Super Bowl commercials unveiled Herb—an actor adorned in horn-rimmed glasses, ill-fitting clothes, and white socks. Shortly after the Super Bowl appearance, the *Chicago Tribune* columnist Bob Greene wrote that, with all of the media exposure, 'Herb is currently one of the most famous men in America.'[16] Herb toured America for the next few weeks, stopping at Burger Kings in each state for surprise Herb-sightings, but the campaign flopped after the Super Bowl advertisements broke the mystery. The Herb promotion had little impact on hamburger sales, but was innovative in its use of the Super Bowl.[17] The commercial narrative began to catch on; CBS ran the first-ever network news story about Super Bowl commercials on 21 January 1987.

The most successful advance promotion of Super Bowl advertisements is the recurring 'Bud Bowl' campaign. The Anheuser-Busch promotion began with the 1989 Super Bowl, and fully embraced its spirit of transforming mundane, inconsequential events into larger-than-life-drama. The Bud Bowls are certainly inconsequential: animated, long-necked beer bottles—Budweiser and Bud Light—play a mock football game in a series of commercials during the Super Bowl. Real sports announcers, such as NBC's Bob Costas, ABC's Keith Jackson, the former ABC Monday Night Football personality Don Meredith, and ESPN's Chris Berman, provide the authentic-sounding drama to pun-filled voice-overs (such as 'This looks like a real brew—haha').

Nevertheless, the first Bud Bowl campaign was elevated into a significant event, if only because of its 'super' status. Consider this lead from a *St. Louis Post-Dispatch* article: 'The world's largest brewer will be the world's largest spender at the world's largest single sporting event."[18] In all, the brewing giant spent $5 million on the first Bud Bowl campaign: about $1 million to make the commercials, $4 million for the Super Bowl advertising time, and another $1 million for store displays and other promotions. For that money Anheuser-Busch gained exclusive beer advertising rights to the 1989 Super Bowl and experienced a jump in January beer sales of 17 per cent that year. One report noted that sales during the cold, post-holiday month of January were once weak, but Super Bowl promotions such as the Bud Bowl had lifted the month to be one of the best-selling beer months of the year.[19] The Bud Bowls have continued in various forms each Super Bowl since 1989, adding Roman numerals to the Bud Bowl name to achieve Super Bowl-style nomenclature. Following the success of the Bud Bowls, many Super Bowl advertisers now run teaser advertisements to build audience anticipation for their brief-but-glorious moments.

Perhaps the most important development in making the Super Bowl commercials a significant cultural story was the advent of the *USA Today* Super Bowl Ad Meter, also in 1989. The Ad Meter moved stories that had previously appeared only in trade journals, such as *Advertising Age,* and made them part of the news media's Super Bowl metanarrative. By social science standards, the Ad Meters are simplistic and sloppy. But the Ad Meter still managed to generate the infinitely valuable stuff that most sports stories are made of: statistics. With these questionable data, *USA Today* could authoritatively determine winners and losers and create a new 'battle' for Super Bowl Sunday. On the debut of the Ad Meter, *USA Today* proclaimed that: 'The real competition at the Super Bowl wasn't on the field. It happened during the commercial breaks. Advertisers spent millions of dollars for commercial ad time in a dazzling and dizzying pitch to the giant Super Bowl audience.'[20] Other news outlets were quick to catch on to this narrative, either by reporting the Ad Meter results, reporting the results of other advertising survey agencies, or at the very least assigning a reporter to review the Super Bowl advertisements.[21]

Like the Bud Bowl, the Ad Meter has deemed itself a Super Bowl tradition, and now counts each yearly appearance with Roman numerals. The surest sign that devices such as the Ad Meter will continue to feed the Super Bowl metanarrative is that blockbuster Super Bowl advertisements themselves have been formally enshrined in a museum. The Museum of Broadcasting in New York presented an hour-long collection of Super Bowl advertisements in a 1995 show appropriately entitled 'The Super Bowl: Super Show case for Commercials'.[22]

Of course, a large number of Americans still tune in to this perennial mega-event to watch the spectacle of the football game, and, obviously, some things about the Super Bowl have not changed since its origins. For example, as a cold war spectacle not unlike the Soviet Union's May Day parade, the Super Bowl operated as a primary site for the display of military nationalism. A *New York Times* account of Super Bowl VI in 1972 noted that the game

> got under way with a patriotic-military display. While a giant U.S. flag, surrounded by smaller U.S. flags, was carried on to the field, Phantom jets roared over the crowd and viewers were requested to say a prayer for those servicemen missing in action or captured in Southeast Asia.[23]

Although the Cold War had ended by 1991, this Vietnam-era symbolic language was recovered in Super Bowl XXV's ritual response to American involvement in the Gulf War. As flags waved (small U.S. flags were provided to each of the 72,500 fans, who had been checked at the gates with a metal detector because of heightened fears of an Arab terrorist attack) and Whitney Houston performed the National Anthem in Tampa Stadium, a jet fly-over added emphasis to the lines 'and the home of the brave.'[24] The fly-over tradition continued in 1999, as the 93rd Fighter Squadron zoomed in the skies above Joe Robbie Stadium in Miami while Cher completed the final notes of the National Anthem.

Yet, as we hope to demonstrate, such continuities are not as decisive as the changes in the Super Bowl experience. Although residual values associated with Fordism and cold war culture are still imprinted in the Super Bowl competition (that is, in the game itself), these values are now the subject of a great deal of controversy and discussion. In fact, the presentation of the game itself has had to acknowledge and accommodate contradictions in the NFL's utopian vision of winning at all costs, as it has expanded into a carnival of multiple narratives. As we have noted elsewhere, Vince Lombardi's professional football credo that 'winning isn't everything, it's the only thing', now competes with a more recent, unofficial doctrine for the way the NFL and the Super Bowl operate: '*Image* isn't everything; it's the only thing.'

The Super Bowl (and its administrators—the NFL and its broadcast partners) has been immensely successful in this difficult cultural balancing act of competing values. The enormous popularity of the Super Bowl—nine of the ten most-watched television programs in American history are Super Bowls (the other is one of the evening skating competitions from the 1994 winter Olympics featuring the dueling of Tonya Harding and Nancy Kerrigan, as described in the essay by Bettina Fabos)—is a testament to how deeply engrained the Super Bowl is in American culture. In 2000 the game drew 130.7 million viewers in the U.S., easily the highest rated program of the year, and the fifth highest program ever (behind four other Super Bowls).[25] But, for the United States to consider the Super Bowl as the most popular *international* sporting event requires both an excessive amount of hype (which the Super Bowl supplies perhaps better than any other event) and an equal amount of solipsism.

The Globalization of the Super Bowl

With the overwhelming dominance of U.S. entertainment content—especially films, television, and music—around the globe, it is no surprise that the National Football League has worked to build a worldwide audience for American football and its premier television event. From the NFL's perspective, it is expanding the market for its product. Don Garber, then senior Vice President of NFL International, explained in 1999: 'We invest in a long-term plan to help the sport grow around the world. The vision is to be a leading global sport. We need to create awareness and encourage involvement.'[26]

But the desire for global dominance of American football extends beyond just the NFL's profit-oriented interests. As an American cultural ritual, it is increasingly relevant (and increasingly common) that the Super Bowl is represented as the greatest and most watched sporting event on the planet. The enormous, *estimated* Super Bowl audience of between 800 million and a billion represents at least two competing ideals. On one hand, the Super Bowl's portrayal in mainstream U.S. news media as the leading international sporting event seems to combat post-cold war fragmentation by emphasizing increasing global unity, via a world-wide, shared Super Bowl experience. On the other, it is significant that this international unity is a unity not focused around World Cup soccer (which is *football* to the majority of the planet), but around *American football,* a U.S.-controlled export. Herein lies the great solipsism of the Super Bowl. To a large extent, Americans (and their mass media) cannot imagine—or do not wish to—the Super Bowl as being anything less than the biggest, 'baddest', and best sporting event in the world.

To imagine the Super Bowl as being this top sporting event is to ignore the counter-evidence of several other major sporting events:

- The estimated audience for the soccer World Cup (held every four years) is more than two billion viewers world-wide for the single-day championship match. In 1998 an estimated cumulative audience of 37 billion people watched some of the 64 games over the month-long event.[27]

- The Cricket World Cup, held every four years (most recently in England in 1999) and involving mostly the countries of the former British Empire, has an estimated two billion viewers world-wide, but receives scant attention in the United States.[28]

- Even the Rugby World Cup, also held every four years (most recently in Wales in 1999), claimed 2.5 billion viewers for its 1995 broadcast from South Africa.[29]

- Canada, perhaps the country outside the U.S. most likely to adopt the Super Bowl as its own favorite sporting event—given Canada's geographic proximity, limited language barriers, and familiarity with the NFL, favors its own sports championship. The Grey Cup, the title game of the Canadian Football League, regularly draws three million viewers, more than the annual broadcasts of the Super Bowl and hockey's Stanley Cup final. Only the Academy Awards generate a larger Canadian television audience each year.[30]

For more empirical evidence of the relative global insignificance of American football in general and of the Super Bowl in particular we turn to another manifestation of the post-modern spirit that has transformed the Super Bowl into a carnival of consumption: the CNN World Report (CNNWR). According to corporate legend, CNNWR is Ted Turner's maverick attempt to correct the distortions of American television news coverage of the global scene. Launched on 25 October 1987, CNNWR was designed to provide an alternative vision of global journalism, a vision that transcends the nationalistic framing that contaminates conventional international reporting by the U.S. broadcasting networks. As the program's founding executive producer, Stuart Looring, describes it, Turner's 'Big Idea' for CNNWR was deceptively simple: 'Our basic role is to be a huge bulletin board in space on which the world's news organizations can tack up their notices, unedited and uncensored.'[31] But while CNN does not edit nor censor the content of the stories submitted to CNNWR, a few ground rules still apply:

- The report must be in English;
- The report can be no longer than 2 1/2 min;
- It must be understandable.

According to Ralph M. Wenge, current executive producer of CNNWR, 'the only time we ever work with any of those reports is if somebody has such a strong accent that we can't understand it; then we retrack it in Atlanta.'[32] Furthermore, in providing this unique 'horizontal news channel', CNN still reserves the right to 'arrange the individual contributor segment packages into the most appealing sequences for maximum viewer interest.'[33]

Our own sampling of World Report programs suggests that the CNNWR has remained just as ungovernable and diversified and refreshingly deviant as when it was launched.[34] A collection of conventional hard news stories, thinly-veiled propaganda, unpaid advertising for tourist industries, funny animal videos, environmental activism, and insightful cultural features, the metaphor that seem most able to capture the meaning and significance of CNNWR is not a carnival, but a circus. With wild animals, clowns, ring masters, and death defying heroics, the CNNWR is an example of post-modern culture in which all truth is a matter of point-of-view—and the distinctions between high and low, strong and weak, professional and amateur, information and entertainment, First World and Third World, friend and foe, no longer matter.

Using the several key-word searches of the CNNWR Archive, we determined that, if coverage in this post-modern, transnational, news venue is any indication, the Super Bowl is a relatively minor blip on the global sports scene. Here are the results:

- The key words 'Super' and 'Bowl' produced only one result. Airing on 22 January 1989, the story was prepared by CNN's own staff and reported on riots that broke out in predominantly black sections of Miami as the city hosted the Super Bowl.
- The key word 'football' produced 37 results. However, only eight of those stories made any reference to American football. The others were about soccer.

Of the eight American football stories:

- Three were from CNN (the Miami riot story, a story on Thanksgiving football games, and a story on the O.J. Simpson murder scandal).

- Two were from Canada (one about financing stadium construction and one on O.J. Simpson).

- One was from France (about entertaining U.S. servicemen during Operation DESERT SHIELD).

- One was from the Netherlands and one from Finland (both about attempts to introduce American football to the two countries).

By way of comparison, consider the preceding results in relation to key-word searches linked to other sports and sporting events:

- The key words 'World' and 'Cup' and 'soccer' produced 18 results from 12 different countries.

- 'Hockey' produced 15 results (but 'Stanley' and 'Cup' produced zero results).

- 'Baseball' produced 30 results (and six were related to the World Series).

- 'Tennis' produced 16 results.

- 'Basketball' produced 18 results.

- 'Olympic' produced 164 results from 56 countries.

Clearly, American football occupies a marginal position in the world of sports reported by CNNWR—a position that puts it in roughly the same place on the hierarchy of world sports as cricket (which produced 11 results in the key-word search of the CNNWR Archive).[35]

Imagining That the U.S. is the Center of Attention

Although the Super Bowl holds second-level status among world sporting events, the National Football League and other organizations have actively promoted American football to an international audience at least since the early 1980s. In England in 1982 the then-new Channel 4 joined with the NFL and the U.S. brewing giant Anheuser-Busch to show a weekly edited highlight program of American football. This program (edited versions of a featured game's highlights with flashy graphics and rock and roll music) offered novel programming for Channel 4 and strategic marketing opportunities to develop a British taste for American football and Budweiser beer. (Anheuser-Busch later even established the Budweiser League that organized a competition of local, American-style, football clubs.) Although the size of the television audience for American football in the United Kingdom grew between 1982 and 1990, its popularity peaked in the mid 1980s and leveled off to a little over two millions for the average game audience by 1990, leading the British sport researcher Joe Maguire to conclude that, 'while American football may be an emergent sport in English society, it certainly has not achieved dominance.'[36]

The first instance of an international audience for the Super Bowl mentioned in the *NFL Record and Fact Book* on-line is for the year 1985.[37] That Super Bowl, notable for President Reagan doing the game's coin toss shortly after he took his second term oath of office, attracted nearly 116 million viewers in the U.S. The *Record and Fact Book* also notes that, in addition, 'six million people watched the Super Bowl in the United Kingdom and a similar number in Italy.' In that same year the NFL adopted a resolution to begin its series of preseason, international, exhibition games, which would field NFL teams in foreign countries to build interest in American football.

In 1986 the *Record and Fact Book* noted, 'Super Bowl XX was televised to 59 foreign countries and beamed via satellite to the *QE II*. An estimated 300 million Chinese viewed a tape delay of the game in March' (more than a month later). The international broadcast remained at about 60 countries for the next several years; but by the end of the cold war the NFL greatly expanded the Super Bowl's reach. In 1993, according to the *Record and Fact Book*, the game was shown live or taped in 101 countries. However, the data for the numbers of countries and viewers are often wildly reported. For the same 1993 Super Bowl (this one was notable for Michael Jackson's 'Heal the World' halftime performance), the *Los Angeles Times* reported that the NFL estimated 'an audience of more than one billion people in the United States and 86 other countries', *USA Weekend* noted 'an estimated one billion viewers in more than 70 countries', and *Amusement Business* (an industry journal concerned with the halftime program) explained the 'television audience is estimated at 1.3 billion in 86 countries, which is one reason Jackson agreed to participate.'[38]

By 1999 the estimates of audience size were smaller, but the scope of the international coverage had expanded to include more nations and more languages. The NFL reported that:

> Nearly 800 million NFL fans around the world are expected to tune in to watch. International broadcasters will televise the game to at least 180 countries and territories in 24 different languages from Pro Player Stadium: Chinese (Mandarin), Danish, Catalan, Dutch, Norwegian, English, French, German, Italian, Japanese, Russian, and Spanish.
>
> In addition, the game will be broadcast in Arabic, Bulgarian, Cantonese, Flemish, Greek, Hebrew, Hindi, Icelandic, Korean, Portuguese, Romanian, Slovak, Thai, and Turkish. Approximately 90 per cent of the international coverage will be through live telecast of Super Bowl XXXIII.
>
> ERA in Taiwan, RDS (Canada), SAT 1 (Austria, Germany, and Switzerland), Sky (United Kingdom), TV-2 (Norway), and TV-2 (Denmark) will be broadcasting on-site for the first time.[39]

On Sunday, 30 January 2000 the *Los Angeles Times* noted that 'the game will be broadcast on 225 television stations, 450 radio stations, and in 180 countries. The cliché about a billion people in China not caring is no longer applicable.'[40] Yet the notion that the entire world pauses to pay homage to the Super Bowl is national mythology, continuously constructed via the NFL and the U.S. mass media. As we shall argue below, it is likely that more than a billion people in China do not even have the opportunity to care about the Super Bowl.

The most interesting element of the international audience claims is that the trend (with the exception of 1993—perhaps a top talent like Michael Jackson was expected to draw a larger audience and thus generate record audience estimates) is always upward. This climbing trajectory, of course, is the trend expected of everything connected to the Super Bowl. Yet the growing number of countries receiving the broadcast and the enormous numbers of the *estimated* or *potential* audience seem to us to be more of a technical achievement than an indication of popularity. In fact, the record of the NFL's appeal beyond the borders of the United States is mixed. The League's exhibition games overseas have often gone well. For example, the first of the so-called 'American Bowls' on 3 August 1986 at Wembley Stadium in London (and co-sponsored by the American football booster, Budweiser beer) drew a sell-out crowd of 82,699. The NFL did not take any chances, and scheduled the Super Bowl champions, the Chicago Bears, to play the high-profile Dallas Cowboys in the game (which the Bears won). In August 1994 a record crowd of 112,376 attended an American Bowl game in Mexico City between Dallas and Houston. By 2000, 34 American Bowls had been played in 11 cities outside the U.S., with an average attendance of 58,474.[41]

Although the one-day American Bowl events do well in local attendance, as the fans watch the very best NFL talent, the NFL's attempts to establish international American football leagues have been mediocre at best. In 1991 the NFL created the World League of American Football, which would be the first sports league to operate with teams in North America and Europe, playing on a weekly basis. In 1995, after a two-year hiatus, the WLAF (an acronym with potentially annoying puns for a struggling league) returned to action with just six teams in Europe. On 23 June of that same year the Frankfurt Galaxy defeated the Amsterdam Admirals 26-22, and won the 1995 World Bowl before a crowd of 23,847 in Amsterdam's Olympic Stadium. There were plenty of empty seats there, and the NFL made no claims to a huge world audience for the World Bowl. By the 1998 season the WLAF was renamed the NFL Europe League, which continues to play with six teams. The NFL's international division—formerly founded as NFL International in 1996—continues its efforts to build grass-roots interest in American football through activities such as sponsored flag football leagues in every NFL Europe city and in Japan, Canada, and Mexico.[42] By 2000 NFL International boasted that more than one million children around the world played NFL Flag Football,[43] and counted Canada, Mexico, Australia, and Japan among its 'priority markets'.[44]

Super Bowl Sunday Everywhere

That reports of the Super Bowl's international appeal are always estimated figures is disconcerting. While it is impossible to get an exact count of the viewers—the United States might have the most technically advanced television ratings systems, yet methodological deficiencies are commonly noted—the number of 800 million viewers is never documented in any way by the NFL nor the news media.

We were curious about this and approached the NFL's public relations department. According to one of the NFL's officials, the figure for the 800 million global audience for the Super Bowl is estimated, based on ratings company figures from the U.S. (Nielsen) and from similar companies in each of the 180 other nations and territories that carried the game.[45] Yet the estimates of the audience always are announced during the pre-game hype, and are never—to the best of our knowledge and research—verified after the game (except for the U.S. numbers). Who could possibly check out these statistics, particularly if the NFL is not forthcoming? (Our NFL source seemed initially surprised that anyone would question the global audience figures, then just recited the same data.) The NFL official did acknowledge that the 800 million means that that number of people tuned in to watch at least a portion of the broadcast, not necessarily the entire one. This, of course, is similar to the American viewing experience; as ratings data indicate, many viewers tune out halfway through the game, particularly if the competition is lopsided.

Although the hyped international audience figures suggest that the whole planet is sharing the same American Super Bowl cultural experience, the time differential (particularly if 90 per cent of the international coverage is via a live feed, as the NFL claims) makes the viewing experience quite different. First of all, Super Bowl Sunday in the United States is Super Bowl Monday for the bulk of the world's population. With a kick-off time at approximately 6 p.m., Eastern Time in the U.S. (the time zone shifts, depending on the annual location of the game) on Sunday evening, game time for European viewers ranges from 12 midnight to 2 a.m., Monday morning. Kick-off is 7 a.m. Monday morning in Beijing, 8 a.m. in Seoul, and 9 a.m. in Brisbane. Thus the Sunday evening weekend party atmosphere that typifies the U.S. experience is awkwardly transplanted to an all-night ordeal in Europe or a Monday morning working day in east Asia and Australia. The Super Bowl's Sunday evening time slot—the evening with the heaviest television viewing in the U.S. each week contributes to the Super Bowl's big viewership. But the Super Bowl's broadcast time in Europe, Asia, and Australia is clearly out of the realm of prime time and is one when few can afford to watch television.

Moreover, while the Super Bowl has free broadcast delivery in the United States, bringing the game to the more than 99 percent of American households that have a television set, in other global markets the program's live distribution often comes only via paid cable or direct broadcast satellite television, both of which have a limited number of subscribers. The global audience is further limited by the fact that significant portions of the world's population are not even served by the cable or satellite signals that carry live feeds of the Super Bowl. For example, ESPN Star Sports, a joint venture between ESPN, Inc. (owned by Disney) and Star TV (owned by the News Corp., Ltd), was the sole carrier of the January 2000 Super Bowl XXXIV game to most Asian nations.[46] In fact, with China, India, Indonesia, Pakistan, Bangladesh, Vietnam, and South Korea among the markets exclusively served by ESPN Star Sports for the Super Bowl broadcast, the company was the provider of the event to a geographic area representing more than three billion people, over half of the world's population. Yet, as of November 1999, ESPN and Star Sports combined to serve fewer than 93 million households in all of its Asian national markets.[47]

The problem of access, however, does little to halt programming that suggests that the whole world stops for the Super Bowl. A 1 $^1/_2$-min, prerecorded television package broadcast in the pre-game program for Super Bowl XXIX in 1995 is the most stunning example to date of U.S. solipsism with regard to the Super Bowl broadcast. The segment begins with a introduction by the ABC television network announcer Brent Musburger [voiced over live video of the shot from an airship of Miami's Joe Robbie Stadium at dusk, which later cuts to a shot of the field, with a pre-game show of balloons, music, and line-kicking women]:

> So there we are. A game that has grown so much over the last 29 years. Remember back in Super Bowl I? There were empty seats in the Los Angeles Coliseum. Seats were priced at $25 a piece. Now we're getting ready in Joe Robbie and the cheapest ticket is $200. The world awaits Super Bowl XXIX. 174 countries will take the feed. And we estimate the audience for this Super Bowl will be in excess of 750 million. We hope everyone enjoys Super Bowl XXIX!

[The program then cuts to the prerecorded package, which begins with a spinning, animated globe and upbeat, suspenseful music. Then Musberger's voice-over resumes over an international montage of seven locations]:

> In Maine, they come in from the shore to watch the Super Bowl. [*Video:* screen text that says 'Cape Elizabeth, Maine' over a shot of a lighthouse on a rocky beach] The DMZ in Korea. Our young soldiers are ready. [*Video:* screen text that says 'The DMZ, Korea' over a shot of an American military check point in South Korea at the demilitarized zone border with North Korea] In San Diego, the Charger fans are euphoric. [*Video:* screen text that says 'San Diego, California' over a shot of whooping partiers on a yacht] Down under, they're ready. [*Video:* screen text that says 'Queensland, Australia' over a shot of a rugged Crocodile Dundee lookalike walking toward the camera] Greybull, Wyoming, where the cowboys come in to watch the game. [*Video:* screen text that says 'Greybull, Wyoming' over several men dismounting from their horses and walking into a barn] And in Antarctica, they're bellying up. [*Video:* screen text that says 'McMurdo Station, Antarctica' over shot where two people dressed in parkas are watching a television outside while a lone penguin in the background falls and slides on his belly] In San Francisco, can the 49ers win it for a fifth time? [*Video:* screen text that says 'San Francisco, California' over a black (we note this because all other subjects shown except for a U.S. serviceman are white) man who puts a 49ers baseball cap on a black boy who is in a hospital bed; the man then turns on the television set; implicitly, they are father and son.]

Musberger then says, 'The stage is set.' The package then builds with a fast montage of each place just visited, as the music modulates to ever-higher keys:

- A night-time shot of Joe Robbie stadium (to give the illusion that this is live)
- A shot of cowboys in a Wyoming barn, crowded around the television set, with the same shot of the stadium on the screen

- The father and son in the hospital, with the same shot of the stadium on the screen
- The Australian takes a seat in his living room, explaining to his wife that this is 'American Footy—the Super Bowl'
- U.S. soldiers in a cafeteria line in Korea
- The mostly male partiers on the San Diego yacht
- The two researchers watching outside in Antarctica, high-fiving each other, and inexplicably drinking what looks like canned beer
- A middle-aged man with a golden retriever dog at his side, in front of a television set, with a warm mug of drink and a roaring fireplace in the background; man, dog, television set; no woman.

Finally, the music shifts to a tympani-heavy crescendo. Close-up shots are edited to the beat, and suggest a world-wide climax in anticipation of this great event:

- A cowboy close-up
- A smiling boy in hospital in a 49ers cap
- A smiling, pretty, young woman in a Chargers cap (the only woman emphasized in this entire package)
- An interested Australian watching the television set
- A captivated Antarctica viewer
- A close-up of the golden retriever's head, being patted by his master.

The montage dissolves to a live aerial shot of the stadium, Musburger says 'Super Bowl XXIX is coming up', and screen text appears that reads, 'SUPER BOWL SUNDAY EVERYWHERE'.[48]

The U.S.-centric thrust of this presumably international Super Bowl promotion is clear. The piece is mired in the old rituals of the Super Bowl: an emphasis on men, on white men, on white men in English-speaking countries and/or U.S. outposts, on U.S. military readiness, on rugged, masculine places like a rocky Maine coast, Wyoming ranches, the Australian outback, the icepack of Antarctica, and the dangerous DMZ. Women appear as the silent wife (Mrs. Aussie) and as a cute, young thing (woman in Chargers cap). It is not surprising that a man's loyal hunting dog gets more screen time than a woman.

Conclusion

In a New World Order and an era of globalization that the U.S. seeks to master, imagining the Super Bowl as the premiere international television sporting event is a way to control 'our' American (U.S.) sport and 'our' superiority. But, in the solipsistic vision of the 1995 ABC television pre-game package, the imagined global audience looks largely like the imagined U.S. audience: people who either are Americans located at various points of the world, or people who look like white, middle-class Americans (the Australian couple), experiencing the telecast from the sofa in the living room, in the appropriate American style. This global vision contradicts the carnivalesque richness of the actual U.S. broadcast of the Super Bowl and the diversity (racial, ethnic, sexual, etc.) in the U.S. and the global population.

The sports historian Allen Guttmann has noted that 'a nation that exercises political and/or economic power usually exercises cultural power as well.'[49] In a way, the symbolic nature of the Super Bowl works in reverse: the Super Bowl's high international stature is constantly reaffirmed in American culture as a self-comforting indication of the United States' political and economic power. Yet the vision of the Super Bowl's global status—particularly with its heavy reliance on symbols of masculinity, whiteness, and U.S. military might—is more Old World Order than New.

The fact that the Super Bowl is not the number one television sporting event may speak volumes about America's overestimation of its global might. It is not surprising, then, that soccer (the world's genuine top televised sporting event) remains a sport to ridicule for many people in the U.S. The *Los Angeles Times* in 2000 wryly stated that:

> the NFL estimates that more than 800 million people will watch the Super Bowl. An estimated 1.3 billion people watched the 1998 World Cup soccer final between Brazil and France. Can you remember the final score? Hint: one of the teams probably had 0.[50]

The comment, a typical joke about soccer's low scoring, which presumably makes it boring for the sporting fan, allows American football fans to dismiss soccer as a sport that does not matter. Meanwhile, soccer continues to diffuse into U.S. culture much more quickly than the American football game extends globally.

Ironically, the hope for extending interest in professional American football in global markets requires the sport itself to be flexible—more malleable than the franchise managed closely by the NFL bureaucracy. But the game is likely to become less American and more internationalized if it should succeed in diffusing widely into other cultures, which is the case with the three leading world team sports—soccer, basketball, and volleyball.[51] Thus the traditional mythic elements of NFL football that are so distinctly American are the same elements that prevent the Super Bowl from becoming the most-watched sporting event in the world.

Notes

1. J.L. Reeves and C.R. Martin, 'ReWriting the Super Bowl: From Cold War Spectacle to Postmodern Carnival', presented at: 'A Comparative Approach to Sport', Texas Tech University's 29th Comparative Literature Symposium, Lubbock, TX, Jan. 1996.
2. R. Martin and J.L. Reeves, 'Re Reading the Super Bowl', presented at the meeting of the Association

for Education in Journalism and Mass Communication, Qualitative Studies Division, Anaheim, CA, August 1996.

3. R. Real, 'The Super Bowl: Mythic Spectacle', in H. Newcornb (ed), *Television: The Critical View* (New York, NY: Oxford University Press, 2nd ed, 1979), pp.170-203.

4. C. Geertz, 'Person, Time, and Conduct in Bali', in Geertz, *The Interpretation of Cultures: Selected Essays* (New York, NY: Basic Books, 1973), pp.443-4.

5. See S. Behrens, 'Technological Convergence: Toward a United State of Media', in *Channels of Communication 1986 Field Guide* (New York: C.C. Publishing, 1986), pp.8-10; J. Miller, 'International Roundup: The Global Picture', ibid., pp.16-18.

6. For a discussion of Fordisim, and post-Fordism, see J.L. Reeves and R. Campbell, *Cracked Coverage* (Durham, NC: Duke University Press, 1994), pp.84-90; also A. Amin (ed), *Post-Fordism: A Reader* (Oxford,: Blackwell, 1994).

7. See G.B. Leonard, 'Winning Isn't Everything. It's Nothing', *Intellectual Digest* (Oct. 1973); reprinted in D.F. Sabo and R. Runfola (eds), *Jock: Sports and Male Identity* (Englewood Cliffs, NJ: Prentice-Hall, 1980), pp.265-6.

8. See M. Sella, 'The Electronic Fishbowl', *New York Times Magazine* (21 May 2000), 50-7, 68, 70, 72, 102, 106.

9. D. Harvey, *The Condition of Postmodernity* (Cambridge, MA: Blackwell, 1989), pp.340-1.

10. Super Bowls are traditionally marked with Roman numerals, which add to the event's sense of pomp.

11. See D. Lieberman, 'The Big-Bucks Ad Battles over TV's Most Expensive Minutes', *TV Guide* (26 Jan. 1991), 11-14; D. Enrico, 'Ad Game Was a Blowout, Too', *USA Today* (30 Jan. 1995), 5B.

12. K. Corliss, 'M*A*S*H, You Were a Smash; After 11 Years of Daring Good Humor, TV's Finest Half-Hour Signs Off', *Time* (28 Feb. 1983), 64ff.

13. S. Elliott, 'Trying to Score Big in "Ad Bowl"', *New York Times on the Web* (28 Jan. 1999), http://www.nytimes.com

14. S. Springer, 'Sure, There's a Football Game Being Played Today but Don't Forget about the Other Stuff', *Los Angeles Times* (30 Jan. 2000), S6.

15. D. Burnham, 'The Computer, the Consumer and Privacy', *New York Times* (4 March 1984), Sectn 4, 8. See also 'The New TV Ads Trying to Wake Up Viewers', *Business Week* (19 March 1984), 46ff.

16. B. Greene, *Chicago Tribune* (2 March 1986), Cl.

17. B. Moran, 'Herb Helped BK Visibility, but Little Else', *Advertising Age* (24 March 1986), 1; also see S. Elliott, 'Super Triumphs and Super Flops', *New York Times* (30 Jan. 1994), Sectn 3, 5.

18. J. VandeWater, 'Anheuser-Busch: Super Advertiser', *St. Louis Post-Dispatch TV Magazine* (9 Jan. 1989), 5. St. Louis is Anheuser-Busch's hometown.

19. Lieberman, 'The Big-Bucks', 14.

20. 'The Super Battle Behind Super Bowl XXIII', *USA Today* (23 Jan. 1989), 4B.

21. Also see M.P. McAllister, 'Super Bowl Advertising as Commercial Celebration', *The Communication Review*, 3(1999), 403-28.

22. 'Remembering the Advertising of the Super Bowls', *New York Times* 8 Jan. 1995, Sectn 13, 9. The Museum of Broadcasting has held subsequent exhibitions of Super Bowl advertisements.

23. J.J. O'Connor, 'TV: Watching Thomas to Astaire to Hope to Bunker', *New York Times* (19 Jan. 1972), 75.

24. See S.C. Jansen, 'Sport/War: the Gender Order, the Persian Gulf War and the New World Order', presented at the International Communication Association Annual Meeting, Miami, FL, May 1992; and C. Scodari, 'Operation Desert Storm as "Wargames": Sport, War, and Media Interrextuality', *Journal of American Culture*, 16(1993), 1-5.

25. R. Huff, 'Tight Contest Pulls Super Ratings', *New York Daily News* (1 Feb. 2000), 82. It is worth noting that the U.S. audience of 130.7 millions represents the total number of people who saw at least part of the game. During the average minute about 88.4 million viewers were tuned in to the game.

26. J. Buckley, 'Football Is Booming around the World' (28 Jan. 1999), http://www.nfl.com/international/990l28future.html

27. 'More than Super Bowl; World Cup Worldwide TV Audience', *Financial Post* [Toronto] (1 June 1994), 82. Also see B. Giussani, 'World Cup Sites Target Ticketless Fans', *New York Times on the Web* (12 May 1998), http://www.nytimes.com; see H. Dauncey and G. Hare (eds), *France the 1998 World Cup: the National Impact of a World Sporting Event* (London and Portland, OR: Frank Cass, 1999) for a book-length treatment of the impact of the World Cup.

28. T. Melville, 'A World in Love with Cricket (Except in US)', *Christian Science Monitor* (14 May 1999), 18.

29. International Rugby Board, 'Off the Field', 16 May 1999, http://www.rwc99.com/offfield/offfield.html

30. 'Game Still an Easy Sell for the CBC', *Toronto Star* (21 Nov 1998).

31. J.E. Fryman and B. Bates, 'By passing the Gateways: International News on CNN CNNWR', *Communication Research Reports* (1993), 3.

32. R.M. Wenge, 'Global Perspectives in Communication: the 1996 Robinson Speech' (Peoria, IL; Department of Communication, Bradley University, 1996), p.3.

33. Fryman and Bates, 'Bypassing the Gateways', 3.

34. J.L. Reeves, 'Ten Years of Achievement on the CNN World Report: A Critical Analysis of an Exemplary Text', in J. Oskam and K. Ward (eds), Proceedings of the International Mass Communications Conference (Lubbock, TX: Texas Tech University, forthcoming).

35. We conducted our search of the Archives in 1999.

36. J. Maguire, 'More than a Sporting Touchdown; The Making of American Football in England 1982-1990', *Sociology of Sport Journal*, 7 (1990), 213-37.

37. See *NFL Record and Fact Book*, 'Chronology: 1981-1990', www.nfl.com/randf/chron90.html

38. See R. Rauzi, 'It's so L.A.: Super Bowl Goes Show Biz', *Los Angeles Times* (26 Jan. 1993), Fl; T. McNichol, 'Will Michael Finally Touch Down?', *USA Weekend* (31 Jan. 1993), 20; Linda Deckard, 'Halftime Show to Blend High-Tech and Traditional Entities', *Amusement Business* (25 Jan. 1993), 15.

39. 'Super Bowl XXXIII Expected to Be Broadcast in 180 Countries in 24 Languages' (22 Jan. 1999), http://www.nfl.com/tvradio/990122sbskedint.html

40. Springer, 'Sure, There's a Football Game', 6.

41. 'NFL Returns to Canada' (27 Jan. 2000), http://www.nfl.com/international/000127.html

42. See Buckley, 'Football Is Booming'.

43. 'NFL International is a Success' (27 Jan. 2000), http://www.nfl.com/international/000125international.html

44. 'Quinn Named Senior VP of NFL International' (7 Oct. 1999), http://www.nfl.com/international/991007quinn.html

45. Interview with Greg Solomon, NFL Public Relations Office, 14 Mar 1999.

46. '1999 Country Table: List of Countries where the NFL Can Be Seen' http://www.nfl.com/international/990512countries.html (2001).

47. ESPN Star Sports, 'Corporate Information', (2001); the company broadcast the NFL to China, India, Indonesia, Pakistan, Bangladesh, Vietnam, South Korea, Myanmar, Nepal, Malaysia, Sri Lanka, Cambodia, Hong Kong, Laos, Papua New Guinea, Singapore, Mongolia, Bhutan, Macau, Brunei, the Maldives, and Guam exclusively, and competed with other NFL broadcasters in the Philippines, Taiwan, and Thailand.

48. The authors thank Prof. Murray Sperber, of Indiana University for additional videotape of this program.

49. See A. Guttmann, 'Sports Diffusion: A Response to Maguire and the Americanization Commentaries', *Sociology of Sport Journal*, 8 (1991), 185 90. Also see B. Kidd, 'How Do We Find Our Own Voices in the "New World Order"? A Commentary on Americanization', ibid., 8(1991), 178-84; E.A. Wagner, 'Sport in Asia and Africa: Americanization or Mundialization', ibid., 7 (1990), 337-402; J. McKay and T. Miller, 'From Old Boys to Men and Women of the Corporation: The Americanization and Commodification of Australian Sport', ibid., 8 (1991), 86-94.

50. T.J. Simers, 'The Super Bowl Will Have a Global Audience of about 800 Million, Many of Whom Are Passionate, Some of Whom are Curious; the Others Just Need a Reason to Party', *Los Angeles*

Times (30 Jan. 2000), DI. For U.S. soccer fans, the victory of the U.S. team in the 1999 Women's World Cup was an enormous event, yet the championship did not have the same cultural impact (nor the television ratings) as the Super Bowl.

51. See Wagner 'Sport in Asia and Africa', 399.

EPILOGUE

The readings in this anthology show us that from the very founding of this country sport has meant different things to different people and a variety of factors such as religion, race, topography, and socioeconomics have influenced its development. Take, for example, the differing conceptions and attitudes toward sport evident among the Puritans of New England and the gentlemen of Colonial Virginia. The Puritans, like some people to this very day, were opposed to many sports as a result of a complex combination of such factors as violation of the Sabbath; violent behavior; evils of gambling; and concerns associated with supposedly frivolous, trivial, and unproductive behavior. There were seemingly no such conflicts among the gentry in early Virginia who participated in sport without a concern for how this participation would negatively affect their standing in the eyes of God or be evidence of a lost soul.

The bifurcated nature of early American sport is still evident in this country, as is the use of sport by individuals and groups to mark themselves off and create and nurture a sense of community. The upper crust in this country continue to make treks and purchase memberships at Pinehurst in North Carolina and other exclusive clubs in search of healthy recreation and opportunities to participate in pastimes and sports that only people with ample time and great wealth could afford.

The search for community through sport was not exclusive to the rich and took place locally, regionally, nationally, and internationally. The bachelor subculture was partly responsible for the growth of boxing, animal sports, and billiards in nineteenth-century New York City. Closely linked with the notion of masculinity and various fraternal organizations and clubs, the bachelor subculture cultivated the aforementioned sports and, by extension, many others. Early American baseball and stock car racing in the more recent South also serve as good examples of the quest for community through sport.

In addition to community, recreation, and competition, sport has been associated with other purposes. Much of its growth and popularity have resulted from the exploits and contributions of individual athletes, coaches, entrepreneurs, and administrators. Prime examples of these individuals are those included in this book, such as Michael Phelan, James Heenan, John Morrissey, Harry Wright, Walter Camp, Henry Chadwick, Joe Louis, Jackie Robinson, Dan Gable, Muhammad Ali, Cal Ripken, Pat Summitt, Tara Van Derveer, Hank Greenberg, and Chris Weller. Through sheer talent, hard work, and dogged determination, these individuals, along with many more not mentioned in these pages, often changed the course of their respective sports and realized national and even international attention and renown.

The lives and careers of many of the aforementioned individuals also make clear the persistent reality of gender and racial inequality in American sport. Although significant progress has been made on these fronts, women and African Americans in particular continue to confront deep-seated stereotypic notions about their ability levels and more blatant forms of discriminatory practices, including the difficulty in assuming managerial and other administrative positions in sport.

In spite of this reality, there is no question that a genuine passion for sport exists in this country as evidenced by the increasing numbers of participants and spectators, idolization of athletes, and popularity of such mega-events as the Olympic Games and annual Super Bowl. In spite of the continued violence, cheating, and performance-enhancing drugs in American sport, people still follow with great fervor their favorite athletes and teams at various levels of competition and in every part of the country. The pursuit of victory, intense competition, striving for physical excellence, inherent symbolism, ritualistic nature, and a host of other factors have contributed to the fascination and national obsession with sport in the United States.

INDEX

ABOUT THE EDITOR

David K. Wiggins, PhD, is director of the School of Recreation, Health and Tourism at George Mason University in Manassas, Virginia. Since earning his PhD from the University of Maryland in 1979, Wiggins has taught undergraduate and graduate courses in sport history at Kansas State University and George Mason University.

Courtesy of David Wiggins

Wiggins is an expert on American sport, particularly as it relates to the involvement of black athletes in sport and physical activity. He has written about sport history since 1980 and published 8 books as well as articles in numerous journals, including *Research Quarterly for Exercise and Sport, Journal of Sport History, Canadian Journal of History of Sport,* and *International Journal of History of Sport.* His work has garnered three Research Writing Awards (1983, 1986, and 1999) from the American Alliance for Health, Physical Education, Recreation and Dance (AAHPERD) and significantly affected subsequent research studies on African American involvement in sport.

In addition to his memberships in AAHPERD, the American Academy of Kinesiology and Physical Education, and the North American Society for Sport History, Wiggins has served as president of the AAHPERD History Academy, editor of the *Journal of Sport History,* and history section editor for the *Research Quarterly for Exercise and Sport.* Wiggins is currently the editor of *Quest.*

In his leisure time, Wiggins enjoys reading, playing golf, and walking. He and his wife, Brenda, reside in Fairfax, Virginia, and have two sons, Jordan and Spencer.

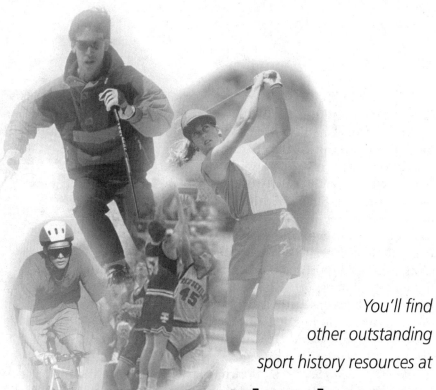